The Selected Journals of
L.M. Montgomery

VOLUME III (1921-1929)

Late in her life, L.M. Montgomery (1874-1942) expressed the wish that, after suitable time had elapsed, her handwritten journals be published. Montgomery—Mrs. Ewan Macdonald in private life—charged her younger son, Dr. E. Stuart Macdonald, with their care. Before his death in 1982, Dr. Macdonald turned over the handwritten volumes of his mother's journals and a much abridged version which she had typed, as well as her scrapbooks and photographic collection, account books and publishing records, personal library and various memorabilia to the University of Guelph.

The journals comprise ten large legal-size volumes of approximately 500 pages each—almost two million words—spanning the years 1889-1942. The first two journals deal with her early life in Prince Edward Island; the others deal primarily with her life in Ontario, at Leaskdale, Norval, and Toronto. This third Oxford volume is a selection of representative entries from the handwritten volumes 5, 6, and 7, showing her activities and preoccupations through the 1920s.

The L.M. Montgomery Collection at the University of Guelph is linked to the University's Scottish Collection, the major archive of Scottish material in North America, and complements holdings in Canadian, women's, and children's literature. Other Montgomery materials are held in Prince Edward Island and at the National Archives of Canada.

L.M. Montgomery, c.1919

The Selected Journals of
L.M. Montgomery

VOLUME III: 1921–1929

EDITED BY
Mary Rubio & Elizabeth Waterston

TORONTO
OXFORD UNIVERSITY PRESS
1992

Oxford University Press, 70 Wynford Drive, Don Mills, Ontario M3C 1J9

Toronto   Oxford   New York   Delhi   Bombay   Calcutta   Madras
Karachi   Petaling Jaya   Singapore   Hong Kong   Tokyo   Nairobi
Dar es Salaam   Cape Town   Melbourne   Auckland   Madrid
and associated companies in
Berlin   Ibadan

DRAWINGS BY ERIC BARTH

CANADIAN CATALOGUING IN PUBLICATION DATA

Montgomery, L.M. (Lucy Maud), 1874-1942
The selected journals of L.M. Montgomery

Includes index.
Partial contents: v. 1. 1889-1910—v. 2. 1910-1921—
v. 3. 1921-1929.
ISBN 0-19-540503-X (v. 1)
ISBN-0-19-540586-2 (v. 2)
ISBN-0-19-540936-1 (v. 3)

1. Montgomery, L.M. (Lucy Maud), 1874-1942–
Diaries.   2. Novelists, Canadian (English)–20th
century – Diaries.*   I. Rubio, Mary, 1939-
II. Waterston, Elizabeth, 1922-   . III. Title.

PS8526.O55Z53 1985   C813'.52   C85-099705-4
PR9199.2.M6Z468 1985

This book is printed on permanent (acid-free) paper ∞ .

Journals copyright © 1992 University of Guelph
Introduction, compilation, selection, illustrations, and notes
copyright © 1992 Mary Rubio and Elizabeth Waterston.

OXFORD is a trademark of Oxford University Press

1   2   3   4   –   95   94   93   92

Printed and bound in Canada by
John Deyell Company Limited.

Contents

Illustrations

Drawings

Acknowledgements

We begin by reiterating our heartfelt gratitude to Gerald Rubio and Douglas Waterston, who have done all that husbands usually do by way of support, and a good deal more. We thank Jennie Rubio for research and for meticulous work with Rebecca Conolly on proofreading and correcting the computer transcription of the relevant journals; Evan W. Siddall for legal research into and the interpretation of Montgomery's litigations; Dan Waterston for help with computer processing; Nick Whistler for early work on the photographs; James Conolly for careful work on manuscript and picture preparation; Rebecca Olivier, Laurie Mazur, and Keyi Jia for early proofreading; Bonnie Hulse for early typing; and Denyse Yeast and Ian Menzies for proofreading the completed manuscript.

Allan McGillivray (Curator, Uxbridge-Scott Historical Society and Museum), Luella Reid Macdonald (Montgomery's daughter-in-law from Norval), George Campbell (great-grandson of Annie Campbell of Park Corner, PEI), John and Jennie Macneill (John is the great-grandson of Alexander and Lucy Macneill), Ruth Macdonald (Montgomery's daughter-in-law from Toronto), and Elizabeth Rollins Epperly (Chair, English Department, Memorial University) have responded over the years to endless queries. Barbara Conolly's help is too ubiquitous to be specified.

For help in the research that produced the notes—a contribution to social, political, theological, familial, and literary contexts—we thank librarians and specialists at the University of Guelph (Nancy Sadek, Archivist; Ellen Morrison, Darlene Wiltsie, Parvin Jahanpour, and Gloria Troyer, staff); the Osborne Collection (Margaret Maloney); Toronto Public Library; London Public Library (Glen Curnoe); College of Physicians and Surgeons (Rose Chiappetta); Knox Theological College (Kim Arnold and Elspeth Reid); the University of Toronto Pharmacy School (Ernest W. Steib, Associate Dean); the Queen Street Mental Health Archives (Jack Griffin and Cyril Greenland); Sunnybrook Hospital (Robert Cleghorn and Margaret Huntley, staff); the Toronto *Star* Archives (Carol Lindsay); the *Globe and Mail* Archives (Amanda Valpy); the City of Toronto Archives (Karen Teeple); the Clarke Institute of Psychiatry (staff members Zindel V. Segal and Steven Hucker; Jean Lowry and Bob Marshall); the University of Toronto Library (Dan Dagostini); McMaster University Archives (Carl Spadoni); Dunwich Museum, England (Ormand Pickard); the British Columbia Provincial Museum (Virginia Careless); the University of Glasgow (Gavin White, Church History); the Mayo Clinic (L. B. Woolner, Emeritus Staff, descended from the Woolner family, PEI); the Boston Public Library; the Public Archives and Records Office, Charlottetown (Harry Holman and Marilyn

Bell); the Prince Edward Island Museum (Douglas Fraser and staff); Parks Canada (Tom Reddin and Barbara Macdonald); Harvard University Archives; Whitby Public Library; Royal Botanical Gardens Library (Shirley Clements); Royal Canadian Yacht Club; Stratford Public Library (Susan Lockhart); Law Society of Upper Canada (Marie Hammond and Marie Langlois); Farrar, Straus & Giroux (Roger Straus, Robert Wohlforth, and Anne Sullivan).

We are also grateful to local historians, specialists, and archivists including Dorothy McLean and Joe Van Leeuwen (Norval); Richard Ruggles (Georgetown); Ivan Sayers (Vancouver); Ken Lamb (Milton); Douglas Worling (St. Andrews College); Doris Clark Ludwig (Media Club); Mary E. Montgomery (PEI); Ronald Rompkey (Newfoundland); Raymond Peringer (Arts and Letters Club); Miss Addison (Trafalgar Castle School, Whitby); Miriam Montgomery Perkins (Clan Montgomery Society Newsletter Editor, USA) and Ken Montgomery (Alberta); Len Taylor (Toronto Press Club); Jack and Linda Hutton (Bala); Mel Andrews (Curator, Railway Museum).

People who dug up extra information or provided resources include Marian Hebb (Lawyer for the L. M. Montgomery Estate); Jack Macdonald, Leonard Conolly, David Murray, and Doug Killam (University of Guelph); Marina Engelsakis (Archivist, St. Michael's Hospital); Carolyn Cannon (Archivist, York University); James Wilson (Skelmorlie Castle, Scotland); David Macdonald (grandson of L. M. Montgomery); Mary Maxwell, Joy Laird, Margaret Russell, Marion Laird, and Joan Carter (all of Norval); Glenys Stow; Dr. Ruth Tatham (Homewood, Guelph); Commodore K.J. Summers; Lieutenant John Whitfield; Arthur Grubbe; Sheila Egoff (Professor Emerita Staff, UBC); Brian Winter; Len Andrews; Isobel Reid; John Middleton, Dorothy MacKay, Robert Jardine, and F.W.P. Bolger (PEI); Elsie Davidson and Wilda Clark (Uxbridge); Asim Masouf (Vancouver); Nina Lunney (Zephyr); James Innes Stewart, Q.C., Faye Thompson, Dr. and Mrs. Richard Braiden and the Rev. Eoin Mackay (all of Toronto); Dorothy Thompson; J. Austin Cook; Kevin McCabe; Ami Lonnroth (Sweden); Barbara Wachowicz (Poland); Gwen Davies and Archivist Patricia Townsend (Acadia); Rea Wilmshurst (Toronto); and W. P. Coues (Boston). Finally, we are grateful to the respondents to the Bill McNeil's CBC "Fresh Air" Program who answered queries and to the lawyers who have offered information on legal history.

At Oxford University Press, we acknowledge the help of Phyllis Wilson, William Toye (who provided the initial design for the published journals and edited volumes one and two), and Olive Koyama, our editor for this volume.

We are especially grateful to artist Erich Barth, who has drawn all of the introductory illustrations for each volume of the journals. For this one, he reconstructed Norval through Women's Institute Books, aerial and historical maps, 1920s pictures of Norval provided through the Russell family, and the memories of many Norval residents. The Radial Railway was researched at the Ontario Electric Railway Historical Association Museum in Rockwood, Ontario.

Finally, we again acknowledge the financial aid given by the Social Sciences and Humanities Research Council of Canada and the use of space and facilities offered by the University of Guelph.

Introduction

In 1921, Lucy Maud Montgomery Macdonald was 46 years old, the mother of two young boys, the wife of a Presbyterian minister, the supporter of church and community activities in an Ontario village—not an extraordinary life for a woman. But this particular woman possessed an extraordinary talent. She was a writer of stories and novels that gripped, absorbed, and impelled readers. She had created a range of imaginary friends; she had developed a language for expressing emotions and responding to the nuances of natural beauty; she tickled funny bones and stirred healing nostalgic tears. As the author of *Anne of Green Gables* and eleven other best-selling books, L.M. Montgomery was a world-known figure. As a professional woman she had already confronted and sued an exploitative publisher. The ordinary and the extraordinary roles of this middle-aged woman brought both pressures and pleasures. Privately, persistently, L.M. Montgomery fingered all the threads of her complex lives and wove them into her journal.

In 1889 she had written in a little notebook, "Life is beginning to get interesting for me—I will soon be fifteen....In *this* journal I am never going to tell what kind of day it is. *And*—I am going to keep this book locked up!" A very private woman, she recorded in that "locked-up book" her ambitions, problems, changing moods, passions, the gradual access of fame, and the sudden possibility of marriage—a tumble of events and emotions which were only unlocked to readers with the publication of *The Selected Journals of L.M. Montgomery, Volume I: 1889-1910* (Toronto: Oxford University Press, 1985).

A dramatic shift in Montgomery's life occurred in 1911, when at the age of 36 she left a single life on the isolated north shore of Prince Edward Island for active involvement in community and family life in mid-Ontario. She packed up her diaries and took them with her. Over the next ten years, with unprecedented frankness and reverence, she recorded in them the experiences of wifehood, pregnancy, and maternity. She also documented her spurts of literary creativity and the satisfaction of her continuing ability to please a large reading public with *The Story Girl*, *The Golden Road*, and a series of sequels to *Anne of Green Gables*—carrying "Anne" and her family through some of the same experiences of romance, marriage, and motherhood. But in those ten years she also had to record both world-wide and personal troubles: the universal tragedy of World War I and the personal trauma of losing her beloved cousin Frederica, victim of the virulent post-W.W.I influenza epidemic. Increasingly, too, entries reflected the strain of balancing the demands of family and her literary vocation against the claims of her husband's profession. As a minister's wife she had to visit members of the Presbyterian church in Leaskdale, Ontario, offer them leadership in women's guilds and youth groups, and comfort them during the devastating war years. Her journal became the repository of her private resentments and her private amusement at village eccentricities. The strains, the sadness, and also the glories and the humour of those years appear in the entries in *The Selected Journals of L.M. Montgomery, Volume II, 1910-1921* (Toronto: Oxford University Press, 1987).

Here now is the third volume: selections from L.M Montgomery's journals for the years 1921 to 1929. These years brought renewed intensity of response to nature—not only to the Prince Edward Island seashore, but to the northern lakes and the picturesque glens of Ontario. Here are new, funny, and touching stories about people and pets: the friends and enemies in Leaskdale and subsequently in Norval, Ontario; the dog Dixie, and the cats Daffy and Pat and Lucky. Here is the hint of a love story. And here is a thorough dissection of a troubled marriage.

L.M. Montgomery's husband, the Reverend Ewan Macdonald, had already shown signs of a long-concealed malady. His depression, traced in its early stages in *The Selected Journals of L.M. Montgomery, Volume II*, now darkened into what was then called "religious melancholy". Distorting the Presbyterian doctrine that certain people, elected by God, are predestined to salvation, Ewan Macdonald became filled with the dreadful contrary certainty that he was damned. He believed that he was predestined to eternal punishment not for his particular sins but as a manifestation of God's power and will. As further attacks of depression alternated with remissions, the married life recorded in the journals became more and more tortured. In 1919, when Ewan Macdonald suffered a major attack and became virtually incapacitated physically and mentally by his melancholia, the Macdonalds had consulted "nerve specialists", *i.e.*, psychiatrists, in Boston. In the years recorded in this volume of the journals, in spite of recurring bouts of debilitating illness, no further psychiatric help was available.

Mental illness constitutes one of Montgomery's recurring themes of this period: references to madness recur both in the journal and in her books. In the 1920s "neurasthenia", "hysteria", and "nervous breakdown" had become familiar phrases, but the modern drugs which could have kept a condition such as Ewan Macdonald's under control were not yet discovered. Melancholy (depression) had been diagnosed as a medical condition for centuries, but no effective treatments were available. Doctor-prescribed doses of hypnotic, addictive drugs like veronal and chloral served as the sole palliative for Ewan's and Maud's own distress.

L.M. Montgomery had long been interested in Freudian theories: she read intensely in psychiatric and medical texts, acting as amateur psychologist regarding her husband's case. She also read about and experimented with thyroid pills and other treatments for mental disorder. Her journals for these years thus contribute specifically to the history of mental illness and the devastation that it could wreak on a family when one member suffered from it.

Meanwhile her own mental state becomes a source of puzzlement and interest for the modern reader. Here is a unique and sophisticated tracing of a relationship triply strained, by ill-matched personalities, by the divisive force of the wife's achievements pitched against the husband's ineptitude, and by general changes in the status of women. A non-intellectual, non-literary man, Ewan Macdonald disparaged his wife's success. The journals record the hurt caused by his resentment whenever reviewers, readers, or (most gallingly) members of his own church honoured her.

Maud Montgomery Macdonald was increasingly in a mood that we would now call feminist. She had read widely in periodical literature when the "Woman Question" was debated in the 1890s. In these later years she takes umbrage at the way men patronize her, praising her lemon pie but not mentioning her literary success. She does more for her husband than many wives would have been able to do, partly because she has excessive energy and talents, partly because her energy and talents have now received material rewards, and partly to compensate for his inadequacies. Her royalty money can make the manse a pretty, well-furnished place and can send the boys off to a good private school. She feels isolated by her husband's failure to appreciate her and resents his envy of her success.

Deciphering the truth about Ewan Macdonald's nature is one of the fascinations of reading the Montgomery journals. A shadowy figure in early volumes concerned with courtship and marriage, in the present volume Ewan becomes a central figure: a worry, an irritant, and a threat. Other observers—parishioners, maids, neighbours—did not always see him as his wife did. Are we to regard the diarist as functioning like the "untrustworthy narrator" in a modern novel? Does she reshape the man in order to strengthen the image of herself as long-suffering, ingenious in hiding his malady from the world? Does her shaping literary instinct lead her to shade him as monstrous? Or is her portrait a true one, revealing the veiled distresses of a marriage difficult in ways that others could not discern?

In middle age, L.M. Montgomery reconnected with many of her childhood friends and relations. In that final era of voluminous correspondence, before the letter-writing habit gave way to long-distance phone calls, she discovered that many of her contemporaries had also undergone traumatic marriages, divorces, loss or alienation of children, mental or physical breakdowns. As she reports her friends' dramas, the journal thus widens to become a catchment of many stories of marriages—stories of life "beyond the happy ending" which all literary romances emphasize. Her journals become an unmatched casebook on the domestic complex in the 1920s. They also record the daily attrition of self-confidence, freedom, joy, and energy in the largely unexplored field of middle-year womanhood.

Women could now vote (Montgomery did), could maintain a separate bank account (she did), could travel alone by train or by car to unfamiliar communities (she did). But patriarchal power in church, state, law, and home seemed undiluted still. In the story of her lawsuit against her publishers, Montgomery records with high drama the waging of one professional woman's battle against that patriarchy. Throughout this period she was involved in a series of law suits against her first publisher, L.C. Page of Boston. The case was significant enough to be carried through a number of legal jurisdictions and eventually to be appealed to the Supreme Court of the United States. It involved the question of the author's right to protest the publisher's misappropriation of her copyrighted material—her "intellectual property". Specifically, L.M. Montgomery protested Page's withholding of royalties and his publication without her permission of materials not revised according to her standards and wishes. More generally she was protesting an unequal power struggle between herself as a creative artist and the rich businessman who was taking advantage of her, a vulnerability emphasized because she was a woman and a non-unionized writer.

Montgomery had the satisfaction of seeing her "Anne" move to ever-greater popularity. She also had the infuriating knowledge that in the process of settling the law suits she had accepted a woefully inadequate sum for all rights to "Anne". Movies and "talkies" were the new entertainment media of the period. (The journals offer references to *Ben Hur*, *The Prisoner of Zenda* and other significant early films.) Montgomery, who loved the movies, did not love the experience of seeing *Anne of Green Gables* on the screen, knowing that none of the money for this highly successful film would come to her.

The record of her lawsuits against her publisher and the frustration of countering his legal appeals against judgements in her favour reflect an issue of general importance. Her story links with the passing of a new Copyright Law in Canada. And her struggle for professional status links her with the new solidarity of writers in the Canadian Authors' Association, Canadian Book Week, the Canadian Women's Press Club—all significantly developing at exactly this time.

Modern readers think of the 1920s as a period obsessed with wealth, get-rich-quick speculation on the stock market, conspicuous consumption of the "Great Gatsby" sort, and the glitter of a jazz-age world of "diamonds as big as the Ritz". L.M. Montgomery's journal for this period reflects some obsession with money, but for idiosyncratic reasons. Partly because of the lawsuits, partly because of either domestic pressures of those from her extended "clan", she became acutely aware of the ups and downs of her royalties.

Against the background of an unsatisfying marriage and professional frustration, however, life in the 1920s presented the novelist with two lively unfolding plots. First, a minor road accident boiled up into a tempest in the township teapot, fanned by surprising gales from Zephyr. Some Methodists in that nearby community were not kindly disposed towards the Presbyterian minister of Leaskdale, his "rich" wife, and their better-than-average car. Second, the nationwide effort to meld Presbyterian, Methodist, and Congregational Protestant churches into a Union in Canada plunged the local congregations into crypto-political campaigns.

In the first of these unfolding dramas, ironic elements were added by the peculiar position of the Macdonalds. As a minister and his wife, they were set by convention apart from the community; but as newcomers to Ontario, to Scott Township, and to Leaskdale and its neighbouring village Zephyr they were doubly outsiders. Both Ewan and Maud Macdonald faced difficulties in fully grasping the tangled web of social connections in the township. This fact underlies the tragi-comedy of the Macdonald-Pickering affair. A very insignificant automobile collision built up into a full-scale legal case, in which witnesses popped up

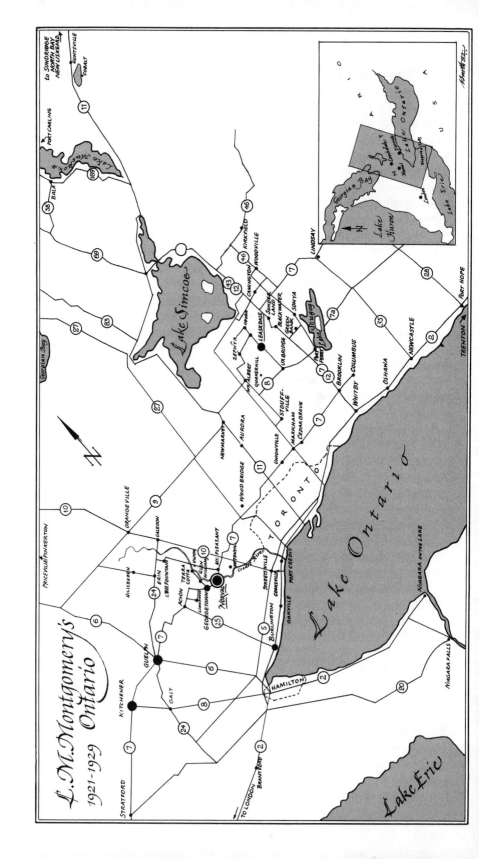

L.M. Montgomery's
1921-1929 Ontario

Lake Ontario

Lake Erie

Lake Simcoe

Georgian Bay

TORONTO

STRATFORD
KITCHENER
GUELPH
GALT
BRANT FORD
TO LONDON
HAMILTON
NIAGARA FALLS
NIAGARA ON THE LAKE
BURLINGTON
OAKVILLE
PORT CREDIT
STREETSVILLE
NORVAL
GEORGETOWN
CHELTENHAM
GLEN WILLIAMS
LIMEHOUSE
ACTON
ERIN
TERRA COTTA
BALLINAFAD
HILLSBURGH
CALEDON
ORANGEVILLE
PRICEVILLE/PINKERTON
MT. PLEASANT
HUTTONVILLE
CREDIT RIVER
WOOD BRIDGE
NEWMARKET
AURORA
UNIONVILLE
MARKHAM
CEDAR GROVE
STOUFF-VILLE
UXBRIDGE
GREEN LAKE RIVER
ZEPHYR
MT. ALBERT
QUAKER HILL
SANDFORD
BLACKWATER
SONYA
SUTTON
LEASKDALE
CANNINGTON
WOODVILLE
KIRKFIELD
LINDSAY
BALSAM LAKE
Port Perry
Scugog
BROOKLIN
COLUMBUS
WHITBY
OSHAWA
NEWCASTLE
PORT HOPE
TRENTON
BOLT
PORT CARLING
Lake Muskoka
COBALT
HUNTSVILLE
to SUNDRIDGE
NORTH BAY
NEW LISKEARD

N

Georgian Bay
Lake Huron
Lake Ontario
Lake Erie
ONTARIO
U.S.
N

and then withdrew—under pressure of extended family connections. The journals record L.M. Montgomery's sharp response to the day-by-day progress of the expanding legal entanglements; in our notes we elucidate some of the interconnections between witnesses for the plaintiff and the defence. For example, the Macdonalds' best witness, the man near whose garage the accident occurred, turned reluctant to go on the stand with his first version of what happened. His son, we discover, was married to the daughter of Marshall Pickering, the antagonist in the case.

Scott Township was a static society. Most of the families around Leaskdale, Zephyr, Uxbridge, Sandford, and Udora lived on the farms settled by their ancestors in the 1830s to 1850s. Those forefathers—and foremothers—had brought sectarian and political allegiances from Scotland, England, Ireland, the United States, and Quebec, causing dissensions remembered by descendants in the 1920s, in spite of intermarriages, shared school memories, and the more recent bonding because of losses during World War I. In Prince Edward Island, Montgomery would have been aware of all these nuances. At home in Cavendish she would have known almost instinctively the cross-connections between Macneills and Simpsons, Mackenzies and Stewarts, Lairds and Clarks. Here in the Ontario world of Lockies and Pickerings, Shiers and Leasks, Mustards and Meyers, she was continually surprised and dismayed by the way witnesses came forward, drew back, and changed their stories under subtle local forces. As a novelist, L.M. Montgomery would use the idea of a "tangled web" of family pressures, resentfully in the Emily books and farcically in *The Blue Castle. A Tangled Web* would in fact become the title of a later novel.

The Pickering case also has a medical aspect. The lawsuit elucidated many myths and misapprehensions with respect to diabetes, held, ironically, at the very moment of the epochal discovery of insulin as a treatment for the condition. The case also reveals the neglect of confidentiality by country doctors of the time: they freely discussed with the defendant (Macdonald) the history and symptoms of the plaintiff (Pickering). It also shows the complications and uncertainty of legal process: how the venue and the personality of the judge can affect the outcome, and how witnesses' motives can affect their testimony.

The second real-life drama staged in this period and reflected with extreme nervous preoccupation in the journal was the hard-fought movement to blend three Protestant sects into one United Church. The fight for or against church union was complicated for L.M. Montgomery by the fact that her unstable husband seemed unlikely to hold his job after a merger, if one did occur. The Presbyterian General Assembly of 1907 had urged a fusion of Protestant churches, a notion accepted by Congregationalists and Methodists. But when it came time to vote on Church Union, the Presbyterians, especially in conservative rural districts, had second thoughts. They dug in their heels to defend their own form of worship and the Presbyterian structure of church government (a democratic system of elected elders acting in local session, regional presbytery, and national assembly to regulate all church matters). They also fought to protect their vested interest in church property and buildings.

The Macdonalds' circle of friends and acquaintances, the people they visited and entertained, were clerical families in hamlets near Leaskdale. Here the resistance to union was particularly strong. This section of her journal records with both humour and acrimony the splits in church congregations as the organizational and political move to union progressed. When the final Union was achieved, although all the professors and most of the students at Knox Presbyterian Theological College in Toronto left the old church for the new United one, people in places like Leaskdale and Mount Pleasant and Wick resisted the change. There was a nation-wide shift in congregations for the ministers who "went Union", and also for those like Ewan Macdonald who stayed in the shrunken but resolute Presbyterian sect. Our notes at the end of this volume give life-dates and church appointments of the Presbyterian ministers named in the journal; many of them underwent radical career changes in 1925-26. Some churches dismissed their ministers; others were left by a preacher "going Union" after a lifetime of Presbyterian leadership. Montgomery's journal records her husband's attitudes—and her own—to the blend of piety and politics torturing Presbyterians in this Post-World War I period. For modern readers in a secularized industrial world where all church force seems diminished, such high ecclesiastic drama reads like a historical romance.

In this unsettled time, Ewan Macdonald, trying to hold one pastoral charge together, was secretly "preaching for a call" to another; his wife, a person who put down deep roots wherever she lived, was secretly facing the probability of another move, almost as traumatic as leaving her native Prince Edward Island to move to Ontario. The move came: to Norval, a very pretty village just west of Toronto, in a glen where the picturesque Credit River flowed.

Here new dramas emerged, new concerns over the maturing sons, new publishing contracts, new experiences—including being presented to the Prime Minister of Great Britain and to the Prince of Wales and Prince George, both future monarchs of the Commonwealth. The journal shifts its tone to accommodate these new colourings as the Macdonalds gain fresh energy from the move to a new community.

If some drama that fills this section of the journals was played out in the lawcourts, in the church Sessions, and at the regal and vice-regal receptions, some was also enacted in the kitchen. Here the action involved co-operative work with a series of maids. These young women were hired to help with the housekeeping while the "mistress of the manse" was involved in the endless round of Guild, Mission Society, and Sunday School meetings, together with parochial visitations, not to mention trips to Toronto on business with publishers and the necessary hours of withdrawal to pen her books and answer unending letters from fans and critics. Given the state of the "mistress's" nerves, it is small wonder that the journal records recurring irritation and furious show-downs with her maids. The young Ontario women who acted as domestic helpers in the 1920s were a far cry from the British "servant class". In the increasingly classless society of rural Canada, most members of the local community were connected by intermarriage as well as by memories of shared experience in school, church, and social events. Many of the maids at the manse came from well-established local families. The first maid, for instance, was the sister-in-law of the local doctor. Most of them subsequently married and raised respectable, ambitious, and talented children.

But L.M. Montgomery, as an over-burdened worker, expected efforts equal to her own from these young women, and she too often assumed they should be as professional and mature as she was. Her feelings were ambivalent. She prided herself on egalitarianism, seating the maid at her own table, but when over-wrought she reveals her strong class consciousness. She writes condescendingly of "servants", reflecting perhaps her immersion in 19th century British literature (likewise, she idealizes the leisured, cultured, "gentlefolk" life of the Barra-cloughs). Furthermore, although genuinely fond of her maids, she was too caught up in her own worries to consider that the young women were distracted by their own problems—problems ironically like her own: fluctuating emotions, inability to sleep, physical maladies, worries about relations with men. She made little allowance for the maids' different upbringing, or for their feelings of pow-erlessness in the domestic employer-employee relationship. The stories of her dealings with the maids are therefore both comic and touching. We have omitted some of the details of these recurring confrontations, keeping only the revealing account of her tussle with the Scottish maid Margaret Mackenzie. In general the relation of maid and employer constitutes an aspect of the life of middle-class women in her era that deserves more attention. The journal here opens a window on yet another facet of the lives of girls and women, and on women's difficulties in balancing a professional life and domestic concerns.

Finally, part of the social drama of these years was still played out in Prince Edward Island. Maud Montgomery Macdonald went "home" whenever possible and she was constantly beset by family problems relayed from the Island by mail or by telegram. She was always loyal to Park Corner, the place of her hap-piest girlhood memories. She remembered that all at Park Corner were good to her in those days. Further back lay the memory that her aunt Annie, alone of all her dead mother's brothers and sisters, was unfailingly kind and supportive. But Park Corner was now a household of women and young children, with no man to keep the farm going. Complaints and pleas for help and money were continu-ous. Her irritation with her Island relatives was intense, but she loved them and helped them when they appealed to her. Her belief that they were part of a great and noble clan, fallen on hard times, increased her own stature.

Her memories of the past perfections of Prince Edward Island were so rich that present-day scenes and people there grated on her nerves. For instance, she was huffy about the Grahams' efforts to send someone to walk home with her—she wanted to be alone—and dismissed their courtesy as insensitivity, capping her criticism by emphasizing that these families lacked the grace of the older inhabitants of earlier days. (This grace is conspicuously absent, by the way, in the hundred-page-long diary kept by old Charles Macneill in the 1870s, labori-ously transcribed by Montgomery in 1925 into her own diary—but omitted from this edition of her journals.) In the mid-20s she felt every change in the old home place like a wound. Perhaps the core of her emotional reactions to Prince Edward Island scenes was their unavoidable reminder of the absence of Frede, whose memory was so much a part of the Island. The thought of Frede was still shattering: every anniversary of her death is marked in the journals, not sadly but bitterly, rebelliously, almost ferociously. Loneliness emerges as a central theme. Montgomery lived increasingly in what she calls the "solitude of unshared thought".

Montgomery took pride in never inflicting her woes on others; in the light of Ewan's melancholy, this seems heroic. She believed that it was the duty of a woman—and especially of a woman who was a minister's wife—to be ever cheerful and uncomplaining. Her irritation was silenced by cultural expectations as to proper womanly behaviour. Montgomery's gender training is firmly inscribed in the journals; yet the journals themselves are in part an anguished cry against the imposed silence, and the forces that insisted she maintain the role of "angel in the house"—serene, uncomplaining, always ready with dignity and grace to cheer and encourage those in her domestic sphere. She did of course express her woes, she did of course complain consistently and eloquently of those exhausting, inexorable demands on her sympathy, but only in her journal. The journals are acts of protest against an ideology that she believes with one part of herself and rejects with another. She writes not as an angel but as an anxious, angry, frustrated woman.

As the years passed, the journal became more and more a necessary confidant—and not only for woe but also for amusement, for self-mockery, for reflective thought, and of course and always, for the flashes of intense response to natural beauty that had called forth surges of passionate comment ever since she was a small girl writing her first diary in the 1880s.

Nature continued to enable the creation of the descriptive passages that were her hallmark. Norval, with its gracefully forked river and its hill of lofty pines beyond the tall church spire, supplemented Prince Edward Island in power to satisfy her hunger for beauty. In these years the journal reflects not only the joys of frequent pilgrimages home to the Island and the daily lift of spirit at sight of the pines on Russells' hill in Norval, but also a brief ecstatic response to the unexpected beauty of the Muskoka lakes. *The Blue Castle*, a novel for adults, reflects the Macdonald family's holiday interlude in Bala, Ontario. From early days her rapt descriptions of nature may have been in part a private escape from a familial and external social code that scorned the expression of emotions; in later years the rapt response carries suggestions of sublimated frustration.

The journals not only record "real" life, but also note reading, movie- and play-going, and intermittent meditations on the past. In the 1920s Montgomery desperately needed recourse to these worlds of imagined experience, in memories and in books. Many of the books get a cursory mention in the journals, but others are dissected. Allusions to Canadian writers—from Isabella Valancy Crawford to Bliss Carman, and from "Marian Keith" to Morley Callaghan—are noteworthy, given the modern assumption that interest in Canadian literature is a recent development. Montgomery read new Canadian authors, especially those published by McClelland & Stewart, her own publisher, for Mr. McClelland sent new books to her in hopes that he could quote her positive responses in future promotional efforts. She also corresponded with and encouraged emerging authors.

She relished re-reading the works of a world of women writers, past and present: Jane Austen, George Eliot, Charlotte Brontë, Mrs. Gaskell, Olive Schreiner, Marie Corelli, Sheila Kaye-Smith. Many of her journal entries became, as our colleague Nick Whistler once said, "the other side of a conversation that began in reading".

Tracing her reading turns out to be an exercise not only in exploring the springs of her activity, but also in uncovering the reading taste of the time. The journals indicate the wide range of books available, in pre-television days, to voracious readers: best-sellers, old favourites, thrillers, mystery stories, scientific popularizations, history books, nostalgic pastorals, poetry, theological texts, and biographies.

All this reading, combined with the social dramas that she and her friends and foes were involuntarily enacting, fuses in the novels produced in the period: *Emily of New Moon*, *Emily Climbs*, *The Blue Castle*, *Emily's Quest*, and *Magic for Marigold*. Montgomery had followed "Anne" in sequels to *Anne of Green Gables* through marriage and motherhood. Now, early in 1921, she had found a new heroine in "Emily". This third volume of the journals illuminates the way life and memories and the experiences of authorship allowed her to explore the psyche of a creative child—a girl who has ever since served as encouragement and model for young women beginning a literary career. (Alice Munro, for instance, assigns to *Emily of New Moon* the experience in reading that first encouraged her to think of herself as a writer.) All the books in the *Emily* series are rich in their presentation of a restrictive cultural network, the central figure being set apart by her sense of herself as a writer. The books recall Cavendish tensions, but these are perceived more clearly and more ironically now because of the double perspective gained in Leaskdale years and Norval years. As for *The Blue Castle*, that strange romance that has gripped the imagination of generations of readers around the world, the journal casts intriguing light on its shadowy sources, in local life and in dreams of a happy marriage. In the novels we see the imaginary correlative of her life in the 1920s, enriched by humour and memories and lifted by romance. But the journal is a powerful counter-narrative. The novels show her positive, witty, up-beat, sentimental side—the side women were supposed to reveal; the journals show the brooding, subtle, questioning, rebellious side—one where she rejected the dominant ideology about woman's perfect behaviour.

By the time she was 54—in 1929, when this volume ends—L.M. Montgomery was still working hard at her novels. She was also more and more absorbed in the journals she had kept so faithfully for forty years, more and more aware of the lasting value of her life records. She had long ago recognized how useful they were to her as a source book on youthful feelings. She had carefully preserved the small, non-uniform diaries dating from the 1890s. As the war years unfolded she had realized that the story of her late-Victorian maturing constituted a record of an epoch gone forever. In the winter of 1918-19 she had begun recopying the earliest diaries into legal-sized ledgers, and she worked on this whenever time permitted. She was well along with copying the journals of her early married life when this volume opens. By 1921 she more and more often

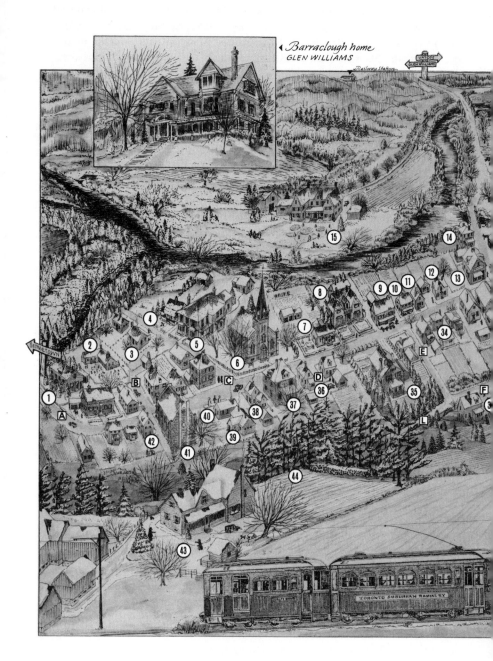

Barraclough home
GLEN WILLIAMS

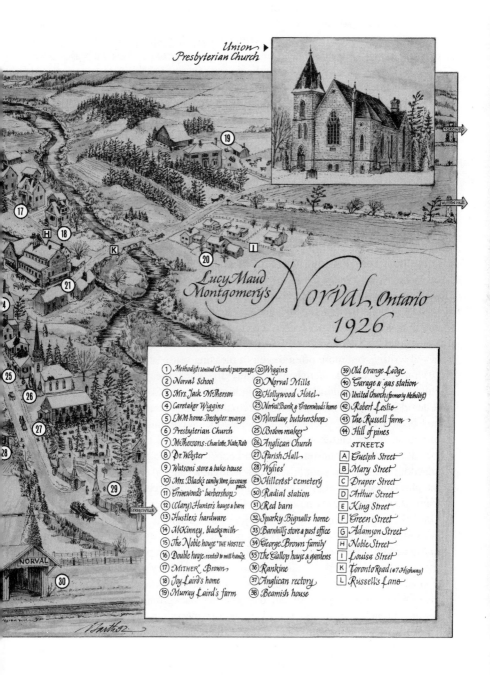

Union Presbyterian Church ▶

Lucy Maud Montgomery's *Norval*, Ontario 1926

① Methodist (United Church) parsonage
② Norval School
③ Mrs. Jack McPherson
④ Caretaker Wiggins
⑤ LMM home: Presbyter. manse
⑥ Presbyterian Church
⑦ McPhersons: Charlotte, Kate, Rob
⑧ Dr. Webster
⑨ Watsons store & bake house
⑩ Mrs. Black's candy store, ice cream parl.
⑪ Grimwoods' barbershop
⑫ (Clary) Hunter's house & barn
⑬ Hustler's hardware
⑭ McKinney, blacksmith
⑮ The Noble house 'THE HOSTEL'
⑯ Double house: rented to mill hands
⑰ MITHER Brown
⑱ Joy Laird's home
⑲ Murray Laird's farm

⑳ Wiggins
㉑ Norval Mills
㉒ Hollywood Hotel
㉓ Norval Bank & Greenwood's home
㉔ Wardlaw, butcher shop
㉕ Broom maker
㉖ Anglican Church
㉗ Parish Hall
㉘ Wylies'
㉙ Hillcrest cemetery
㉚ Radial station
㉛ Red barn
㉜ Sparky Bignall's home
㉝ Barnhill's store & post office
㉞ George Brown family
㉟ The Gallop house & gardens
㊱ Rankine
㊲ Anglican rectory
㊳ Beamish house

㊴ Old Orange Lodge
㊵ Garage & gas station
㊶ United Church (formerly Methodist)
㊷ Robert Leslie
㊸ The Russell farm
㊹ Hill of pines

STREETS

Ⓐ Guelph Street
Ⓑ Mary Street
Ⓒ Draper Street
Ⓓ Arthur Street
Ⓔ King Street
Ⓕ Green Street
Ⓖ Adamson Street
Ⓗ Noble Street
Ⓘ Louisa Street
Ⓚ Toronto Road (#7 Highway)
Ⓛ Russell's Lane

needed the refuge and outlet they provided. The old journals kept memories fresh—too fresh, sometimes—and the desire to keep the journalizing habit going supplied a mechanical exercise in writing even when immediate life seemed too dark or too pale to warrant an entry. Her new journal entries increase in frequency. Under these strains, journal entries sometimes shrink into barren recording of weather—"Another gray day", "The bitter cold continues" or occasionally "A lovely day. Fine and cool"—the kind of diarizing she once swore she would never stoop to. In this edition we have dropped some of these flat initial phrases, marking their omission with ellipses (. . .), but have kept some to show the way the journal resumes its spell. Sharp, focused comments flow from her pen, keeping depression and inanition at bay.

Some such editing she no doubt did herself. When she initially wrote her journal notes on odd pieces of paper, she fiercely clung to her intention to keep the life record whole—growls and all, despair and all, malice and all. But as she assembled her notes and turned them into clean copy, no doubt her story-shaping instinct came into play; a writer cannot put pen to paper without the mind doing both conscious and unconscious shaping. As she assembled and copied her notes Montgomery tended to balance the moods between entries, and artistically to pick up on a final phrase in one entry in order to shift the tone of the next. She does thumbnail introductory sketches of people just entering her life and makes sure she has recorded the conclusion or aftermath of earlier incidents. Sometimes the deliberate effort to revive interest results in strained and contrived writing, but more often there is a pleasing sense of variety and range.

Montgomery was increasingly ready to shape the journal consciously, to emphasize its continuities and to highlight its climaxes. Like all of us, she ordered her reflections by the intellectual-emotional framework into which she had been socialized. Hers was a framework of community gossip and of oral narrative. In her childhood home people had gathered to collect mail from her grandfather the postmaster—who also happened to be a past master in the art of anecdote. He regaled people with his own gatherings of village lore, sharpening the phrasing with retellings. Further, gossip characterized women's gatherings in Cavendish, Charlottetown, and Park Corner. In an alien Ontario world with no kindred spirits to share remembered jokes and scandals, Montgomery turned to her journal as to a listener. Every day produces a little story, every visit a potential anecdote, every encounter a little dialogue. She reports in a gossippy way the actuality of people's talk and movement as they cope with momentary events. She notes her own immediate reactions. She reveals some of the prejudices which were typical of her day and her background—a snobbish attitude toward French-Canadians, for example: to marry an Acadian or a Roman Catholic was unthinkable. She worries about her children, keeping a terrified eye on any traits that may betray the genetic transmission of Ewan's maladies. She complains of being put upon and bored, and she chuckles over her neighbours' eccentricities and inconsistencies. In every case she catches the freshness of an age before mass media had universalized pat phrases and clichéd gestures as substitutes for idiosyncratic response to experience. The journals read like the voice of a confidant amusing a good friend.

As a novelist Montgomery was driven by expectations of plot, of event, of rising and falling action. In retelling the events of her days, that shaping craft could not be set aside. Her novels were written in short self-contained chapters, like Dickens's; the entries in her recopied journal tend to shape themselves in the same cohesive way. As she sits in the evening recounting her day or week or month, each incident unfolds like an instalment in a serial. Perhaps to compensate for the flatness of everyday life and the dullness of domesticity, further sapped by the company of a moody and inefficient maid, she heightens the rhetoric. The delay in writing up the final version from her scraps of notes allowed her to see which events held most potential drama.

But the essential difference between a novel and a diary is that the diarist cannot control all the lines her life will take. The essence of an autobiography written in process, while life is still ravelling, is its unfinishedness, its openness to unpredictable twists. L.M. Montgomery was artist enough to be aware that she was working at a loom for which all the threads were not yet given. Her fascination with the unfinished quality of her story counters her despair at the experiences themselves. She turns in on herself, pondering why her life is taking the shape it does and testing strategies for coping. For modern readers, this is part of the appeal of the journal. Montgomery communicates her sense of the mystery of individual action in an open-ended reality, powerful reading for a generation increasingly constrained, bound socially and technologically.

The set pieces in the journal—the bits of gossip worked up into formed stories—are like the design in a tapestry or a quilt, still being added to, its colour balance still being adjusted. Montgomery lived in an imaginative world impelled by female modes of discourse. She was not bound, as a male diarist would be, by androcentric paradigms of self-representation. Her world announced itself in terms very different from those of male, conclusion-oriented thinking. She was always shaping, making over, making up, making do. Nothing is finished in her mind; she is speaking to the journal, out of a moment in process. Long before a thought becomes conscious, the shaping and colouring process begins. She works partly as any woman does in creating or choosing a dress or a roomful of furniture. Learning to choose colours and textures that will set off one's complexion and figure is much more a part of growing up and becoming socialized for girls than for men. L.M. Montgomery's journals set her off as a fascinating persona in her own story, partly because she is adept at both character development and self-presentation.

Not only the individual entries or series of entries, but also the volumes of the journals, contained physically in the legal-sized ledgers she wrote in, aroused her shaping instinct. Each of her volumes begins provocatively; most also round off at the ending. Yet each framing moment maintains the old story teller's element of suspense: "What next?"

She tinkered with the manuscript. In the record of her life, pages are carefully razored out and painstakingly replaced with substitute sheets on which she writes passages to replace those she considered not proper for eyes other than her own. Other passages are heavily inked over; still others are erased and overwritten, probably at a time later than the first period of copying.

She did, then, rework the journals. The question arises: how valid are they as a direct and complete record of her life? The answer is that at every given moment of writing in her journal she presents a truth as she sees it *at that moment*, but that truth may include a distortion of what actually happened, and it may be different from how she saw it earlier. The reshaping adds interest and literary quality, but does not destroy the essential quality of process, of suspense.

Increasingly confident that her diary was a literary creation in itself, she inserted into it at intervals directions to those who would read it in the future: her sons and her descendants, but also a wider audience. She records her own conviction of the worth of her journal:

> This journal is a faithful record of one human being's life
> and so should have a certain literary value. My heirs might
> publish an *abridged volume* after my death, if I do not
> myself do it before (16 April 1922).

But she also accepts the need for some editorial intervention. Several times she speaks directly to those who will eventually publish her life record. With respect to parts of this same entry, she exhorts, "Cut it out, descendants!"

We as editors consider ourselves her "descendants" in the sense that she has contributed powerfully to our moral, intellectual, aesthetic, and emotional fibres, both through her novels and now through the journals. In editing this volume we also had at the outset the advice of a literal "descendant", the late Dr Stuart Macdonald, L.M. Montgomery's son. He suggested that we should "cut out" as much as possible of gratuitous criticism that would hurt living people who were peripheral to her story, otherwise leaving a full record of his mother's life, times, and thoughts. He recognized regretfully that the publication of the journal would affect the privacy of all family members, including his own, but he saw his mother's journals as important social and historical documents.

With the passage of years and the ever-widening interest in L.M. Montgomery's life and works, we have become even more aware than either Montgomery or her son could have been of the value of her journal. It remains as an eminently readable and re-readable document on social, theological, and political life, customs, costumes, marriages, reading habits, games, home decoration, educational practice and technological changes during a pivotal era. It remains also as the amazing record of the life of a complex, sensitive, disturbed, influential woman—gifted with an unmatched power of reporting her society and expressing her self.

A Note on the Text

The original text of the handwritten journals covering this period fills approximately three large legal-sized ledgers written on both sides of the page and illustrated with inserted photographs, most taken by Montgomery herself. This original text (the copy text) has been carefully scrutinized and collated with the abridged typescript which she herself prepared still later in her life. In this present edition, inconsistencies in names and dates have been regularized, and editorial changes are specified in notes at the end of the book. Our notes mention some of her idiosyncrasies of spelling: she always misspells the name of one favourite author, George "Elliot", for instance, and is inconsistent in spelling Scottish names, "McPherson" or "MacPherson". She rarely uses French accents, and she even more rarely places a question mark after a rhetorical question: we have preserved these habits in the text. When Montgomery misquotes (as she does fairly frequently in this section of her journals) we reproduce her versions of the phrasing, to show how her once-extraordinary memory for details was weakening.

Other notes relate to the content; as far as possible they explain allusions and quotations, and place the people and events mentioned in a historical, local, social, theological, or familial context.

As editors of this volume, we have continued the same process of selection that we used in the previous two volumes. We have preserved all the narrative lines which Montgomery has been threading through the journals. When cutting non-essential and repetitive materials we have attempted to maintain the narrative flow of Montgomery's rhythms in storytelling. We have added nothing to the words written by Montgomery. We have selected what we consider representative passages, keeping the flavour of the journals as a whole but highlighting material of most general interest. For instance, we have included a minimum of entries in which fatigue and depression result in sentence fragments of the "Had a letter from Stella. Full of complaints as usual" variety. We emphasize that a fuller understanding of Montgomery would of course necessitate recognition of the very qualities of repetitiveness, blurring, and occasional flatness that we have set aside in order to make this volume of selections more accessible for the general reader.

As in the previous volumes, we have dropped many of Montgomery's accounts of her dreams, the catalogues of friends visited in Prince Edward Island and some of her effusions over the landscape there, and the detailed analyses of some of the books she read. We have omitted regretfully some of the threnodies of grief which pour out of each year on the anniversary of Frederica Campbell's death, as well as repeated celebrations of the charm and beauty of the grey-and-white striped cat "Good Luck". We append a list of the entries where material has been excised. All these omitted sections of the journals are of course preserved in the original handwritten text held at the University of Guelph.

Mary Rubio/Elizabeth Waterston

1921

Friday, April 8, 1921
The Manse, Leaskdale, Ont.
We have had a very early spring. This week has been summer-warm; the grass is green and the leaves coming out....Ewan has been pretty well and life has been very stimulating and agreeable.

Tonight I finished Grote's *History of Greece*—twelve volumes. This is the second time I have read it through and I think it will be the last. I shall not be able to spare the time for it again. But I'm glad I've read it twice—though the reading of history always makes me feel somewhat cynical and very dubious as to the "uplift" moments of our time....

Tuesday, April 12, 1921
The Manse, Leaskdale
There is nothing like perseverance. It must be all of twenty years since I wrote a screed of verse called "Premonitions." I've been sending it out at intervals all these years and getting it back. Today a magazine took it; the verses are trash but I've had many no better accepted long ago.

Today we went to Uxbridge to attend the induction of Mr. Bennie, the new minister. When I came here Mr. Fraser was minister in Uxbridge. He was a widower, with a small son and daughter, a middle-aged man, slightly lame, very clever and well-read. We have always been good friends and he has often been here. I always enjoyed his visits. Despite his cleverness, he had no charm and he somehow mopped up all the conversation himself. He not only talked a great deal but he left his hearers with nothing to say. Yet I liked him very well and always liked to see him come. He was very much interested in Frede at one time but she did not respond and so nothing came of it. He has somehow been linked with our life here during the past nine years. But last fall he did a mean thing— mean from a professional point of view as well as a personal one.

He resigned from Uxbridge in the spring, but his resignation was not to take effect until the end of the year. This left him free to "candidate" when and where he wished. He preached in a great many vacancies but no call came. This was rather odd; but I suppose his lameness and widowerhood were rather against him.

Last fall the congregation of Columbus and Brooklyn became vacant. Ewan asked the moderator for a Sunday and was given the last one of the leet. He preached, made a good impression, and it was reasonably certain that he would get the call. We were both pleased. It is not an easy thing for a settled minister to get away "to preach for a call." I have always felt satisfied in Leaskdale and never hankered for a change. But Ewan has not been contented here for some time, owing mainly to the unsatisfactory conditions in Zephyr. And as he was anxious to make a change I was very glad that we had the chance of going to a place we would like. There was a nice large manse and it was near Whitby. Besides, I have always had a feeling that if Ewan got a call to a place he liked he might get quite well. Looking back over his attacks I find that they have always come on suddenly when he was disappointed or homesick. Evidently his disappointment and loneliness were repressed into his subconscious mind and began playing tricks with his nerves, as psycho-analysis has recently discovered such things do. Two years ago Ewan preached in Pinkerton and Priceville. Priceville did not call him: Pinkerton wanted to but after being there he did not like it and declined. But all the same he was disappointed that his efforts had been fruitless and a few weeks later I am convinced that his suppressed disappointment brought on his last and worst attack. If he were now to get a call to a place he liked this old rankling disappointment might be rooted out and he would be perfectly well.

We had never thought of Fraser trying for Columbus and Brooklyn. It was not in his "class," being a straggling double rural charge. Besides, he knew Ewan was trying for it. But he wrote and asked the moderator for a day and when the moderator refused, saying that it was not a congregation he would really like, Fraser wrote again and *pleaded* for a Sunday. Also, he got it.

From the time I heard Fraser was to preach there I lost all hope of Ewan getting the call. For Fraser can preach quite brilliantly when he likes. He got the call—and accepted it.

Ewan and I resented his behavior very keenly and we did not try to hide from him the fact that we thought he had behaved very meanly and unkindly towards us. As a result we parted very coolly. It hurt me a little and has left a bit of a soreness. As for Fraser, he felt *galled*. It hurt his pride woefully to be the rival of Ewan for a little country charge. The whole affair is one of those things that leave a bruise—as if our past friendship and social hours had all been stained and discolored by it.

As for the Bennies I don't think I shall find either of them at all congenial. I dislike him; and she is a pretty, dull girl.

I have been reading May Sinclair's *Mary Oliver* and *The Romantic*. *Mary* is a strong gripping book without a particle of charm or atmosphere and defaced by some disagreeable mannerisms. Life can have neither charm nor atmosphere when you strip it to the bare bones. As for *The Romantic* it is a disagreeable, unnecessary piece of work, and it is hard to see just why anybody should have written it or wanted to write it—unless to show the difference—the unfathomable gulf—between the heroines of the Victorian age and the "heroines" of today. Certainly there is some difference between "Amelia" and "Charlotte Redhead"—even between "Jane Eyre" and "Charlotte." But at least "Amelia" was sweet and "Jane Eyre" vivid and womanly while "Charlotte" is something you wouldn't like to have around—and all Miss Sinclair's cleverness can't alter the fact.

Sunday, April 17, 1921
The Manse, Leaskdale

Yesterday was an abominable day—inside and out. Outdoors, it was bitterly cold, with an ice-storm—a return of winter entirely unexpected after the two weeks of summer we've had—weeks that have brought the leaves out and turned the fields green.

Inside matters were worse. Lily flew into an utterly unprovoked and unjustifiable tantrum this morning and was insolent and absurd. I felt that the time had come when she must be taught a lesson. I rebuked her sharply and ignored her absolutely for the rest of the day. It made me unhappy—I cannot bear to be "out" with anyone in the house with me. It poisons everything. But I held out resolutely for I knew if I thawed too soon she would not be taught the necessary lesson. I think she *has* learned it and will be careful for a time at least not to make a similar mistake. But these things blister my soul somehow.

Today was cold, with the world coated in ice—trees, ground, everything. We seem to have been pitchforked bodily back into winter.

Thursday, April 21, 1921
Leaskdale, Ont.

Today I carried about 1,200 books out of the library into the parlor—preparatory to cleaning the room. This left me by nightfall feeling that the world was a wilderness of woe. But after I got the boys to bed I curled up on my own bed with a bag of chocolates and read *The Tiger In The House* until I forgot all about the woes of the flesh. It's a very fascinating book, all about cats by a man who loves them. Some of it made my blood run cold.

Grandfather and Grandmother hated cats. I always loved them. Just where I got my fondness for them would be hard to say since my "forbears" on both sides, back to the third generation at least, detested them. But love them I did; and I was also convinced that it was very reprehensible in me to love them, since Grandfather and Grandmother condemned them so harshly, that I felt it was somehow a shameful thing to find pleasure in pussies. Nevertheless I went on loving them and love them to this day. Yet I have never been able quite to throw off a sort of apologetic attitude regarding my affection for them. I always say I like cats a little defiantly, as if I were adding in effect—"and I don't care if you do think it disgraceful."

As for those people who say they "like cats in their place" I know *all* about them from that one phrase!

Having had it so grained into me in youth that a love for cats betokened utter depravity and weakness of intellect, I was rather surprised and pleased to learn from *The Tiger In The House* how many eminent and admirable individuals of both sexes were lovers of puss—Petrarch, Mohammed, Cardinal Richelieu, Chateaubriand, Zola, Dr. Johnson, Dickens, Victor Hugo, Sir Walter Scott, Montaigne, Charlotte Brontë, Carlyle (I have a better opinion of Carlyle than I ever had before), Walter Pater, Andrew Lang, Edgar Allan Poe, Mark Twain, Sara Orne Jewett, Mary E. Wilkins and many more. Verily, 'tis no company to be ashamed of.

4

I miss Daffy this spring. When he died last summer I thought I could never care for another pussy. Yet, as Samuel Butler says, I have "catted" again. I am becoming fond of the boys' *Paddy* and find pleasure in him. Yet he will never have the personality of Daff. Daffy never got over the Bubastis habit of godship. Pat is a nice puss but he has forgotten the worship of the Nile.

Sunday, May 1, 1921
Leaskdale, Ont.
....On Wednesday I went to London and was the guest of Mrs. Dr. Hughes during my stay there. On Thursday I lunched with Mrs. MacGregor ("Marian Keith") and Miss Wilson (Anison North), then had a motor drive round London which is a clean, pretty, tree-y town. Then I gave readings to the Canadian Club, got a bouquet of roses, went to the Girls' Canadian Club in the evening and read to them and got another bouquet of roses. Then went to the home of Miss Grace Blackburn, a clever journalist, to meet the Woman's Press Club, and got another bouquet of daffodils and narcissus.

I admit I enjoy these excursions very much. I am always treated beautifully and meet many clever and interesting women, besides seeing the different parts of the country.

That evening at the Press Club I happened to say of some book that I "always read it when I felt blue and despondent."

"Oh," said Miss Blackburn, "I do not believe you ever feel blue or despondent. You are too full of humor and philosophy."

I wonder what she would think if she could read some of the pages of this journal. But perhaps it may be accounted unto me for righteousness that I confine my blues to my journal and don't scatter them abroad in my household or community.

I came back to Toronto Friday, in a pouring rain, shopped all day Saturday and came home in the evening to find that Ewan had sold our Chevrolet car and bought a new Gray-Dort. It's a very nice car.

Saturday, May 8, 1921
The Manse, Leaskdale
Cleaned house all week and are through all but kitchen—for which I'm glad. Housecleaning has been unpleasant this year owing to Lily's grouchiness, and doubly hard because of her inability to systematize her work, or let me systematize it for her.

Friday was a lovely day. Captain Smith called and I went down with him to Whitby. We motored through a spring world of young leaf and blossom and had a wonderful drive. In the evening I gave a programme of readings to the girls in the Ladies' College and there was a little reception afterwards and we all had a very nice time.

Ewan and the boys came down this morning for me and we motored home, to find Lily crankier than ever and full of complaints. I can't decide whether the girl is really sick or not. By times I think she is; but she is always able to go out on the road or to a dance, no matter how much she has complained through the day, so I believe her malady is mainly nervous, induced by her secret bitterness and disappointment.

I have been reading Scott's *Betrothed* this week. It is one of his poorest novels. But I was struck by his immeasurable superiority to the novel-writers of today—even those who are acclaimed as the strongest and most virile. Compared to Scott they seem like a feverish nightmare of unrest and chaos. To go from them to him is to go to sanity and breadth and perspective. The novel-writers of today have no perspective. They will spend pages describing a character's

"Captain Smith"

Ontario Ladies' College

passing emotion of lust and greed—as if lust and greed were something uncommon, instead of being passions we all experience more or less all through our mature lives.

Stuart and Chester were gathering trilliums today and brought me big bunches of them. Stuart is especially thoughtful about bringing me posies. He is very fond of flowers. Chester does not care much for them I think.

Wednesday, May 11, 1921
The Manse, Leaskdale
Captain Smith was here tonight. Our plans for summer vacation have assumed a definite form. We have decided to motor down East and the Smiths are going too in their car. I am not very enthusiastic about it. It is a long distance to motor and I think I will be frightfully tired. I can imagine an auto trip being very delightful under certain conditions but these conditions will all be absent in this case.

Had a letter from Stokes today re my new book-series. I suggested calling it *The New Moon Series*, making the first book *Emily of New Moon*. They like the idea but want "a more attractive name than Emily." I have written them my ultimatum on this. "Emily" is a quaint, delightful name, and hasn't been worn threadbare in recent fiction as almost every other name has. Besides, my heroine *is* Emily, just as Anne was Anne. She has been "Emily" for the past ten years during which time I have been carrying her in my mind, waiting for the time when I could put her into a book. She has "grown" just as "Anne" did and so ought to be just as well-beloved. And "Emily" she shall remain.

Monday, May 16, 1921
Leaskdale, Ont.
Ewan has had another attack. He has been pretty well ever since early in April. He has not been so well since that interval in the fall of 1919. Once more, in spite of past experience, I let myself hope that his recovery was permanent. But he is very bad just at present—restless and melancholy. I seem to have grown *hardened* to it and don't worry over it quite as much as I used to. But my heart sinks at the idea of a third summer like the last two. Our trip down East will be no pleasure to either of us if he is like he was last summer, poor fellow. What an awful curse melancholia is to all concerned! I cringe sometimes with the fear that Chester or Stuart may inherit the tendency—especially the former, who resembles his father very strongly in physical appearance. He is subject to occasional headaches and this worries me. But they seem to be connected with his stomach and to be more like my sick headaches. They disappear after he vomits. So very likely they indicate nothing worse than some digestive disturbance. Yet I will always have my little secret dread.

I had a letter from Stell today—the first cheerful epistle for many moons. She is out of her troubles—or fancies she is. The U.S. Gov't is going to lend money to the soldiers to give them a start, so Lowry and she expect to get a loan, repay me, and make a fortune out of the rest. I shall be very glad if it is so; but I'll wait until I see the cash before rejoicing. Stell has been going to do wonders so many times. Poor old Stell! But she's one of the "old gang"—and there are not so many of us left.

Wednesday, May 18, 1921
The Manse, Leaskdale
I wonder if I shall ever again have a pleasant spring. Since 1914 I have not known one. Every spring of the war was an anguish of suspense and worry; and when the war was over Ewan's malady has darkened every spring since. Poor fellow, he is good and kind and never did wilful harm or wrong to anyone in his life. Yet he is most miserable. Yes, it is weakness that suffers in this world—not wickedness.

But I suppose I am inclined to take the gloomiest view of everything tonight, for this has been a hard day. Ewan could not sleep at all last night and has been very bad all day—nearly as bad as any attack yet I think. Then Lily was exceedingly cranky all day—for no reason at all that I could see—except that the cistern pump was acting badly, which was nobody's fault and inconvenienced us all as much as it did her.

Ewan and I went to Quaker Hill manse for tea, as we had promised to. The Millers are bores, I was physically wretched with a cold in the head and Ewan was so dull that everything dragged. Then we came home and went to Guild. The subject tonight was a literary one—"Masterpieces of Poetry." I had arranged a good programme but Lord ha' mercy! How those masterpieces were murdered by the readers thereof. It was agony to sit and listen. What are the public schools of Ontario about that they turn out such readers? The meaning of the poems was wholly lost and not a creature there was any the better or wiser in any way for them.

I came home alone through a night of magic spring moonlight and sought refuge from unhappy realities and vexations in imagining something very wonderful and delightful and impossible. It kept me from ending up my day with a fit of tears and I'll go to bed now and sleep.

Tuesday, May 31, 1921
The Manse, Leaskdale
....Tonight was cool and I had a very happy evening—one of the kind I delight in. I spent it on the lawn setting out my geranium bed. It was clear and cool, with a beautiful sunset behind the trees. Stuart and Chester were delightedly mowing the lawn which they consider great fun. Neighbors passed by and called greetings over the gate. Ewan strolled about and seemed fairly cheerful. It was so delightful that I wondered what I would have to pay for it.

Thursday, June 16, 1921
We had a terrible accident last Sunday. It might have been a thousand-fold worse. I am thankful we escaped as we did. But it was horrible—horrible. This is the first day I have felt at all like myself.

We went to Zephyr last Sunday afternoon—Ewan, the boys and I. After service Mrs. Jake Meyers asked us to go there to tea and she and her little girl got in behind with Stuart and me. Ewan and Chester were in the front seat. We stopped at the garage for gas. After we pulled out from the tank Ewan turned to cut the corner. Then I looked up and saw a car in the middle of the road and going very fast—Marshall Pickering's car, as it turned out. I said to Ewan "Look out for that car" but it seems he did not hear me. Neither did he see the car, although it was right in front of us and only a few yards away. *He turned northwest across the road in front of the oncoming car*, meaning to turn up the side road.

Why he did such a thing without looking to see if the road was clear is inexplicable, unless—unless—oh, I fear that his mind was so fastened on the one gloomy idea of his melancholy dread that he was not thinking about anything else. Too late he saw the other car. There was one awful moment when I saw that a collision was inevitable and felt that it was impossible to escape without someone being killed. Then the cars crashed together.

What saved us was the fact that we were still on low gear and going very slow. The whole thing was like a nightmare. There was a tremendous crash, the sound of breaking glass—screams—then the cars were still. I said, "Thank God, nobody is killed." Then I sat there in a curious kind of numbness. Our new car was badly done up—the Pickering car was worse—Mrs. Pickering was being taken out her face bleeding from a cut on the windshield—which looked very bad though it afterwards turned out to be very slight—and yet all that I was worrying over was how Mrs. Meyers and her little girl were to get home!

The sight of the blood on Mrs. Pickering's face broke up this abnormal calm. I began to cry and shake. Mrs. Law took me up to her house and I stayed there an hour and cried all the time—just nervous crying that I couldn't stop. Mr. Law brought us home and I went to bed and stayed there for two days unable to eat or sleep.

The damage done our car has been fixed up—axle straightened, new fender and lamp post put on. But the affair has left me very nervous and I fear has spoiled my summer. I can't go in the car again without fear of another accident. For if Ewan did not see that car simply because of his obsession the same thing or worse may happen again.

Of course Marshall Pickering was equally to blame. He is notorious as a speeder and road-hog. If he had been on his own side of the road as he should have been—since according to his own admission he saw our car in plenty of time to turn out—nothing would have happened. We would have crossed to the sideroad behind him. But when I recall that moment when, as it seemed to me, Ewan turned our car deliberately across before that other car in plain sight—oh, I thought he had gone violently insane at last and was taking us all to destruction with him.

I am sick of the talk it has made. Everywhere we go we have to talk of it and explain. A hundred exaggerated reports have gone abroad concerning it. This is the third nasty automobile accident I have been in and I feel as if I had had enough.

Sunday, July 3, 1921
Leaskdale, Ont.

The last two weeks of June were dreadfully hot. I have been very busy. All the boys' clothes had to be got in order for our trip. I weeded the garden for the fourth time from one end to the other. We had men here putting a cement floor in the garage. Stuart ran a rusty nail in his foot and was laid up for three days. There was a Sunday School picnic. I had cherries and strawberries to preserve. Lily has been in a vile temper most of the time—and the heat day and night has been dreadful. Nevertheless, I have felt well and cheerful also, since Ewan has been pretty well. We leave tomorrow night on our long drive. Goodness knows how we'll get along. Chester and Stuart are wild with delight and anticipation. Nothing clouds their horizon, thanks be. I hope we'll strike a cooler zone erelong.

Yesterday I finished reading Dr. Prince's *Dissociation of a Personality*. It is one of the most fascinating, extraordinary and illuminating books I have ever read. Today I began to read *Human Personality and Its Survival of Bodily Death*. I am intensely interested in these psychical subjects.

I hate to leave my garden. It is just coming into bloom and is the first good garden I have had for three years since it was neither washed out nor given over to weeds because of my absence. I shall miss all its best. Lily is supposed to keep it weeded but goodness knows whether she will or not. She was in a terrible temper yesterday forenoon but is quite amiable today.

Thursday, Aug. 11, 1921
The Manse, Leaskdale

We got home last Friday after what was, on the whole, a disapointing trip—at least, to me. There were a few odd hours and days of enjoyment in it but not enough to make up for the many that were downright miserable. It seemed to me that almost every day brought something that spoiled it; I was very tired and never seemed to get really rested; and the obligation we were under to be back by a certain date compelled us to "make" so many miles per day and so spoiled our pleasure to a great extent.

Monday July 4th, was exceedingly hot and exceedingly busy. I packed, put the house in order and made all the final arrangements. After tea we motored to Whitby and spent the night at Capt. Smith's....

When we reached Boston the Smith party went to their friends and we went on to Braintree. I was almost exhausted when we got to Flora's but a cool lovely breeze blew up in the evening and I looked forward to a good sleep and a pleasant, restful visit. It was not to be. East Braintree is certainly a place of evil omen for me. Nothing good can come out of it.

To begin with, that night there happened the worst electric storm that has been known in New England since 1837. I never saw anything like it. Sleep was impossible. The house next Aunt Flora's was struck. One could have read by the incessant glare of the lightning, and the crash of thunder was continuous. It lasted all night and rained at intervals all day Saturday.

Saturday forenoon I washed out our laundry. After dinner Ewan said he was going to take the car to a garage for overhauling and the boys wanted to go with him. I ought not to have let them go—I knew well enough that Ewan, when getting anything done to the car, pays no attention to anything else. But Flora was going, too—the garage was just at the foot of the hill, and I was woefully tired and wanted to get a little rest that afternoon if it were possible. So I let them go.

"Breakfast on the road" [Captain and Mrs. Edwin Smith, Mr. and Mrs. Alonzo Smith, Ewan Macdonald and boys]

About an hour or so later I went to the street door and to my amazement found Stuart there, playing with a neighbor's boy. I asked him where Chester was and he said, "Oh, just down the hill." I supposed Chester had stayed with his father at the garage and thought no more about it. The afternoon went by—it began to rain heavily again and thunder growled ominously. Just before six I heard the car and the next minute Ewan and Flora rushed in, demanding,

"Are the boys here?"

I stared at them in amazement.

"Stuart is here," I said. "Where is Chester?"

They gasped out a tale that almost made my heart stop. Not finding the garage at the foot of the hill up to requirements, they had gone to Quincy, two and a half miles away. While there they had suddenly missed the children. Search proved fruitless. They had been searching frantically for an hour, then had come home in desperation.

We hastened to question Stuart. His tale was as follows:—

He and Chester had grown tired waiting round the garage and wanted to come home. They had told their father so, and started. Ewan had not heard or noticed them. The extraordinary thing is that those two boys, one only nine and the other not yet six, *did* find their way home over two and a half miles of thronged and twisted city streets which they had only traversed once and that in a car. They got to the street at the foot of the hill and here Chester made his first mistake and went on round a curve of the East Weymouth road. Stuart was lagging behind and turned up the right street and came home, thinking Chester would soon be after him.

This was all. *Where was Chester?* It was growing dark and beginning to pour in torrents. I was nearly crazy. I could do nothing—except walk the floor! Taking one time with another I must have walked a hundred miles on the floor of that Braintree bungalow.

Amos, who was nettled over the bother of it all, vexed because his supper was delayed, and who has no liking for nor patience with children, remarked sharply that Chester ought to be whipped within an inch of his life. I retorted that such would be a sufficient punishment if Chester had set fire to the house. Flora was upset because her heart is weak. Ewan was distracted—though the real trouble pulled him out of his melancholy rut of brooding over unpardonable sins for the time being, so that he was quite well for a week.

The police of Braintree, Quincy and Weymouth were notified. The East Braintree men organized themselves into a posse to comb the streets. Ewan went to a small store below the hill and found that Chester had been seen passing it, apparently on the way back to Quincy, about half an hour before. When I heard this I said,

"If Chester found his way home from Quincy he is not lost. I know what has happened. When he looked back and saw that Stuart was not in sight he would go back to look for him and not finding him would think he was lost. He would be afraid to come home without Stuart. He is looking for Stuart and won't come home without him."

Ewan decided to go back to Quincy and see if he could find Chester on the road. Back he went—I walked the floor. Half an hour passed—it was pitch dark—it was pouring rain. I pictured my poor little son, lost, terrified, broken–hearted over Stuart, wandering about in strange streets, not knowing where to go. For Chester is such an odd, independent little chap that he would never stop anybody and ask to be shown the road home.

Then Ewan returned—*with Chester*. The poor child had gone all the way back to the Quincy garage to get his father to come and find Stuart. The garage man at once 'phoned the police station and a policeman came and took him over.

I was so thankful I cried; but that night I couldn't sleep again after the worry and excitement. I had seen Chester, in imagination, crushed beneath the wheels of a motor car.

We left next day after dinner, met the Smiths at the State House and set out for Portland. That afternoon was delightful—one of the few times when I really enjoyed the journey. It was deliciously cool and gray; the road was splendid and much of it was along the New England coast where the Atlantic waves were rolling in in great gray misty breakers.

But our luck did not last. Just at dark, when we were about six miles from Portland it began to rain heavily—and our lights went out! Ewan had to get out and put a new fuse in. I had to get out and hold the flashlight. I got soaked to the skin and arrived at Portland with ruined hat and clothes, very disgruntled.

The next day went fairly well until we reached Belfast. Then we got separated from the Smiths and passed them owing to their taking a wrong road. We had to make a long detour over a terrible mountain road. Fortunately, we *did* get over it, crossed Bucksport Ferry, and an hour later got to Ellsworth—and found no sign of the Smiths. And then our car broke down! Some of the interior mechanism connected with the clutch had been broken on that dreadful road. There we had to stay. The Smith party turned up. We refused to let them wait for us, as they could not help us and it would only worry us to feel we were holding them up, too. So, in the end they went on. We had to stay there nearly two days. It was a dull little town and the time seemed endless. But at last at two o'clock Wednesday, we got away and had a pleasant drive to St. Stephen's, New Brunswick, which we reached a little after eight Wednesday evening. We found out that the last boat left Cape Tormentine for the Island at 7.30 o'clock P.M. and Ewan said he believed we could catch it if I could be ready to start at 5.30. I *was* ready. We left in a fog cold enough to freeze the marrow. We had an *awful* road to St. John. Most of it was under construction and we *wallowed* through miles of gravel and had constant trouble with our clutch. From St. John on the road was quite good and we literally tore across New Brunswick. It grew very hot and terribly dusty. Chester developed a headache. But on we rushed. We reached Sackville at seven and discovered we had a punctured tire! I was so tired that I was really pleased.

I went to the hotel and asked for a room with a bath. The clerk did not *say* but he *looked* "You need it." I certainly did. Never in my life did I look so disreputable. My hair was hanging in strings around my neck and I was gray with dust from head to foot. But I got my bath room. I got Chester bathed and dosed and put to bed—then Stuart—then myself. I got a good sleep—there was a nice rain in the night—and the world was quite a different place in the morning.

We had a delightful run down to the Cape. It was cool and dustless and pleasant. When we got to Point Borden we motored up to Breadalbane. The roads—the dear old red roads—were very bad after the recent rain; but they were the Island roads, green-bordered, vivid, and lovely....we went out to Winsloe and had tea with Mary Campbell. I have not seen Mary for eight years. They have moved to Winsloe, since then and have a very nice place. Mary looks old—thin and pale and gray. She has not had a very happy life I think. Maud Beaton is eighteen, very tall, and quite nice-looking, though not pretty, and a nice girl.

We had a dear drive up to Alec Macneill's that evening over the old "town road" I knew so well in childhood. It was cool, and a gray mist came in from the sea on the wings of the north easter. When we got to Alec's and I went up to put the children to bed the same north easter was keening around the eaves and down below on the shore was the boom of the surf. How I loved that sonorous old music—how I loved that windy, dark-gray night on the old north shore.

We stayed till Friday night at Alec's and at Myrtle's till Sunday night. There were pleasant things in those four days but we had too many people to visit and we all got tired and disgruntled. We had some good hours at Alec's. May

[The Webb family (clockwise): Mrs. Myrtle Webb, baby Pauline, Marion,
Mr. Ernest Webb, Keith Webb, Chester Macdonald,
Lorraine Webb, Stuart Macdonald, Anita Webb]

cooked us the most gorgeous meals and we sat and talked and laughed over them—really, they were the pleasantest parts of our stay. We saw changes everywhere—in people and places. It hurts. But I suppose if there were never any change there would be no progress. And we would probably in time get bored with the everlasting sameness. Just the same—it *does* hurt.

Next morning I walked through Lover's Lane. Alas—alas! Lover's Lane has grown old. That I should have to say it! It hurt—oh, how it hurt. It is three years since I saw it in summer and it had changed more in those three years than in all the years of my remembrance. So many of the trees have died. And all the spruces which were young and green a few years ago have grown so tall that their lower boughs along the lane are dead. The woods around it are growing thin, too. I suppose the dry summer has also robbed it of some beauty there was no growth of fern or waving grass to cloak the bareness. I came back—and I did not go again.

We went over to Park Corner Sunday night and stayed there until Thursday. I had a rest and many pleasant hours. But, as everywhere else on the Island, there was an undercurrent of worry and misery because of Ewan's malady. His melancholy and restlessness returned soon after we got to the Island and clouded all our time there. In company he generally brightened up and talked with some cheerfulness; but I knew that all the time he was troubled with that wretched obsession of guilt and punishment. The only time he seemed free from it was when we were in the car. The necessity of concentrating his mind on the business of driving banished for a time his haunting spectre of worry and his headaches ceased.

Oh, how I missed Frede at Park Corner! The last summer I was there she was, too. Somehow, I missed her even more than last fall. She seemed to belong to Park Corner in summer time. Oh, Frede, dear old comrade, whither have you strayed? Do you still *know*—and understand?

Aunt Annie is wonderfully smart and energetic. Dan is almost grown up. He is smart, too, and seems to be taking an interest in the place. Chester and Stuart had a glorious time at Park Corner. They "ring in" with their cousins and enjoy

[Stuart Macdonald and Maudie Campbell]

playing with them. They "got on" very well with the Webb children but never seemed to have very much fun with them. How the house and yard are ringing with shouts and laughter from morning to night—just as they rang years ago for other children!

Thursday, July 28, we went to Breadalbane and stayed all night with the Stirlings. We left at six the next morning and had a lovely drive to Borden. I hated to leave the Island—somehow I had a nasty feeling that it would be long ere I saw it again. I have learned to shrink from these presentiments. Too many of them have come true.

We met Capt. and Mrs. Smith at Sackville....We got to St. John that night and stayed with Dr. and Mrs. Mahoney—the latter being "little Maudie Estey" of the old Bideford days. She is anything but little now—a big, fat, "sonsy" woman of 160 lbs. I couldn't see any resemblance to the little pale, fairylike maiden of long ago. Mrs. Estey was there, too, and we had a gay evening. Next day we motored up the St. John river to Woodstock where I arrived sinfully tired, partly because of bad roads, partly because of constant worry over the car, which didn't act right, partly too, because Ewan was morose and contrary. This is a phase of his malady, of course, and it spoiled all pleasure in the day for me.

Things were better next day. It was cool and pleasant and most of our road was through the wonderful pine woods of Maine. I never tired of them....I was thankful to get...back to work after my disappointing trip. Lily was here—didn't seem overjoyed to see us. I suppose she didn't like the idea of getting down to work under a mistress again. Perhaps that is natural enough but she need not have vented it on us. I am not responsible for the fact that she has to work out. I give her good wages and much consideration. She is treated like one of the family. So I thought I hardly deserved my cool reception. As for poor Chester, he wasn't out of the car before she began heckling him and she did not speak a kind word either to him or Stuart. She has not been quite so cranky since we came back, however, but even more untidy, "feckless" and gadding. Her work is never done on time or completely. Something is always at loose ends—everything in a muddle. When she first came she was willing to let me plan out the work but now she resents this and rather than have her in a temper I let her alone. But the result is a fearful muddle as a rule.

I was ill for three days after getting home with stomach and bowel trouble. Since then I've got settled down again. In the evenings I have been copying my old journal of the summer of Chester's birth. It hurt me. I was so happy then. Frede was here and I had my dear little chubby baby and Ewan was well. Those two years after Chester's birth were the happiest of my life. After that the war came and the loss of dear "little Hugh"; and when the war was over Frede died and life changed forever; and then Ewan's malady came upon him and all happiness left my life. I do not suppose it will ever return. Sometimes Ewan is so much better that I almost think he is as he used to be. But as I wrote over that old journal I realized how unlike his old self he is, even in the days when his trouble grows lighter. It is only in contrast with his dark days that he seems well.

Wednesday, Aug. 17, 1921
Leaskdale, Ont.
This has been a miserable sort of day, so I come to my old journal to get it out of my system. I really feel blue and discouraged. It poured rain all day. Ewan was terribly miserable. Lily was cranky. Then I had a letter from Mr. Rollins with a copy of the Master's report which was on the whole decidedly adverse. I never expected anything else, after the false statements sworn to by the Pages, yet the injustice of it all hurt me. Of course the Judge has to pronounce on the case yet but it is not at all likely he will reverse the Master's findings. Rollins sent another bill for $3,000. Six thousand so far thrown away for nothing. And the end is not yet.

One cheering item in his letter, however, was that the Page suit against me was dismissed August 11th on the ground that it was illegal. French threatens to carry it to the Supreme Court. I suppose he does not like to rest under the imputation of doing an illegal thing.

Yes, I'm blue!

Thursday, Aug. 18, 1921
The Manse, Leaskdale

I had a bad night—couldn't sleep. But I feel a bit pluckier today, though I couldn't settle down to writing. Had a letter from McClelland. He is going to give *Rilla* to Hodder and Stoughton in England, Constable not having "measured up." I hate changing publishers like this.

Hattie Harrison and her mother were here to tea tonight. The mother is a very sweet and quite brainy little old lady whom I have always liked. When I went up to the spare room with her she put her arms around me and said,

"Mrs. Macdonald, you have done a great deal for our little church."

I was touched and pleased—and surprised. For in all the ten years I have been here and hard as I have worked in all the societies no living soul has ever said to me a word of similar appreciation. It has often hurt—but among other deeper pangs did not seem worth noticing.

"And you always seem so bright and happy that it heartens us up to see you," she went on.

Happy! With my heart wrung as it is! With a constant ache of loneliness in my being. With no one to help me guide and train and control my sons! With my husband at that very moment lying on his bed, gazing at the ceiling and worrying over having committed the unpardonable sin! Well, I must be a good actress. I wonder how many

[Frontispiece from Rilla of Ingleside*]*

other women I know, who seem "bright and happy," have likewise a closet full of skeletons. Plenty of them, I daresay.

Yet today was not wholly unpleasant. After the Harrisons went away I coaxed Ewan to go out for a little drive to call on some sick people. As always when in the car he brightened up and was better. It was a perfect evening—clear, sunset-lit and cool, with a big lucent "harvest moon" floating over the golden fields. For a little while I forgot care and enjoyed it.

Saturday, Aug. 20, 1921
The Manse, Leaskdale

This morning I wrote the first chapter of my new book—*Emily of New Moon*. It ought to be good. "Emily" is a dear little soul and I have some good experiences waiting for her. And it is such a relief to be done of the "Anne gang." I had gone so stale on them....

Saturday, Sept. 3, 1921
Rilla of Ingleside came today—my eleventh book! It looks very well. I don't suppose it will be much of a success, for the public are said to be sick of anything connected with the war. But at least I did my best to reflect the life we lived in Canada during those four years. It is dedicated to Frede's memory. I wish she could have read it. It is the first one I have written with a purpose....

Sunday, Sept. 11, 1921
Leaskdale, Ont.
Another busy week, with much strain. It has been unseasonably hot for September—hot as many Julys. Monday was a muggy day. Ewan and I went to Cannington and had dinner with the Kennedys. In the evening we went to Woodville to the opening services of the new church there. The programme didn't begin till nine and continued till twelve. We didn't get home till nearly two. Mr. Fraser came with us—the first time he has been here since he left Uxbridge. I made no difference and he appeared to make none; but I shall never feel the same to him again. He behaved contemptibly in that matter.

I got the men a lunch and we got to bed at three. Got up early as Fraser had to be taken to Uxbridge. Chester began school again. There is a new teacher—I hope she will be better than the former. All the teachers they ever get here are inexperienced girls of sixteen or seventeen. Yet they are paid a thousand dollars a year. I taught school for $180 a year plus $10—"supplement." Well, "the world do move"—also prices. On Wednesday Miss Mitchell came to address the W.M.S. at Zephyr and was here all night. Mr. Curtiss of Uxbridge came up to give a talk to the Guild and I got lunch for him after it—and then had the only pleasant thing this week—an hour's chat with intelligent people as we sat over our cake and cocoa.

Thursday was a hard day. I had a nasty cold in my head, Ewan developed the opening symptoms of another attack of melancholia and I felt blue and discouraged, also a little worried over Chester's operation on the morrow.

Friday Dr. Shier came up and removed Chester's tonsils. When Chester was three years old Dr. Shier told me he had enlarged tonsils. But he was too young then to have them removed and as Ewan was much opposed to the operation nothing has been done. They have never seemed to trouble him—he never has sore throats or anything like that. But lately the increasing frequency of his headaches has led me to wonder if his diseased tonsils might be causing it. Shier said not, but thought the operation should be performed as one side of his throat was almost closed. So I prevailed on Ewan to consent and it was done on Friday morning. I stood by and watched it—which shows how much my nerves have improved since two years ago when Chester had to have chloroform for his eyes. Well, they have—thanks to vitamins. Ewan tried to watch, but broke down, cried, and started a headache. Chester was found to have some adenoids also. Miss Payne, the nurse, stayed till yesterday morning. Chester was plucky and patient. His stomach was not settled until yesterday at noon. Today he is up and about, eating as usual. I am glad it is over....

Tonight I am alone. The boys are in bed. I feel lonely and depressed. I am sitting in the dining room. Outside in the September darkness the crickets are chirping. It is close and muggy. I wish somebody would come in and make me laugh. But there is nobody to come in. There isn't a single interesting person in this village—not one who makes you feel better just because of a chat. I really never saw such a collection of stupid, uninteresting people. They know nothing but gossip and malicious gossip at that. They are all old or elderly, not only in body but in mind—old maids or retired farmers and farmeresses. When I am feeling normal I suffer them gladly and find some amusement in their very stupidity but when I'm below par I'd like to blow them all up with gunpowder.

Saturday, October 1, 1921
The Manse, Leaskdale

I have had a fortnight so quiet and orderly that it has seemed uncanny. On September 17th Lily went away for her fortnight's vacation and the next day Ewan left for a motor trip to Warsaw to visit his brother Angus. Monro of Cannington went with him. The boys and I were left alone.

The first thing I did was to put everything in complete order, especially the kitchen and pantry—which under Lily's regime are commonly in awful disorder. I keep the rest of the house fairly tidy but I haven't time for the kitchen and if I had Lily would resent it. But by Monday night everything was in order. Then I mapped out my work on a system and followed it. As a result it was all done early every day leaving me from three o'clock free. There was no "visiting" to do—or endure—I went nowhere—nobody came. I could read or sew or dream. And I've had a glorious two weeks of it. It was lovely to have no alien about— and a cranky alien at that. I can't do without a maid—but I wish I could. But at least I've had two good weeks without one. Lily at present is laid up with tonsillitis and can't come back for another week. It is such a full week that I must have help, so I've got a young girl to come and help out.

Ewan returned Thursday. He had a good trip and seems very well. He has been well every fall for awhile so probably it will be the same way this year. It is a relief to have him well even for a few weeks. And what a relief it must be for him to be free from that torturing fear of "eternal damnation." I do not think normal people, who are not the victims of such a delusion, can have any real idea of the full horror of it.

I am keeping one eye on my writing and the other on the filling for my lemon pie. Which reminds me of a compliment I got last Sunday—an Englishman's compliment and such as only an Englishman could pay. We had Dr. Schofield supplying last Sunday—a medical missionary from Korea—a clever tactless man who certainly isn't afraid of man or devil. He seemed to have the Englishman's customary contempt of crude colonials, but when he had eaten his section of lemon pie at dinner he said,

"Well, *at least*, you certainly do know how to make lemon pie."

The italics are mine!

I remember that the only compliment Uncle Leander ever paid me in his life was to say that my lemon pies couldn't be beat. Who says that the way to a man's heart *isn't* through his stomach? I might have talked with the tongues of men and angels—I didn't—and it would not have extorted approval from Dr. Schofield. But the pie did the trick.

Stuart and Chester were delightfully good those two weeks. Ordinarily Lily rags them so unceasingly that she keeps the poor little monkeys cross and contrary. But they've been lovely. Chester has picked up finely since his operation and is getting rosy and plump again. Stuart is always rosy and plump and adorable. I never saw a sweeter child. He has never from birth given me a moment's care or worry.

Several mornings the two little chaps sneaked down and had the breakfast table set when I came down. Stuart generally set the dinner table for me—and did it beautifully, too.

The reviews of *Rilla* are beginning to come in. So far they are good.

Monday, October 3, 1921
The Manse, Leaskdale
Had my semi-annual report from Stokes today, dealing with sales of *House of Dreams* and *Rainbow Valley*. It's the poorest one I ever got—probably owing to the extreme financial depression in the States, printers' strikes etc. I shall not find it any too easy to get through the winter without drawing on my capital. That three thousand I had to send Rollins would have made a good deal of difference to me if I could have kept it. Well, I never cry over spilt milk; and if I can get along until spring when the *Rilla* reports come in I ought to come through all right.

I had a letter from poor Aunt Annie today full of complaints and groans. I wonder what the Campbell family would do without me to unload their miseries on. I don't mind Aunt Annie doing it. She is old and overworked and *has* a hard time of it. If it is any solace to her to pour out her woes to me she is welcome to do it and I am ready to give what aid and sympathy I can. But Stella and Clara do the same. I never get a letter from either of them which is not full of complaints and grumbles. Yet they are young women with no more worries and troubles than I have or than most people have. And I *do* get tired, amid all my own troubles and anxieties, of their endless shrieks of despair.

But Park Corner was very good to me long ago. So for "old sake's sake" I must try to keep the Park Corner folks now....

Friday, Oct. 7, 1921
This is Stuart's birthday; he is six years old today—six beautiful years. And every year seems to make him smarter and more lovable. And it is not because he is my own child that I think him so. Chester is my own and first-born and exceedingly dear and precious to me. Yet I see qualities in him that may interfere seriously not only with his success in life but with his happiness and the happiness of those he lives with. He has some very engaging qualities but there is the same curious little streak of contrariness in him that there is in Ewan. He may outgrow this—I hope he will; but its presence has always made him an exceedingly difficult child to train, especially in the more superficial aspects of existence—table manners, social observances etc. Stuart, on the other hand, is

not only easily taught but seems to possess the social graces as a natural endowment. It "comes natural" to him to be courteous and polite and engaging. In the detestable slang of the day he is "a good mixer." Chester is not. Perhaps it is not an unmixed blessing for Stuart. He will be as easily influenced for evil as for good. Chester is, perhaps in this respect, the less likely to be swayed by others. But he is a blunt reserved little fellow while Stuart, with his angel face and joyous pervasive smile, is the friend of all the world.

Stuart, too, is a quite wonderful worker and always has been. He is a most industrious little mortal. Chester doesn't like work; he is a bookworm; but Stuart eats it. Today he went over to Richard Oxtoby's and picked potatoes the whole day, coming joyfully home at night with fifty cents which Mr. Oxtoby had given him and which I have no doubt he fully earned.

He possesses a weird liking for the medicine known as "Emulsion of Cod Liver Oil"—which most people take when they have to and not otherwise. I have been giving a bottle of it to Chester to build him up after his operation and Stuart always pleads for some, too, but has been refused, as he did not need it. This morning he said, gravely and earnestly, lifting his large brilliant blue eyes to me, "Mother dear, since this is my birthday can't I have a dose of emulsion as a *special treat?*"

He got it!

Six years old! I have no baby now.

Tuesday, October 18, 1921
Leaskdale, Ont.

Lily has been back for a week. Her throat isn't very well yet, but that doesn't prevent her from going out every evening, fine or wet. However, she has been much better tempered. I think she had imagined that I would put up with everything because I could not get other help. But now that she has found out that I can fall back on Elsie at a pinch she has decided that it will be safer to be amiable.

A small village like this, is, I think, the pettiest place in the world. The "retired" folk have little to do except "keep tabs" on their neighbors. And they are all devouringly curious as to what goes on in "the manse"—curious about details that it would never enter into my head to think of. They even count the mats that we hang out on the backyard fence on sweeping day—count them and tell their neighbors about them. They know the exact moment our washing is hung out, the number of pieces, and everything else that is done in our back yard. As to what goes on indoors, where they can't see, I fear their agony of curiosity about it will shorten their lives....

Chester came to me the other day and said he wanted to read *Green Gables.* He has lately been awakening to a realization that he has an author for a mother. So he is poring over it now and seems to find it fairly interesting—though I think in his soul he prefers *Granny Fox* and *The Cockhouse at Fellsgarth* which is natural enough.

I have finished reading McCarthy's *History of our Own Times.* I have read it many times since I was a child of 12, when I read it first. Then and now I found it fascinating. McCarthy had a style almost equal to Macaulay and most of his opinions have stood pretty well the test of time. I doubt if I shall ever have time to read the book again—there are too many new ones coming out all the time which I want to read. Yet an old book has something for me which no new book can ever have—for at every reading the memories and atmosphere of other readings come back and I am reading old years as well as an old book.

Friday, October 21, 1921
Leaskdale, Ont.

The weather this October has been an atrocious mixture of rain and wind. I have finished the ninth chapter of *Emily*. I should have more finished, considering the weeks I have been at it, but it is very hard to get all the time I should. However, I feel pretty well satisfied with the quality. I think *Emily* will be a good bit of work.

A little incident that happened this evening in connection with Stuart reminded me, by the law of association, of a long unthought-of happening of my early childhood. I was about five or six and Grandma was teaching me a spelling lesson. I don't remember the lesson—I don't remember what I did that annoyed her—but I *do* remember the punishment she made me undergo and the humiliation and anger and disgust with which it filled me to the core of my soul. Grandma "meant well" of course but she did a terrible thing. She made me kneel down on the floor before her and pray to God to forgive me for being such a bad girl—that is, she made me utter the words with my lips. There was of course nothing of *real* prayer in them—for I only uttered them because I was compelled to do so, sorely against my will, and with a soul filled with humiliation, impotent anger, and a queer sense of degradation as if something in me was outraged. And truly something was—something sacred and inalienable. It was a dreadful thing for her—for anyone—to do. To force a human soul to utter words of prayer when it was not in a fit state to do so—when stormy rebellion and bitterness filled it. Grandmother never realized what she had done but she filled me with a lasting sense of disgust with and hatred for prayer and religion—what she called prayer and religion at least. It never left me. From that day I loathed it. It was not until I grew old enough to think for myself and began to realize that real prayer—real religion—was something very different from pattering formulas and going blindly through certain meaningless ceremonies that I escaped from the influence of that day. And indeed I never fully escaped from it. My conscious mind cast it off at the bidding of reason; but that subconscious mind over which we have little, if any, control, retained it—retains it still. To this day, the humiliation of that hour manifests itself in a *feeling* which lurks under all the beliefs and conclusions of my reason, that "religion" and all connected with it was something which—like sex—one had to have but was ashamed of for all that.

I suppose I am like most people in being a helpless victim to impressions made in early years. Perhaps I am more helpless than some owing to the exceeding sharpness and depth of the impressions made on a somewhat unusually sensitive nature. But in that same subconscious mind I carry an irrational detestation of "being a Christian."

When I was a child a certain Mr. Secord travelled over the Island as a Bible Society Colporteur. He came around about twice a year and I always hailed his arrival with delight since it generally meant a new volume of *Talmage's Sermons* and perhaps a *Pansy* Book or something similar where the so-called religion was sugar-coated with an interesting story. But for Mr. Secord himself I felt no enthusiasm. He was a thin, anaemic individual with a straggling pointed beard and pale, indeterminate eyes.

One evening in late November he arrived at twilight, chilled to the bone. He sat hunched up in front of the kitchen stove, trying to get warm and evidently bent on sowing good seed in season and out of season, for he said to me, as I stood in the corner by the stove, watching him curiously, in his thin, squeaky voice,

"Little girl, isn't it nice to be a Christian?"

I looked at him—at his shivering form, his pinched blue face, his claw-like hands spread over the stove, and I thought that *he* was a Christian and that I certainly didn't want to be one! I have never been able really to divorce the two ideas that were so incongruously wedded at that moment. To this day, a *Christian* really means to me, *not* an individual who is trying to carry the ideas and ideals of Jesus into the practical life of community and state, as my reason tells me—but a creature like "old Secord"—and I can't separate myself from the deeply-rooted idea of repugnance to the *name* "Christian," born in me by that unlucky incident.

Another thing that I dislike is the *name* "Jesus" itself. I do not know exactly why—at least, I cannot recall any such specific cause as the Secord one to account for my feeling about it. I believe it was because I used to hear it howled forth so frequently in absurd, meaningless "gospel hymns" by unctuous evangelists and revivalists. Perhaps because the name itself, like so many of the Hebrew names, was disagreeable to me. Until I learned to think of the man, apart from the name. I felt repulsion towards both. Eventually I did accomplish this and came into my heritage for love and reverence for that unique and wonderful Personality with its lofty aspirations, its pure conceptions of truth, its radical scorn for outworn conventions and laws. I never call him "Jesus" but always Christ, though I know the latter is a title and not a name. But to me it seems a beautiful word with none of the obscurely disagreeable suggestions of "Jesus."

I wish I could protect my children against false and ugly conceptions of these matters. I try to do so. But in dealing with children who "blurt out" things, I have to be careful for Ewan's sake. And they have to go to Sunday School where they are taught by a couple of crude, ignorant old women who never had an original thought in their lives and who would think anyone who didn't believe in the literal existence of Adam and Eve and a talking snake as an infidel of deepest dye.

Stuart was learning his catechism question the other evening, "Why did God make all things?"; the answer being, "For his own glory."

This has always seemed to me an abominable libel on God—seeming to present him in the light of a monstrous egotist. I resolved to dare the Leaskdale grundyites for once, and I said to Stuart,

"That is not how that question should be answered. God made all things for the love and pleasure of creating them—of doing good work—of bringing beauty into existence."

That seems to me a very much higher conception of God's creation than the other.

Monday, October 24, 1921
Leaskdale, Ont.
"To him that hath shall be given." Recently I sent a short story of 5,000 words to a New York Magazine and it sent me $270 for it. In other years I wrote dozens of stories every bit as good and some really much better for $30 apiece—and thought myself lucky to get that. Even for the best short story I ever wrote—when it was published in *Chronicles of Avonlea* a reviewer said it was "one of the finest short stories in the world"—I got only a hundred.

Yet after all it was not really for the story they paid the price but for the name, and that name was won by the long toil of the obscure years—a toil that blossoms now.

We have been housecleaning lately and doing a hundred other things. I work from seven to eleven with hand or head and sometimes both. Yet I never feel worse than nominally tired and then I sleep like a top and waken fresh as paint. This to me is quite wonderful, who for years felt tired half the time. I am as fat as a seal, rosy as an apple, and fuller of "ginger," "pep" and "vim" than I ever was since I was twenty. There is no very deep-seated reason for this—instead a very prosaic one indeed—*yeast cakes.*

One of the recent discoveries of science is *vitamins.* Yeast cakes are full of them. For over a year I've been taking a yeast cake every day—and this is the result. It aggravates me to think of how much I might have been spared if I had known this years ago. I always had good health; but I felt, much of the time, horribly *tired* in body and soul. I never feel that way now, even amid all the hard work and worry of my present life. I really feel as if I had been reborn. It is delightful to feel so. I believe if I had known of yeast cake magic I should have escaped many of those terrible months in the winter after Grandfather's death. Our winter diet, I realize now, was sadly lacking in "vitamins." It is not only an army that moves on its stomach!

Tuesday, Nov. 1, 1921
Leaskdale, Ont.
I have been having a dreadful week of it. Ewan has had one of the worst attacks of his malady he has ever had—by far the worst this year. It came on last Wednesday and increased in intensity until yesterday. When he came home from church on Sunday he said to me, "I was preaching to the people today—and they should be preaching to me."

I said, "Would you call it rational if a minister who was delirious with the delusions of typhoid fever should say that he was not fit to preach to his people?"

"No."

"Well, then, can't you see that it is just as irrational for you, in the delusions of your malady to imagine the same thing?" But, no, he couldn't see it. Poor Ewan, in these attacks, doesn't believe that he *has* any malady.

"I am perfectly well; but I am outcast from God. *That* is my trouble. You do not sympathize with me."

That is Ewan's attitude. Because I cannot believe that he is a lost soul I have "no sympathy." Dr. Garrick told me I must not argue with him on the subject but that, on the other hand, I must be careful not to say anything that would confirm it. I never do. And yet, so well do I know a certain ingrained contrariness in Ewan's personality which has always seemed to drive him into opposition to any opinion held or expressed by other people, that I verily believe that if I were to agree with him and say bluntly, "Yes, I *do* think you are lost and that there is no hope for you," that very quality of his would assert itself and oppose me, to the auto-banishment of his obsession. But I dare not make the experiment.

He slept better last night and seemed more restful today, though dull. Tonight he was lying on the bed in our room after supper, and I was brushing my hair, when he said suddenly, "Maud, there are times when I am afraid of myself."

I knew too well what he meant but I said, "What do you mean?"

He said, "I am afraid of what I may do."

I said, "My dear, put your meaning into plain blunt words. It will help you to do so—it will take it out of your mind. Do you mean suicide or anything like that?"

He nodded. I felt aghast but I took his hand and said earnestly, "Ewan, promise me that you will *never* do anything like that."

He said, "Oh, I won't do it—I am too much of a coward."

I feel sick at heart. During the first summer of his melancholia I knew he was tortured by such thoughts but I did not think they had troubled him since. Oh, *can* I go on like this, with no one to advise or share the burden? I have been living on the hope that he would have a normal interval this fall again—but we are not to have even that short respite. Oh, religious melancholy is a hideous thing. A man who is physically ill is still the same man: but a man in Ewan's case is *not*. Ewan seems to me like an absolute stranger in these attacks. He is no more like the man I married than—he is *not* the man I married. An altogether different personality is there—and a personality which is repulsive and abhorrent to me. And yet to this personality I must be a wife. It is horrible—it is indecent—it should not be. I feel degraded and unclean.

Thursday, Nov. 17, 1921
The Manse, Leaskdale
The weather has been mild but abominably messy. I have been very busy, and have sat up till twelve or one every night writing letters and publicity articles for the Canadian Book Week which begins Saturday. I am going into Toronto for it.

Ewan is much better and seems fairly normal but I take anxiety with me. And yet I want to get away for just a few days and have a sort of *change of tribulation*—use a different set of nerve cells.

Friday, Nov. 18, 1921
2 Nina Ave., Toronto
It used to be an old family joke that "Maud always takes rain when she goes." It really does seem so. I came in today and it has poured all the time. Mary and I went to the Authors' Association Dinner in honor of Nellie McClung at the Arts and Letters Club tonight. There were about 80 there and I had a seat at the head table next the president and guest of honor—which didn't make a very poor menu taste any better. But the evening was enjoyable and I met heaps of clever people. Basil King was on my left. I haven't seen him since that evening of the reception at his home eleven years ago in Cambridge. Nellie is a handsome woman in a stunning dress, glib of tongue. She made a speech full of obvious platitudes and amusing little stories which made everyone laugh and deluded us into thinking it was quite a fine thing—until we began to think it over. And she told one story, as happening to herself which is a hoary old jokes-column chestnut. *Why* will people do things like that? There is sure to be one person in the audience who will know its genesis.

Basil King made an excellent speech, full of good ideas, with no superfluities or frills or gallery plays.

Old James S. Hughes was there and told me "*Anne*" was "the finest piece of literature we had in Canada." This may be an absurd statement but at least he meant it for he is a terribly outspoken old fellow and pays no idle compliments.

Saturday, Nov. 19, 1921
Toronto, Ont.
Still rainy. This afternoon Mary and I went to hear Basil King speak in the auditorium in the Robert Simpson Co. store. Then we went to the big reception given by the Press Club to the Authors' Association. A horrible mob! Twelve hundred people packed together—nothing much to eat. But I met Jen Fraser, Frede's old Macdonald crony who is in Toronto now, organizing the Commissariat of the Bell Telephone. We had never met before but seemed old friends because of hearing so much about each other from Frede. Jen seemed to bring Frede back to me—I felt that she *must* be there too—and the feeling was so compounded of pain and sweetness that I did not know whether to smile or cry—and finally cried, there in that swarming mob where I felt like a maggot in a swarm of inane maggots—at least they seemed inane in that personality smothering mass—coming and going and repeating endlessly, "I love your books"—"Was "Anne" a real girl?"——. etc. etc.

Mary and Norman and I went to Hart House tonight to see the Community players of Montreal put on a couple of plays. I enjoyed them. Good amateur acting is always enjoyable, all the more so from the absence of stage mannerisms and too-great skill. There is more reality about it....

Monday, Nov. 21, 1921
2 Nina Ave., Toronto
The weather has cleared up. I shopped all the morning, since my family must eat and be clothed. Then I had lunch with Jen Fraser at Simpsons—with Cam's doings and peculiarities for sauce. Jen's opinion of him is the same as mine. She says the only excuse for his behavior is the possibility that the war affected his mind in some way. She did not know him before his marriage, so couldn't tell me if he were always like that. She says he was running around with all sorts of girls last summer. Well, Frede has gone beyond it—and those of us who loved her—who *love* her——.

Jen told me a little story of Frede so characteristic of her that I must record it here. When Jen and Frede first met at Macdonald Frede looked at her across the room and said briefly, "Maritime."

"Yes," said Jen.

"Presbyterian?"

"Yes."

"Shake," said Frede. "They're the only decent things to be!"

In the afternoon I went to Jarvis St. Collegiate and read and talked to an audience of about 800 girls. I enjoyed it. They were so eager, so appreciative, so enthusiastic. I felt at one with them from the start. I autographed about a hundred books and cards and then went to an I.O.D.E. meeting in Parkdale, gave a reading, answered innumerable questions, met some charming women and some very foolish ones. Came home to dinner, then went to Victoria College and spent a very dull evening listening to a couple of literary papers by erudite authors who could not stoop to be interesting as well as erudite.

The thing *has* been done—but they didn't do it. I nearly fell asleep. But at least the evening was restful!

Tuesday, Nov. 22, 1921
A full day—full of something at least. This morning I went to Moulton College and gave a reading and a brief talk to the girls thereof, writing a hundred autographs afterwards. I shopped the rest of the forenoon and after lunch went with Mary to see *Quo Vadis* on the screen. I don't know why I keep on going to see my favorite books screened. The result is always a disappointment. And yet I suppose I will keep on doing it whenever the chance comes my way. At 4.30 I went to give readings in the auditorium of the Simpson store. I had a bumper audience. The room was packed and half as many more couldn't get in. It was not an easy place to read in—the acoustic properties were poor and the noises of the street outside disturbed me. I was told my audience heard me well, however. After it came the usual autographing and handshaking. Two men came up to me and asked me to speak next Sunday at the Dunn Avenue Methodist Sunday School. At first I refused: but they would not take no for an answer. They stood there and pleaded, holding up the line and keeping everything at a standstill, so finally I said yes to get rid of them. I couldn't give readings on Sunday to a Sunday School—I hadn't a thing to talk on to such an audience. The whole thing

worried me until after dinner tonight when it suddenly occurred to me that I could give a talk on "The *Bible* as Literature."

An amusing coincidence happened in the store today. I passed two women at a counter, evidently women of refinement and culture, and as I went by I heard one say, evidently *apropos* of some person they had been discussing, "Oh, she has a *perfectly wonderful* husband." About half an hour later I was going down in an elevator and two women, evidently of a very different class, were talking behind me and one said emphatically, "Gosh, but she's got a swell man."

The colonel's lady and Judy O'Grady!

Wednesday, Nov. 23, 1921
Toronto, Ont.
Last night I went to bed very tired, and should have gone right to sleep like a sensible person. But frequently I am not a sensible person. I let myself begin thinking out my address to that Sunday School and got so interested in it that sleepiness fled and I kept at it until two o'clock when I had it complete in my mind. But I felt quite differently at 7.30 this morning when I had to crawl out in the chill of the gray dawn.

I went to Oakwood where I gave readings to an audience of 1,300 boys and girls. I felt rather nervous for I had never read to boys before and did not know if I could appeal to them. I gave the story of *Dog Monday* from *Rilla*, arranged to form a continued reading and my audience seemed to like it very much. I autographed 91 books. In the afternoon I went to the School of Commerce to read to the High School girls of Toronto. I had a very enthusiastic audience of about 1,500. Before I began to read they gave me a magnificent basket of big white and pale pink "'mums" in the "name of the girls of Toronto," which was very sweet of them. Afterwards I was nearly mobbed by a sea of girls wanting autographs. They nearly smothered me. I wrote about 400 autographs in half an hour. I was so tired that evening that everything seemed vanity and schoolgirls the vainest things of all.

Thursday, Nov. 24, 1921
2 Nina Ave., Toronto
Today I got a letter from Mr. Douglas of the Carnegie Library, Vancouver, which warmed and illumined the whole day. He says of *Rilla:* "You have written a very wonderful book—a book that will live, I think, when most of the ephemeral literature of the time will be forgotten. You have visualized the soul of the Canadian people in the war; you have given a true picture of what we went through during five long years of agony, and you have lighted up the canvas with gleams of humor which no other living writer could have excelled....The storm and stress of home life during those anxious days have never received audible expression, except in your wonderful book."

I was especially pleased with this because that is exactly what I tried to do in my book and this is the first competent testimony that I had succeeded.

Mary gave an At Home for me today—the usual thing. One guest was interesting to me—Mrs. Rochester who came to Prince Albert as a bride with her young husband thirty years ago. I knew her well then but have never seen her since. She has changed beyond recognition. Naturally there would be a change between the bride of about twenty and the woman of fifty. But she looks so much older than that, with her white hair and shrivelled face. Two of her sons were killed in the war and a third has been an invalid ever since. Probably that is the reason of her aged appearance.

This evening Norman and Mary and I went to see *Biff-Bing-Bang*. It was incredibly funny and well done, and I laughed as I haven't laughed for years. The female parts were all played by men and three of them were the most stunning beauties I ever beheld. When I read that in the days of Shakespeare the parts of women on the stage were all played by men I used to think that the result must be ludicrous and unpleasing. But I think so no longer. The ladies of *Biff-Bing-Bang* were wonderful creations, with their snowy shoulders, jewelled breasts and rose bloom cheeks. The only thing that gave them away was their thick ankles!

I am fogging up with an abominable cold.

Friday, Nov. 25, 1921
Toronto, Ont.
Shopped all the morning and picked up an adorable Chessy-cat brass knocker for my bedroom door at Ryries. I was delighted over my find for it had an interest for me entirely apart from its own quaint charm. In the summer of 1918 when Frede and I were at Park Corner she showed me with great delight a chessy-cat knocker exactly like this one which Cam had picked up in England and sent her. We laughed and gloated over it and I told her to put it out of sight lest I be tempted to poison her tea for the chance of falling heir to it! Frede howled and declared she would lock it up instanter.

The next time I saw it was in her room at Macdonald after her death. I packed it away with Cam's things, crying my heart out. Yet I would have liked to have had the thing—it was so expressive of Frede—the very spirit of all our old jokes and traditions was in it. It was impossible to look at the grin on the face of that cat without a responsive grin. When Cam was here I admit I did give him a hint—for I thought Frede would have liked me to have had that knocker. I told him how we had laughed together over it and how quaint and wholly delightful I thought it. But he did not say, as I thought he might have, "Would you like to have it, Maud?" So today I was much pleased to find an exactly similar cat at Ryries among some English brasses they had imported for Xmas. I shall put it on my room door. I have been trying to train Chester and Stuart always to rap on my door before entering; but they have been so long used to rushing in in baby days that they find it hard to remember. I think they will get into the habit now for they will want to rap with the chessy for the fun of it. And every time I see it I will see Frede, too, with her laughing face and pleased eyes, and she will not seem altogether gone from me....

This afternoon I went to Hamilton to autograph books....

Saturday, Nov. 26, 1921
Toronto, Ont.

I am beginning to get desperately homesick for the children. Hitherto I have been so drugged by the rapid succession of the crowded days that I haven't really thought of home at all. But now the effects of the drug have worn off and last night my hunger for Stuart and Chester seemed absolutely physical in its intensity. I could not sleep for thinking of them and longing for them—my darling little boys!

Today Mr. Stewart gave a luncheon for me at the National. Mrs. Stewart and Mr. and Mrs. Brady were also there and we had a jolly time. Mr. Mac is over in England at present. After luncheon I went to Sherbourne House and gave readings to a mob of school teachers who may have been very nice individually but were bores *en masse*....

Sunday, Nov. 28, 1921
2 Nina Ave., Toronto

This afternoon I spoke to the Dunn Ave. Methodist Church Sunday School for half an hour. It is really the first "honest-to-goodness" speech I ever made in my life—for when I have "spoken" before I have read my speech or had notes. I was nervous before I began but forgot it and found myself enjoying it. As 600 S.S. pupils, half of them boys of all ages, kept perfect order they must have found it fairly interesting. If I had had the proper training in early life I think I could have made a fairly good speaker. But it is too late now and I don't want to bother with it anyway. I have one work to do and have no time to take up another. Besides, the country is lousy with amateur speakers.

Tuesday, Nov. 29, 1921
The Manse, Leaskdale

Yesterday I was one of the guests at a Business Women's Club luncheon. My fellow guest was Mrs. Pankhurst of suffragette fame—the redoubtable "Emmeline" in the flesh. As I looked at her I could not see the smasher of London windows and the hunger striker forcibly fed in Holloway jail. She had a sweet, tired, gentle face—looked like some Presbyterian elder's wife in a country village who had done nothing more strenuous in her life than putting up with the elder and running the W.M.S.

After the luncheon Mary and I dressed and went to the Press Club reception of Lady Byng. It was a pleasant affair. Lady B. is not handsome. She has an enormous nose, but fine eyes, and is rather stately in appearance. I liked her. She was jolly and democratic—which is a new thing in vice-reines. She is a novelist also, having written two novels. They are readable books of the kind almost any clever English woman seems able to turn out.

Tonight I came home—a little fearful of what might await me. But Ewan met me in pretty good spirits and after a dull, dark drive home which seemed intolerably slow after our car we got here and I had my darling boys again.

Thursday, Dec. 1, 1921
Leaskdale, Ont.

This dull foggy day was *not* enlivened by a letter from poor Aunt Annie full of woes and complaints. She told me all over again everything in her last letter and then some. At the end she wound up by entreating me not to "tell Clara or Stella anything of this because it would worry them."

Of course, it does not matter about worrying me!

But poor old Aunty *has* a hard time of it—and will have it harder I fear. She is getting too much like Grandma for her own good. The crop was not good this year and I think she is pretty hard up for a little ready cash. I must send her a check for Christmas. It will not occur to Stella or Clara to do anything of the sort.

I must "hoe in" now. Christmas is in the air and I have no preparations made. I shall have to do some planning and hustling. Fortunately Lily is a changed creature. All last year she was almost unbearable with crankiness and bad temper. But ever since she came back after her tonsillitis she has been like her old self—good-tempered, obliging and respectful. I can't account for it. Perhaps her nerves are better....

Wednesday, Dec. 7, 1921
The Manse, Leaskdale

Yesterday was election day. I have not been able to get up the slightest excitement about it. There does not seem to be any vital difference between the parties. In our riding there was no Liberal Candidate—only a Conservative and a "U.F.O." I have no use for the U.F.O's in general and the candidate here in particular. He is an ignorant boor. So I voted for the Conservative because he is a fine fellow. But I "lost my vote" for Halbert went in after all. But the Liberals are in at Ottawa. I was, however, much more excited over the *Globe* announcement that "the peace treaty" between Ireland and England had been signed at last. Lloyd George has pulled it off. That little Welshman is a wonder. As for the Irish, I predict fun. They have been fighting England for 700 years. Now they will fight each other—for fight they must.

Tuesday, Dec. 13, 1921
Leaskdale, Ont.

Last night I got back from a trip to Cleveland, Ohio, where I went at Stokes' request to attend a reception in the book dep't of the Halle Bros. big store. I had good weather and a good time.

I reached Cleveland at 6.30 on Friday evening and was met by Miss Hutchinson, head of the Book Dep't, and young Mr. Stokes who took us, with Mr. Claggett of Lippincott's to dinner at the Carlton Terrace, a high-class cabaret where we "dined" from seven to twelve, listened to "jazz" music and watched the modern dances concerning which there are such skirls of wrath in the magazines of the period. I hardly wondered. I have always liked dancing, but truth to tell, some of the couples I saw there (*not* all—the majority really danced unobjectionably) reminded me of Byron's biting line,

"Nor leave much mystery for the nuptial night."

However, I enjoyed the evening as a variety. Soft and mellow light, delicious food, agreeable music—"jazz" may "appeal to the baser passions" perhaps, but I liked it although I had not expected to like it—and most of all, conversation with intellectual and cultured people were very delightful.

Saturday Miss Hutchinson and I went to Luncheon at a Women's Club where I spoke, giving P.E. Island a good boost—and then I spent the afternoon in the store talking to customers and autographing endless books. Miss H. and I then dined together and went to a movie. I left for home at 11.30 and arrived in Toronto Sunday morning. Got home yesternight to find Ewan very blue and miserable again. I am glad my journeyings are over for a while....

Saturday, Dec. 24, 1921

We celebrated Christmas today—and it was quite a pleasant one after all. I say "after all" for until this morning I did not expect it would be pleasant. Ewan seemed very miserable yesterday. I was busy all day making preparations for Christmas and for the concert at night. Among other things I made our custom-ary Christmas pudding—the delicious old Park Corner "Lemon Bread Pud-ding"—and cried as I made it, for it reminded me so of Frede. I always made it for her. She loved it—and never got at Macdonald any pudding so deliciously extravagant in eggs. I generally made it on the day I expected her. Oh, the change! Will I ever be able to think of her without this pain and longing? Frede, it is five years since that last Christmas of ours together in 1916. Oh, we little dreamed then it was our last. Frede—Frede.

Our S.S. concert came off at night. Stuart recited "Just Afore Christmas" splendidly. He was the best number on the programme. He has inherited my knack of elocution with a frank, charming roguishness of delivery which I never possessed, so he carried his audience along with him and enjoyed himself as much as they did.

When we came home I got the boys to bed. Then I stayed up till one dressing up the tree. Last year Ewan kept putting off getting the tree till it was too late. A storm came up the day before Christmas and he could not get it. This year I was determined to have one, so I began early and kept at him until he got one in good time. It looked very pretty when I got through. But I had bought a "rail-road" for the boys in Toronto and wanted to put it together to have it ready. But I could *not* get it to work. I tried for an hour and a half, got all tired out, and went to bed too weary to sleep and thoroughly down and out. I lay there for hours and *everything* was absurdly black. Ewan would *never* be better—every-thing I tried to do was a failure—Chester and Stuart would be unhappy fail-ures—and so on and so on. Nothing good could come out of the Nazareth of my future. That was at three o'clock. Then I fell asleep. And even three hours' sleep made the world over for me. The boys were delighted with the tree and their gifts. That perverse railroad worked without a hitch. Lily—whose people do not celebrate till Monday—was here, so for the first time since 1916 I was not alone and did not have to spend the most of the day cooking meals and cleaning up. The boys had good fun and I had a glorious "read," Mr. McClelland having sent

us his usual generous parcel of books. Ewan, too, seemed much better today—
the first Christmas day since 1918 that he was at all well.

Thursday, Dec. 29, 1921
The Manse, Leaskdale

For the eleventh time I entertained the Guild executive tonight. I have done so
every Xmas week since I came. The personnel of the Guild has wholly changed.
We had a nice time tonight. For the first time for three years Ewan happened to
feel well on this occasion and enjoyed it all, instead of trying to slip away and
indulge his broodings alone as formerly.

I took a couple of flashlights of the crowd, gave them a tip top lunch, and we
got out a good guild programme. Reading something in today's paper about
Miss Agnes MacPhail, the first woman to be elected to the Dominion Parliament, reminded me of one of the "dream lives" I was fond of living when I was
a child. I have lived a great many "dream" lives—I live them yet. But this was a
great favorite. In it I was "Lady Trevanion" and a member of the British House
of Commons to boot. Also a famous novelist. There was a "Lord Trevanion" but
he was a very nebulous personage and didn't cut much ice. One of the favorite
scenes in this dream was when another M.P. made a contemptuous reference to
me as a *woman*. A thousand times have I bounded to my feet and burst into a
vehement speech in my own defence. This speech was not original. I took "Pitt's
Reply to Walpole" and hurled it at my sneerer—only of course in the dream it
was original—changed to suit the circumstance.

"Sir, the atrocious crime of being a *woman* which the honorable gentleman
has, with such spirit and decency charged upon me, I shall attempt neither to
palliate nor deny but shall content myself with wishing that I may be one of
those whose follies cease with their *sex* and not one of that number who are
ignorant in spite of *manhood* and experience."

Here I was always interrupted by thunders of applause. And nobody ever
again dared to sneer at "Lady Trevanion."

My, what fun I got out of that!—hundreds of nights when my small body was
cuddled between the blankets in that old P.E.I. farmhouse!

The time of the South African war I began living a dream life in South
Africa—and have lived it to this day. Side by side with my real life the current
has flowed on. An idealized *Cecil Rhodes* has shared it with me in various plots
and developments some widely differing from the other.

Chester is reading *Midshipman Easy* and finds it very enthralling. I can recall
how delightedly I revelled in it when a child and how I laughed over Jack's
green silk petticoat banner. By the law of association this reminds me of the
green silk petticoat I am at present making for myself—out of my mother's wedding dress.

My mother was married in the fashionable taffeta silk of the time. And the silk
was the brightest, vividest green imaginable! When I was a child the dress hung
on the wall of the north room. It was made with the full crinoline skirt of the
'74's, the sloping shoulders and large, loose sleeves, trimmed with green satin
bands and green silk fringe. I would give much if I had that dress today just as it

was. It would be a valuable heirloom. But Grandma was always saying that when I grew up it was to be made over for me. I was too young then to realize how much better it would be to keep it as it was, and I rather looked forward to the time when I could wear it. When I was about fourteen Grandmother ripped it to pieces and discarded everything but the sleeves and skirt breadths. Then these were rolled up and stowed away to await the day when they should be made up for me. That day never came. When I was old enough to wear silk dresses the fashion of silks had changed. I was secretly aghast at the idea of appearing out in that brilliant green silk—so I never said anything about it and Grandmother appeared to forget it. As the years went by I cherished a design of having the dress made up with a black lace overdress to tone it down or something of the sort. But somehow the years came and went and I never did it. When I came here I brought the rolls of silk with me and they have lain in my trunk ever since. Not long ago, I decided to make a couple of silk petticoats out of it....

The petticoats are going to be very pretty. The silk must have been a wonderful stuff. It is 48 years old but there is never a sign of cut about it. It is as soft and glossy as ever. Last night I tried the petticoat on—and as I did so I thought of how, forty-eight years ago the beautiful young Clara Macneill must have tried it on, too—her wedding dress. It would become her fair beauty. It made her seem a little real to me for the moment. It is very seldom mother has seemed *real* to me. If she were alive she would be sixty-eight—quite an old woman. I wonder if she would be proud of her daughter's success. I suppose my life would have been absolutely different if she had lived—perhaps a happier life. How I wish I could remember her as she was in her young womanhood. I have not even a good picture of her. Grandmother and Grandfather never talked of her—Aunt Annie and Aunt Emily never talked of her. It was only by casual remarks dropped here and there that I picked up any idea of her. I know nothing of her childhood—her girlhood—except that she was thought very beautiful—a tall, fair girl—and had a great many admirers. William Clark was always supposed to have gone insane and hanged himself because she did not care for him. I never heard her parents or her brothers and sisters talk of her in their family gatherings. Yet she must have been a gay, lively, mischievous little lass. I have an old daguerreotype taken of her when she was twelve. She looks sad in it. I think she was always "fey"—that people always felt she was not to live very long. Yet she was not considered delicate. She caught cold after I was born, when she was run down from nursing me, and developed consumption very rapidly. She was not ill very long. I fear her death was hastened by worry. Father had failed as a merchant in Clifton, owing to the extravagance and dissipation of his partner, Duncan McIntyre—and things were very hard for mother. I am afraid she must have been not unwilling to die. But I *know* nothing—I have never heard *anything* of what she thought or felt after her illness came on. Did she grieve to leave me? Does she live yet? Will I ever see her? Will we be anything to each other if I do? Somehow, I have an odd feeling that mother is *very near* me as I write. *Does* human personality survive death? And is it possible that when we *think* of our dead it summons them irresistibly to us? Oh, we *know* nothing. We are lost in the blackest ignorance of *everything* we *should* know—

we stumble blindly in the night of the universe and the dawn of a new day will not be in the lifetime of our planet!

Mother, I can see you on your bridal night, flushed and lovely and radiant in your flowing green silk dress, with its point lace collar, in the old parlor in Cavendish. Father stands beside you, a handsome young man of thirty-two—handsome, in spite of fine, dark, side-whiskers! For to the taste of the '70's side whiskers were the hallmark of a handsome man. And, if one could tolerate whiskers at all, side whiskers were the best kind. They certainly became father. I always liked them much better than the full beard he afterwards wore. It is the *name* that is against them. "Side-whiskers"—could anything sound more ridiculous? Romance and sentiment wither away beside such a name. Yet father and mother were a handsome couple and mother was doubtless a radiantly happy bride in that green silk dress.

I have not even a letter of mother's—no scrap of her writing save one or two copied poems in an old album—nothing that would savor of her personality to me. I would give anything if mother had only thought of writing a letter to *me* before she died and giving it to someone to keep for me until I was grown-up. Failing that, I wish I had a letter she had written to anybody. There would be something of *herself* in it. I have a letter written *to* her, which I treasure, but nothing *from* her.

I will paste a little scrap of her wedding dress here.

1922

Sunday, Jan. 1, 1922
Leaskdale, Ont.
Nineteen-twenty-two should have a gallant heart. It has a hard task before it.
The world is, as I heard a man on the train say the other day, "upside down and inside out." Such a world is in a bad plight. Will 1922 be able to put it right—or even start putting it right?

Well, Lloyd George will do what he can to help it!

Chester has been reading *Midshipman Easy*—and has announced to me that when he grows up he is going to sea. I am quite accustomed to hearing him say he will be this or that—farmer, livery-keeper, garageman—according to the whim of the moment. I always laugh and say "All right, if you want to be." I said it today but I found it a little harder to laugh. For, some how, it gave me a nasty little sensation. Ewan's mother was a Cameron and the sea is in the Cameron blood. I wonder if Chester has it. I hope not. But I swear if he feels that way when the time comes to choose a career I won't try to hinder him. I have seen too much ruin and havoc come from parents forcing square pegs into round holes because of some selfish ambition of their own. But I sincerely hope it is only a passing whim born of *Midshipman Easy*. I shall put no more sea-tales in Chester's way—and I shall not fan the flame by any opposition.

I was helping Chester with some of the sums of his home work the other day. It amused me to find the problems dealing with the speed of automobiles passing each other. In my time it was railway trains. I suppose Chester's children will be ciphering out the speed of aeroplanes.

Friday, Jan. 6, 1922
The Manse, Leaskdale
I am famous—no longer is there any doubt of it! I have reached the stage where orphaned anecdotes in search of a parent are "mothered" on me, in the newspaper paragraphs. A friend sent me today a clipping from a western paper running thus:—

> *"Why She Refused to Offer Her Opinions."*
> *Miss L.M. Montgomery Wanted to Remain Friends.*

Miss L.M. Montgomery, now Mrs. Macdonald, the well-known Canadian author, was once sitting in an editor's office when a young novelist entered.

"Miss Montgomery," said the novelist eagerly. "I value your opinion very much. Now, I want you to tell me candidly what you think of my new book?"

Miss Montgomery smiled. "No, no," she hurriedly replied, "let us remain friends."

I was never guilty of this *bon mot!*

I also got two other amusing clippings....

There exists in New Glasgow, Nova Scotia, an editor named James Fraser—*en passant*, the father of Jen. He edits the New Glasgow *Chronicle*, is a rampant Liberal, a virulent anti-Unionist, and easily first in the gentle art of making enemies. In journalism he is a hangover from the days of the *Eatonsville Gazette*, and makes vitriolic abuse take the place of argument. Anyone who is opposed to him is on the side of the devil—nay, *is* the devil incarnate. Hitherto he has rather liked my books and has mentioned them favorably. But in the case of *Rilla* he sees red. From one brief sentence in the book, written by way of a joke on one of the characters, he infers that I am Unionist, likewise my husband. From another paragraph dealing with the Khaki election in 1917, he deduces that I am a Tory and he gets after me loaded for bear. I just howled over the editorials. They do not belong to the kind that can really "get under my skin," so I must confess I found a sinful enjoyment in them.

Here are some choice tid-bits from them:—

"Possibly if there were more prayers and less stories in the Unionist minister's homes there would be less desire to throw away the church of their fathers—less of the spirit of Babel and more of Christ."

(Wonder what kind of prayers Jimmy F. puts up!)

"The series of Anne stories which are referred to *now and then* in the *cheaper* reviews." (The italics are mine.)

"She is the wife of one of those transmogrified ministers who clutter up the once proud and exclusive Presbyterian church in Canada."

What *is* a "transmogrified minister?" And could the bitterest enemy of the Presbyterian church say of it anything harsher than that it was "proud and exclusive." Shade of the meek and lowly Founder!

"The writer alleges that Whiskers-on-the-Moon was the only Liberal in the valley where they lived."

Where do I allege it?

"The story is machine made and reads as if the machine was getting out of repair and consequently slipping cogs. But as the author has removed to Tory Ontario it is probable that if she does not improve as a story writer she will at least enjoy her days in a bath of that Toryism in which she so delights to take readers and do lots of splashing. Well, let her splash in her own mud-puddle to her heart's content."

The joke is that I have always been a fervent Liberal and as bitter an anti-Unionist as Jimmy F. himself. But I think I'll have to turn now. I don't want to be on the same side as he is.

Stuart is very indignant because the hens won't lay as fast as he wants them to. Today he came in and said despairingly, "Mother, can't you *make* those hens lay?" "*I* can't make them lay!" I said. "Why don't *you* make Paddy lay you some eggs?"

Stuart looked at me in disdain.

"Why, mother, Pat can't lay eggs," he explained. "*He* lays kittens."

Tuesday, Jan. 17, 1922
Leaskdale, Ont.

Last night we had our anniversary concert. Stuart recited "Seeing Things At Night." It is an old piece and nearly everybody there had heard it two or three times. But he brought down the house. They clapped him back and he recited "A Little Boy Snake" concluding in a storm of laughter. He is really quite wonderful for six years of age. There he stood, rosy, handsome, perfectly at ease, smiling at everyone as if they were bosom friends with whom he was sharing a jolly little secret. What is before him, the little, loving starry-eyed fellow? Somehow I have always felt vaguely anxious about his future. He is so sensitive. Will the world use him gently? Will it love him too much—or not enough?

Friday, Jan. 27, 1922
The Manse, Leaskdale

I went in to Toronto Wednesday and came home tonight. I attended the Press Club dinner, at which I was guest of honor and spoke. I gave a talk on my experiences in climbing the ladder and some good advice born of my sorrows with the Page Co.

In my task of copying my journals into uniform volumes I have reached the summer of 1918. Today a line, written blithely then, gave me a stab of bitter pain. Speaking of Frede I said, "She goes soon to P.E. Island and we are hoping for one more happy vacation in the dear old spot."

We had it—it "was our blithest and our last."

That summer of 1918 was, I think, the pleasantest summer of my life. Never did I have such a delightful vacation as those six weeks on the Island—never can I have as dear a one again—for never can I have one with Frede. It will soon be three years since she went out that winter morning at Macdonald—Oh God, when I recall it I turn sick with pain.

Today I had a nice letter from Sir Ernest Hodder Williams (of Hodder and Stoughton) and some English reviews of *Rilla*. All were kind but one which sneered at my "sentiment." The attitude of some English critics towards anything that savors of sentiment amuses me. It is to them as the proverbial red rag to a bull. They are very silly. Can't they see that civilization is founded on and held together by sentiment. Passion is transient and quite as often destructive as not. Sentiment remains and binds. Perhaps what they really mean is sentimentality, which *is* an abominable thing. But my books are not sentimental. I have always tried in them to register normal and ordinary emotions—not merely passionate or unique episodes.

I had also two curious letters, one from a male prig and one from a female prig. The most humiliating thing about these letters is that the writers like my books. I wish they loathed them. The male prig says that my books have convinced him that "a real Christian can still write books" but goes on to solemnly warn me that my nefarious habit of marrying off my characters "tends to lower the conception of the holy state of matrimony." Whew! I wonder if he thinks it would be better if I let them mate up without marrying, or sent them into convents.

The female prig thinks "Mary Vance's" talk is "vulgar" and that it should not be found in a book "written to influence young people." But then I don't write books for the purpose of influencing young people and I don't make children of the antecedents and upbringing of "Mary Vance" talk like "Elsie."

The said prig also rebukes me gravely for letting "Susan" call the cat she "tried to kick with both feet" a *darned* cat. But the real old lady of the anecdote said bluntly that the animal was damned. Yet this terrible example did no harm that I know of.

I shall not bother replying to the male prig. But I intend to write a polite, carefully ironic letter to the female of the species.

I am re-reading Froude's *Elizabeth*. His unsurpassable description of the long duel between her and Mary Stuart is as fascinating as fiction. He makes Elizabeth and Mary *live*—I feel as if I knew them both intimately. Whether his Elizabeth and Mary are the *real* Elizabeth and Mary cannot now be told but I believe they are, judging from the evidence of their letters and words.

It is odd—but I have always been on Elizabeth's side in that famous struggle. Why I can't say. Most people seem to incline to Mary even those who admit her crimes. And I don't think I would have liked Elizabeth at all in the flesh. Nevertheless, I have always been on her side—have always felt sorry for her. Mary Stuart has intrigued the world's fancy by her charm, her passion, her tragedies, her misfortunes. Elizabeth, by contrast, seems sordid and shrewish. Yet in spite of all this I am glad she won. I think, though, she made a mistake in executing Mary. By so doing she set her up as a world's tragedy queen forever. Mary's death wiped out of recollection the crimes of her life and made a martyr of her. There is a fatal contrast between her dramatic exit and Elizabeth's pitiful death in old age.

Twenty years ago a travelling lecturer gave an entertainment in Cavendish Hall. I was not there, but later on I heard that one of the pictures he showed was Mary, Queen of Scots, and when it flashed on the screen, half the people in the audience exclaimed, "Why, that is Maud Montgomery."

I don't know which of the pictures of Mary it was. None that I have seen resemble in the least my face as I see it in the glass. And though Mary Stuart was a beautiful woman I have never seen any picture of her which I thought beautiful.

They certainly had colorful sovereigns in those days. What a difference between the Tudors and "Farmer George." What a contrast between "Queen Bess" and "Victoria." Nor do I think the contrast all, or even largely, in the latter's favor. Somehow, that splendid, impervious, stately, *human* Elizabeth is a very striking figure in history even if possessing none of the strange fascination that hangs around the name of Mary Stuart.

Monday, Feb. 13, 1922
For twenty-five years I have been trying to get into the *Ladies' Home Journal*. At last I have succeeded. Years ago I used to try them vainly with stories. I have not sent them a story for fifteen years because I had not the leisure to write the type of story they want. But I have dangled a tidbit of verse before them now and again. Bite they would not. And now they have accepted a poem—"Farewell To An Old Room"—and asked me for stories, assuring me that whatever I send them will be "carefully considered."

I feel a certain amount of quite childish triumph. It does not mean to me now anything as much as it would have meant fifteen years ago. The "wished-for comes too late," as the French proverb says. But it always gives me an intense satisfaction to succeed finally in anything I have tried for a long time to do....

Wednesday, Feb. 15, 1922
Today I finished *Emily of New Moon*, after six months writing. It is the best book I have ever written—and I have had more intense pleasure in writing it than any of the others—not even excepting *Green Gables*. I have *lived* it, and I hated to pen the last line and write *finis*. Of course, I'll have to write several sequels but they will be more or less hackwork I fear. They cannot be to me what this book has been.

Tuesday, Feb. 28, 1922
I have been considerably upset lately over several things. There is never any end to worry, it seems. If it doesn't come in one form it does in another. But there have been some pleasant things, too.

Ewan was away last Sunday and Capt. Smith preached for him. He was here both Saturday and Sunday nights and we spent both evenings talking of a thousand subjects. It is such a delight to have a real conversation with a companion of intellect and sympathy. Captain Smith is one of the few people I have met with whom I can discuss with absolute frankness, any and every subject, even the delicate ones of sex. Sex is to men and women one of the most vital subjects in the world—perhaps *the* most vital subject since our total existence is based on and centres around it. Yet with how few, even of women, can this vital subject be frankly and intelligently discussed. It is so overlaid with conventions, inhibitions and taboos that it is almost impossible for anyone to see it as it really is.

Monday afternoon we went to Toronto, met Ewan and Mrs. Smith there, and went to hear Margot Asquith speak in Massey Hall. She was not worth listening to and I had not expected she would be but I was extremely anxious to see her, after reading that amazing biography of hers. She was not worth looking at either. I never saw so witch-like a profile; and she was so flat you couldn't have told her front from her back if she had been headless. Nevertheless, she was— Margot Asquith! She is a personality. You may hate—despise—deride—but you cannot ignore her.

We stayed all night in Toronto and came home next day.

Ewan was preaching in Markham. It is vacant. It seems to me rather too good to be true that he could get a call there, but I heartily wish it for many reasons. I would hate to leave this dear old manse, my first *home* and my children's birth-place; but we will have to leave it some day and it would be wiser to go while the going is good. Ewan has not been contented here for a long time. The congregation is not as strong as it was owing to deaths and removals. Zephyr, for one reason or another, has never been satisfactory. We have lost our best man in both sections and so find the work much harder. "Union" seems to be "in the air" at Zephyr and if that should come to pass the congregation will be disrupted and we would have to leave, not knowing where to go—a prospect that always haunts me in my pessimistic, three-o'clock-in-the-morning moods. Ewan has been here twelve years—there is no one else in Lindsay Presbytery who was in it when he came save one and that one has changed congregations. I think he has begun to feel an uneasy suspicion that people think he stays because he can't get any other place. This isn't so, of course—yet! Three years ago the Pinkerton congregation asked him if he would accept a call. I was willing to go, though not enthusiastic, but he refused, for what reason I never could fully fathom. But it was well he did for it was only three months after that when his mental malady struck him down. It would have been much harder for me if we had just moved to a new place.

Then a year ago he would have got the call to Brooklyn and Columbus if Fraser had not behaved so meanly. I shall never really forgive Fraser for that....

Then, too, if Ewan "got a call" to a nice place the pleasant sensation might cure his malady. He has really been much better this winter and a "shock of joy" I verily believe might complete the cure and render it permanent.

All these things make me feel quite willing to "move," if we could go to a place at least as good as Leaskdale. I have never felt that it would be any use to hope or try for a much better place. There is too keen a competition in such places for a man of Ewan's limitations to have much chance of success.

Markham and Cedar Grove would, so far as we know, be a very nice place. Markham is a little town, or rather a large village, not so large as to preclude all hope of Ewan's being acceptable to it. The manse is fairly satisfactory and has electric light in it. Markham has a station and is only 25 miles from Toronto which would mean much to me. But the great thing which made me wish to go there was the fact that it possessed a High School. Thanks to this wretched school system of Ontario Chester will have to leave home in two or three years more to attend High School and this thought haunts me and worries me, because he will need home surroundings and restraints for several years more. If we could get to a place where there is a High School his inevitable going from home would be postponed several years—at least, until he is old enough to govern himself properly.

Mr. Rae of Unionville, whom we know, is the moderator of Markham and so Ewan easily got a "hearing"—which is a hard thing to get in Ontario when this matter too often goes by "pull"—something which Ewan does not possess in many quarters.

Mr. Rae gave Ewan the first Sunday after the vacancy. I was disappointed in this. Mr. Rae seemed to think that he was thus giving him the best chance but Mr. Rae is a Scotchman and evidently does not understand how things go in

Canada. It is very seldom that the first man on a leet is called unless he is a very outstanding man. The last man has by far the best chance. Even though the people liked the first man the memory is blurred by succeeding candidates.

However, so it was and Ewan preached there last Sunday. We kept it secret of course. Owing to the system of settling ministers which obtains in the Presbyterian church—surely the worst system that was ever devised by the intellect of rational beings—it does a minister harm if it is known in his congregation that he has been "preaching for a call" and hasn't got it.

Ewan was quite encouraged by his day in Markham. He received so many compliments on his sermons that he thinks he may hope for a call. I cannot help hoping, too, though I try to suppress it, dreading increased disappointment. And now, I suppose, we must spend weeks in suspense, hampered in every respect by our uncertainty.

And now for the unpleasant things.

When we came home today we found a letter for Ewan from Marshall Pickering!

Marshall Pickering is the man whose car collided with ours that unfortunate Sunday last June. For this collision I consider that both men were to blame but that Pickering was more to blame than Ewan. And this I think is the opinion held

[Zephyr corner where accident occurred: wheelwright's shop at crossroads in countryside, with Marshall Pickering's house on left]

by almost everyone. Ewan was guilty of decided carelessness in turning towards the side road without looking a *second* time to see if a car was coming from the north. He *had* looked once just before starting his car and, seeing no one, thought there was plenty of time to cross the road before any car came—and so there would have been were it not for Pickering's furious driving. Pickering, on the other hand, was going at a furious rate—his own son when he heard of the accident said, "I suppose he was driving like the devil as usual"—right in the middle of the road and never slowed down or turned out an inch although by his own admission he had seen us for several minutes before we pulled out to the middle of the road.

Consequently the fair thing to do was for each man to pay for the damage of his own car. Eventually this proved to be about $50 for ours and $85 for his, ours being much lighter because we were on low gear, going very slowly, while he was tearing along at fully 30 miles an hour.

The morning after the accident we heard that Pickering had been taken ill in the night with stoppage of urine and had been taken to the hospital in the morning. Mrs. Meyers, who told me this over the 'phone, added that Pickering had had several of these attacks before. We heard this from several people afterwards also. Ewan went to see Mrs. Pickering that evening. She is a very ignorant, insolent, vulgar woman and was very insulting to Ewan but she never even hinted that the accident caused the attack nor did Pickering himself when Ewan went to call on him in the hospital. Moreover, a son of Pickering's, Wellington by name, was at the hospital and when he was talking to Ewan told him that his father *had intended to have the operation anyhow* the next week and had written him four weeks before asking him to come home for the summer and look after things while he was in the hospital. Ewan told me this when he came home from the hospital that night. Our minds were completely relieved and we heard no more of the matter.

One night early in December I had one of my queer "symbolic" dreams. I dreamed that I came home from Toronto and was told that Ewan had been *hanged* in the church shed by some unknown man and been cut down for dead but had come back to life after having been so cut down! I felt sure that some kind of trouble was impending of which my subconscious mind was trying to warn me but I supposed it was connected with Ewan's malady and perhaps portended a new and unusually bad attack. None followed; but ten days later Ewan got a letter from Pickering stating that the accident had caused the operation, that it had cost him a thousand dollars, and coolly demanding that Ewan pay $500 of it.

I have seldom heard of such effrontery. If he had asked us to pay for the damages to his car there might have been some reason in it, and we would have done so to avoid trouble, even though he was equally to blame and a well-to-do farmer quite able to pay for his own car. But it was outrageous to ask Ewan to pay for the expenses of an operation which he intended to have anyhow—though *he* didn't know we knew that, I suppose, not having heard his son's conversation with Ewan. I suppose he thought he could "put it over us" quite easily. I might here say that the "operation" was the removal of an enlarged prostate gland which of course had been coming on for years.

Ewan wrote him back a temperate letter stating that as he considered they were both equally to blame for the accident he considered that it was only fair that each should pay his own damages. As for the operation he told Pickering that it was well-known that he had those attacks before and had intended to have the operation anyhow. Probably this put Pickering into the rage of a man who has tried to do a detestable thing and has been found out. He is a very conceited, arrogant, bumptious man who cannot brook contradiction in anything.

But until today we had heard nothing more from him and had come to the conclusion that we never would. But today another letter came—the letter of a very angry man. I should not have been surprised at its coming for that morning in the hotel just as I woke up I heard a voice say distinctly "Marshall Pickering *has won his lawsuit.*" Evidently I had caught a thought wave!

Pickering denied that he had ever been ill before, said he would "prove by the doctors" that the accident had caused the operation and raved on generally and abusively through several very badly written and badly spelled pages. Among other things he said that he was "fourteen feet over on his own side of the road and going only at 15 miles as 20 witnesses could prove." This, of course, is absolutely false. Finally he wound up by declaring that if Ewan didn't settle for $500 before "a month from date" it would be settled in the courts.

The whole letter was evidently his own confused, ungrammatical, contradictory composition; but, as he stated fore and aft that it was "written without prejudice" it is evident that he has talked to some lawyer about it. I suppose he imagines that Ewan, being a minister, will submit to blackmail rather than be dragged into the worry and notoriety of a lawsuit. If so he does not know either of us. If, instead of writing insolent letters he had come frankly, as man to man, and asked for some assistance because of having been put to considerable expense, we would both have gladly done something for him. But this barefaced lie and demand is something neither of us can tolerate.

We will not be frightened into paying his bills. Nevertheless it has worried and upset me. I can never take things with the "easy-goingness" of Ewan. Ewan never worries over anything—except eternal damnation—but I do. It seems as if there could never be any end of worry for me. Just as soon as one thing passes, or grows easier, something else comes. I am somehow beginning to feel very restive and rebellious under it.

My own mail was not exhilarating. Mac sent royalty reports and the sales of *Rilla* are two or three thousand short of the sales of the other books. I had expected this. It couldn't be anything else in view of the terrible business depression all over Canada this past year. Nevertheless, it was a bit disappointing.

Ewan went over to Zephyr to see Mr. Law, the car agent and owner of the gas tank where we stopped. He is one of the two men who saw the accident. He told Ewan that Pickering was in the middle of the road and that he was willing to testify to that.

Now for weeks of worry!....

Thursday, March 2, 1922

I slept poorly last night. Woke at four and couldn't sleep again—instead, I went through the details of several lawsuits with Marshall Pickering and was crossed–examined by lawyers without pity and without remorse. I saw Pickering producing hosts of doctors who swore that the smash caused the operation—saw endless notoriety and unpleasantness—saw everything black and hopeless—but *still* said, away back inside, "We *won't* be bull-dozed."

Ewan is troubled with headache again. I had a touch of it myself all day.

This morning when I went to call the boys I found a placard hanging on their door whereon in big black homemade letters was inscribed the legend, "No entrance without our consent."

They are delicious. I was afterwards informed that *I* was not debarred, neither father. The prohibition was for Lily, whom they both detest—for which fact I cannot greatly blame them. She is occasionally—*very* occasionally—half decent to Stuart but she never ceases to nag and persecute Chester. She has never said a kind word to him since she came. And he was such a pet with Lily Reid and Frede. But he is too independent to suit Miss Meyers.

Monday, March 6, 1922
Leaskdale, Ont.

Friday night I took ill with an attack of flu and was in bed Saturday and yesterday. I crawled up today but am very shaky. I was not, of course, anything like as ill as I was when I had the flu in 1918. But neither then nor any other time did I ever feel such bottomless depression as I have experienced in this attack. It is a frequent accompaniment of influenza but has never been among my symptoms before. Never have I felt so utterly discouraged and pessimistic as during these past three days. Ewan is dull, too, so I am afraid another of his attacks is coming on. This, and the Pickering matter, intensifies my gloom. I can't see a ray of light—Ewan will never get a call anywhere—he will never be well—my children will be failures or worse—I shall be involved in lawsuits all my life—it is all dark and it will never be dawn. That is my feeling. I try to reason it away, but reason has no effect on it, any more than on Ewan's attacks of melancholy.

Tonight, as I sat in my room, feeling utterly wretched, Stuart, who was playing with Chester in the hall, came running in, his eyes shining, his cheeks flushed.

Stuart

"Oh mother," he exclaimed, throwing his arms around me, "this is a happy life! I hope it will last always."

The contrast between my mood and his struck me rather bitterly. Dear little fellow, neither he nor anyone else can wholly escape unhappiness in life. But I do desire deeply that he may have on the whole a happy life. I try at least to give him a happy childhood. But is it any use trying to accomplish *anything* in this world! Are we not only puppets in the hands of destiny?

Tuesday, March 7, 1922
Leaskdale, Ont.
This has been a dark dull day, gloomy in every way. It has poured rain—the skies have been obscured by heavy clouds—the house seemed filled with shadows. Ewan is dull. I was too weak to work, so read Froude's history of *Bloody Mary* all day. It was not a cheerful book but in my present mood I don't care for cheerful books. They are insulting. Poor Mary. In schooldays I learned to hate her; but now I think she was to be pitied. How very unhappy she was! If she had been happier she might have been kinder. On the other hand it might be as true to say that if she had been kinder she might have been happier. And can *anything* excuse the Smithfield fires? To *burn* a human being alive because he believed something different from you! It seems to us now inexcusable. But is not that because we have ceased to believe in the reality of hell fire and ceased to believe that God would doom his creatures to everlasting torment because of an error in judgment or belief? Therefore it seems to us now incredibly hellish and cruel to torture to death anyone guilty of such error. But let us try to put ourselves in the place of one who did so believe. Come! *I* am a Catholic—I believe in everlasting hell—I believe that anyone who is not a Catholic will go there. I love my boys Stuart and Chester. A man comes who does not believe Catholic doctrine. He teaches what I believe a false religion. If Chester and Stuart should be led away into it I believe they will burn in horrible tortures for all eternity. Would I not feel that, in order to save *them* I *must* root out the abominable heresy? And, since ordinary death has no terror for the teachers thereof, I must terrorize them by the most hideous death possible—to save Chester and Stuart.

Yes, I think I can understand poor Mary Tudor.

Saturday, March 11, 1922
Leaskdale, Ont.
Ewan seems better. I am a little better too and have begun to write again. I had one of Ella's hysterical letters again Thursday. She has not inflicted any of the kind on me since I pulled her up three years ago. I shall have to write her another bracer. If she goes on brooding in this way over old things she will go out of her mind. This letter, several pages long, seems to have been produced by the following facts:—Recently I sent Amy a check for $8 to pay for a quarter's music lessons for her. This seems to have overwhelmed Ella and brought on an acute attack of remorse of conscience which in turn was responsible for the letter. It seems that, when I was down at Park Corner in the fall of 1920, helping Aunt Annie out with her business as administratrix of George's "estate," one night Ella chose, after her habit, to feel slighted over something that had been said or done—or *not* said or done—and had not "gone into the spareroom to kiss me good night as usual." This offence is now preying on her mind and must be confessed and pardoned before she can feel comfortable over accepting the money. In a child this would be natural but in a woman of nearly fifty it betrays

the weakness of mind that has always characterized poor Ella. The amusing part is that I never noticed the omission of which she was guilty, so little impression did her nightly pilgrimages to my room to kiss me good night after I was in bed make on me. Truth to tell, I dislike such sentimentalities in mature women and had I noticed an absence at all I would have been relieved by it.

I shall write her, forgiving her fully and freely and give her a little plain advice about brooding over old shortcomings as she does.

Saturday, March 18, 1922
....Tonight, when I was pouring the tea something I happened to do suddenly recalled to me the memory of Amanda's mother—Mrs. Wm. C. Macneill.

I happened to pour the cream into the tea-cups *before* grace was said. Instantly I remembered that Mrs. Macneill *always* poured the cream into the cups and then gave Wm. C. the signal for grace. It always seemed a bit strange to me in those days because everywhere else in my somewhat limited experience the ladies of the table waited until grace was said before doing anything.

Instantly I was back thirty or thirty-five years ago. I was sitting on the old sofa—I could see the very pattern of the brown-and-white cretonne that covered it—in the sitting room of that old house. I always sat in its corner when I was there to tea. Behind me was the window with its muslin "lambrequin" and the house plants on the sill. Before me was the table, set out with "Aunt Caroline's" famous old china set which they always used when they had company. I saw the quaint delightful shapes of cups and saucers and the peculiar ornamentation of spears and battle axes which were so arranged that a little distance away they looked like a conventional flower. I saw the dish of raspberry preserve, the little pat of butter on a small plate, the little cubes of cheese, the glass plateful of small squares of fruit cake and the invariable round thin cookies which completed the unchanging menu of a supper there—and always tasted good, too.

Old wrinkled Caroline was sitting opposite to me, Amanda was beside me, young and girlish and ungnarled. Old William C. was at one end, making the grimaces for which he was noted—and close to me on my right hand at the other end sat Mrs. Macneill, pouring the cream into the cups with the air of a high priestess performing duly some significant rite. I could see her pale gentle face, hear her pale, gentle voice. Her voice *was* pale—her whole personality was colorless. I never heard her laugh in my life; and yet there was something about her I always loved. She *lived* for me tonight for a few seconds—she who has slept for over twenty years in the old Cavendish graveyard. She sat at the head of her table and poured tea in that quaint, prim, neat old room—a room which in spite of its quaintness and primness, had a dignity and reserve and charm which I never find in any modern room—and poured spectral cream into ghostly cups for me again tonight—that tall fair faded woman who never laughed and yet whom I remember so much more lovingly than many who were gay and mirthful.

Just a few seconds—then I was back again in the year of grace 1922, sitting at the head of my own table in Leaskdale manse and no one here knew of my flight over a thousand miles of space and an abyss of time....

Saturday, Mar. 25, 1922
Leaskdale, Ont.

....I feel horribly *stale* on everything this spring. It is just as if everything in life had gone utterly *flat*. I suppose it is the aftermath of the flu coupled with worry. But one pleasant thing did happen on Wednesday evening which sent a little thrill of courage and hope through my veins. It was Guild night and the subject was "Canadian Authors" which had been put on the programme at the suggestion of Margaret Leask. I had written a paper on the subject and selected a programme of readings. I went to the church feeling very dull. It was a cold "dour" night, the walking was bad and I supposed there would be only the usual 18 or 20 of an audience. To my amazement the basement was full. The whole congregation had turned out. And when the programme was ended Margaret read to me a very nice address and Dorothy Lapp presented me with a bouquet of pink roses in the name of the Guild and as a tribute to their "Canadian Author."

The "address" read as follows:—

"Dear Mrs. Macdonald:—

The members of the Guild decided that since this was to be "Canadian Authors' night" it would be a most fitting time to pay tribute to you as a Canadian authoress and also to show in some degree our appreciation of the wonderful interest which you take in our welfare.

As an Authoress, celebrated throughout the world, we are proud to know you and honored to have you as the leader in our activities. Your leadership is a source of inspiration to all of us and under your leadership the meetings of the Guild are both interesting and instructive.

The outside world knows you as a brilliant writer but we know you not only as a writer but as a woman who has deservedly won respect and admiration.

Leaskdale Church

We have met here many times during the years you have been with us and we have spent many hours in your home where we have enjoyed your gracious hospitality. We as a Guild ask you, Mrs. Macdonald, to accept this gift of roses with our best wishes for a long and happy life crowned with the glory your efforts deserve.

In future we want to show our appreciation not only with roses but with a happy willingness to assist you in every way in making our guild a success."

I confess I was pleased. I have worked hard, and with very little assistance, for ten years, to keep the Guild up; and I have thought sometimes that it was very little appreciated—at least, if appreciation was felt it was never uttered. So tonight's little tribute was very pleasant.

And yet there was a fly in the ointment, too. The plain truth is that Ewan wasn't overly pleased about it. He would deny this flatly—he would not admit it even to himself—but it is a fact for all that. I have always felt that Ewan never sympathized with or was pleased over any little compliment paid to me or my work in any department. I can't quite account for it but it is there and I have all too often felt the sting of it. Whenever we have been anywhere that an allusion was made to my literary success Ewan has invariably greeted it with a little jibe or deprecating joke—quite good-naturedly—such as a parent might utter when a precocious child is praised. The child mustn't be made conceited—mustn't be allowed to think that it is really of any importance. Ewan's attitude to women— though I believe he is quite unconscious of this himself—is that of the mediaeval mind. A woman is a thing of no importance intellectually—the plaything and servant of man—and couldn't possibly do anything that would be worthy of a real tribute.

I *felt* this as we walked home together and something he said when we went to our room confirmed it. It gave me a very lonely feeling. It was not a pleasant thing to feel that my husband did not enter whole-heartedly into my little triumph—did not even say "You have deserved it" or something of the sort. Of course I have always known that Ewan has never had any real sympathy with or intelligent interest in my literary work and has always seemed either incredulous or resentful when anyone has attributed to me any importance on the score of it. But as he never sought to interfere with it in any way I would not let myself feel badly over this and have simply kept that side of my life and aspirations to myself and made it as unobtrusive as possible. But his attitude tonight hurt me and made me feel very solitary.

Monday, Mar. 27, 1922
A miserable day—wet—raw—cold. The house was cold and uncomfortable all day. Ewan went to Whitby to consult a lawyer *re* the Pickering affair. At first he declared that if it came to a suit he would "conduct his case himself" but eventually I have been able to make him see the absurdity of this attitude and he has consented to see a lawyer.

Today I had a sharp, sudden spasm of *rebellion*—rebellion against worry! Everyone must have some worry in life—I am not such a fool as to be rebellious because I must endure my allotted share. But for the past twenty-three years—

with the exception of the first three years of my marriage—I have had *ceaseless* worry. And today I felt as if I had reached the limit of endurance. I stood up and stamped my foot and flung defiance at the Powers That Govern, whatever they may be. I may have to go on suffering but I am not any longer going to believe that it is for my good. No; the Prince of Evil rules in *this* universe and when he tortures me I shall not insult God by attributing it to Him and "submit" in resignation. I shall stand up to and defy that Evil Spirit.

Sunday, April 2, 1922
The Manse, Leaskdale, Ont.
When Ewan came home on Tuesday he said that he had been advised by Judge McGillivray to retain a certain Mr. McCullough of Toronto and had gone to him. He said McCullough heard his story and said, "If you can prove this Pickering hasn't the ghost of a chance."

So far, encouraging. But *can* we prove it satisfactorily? That is the point. And in any case even a successful lawsuit will be a worry and a very unpleasant thing for people in our position to undergo.

I was in Toronto for a few days shopping last week. Saw McClelland and he told me that Wanamakers had closed their account with Page. This firm was his best customer and the loss will be a terrible blow to him.

Up to date we have had no bad news—and no good news. That is, Pickering has made no sign—and we have heard no word from Markham. I wish we knew definitely whether they will call us or not. I cannot make any spring plans....

Monday, April 3, 1922
The Manse, Leaskdale, Ont.
Ewan had his handkerchief tied round his head again today. This always worries me. His attacks recently have been very light but one can never tell when a bad one will come again.

Stokes' royalty report came, too, and was not precisely cheering. *Rilla* fell a little short of my other books, but not, after all, as much as I had feared, considering the state of the business world.

Thursday, April 6, 1922
We were at Wm. Lockie's to tea tonight. It was a sort of martyrdom. Mrs. Lockie is a woman with whom I always feel wretchedly uncomfortable, as if I were in the presence of something essentially antagonistic. And her husband is the same type. They are both abnormal and their abnormality takes the form of their peculiar brand of so-called religion. Wm. Lockie is one of the two "leading men" in Zephyr church, because he is an elder and a large giver. Yet his giving does not spring from real liberality but from the same root as his abnormal views. He gives from a certain form of ostentation—"for his own glory" in short. He has done far more harm to Zephyr church than the most indifferent member in it. He will not accept any leadership or suggestion, even from his minister, but wishes to force his own peculiar viewpoint on everyone else. For instance—he thinks it wrong to run a church on business principles. There

should be no "guaranteed" salary, no reports etc. People "should give as the Lord prospers them." In theory this position is quite correct and Will Lockie *does* carry it out. But human nature being what it is, a church would very soon die financially if run on that basis; and Zephyr church *is* dying financially because of it. Will Lockie has stubbornly blocked for years all effort to have it organized on a proper basis. The majority of the people realize this but are afraid to antagonize Will lest he withdraw his givings—as he always threatens to do when opposed—and leave them with a deficit to make up. He doesn't believe in prayer meetings, Guilds, Missionary societies or any organizations of that sort and has always opposed them. He has a colossal conceit and thinks he understands the Scriptures, church law, and church procedure far better than an educated and experienced minister. He has some of the most absurd ideas possible and I could shriek with laughter over them if the consequences of them were not so serious. I remember during the war hearing him berating the allies because they bombarded the German trenches before an attack, thereby giving the Germans due notice of their intentions. "Why," William used to demand, "don't they just slip over quietly by night and *take* the trenches?" At other times he would ask the world why the Allied aviators didn't set the Allied prisoners in the internment camps free by flying over the prisons and blowing them to pieces with bombs. It evidently never occurred to him that the prisoners would probably be blown to pieces too!

As for Mrs. Lockie, while she was airing some of her "religious" views I was mentally recalling some tales I had heard of her from a lady in whose family Mrs. L. was a servant in her girlhood. She was a persistent thief of their jams and preserves—they could never be sure of finding a full jar in their cupboards. They had a terrible time with her. Yet this woman sets herself up as a model Christian and condemns anyone who doesn't agree with her on all points. I try to treat her courteously because if I offended her she would certainly try to make things unpleasant for Ewan; yet I question if it is not wasted patience. She *must* feel as I do the radical antagonism of our natures and dislike me quite as much as she could in any case.

Tonight William told us that they had given up the use of pork almost totally because it was contrary to Scripture, and that he never sowed mixed seed because it was forbidden somewhere in the Old Testament!

I was thankful when we got away. It was pouring rain and the roads were bad and our horse slow and we had seven miles of hills before us. But anything was preferable to the Lockies.

Sunday, April 16, 1922
The Manse, Leaskdale, Ont.
I had one of my queer symbolical dreams last night and I take it to mean that we shall not get the Markham call, especially as I had directed my subconscious mind, when I was dropping off to sleep, to "listen in" at Markham and tell me what was in the people's minds.

I dreamed that I was pregnant and expecting the hour of confinement. It came. I seemed to be ill for hours but no birth occurred. Then it was over but I had no child. I said to the doctor, "Am I going to have a child?" "No," he said. "It was a *false pregnancy* then?" I said. "Yes," he replied. I felt terribly disappointed—and then I woke with the thought of Markham in my mind. I never have those clear-cut symbolical dreams for nothing. I feel that I have been cherishing a false hope and the conviction has kept me feeling depressed and disappointed all day.

But today I finished copying my journal into uniform volumes. It has been a long piece of work but an interesting one....

This journal is a faithful record of one human being's life and so should have a certain literary value. My heirs might publish an *abridged volume* after my death, if I do not myself do it before....

I desire that these journals never be destroyed but kept as long as the leaves hold together. I leave this to my descendants or my literary heirs as a sacred charge and invoke a Shakespearean curse on them if they disregard it. There is so much of myself in

L.M.M. picking flowers

these volumes that I cannot bear the thought of their ever being destroyed. It would seem to me like a sort of murder....

Thursday, April 20, 1922
The Manse, Leaskdale, Ont.
....When the mail came Ewan took the Uxbridge *Times* and the *Presbyterian Witness* and sat down in the kitchen rocker to read them. I was working at the dining room table. Happening to glance up I was arrested by the expression on Ewan's face—an expression it rarely wears but which I have seen on it sometimes when he had heard or seen something that annoyed him very much, especially something that had ruffled his *amour propre*. It was evidently produced by something he had read and I wondered curiously what it could be. When he finished with the papers he threw them down and went out silently, still with that expression on his face. I was curious enough to go out and scan the *Presbyterian*, thinking perhaps there was something in it regarding Markham. But though I searched it from cover to cover I could not find anything to account for that bitter, disdainful, contemptuous look I had seen so plainly on his face and mouth. Then I looked through the *Times*. And there I found it—a brief little paragraph in the *Leaskdale Notes*.

"A pleasing event took place in our Guild lately when Mrs. Macdonald "Our Canadian Authoress" was presented with a bouquet of roses. Mrs. Macdonald since coming to our midst has always given herself to everything that was worthy."

I went upstairs feeling very bitter. I was hurt—and I was worse than hurt—I was *ashamed* that my husband could be so small and petty as to look as Ewan had looked because his wife had been given a small tribute which in no way detracted from him. I wonder if other ministers feel that way when their wives are praised. I read recently an account of the presentation of an address and purse to some minister. In his reply to the address he said that he owed much to the assistance and sympathy of his wife. Ewan would *never* say such a thing to or about me—would never *think* it. And when others say something like that he is annoyed.

It has made me feel very lonely in soul.

I remember a bitter little experience early in our married life—one of those things that leave a scar forever. It was just after we came to Leaskdale and were getting the manse in order. One day Ewan came up from the Post Office with a letter from some stranger addressed to "Miss L.M. Montgomery."

He looked just about as he did today. "If you are going to go on receiving letters addressed like that you can get away from me," he said.

I was amazed. The thing seemed to me so trifling. And surely he had sense enough to realize that strangers who knew me only by the name on my books must so address me if they wrote at all. But he seemed to be absolutely blind to this; he sulked for three days. I let him sulk, too, for I myself was angry and disgusted. But I was also deeply hurt and it was long before I forgot it and the crude contemptuous way he had spoken to me. Eventually he got over his pet and resigned himself to seeing such letters occasionally. Less than a year ago something occurred that brought the matter up for discussion and Ewan owned quite frankly that he had been wrong and foolish—"I didn't know any better" he said.

But there is evidently some of the same feeling at the bottom of his mind yet— the mediaeval feeling that a woman has no business to have any separate individuality in name or attainment from her lord and master. I feel hurt—hurt. I have tried so hard ever since I came here to help Ewan in *his* work in every way in my power—and yet he feels and looks like this when a compliment is paid me on it.

Tuesday, Apr. 25, 1922
The Manse, Leaskdale, Ont.
Some malicious demon seems to delight in torturing me this spring. Life has been bitter of late. Last Saturday I took ill again with another attack of flu and I was horribly sick at night. I lay alone on the lounge in the dining room all the evening. Lily had gone home for Sunday before I became so ill and Ewan had gone out to spend the evening somewhere. If I had said to him, "I am sick and lonely. I want someone in the house to get me a drink when I need one or phone for the doctor if I get worse" Ewan would have stayed home willingly and been all kindness. But he never seems to *think* of anything unless it is suggested to

him. When I was so ill with flu for three days in 1918 he never thought of suggesting a doctor until I roused from my stupor to ask for one myself.

I did not know he was going out until he had gone. Then I felt like *giving up*. I was so sick that I suddenly took it into my head that I was taking pneumonia—that deadly foe of my family. And if I did I would never recover—I would die and there would be no one to look after my children properly. I know now that I was a little lightheaded with fever. I ached all over; my throat was sore. I just got absolutely *babyish*. I wanted to be petted and waited on. I wanted someone to talk to me and cheer me up and make me laugh. I was so blue and lonely I cried pitifully. I had a miserable night but on Sunday I was able to get up and drag around to get meals. The fever was gone and I was no longer afraid of pneumonia but I was weak and wretched and hopeless. Yesterday I was a little better but very dull. Yet a letter that came—addressed to "Mrs. L.M. Montgomery" by the way!—made me feel ashamed of my depression. It was from a little girl of thirteen who had been thrown from a horse and had to lie on her back for five months, with the prospect of so lying for seven more. And she had read my books *forty-two times over* and wanted to write and tell me that she could never have endured her lot if it were not for those books. Surely, when I can help and encourage people like this I can't be altogether useless and superfluous.

We had never heard anything from Pickering and were beginning to think he had come to his senses. But yesterday Ewan got a letter from Greig, a scratch lawyer at Uxbridge, demanding immediate payment of "$1,500" under threat of a writ. He has raised Pickering's original demand considerably—hoping to scare us a bit more I suppose. We are not so easily scarable. Moreover, we both feel that it is a matter of principle that is at stake. I suppose we are in for a lawsuit now and in my present condition of weakness it upset me. I couldn't sleep all night but managed to go on with my work today. Yet tonight I feel a sort of desperation over my loneliness, problems, and lack of prospect. I can't *see beyond anything*. The landscape is blocked up and blocked out by these things.

Ewan went to see Law today. He is our main witness but is desperately anxious not to get mixed up in a suit. Last week when he thought Pickering had given up he said to Ewan, "You were both in the middle of the road." Now he is not "certain that it was the middle of the road." It is all rather sickening. But we will not be blackmailed for all that.

Thursday, Apr. 27, 1922
The Manse, Leaskdale, Ont.

I have not been very well these two days—I have a racking cough and get tired so easily. The weather is bad and everything seems discouraging.

Ewan went to Toronto yesterday and saw McCullough. In order to put ourselves in a good position McCullough advised a small offer of settlement. So he has written Greig saying that both were equally to blame for the collision. Ewan will agree to pool the damages and each pay half. As Pickering's were about $100 and ours about $40 this would mean that we would pay him about $30. I feel sure Pickering won't accept it. To demand $1,500 and accept $30 would be practically to admit a frame-up and he will never do it. He will either send the writ or drop the case altogether.

Ewan saw young Horner in Toronto. He is a law-student there and was standing by Law at the time of the accident. He was not willing to give evidence, though he said Pickering was going at a furious rate. McCullough said he would do more harm than good as he seemed to have an entirely mistaken impression that Ewan turned his car to the left *after* he saw Pickering. This is absurd of course. Ewan had no time to do anything after he saw Pickering. Pickering's car struck ours and slewed it around to the left.

It is to be hoped Pickering won't get him. Old Horner, his father, a notorious old character, is very intimate with Pickering. But young Horner and his father are or have been on bad terms owing to the former's marriage. Young Horner doesn't want to be mixed up in the affair at all so may not tell the Pickerings what he thinks. I sincerely hope so, for if he swore to his statement regarding Ewan's turn it might do us a great deal of harm.

Friday, April 28, 1922
....Ewan went to Zephyr and he and Mr. Law measured the road. They found that where the cars were was *not* in the middle of the road but better still, several inches over on our side. This is fine. Law seems quite willing to testify now. Ewan also heard of some man in Mt. Albert to whom Pickering told that he was going to have the operation anyhow. If this be so and we can get him it will be a good point for us. But rumor and witnesses are very uncertain. Of course we *know* Pickering meant to have it—his son told us all about it. But in the eyes of the law that is "hearsay evidence" and we cannot get it in.

Anyhow, we will soon know the worst since Greig stated that he would send the writ in a week unless the claim was paid. The suspense will be over then and that is always the hardest to bear. But our whole summer will be spoiled. The trial will likely be in August and we can make no plans for any vacation or trip. Well, poor Ewan has paid bitterly for that carelessness of his on that fatal Sunday; and I have to pay, too.

Wednesday, May 9, 1922
A few days ago Ewan, who has seemed almost well for two months, had a return of headache and melancholia....

We are not to get to Markham. In the *Presbyterian Witness* today it was announced that they had called a young Mr. Auld—who, oddly enough, is a P.E. Islander too. Middle aged men have little chance against young men in the Presbyterian ministry. Hope has been ebbing steadily this past month when no news came so it was not really such a disappointment to me as if it had come earlier. Besides, I never had any *real* hope since my dream.

Ewan seemed to take it lightly enough. But then he always takes disappointments lightly. The trouble is, I believe, that he won't *admit* they are disappointments. In the jargon of the psycho-analysts he suppresses them into his subconscious mind and later on they work out trouble for him. I can't help dreading the ultimate effect of this on him. Yet it may not have any at all. Ewan's reactions to anything are never those of the normal human being....

Thursday, May 10, 1922
The Manse, Leaskdale, Ont.
...I had an hour of reading Lecky's *Rise of European Morals*. His discussion of the origin of conscience is interesting. He is opposed to the utilitarian theory and thinks conscience is divinely implanted. Somehow, I cannot accept either of the theories *in toto*. It seems to me that there *is* implanted in us a certain feeling that we *ought* to do right and ought *not* to do wrong. So far I go with Lecky. But I believe that what we consider to be right and wrong is wholly a matter of education. We are trained to believe that a certain thing is wrong; when we do it therefore, *believing* it to be wrong, our innate sense that we ought not to do it vexes and reproaches us. Yet the thing in itself may not be wrong—may be absolutely right. Conscience is merely the result of our education in so called right and wrong and is not in itself an infallible guide, though, since bitter experience has taught the human race the unpleasant results of certain deeds and courses of action (here I agree with the Utilitarians) it is a pretty safe guide, broadly speaking. Yet

"Christians have burnt each other, quite persuaded
That the apostles would have done as they did."

Lecky, too, discusses suicide in full. Personally, I have never felt the horror in regard to suicide that some feel. My attitude towards it is much what I found in Lecky, as quoted of someone.

"Life is forced on us; we did not ask for it; therefore, if it becomes too hard we have a right to lay it down."

But it is a cowardly thing to do if the doing of it leaves our burden upon others—ay, and a wicked thing. But if it does *not* I cannot see that it is wicked. It is a wicked and immoral thing to take *another* person's life, just as it is wicked and immoral to steal another person's money. But if the money is my *own*, and if I only will suffer from destroying it, it is *not* wicked to destroy it, though it may be a foolish thing to do.

I don't think *I* would ever be *really* tempted to commit suicide as long as I could get enough to eat and wear by any means short of begging. Life, with all its problems has always been an extremely interesting thing to me.

Saturday, May 13, 1922
We finished cleaning the kitchen today, so housecleaning is over for another year. I am gardening now—I am glad—I love that. Ewan seems fairly well again. His attacks certainly *are* growing lighter. My tulips are out in full glory under the parlor windows.

We were out calling this evening. It was a perfect spring evening—the world was young and green and beautiful—and *clean*. Everything is always so clean in spring—no weeds—no long grass—no fallen leaves. Think how many million springs there have been since "Creation's dawn" and all of them beautiful....

Friday, May 20, 1922
The Manse, Leaskdale, Ont.

I went in to Toronto yesterday. After shopping all day I went for a drive with friends out to Oakville through the misty spring evening. It was delightful—the white blossom glory of cherry and plum—the greenness—the cool gray mist—and the perfect comradeship. Next morning the drive back was just as lovely in the golden, fresh, dancing air.

Sunday, May 21, 1922

Today at dinner in the presence of a staid, solemn old minister Stuart looked up during a pause and said gravely, "Mother, do you think you'll ever have another baby?"

!!!

No, I never will. And as things are it is best. Yet that little unborn daughter of mine—how I would love her in the flesh. What would she have been like? Would I have seen my own girlhood again in her? Well, I shall have to hope for it in some little granddaughter—whom I may not live to see.

I wish I had at least half a dozen children—or I would wish it if it were not for Ewan's terrible malady.

Monday, May 22, 1922

Began work today collecting material for *Emily II*. I am sure I won't be able to make it anything as good as *Emily I* but the publishers want a series and it pays and so I'll carry it on. But I've a good idea for an adult novel, of the light fairy-land kind, and I'm going to go to work at it in the fall and see if I can go on with both at the same time. The experiment *may* be disastrous—I may "hate the one and despise the other." But I mean to try it.

There has been no word from Pickering yet. We expect it every day and it spoils the half hour before the mail. It is strange they don't either accept the offer or send the writ. We have found *two* men at Mt. Albert who were told by Pickering after the operation last summer that "the collision didn't cause his operation—he was going to have that anyway." They are reliable men and are quite ready to swear to this. This will be an immense help to our case and my mind has been much easier since we found it out.

This evening I spent gardening. Our lawn was green and blossomy. The sunset was exquisite behind the big maple trees. A peace long unknown to my troubled soul seemed to possess me. It shut out the world and corroding worries and discontents.

Paddy frisked about among the shadows. In the twilight—appropriately called the cat's light—is the only time when a cat reveals himself. At all other times he is inscrutable but in the hour of dusk and dew we can catch a glimpse of the tantalizing secret of his personality.

It was all so lovely that I loved the place and felt a foolish, irrational gladness that we had not been called to Markham and compelled to leave it. I had not only the beauty of this spring but of all the old springs here—especially my first spring here, I always remember that spring especially for the delight of having a garden again after having none for so long, mingled with the joy of my baby's anticipated coming. Yes, for a few hours tonight I was very happy.

I am feeling better anyhow. I seem at last to have shaken off the stubborn depression of the flu and am full of "pep" again. The old illusion that there is something good around the bend has come back to me. I know now that it *is* only an illusion but it helps me to live for all that.

Union is in the air at Zephyr. I don't know what the outcome will be. The Zephyr people want Union on a general scale but are with a few exceptions bitterly averse to Union with the local Methodist church. I am not going to worry over it. We have plenty to live on no matter what happens. This "Union" matter has been a Dweller On My Threshold for years and now I'm just going to kick it out.

Thursday, June 8, 1922
The Manse, Leaskdale, Ont.
...There is one thing that has always been a matter of amazement to me—the wholly foundationless and absurd yarns that occasionally get into circulation in this community concerning me—yarns which have almost invariably had their source or their first circulation in Mrs. Alec Leask, who, although she is friendly enough to me, has really caused me more annoyance than if she were my enemy. A few years ago she circulated a weird yarn that I was writing a book on *stepmothers* and meant to have it published *after my death*. I had never mentioned *my* stepmother to a soul in this province so what was the origin of the yarn I cannot imagine—if it had any origin outside of Mrs. Alec Leask's silly head. Soon after I came here the story was told everywhere that I had been born and brought up in the Anglican church and had told someone that I would "*never feel at home in the Presbyterian church.*" The genesis of this *may* have been some joking remark of mine that "if Union went through I'd go over to the Anglicans."

Another of Mrs. Alec's fictions was that one day I had been informed over the 'phone that a certain check was coming to me and that I at once told the person 'phoning to "send it away for jewelry." This, of course, had no shred of foundation. I have never since coming to Leaskdale bought *any* jewelry except a pearl and aquamarine ring, price $14, and some bead necklets and pearl-bead earrings. And I did not order these over the 'phone!!

But the latest tale annoys me. It is to the effect that I have recently been left "a millionaire's estate" by the death of a relative. Mrs. A. Leask, it seems, was told during a recent visit in Toronto, that "a prominent Canadian author" had been left this and seems to have jumped to the conclusion that I was the lucky party. She has accordingly been diligently circulating the same. It is vexatious. Such a yarn will do neither me nor Ewan any good in the congregation. If a minister's wife "has money" some people seem to think that *he* doesn't need a salary at all. I have always been careful never to let anyone know how much money I really have made on this account. But this prudence has been defeated by the fictions that people make up. I could wring Mrs. Leask's neck with unholy pleasure—as well as those of all curiosity mongers.

I have been having a little trouble of late over some incidents in connection with Chester at school. Our teacher is a somewhat weak and inexperienced young girl and some of the older boys in school have been putting Chester and his classmates up to pranks. In some respects Chester is not an easy boy to train and Ewan makes no attempt whatever to help me in this matter. I told him he would *have* to help me in this affair and talk to Chester; he did so very reluctantly but in the end the disciplining was as usual left to me. There is nothing I miss more in my life than the aid of a wise and competent father in the bringing up of my children. It is absolutely lacking.

I had to "outlaw" Chester for a few days—that is, he was cut off from all the privileges of a son. I have found that this punishment is more effective than any other. Tonight I heard him crying in his bed. I went in and we "made up" and he promised to do better.

But these incidents make me very unhappy. I am afraid that my sons will come to regard me as the parent who is always correcting and punishing them and Ewan as the parent who indulges them and never punishes. It is not fair—and at times I feel very bitter about it.

Ewan went to Sutton today to consult with Dr. Boynton, who a friend told us might have been the doctor consulted by Marshall Pickering *before* the collision. He found out that Pickering had been to see Boynton in the middle of May, a month before the operation, and Boynton then diagnosed his trouble as enlarged prostate gland and advised an operation. This tallies with what Pickering's son told Ewan.

I think Pickering wishes he were out of it. "Bill" Horner, his crony, went to Mr. McCullough the other day and asked him to get us to "settle" it—a most extraordinary thing to do from every point of view....

Monday, June 12, 1922
Ewan has been very dull and moody of late and that horrible sense of a *change of personality* in him has made itself felt these last two or three days. I can hardly bear to be in his company when I feel this. There is something in him then that is utterly repellent to me and I cannot overcome or smother the repugnance.

We were out calling this evening. The old lady of the house said some very nice things to me and I felt a warm glow steal over my forlorn soul, especially as Ewan was in another room and so could neither be annoyed nor derisive over her compliments. To be sure, she rather spoiled it by remarking, "Nobody ever need say anything against you or Mr. Macdonald to me"—thereby giving me the unpleasant feeling that people *had* been saying something to her. Probably she saw this significance herself for she added hastily, "They don't say anything—they don't dare to"—which didn't make it any better. I came away feeling that a thistle was sticking in my soul. My philosophy tells me that we can't please everybody and that it doesn't matter. But still the thistle pricks.

Tuesday, June 13, 1922
The Manse, Leaskdale, Ont.
Today was pleasant. I forgot all thistle pricks. We motored to Cannington where

I addressed the I.O.D.E. on Canadian literature. Later on we had tea with Mrs. McKinnon, the widow of a second cousin of Ewan's who was also a Presbyterian minister. Ewan seemed much better again and even seemed able to bear Mrs. McKinnon's telling him he had "an ideal wife" without resentment. I am very far from being an ideal wife and Mrs. McKinnon is a rather silly woman.

When I got home I found a letter from a woman in Oshawa who wanted me to "select a verse that 'Anne' would have liked" for her darling baby's gravestone! There is a pathetic side to this—and I've written her a nice letter; and yet it is an absurd thing to do.

Tuesday, June 20, 1922
The Manse, Leaskdale, Ont.
Marshall Pickering is like Ewan's melancholia. Just as soon as we begin to hope there is an end of him he comes back. Today Ewan got a letter from McCullough saying he had received the writ. Well, the suspense is over and we know the worst. The trial will not come off until the fall. I think Boynton's evidence will settle it in our favor—though I never recall that dream of mine without a qualm. We will just put it out of our minds till autumn and not let it spoil our summer. The talk and gossip it will make—and has made—is really the most disagreeable part. Almost everyone seems to sympathize with us and Marshall Pickering is universally condemned; but to feel that we are the centre of a whirlpool of gossip and surmise is very annoying—a whole bed of thistles.

Sunday, July 2, 1922
Cars are decent things—when they behave decently. After Zephyr service Ewan went to Mt. Albert and Mr. Dyer of Mt. Albert came back here in our car with his wife to speak at our missionary service this evening. Service was over at nine o'clock and the evening fine. I decided to "run over" to Mt. Albert with them to have the fun of coming back with Ewan. Which I did—and enjoyed it all very much and got back at eleven. But twenty years ago in the days of horses and buggies who would have thought of starting on a twenty-five mile drive after preaching "just for the fun of it?"

But the old days had their good points, too. And a six mile moonlit or starlit drive behind a spirited horse, with a pleasant companion, through the old fragrant Island woods, past the dim orchards and the dreaming fields, with the moan of the sea on a faraway shore sounding through the air, was a very pleasant thing. For, as Einstein says, Time is only relative.

We leave for Niagara in the morning, having promised the boys the trip all winter.

Saturday, July 8, 1922
The Manse, Leaskdale, Ont.
We had a splendid Niagara trip—good roads, good weather, and Lady Jane Grey-Dort behaved herself much better than she usually does. We spent Monday night at Streetsville with the McKays. The traditions of the pantry seem to be as lean as ever in that ménage. I cannot understand how people can invite

people to visit them, be, or appear to be, glad to see them, and then literally starve them. Seven of us sat down to a table whereon was just about enough food to supply three....

We got to Niagara the next evening. After dinner we walked out and looked into that stupendous gorge where the maddened waters of the tortured river make their leap of supreme agony and the smoke of their torment goes up forever. Niagara is something it is futile to talk or write about.

We all went over the toll-bridge to the United States at night and saw two excellent movies. Next day we motored to Buffalo and back—a delightful drive—and then came as far as St. Catherines on the road home. Next night we reached Oshawa where the Smiths are living now and stayed all night there. We came home last night after a very enjoyable trip. Ewan was well, the boys good and interested, the weather perfect.

Saturday, July 15, 1922

I had a letter from Mr. Rollins yesterday—like a voice from the tomb or an echo from ancient history. He says that "after long continued oral and written argument"—which is of ominous sound as bearing upon fees—he got the master to file a much better report than the first one but could not get him to file a really fair report (which is a euphemistic way of saying that the report was against us). The case was argued before Judge Hammond in May and though the Judge said nothing either way he—Rollins—had a feeling that "he was impressed with our side of the case." But as the said Judge has gone to Europe there will be no decision till the fall.

Also, the Page Co. have appealed their libel suit against me to the Supreme Court.

But I am not worrying over it. I got through with all that at once in those bad months two years ago. Herewith I dismiss the whole affair until the next letter from Rollins. Whiff—pooh—away it goes!

Tonight I was re-reading Mrs. Asquith's biography, keeping before me as I read the picture of that thin, witch-profiled woman on the platform of Massey Hall. The book is in bad taste of course—but things that are in bad taste are always intensely interesting. And some parts of it are very touching and beautiful. Tonight I read the chapter in which she watches at her sister Laura's deathbed. It reminded me so deeply of Frede's—once more I stood in that dim sunrise room at Macdonald—once more I watched my darling's ebbing breath— saw it falter—fail—stop—once more my heart was rent with the torture of that awful hour—I flung the book away—turned out the light—cried myself to sleep. Oh, Frede—Frede! No, the dead never come back—or you would have come to me!

On every page of Mrs. Asquith's book I found myself wishing that Frede and I could have read it together. How we would have enjoyed talking it over—it is the sort of a book we could have discussed endlessly. It is at such moments I realize horribly how much Frede's death took out of my life on its intellectual side and how bare and desolate the finest chambers of my soul have ever since been.

Thursday, July 20, 1922
The Manse, Leaskdale, Ont.

Stokes' letter came today asking for the MS. of my new book. So I packed *Emily* off on her journey to the portals of the world—dear little "Emily" whom I love far better than I ever loved "Anne." I felt as if I were sending part of myself. Will she win a welcome? My original MS. of *Emily* I have put away. Some day it may have a certain value. I have the original MS. of *Anne of Green Gables* but not of some of its successors. I wish now that I had kept them all....

Tonight I was sitting on the veranda. Chester was playing about with a couple of girl chums and Lily was also there. Chester attempted to spring over the hammock in a running jump, caught his foot and fell, striking his head against the hard ground. I expected a howl of anguish for it must have hurt terribly. I exclaimed, "Chester, what have you done?" But Chester sprang up with a gay laugh—"Oh, nothing much, I guess"—and then bolted through the front door. I stepped in and heard muffled sobs in the library. He was curled up on the davenport crying into the pillows. The spunky little chap had braved it off before others but as I sat down beside him and took his poor little head close to my heart he said piteously, "Oh, mother, it hurts!" So I cuddled him and kissed him and told him I was proud of him for hiding it from the world—and felt that this was what mothers are made for—to comfort behind the scenes.

Sunday, July 30, 1922
"Roselawn" Bala, Muskoka

We motored up here—85 miles—last Monday morning. Roselawn is a boarding house on the Muskosh river, kept by a Miss *Toms*. Old Mr. Toms, her father, is here too and her sister, Mrs. Brackinridge. They are very nice people.

We only room here. We get our meals up the street at a certain Mrs. Pykes who is a lady cumbered with much serving. The situation here is very lovely.

[Starting for Bala: Ewan, Chester, Maud and Stuart]

The lawn runs down to the river where the bank is fringed by trees. It is beautiful at all times but especially at night when the river silvers under the moon, the lights of the cottages twinkle out in the woods along the opposite bank, bonfires blaze with all the old allure of the camp fire, and music and laughter drift across from the innumerable canoes and launches on the river.

Bala is a dear spot—somehow I love it. It has the flavor of home—perhaps because of its pines which are plentiful hereabout. The only drawback to the place is our terrible beds. They are those vile things—mattresses that have a hollow in the middle towards which sleepers insistently roll; and if we put something between us to prevent this the beds are so narrow that the remaining space is too "cabined, cribbed, confined" for any comfort. I haven't had a decent

"Fringed with trees" [Bala]

night's sleep since I came. Stuart was sick the first three days with an upset stomach and I had a secret fear that he was taking the measles, having been exposed to them two weeks ago. But luckily it was not measles and he is all right again and bathes in the Muskosh every day. Ewan has been rather dull, too, bothered by headache and depression but seems better now. I read—do fancy work—correct a second MS. of *Emily* for my English publisher—and dream— lost but immortal dreams. I find that I can dream even yet in Muskoka.

What a lovely name is Muskoka! Music—charm—wonder—it suggests them all. Shakespeare nodded when he suggested that there was nothing in a name. There's a tremendous lot in it. Suppose Muskoka were called Udora! Or Stouffville?

Yesterday we motored up to Dudley and spent the day with John Mustard and his wife. They have a cottage in an ideal spot on the bank of Lake Muskoka, buried in maple and oak trees. I loved it. The hot, noisy world was far away— cool silence was all around me—the gods of the wild wood welcomed back their own.

We had a nice afternoon. In the later part of it Ewan and the boys and Mrs. Mustard went fishing. I didn't want to go so I said I'd sit on the veranda and do fancy work. I wanted to be there *alone* in that lovely spot—to listen to the wind sighing and singing in the tree-tops—to watch the beautiful zones of color on the lake—to dream out something very delightful. But John Mustard evidently supposed it wouldn't do to leave a guest alone and stayed, too. He bored me horribly; and, besides, I was rather disagreeably conscious of the *last* time we were alone together—that evening in the twilight in Eglinton Villa, Prince Albert, when he asked me to marry him. I wonder if he remembered it, too. There isn't the slightest thing about John Mustard to suggest that he recalls anything connected with those days—except *one* thing—the fact that he *never refers to them in any way*. If he were *not* self-conscious it would be the most natural thing in the world to recall a lot of the incidents of that year which had no connection with our "affair." *I* never refer to them—*he* never refers to them; the reason is the same in both cases.

Well, the world has changed so much since the last time we were alone together that it is rather hard to think it ever happened. It is rather as if two souls met in Eternity and thought but spoke not of some happening in some incarnation a score of lives before.

One thing I love about Bala is the roar of its falls. When I lie in bed at night it sounds exactly like the old surge roar of the Atlantic on some windy, dark-gray night on the old north shore.

Monday, July 31, 1922
Bala, Muskoka
Today we spent in making a boat trip over Lakes Muskoka and Rosseau. It was very lovely. The continuous panorama of lake and river and island made me think of Stevenson's lines.

> "Where all the ways on every hand
> Lead onwards into fairyland."

I had a very lovely forenoon. The boys were with Ewan so I sat alone—and—dreamed. I picked out an island that just suited me. I built thereon a summer cottage and furnished it *de luxe*. I set up a boat-house and a motor launch. I peopled it with summer guests—Frede, Aunt Annie, Stella, Bertie—Mr. MacMillan (to whom I engaged Bertie!). We spent a whole idyllic summer there together. Youth—mystery—delight, were all ours once more. I lived it all out in every detail; we swam and sailed and fished and read and built camp fires under the pines—I saw to it that I had an island with pines—and dined gloriously at sunset *al fresco*, and then sat out on moonlit porches (well-screened from Muskoka mosquitoes!)—and always we talked—the soul-satisfying talk of kindred spirits, asking all the old, unanswered questions, caring not though there were no answers so long as we were all ignorant together.

Sometimes we varied it by going out to dinners and dances (for in my dream Ewan was *not* a minister!) at neighboring islands, enjoying them tremendously but always glad to skim back home over moonlit wonder-ways of soft, mysterious, dim silver, to our own dear bit of an island.

"Dreaming" [Bala]

Some of us slept in the porches at night and some of us slept in the open, with the dark pines all about us, their crests in communion with the stars. (I don't know how we managed about the mosquitoes there but in a fairy dream one does not have to bother about things like that.) And what a perennial fascination there is in the thought of sleeping in the open under the stars for the heart of mankind!

I dreamed it all out to the end of September. Then one night a storm came up. Our men and boys and Frede and Bertie had gone to the mainland in the motor launch early in the day. Aunt Annie and Stella and I waited in alarm for their return through the wild night while the hurricane shrieked through the channels and the waves dashed over the rocks to our very doors. At last, after anxious hours, they came, drenched and cold, but safe. And we joyfully pulled them in and shut the door on the storm; and we all sat down to a hot supper before the blazing fire in our big, timbered living-room, made all the cosier by the baffled, raging wind outside. And we talked—and drank of laughter—and were happy and triumphant, surrounded by the black legions of the storm. But under all our gayety we knew that our summer was over.

How silly it all seems written out! And how vital and delightful it all was in my dream! I woke from it when we reached Rosseau. And there was no enchanted island—Bertie and Stella were in different lands—Frede slept dreamlessly in her grave by a far-off ocean. Yet not two minutes before she had been laughing at me across our supper table in the firelight and I had heard the very cadences of her voice as she described their wild buffet through the storm and how she had been the first to see the lantern light I had hung on the pine tree by the boathouse for their guidance!

Thursday, Aug. 3, 1922
Bala, Muskoka
Today we motored to Pt. Sandfield, taking Father Toms and Mrs. Brackinridge with us to see a certain garden there of which we had heard. It was an awful

place to get to—I thought our car would be ruined. But it *was* lovely when we got there—as lovely as my dream-built castle of last Monday. The view from the veranda looking over garden and lake was so lovely that it hurt me.

Friday, Aug. 4, 1922
Eight years ago today the world in which I spent my girlhood and young womanhood passed away forever in one sudden, overwhelming cataclysm. It seems impossible that it can be eight years. It seems as yesterday—it will always seem as yesterday—as the mountain always looks near though ever lengthening miles intervene. To me, those four years of agony seem an ever present thing. Yet in a letter I received the other day from a fifteen-year-old reader (who would of course be only seven when the war broke out) she told me how *Rilla* had made the years of the great war (which she only remembered dimly) "seem so real to her." She belongs to a generation to which the Great War is only a name as well as all the other wars of the past.

The Manse, Leaskdale, Ont.
Aug. 6, 1922
We motored home yesterday, leaving "Roselawn" with real regret. Our vacation has been—as most vacations are—a compound of pleasures and discomforts. But the pleasures far outweighed the discomforts and we were sorry to come

"Roselawn" [Bala]

away—and then when we got home we were glad to get home. I was, anyway. It was so nice to see my own green lawn and maple trees again—my garden, my flowers, my house.

And *so* nice to lie gratefully down on a *good* bed at night....

Something that was said in our supper table conversation tonight reminded me of "Mad MacKinley."

"Mad MacKinley" was one of those eccentric creatures with which the P.E. Island country side used to abound in my childhood. They are never seen now. Mad MacKinley was a very striking and picturesque figure.

He was one of the North River MacKinleys—an old and good family. In his youth he was brilliant and studied for the Baptist ministry, teaching school in order to pay his way through college and studying so hard at the same time that his mind gave way—and he became "Mad MacKinley." The insanity was concerned only with religion. In every other respect he seemed absolutely normal. But he conceived the idea that immersion was absolutely necessary to salvation and that anyone not immersed was damned. It followed that he must go forth and preach this to all at sundry times and in divers places.

His relatives had put him in the asylum once or twice but he always escaped; and finally, as he was quite harmless—they ceased to try to restrain him and for many years he wandered over the Island continually preaching his warning—and he *could* preach, with a flood of eloquence and rhetoric.

He came very often to Cavendish, as several Cavendish people were married to North River people and he found a congenial atmosphere among the Cavendish Baptists, who were at that time very narrow and bigoted—believing, I think, in their secret souls just exactly as he did, although they were always ashamed of "Mad MacKinley" and his ranting.

"Old Presbyterian Church" [Cavendish]

We would be coming out of the old Presbyterian church some fine Sunday morning. Long before we who sat near the top got out, we would hear shouts of exhortation rolling in—for Mad MacKinley always preached at the top of a sonorous voice. And when we reached the door there he would be, standing in the graveyard, haranguing the doomed Presbyterians eloquently.

He always took up his position in the graveyard because no one could molest him there. At first he had occupied the church green but some of the old Simpsons and Macneills, who were as bigoted as the Baptists—and who had not sense enough to leave a madman alone, had once hustled him roughly away. Then he resorted to the graveyard, standing just before the church door. He was quite an imposing figure, tall, always neatly dressed in a long black coat, with long gray hair and beard, clear-cut, intellectual features, and fine eyes where the light of frenzy burned. He would preach until the last straggler had gone. Then he would tuck under his arm the umbrella which he always carried—and which he waved wildly while preaching—and stalk off down the hill.

He would generally hang about the community for a week or so after that. He always visited the school and harangued the pupils on immersion. I remember two of these visits with especial clearness. One day he preached so long that the teacher became impatient and intimated that enough time had been lost. Mad MacKinley was very indignant. He turned and went out and ran around the school seven times. It was a very windy day and as he flashed repeatedly past the four low windows his long gray "duster" and long gray hair streamed out behind him like the robe and hair of some irate Hebrew prophet.

The other incident was still more comical.

It was the custom to have "Testament Reading" every morning at the opening of school and each scholar had a "Testament." These Testaments, being very cheap affairs, wore out rapidly and were replaced by new ones, but the old ones remained in the desks. One spring Sarah Jack cleaned the school and collected about a bushel of old, torn, dog-eared, absolutely useless "testaments" and parts thereof out of the desks and carried them down into the bush where she dumped them under a tree. The very next week Mad MacKinley came around and, wandering through the bush, found this heap. He gathered all the Testaments up in the skirt of his gray duster, stalked up to and into the school and emptied the testaments down on the floor at the feet of the amazed teacher, exclaiming wrathfully,

"Behold how you Presbyterians treat the word of God!"

As there were as many Baptists as Presbyterians among the pupils, we Presbyterians felt very indignant!

Mad MacKinley often came to our place for his mail and frequently stayed for hours talking to Grandfather. Grandfather had once said to him, "Mr. MacKinley, you are welcome to come here whenever you like. But not one word are you to say of or about immersion under this roof." Mad MacKinley never did say one word; and he conversed with Grandfather on all subjects of world interest as rationally as anyone could. One day he came in and asked Grandmother if he might see a *Patriot*. Grandmother gave him one and he sat down in the kitchen to read it. He read silently for some time, neither speaking nor being spoken to; suddenly he gave a shout, threw the paper down, and rushed out of the house. He never came back again and we never knew why. Possibly he had seen something in the paper that displeased or upset him.

Mad MacKinley was a source of amusement to us young fry. We were delighted when he appeared, howling out his anathemas in the graveyard. We were too young to realize the tragedy in this wreck of a once brilliant intellect. To us, "Mad MacKinley" was a Roman holiday and nothing else.

He has been dead these many years. During his life he wanted his brother at North River to sell him a little bit of land on his farm and bury him there when he died, erecting a tombstone bearing nothing but the sole word "*Commissioned.*" This was not done, however.

I am reading Mommsenn's *Rome.* The scholarship is no doubt amazing but the history is deadly dull. There is not one spark of imagination or insight to clothe the dry bones with life.

I had a delightful letter from a young girl in Washington State today. She lost her mother when a baby and said to me, "Your books are to me the mother I have never known." Could anything nicer be said? It means much to me to know that my books have helped one human being as much as that.

I got another compliment tonight, too—Stuart looked up gravely into my face as I kissed him good-night and said,

"Mother, if you were a girl and would wait for me I'd marry you when I grew up."

Stuart is always saying funny little unexpected things. The other day he was going away for the afternoon and he said earnestly, "Good-bye, dear mother. Oh, I *hope you won't die before I get back!*"

Leaskdale, Ont.
Saturday, Aug. 26, 1922
....I was in Toronto last Monday to discuss the new Stokes contract with Mac, missed my train—the very first time I ever missed a train in my life—and had to stay in over night. So I went to see the film *Orphans of the Storm.* It was really the most wonderful thing of its kind I ever saw. I felt when I came out that I had *seen* the French Revolution. The guillotine scene, the storming of the Bastille, and the dance of the Carmagnole through the streets of Paris were very realistic and horrible.

What a way this will be to teach history to children when the Powers that run the schools wake up to it—in another hundred years!

Saturday, Sept. 2, 1922
A busy week. Monday we were occupied in preparing for the ministerial association which met here on Tuesday. On Wednesday we rose at 5:30 and left at seven, to have a day at the Exhibition for the children's sake. For the same sake we waited for the Grand Stand show in the evening—which was good. I enjoyed the fireworks as much as the boys did. We left the grounds at eleven and got home at 1:30. I enjoyed the drive home. The night was fine—Lady Jane behaved well for a wonder. I like travelling by night in a car that acts well. It always gives me the delightful sensation of being a comet, rushing through the darkness of space by my own light....

Last night I heard an owl laughing out on one of the trees of the lawn. I shall never forget the first time I heard owl's laughter. I had often read of it but had never heard it. One night about eight years ago I was going up the road to make a call. It was a dark, still, autumn night with the first fine tang of frost in the air. Suddenly in the little copse of cedar trees on the side of the road to my right I heard chuckles of laughter. I thought it must be some of the village boys hiding there and felt annoyed at the thought that I might be the butt of their clownish amusement. But then it occurred to me that the laughter had in it something not quite human—some weird indescribable quality alien to our laughter—more akin to the Puckish mirth of fairy folk or fauns—with just a faint hint of malice in it. Now, unfortunately I can no longer believe in wood elves, so this laughter puzzled me. Until suddenly I thought of owls and knew it for what it was—a truly, delightful intriguing sound as if some unearthly survival of the Golden Age was chuckling to itself on a dark night.

Last night there was but one owl and he was certainly having a good time all alone over some owlish joke.

The Manse, Leaskdale, Ont.
Sept. 10, 1922
Cars sometimes become possessed of the devil—no doubt at all about that. Lady Jane had seven in her this week. She has worried our lives out. Of course she has never been really right since Pickering ran into us that unlucky Sunday last year. Besides the smashing up she got, everything else was jarred and loosened so that something has been continually going wrong ever since. But this week has beaten all records. It began last Wednesday when we went to Uxbridge. She stopped seven times on the way down without any reason that we could discover. Nothing we could do availed to budge her but always after about ten minutes she would apparently start of her own accord. Really, for all the world she acted just like a balky horse. At Uxbridge, a garage man thought, or pretended to think, that he had located the trouble and fixed it. Lady Jane came home properly. Thursday morning we had planned to go in to Toronto. The *Prisoner of Zenda* was being screened in Massey Hall and the manager had sent me four tickets. So I asked Mrs. Leask and Margaret to go in with us, desiring to put this treat in Margaret's way because she has always been such a cheerful, efficient helper in our Guild.

Lady Jane, however, had her own opinion on the matter and wouldn't start. It was noon before Ewan got her running and then she stopped three times on the road in. However, we did get there and Ewan took her to the Gray-Dort headquarters, thinking that they could surely discover there what was the matter with her. Mrs. Leask, Margaret and I got our dinners and went to Massey Hall.

I don't know whether I shall *ever* become sensible enough *not* to go to see screen versions of my favorite books. I am afraid I won't because I have been disappointed often enough to cure me of the foolishness if I were curable. I was very much disappointed in the film. "Rudolf" wasn't even good-looking and "Flavia" was merely a curly-headed doll with "goo-goo" eyes. The only live character was old "Sapt" who looked uncannily like what the real "Sapt" must have looked. He was convincing but nothing else was. I would resolve never to go to see another book-film if I thought I could keep it but I know I cannot. I will always go to them when occasion offers and always be sorry I did.

We got out at ten and tried to start for home. The Gray-Dort people had over-hauled "Lady Jane" and charged Ewan nine dollars—and she wouldn't even start. Ewan worked over her an hour but in vain. The Gray-Dort garage was closed and no other was near except a little Ford all-night service station. Ewan got her towed there and then took the Leasks up-town to relatives, while I waited in the *Iroquois* lobby and vowed that I'd never again invite anyone to go with us in a car—though I probably won't keep *that* resolution anyhow.

Next morning Ewan got Lady Jane overhauled again, paid some more cash and got away at ten. The brute stopped twice on the road home and we had four flat tires—or rather the same tire went flat for four times and no garage could discover what was wrong. However, we did eventually get home.

Tonight we started for Zephyr to attend a christening. Lady Jane stopped *eleven* times on the way over—and a thunderstorm came up and torrents of rain poured down. I was worn out when we reached there and dreaded the return home. But that absurd car came home without a spark of trouble. Of course she is possessed—not a doubt of it. The Old Scratch himself is in her.

Tired? It is to laugh.

Sunday, Sept. 17, 1922
Leaskdale, Ont.
I have had a beautiful week. Really, I haven't had such a delightful ten days for many a moon.

Ewan left last Monday for a motor trip to Warsaw. (This is not exactly the reason for my beautiful week!) He took Rev. Macdonald of Wick with him and if dear Lady Jane kept on with her antics as she did last week they'd have a charming trip but on the knees of the gods be it.

Lily also departed for her vacation and *this* is why I've had a nice time. Lily has really been intolerable for the past few months again. She was very good all winter, but by spring the salutary effect of the fact of Elsie and its implications had begun to wear off and she slipped back gradually into her pre-Elsie habits. She was forget-ful, lazy, neglectful, cranky and impertinent. So I hailed her departure with a secret exultation. The minute she was out of the house I fell upon kitchen, pantry and cellar cupboard. I

"Kitchen"

put them in order and kept them so. I have had an orderly, peaceful, enjoyable week of it, with plenty of leisure made possible by system and the absence of any one to clutter up.

I got up in the morning, got breakfast and "got" the boys off to school. Then I washed my dishes and sat down for a forenoon of writing. That done I got myself a "pantry bite," did what little tidying was necessary, dressed, did what tasks I had allotted to the day, cooked dinner at night, and then had a good evening of reading and fancy work. There was no abominable "visiting" to do and I was not plagued with aimless callers. When I felt so disposed I did a lot of fancy cooking by way of seeing if my hand had lost its culinary skill—it hadn't! I revelled in my garden—which is splendid this year. All in all, I've had, as I remarked in the beginning, a beautiful week, with no alien spirit in the house to poison the atmosphere.

Monday, Sept. 18, 1922
The Manse, Leaskdale, Ont.
We had Mr. Carswell for Sunday—a nice, ladylike old man of irreproachable soundness of theology. It would be impossible to dislike so harmless a creature but he bored me.

Today I wrote a poem, canned six jars of tomatoes and re-read *Trilby*. One never hears *Trilby* mentioned now. It made the most tremendous sensation twenty years ago. One minister denounced it from his pulpit as "the apotheosis of the scarlet letter." Yet beside some of the heroines of today's novels *Trilby* was chaste as ice and pure as snow. Whatever she was, she was adorable and the book is full of charm from cover to cover and worth a thousand of the arid, sex-obsessed, novels of today.

A question Stuart has just asked me reminded me of the hoods that were worn by children in my day. One never sees hoods now—except on young babies and then they are called bonnets. They are as out-of-date as crinolines. Youngsters now wear "tams," which are really not half so pretty and can't, I'm sure, be as warm. Those old hoods were cosy things. Mine, I remember, were generally crocheted out of "cardinal" wool, with cardinal satin ribbon run through the holes, a perky bow of ribbon just over the forehead, and ties of ribbon. The last hood I ever wore was when I was twelve. Father sent it to me from the west. It was of cream wool and was very becoming. Really, I never looked nicer in anything.

I think it is a pity bonnets for elderly women have gone out. They were more dignified than the hats of today and much kinder to faded, wrinkled faces. Hats seem to emphasize hollow necks and sagging contours while bonnets minimized them. I remember that I liked very much to try on Grandmother's bonnets in the secrecy of the spare room. Grandma had irreproachable taste in bonnets and I thought they became me beautifully and looked forward with pleasure to wearing them when I grew up and married. Alas, I never did wear a bonnet— although the dressy little "toques" which were in style in my early twenties were bonnets in every essential respect, lacking only strings. I remember one especially pretty one I had of black lace with a wreath of flowers. Those "toques" were very becoming to me and I have always cherished a hope that they would "come in" again. They never have. The vogue of big hats and engulfing turbans has continued for years and seems likely to continue—if hats don't "go out" altogether.

I have also been reading Emile Coué's book on "Suggestion." I can hardly believe in all his miracles. If one could make oneself well and good by repeating over and over before going to sleep the mystic formula, "every day in every way I'm growing better and better" why couldn't one make oneself perfect or immortal? Still, I have proved in my own experiments that there is a great power in suggestion. I believe I have cured Chester of some annoying little nervous habits—blinking his eyes and tapping his teeth with nail of his forefinger for example—by bending over him every night after he had gone to sleep and suggesting to him aloud, three times, that he wouldn't do it anymore. At any rate the habits ceased abruptly after two or three nights. The headaches, too, from which he has suffered for years seem to have almost disappeared. Perhaps it was my "suggestion"—perhaps he is simply growing out of them. One cannot *prove* these things. I have been conducting a series of experiments on myself also but cannot as yet say whether they have effected anything or not. Some things happened—but then they might have happened anyway.

Last Friday a letter came from Rev. Mr. Lindsay of Erin, telling Ewan that he could have the last Sunday in September in Hillsburg—a vacant congregation in the Orangeville Presbytery. He had applied for a hearing sometime ago and had given up hope of getting it. I at once telegraphed him and Saturday I had a wire saying he had sent word to Mr. Lindsay that he would go. From all we have heard of it I think it would be a nice place with some advantages that Leaskdale does not possess—and doubtless with some disadvantages. But there is a nice manse and quite a strong congregation where one would not have to worry over the removal of a family.

I had a letter from Ewan today. They reached Warsaw all right. Lady Jane behaved herself badly as far as Ingersoll where E. consulted an electrical expert who located the trouble in the coil. A new coil was put in and Lady Jane's insides troubled her no more. Ewan writes cheerfully and does not seem troubled by headaches or melancholy obsessions.

Saturday, Sept. 23, 1922
Leaskdale, Ont.
I feel as flat as a punctured tire, after the worry of the last twenty-four hours. Yesterday I expected Ewan home all day. He *had* to get back yesterday in order to catch the train to Hillsburg today. But the day passed and he did not come. I made pickles, canned tomatoes, cooked dinner for the boys and two of their school chums, and did not feel anxious until dusk. Then I began to feel anxious and continued to feel anxious until ten, when my anxiety passed into worry which deepened into a brainstorm as the hours crawled by and no one appeared. I had a wretched night. I was worried about the Hillsburg appointment but I was far more worried over the reason of Ewan's non-appearance for I felt sure some accident must have happened to delay him.

I stayed up till three when I took veronal and went to bed. But even the veronal could not keep me soundly asleep. Every time a belated car purred past I sprang up listening, thinking it might be E. But morning came—no E.—noon—no E.! By this time I was really crazy—couldn't work—couldn't do anything but walk the floor.

At four o'clock Ewan walked in, tired, dusty, dishevelled.

On Wednesday night he had had a bad accident—an accident that might have been ten times worse. A car, *without lights* and on the wrong side of the road, had run right into him! Fortunately nobody was injured but Lady Jane was badly knocked up. It cost him seventy five dollars, two days' delay and no end of worry to get her put into shape again. This accident was certainly not his fault in any way. Nevertheless it is enough to make one superstitious. Ewan *has* dreadful luck in the matter of cars. I think it is because he is a man who is slow of thought and cannot think quickly enough what to do in a sudden emergency.

Well, it boots not! The smash took place—and now what about Hillsburg? Ewan declared that he would motor there that night—84 miles—and keep his appointment. I flew round, got his supper, got out his clothes and hunted out his best sermons, while he washed and dressed. Then he started again on his long drive. But I have given up all hope of Hillsburg. He has a bad cold, is very hoarse, and is tired out. He will be very far from his best tomorrow and will not likely make a favorable impression. Well, so be it. In moments like this when I am at my last gasp I fall back on kismet. What is to be will be! Why worry?

Monday, Sept. 25, 1922
The Manse, Leaskdale, Ont.

It is late but I am going to sit up and write in this doomed book. I might as well for I couldn't sleep if I did go to bed.

Talk of blue Monday!

To deal with minor matters first:—Ewan came home tonight feeling quite sure that he had lost out in Hillsburg. And why? *Because he motored there*—or rather, because he has a car. It seems their last minister kept a car and by reason of it *spent too much time in Toronto*. So the people are prejudiced against a minister who has a car! The old folks with whom Ewan stayed were very bitter on the subject and plainly thought motoring a dreadful shortcoming in a minister.

Is it any wonder that young men are not crowding into the ministry?

But after all I suppose it is as well that Hillsburg is no longer one of our problems. For we have before us a fall of misery and worry.

Ewan was in Toronto on his way home and saw McCullough. Pickering is going ahead with his lawsuit and is claiming *eight thousand* dollars damages—one thousand for his operation, five thousand for his "sufferings" and two thousand for "injuries to his wife."

It is simply a conspiracy to get money out of us, nothing more or less. This man who wants five thousand for his "sufferings" is a well man today where for years before the accident he was miserable; his *own son* told Ewan that he had planned to have the operation the next week; as for Mrs. Pickering this is the first heard of *her* injuries. Pickering never referred to her in his letters. It is evidently a device of the lawyers who know that if Pickering was negligent *he* cannot get damages but that *his* negligence will not prevent *her* from getting them. Nobody heard of Mrs. Pickering complaining of any lasting injury before. At the time of the collision she had a tiny two-inch cut on her forehead which healed up in a week. On the other hand it is well-known that she had been complaining of her health for years before the accident. Two thousand dollars is quite a large sum for a scratch that did not even leave a scar! But the woman is such a notorious person that she is capable of anything, so I feel more worried over this than over her husband's claims. Yet surely no court would give her damages without medical evidence to her injuries. I would not think it possible, yet McCullough is evidently worried.

Well, we must fight. It is a hideous sort of predicament to be in but we are not going to pay the hospital bills of a man like Pickering unless we are compelled to. It is sheer blackmail and we will not submit to it as a matter of principle if nothing else. One comfort is that every soul in the community, outside of the Pickering clan—and indeed some in it—is on our side. Pickering is universally condemned and we will not lose either caste or repute by fighting him when he drags us into law like this. Everyone knows that he has been ill for years and everyone knows, too, that he tore up Zephyr street like a madman and ran right into us, although he saw us plainly by his own admission. Of course Ewan should have looked a second time before he turned to cut the corner—and of course he shouldn't have been cutting the corner at all but that does not excuse Pickering for hogging the road at the rate of thirty to thirty-five miles an hour.

But oh, what a wretched fall I foresee!

Wednesday, Sept. 27, 1922
The Manse, Leaskdale, Ont.
Poor Ewan has begun his task of getting all possible evidence. We have already Mr. Law who will say that Pickering was in the middle of the road, did not turn out, did not sound his horn, was going very fast and was equally to blame. Then we have two men at Mt. Albert, Mr. Hugh Evans and Mr. Robert Wilson, both respected and reputable men who will testify that Pickering said to them shortly after he came out of the hospital, "The accident didn't cause my operation. I had to have that anyway."

Ewan also got several new witnesses today. Mrs. Jake Meyers, who was with us, says he was in the middle of the road—never tooted—and was going very fast. Another Mr. Meyers and a Mrs. Smith who saw him pass just before the crash say the same.

The Manse, Leaskdale, Ont.
Saturday, Sept. 30, 1922
We are having such lovely weather. If only we had "minds at leisure from themselves" to enjoy it! But I can think of nothing but the Pickering affair.

Many people in Zephyr think that it is Mrs. Pickering that put Pickering up to this. She is a woman notorious for bad temper, tyranny and stubbornness. She looks it—her very face is obscene. She doesn't seem to have a friend. She is

Pickering's second wife—by the way, he "had to get married" as the country phrase goes, both times.

Other people think it is Greig who has put Pickering up to it. Greig has the reputation of taking up and pushing dirty cases. *I* think it is probably both Mrs. Pickering and Greig. The latter evidently thinks, from things he has said, that *I* will settle the case rather than go to court. He little knows me. I have fought bigger and more hopeless cases than this rather than give in tamely to imposition.

Ewan went to Zephyr today to meet Mr. McCullough who wanted to see the ground for himself. He brought home two good bits of news. In the first place, there is no law against cutting a corner in the country. That is only a city ordinance. So Pickering can't catch us there. In the second place, the corner at Zephyr is a "blind" corner and the law is that anyone approaching such a corner

"The blind corner" [Zephyr]

must slow down to twelve and a half miles and blow his horn. Pickering certainly didn't do either. If he had the accident wouldn't have happened.

If—if—if! It's the most fateful word in the language. *If* I hadn't gone to Zephyr that Sunday—*if* Mrs. Meyers hadn't asked us to tea—*if* we hadn't been short of gas—*if* Ewan had looked a second time—*if* Marshall Pickering were a straight man instead of a crook—well, *if* Eve had never eaten the apple. Or, if you like it better, *if* the first ape who twisted off a bough and used it as a club had never thought of doing the thing. You can go very far back with your "ifs." But for all I'm glad the first ape *did* think of it—I don't know whether I'm even sorry that Eve ate the apple! After all, isn't it well "to know good and evil?" If we didn't what better would we be than babies or vegetables?

The Manse, Leaskdale, Ont.
October 1, 1922
Eleven years ago October first also fell on a Sunday. It was a day of pouring rain and I was blue and homesick. Eleven years—in those eleven years the world in which I was brought up has utterly passed away—humanity has had its heart

broken—and Marshall Pickering has developed and lost an enlarged prostate gland!!

This fact just now looms largest in my consciousness, as a five-cent bit held close to the eye will blot out the hosts of heaven.

A man at Mt. Albert, said, when he heard that Pickering was suing us for $8,000, "Eight thousand! It's more than his whole damned carcass is worth, let alone his prostate gland."

Of course Ewan and I know that even if Pickering won his suit he would never get anything like $8,000—that it is the usual legal dodge to ask about four times what you have any real chance of getting. But our simple country folk, unacquainted with legal dodges, believe that if Pickering wins he will get the whole amount and they are horror stricken.

And they are also horrified at his suing "a *minister*." Evidently reverence for "the cloth" is not yet totally extinct in our land!

Mac writes me that *Emily* is a fine piece of work and "a great story." Let us hope my dear public will think so.

Wednesday, October 4, 1922
I felt very tired and depressed all day. But I fussed up a tea for two schoolteachers—Miss Buckham of the North School and Olive Blanchard of our own.

Ewan went to Toronto today to see his lawyer. Before he went he remarked on how well he was feeling this fall. And he *is*. He has never had a headache or any sign of mental trouble since August. He *seems* perfectly well but I have hoped too often to dare hope again. If the improvement only lasts until our lawsuit is over I will be thankful. I really think the fact that his mind is so taken up with the suit accounts in a great measure for the improvement. He cannot brood over religious phobias when he *has* to contemplate Marshall Pickering and his doings.

Saturday, October 7, 1922
I had a nasty dream last night—one of my vivid, symbolic dreams that always mean something. I don't like it at all. I am sure it means trouble ahead.

I dreamed that Ewan was standing out on the road in front of Mr. Warner's house, talking to two men who were strangers to me. He was making some request of them which they seemed to grant, for he shook hands, smiled, and bade them good-bye. Then, as he turned away, the taller of the two men struck him a blow from behind and stretched him on the dusty road. Ewan sprang up at once and I had just time to think, "Oh, what a humiliation before the congregation," when I woke.

Every one of these vivid dreams that I have ever had has "come true" and I know this is a warning, let who will laugh....

Stuart, reading in a book today came across the statement that all insects were hatched from the egg. He asked me if this were true. When I replied "yes" he said, "But where would they get an insect to lay the *first* egg?"

Ay, there's the rub!

The Manse, Leaskdale, Ont.
Wednesday, Oct. 11, 1922

We have been shivering for two weeks for it has been quite cold and we have been unable to have a fire in the furnace because of some repairs that have to be made. But the man came up from Uxbridge today and finished the job. So we have a fire tonight and are physically comfortable, for which praise be. It is a little easier to bear one's worries when one is free from goose-flesh.

Ewan went to Toronto today. The "examination for discovery," as they call it, takes place tomorrow. Pickering's Toronto lawyer—Phelan, K.C., who is said to be one of the best lawyers in Toronto. I am afraid Pickering has got ahead of us *there*—will examine Ewan and McCullough will examine Pickering and his Sarah. We will then know what they mean to assert and try to prove. I wonder if Marshall Pickering will really swear to his falsehoods when it comes to a show down. Ewan thinks he won't but I feel quite sure he will. What else is there for him to do unless he backs down altogether which he certainly won't do now.

I have been writing every morning up to now but this morning I couldn't settle my mind to it. I kept worrying over tomorrow. Oh, if it were only over! I dread Ewan's return home.

The Manse, Leaskdale, Ont.
Thursday, Oct. 12, 1922

This has been a wretched day—dull, cold, showery. When I woke I said, "How can I get through this day?"

But I can always get through today. It is only tomorrow that I can't get through.

The day was one of silent worry—silent because I had no one to talk to. We cleaned the spare room. My worry deepened as the day wore on, closing down into the early darkness of a rainy night. At twilight I looked out over the dim landscape and shivered. The rain on autumn fields is a very sorrowful thing.

I helped Chester with his arithmetic and played dominoes with him and Stuart—and all the time I was fairly trembling with nervous dread. *Why* I should have been so nervous I don't know—I *knew* perfectly well what Marshall Pickering would say. I think at bottom I must have had a faint unacknowledged hope that after all he might back down when he saw Ewan would not buy him off and that I dreaded the extinction of that hope, even while I believed I did not possess it. At such times our minds seem split in two parts—one part a rational one which recognizes facts as they present themselves—the other an irrational one which persists in clinging to a blind, instinctive hope that *something* will turn up to avert the evil we shrink from and which trembles lest its hope be destroyed.

I was really cold with dread. I expected Ewan home by eight and got the boys off to bed that we might have an uninterrupted conversation. But he did not come. It was pouring rain and I feared some accident for I couldn't see what else could delay him. I compelled myself to sit and sew until ten. Then I could not sit still any longer—neither could I read. So I fell to swatting flies! We have a fearful dose of them at present owing to the fact that Stuart left the screen door open today. For an hour I dealt death and destruction. Marshall Pickering was the doom of hundreds of flies tonight who might otherwise have lived several fly-years longer. At eleven the carcases of flies lay in drifts on the floor—the house was free from them—and Ewan came home.

He was blue enough, too. Like myself he had evidently been cherishing irrational hopes. Pickering swore to a whole catalogue of lies. He swore that he had never had *any* trouble before the collision—that he had never complained to anyone—that he had never consulted a doctor—in short that, as far as he knew, he was a perfectly well man until the night after the collision. When one recalls what his son told Ewan in the hospital it makes one wonder how a man *could* swear to such lies.

But that was not the limit of Marshall Pickering's fictions. He told an even more barefaced lie than that. He deliberately said that after the collision Ewan went up to him and said,

"This was my fault, Mr. Pickering, and I want to make it right"—that Ewan then reckoned up the damages—"the radiator will cost so much etc. etc." and that *he*, Pickering, then said,

"Well, Mr. Macdonald, this is Sunday night and we won't talk about it now."

Nice little dose of hypocrisy that!

Now, I was there and I heard every word that Ewan and Pickering said to each other. When they got out of the cars Ewan said, "Why, Mr. Pickering, is this you? I didn't know it was you."

"Neither did I know it was you," said Pickering.

"How was it we didn't see each other?" asked Ewan.

"Oh, I saw you—I saw you," exclaimed Pickering. "I saw you from the time you started from the tank."

"Are you hurt?" asked Ewan.

"No, *I'm all right*," said Pickering, "but Mrs. Pickering is a little hurt."

Then Ewan said,

"Well, that is the worst feature of this. As far as the damage to the cars go we can repair them in the garage."

Then Pickering went away with his wife and had no further conversation with Ewan. That is every word that was said—and yet he could go and swear—but there! He is a man who will stick at nothing!

Then Mrs. Pickering had her turn. She swore she was quite well before the collision and had never been well since. Questioned, she said "she had no ambition and had to keep her daughters who had been working out, home to do the work." Admitted that she had not been to a doctor but was taking "a tonic." Both she and Pickering swore he was going "fifteen to twenty miles." Evidently their lawyers haven't yet seen the corner and don't know it is blind or they wouldn't have let him admit even that much. Pickering and his wife—they were examined separately of course—told different stories as to where their car was at the moment of collision—she saying they were away off on their own side of the road, he saying that he was on the middle of the road but turned out as much as the law required. This is just the opposite of what he said in his letters last winter. That man will say *anything* and if we cannot prove he is lying we will lose our case. The worst of it is that we cannot get what his son told Ewan in evidence. It is "hearsay" and so will not be allowed in. I daresay Pickering himself does not know that his son told Ewan that. If he *had* known I think even he could hardly have the face to make the claims he did. When he wrote his first letter to Ewan he thought Ewan knew nothing at all of his previous trouble or intentions and when Ewan wrote him that he knew (but didn't say who had told him) Marshall Pickering was so wild with shame over the thought that he had made such claims when Ewan knew the truth all along that he determined to stick to his lie to save his face if he could. He is a notoriously conceited man and it would make him writhe to think that Ewan *knew* he had to have an operation and that he was just putting a conspiracy over on us. So he has gone on, deeper and deeper, thinking Ewan would eventually pay something rather than be dragged into a lawsuit until he got in so deep that he could not back out without humiliation he could not bear. I think that is the real truth of the matter and explains the long delays that took place between each of his moves. He was afraid to go on and ashamed to go back. People in Zephyr, too, were constantly twitting him about it—asking him if he had given up the notion of suing Macdonald etc, and all this goaded him to carry out his threats.

Well, there is not much likelihood that he will retract now; and we will not. If he had not lied—if he had confined his demands to the hundred dollars that his car cost him—we would have paid the whole hundred without hesitation rather than be dragged into the courts, even though he was more to blame for the collision than we were. But when he tried to make us pay his hospital bills we simply would not do it and we both feel the same way about it. There is something in us both that will not submit to injustice even for the sake of peace.

But I will not sleep tonight.

The Manse, Leaskdale, Ont.
Friday, Oct. 13, 1922
This morning we went to Zephyr and I stayed with Lily Shier while Ewan was hunting evidence. Rob said Dr. Johnson was a witness for Pickering—having said that in his opinion the collision "produced congestion of the gland" and necessitated the operation. This is bad.

I went to see Mrs. Heath and when I told her that Marshall Pickering had sworn that he never had any trouble before the collision she threw up her hands and said, "Oh, Mrs. Macdonald, surely Marshall Pickering could never have sworn *that*. Why, he has been complaining and doctoring for years. And the morning after the collision my daughter, Mrs. Burnham, telephoned over to Pickerings and asked his daughter Verna how he was. When she heard he had gone to the hospital she asked if this was the result of the collision Verna said, "Oh, no, it's only just pa's old trouble back again. He had to have the operation anyway."

I asked Mrs. Heath if Mrs. Burnham would give evidence to this. Likely Verna P. will be on the stand and we will be able to get it in. Mrs. Heath said she felt sure she would. So I came home in better spirits than I expected to.

This evening we went to a "Hypatia" social at Uxbridge, held in Minnie Gould's house. I had expected I would be too worried to enjoy it but somehow I wasn't. To put on a pretty evening dress and then spin down to town over the good roads in the clear evening air, under a cloudless silvery sky was so exhilarating that it made me feel almost happy for the time being. Besides, riding in a car always seems to cheer me up. It is as if we went so fast that we *left worry behind.* This impression seems to seize upon the imagination and produce for a time the effects of reality. I think this is why Ewan, when his attacks of melancholia come on, always seems to be so much better in the car.

The old Gould house is a spacious dwelling built in the days of large families, cheap lumber and cheap labor. We had a delightful evening. It was wonderful to have an evening with intelligent people who could really *talk* about something besides local gossip and politics. We had a good programme, a good supper and a jolly hour of after dinner speeches.

But of course this couldn't last all the way through. We left for home at one and just out of Uxbridge poor unlucky Lady Jane began to "act up." Out went our lights. Ewan couldn't locate the trouble and at that hour no help could be obtained. Luckily—yes, there *must* be such a thing as luck. Jacques Loeb says the universe and all therein is the product of chance and at times I agree with him—there was clouded moonlight, so we managed to get home all in one piece by driving slowly. Luckily again we did not meet anyone. Yes, it was a charming evening and has restored my sadly impaired morale.

The Manse, Leaskdale, Ont.
Saturday, Oct. 14, 1922
This windy morning we went to Stouffville to confer with Mr. McCullough who was to meet us there. We called at Zephyr where Ewan asked Rob Shier just what Dr. Johnson said. It seems he said that he *thought* the accident must have caused Pickering's "spasm" that night but said he could not say so positively— many other things might have brought it on. This is not so bad as we feared.

We called for Mrs. Jake Meyers and then went to Mt. Albert where E. saw Mrs. Burnham. She was not very willing to testify. Her husband was away but she seemed to think he would be averse to it. However, E. pointed out how much it might mean to us and eventually she consented.

At Stouffville Mr. McCullough examined Mrs. Meyers and me and was pleased with what we could say.

I was woefully tired when I came home. The worst of it is that Ewan and I cannot stop talking about the case continually and discussing it from every angle. We vow we will not—and three minutes later break the vow. Day and night, out and in, at board and in bed, it haunts us. It is The Dweller On The Threshold and we cannot forget its grisly presence for an instant.

Sunday, Oct. 15, 1922
We have got an important piece of evidence. After church service in Zephyr today we went to see old Mrs. Alex Lockie who used to live across the road from Pickerings and is well acquainted with him. When I told her that Pickering had sworn that he had never had any trouble before the collision she stared.

"Why," she said, "in March 1919 he came to see my husband who was ill and when I asked him how he was he said, `I feel very miserable. I am afraid I am going the same way my father did.' (His father died under an operation for enlarged prostate gland complicated with Bright's disease)."

We must get Mrs. Lockie as a witness.

Tonight I read Thomas Hardy's *Two on a Tower*. I think I would like it very much if my mind was at leisure from itself. But the story ends abominably. When I am reasonably comfortable in mind and body I can endure a tale that ends sadly. But when, as now, I am in a chronic state of unrest and dread I want a fairy story where everything ends happily—something that will create in me the temporary illusion that there *is* "a destiny that shapes our ends" and occasionally brings good out of evil.

The Manse, Leaskdale, Ont.
Monday, Oct. 16, 1922

This morning we went to Uxbridge and Ewan went to see Dr. McClintock. He was the doctor Johnson called in to help him when he found that he couldn't "relieve" Pickering. We have been afraid of McClintock for we have had the impression for some time that he was antagonistic to us. But it seems he is not. He said that the prostate gland couldn't have been injured by the collision and that in his opinion the latter had nothing whatever to do with it. We will subpoena him—it will offset Johnson.

Nevertheless I am tonight tired, worried, blue, and about as composed as a flea. Ewan is away, having gone to Sutton on an evidence hunt. I don't know which is worse—talking about the affair to him or threshing it over in my own thoughts.

Tuesday, Oct. 17, 1922

I am excited tonight—happily excited. Ewan is home with a fine "kill" of evidence. One bit of it ought to win our case for us.

I was housecleaning all day, working feverishly to drug my worry. In the evening I put the boys to bed. Lily was out and I settled down to wait until Ewan came home. I trembled with suspense when I heard Lady Jane purring in. But Ewan came in, smiling.

"My search has not been fruitless," he said triumphantly.

We had been told by one of our people—who, by the way, are all eagerly hunting evidence for us—that she believed Pickering had been to Dr. Boynton of Sutton. So Ewan went to see him. And Pickering *was* there, in May 1922, about a month before the collision.

Boynton said,

"I didn't examine him but from the symptoms he described I diagnosed his trouble as an enlarged prostate gland and I advised an operation."

Moreover, Boynton has the date and name of Marshall Pickering entered in his ledger, though not, unfortunately, the nature of his complaint. But even so it is very good.

And Pickering swore that he never consulted a doctor. If this holds good—and it is documentary evidence—we can convict him of perjury.

Lily also tells me that her father went to consult Boynton in the spring of 1922 and saw Pickering in the office at the same time. He spoke of it to his family when he went home. But he is now dead so that is no help to us.

Another bit of good news was that Mrs. Alex Lockie is quite willing to give evidence. Joe Taylor saw the Pickering car pass "at thirty miles an hour if an inch" a second or two before the collision. And Mrs. Bingham told Ewan that in 1917 Verna Pickering told her that her mother had been to a specialist in Toronto and had been told that she had diabetes—the "sugar diabetes" as it is called.

Now, if we can establish this surely we can corner Mrs. P. Yet that woman said in the examination for discovery that she never was ill before the collision. Surely, if we can show by medical evidence that both Pickering and his wife have sworn falsely the Judge will not believe that any of their tale is true.

Thursday, Oct. 19, 1922

More ups and downs—fortunately the "ups" came after the "down." We had a letter from Mrs. Burnham imploring us not to subpoena her as a witness. Her husband she says will be dreadfully angry because their daughter is married to "the brother of the husband of a daughter of Marshall Pickering's." It will, she declares, brew up all kinds of family trouble for her. Well, it is hard on us but we will not take an unwilling witness. Anyway, Boynton's evidence is worth all the others put together. And Ewan has got another witness in Mrs. Burnham's place—Mrs. Bingham to whom Verna Pickering said the same thing....All our pastoral work is being hung up this fall because of this wretched worry. Fortunately our people understand. Everyone far and near is on our side, outside half a dozen birds-of-a-feather who herd with the Pickering crew. But "everyone" is not the Judge who will try our case....

The Manse, Leaskdale, Ont.
Friday, Oct. 20, 1922

Busy all day housecleaning, burning leaves—I do love the pungent reek of burning autumn leaves—and harvesting gladiolus bulbs. My glads were wonderful this summer. My rooms were full of them for nearly three months and I luxuriated in their exotic beauty. But this is the end of it for this season—and sometimes I feel drearily for all time. Will there ever be any beauty in life for me again?

Ewan came home tonight. He saw Dr. Johnson and Dr. J. said that in 1917 Mrs. Pickering consulted him in regard to certain symptoms. He diagnosed her trouble as sugar diabetes and sent her to a specialist in Toronto who confirmed the diagnosis. We have the address of this specialist and Ewan will see him.

One item of Ewan's report troubled me. Dr. Stephens, an expert who is interested in our case, saw Dr. Jones, who performed the operation on Pickering and said to him, "Mr. Pickering is suing for damages for that affair." "Yes, and he'll get them too," said Jones.

This must mean that Jones' opinion is adverse to us and he will be on their side.

Long ago I read in D'Aubigny's *History of the Reformation in France* a horrible tale of some poor creature who was tortured at an *auto da fe* by being lowered from a beam into a slow fire for a few minutes and then hoisted up again and so on. I think I have some idea of what he suffered. My torture at present is of the same nature.

Nevertheless I have never been able to agree that mental anguish is harder to endure than bodily anguish—that is, if it is of the same degree. Many people declare that it is—but it is my opinion that such people, while they may have suffered extreme mental pain have never suffered any extreme physical pain and so have no proper standard of comparison. I cannot believe that *any* mental anguish could equal the agony of a human being being broiled alive over a slow fire.

There *is* a devil and he is the Spirit of Cruelty that is rampant in the whole universe and that drags its bestial trail over every page of history. Cruelty is the very essence of sin.

The Manse, Leaskdale, Ont.
Sat. Oct. 21, 1922
The Lloyd George Government has gone down—rather unexpectedly after all. He has weathered so many crises that one expected him to weather this one also. But the man who has been the virtual ruler of the British Empire since the terrible autumn of 1917 has fallen. Perhaps it is well. Lloyd George was an indomitable fighter. He was the man for leadership in a great war. But I do not think he is a constructive statesman and that is what heaven and earth are shrieking for now—and failing to find.

But just now I am not interested in Lloyd George. Marshall Pickering is the man of the hour for me—the old devil!

Ewan talks of him continually. But it is better for his mind to be taken up with this than with his melancholic phobias. Even Marshall Pickering is not so bad as a dread that you have committed the unpardonable sin.

This morning Stuart gave us a laugh at the breakfast table. I was speaking of some woman whose badly spoiled children were dreadful nuisances. Where upon Stuart remarked gravely, "When I grow up I think I'll marry a wife without children."!

Thursday, Oct. 24, 1922
This has been a most unpleasant day. For the first time since I began housekeeping here eleven years ago I have had a quarrel with my maid. I have known for sometime that it was bound to come sooner or later....I could have put up with her untidiness and forgetfulness but her bad temper and impertinence could not be endured and I knew that very soon we would have to have "a showdown." Lily must either be taught her place or leave.

I shrank from it. I hate to quarrel with a person I am living with. But Lily was making life so bitter for me in a hundred petty ways—and this, too, at a time when I am so harassed and worried—that I realized this sort of thing could not go on much longer. Lily had evidently come to the conclusion that I would put up with anything and that she could rule the house because I dared not quarrel with or dismiss her.

The limit of my endurance was reached one morning about a fortnight ago. Ewan and I had been away until late at night and Chester had forgotten to go to

"Pat" [and Lily Meyers]

Mr. Leask's for the milk in the evening. Lily should have reminded him of course but she did not do so. When she came down in the morning there was no milk or cream for breakfast and she had to go over for it. One would have thought that to step across the road on a fine bright morning and carry back a quart of milk could not have been such a terrible thing; and one would also have thought that a person so forgetful as Lily herself should make a little allowance when other people forgot. But Lily has got into the habit of coming down *every* morning in a bad temper and she welcomes any kind of excuse for it. She was so unbearable that my fingers tingled to give her a right good box on her sullen face. My patience suddenly gave way. I decided then and there that I would put an end to this sort of thing. I have been patient for several reasons. Help is hard to get here; and Lily is the sort of girl who, if sent away from a place, would revenge herself by telling lies everywhere about the menage she had left.

But now nothing mattered except to rid myself of a nuisance that had become absolutely intolerable.

However, I did not say anything just then. I thought I could not have a domestic explosion when I am so upset over this lawsuit. It was unthinkable. So I decided that I would wait until the trial was over and then I would tell Lily plainly that she must behave herself or leave.

I felt very bitterly towards her. I have been very good to her—very thoughtful of her comfort and feelings. She is treated as one of the family and paid good wages for doing—and often doing very poorly—much lighter work than she had on the farms where she used to be hired. And yet now, when I am having such a hard and anxious time, she will not even refrain from adding to the misery and discomfort of my life by her unreasonable tantrums.

So I said nothing that day but events have forced my hand, and the long overdue storm burst today....

We were cleaning the library yesterday and just before supper I asked Lily to wash the south window so that I could put the plants back on the sill, as I wanted them out of the way before I set the supper table. Lily answered in a rather impertinent tone that she wanted to finish rubbing down the furniture on the veranda and bring it in before dark. I ignored her tone, since her request in itself was reasonable enough.

"Oh, very well," I said pleasantly. "You can finish that first."

But Lily did not go back to the furniture. Whether she misunderstood me or not, she hurled herself out to the kitchen, got water, and went at the window in a rage. I shrugged my shoulders and said no more but went to get a light by which to set the table. As usual I found that the lamps had not been cleaned or filled. I went to work and cleaned them. Lily saw me and seemed to be angrier than ever—because she felt, I suppose, that it put her in the wrong. Finally she came out—the window was only a ten minute job—and said in a voice that fairly trembled with rage, "Your window is ready for you."

Still preserving silence I put the plants back, while Lily made the pancakes for supper—and spoiled them also. They were scorched, and heavy as lead when she put them on the table. She slammed into her chair and began to drink a cup of tea. Stuart, who loves pancakes, said innocently, "Don't you want some pancakes, Lily?" "No," she snapped, "I don't feel much like eating anything."

Still I said nothing. I ate my supper, attended to the boys and ignored her—a proceeding that seemed to aggravate her still further. After supper she washed the dishes and went out as usual. I drew a relieved breath. The house seemed released from an incubus.

This morning I came down and found that Lily, having gone to bed in a bad temper had evidently got up in a worse one. I was preparing Chester's school lunch and I asked Lily where she had put the butter. She gave me an impudent answer.

I laid down my knife and turned around. It was the last straw. I said, in a cold, measured voice,

"Lily, I have come to the end of my patience with you. I do not wish to quarrel with anyone but the time has come when you compel me to say to you that if you cannot behave yourself a little better than you have been behaving here for months you must find a place where the mistress will put up with that sort of thing, because *I* will not."

Lily's face turned crimson. I think she was utterly amazed at this turning of the worm. At first she attempted to speak but I silenced her and went on. I gave her such a dressing down as she richly deserved. She muttered sullenly that the boys wouldn't "obey her"—that she "couldn't get to sleep till all hours" because Mr. Macdonald and I were out late so often or sat up so late and that was why she was out of sorts in the morning—"you don't feel very good yourself when you don't get your sleep."

"No, I do not," I said, "but I do not visit it on those who live in the house with me and are not to blame for it. You are out late far oftener than we are. You knew when you came here that you were coming to the house of a minister and student who could not go to bed at nine o'clock as farmers do. You knew that Mr. Macdonald and I had to visit—and sit up when we were home to study and write. We make no loud noise when we come in and go to bed—there is no reason why it should disturb you."

"Even a person moving about the house keeps me awake."

"Then you must go where no one will move about the house. You cannot find such conditions here. As for the boys, if you treated them decently you would have no trouble with them. You never say a kind word to them—you nag and rail at them from morning till night. You cannot even speak civilly to them when they are not meddling with you at all. It is no wonder they will not try to please you. You have neglected your work recently to a ridiculous extent. In short we have come to the point where I must tell you plainly that you must either behave yourself or go."

"Perhaps I'd better go then if you're not satisfied," she muttered.

"You can please yourself about that," I said coolly. "I am not sending you away. I simply say that I will not have a maid in this house who isn't contented with her position. I have nothing to reproach myself with. I have been a good mistress to you. If you know of a place where you will have no inconveniences to put up with you had better go to it. *I* have never found such a place. But if you want to stay here I repeat for the last time that you must behave yourself properly and have done with these continual tantrums of yours and neglect of your work."

I left her there and went upstairs. I felt a great relief and I only regret that I did not speak just so to her long ago. Of course it has been a most unpleasant day. Lily has been very down but she has worked with a vengeance, doing everything quickly and thoroughly and in due season—as she *can* when she likes. I have ignored her completely.

I do not know what she will do. I think she will stay. She knows perfectly well that she cannot get another place like this, with no outside work, near her home, good wages, and steady employment. But I would be just as well pleased if she did go. I shall never feel the same to her again.

Ay, di me! Life seems a very prickly, thorny wilderness to me at present with no oasis anywhere in sight.

Thursday, October 26, 1922
The Manse, Leaskdale, Ont.

For the first time in three weeks our house is warm—and consequently life is tolerable. We could not light a fire in the furnace because part of it was burned out and had to be replaced. And the evenings have been very cold of late. We have continued to exist by the grace of our coal oil heater. Said heater has saved our lives several times since its purchase, so I ought to be grateful to it. But I am not—I detest it.

All my life I have longed for an open fireplace. I suppose all my life I shall long for it and never get it—at least, until it is too late. If this house were our own I would have had one built in long ago. But in a manse this is almost out of the question. Though, had I known eleven years ago that we would be this long I would have put one in and felt that the delight of a fireplace for so many years would be sufficient recompense even if we did "move on" then. But one cannot know—and to go to all the trouble and expense of building a fireplace into a house and then possibly leave it in a year or so seems foolish. If the expense were all I would put it in—but it would mean so much bother and tearing to pieces. No, I am afraid I can never have my fireplace—can never sit before it on a cold evening, with my children and my friends, and talk as people *can* talk only before an open fire. A house without an open fire is a house without a soul. A black hole in the floor—ugh!

In the old home we had no fireplaces—they had been done away with when Grandpa remodelled the house. But we had what was almost quite as good—the old-fashioned coal stoves whose open doors let out all the glow and warmth and friendliness within. Even the kitchen stove had a grate which radiated light and cheer. Nowadays there are no such stoves—even the kitchen ranges are ugly black boxes in which you cannot catch a glimpse of flame.

But at any rate we got the furnace fixed today and there is a very different atmosphere in the house tonight. I fear we shall have to burn wood this winter, owing to the coal strike in the U.S. and that will mean a good deal of annoyance from smoke since our furnace is not well adapted to wood.

Ewan has been talking lately of how well he is feeling. And he *is* well—perfectly well, whether it lasts or not. I am afraid to hope it will last but at any rate he is absolutely well now. I know this from a queer enough reason—*he doesn't "say his prayers"* any more!!

When I married I had a touching belief that ministers always prayed. Even I, who no longer believed many things of the old creeds, had never given up my habit of nightly prayer or lost a certain faith that there *was* a Power who would hear it. How much more, then, should a minister, who *did* believe the old creeds fully, still pray. It was a distinct shock to me to find that Ewan never prayed, except for the prayer at family worship. I think the truth is that he was never taught to pray in childhood and so never formed the habit. His parents were poor, his mother overworked and the whole atmosphere and tradition of the family the reverse of spiritual. Ewan, himself, normally has not an atom of spirituality about him, being a jolly, practical sort of man.

But from the moment his attack of melancholia came on in the spring of 1919, three and a half years ago, he has prayed, morning and night and often, when the recurring attacks were at their worst, through the day. Such prayers of course, did him no good and were only the instinctive cries of his irrational fear. Lately he has stopped them completely—never seems to think of praying. So I know that he is perfectly well for the first time since 1919. Oh, if it would only continue! If I thought the real worry he has had lately was the cause of his cure I would bless even Marshall Pickering. But it is probably a mere coincidence.

Friday, October 27, 1922
….Lily, after sulking for two days—but *not* going—has suddenly become quite angelic and no one would ever imagine that there had been a word between us. I should have "spoken out in meeting" long ago.

I have the proofs of *Emily* to read but so far I have not been able to read them. I cannot settle down to mental effort of any sort. I am getting no work at all done this fall.

Monday, Oct. 30, 1922
Leaskdale, Ont.

I am terribly upset and cannot sleep or rest. We went over to Zephyr this morning and I stayed at Rob Shier's while Ewan went up to take Boynton his subpoena. I soon made a ghastly discovery, which was confirmed when I returned.

It seems that Pickering heard in some way that Boynton was to be our witness—Boynton himself very foolishly told it. Pickering went to Sutton yesterday afternoon and told Boynton that he had never consulted him.

"Oh, yes, you did," said Boynton. "I have the record of your visit in my book"—and then, more foolishly still, he showed it to him.

Pickering looked staggered at first—then said,

"That must be my nephew, young Marshall Pickering."

This said young Marshall is a notorious scamp who got into some scrape this summer and has decamped no one knows where, so we cannot find him to disprove this. If we *could* find him I daresay he would be quite willing to help us for he hates his uncle. He is a young man of twenty-two and, as Boynton says, would never have an enlarged prostate gland, which is an old man's disease. But the trouble is that Boynton has been so befuddled by Pickering's positive assertion that he had never consulted him that he cannot swear to anything now. He told Ewan that he cannot remember the *face* of the man who consulted him and though he is "quite certain" in his own mind that it was Pickering he says he can't go on the stand and take oath to it. The entry itself proves nothing since there is nothing in it that shows *which* Marshall Pickering was there. Boynton says he is positive young Marshall never was to see him about anything.

We know old Marshall Pickering *was* there for Lily's father saw him in Boynton's office a month before the collision and mentioned it to his family when he came home. But he is dead and so we cannot bring the lie home to Pickering....

I shall not sleep again tonight. And there are two weeks yet before the trial comes on. It seems to me just now that I *cannot* live through them. When the worst comes I'll be able to bear it. But this suspense!

Tuesday, October 31, 1922
The Manse, Leaskdale, Ont.

I had a bad night—even veronal could not give me oblivion—and I had a worse day until dusk. I felt dreadfully worn-out physically and upset mentally. Ewan went to Zephyr in the forenoon to meet Mr. Button—McCullough's partner—and a surveyor who were coming out to make a chart of the road. I worked at routine tasks, sewed, mended, and tried to read proof but couldn't. Always I have taken delight in reading my proofs but this time I read them in torment.

Then the boys came home from school bent on having Jack-o-lanterns made for Hallowe'en festivities tonight. I couldn't disappoint them, so I went to work with two pumpkins and made jackies out of them, while I lived over the trial in my mind, saw our case lost, saw us having to pay out anywhere from three to six thousand dollars, and saw Marshall Pickering and that demon of a wife of his triumphant and boasting—which was the worst anticipation of all.

Then Ewan came home and beckoned me into the library.

"I have good news for you." he said. "Mr. Button told me that McCullough had 'phoned out to him that Dr. Stevenson had managed to obtain a peep at the record of the case in the hospital and that it was *very favorable to us.*"

I felt as if I had been released from the rack. If there is a record of the case in the hospital—something we did not know before—I cannot believe that Pickering even now will really take this case into court after all. If he did and this record were produced it would prove him a perjuror. If the record is "very favorable"—and McCullough is not the man to overstate his case—he will indeed be a fool to go on with this. Unless he has actually, through the effects of pain and ether, forgotten there was such a thing.

I haven't felt so care-free for a month as I felt tonight. Everything was transformed in the wink of an eye. An intolerable burden of worry and unrest seemed lifted from my soul. I was a child with the children and flung myself into the Hallowe'en sports without reservation. The village boys came in and Lily and I rigged them up in masks and ridiculous costumes and started them off. We had our gate posts adorned with two fine fiendish jacks and we went out into the crisp moonlit night and raked up fallen leaves and had a bonfire. I could hardly believe I was the same creature I was in the afternoon—I felt so light-hearted, so joyful, so seized with the beauty of the night.

Then, when the fun was over and the boys in bed, I sat down and read my proof in enjoyment. Oh, I'm going to have a delightful sleep tonight.

This day week is the day of the trial. It will be over this night week. It seems impossible of belief.

Wednesday, November 1, 1922
Leaskdale, Ont.
I had my good sleep. It knit up my ravelled sleeve of care beautifully and I have enjoyed the day and my work. We went to Uxbridge and E. subpoenaed McClintock. No doubt we will have Johnson and Jones against us but still he will help us a lot.

This afternoon Ewan went away after another hunt for evidence. He is not back yet. I always dread his coming for I am always in dread of bad news—such as the slump of another witness *à la* Boynton.

Thursday, Nov. 2, 1922
....This agony seems so long drawn out. For two months my very meat and drink have been flavored with Marshall Pickering—and a more odious flavor could not be imagined. Ugh!

Friday, Nov. 3, 1922
There are two adjectives that are never separated in regard to a November day—dull and gloomy. They were wedded together in the dawn of language and I shall not divorce them now. Today *was* dull and gloomy. And as night drew on my feeling of worry and unrest again became almost intolerable. I expected Ewan back this evening—and dreaded it lest he have bad news—but when Dr. Shier 'phoned up at dark to say Ewan had 'phoned him he wouldn't be out

tonight that was even worse, for I tortured myself with reasons as to why he had not come.

A spasm of rebellion seized me tonight—fierce rebellion that I should have been dragged into this wretched affair—forced into court and held up to the ribald gaze of a vulgar curious crowd—for, from all reports, the whole country side is going to the trial. It is true most of the onlookers are on our side and their curiosity friendly. It *is* curiosity, just the same, and I will be mouthed over afterwards in a hundred assemblages of gossip, and my looks, bearing, and evidence canvassed and detailed. It is indecent—indecent!....

This night week the torture scene will be over and there will be, whatever way it goes, an end of suspense—which is always the hardest thing to bear.

The Manse, Leaskdale
Saturday, Nov. 4, 1922
I had a nasty dream last night that Ewan came home and when I asked him about "the history of the case" said, "There is nothing in it." It was so vivid that it worried and depressed me and I was not surprised at the contents of a letter from Ewan at noon, saying that there was no history of the case after all, such being only taken when patients are in the wards. What Dr. Stevenson had seen was the report of the pathologist of Toronto University who dissected the gland and found that there was no congestion in it. As McClintock told us that if there were no congestion in the gland the accident had nothing to do with it, this is good: but the Pickering side knows nothing of this, so it will not prevent them from taking the case into court which was what I hoped....

As soon as we got a bit of supper we started for Zephyr, as Mrs. Jas. Lockie had 'phoned over in the afternoon that she wanted to see Mr. Macdonald as soon as possible. I had been half wild with nervousness before we started, after being cooped up here alone for three dark days with no one to talk to; but the cool fresh air and the agreeable sense of flying away from all earthly affairs which the car gave, did me a heap of good and made me feel quite full of spunk again. The tall mulleins stood up along our road in stiff, orderly ranks like companies of soldiers. I like best their vernacular name, "*devil's* candle-sticks." It is full of savor. And the trees and fields and groves were pleasantly suggestive and eerie as if full of elfish secrets. For a blessed short time I forgot everything but the lure of the night.

Mrs. Lockie's news didn't amount to anything much. It was only a wild yarn that has got around to the effect that Boynton has been "bought off" by Pickering. I don't believe *that*. He told Ewan that Pickering's act in bringing suit against us was "a dastardly deed" and hoped earnestly that we would "beat him." He told Mrs. Lockie some time ago that Pickering had been to him for treatment and that Mrs. Pickering had been to him in 1919 for diabetes....

Sunday, November 5, 1922
Leaskdale, Ont.
By next Sunday the suspense will be over. Ewan preached well today. One would not think any worry was hanging over him. But Ewan never worries over

anything, except the things normal people do *not* worry over. I suppose it is as well; and yet I think it is better to worry a little more over real things and less about unreal things. It is not quite normal for anyone not to worry *at all* over troubles, even though they may not feel them so deeply as others do. Any normal person worries a little over real difficulties.

Monday, Nov. 6, 1922
This was Thanksgiving but I can't say the atmosphere of Leaskdale manse was exactly in accord with the spirit of the day. The weather was abominable. Showers of snow fell constantly and it was so dark that we had to light the lamps at 3.30. Ewan was not home either, having gone away on the trail of another witness. He got him, too—Lance Copeland, who asked Pickering after he came out of the hospital if the accident caused the operation and was told it had not.

Mr. Button 'phoned today that the trial would not likely be until Tuesday—another two days of suspense.

We also heard a rumor that Pickering has "a lot" of witnesses. We can hardly credit this. We know he has four—Mason Horner, Harry Risley, John Urquhart and "old Joe Profit." But still the rumor is a worrying one.

Mason Horner is the son of "old Bill Horner," Pickering's intimate friend. We know what Mason will swear to but we cannot find out what the others are going for. They are a fine assortment. Risley is a "home boy" who used to work in Law's garage and was discharged last fall. He is notorious for his wild lies so will doubtless be quite ready to swear to anything he is wanted to. We will see if the boast I have heard so many lawyers make that "they can always tell when a witness is lying" is justified by facts. Joe Profit is an old "bum" who has been living all his life on his wife's earnings as a scrubwoman. John Urquhart was in a scrape a few years ago for stealing oats out of the mill at Zephyr. A nice lot of witnesses! But they will stick at no lies and so are better for Pickering's purposes than truthful or honest people. This worries me for I have no faith in judges being able to tell when witnesses are lying anymore than other people. I have seen judges fooled by the lies the Pages told half a dozen times.

Wednesday, Nov. 8, 1922
....Mr. Button 'phoned today that our case may not go on before Monday. Worse and worse! These repeated postponements are hard on the nerves. I spend these days listening miserably for 'phone calls—but I am thankful they *can* call us. Last week the line was out and nobody could get us and the worry of it added considerably to the sum total of all our other worries at present.

I am too restless these days to do any work requiring thought or concentration but I am getting a whole lot of odd jobs done that have hung fire for months waiting until I could finish them up. So thanks to M. P. for *that*.

Ewan went to Zephyr tonight...and fortunately got back without any fresh mishap but with no new witnesses. But we picked up a couple of bits of gossip which agreed with us. Mrs. Lockie was listening on the phone the other day when Pickering was talking to his married daughter Mrs. Pete Arnold. (I fancy the Pickering ring is seldom heard these days when someone is *not* listening in.)

Mrs. Pete asked him how he was. "Oh, I'm all in," he said. "Oh, don't worry over this," she said soothingly. "It is pretty hard to keep from worrying," was his response.

So *we* are not doing all the worrying. And if *he* is worrying so much he cannot be very sure of his case.

Then Marshall Pickering has been tampering with our witnesses. He has been to three of them and asked them out and out "not to tell any more than they could help." Surely this will score against him in the court's opinion.

Oh, if this were only over! Sometimes I feel that I *cannot* bear it a minute longer. Of course I *do*—and after all I've borne far worse things. And I don't think the outside world knows much of my worry. I keep a cool unmoved front outwardly. It is much to be thankful for that Ewan is so well—and I *will* be thankful for it when the smoke of conflict clears away and lets me see the stars that *are* shining in my dark sky.

Friday, November 10, 1922

We had the garage man from Uxbridge come up this morning and induce Lady Jane to go. When I cast up my accounts at the end of the year I feel sure the sum total of the upkeep expense of Lady Jane will drive me to home brew.

The trial is put off again until November 20th and is to be in Toronto instead of Whitby. These repeated postponements are hard to endure philosophically. As for the change of venue, it is more convenient for us in some ways but I believe we would have stood a better chance in Whitby. Our consolation is—not so many people will be able to go down from hereabouts.

Dr. Johnson seems to be out of conceit with Pickering at last. He has been rather backing him right along but he has found him out. Pickering disgusted him lately by going to him and begging him not to tell on the witness stand that Mrs. Pickering had diabetes! Johnson angrily told him that he would tell the truth to whatever was asked of him. Dr. Johnson himself told Rob Shier this.

We have subpoenaed another witness on our lawyer's advice but I don't know if it will do us any good. There is a certain Mrs. Taylor up at Shiloh who is a Methodist and rather intimate with the Pickering clique. Soon after the collision this woman was at a Ladies' Aid meeting in Zephyr and said that she was sorry she had not insisted on the Pickerings staying to tea that afternoon—they had called at her place—because then the collision would not have taken place. But Mrs. Pickering had said, in refusing, that they must hurry home because Mr. Pickering was *feeling so miserable*. When we heard this Ewan went to see her but she would not admit she knew anything. But another Mr. Taylor there, a friend of ours, said to Ewan, "Take her down. She is a good woman and will tell the truth on the stand."

If she would give this evidence it would be very valuable as showing that Pickering's attack was coming on before the accident.

Saturday, Nov. 11, 1922
The Manse, Leaskdale, Ont.

Old Joe Profit has been forbidden by doctor to go on witness stand, owing to "a bad heart," so was examined by commission this afternoon. He told an undiluted lie. He said that he and Risley had heard Ewan say at Zephyr garage the morning after the accident, "*If I had been minding my business instead of talking to Law the accident would never have happened.*"

Old Joe couldn't remember *anything* else—the time of the accident, whether it was spring or fall, not even the year it took place. His memory only retained one thing apparently. Risley, of course, will testify to the same lie. But Mr. Law says Ewan never looked at or spoke to him after he started the car and Rob Shier was in the garage next morning all the time Risley and Profit were there and says that Ewan never said such words or anything like them. So it will be Ewan, Mr. Law, Mr. Shier, Mrs. Meyers and myself against Risley, the offspring of the London gutters, and the old village bum Joe Profit. And if the Judge believes them against us there is no such thing as justice!

Monday, November 13, 1922
I had a letter from Stell today which is in the nature of a portent. It was absolutely cheerful. She said in it that she was feeling fine—better than she had felt for ten years.

I suspect the recent rise in cotton has something to do with her cheerfulness. But whatever the cause I hailed it thankfully. One of Stell's howls of despair coming on top of all my present worries would be the proverbial last straw.

Lawyer Ormiston told Ewan in Uxbridge today that Pickering has subpoenaed McClintock and that he told Ormiston he was "going to contradict everything Johnson said." That is good, because it will come from Pickering's own witness. Though likely Greig will find it out before he puts him on the stand.

Ormiston also told E. that he had asked Greig why he didn't have a jury on the case. Greig responded, "Do you suppose a jury would ever find against a Presbyterian minister?"

This convinces me of what I have felt all along—that we *should* have asked for a jury. But our lawyers thought a judge would be better, saying that a jury would be more apt to sympathize with Pickering's tale of woe etc. than a judge would. I have my doubts. But it is too late now.

Tuesday, Nov. 14, 1922
I have had another dream that means something. I dreamed I was in the old kitchen in Cavendish looking out of the west window at a hideous, pitch-black cloud that covered the whole western sky. I was dreadfully frightened of it, believing that some terrible destruction was coming upon me from it. But just as my dread was at its height—presto, there was no cloud—the sky was aswim with sunshine. I was in an incredulous daze. "It is impossible," I said, "that there was not even a drop of rain out of so black a cloud."

Then I woke. The dream has worried me. I believe it means we are to lose the suit. But in that case, how about the disappearance of the cloud and the absence of any evil consequences? To have to pay out anywhere from three to six thousand dollars would not agree with that. I can't understand it. But I feel sure trouble of some kind is ahead....

Thursday, Nov. 16, 1922
The Manse, Leaskdale

Ewan met Marshall Pickering on the road today and was amazed to see how thin he had grown. We had been told this before but I thought people were perhaps exaggerating it to please us. It is true, however.

There was a cottage prayer-meeting at John Lockie's tonight and I permitted myself the satisfaction of snubbing Mrs. Will Lockie, as I have long yearned to do. I cannot make her any more my enemy than she really is and I consider that the time has come to put her in her place.

She was sitting beside me on the sofa. I happened to remark to one of the men on the fact of the Labour group in England having made such striking gains in the recent elections. Mrs. Will struck in:—"Well, I think Labour had better do something in this country. I'm getting tired working for nothing. I think I'll go to Toronto, too, and see if I can't get something done for the workers."

Mrs. Lockie is *jealous* of me because *I* keep a maid and so—as she fondly imagines—can "live without working." She was jealous when my children were born because I had a trained nurse. I remember the first time I was there after Chester was born she said, "We country women can't get a trained nurse. *We have to die*."

I wanted to ask, "Has anybody died around here for lack of a trained nurse"—but I didn't. Neither did I say, "*You* have had three children. Yet you are alive." But tonight I turned and looked Mrs. Will squarely in the face. "You have your U.F.O. government," I said. "I thought when you put it in it would do away with all the farmer's grievances."

There was a general laugh in which even Will joined. Mrs. Will is a great U.F.O. woman. She looked very silly and said nothing more. I ignored her for the rest of the evening.

I think little except our suit is talked of around here for a radius of twenty miles where two or three are gathered together. I can't exactly blame people. The fact of a minister being sued is a dramatic event to them—a veritable god-send in their humdrum, colorless lives. It is only natural they should make the most of it. But it is hard that Ewan and I should be butchered to make a Roman holiday! I feel all raw and bleeding, mentally and physically.

Friday, Nov. 17, 1922

Ewan was in Toronto today for a final trip before the trial. Mr. McCullough says that *if* our witnesses stand by what they have said we will win our case. This is encouraging. But one can never tell. I remember my dream of the cloud....

I have just had a bed-time snack of home-cured pork ham. After all, Marshall Pickering can't embitter everything. A good bit of pork ham still has some savor.

Tuesday, November 21, 1922

I am feeling restless and worried. I do not know just why I should feel like this so much of the time. Even if we lose it will not ruin us. I think much of the unrest I feel and have felt all the fall, especially in the evenings, comes from the effect of the old Page lawsuits on my subconscious mind. All that old unrest I felt in Boston is registered there and gets stirred up when a similar worry arises.

It seems impossible that by this night week the trial will be over and the worst or best known....We have got another witness—John Hall to whom Pickering also told after his return from the hospital that the accident did not cause his operation. He told him, "The trouble was coming on for some time—the collision may have hastened it a little." This makes eight good reliable witnesses to statements from Marshall Pickering's own lips.

We leave for Toronto tomorrow....

Ewan looks very tired. He has had a strenuous fall. Yet he has been well and jolly through it all. If it only continues! I think if we win the trial the sense of success will scatter that dark complex of inadequacy in his subconscious mind which I believe is responsible for much of his trouble. But if we lose the opposite effect may be produced, and the complex intensified.

Sunday, November 26, 1922
The Manse, Leaskdale, Ont.
The suit is over—and we have *lost*, after a most unfair trial!

I suppose most people who have lost a suit are inclined to think that the Judge was unfair or prejudiced. That is natural enough. But I do not really think I am like that. When the Master, in my Page lawsuit, gave in a report that was mainly adverse to me I was disappointed but I did not think he had been unfair. He had listened to and weighed all my evidence, and when he believed the two Pages against my solitary assertion, unsupported by any other evidence, I did not blame him. The Pages were strangers to him and he had not the means of knowing them to be the liars they were. But in this case the Judge *was* unfair. Everyone who heard the trial says the same thing. People who are absolute strangers to us and merely happened to be there said it. Even Mason Horner, a law-student and Pickering's star witness, said in Zephyr yesterday that it was "a very one-sided trial."

One-sided! I should say so. We simply did not have the ghost of a show. As soon as Judge Riddell heard Pickering's story he made up his mind then and there, as everyone saw, and was determined not to change it. His conduct showed that plainly.

On Wednesday we motored into Toronto and took with us Edith, Mrs. Alexander Lockie and Mrs. Meyers. We spent the evening in John McCullough's law office where all our witnesses were examined. I was dreadfully tired when it was all over and slept little that night.

Thursday morning we went to the court house but an unfinished trial took up the forenoon. I sat and listened to it. I did not just like Judge Riddell even then. He is a very eminent legal light but he is plainly a colossal egotist and thinks his own judgment quite infallible.

Our trial began in the afternoon. It all seemed a nightmare to me. The big courtroom was filled with people, nearly all of them Zephyr and Leaskdale people. Pickering went on the stand first and told the same string of lies as in his examination for discovery but made an important change in one respect. In the former examination he had stated that he had seen our car one hundred rods away. This time he said *Twenty rods*. Confronted by Mr. McCullough with his preliminary answer he said, "*Well, if I said that I was wrong.*" I suppose his lawyer has told him that his former answer (which was the true one—or at least what he has said many times heretofore) was prejudicial to his case. One would think that a judge would conclude from this that a man who would swear to one thing in his preliminary exam and then contradict himself in the next examination, would very likely be "wrong" on other points also. But not so Judge Riddell.

Pickering swore he was going only 20 miles an hour. Asked by our lawyer if he didn't know that the law required a slowing down to 12 1/2 miles at a blind corner he retorted that it wasn't a blind corner. He said he had sounded his horn four times (another absolute lie) and he repeated his former falsehoods as to what Ewan said to him after the collision. He said that he had to be operated on not for *enlarged* gland but *for congested* gland and that the congestion was caused by the accident. He also said that he had *never* spoken of or thought of an operation!

Then Mr. McCullough began to cross-question him: "Did you say such-and-such to So-and-So etc.," as the laws of evidence require. Pickering denied flatly every allegation—he had never told Mr. Meyers he was going to have an operation—he had never complained to Mrs. Lockie—he had never told anyone that the accident hadn't caused his operation etc. At first he did it very brazenly but as the long string of witnesses was named off he began to go to pieces and finally admitted that he "might have said he had a burning sensation at times"—which of course was exactly opposite to what he said in the examination for discovery.

Then Mr. McCullough asked him if his wife ever had, or had been treated for, diabetes. He said nervously, "She *had a little* of it a few years ago but she got some medicine from the States that cured her."

He was also compelled to admit that if he had slowed down to 12 1/2 miles he could have avoided the accident.

All through his cross-examination the Judge plainly favored him and checked Mr. McCullough repeatedly although Mr. McCullough asked nothing he had not a right to ask. When he began to ask Pickering about tampering with our witnesses the Judge stopped him at once and declared "it didn't matter." "Not matter?" said McCullough. "I think it was a most improper thing." "Not at all—not at all," said the Judge.

This was the first moment that I said to myself "The suit will go against us." A judge who could say that there was nothing improper in Pickering's going to our witnesses and asking them to keep back part of the truth was not a judge who would listen to *anything* that contradicted his pre-conception of the case, if he could get any legal excuse for refusing to listen.

When Pickering left the stand the Judge said to Mr. McCullough,

"I suggest that you do not put on those witnesses you mentioned," or words to that effect.

I felt thunderstruck. Mr. McCullough, too, was amazed and protested.

"Of course I don't tell you you can't put them on," said Riddell. "I merely suggest that you will save time by not doing it. I *shall give very little attention to such evidence.*"

I found it hard to believe my ears. This man was practically saying that he would not believe our witnesses, although he had not seen or heard one of them.

The Judge then went on to say, "The man has admitted that he had some trouble before the accident. What more do you want?"

Mr. McCullough was not quite quick enough here. He should have said, "I want to prove that he intended, before the collision, to have an operation."

Not that it mattered—not that anything he could have said would have mattered. The Judge had already made up his mind and decided the case.

But Mr. McCullough was so taken aback by the Judge practically barring out the very witnesses upon whom we depended to win our case that he was a bit rattled and said, "I want to test the credibility of the witness."

"Oh, I believe the witness. He is an honest man," said the Judge.

I knew that we had lost then and so did everyone else in the room. The Judge believed Pickering's story—that tissue of lies—and was evidently determined that we should have no chance of disproving it. He impressed me all through the trial as being determined to keep out or minimize *any* evidence that would make him doubtful, in his own despite, of the truth of the Pickerings' tale or render it difficult for him to decide in their favor.

"Call the doctors," said the Judge. "I see some of them here. Put them on."

It was evident that the Judge supposed the doctors were all on Pickering's side. Dr. Johnson went on first. He said he had been called in by Pickering, had "found some congestion in the gland" and thought it must have been caused by the accident as he could find no other reason for it. When it came to Mrs. Pickering he said he had treated her for diabetes and had sent her to a Toronto specialist who had confirmed his diagnosis.

We expected that Dr. Jones would be called after Johnson. One would have imagined that the specialist who performed the operation would be called on for evidence, whoever else was not. But he was not there at all. This shows, of course, that his evidence would not have been favorable to them. I wish now that we had subpoenaed him; but after his saying of Pickering, "He'll get it, too," we did not dare, supposing him to be on Pickering's side. I suppose he said that on purpose to prevent our subpoenaing him. They did not have McClintock either, evidently having found out that he was not on their side. Our lawyer did not call him either then, which I think was a mistake.

Johnson was the only doctor Pickering had there. Then Dr. Robinson, the Pathologist of Toronto University and the leading authority in his line in Canada, went on. He stated that there was no congestion whatever in the gland and had the section of the gland there to prove it. Phelan quite lost his calm at this point. This evidence was evidently something totally unexpected by him, and it completely upset his plea that the congestion of the gland necessitated the operation. He asked angrily, "Is it customary to dissect the glands like that?"

"Yes." "And are they open to the inspection of the public?" "Yes." Dr. Robinson furthermore said that an operation would have been necessary in any case in two or three months.

Then we had Dr. Powell and Dr. Stevenson, both kidney disease experts, who said that diabetes was incurable and that the symptoms of Mrs. Pickering's complaint were the symptoms of diabetes. Then the court adjourned.

We did not know what to think. The Clerk of the Court, who seemed strongly in our favor, told us he could see plainly it was just a conspiracy to get money out of us. He said he believed Riddell would decide for us. He said he believed the reason Riddell had barred out the witnesses was simply that he had made up his mind that Pickering was negligent in not slowing down to the required legal speed and that therefore it did not matter whether the collision caused the operation or not—he could not claim damages. This encouraged us a little but I had a miserable night. I thought of my dream of the black cloud and felt sure it meant the loss of the suit.

Next morning court opened at ten. The first thing the Judge did was to make a suggestion that Ewan and Pickering go into a room together and try to settle the dispute "in Christian amity." Then I gave up hope utterly. If the Judge had not already decided in Pickering's favor he would not have suggested "settling." That is, he had made up his mind to give P. the verdict *before* he had heard a single one of our witnesses, except the doctors. For anything he knew we might have been able to prove that the collision was wholly Pickering's fault and in that case to ask Ewan to "settle" would have been rank injustice. It is incredible to me that a judge could do such a thing.

Ewan went in with Pickering for form's sake but Pickering's "terms"—all the expenses and a thousand dollars besides—were not to be considered.

Mrs. Pickering then was put on the stand. She swore that she had not been "able to work" since the collision—had "no ambition" etc. etc. It really sounded awfully funny in that whining voice of hers—a voice assumed for the occasion as it is not her natural tone at all. In her preliminary examination she had sworn that her daughters had worked out *before* and had to stay home *after* the collision. She did not dare to repeat this lie, as she knew we had witnesses there to prove that such a statement was an absolute falsehood. Under cross-examination she admitted that she had never had a doctor or consulted one since the collision—which was rather odd in a woman as ill as she made herself out to be—and simply denied flatly that she ever had diabetes, although Pickering himself had admitted she had. *One* of them must have been lying, as any judge must have seen.

When Mr. McCullough tried to cross-question her about consulting various doctors for diabetes the Judge headed him off every time. When he referred to the specialist the Judge said, "This is the first time we have heard of the specialist"—although Dr. Johnson had told the whole story of sending her to the specialist on the stand. When Mr. McCullough persisted in asking her the Judge said, "I don't believe she ever had diabetes or if she had she is cured," and then he said to her, "You needn't answer any more of those questions."

I could never have believed any reputable judge would say such a thing. It was incredible. Dr. Johnson, Pickering's own witness, not ours, had sworn she had diabetes and that her specialist had confirmed it; two experts had sworn that the symptoms she complained of were diabetic; her own husband had said she had it once. And everyone knows diabetes is an incurable disease—or was up to a few weeks ago when Dr. Banting's discovery was given to the world. And nobody pretends that Mrs. P. had taken the insulin treatment. And yet the Judge could say "She never had diabetes or if she had she is cured!!!"

Mason Horner was next put on the stand. He swore that Ewan turned the *second* time across the road. Of course Ewan did nothing of the sort. Pickering's car struck ours and knocked it round. Mason Horner *may* have honestly thought that Ewan turned the car—but it is a little suspicious when Horner is the son of "old Bill Horner" who is supposed to have put Pickering up to the whole thing. Horner is a law student and couched his testimony in clear-cut legal language which seemed to make a very favorable impression on the Judge. Besides, Phelan staged a piece of acting in pretending that Mason Horner was "an unwilling witness." *We* knew all about what was behind this pretence for Horner is in the office next to McCullough's; but Riddell swallowed it whole and believed it.

Then Risley swore to his lie and old Jack Urquhart, the oat-stealer, swore to another, saying he had seen Ewan talking to Law *after* the car had started.

Our side went on then. Ewan went first and did very well—and *told the truth.* Then my turn came. It was the most horrible ordeal I had ever endured, standing there before that crowded courtroom of curious Zephyr gossips—even though they were on our side. I felt very nervous but I did not make any mistakes and Phelan let me off surprisingly easy in his cross-examination. Law gave very good evidence and Mrs. Meyers, but Joe Taylor made an absurd mistake through nervousness which robbed his evidence of all value. The rest of our witnesses were not put on. John McCullough wanted to put them on, but James McCullough did not because he thought the Judge would only be exasperated and besides, he, McCullough, was sure the Judge would give *us* the verdict because of Pickering's admission of not slowing down at the corner. I wish now we had insisted on their being heard but it is always easy to be wise after the event. Then Riddell summed up and gave Pickering his verdict saying that his negligence in not slowing down was negligence to the public at large, or something like that, and not towards us, and that if it hadn't been for the collision he might have "gone on for years" without an operation. He gave Pickering a thousand for his operation expenses and five hundred for his "*sufferings*"—Pickering, who is perfectly well today after suffering for years!—five hundred for Mrs. Pickering, and "expenses."

We got up and left the court. We smiled gallantly and I don't think anyone saw much in our faces. But it was the most trying and humiliating moment of all. I bore up until we got to our room at the hotel and then I broke down and cried bitterly. I knew I would have to pay the three thousand for Ewan has only his $1,000 Victory Bond and our own expenses would amount to that. To pay out three or four thousand of my hard-earned money was not a pleasant prospect but I would have done it cheerfully for an honest debt and never given it another thought; but it was the horrible *injustice* of it all that hurt me. This was just a conspiracy on the part of the Pickerings and old Horner to get money out of me. Everybody knows it—and there is something in me that revolts against it.

Then Ewan came in and said, "I shall never pay or let you pay a cent of money to Marshall Pickering."

"You'll have to," I said despairingly. "If you don't they'll sell up our furniture and garnishee the salary. You know we can't let *that* happen."

"The furniture is yours," he said.

"Not in the eyes of the law," I said, believing this at the time.

When we were married Ewan had no money. He had had to pay some college debts after he got through and he had moved about a good deal. Besides, Ewan has certainly no "knack" of saving money. So I paid for all the furniture. I lent him the money for the Victory bond, too, but he paid *all* our living expense;—not merely *half*, as was our arrangement—until that was paid back. So the bond was his morally as well as legally. But I thought the furniture would be considered *legally* his and so could be seized.

"Well, I'm not going to pay it," said Ewan stubbornly. "If he garnishees my salary I'll give up the ministry and go into something else, before I will bow to such injustice. And not one cent of your money shall go for what was not *your* fault, whoever was to blame."

But I had no fight left in me just then.

We went up to our lawyer's office. Ewan told them how matters stood. Mr. McCullough laughed. "I'm *glad*," he said—"not glad, of course that you haven't anything but glad that scoundrel can't get it."

"What about the furniture?" I said. "It is really mine but can we prove it?"

"How was it paid for?" he said.

"By my personal check."

"Oh, then it is all right—that check can be got from the bank any time."

"What about my salary?" asked Ewan.

"Let your congregation pay it monthly in advance and they can't touch it."

This was news to me and gave me some courage to go on fighting. I know it will mean a lot of worry for us, perhaps for years, but as long as Ewan feels like fighting them I will do anything in my power to get the better of that pair of plotters and perjurers.

We decided to appeal. Of course there isn't much chance, since we haven't got our evidence in. McCullough said there was one chance in ten—which is probably an over-favorable estimate. But the point is—we'll get time to open the congregation's eyes diplomatically to what must be done; *and* we'll give Mr. Pickering enough law to satisfy him. He must learn that man can go to law when he likes but can't always stop when he likes.

When we left the lawyer's office it was five o'clock and beginning to snow. I suppose the sensible thing would have been to stay in Toronto all night. But Edith wanted to get home that night to her children; and I had the instinctive and imperative desire of the wounded animal to crawl away and hide. So we started, having telephoned our party to meet us at an uptown garage—they were all staying far out in a suburb. About four or five miles up town in a residential district

Lady Jane, true to form, stopped. Ewan discovered that the little reservoir in front was empty of gas. We could not get any from our tank so there was nothing to do but go for gas. He had to go a long way. I stayed there, alone and cold—for it was turning very cold. It was snowing thickly. Cars of gay people streamed past. I felt so wretched and crushed that I was numb. After about an hour Ewan returned with gas and filled the reservoir. Even then Lady Jane wouldn't go. He had to work with her for over half an hour before she would start. I stood and held the flashlight with freezing hands and feet. The snow was getting thicker—I began to fear we would be stuck on the road home. And at that moment Marshall Pickering was probably spinning homeward in great spirits. Well, never mind, Mr. Pickering. He laughs best who laughs last. You may find, dear Mr. Pickering, that getting a verdict is not quite the same thing as getting my money!

Finally Lady Jane consented to go. We reached the garage where our party was to have met us. They were not there—nor did they come for two whole hours, having waited to get their suppers. If they had told us they were going to do this *we* might have got something, too—but they hadn't. I went into a neighboring drug store and paced the floor, wishing sickly that I could get home— only get home. Ewan was cool, composed and in good spirits. When Ewan is normal *nothing* upsets him. He has a most enviable equanimity. And when he isn't normal he is entirely the opposite.

At last they did come. We started—the lights of the city slipped past us like the gleaming, hungry eyes of hundreds of great stealthy panthers. It was nine o'clock; I had dismal forebodings; the snow was thick and if Lady Jane "acted up" again on that desolate road at that hour of the night what could we do—especially with old Mrs. Lockie?

But our evil genius had decided to take a rest. All went well. The snow stopped, the road was good, Lady Jane skimmed along like a bird. And, as always in a car, my spirits rose. I ceased to feel tired—or rather, my tiredness showed itself in a certain exaltation of feeling and imagination such as I sometimes experience when I am much fatigued. I felt suddenly full of vim and *fight* again. We would get the better of Marshall Pickering yet.

The drive home was not the nightmare it had promised to be. But still I was very thankful when we got home. I got our guests a lunch and got them to bed. Then I went to bed, too. I can't say I slept much but I rested at least. Ewan, strange man, slept like a top.

In the morning Ewan took Mrs. Lockie and Mrs. Meyers home. He came back with the news that Zephyr was in a ferment. The people are furious. They are ready to tear the Pickerings in pieces. When Marshall Pickering phoned to someone that morning that he had won the suit a listening woman cut in with, "Yes, you've won the suit but *you've lost your soul*." I don't envy Marshall Pickering his existence in that community after this. He is so hated that everyone will be glad to cast things up to him. After the trial Law went up to Pickering and said to him on the steps of the courthouse, "You *lied* on the witness stand." Pickering, it is said, made no reply.

Today was fine but cold. We had the ordeal of going out to church and endur-ing *sympathy*—or rather the expression of sympathy. I mean, by that, that one likes to feel that people *do* sympathize but it *is* an ordeal to listen to their attempts at voicing it. But Ewan preached a splendid sermon and I think a cer-tain family of Methodists who came to hear what they could got an earful. One of the sons is engaged to Verna Pickering—who has a very rank reputation, it is said. So of course they are on Pickering's side.

When Ewan came back from Zephyr he had some more news. Mason Horner was out yesterday and was nearly mobbed. The boys of Zephyr shouted "*Lie*-yer—*lie*-yer," after him every time he was seen out. He himself said to someone that "the trial was very one-sided."

The Pickering gang are telling that *I* "tore my handkerchief to pieces when I heard the verdict." Their genius for lying is not confined to the stand, it seems.

Ewan still talks continually of the trial—its injustice and absurdities. But I feel as if I couldn't *bear* to talk of it, now that it is over and talking can do no good. It hurts me. I want to forget it and so be able to go on with my regular work, putting the devilish thing behind me. I am feeling very flat and spiritless in the reaction after the long strain. I am as firmly resolved to fight as ever but I have no stomach for it. Tonight for the first time since the trial I cried bitterly. It seems to me this thing will hang over us all our lives and in my present mood I cannot bear the thought of it. If Ewan would agree I would give in now, pay the money and be free. But Ewan is resolved and I know by experience that it is no use to try to move him.

Poor little Stuart! Yesterday morning at breakfast, when our visitors were jok-ing over Marshall Pickering, saying he would have to seize the old cutter and Ewan's books, Stuart threw his arms around me and exclaimed, "Never mind, mother, Mr. Pickering can't take *me* from you."

No, he can't, darling. And I ought not to worry when he can't touch anything vital. But I've had so much worry and grief in these hard last five years that at times I feel as if I could not bear even an added pinprick. But these moods pass and I can always pick up and go on. What a blessing Ewan is so well this fall! If he had been as he was last fall what could we have done—except knuckled under and paid him all he wanted to get out of trouble,—him, the perjurer and blackmailer!

Monday, November 27, 1922
Leaskdale, Ont.

I slept better last night and felt today as if I were getting back to normal but still so tired—too tired even to realize yet that the trial is *over* and that no matter what comes the worst is past. I can't *feel* that yet; its incubus still burdens me. Tonight I could not help going over the trial in my mind and raging at the injus-tice of it. *That* is what hurts. If we had had *no* evidence I would not feel that the Judge had been unfair, but we *had* and he either barred it out practically or totally disregarded it. He gave that woman damages on her own say-so, although she had *no* medical testimony in her favor and we had the best against it. I have always heard that the plaintiff had to *prove* his injuries but in her case there was no proof of any kind. So I *do* feel that Riddell was very unfair.

Ewan went to Toronto today and Lily went home, so I am all alone and very heartsick. If I only had Frede to talk this out to! I could not talk of it to any other creature.

Tuesday, Nov. 28, 1922

I began writing again today and found that while I was at it I could abstract my mind from the real and live in the ideal. But as soon as I stop writing the real confronts me again.

Lily came back today bringing a flood of gossip about Pickering. One tale is that he had to borrow the money from old Horner to pay his lawyer....

Ewan isn't home yet. I feel very lonely.

Wednesday, Nov. 29, 1922

Ewan got home last night at twelve. We have entered our appeal. He also says that if it fails he will take the case to the Supreme Court at Ottawa....

Saturday, Dec. 2, 1922
Leaskdale, Ont.

Thursday I went to Toronto to shop and stayed in until this evening. I had a rather miserable time. I can't as yet shake off the *effects* of over worry. I am nervous and restless much of the time, especially if I am away from home; and can't enjoy anything. The crowds of shoppers made me still wearier and I wandered around and did my buying without any of my usual pleasure in it. I stayed at a hotel, feeling that I *couldn't* visit friends and be asked about the trial a dozen times over. Ewan met me at Uxbridge this evening and we had a pleasant drive home in the mild wintery twilight. He said he had been to see James Mustard, the Leaskdale treasurer, and Mr. Mustard said that if Pickering tried to garnishee our salary he could be "easily outwitted there." This raised my spirits. In my depressed state I had got it into my head that perhaps our people wouldn't back us up—a foolish fear, for I know exactly how they feel about it. But I knew Leaskdale would be all right. I wish I felt as sure about Zephyr. Of course, the Zephyr people are even more indignant at Pickering than the Leaskdale people, being nearer and hating him personally. But Will Lockie is treasurer there and he is such an oddity that there is no counting on what he will or will not do.

Monday, December 4, 1922

....I was in Uxbridge today and met old George Allan Smith who had to stop me and ask all about the trial. I do hate talking about it. I would forget it—let it heal over—if people would let me—wouldn't tear the wound open with questions.

"Well," said old George, when I finished, "everybody says he just tore up the street and run right into you. It's a funny thing that he could get damages for *that.*"

Natheless, he did. The thing is so un-understandable to the simple country folk that they are all asserting that "Pickering bribed the Judge." This is absurd, of course. I do not think that Riddell, though egotistic and prejudiced, is the kind of judge who could be bribed—certainly not by any sum Pickering could be likely to offer. But the story shows how puzzled the people are over the verdict when they can only account for it by such a supposition.

Tuesday, Dec. 5, 1922
Leaskdale, Ont.
I am beginning to be able to *forget* for a few minutes at a time, which is a hopeful sign....

The most interesting department of *The Globe* now is the report of the appeals at Osgoode Hall. I study them with painful interest. I note that more of Riddell's cases are appealed than any other judge's. I note also that in almost every case he has given the plaintiff the verdict. It seems to be a habit of his.

Thursday, Dec. 7, 1922
Tonight we were at Richard Curl's in Zephyr and supped gloriously on venison steak—the said Richard being a mighty hunter in the season. He is also a bitter hater of Pickering and said "Don't you pay him one cent. Everybody round here knows that man and his wife have been doctoring for years. He always has been a notorious liar anyhow."

Saturday, Dec. 9, 1922
Last night I had my last ride in old Lady Jane. Today Ewan took her to Cannington and sold her. I saw her go with no regret. From first to last she has been a hoodooed car.

She really was my car of course, since I paid for her. But luckily she was registered in Ewan's name so was legally his. If she had been in my name Pickering could have come on me for his damages. I fancy his lawyers were a little disappointed when they found out she was in Ewan's name.

Wednesday, Dec. 13, 1922
Every time we go to Zephyr we pick up some new bits of gossip. Today Mrs. Bingham told us that Dr. Johnson told her that if the medical men who were at the trial banded together they could "make it hot" for the Judge. Of course I don't think they could do anything of the sort but it shows Johnson's opinion—and he was Pickering's witness. He is furious because the Judge believed Mrs. Pickering and not him in regard to her diabetes. In nothing more than in his treatment of Johnson's evidence was the Judge's bias so clearly shown. He believed the part that testified to congestion in Pickering's notorious gland and rejected the part that testified to her diabetes. Mrs. Bingham also said that the Zephyr boys would have pelted Mason Horner that day he was out with rotten eggs if they could have found any.

We hear that Mr. Pickering is "very mad" because we have appealed. Poor Mr. Pickering! I suppose he fondly dreams that no one should appeal to the law for justice but him. I expect he will be "madder" still before spring.

Saturday, December 16, 1922
The Manse, Leaskdale, Ont.

Stuart has had a cold and sore throat for a couple of weeks and today I discovered that the gland under his ear was badly swollen. It worries me—although I remember that my worry over a similar gland in Chester's neck that terrible winter seven years ago was needless and I tell myself I am foolish. I was alone this evening and got very restless and depressed. I wildly wanted some of *my own gang* to talk to and laugh with—Bertie or Stell or Margaret. "Oh, for one hour" of any of them! But it cannot be!

The papers nowadays are filled with *radio*. Dr. Shier has a set and he told me recently that last Sunday morning he heard a sermon preached in Pittsburg, Pa. in the morning and one in Chicago in the evening. It is all very wonderful—and I find it a little depressing. Is it because I'm getting on in life that all these wonderful inventions and discoveries, treading on each other's heels, give me a sense of weariness and a longing to go back to the slower years of old. Doubtless that has something to do with it. But I do really think we are rushing on rather fast. It keeps humanity on tiptoe. And all these things don't make the world or the people in it any *happier*. But I think this will go on for two or three hundred years—I mean the flood of great discoveries and inventions. Then probably the Zeit Geist will get tired and take a rest for a few centuries and allow humanity to rest with him. But those of us living now have to speed on with him willy nilly.

In a generation or two *letters* will be obsolete. Everyone will talk to absent friends the world over by *radio*. It will be nice; but something will be lost with letters. The world can't eat its cake and have it, too. And none of these things really "save time." They only fill it more breathlessly full. That is all right for the young. But I look back to the old '90's with a feeling that they were a nice unhurried leisurely time. But perhaps that is only because I lived in a remote little country place eleven miles from a railway. Even today life is very unhurried and peaceful in Cavendish. Yes, I daresay that is the explanation.

I have recently been reading the life of Tennyson by his son. It is a delightful book because of its atmosphere and background. It has always seemed to me that life among the "gentlefolk" of England must be—or was then—as nearly an ideal existence as can be found on this planet. I have always felt, when reading books reflecting it, that it was above all others the sort of life I should have liked to live—the one that most appeals to me. Today my reading Tennyson's life filled me with a sort of envy of that intercourse with congenial souls that was always his—going and coming. That is so wholly lacking in my life.

But if Ewan only keeps well I will be content—I will not complain of what is lacking. After all, books are wonderful companions.

I have been busy lately decanting "home brew." Last summer I made some red currant wine and some raspberry wine, from my recollection of Grandmother's method. Grandmother was famed for her currant wine. It *was* delicious—even Chateau Yquem was not much its superior. I was doubtful of my success for I was not sure I remembered her whole process and I knew of many folk who had followed her recipe straightly and produced but a sorry beverage.

But either I had good luck or I have inherited some of her brain cells for my "brew" is delicious—clear, ruby, sparkling with a quite sufficient "bite." I made it mainly for Ewan who seems to feel better and brighter after an occasional glass of it. But he doesn't need it now for he keeps perfectly well. Oh, if it only continues!

Friday, December 22, 1922
Leaskdale, Ont.
...Chester has finished his school exams and got honors—78%. He started in by getting only 50% for writing and 56 for arithmetic—his poorest subjects—and I felt discouraged but after that he came right along. But, though a great reader, he isn't a student at all—at least as yet. Perhaps the desire will waken later—it did in both Ewan and me.

Tuesday, December 26, 1922
Christmas is over—a pleasanter Christmas than I have had for several years, as Ewan was well and cheerful. Stuart's neck is getting all right, too.

Lily was home for Xmas and brought back some gossip about Pickering. He is said to be "a changed man"—"looks miserable"—"doesn't want to talk" etc. I have heard this from other sources. I fancy he is feeling his loss of caste and standing. They say his perjury is constantly cast up to him and the boys hoot it after him on the streets. Many members of his Bible class have stopped attending, averring that they will not be "taught by a perjurer," etc. All this seems to have pierced even his iron hide....

Thursday, December 28, 1922
Leaskdale, Ont.
I am feeling like myself again. Today for the first time in months I felt my old rapturous, *indwelling* sense of the imperishable beauty in life and in the world. It was glorious to experience it again.

We were out to supper tonight with a nice family and had a pleasant time. Mr. Barton talked of the trial and said that he had never known a trial concerning which there was such absolute unanimity of opinion. In most trials, he said, some would be on one side, some on the other, but in this everywhere there was just the one thing said.

"A trial like this," he said, "should be held in a place where a man is known. Up in Toronto they didn't know what sort of a couple Pickering and his wife are, so the Judge believed them. If that had been tried where they were known you would have won."

Sunday, Dec. 31, 1922
The last day of the old year—the old miserable worried year. It closes in gloom again. All Friday Ewan's head trouble and melancholia returned with the uncanny suddenness of all his attacks. No doubt he will be miserable all winter now, in addition to all our other worries. I feel disheartened. It is all the harder to endure after this long time when he has seemed quite well and which led me

to hope, in spite of the repeated experiences of the past four years, that this time he was really well. I have even dared to think that this Pickering trial was a blessing in disguise, since it cured him—a device of Ormuzd to hoodwink Ahrimanes! I feel that I *can't* face the winter. But of course I *will* face it—and live through it somehow. One has to.

1923

....The holidays are over and the boys started to school again. I get up before daylight to get them and Lily up, prepare their lunch and get them off. If I were not unhappy and worried I wouldn't mind this. But somehow, as it is, it seems unreasonably nasty to get up thus in the dark and cold—a dark that reluctantly fades out into dull bitter gray. The manse is always bitterly cold these mornings. Owing to the coal strike last fall we could not get any hard coal and have to burn wood and soft coal. The furnace is not suited to this and the result is discomfort every way—a cold house—gas—smoke—dirt. Everything has a smear of fine black grime over it and the curtains and silver turn as yellow as brass in a few days. These in themselves are small things but it makes the big troubles harder to endure cheerfully when your flesh is goosey and your eyes are smarting with smoke.

I have been desperately lonely this evening. It is a cold stormy night and the snow is heaping up around the manse. I was all alone as usual after the boys had gone to bed—and I was tired after working hard all day and wanted some companionship. But there is none. Ewan in the grip of this horrible malady is as a stranger. He is interested in *nothing*—he is absolutely indifferent to me and the children. We mean nothing to him—in fact, I feel that he thinks our presence and existence irksome to him, as reminders of responsibilities he wants to forget or ignore. He has never actually turned against us—so far I have been spared *that*. He is simply indifferent to us and to all that concerns us and our home.

> The heart asks pleasure first,
> And then—excuse from pain,
> And then—those little anodynes
> That deaden suffering
> And then—to go to sleep,
> And then—if it should be the will
> Of its inquisitor
> The liberty to die.

So wrote Emily Dickinson bitterly—and I fear truly. I have got along to humbly asking for the "anodynes." Not yet have I asked to go to sleep or to die—no, life is too interesting in spite of its torture. And I want to live until my children can do without me. Sometimes when I get disheartened and discouraged in these gray, merciless days and worried nights I fear that I will not live—

will have to leave my children without any real protector or guide. This is all foolish. So far as I know I am perfectly healthy and never felt better in my life. But at present I cannot believe that the "Inquisitor" is anything but capricious Cruelty.

Saturday, Jan. 6, 1923
The Manse, Leaskdale, Ont.
This has been a week of intense cold. Ewan has been very dull—much worse than last week. I have especially noticed this week the *repulsive* expression his features assume in these attacks. It changes his whole face. He is like a stranger. I cannot bear to look at him. That dull, sullen face, with its wild, haunted eyes, is so miserably unlike his normal cheerful smiling face with its dimples and roguish eyes. The change seems incredible.

Monday, Jan. 8, 1923
The bitter cold continues unbrokenly. But Ewan seems a little brighter and Stuart's neck is almost well.

Tonight I have been studying Emile Coué's book on "Auto Suggestion"....I believe Auto Suggestion would help Ewan if he would try it. But he will not. This is the difficulty in his case. He will *not* believe there is anything the matter with him—he is, he insists, simply unforgiven for sin—and he will not try *any* method of curing himself. Besides, he seems incapable of making any continued mental effort. I have tried to "suggest" helpful ideas to him when he is asleep but the trouble is he always wakes up at once, he sleeps so lightly and my "suggestions" have no chance to work. Not that it matters much. I feel that Ewan's trouble is constitutional and too deeply rooted to be charmed away by formulae....

Lately I re-read *Kate Carnegie*. I don't think I've read it for fifteen years. The "Ian MacLaren" books had a tremendous vogue twenty years ago—and deserved it. There is a great gulf fixed between them and the nauseous sex stuff that pours from the press today. The atmosphere of *Kate* is delightful. I seemed to be back in the Cavendish of my childhood. There was the same tang and charm and simplicity in people, place and religion. One had a sense of "time to grow."

Friday, Jan. 19, 1923
....I had a dear bit of a walk all by myself tonight—in a soft white twilight under a young moon. The night was all my own and it was very kind to me. I bowed me down to my ancient gods. It was like a bit out of the olden years and lightened a little my present disgust of life. But the walk ended in an evening spent, in Jane Welsh Carlyle's splendid phrase "under a harrow." We were visiting a family where the ill-trained youngsters kept up such a ceaseless riot of yells and pursuit that I could hardly hear a word anyone was saying. And the people talked of Marshall Pickering *ad nauseam*. To be sure, they abused him whole heartedly but we have heard so much of that and it doesn't get us anywhere and keeps us all raw and sore. If only I might never hear Marshall Pickering's name again!

Towards the end of the evening I abstracted myself behind my knitting and while the children romped and yelled and their mother scolded them ceaselessly and ineffectively I deadened unpleasant sensations by formulating a theory of my own concerning *life*—what it was and how it entered into matter. But I shall not write it here. My descendants and readers can guess at it....

Sunday, Jan. 21, 1923
The Manse, Leaskdale
Ewan was at David Graham's in Zephyr this evening for tea and picked up some Pickeringiana. Marshall P. complained to Mrs. Graham not long ago that "No one congratulated him after the trial"—"they all crowded around Macdonald."

Poor Pickering! What could they congratulate him on—committing perjury? Mrs. Graham told him she had heard "Mr. Macdonald was so fixed he couldn't pay." "Oh," said Pickering. "Mrs. Macdonald will pay rather than have the judgment hanging over them. If Mr. Macdonald had had nothing but his salary I wouldn't have sued him. But I knew Mrs. Macdonald had money"....

Wednesday, Jan. 24, 1923
Leaskdale, Ont.
....This evening we went out visiting. When we started I felt dreadfully depressed and down-hearted. But as we drove on through the woods my spirits rose. It was a strange weird night—cloudy but with a moon behind the clouds— snowing softly and wetly but quite calm. We drove through woods and swamps where the trees were covered with white and looked like great ranks of spectres standing in sorrowful enchantment. There was something in the eerie beauty of the landscape that thrilled a chord in my spirit and my being responded to the music. So that, in spite of Ewan's gloomy silence and the monotonous evening with a family so dull that they make others dull sandwiched between our drives, I felt oddly happy and delighted, with a secret inner happiness and delight—as of a "fountain sealed" somewhere deep in my soul where no drop of poison from the outward universe could distil. "The kingdom of God is within you."

We came home early. Ewan went to bed but I settled down for a bit of reading. Something I read suddenly recalled to mind a curious little incident of my childhood. I was I think about eleven or twelve. I was up in the loft of our "new barn," playing with a kitten. The loft was filled almost to the roof with wheat straw and I was on top of it about forty feet from the floor. I made a dive to catch my kitten, the slippery straw slid from under my feet and I shot head downward to the floor. Now, the curious thing about the experience was this. I could only have been one or two seconds in falling. Yet in that time I thought *five* distinct and deliberate thoughts with, so it seemed to me, quite a long interval between them. The first thought, as I felt myself falling was, "What has happened?" After what seemed an appreciable interval another part of me answered, "I am falling." Then I asked, "What will become of me when I strike the floor?" A second interval. The other part again answered, "I will be killed." A third interval. Then I thought clearly and unhurriedly, "Well, I do not care."

And neither did I. I knew I was going to be killed and it did not alarm me in the least. I was absolutely indifferent. Then I struck—not on the floor but on a huge pile of chaff. I was almost buried in it but I was not at all hurt save for the discomfort of chaff grains down my neck and in eyes, nose and hair.

I have never forgotten the experience and the strange leisurely way those questions and answers seemed to come in that brief moment. And the memory has always been a comfort to me. I do not think I will be afraid of death when it really comes. It will be just the same as it was then.

I think this explains the calmness and courage with which many have faced death in the past—as for instance the great Argyle found soundly sleeping when the executioner came to call him....

Thursday, Jan. 25, 1923
The Manse, Leaskdale, Ont.
It is four years today since Frede died. And tonight how fierce is my yearning for her. Oh, if I could only see that door open and Frede enter—sit down here beside me—talk, laugh. Oh, surely the jests of heaven have had more spice since she has shared in them. She can never come—the door can never open to her. Oh, my God, what a stab of pain comes with the thought! Oh, my friend—my friend! There isn't any *you*. You may be here in the spirit—but I want you in the flesh. I want you to grow old with me. Now, in old age, if I ever reach it, I shall have to remember things alone.

Sunday, Jan. 28, 1923
The bitter cold continues without any cessation. Ewan has been very miserable. On Friday he was about as bad as I have ever seen him. He could not even read—he walked the floor restlessly and looked wild and tortured. And there is no help. What help is there for a man who believes or fears that he is eternally lost?

Yet he preached quite well this morning. It is curious how he can. When he is compelled to do a thing he can do it and while doing it forgets all his dreads and terrors. Then, when it is finished, they return. While he is preaching or when he is out in company he can banish or control them. No one would then suspect his real condition.

The other day I received a letter from the Secretary of the Royal Society of Arts of Great Britain, telling me that "the Council" had decided to invite me to become a "Fellow." This is a great compliment and one I certainly never dreamed of receiving. I am, it seems, the first Canadian woman to whom this honor has been offered. I wish Frede could have known of it. There is no one else to care very much, since my sons are not old enough to feel proud of it. Years ago I wrote in my portfolio that I meant "to climb the Alpine Path" and "write upon its shining scroll a woman's humble name." I suppose I may say I have climbed it. After that humble name I shall henceforth have the right to write "F.R.S.A." But the real reward of the climb has not been the attainment of the crest but the wood violets and mountain fern gathered by the way—and the glimpses along the path of shining heights and golden valleys afar.

I have to go next week to Stratford and Mitchell to give readings....

Saturday, Feb. 3, 1923
Leaskdale, Ont.

I am home again. I had a delightful time while away and feel ever so much better, brighter and braver. I got back my proper perspective while away and can see *around* things now that have been blocking up my vision. The uplift of this ought to carry me through February at least. I felt dull enough when I left home last Tuesday. But I resolved that since I had to go I would *not* take my worries with me—I could leave them behind. Sometimes I cannot do this. At other times I can. This was one of the other times. I seemed to turn a lock on certain rooms in my house of life and did not enter them while I was away. The result was that I had a very happy and pleasant four days. Wednesday I spent in Toronto shopping and had lunch at the National Club with Mr. McClelland and Mr. Stewart. This is something I always enjoy. The National is a nice place to eat and Messrs Mac. and S. are always agreeable companions. I went to Stratford that afternoon and spent the night at the manse there with Mr. and Mrs. Finlay Matheson—a delightful pair of people. Thursday morning I went to Mitchell a town twelve miles from Stratford. In the afternoon I spoke and read to the High School Students and in the evening at a "banquet" given by the I.O.D.E. About one hundred and fifty were present, half of course being men. I had never spoken to an audience of men before and I felt rather nervous at first but got on all right and everyone seemed pleased. We had a "spluxious" dinner and the Regent of the Chapter presented me with a bouquet of roses. On Friday morning I returned to Stratford and the Executive of the Canadian Club gave me a luncheon at the Windsor and another bouquet of roses. In the afternoon I addressed the Club and enjoyed it. The audience seemed to also. But one lady told my hostess afterwards that she "really had not been able to listen" to what I was saying because she was "so taken up with *watching my beautiful hands and feet*"! Poor soul! I ought to wear brogans and fur mitts the next time I speak.

I left Stratford—which must in summer be a wonderfully pretty place—at six and reached Toronto at 9.30 exceedingly tired. But I got a magazine and a box of my favorite candy (pecan roll, for the information of readers two hundred years hence!) and had a gorgeous revel of reading before I went to sleep. I came home this morning and on the train out unlocked the doors of my skeleton closet. I dreaded coming home. But Ewan seemed quite cheerful again and the appeal has not yet been heard so, if no news of success met me, I did not at least have to brace up against defeat.

I *wish* the appeal was over. We are awaiting it from day to day now and the suspense embitters life.

Tuesday, Feb. 6, 1923
Leaskdale, Ont.

I had a curious dream last night. I dreamed that a big box was delivered at our door "from Zephyr." I opened it and found therein a *coffin*. I opened the coffin and found it packed full of *candy*. I said, "Why, this is not a coffin at all. It is a Christmas box." Then I found myself in a strange room looking at another coffin which was on the table and which someone in the room told me "came from the direction of Peterboro." But as I looked at it it faded away like mist.

The symbolism of the first coffin is plain enough. We will lose the appeal but the result will not injure us. But the meaning of the second coffin, which must refer to the appeal to Ottawa is not so clear. Why did it fade away?

In a magazine I was reading today I found a poem on a woman's favorite dresses—and a very dainty fanciful little bit of verse it was, too. It set me thinking of all the dresses I have had—and my favorites among them. Most of my dresses have been pretty ones. Grandmother had good taste in materials and I, myself, am not supposed to be lacking in the quality. But of course some I liked better than others. My first "favorite" dress was a silver-gray "pongee," trimmed with black velvet ribbon, which I had when I was about eleven. It was one of the prettiest dresses I ever had and I loved it all the more because it was a welcome change from the red cashmere which was the fashionable thing for little girls in my childhood. I had had several red cashmere dresses trimmed with plush or velvet—very nice dresses they were as dresses went then but I really never liked them, never having cared for red as a color. My shining silvery dress was very dear to my heart. My next favorite was a cream delaine with a blue spot, trimmed with lace, which father sent me, followed in my affections by a dress of golden-brown material which I had when I went out west—very pretty material made in a very pretty way. I did not again have a favorite dress until my year at P.W.C. when I had a cream challie blouse with a spray of purple violets in it, which, with its daintily puffed sleeves and lace bertha was one of the prettiest and most becoming things I ever had. It was made by Maggie Stuart, a Cavendish dressmaker who never had any training but was a born artist in her line. I've never seen her dresses equalled anywhere; and in those days of tightly fitting robes her ability to make "a perfect fit" was something uncanny. Her dresses always made you, in the country phrase, look as if you had been melted and poured into them. She, too, made my next favorite—a dress I had that miserable spring in Belmont, of some silvery-blue figured goods, with "bell" skirt and "butterfly" sleeves. It would no doubt look very funny nowadays but it was a beautiful dress in its time. My next dress love was a flowered organdy made up over yellow sateen—a lovely thing and very becoming. Later on I had another something like it—my bridesmaid dress when Bertha was married—an organdy with a purple flower and silk stripe. Two dresses that I got in Boston were lovely—my old rose "hobble skirt" dress and my apricot evening one. My trousseau dresses were all pretty and smart but the only one I really call a favorite was a black one of silk striped net. Two years later I had a lovely thing of brown charmeuse with a jacket of heavy cream lace. My latest favorite was the French evening dress of shot old-rose-and-pale-green and Honiton lace I got five years ago. I've never had anything since that I loved though I've had many pretty and becoming dresses. I think the fashions of today are very beautiful— the simple lines and classical effects which never look odd or queer—as do the crinolines, polonaises, bustles and huge puffed sleeves and similar monstrosities of Victorian days—though some of the extremely short skirts look foolish enough on tall or stout figures. Well, most of those dresses of mine have been long outworn and gone into the limbo of forgotten things, with all their daintiness and beauty, along with the passions and hopes and fears of the years in which they were worn. *Sic transit gloria mundi!*

My day for the frilly gowns of organdy and lace is over—henceforth I must wear the richer hues and materials of the matron. But I shall never be indifferent to dress. It is a very foolish woman who is—just as foolish as the one who makes it the foremost and only thing. Both are badly mistaken.

Monday, Feb. 12, 1923

Our intense cold continues and tonight is wild and stormy, with the wind howling around the windows and wraith-like whirls of snow. Somehow, though, I like a night like this and always have. I've always loved to cuddle down in a cosy lighted room or between warm blankets and listen to a storm. It seems to give me an exhilarating sense of victory—as if I were getting the better of some mighty foe. I even like being out in a storm if I can keep warm. It is pleasant to look forward through it to a warm shelter and a good table and a restful bed. It is pleasant to look at the houses we pass with their lights shining out through the tempest and picture the folks inside them as comfortable and safe, and little children, rosy and warm, their dear hands folded in exquisite slumber. And, apart from all this and under it all is some dramatic enjoyment of contrast which is too instinctive to be defined or expressed.

Sunday, Feb. 18, 1923

This has been a very dreary week—so dreary that my courage has ebbed low. It has been extremely cold; we are burning soft coal now, our wood being exhausted, and it is abominable stuff; it is a wonder we have not been asphyxiated with coal gas or blinded by smoke. Our hard-coal furnace hasn't sufficient draft for soft coal; then everybody around us is sick in a widespread epidemic of "flu." I suppose we will all have it and I dread it. Two days we had no mail and the 'phone lines are all out owing to the storm. But then our 'phone service has been abominable all winter. Half the time we cannot get Central and the other half Central can't get us. Sometimes even the rings on our own line can't get in.

Then on Friday evening we got word that our appeal was lost. We had expected this but it didn't lighten the week's gloom any. All this was depressing enough but by far the worst is that Ewan has been very miserable all the week. It is the worst attack he has had for a year and a half and for a couple of days he was almost as bad as I have ever seen him—walked the floor, looked wild and haunted, declared he "wasn't worthy to speak to the people" when I reminded him that it was prayer meeting night in Zephyr. Poor Ewan! To hear him talking about not being worthy to speak to the Zephyrites would be ludicrous if it were not so hideously tragic. In his normal condition of mind he would laugh at the idea as a joke. But it is no joke now but horrible reality that for the time being he really feels that it is so, poor unhappy tormented soul.

When his attack came on in that spring of 1919—nearly four years ago now— he admitted to me that he had had three similar attacks. One in Glasgow—one when he went to Dalhousie—and one when he went to Prince of Wales. Yesterday, however, he admitted that he had had four, the first one being when he was about sixteen. It was induced, he said, by a sermon he heard on hell, preached by an old-style believer in fire and brimstone. It is useless to blame the preacher. He preached as he was taught by the church of his time. If the constitutional weakness had not been in Ewan the sermon would not have produced such an effect; and if the sermon had not done it probably something else would—he would at least have had the headaches and sleeplessness, with the depression, whether he had any definite "phobia" or not.

It has just occurred to me that when my sons read this journal after I am dead, if they ever do, they may possibly be inclined to blame their father for not telling me before our marriage that he was subject to recurrent constitutional melancholia. I do not want them to do this. I have never done so. Ewan did not *know* what his malady was—did not even realize that he had a malady. He believed—and believes still—that his attacks were—and are—the quite natural feelings of a soul under the wrath of God. He does not believe that his trouble is either mental or physical, save for his headaches,—does not believe, in short, that he is the victim of any mental unsoundness at all—and before the spring of 1919, when I insisted on his consulting a doctor, such an idea never presented itself to him. When he has recovered from an attack he believes firmly that he will "never feel that way again" and, indeed, seems absolutely to forget that he has had such attacks.

So I do not blame him for not telling me. I *do* think, however, that it was a very strange thing that his parents never discovered his real malady or obtained any medical advice for him. His father, at least, knew of his condition during the two years at Dalhousie which it lasted, but never seems to have taken any notice of it beyond telling him "he would feel better soon." I simply cannot understand such conduct, except on the ground that old Mr. Macdonald, who was certainly a man of very mediocre intellect and narrow experience did not know enough to realize what the trouble was, and that his mother who in her younger days was quite a bright woman naturally though with no advantages and little education, was so driven and harassed with the care of a large family and small means that she had not time to think about the minds or feelings of her children. At all events, whatever was the reason, nothing was done for him, although it is possible that proper treatment at the outset might have eradicated or subdued the evil tendency and prevented recurrence.

Therefore, as I have said, I do not blame Ewan for not telling me of his malady. Nor can I find it in my heart to wish he had, in spite of the agony I have endured in the past four years and the gloomy outlook of the future. If he *had* told me, of course I would not have married him. I could never have had the courage to marry a man under such a doom; nor, if I could have dared, would I have thought it right to do so because I hold that no man or woman ought to bring children into the world under the curse of such a hereditary tendency. And so Chester and Stuart would never have come to me and, under everything, is the basic conviction that that would have been terrible and that the fact that I have them makes up for everything else. If they escape their father's malady and grow up into good and useful men I shall always feel so, and be glad that Ewan did not tell me. But if they develop mental trouble as they mature or break my heart in some other way, as children so often do—oh, then I shall feel very differently about the matter....

Ewan heard in Zephyr yesterday that Mrs. Pickering had been sick in bed for two weeks with "Bright's Disease." I suppose they can't conceal the fact that she is ill and dare not call it diabetes after what she swore to in the witness box. That perjury may cost her her life yet. If she had not been guilty of it she might go openly to Toronto now and take the new insulin treatment for diabetes and be cured. But now, if she does that, she must do it secretly and that is not easy or perhaps even possible. In spite of the fact that she is confined to bed they have not had a doctor for her—for fear, I suppose, that he would tell other people what her real ailment is. Certainly people are sometimes caught in their own trap.

This morning when we woke a snowstorm was raging and I got up prepared to face a lonely sunless day. But after all it has been a pleasant day. Owing to the storm there was no service and I, being exceedingly tired, resolved to make it a real day of rest. Ewan stayed in bed, the boys were both absorbed in a book, so I was free after a fashion. So I took the book Mr. MacMillan sent me at Christmas, and which I have never even had time to look over, and settled down for "a good read." I had it. The storm raged outside and the gray day wore to its sullen close but I was far away, a free soul, roaming amid the delights of *A Flower Patch In The Hills*. It is one of a kind of books which seem to be quite common in England and Scotland but which United States and Canadian writers cannot or do not produce. I have often felt that I would like to write such a book and that I *could* do it but hitherto I have never had the time—for such a book would be a labor of love with love as its reward. It wouldn't "sell" here. Mr. MacMillan has sent me several of these books and I love them all but I think *The Flower Patch* is the best.

Monday Feb. 19, 1923
The Manse, Leaskdale, Ont.
Today was milder and Lily and I went to work to clean our pipes ourselves, driven thereto by the absolutely unbearable smoking of range and furnace. The pipes fill up so quickly as the result of burning soft coal. This being done and the pipes put up again we had some comfort the rest of the day.

Ewan went to Toronto today to see about carrying our case to the Supreme Court but came back this evening with the news that they had decided not to because in order to do so we would have to give a bond to pay Pickering's expenses if we lost. As we have no hope of winning it, since our evidence was not half in, and only meant to take it there to give Marshall Pickering a full dose of the law he likes so much, we will not do this. McCullough should have told us of this condition before. He does not seem to have known of it himself, as he told us some weeks ago that it would be better to go to Ottawa than England because in the latter case we would have to give a bond. We have told several people that we meant to go to Ottawa and now we are put in a silly position which I resent. Besides, thinking there was plenty of time, Ewan had not yet concluded arrangements with the congregation for the payment of the salary in advance. This must be done right away. Also it is possible that Pickering will send the sheriff here at once. He can do it legally. Of course, he can't get anything if he does come since everything is mine but I hate the thought of it....

Wednesday, Feb. 22, 1923
The Manse, Leaskdale, Ont.
In spite of our pipe cleaning Monday the furnace and range began to pour out smoke today so we burned the flue out—a horrible job. If Ewan won't see to getting it properly cleaned soon I'll have to. Perhaps we will now have at least one smokeless week.

I've been receiving several letters recently congratulating me on being elected to the F.R.S.A. Well, I wish being a "Fellow" conferred immunity from smoking furnaces, malicious law-suits, "flu" and bad 'phone service. But alas, it doesn't. I shall still have to shake down, and shovel coal into, the furnace o'mornings and o'nights just the same.

Ewan has been very dull lately. I have resolved to accept one fact—viz:—he will probably never again be really well. Intervals may come, when like last fall, he may seem almost or quite well; but these will be temporary and I must henceforth live my life alone as far as any real companionship and assistance from my husband goes and as far as the care and training of my sons is concerned. I refuse any longer to be tortured by alternate hope and fear and disappointment and suspense. "Despair is a free man, Hope is a slave"....

Saturday, Feb. 24, 1923
This week has been intensely cold and I am truly terrified lest we be found some morning all asphyxiated by coal gas. I read of similar catastrophes every day in the papers. I keep all the windows open at night but that in this 20-below-zero weather is a choice of evils.

The managers of both Zephyr and Leaskdale have paid Ewan's salary a month ahead and will continue to do so. They are all as anxious as we are to get the better of Pickering. This is a great relief to us. Now the next thing, I suppose, will be that Ewan will be summoned to examination as to why he did not pay up. After that they can do no more—except drag him up for examination every now and then. They would gladly do this to annoy him no doubt but they may be restrained by the fact that it will cost them a good bit!

Stuart, bless his sunny face, ensures us a laugh per day. Tonight at supper when Chester took a third tart Stuart looked at him and said severely,

"Chester, if you don't learn to stop eating when you've had enough you won't be a husband long to the person you are going to marry."

I *wish* it would get milder. We have hardly had a day above zero since December. The house is so bitterly cold in the mornings as we can't check the furnace, owing to the gas, so it burns out.

My geraniums are all dying from the effects of the gas.

Wednesday, Feb. 28, 1923
The Manse, Leaskdale, Ont.
It has been quite fine and mild since Sunday and consequently life has not been such a valley of dry bones. Ewan was in Toronto yesterday and brought home the typed evidence of our trial. We have been reading it. The amazing bias of the Judge is even more evident than it seemed during the trial. He asked several "leading questions" himself of Pickering and helped him out whenever he got cornered—also Mrs. Pickering. But he did not so help any of our side. But then *we* were *not* cornered. We were telling the truth so didn't have to cover up and explain. Every one of our witnesses told a plain straight tale and never once tried to hedge during cross examination. The Judge minimized our evidence all he possibly could and brushed aside what he couldn't. It is certainly all very curious. The medical testimony was all in our favor except Johnson's in regard to congestion and this was contradicted by Dr. Robinson's evidence and the gland itself—and yet the Judge paid no attention to it at all. I simply cannot understand it.

But oh, I am dreadfully sick of the subject and wish woefully that I might never hear it mentioned again. And Ewan, since he has been reading the evidence, talks about it unceasingly. I am glad of this, of course, because it is much better that he should be thinking of this than of his morbid terrors, and so I discuss it with him readily—but all the time I feel as if I were being flicked and teased on some raw surface. The whole thing has been such a wretched, sordid, humiliating affair. I feel as if I had been dragged through a cess-pool....

Well, never mind. Life will be easier when spring comes; and meanwhile it is very nice to have a small, blue-eyed son say to you as Stuart said today, "I hope if I am born again *you* will be born again as my mother"....

Monday, March 5, 1923
The Manse, Leaskdale, Ont.
Went to the Hypatia club today and read a paper on The Goddess Pasht....

Monday, March 12, 1923
The Manse, Leaskdale, Ont.
No sign of spring yet. This is unusual for Ontario. I feel quietly happy tonight—because of something I was able to do today.

This afternoon a certain Mrs. Widdifield of Sandford came here—coming herself because her husband was just recovering from flu pneumonia. She had a pitiful tale to tell. There was a mortgage on the farm for $5,000. Up to this year they had always paid the interest. Then a succession of misfortunes befell them—poor crop, poor prices, an operation on a daughter costing five hundred dollars. Consequently, they were six months behind with the interest and the mortgagor—backed by *Greig*—was going to foreclose at once. A forced auction sale now, when the farmer's market is so low, would not bring more than two thirds of the value of the place and they would be turned out with nowhere to go. Her husband was worrying so over it that his recovery was retarded. She could not get aid anywhere in the present dearth of ready money in these parts and in her despair came to me. Would I lend them the money for principal and interest—five thousand five hundred in all—and take over the mortgage?

I felt really aghast. I could not do it. I would have to sell out Victory bonds to get the money now and I will not do that for these Victory bonds are for my children, or for us to live on if anything should occur to prevent me from writing and I will take no risks with them. Besides I hate the thought of tying up any more money in mortgages. I have $5,000 in two mortgages now that have never paid a cent of interest for five to eight years and I doubt if I ever get even the principal back. I could not tie up another five thousand so. These people are honest; but their ill-luck might continue. I could *never* foreclose a mortgage and sell people out if I lost every cent. So the only thing to do was to tell her I couldn't and it was the hardest thing I ever did for there was something about this woman I liked. She tried to be brave—thanked me with a quivering lip for having listened so kindly to her story—and then broke down and sobbed. "I thought God would not let us be"—and stopped, unable to speak.

Well, I had to do something. I could not let that woman leave my door without some assistance—I could not nullify her faith in God. I would not have slept a wink tonight if I had done so. I had a sudden inspiration.

"I cannot take over your mortgage," I said, "but I will tell you what I will do. I will lend you enough money on your note of hand to pay the interest up to November. Then they cannot foreclose until the mortgage falls due and you will have time to get another crop and time to look about you to find someone who can take over the mortgage, with a better chance of succeeding, since you can say that you have always paid up the interest."

The change in poor Mrs. Widdifield almost made me cry myself. She tried to thank me, broke down again, sobbed out "God bless you" two or three times. When she went away she turned to me at the door and said, "Oh, Mrs. Macdonald, *I feel as if I could fly.*"

I have felt so happy all the evening that I was able to lift the worst of her burden from her and so thankful I could do it. Even if I never saw a cent of the loan again I would not regret giving it to the poor soul.

Stuart gave us another laugh at supper tonight. He was sitting, looking very grave; suddenly he drew a long sigh and said, "Oh, mother, I wish I was grown up and married and *had it over with.*"

It was very funny and yet I sighed a little behind my laughter. Stuart evidently has my tendency to cross bridges before he comes to them. It means a lot of unnecessary worry through life. And yet—I don't know. Perhaps it is the foresight and preparation induced by the worry that makes the bridge safe....

Saturday, March 17, 1923
Yesterday, driven to desperation, I went out myself and got two Leaskdale boys to come and clean our chimney. It was almost full up. We soon had it cleaned. It left us with a filthy house but we have cleaned that up and are free from smoke once more.

Yesterday a big envelope came from Mr. Rollins. Dreading some ill news I did not open it till tonight—for we had to go out to tea last night and I didn't want to be upset for that and for the work I had to do today. So tonight after the boys were in bed and I was alone I set my teeth and opened it. But there was nothing definite. Last Tuesday the Page suit was argued in the Supreme Court of the United States but the decision will not likely be given for some months. Rollins says he "had a feeling" that the hearing went on "pretty well." I found the reading of the briefs and pleadings very interesting. The Deputy Marshall made affidavit that he had attached a "chip" as my property. I didn't know I owned a chip in Massachusetts!

In regard to *my* suit there is no decision yet. Rollins says it is most unusual for a judge to be so long in handing down a decision. He says French wrote the Judge the other day asking if he could not soon give his decision. It is possible that the delay means that the Judge finds a decision difficult and may give it in *my* favor. But I long ago gave up any hope that I could win the suit. Nor does it matter much now. The sale of the book has ceased now, and the injunction, which was all I ever expected to get, means nothing now. I only want to have it over with and wiped off the slate. It has been hanging over me, like a veritable sword of Damocles, for three years and I never know where I stand or what bills I will be called on to pay.

Poor Ewan remarked today that he "felt no interest in anything." That is terribly true. He has never actually turned against me or the children—he is just absolutely indifferent to us. And if I did not insist on his doing certain things—visiting, going to Guild meetings etc.—he would never stir finger or foot to do them. The strange thing is that after I make him do them he feels much better for the time being and admits it. Yet next time it is just the same....Sometimes I get so disheartened that I feel it would be better to give up, get him to resign and cut him free from every obligation and responsibility. That would be by far the easier way. But from what Dr. Garrick told me I fear it would not be the best thing for Ewan. So I struggle on, do what I can myself and *make* Ewan do what I can't do....

Sunday, April 1, 1923
The Manse, Leaskdale, Ont.
....I went to Toronto last Monday and stayed in till yesterday, shopping and having a pleasant change from the sordid life of the past months—though under it all I was haunted by the worry that the bailiff might come while I was away etc.

However, I had a pleasant time. While I was in, the Toronto *Star* published the results of a voting contest it recently had. "Who Are the Twelve Greatest Women in Canada?" I was one of the twelve! Such competitions are very silly and this is sillier than most for greatness has no necessary connection with fame. I am not "great" and neither are most of the twelve. But of course if the competition had been avowedly what it really was, a questionnaire as to the most *widely-known* women in Canada. I certainly am one and perhaps *the* most widely known.

I froze my ears going down Yonge St. on the 28th of March. This hasn't happened to me since Cavendish school days.

I had a talk with Mr. McCullough who is altering my will so that Mr. Pickering wouldn't be the gainer if I should suddenly drop out. I think we have got it fixed so that Ewan will really have what I want him to have and yet no one be able to touch it.

In speaking of the examination McCullough said rather doubtfully that he hoped we would be able to "maintain the ground we have taken." His uncertainty depressed me. There is one question which will be awkward if Phelan asks it—and ask it he certainly will.

The matter is this: When the big "fox boom" was in swing on the Island and fortunes were being made over night I lent Ewan a couple of thousand dollars to invest. He expected to double his money in the fall and pay me back. And he would have if the heir to the Austrian throne had not been assassinated at Sarajevo. The war came—the boom slumped—and Ewan was left with a lot of doubtful fox stock on his hands. It was thereupon agreed between us that I was to take the fox stock. I got whatever dividends were paid since—very few—but we never bothered with having them transferred to my name. This winter we *have* had them transferred. They are morally mine and McCullough says the fact that I have had the dividends will prove them legally mine, he thinks. Now, if Ewan is asked "Did you transfer any of your property to your wife since the accident" he will say "no," because that is the truth. But if Phelan asks, "Did you transfer any property from your name to your wife's," Ewan will have to say "yes." The fox stock is worth so little that it is hardly likely they will go to the expense of trying to get it; still they might, and even if we can "maintain our ground" as McCullough says, it will mean more trouble, worry and expense.

Chester MacClure, a second cousin of mine, was in Toronto visiting his daughter who is at the Conservatory of Music....We had dinner at the King Edward. He told me he had been talking to a *Mail-and-Empire* editor who had been in court during our trial and who told him that anyone could see it was a framed-up job and that it was a shame that such a miscarriage of justice should be permitted.

Norman Beal tells me that Riddell is said to be "crooked" and has been suspected more than once of accepting bribes. But I can't believe that Marshall Pickering could afford to give a big enough bribe to influence a man of Riddell's standing—unless Riddell was dreadfully hard up—which isn't likely. Riddell is known to have a keen grasp of "points of law" and he certainly used his knowledge to wrest his verdict in Pickering's favor, but I think it was through prejudice, not bribery.

Monday, April 2, 1923
The Manse, Leaskdale, Ont.
This morning when I got up I said to Ewan, "You are going to hear from Pickering soon. I dreamed last night that the bailiff came." Ewan laughed as usual but I felt quite sure. There was also something in the dream about "Tuesday or Thursday," but it was so confused I couldn't make that part out.

But this afternoon the bailiff did come at last—Mr. McCully from Blackwater whom we know. He was smiling broadly and seemed to look on the affair as a joke. He said he was deputed to come in the place of Sheriff Paxton of Whitby who was ill. Perhaps the Sheriff *was* ill but I fancy he didn't like coming to a minister's house on such an errand, so shunted it over on McCully. McCully asked Ewan if he were going to pay the damages. Ewan gravely said he couldn't. Mr. McCully, with a twinkle in his eye, asked if he had any property. Ewan said "An old cutter and some theological books." This being done, Mr. McCully laughed over it all and said the story he had heard was that Pickering ran into us as we were backing out of a yard in Zephyr. This is a little more favorable to us than the real truth but shows the trend of public opinion.

Well, this is over. The next thing will be the exam. and the sooner it comes the better. *Anything* is better than suspense.

Sunday, April 8, 1923
....This evening I read Gertrude Atherton's *Black Oxen*. Like all her books it was charmless. She has neither atmosphere nor distinction of style but she can write an interesting yarn. In *Black Oxen* her heroine is a woman of sixty, who has been made young again by a certain gland treatment—which I believe is really being practised successfully in Austria. This woman becomes again beautiful and charming but alas, it is only her body that is rejuvenated. Her mind—her cynical, disillusioned mind—is still sixty years old. It works out very consistently.

Suppose I were able to take that gland treatment and be physically twenty years old again. Would I do it? Decide carefully. To be twenty again—oh, beautiful! But wait. Twenty—with a middle-aged mind—a *déclassé*—cast out of my own generation because of my seeming youth—unable to find real companionship among the young because of my old mind. It would be horrible. No, no. I would not be twenty again unless all my friends could be twenty also. And even then—unless the clever surgeons of Vienna could blot out memory as well as years—I fear it would be but a sorry state of affairs.

Monday, April 9, 1923
Leaskdale, Ont.
This evening the constable of Uxbridge, yclept Smith, came up and gave Ewan a summons to examination at Whitby on *Thursday*. (So much for my dream!) The joke is that he had also to give him six dollars of Marshall Pickering's cash, as it seems the law demands that the "judgment creditor" must pay the expenses of the "judgment debtor" to examination! This is really funny. It seems that Ewan will get more out of Pickering than Pickering will get out of him.

Ewan laughs over this. I can't. The whole thing is a nightmare and I dare not laugh till that examination is over. I am so afraid Phelan will ensnare Ewan into some answer that they can take hold of. And yet, in my dream of last fall, there was not a "single drop" out of the black cloud. If I could believe this absolutely I would not worry. And I should be able to believe in it for all my dreams of that kind have come true....

Wednesday, April 11, 1923
The Manse, Leaskdale
Mr. Cook has been here for two days painting and staining hall and dining room. Consequently the house has been upset. And I have been upset. Now that the examination is drawing near I cannot settle to anything. I have worked hard both evenings making out an itemized statement of all money expended since last fall so that Ewan can account for every cent. I thank my stars that I have always kept a rigid account of all our expenditures every day. I have day books back to our marriage. We can show that the money we spent came to more than Ewan had from all sources and yet the expenditures are all entirely reasonable for a family like ours. Mr. Greig may suspect that under ordinary circumstances Ewan would not have to pay all this—that I would pay at least half. But I am not compelled to pay half. If I choose to say sternly to Ewan, "You should wholly support your family as other men have to do. I will not pay for such support," no lawyer or judge on earth can condemn *me* for such a reasonable attitude! *I* don't owe Pickering anything—*I* am not responsible for his enlarged prostate gland! And if poor Ewan is cursed with a miserly wife who ties up her purse strings and makes him expend *all* his salary on keeping her and her children what can Mr. Greig do but sympathize with him!!!

Moreover, if said miserly wife sometimes feels compunction and puts a certain sum aside in the bank for her husband to make use of if he will, said sum being equivalent to half our living expenses, that is still nobody's business but my own. *I* haven't got to account to Pickering in regard to how I spend my cash, whether wisely or foolishly....

Saturday, April 14, 1923
The Manse, Leaskdale, Ont.
....All day Thursday I was upset and could settle to no steady work, so did odd jobs. The mail came. There was a letter from Mr. Rollins. Instantly I knew that the Judge had given his decision at last on my suit—after three years!
....I looked at it a little while before I opened it, telling myself that it really did not matter in the least that I had lost—nay, that, all things considered, it would be *better* if I lost. Then the thing would be ended for good and all, I would pay another big fee, charge up my expenses to profit and loss, and know where I stood at last. I would be *free*. On the other hand if I won—what? The injunction would be all I would likely get. After three years it would be a barren victory for the sale of the book is practically over. For all my expense and worry I should only have the satisfaction of beating the Pages. Then they would, of course, appeal—and that would mean more expense and worry. Yes, it would be much better to lose—swallow the bitter dose—and henceforth be at peace. Yet there was something in me that grimaced at the thought of swallowing that draught of humiliation after my long fight.

"Well," I said, "let's take it and get it over."

I opened the envelope. There were two letters in it. The first—...

"Dear Mrs. Macdonald:—

Judge Hammond handed down a memorandum of finding yesterday construing the contract in your favor and directing a decree in accordance with the memorandum which I enclose. This decree will direct that the defendants pay you all profits made from the sales of the book.

I congratulate you on being at length successful in this long litigation and I trust that the profits will turn out to be something substantial. The defendant however takes the ground that there have been no profits...."

The second letter, evidently written a little later in the day than the other, read:—

"Dear Mrs. Macdonald:—

I have just heard that, oddly enough, the Supreme Court in Washington also decided its case yesterday, this also being in your favor. I am not surprised that the decision should be in your favor but it is truly remarkable that two courts should decide the cases both on the same day after this great lapse of time. I am very much pleased that we are winning out."

At first I couldn't believe it. It must be a dream. Such things didn't happen in real life—not in my life anyhow. Then I went a little crazy I guess. I felt as I haven't felt for years—I felt *free*—I felt as if *all* my shackles had dropped off! They hadn't, of course—I knew that; the heaviest were still on me. But I did not feel their weight. I had wings for a few hours....

This morning my wings had gone. I was back on earth again. The Page suit against me is done with; but they will certainly appeal the other and there will be more *ex*pense and *sus*pense.

As for the profits, the book sold about 13,000 copies before the trial and they brought out a new edition while the trial was going on. But I feel sure the Pages will garble the accounts in some way and I doubt if I ever get a cent. Meanwhile, I know there will be another big bill of Rollins to pay.

It certainly was an odd coincidence that the suits should be settled the same day. My dream of losing my bad luck seems to have come true. But I am afraid the bad luck won't *stay* lost. The past four years have robbed me of most of my old optimism.

And then there was Ewan and his examination at Whitby. *It* couldn't have gone well, too. *That* would be too much good fortune to come all at once. There was a letter from him in the mail which I was afraid to open. If all had gone well and he was coming home that night why should he have written? I tore it open shrinkingly. It contained nothing but the cryptic announcement that "nothing had been done at Whitby." So I was left in suspense till tonight when he came home. It seems that ass, Greig, had sent him merely a copy of the summons, not the summons itself. This wasn't legal and McCullough wouldn't let Ewan appear on it. The examination is put off till next Thursday. The joke is that yesterday would cost them about $25 for nothing. *And* they have to give Ewan another six dollars for next trip!...

Phelan wasn't at Whitby, so it is evident that Greig means to conduct the examination himself. I am very glad of this. Phelan is a keen clever lawyer but Greig is an ass....

It is not enough that we have our own worries. Others must dump their financial troubles on us too. We had a pitiful letter today from Ewan's sister Christie. They seem to be in a bad plight. I can't go into details—indeed, it was hard to make out what was the real trouble. It is because of their son Leavitt's doings. Poor Christie seems almost distracted. Her husband is very ill, too. She asked for a loan of $100. I sent it to her as a gift not a loan. I am glad to be able to help Christie. But she has two brothers, Angus and Alec, who are reputed to be worth a great deal of money. One wonders she would not apply to them instead of Ewan. And one more than suspects that it is because they know how to hold on to their money and are not remarkable for clannishness.

Tonight, after a long day's work was done I read an hour in *Tommy and Grizel*. The book has all its old charm....especially as one can't help hoping all the way through—yes, though it were at the twentieth reading—that Barrie will "find a way" to end it happily. Barrie has to a superlative degree the power of creating atmosphere and character, so that his books give us the sensation of reading about people and places we have known well, and consequently have all the charm of a newsy letter from home. In a much smaller degree I have the same knack myself and that is why my books are liked.

I cannot help thinking that it was a great pity that Barrie forsook writing books and took to writing plays. His audience is much smaller and the life of a play short. He has cheated the world.

Somehow, I can never rid myself of the idea that Barrie was depicting *himself* in "Tommy." And was his wife drawn from "Grizel"? She divorced him—why, has never been satisfactorily explained. I hope I will live long enough to read a truthful biography (if there is such a thing!) of his life. Perhaps it will clear the mystery up.

Wednesday, April 18, 1923
The Manse, Leaskdale, Ont.
....I gave myself the satisfaction of phoning the news of my successful suit to the two Uxbridge papers. I do not usually air my private affairs thus. But at the time of the suit it got out and ever since at intervals someone asks me how it ended. So it will be just as well to let them know the result. If I lose the appeal they needn't know *that*.

And I think it will be a pill for Messrs. Greig and Pickering! At least, it will show them that I am not afraid of litigation and do not easily submit to blackmail or threats.

Friday, April 20, 1923
Leaskdale, Ont., Can.
The long nightmare is ended....Greig never asked the question we dreaded. He must be an ass *not* to have asked it, but the lucky fact remains that he did not. And he *did* ask some absurd questions. For instance he asked *three* times, "Had

you any money in the *Leaskdale* bank?" When he asked it the third time Mr. McCullough said impatiently, "Mr. Greig, Mr. Macdonald has told you twice that there is no bank in Leaskdale. Surely you ought to know that yourself after living only seven miles from it for several years."

It shows Greig's calibre that he should ask such a question. I foresee that the Leaskdale bank will be a family joke in the House of Macdonald henceforth.

Greig seemed to have the fixed idea that Ewan had had a lot of money in some bank—something he *never* had—and spent most of his time questioning along this line, after Ewan had repeatedly told him he had none. I feel a primitive desire to slap Greig's insignificant face for him. Insolent cub, to doubt the oath or even the word of a Presbyterian minister. After he gave up the bank line in despair he began on the salary. When he was told that it was paid monthly in advance he was furious and could not hide it. I believe the idea had never occurred to him that the congregation would do that. I fancy Mr. Greig is a sore and angry man tonight—and I don't envy him when he has got to tell his tale to Pickering. Some say he isn't paid in full by Pickering yet. If this be so, the odds are against his ever getting it.

I feel so relieved. It really seems too good to be true that Greig never asked that one awkward question.

Nevertheless I shall feel uneasy for a time. They will leave no stone unturned to harass us. Pickering will be furious. And the announcement of *my* successful suit coming the same day will fill up the bitterness of his cup. He will be sure to imagine I have got thousands out of it.

I had a letter from Rollins today. He seems a bit downhearted. It seems he did not think the Pages would appeal because the expense of printing so much evidence would cost as much as they would have to pay us in profits. He does not yet know the Pages as I do. They would rather pay a lawyer ten thousand than me one thousand. They are going to appeal by a "bill of exceptions" which it seems is a tedious process and is a rare procedure. Rollins is so blue he suggests a compromise. I will not agree to this. For one thing I feel sure Page wouldn't compromise on any terms. For another I'm not going to back down now after fighting so long and winning the first round. Rollins was so down three years ago that he wanted to settle because he thought Nay's evidence would kill our case. But I refused and as a result I won despite Nay's evidence. Very likely I'll lose in the appeal but I will *not* knuckle down to Page.

Saturday, April 22, 1923
The Manse, Leaskdale, Ont.

I am feeling the reaction from the long strain of recent weeks. Today instead of feeling relieved that the exam. was finally over I felt restless, unhappy, upset. Everything worried me. I expected the worst of everything. Marshall Pickering would sue us for conspiracy—or begin to worry our treasurers. Rollins' attitude got on my nerves, too. To add to the tension another distracted letter came from poor Christie. It is impossible to make out the rights of the matter but it is evident that Leavitt has landed them in a dreadful scrape of some kind. She wants me to lend them $5,000 on a mortgage. I simply can't do it. Poor Alex is dying—I have no confidence in Leavitt—if they failed to pay interest or principal I could never foreclose. I have $10,000 out now, some in mortgages and the rest on notes, from which I have never received one cent of interest and will not likely ever see a cent of my principal. I cannot tie up any more. One does not know what might happen.

Ewan has decided to run down to the Island for a few days and see how things are. He seems to think I should lend the money. I can't see it so. Angus is Christie's brother and has three times as much as I have and he is the one who should lend it.

I went from bad to worse until the evening when I fled to my room, broke down and had a long cry. This served as a "went" and I felt ten times better afterwards—snapped my fingers at Marshall Pickering and wrote Rollins an order for full steam ahead. I even began to think that, since poor Christie had to be rescued, I must see what I could do.

Thursday, April 26, 1923
Leaskdale, Ont.
Our new car came today—a Dodge. It is no more mine than the others were of course but it is in my name. Mr. Pickering will be furious when he sees us in it....

I hope we will have better luck with Dodgie than with poor Lady Jane. The trouble is Ewan can't take proper care of *anything*—from a pen knife to a car. He seems to have absolutely no idea of it naturally and was never trained to it. So we will likely have some trouble with it but surely not so much as Lady Jane.

Sometimes when I am working away at some prosaic task—as for instance today when I was washing paint—a memory picture and sensation comes vividly back to me—for no reason that I can perceive. Today I was looking from my window at home on a spring evening when the world seemed holding its breath over a sudden perception of its own beauty. I saw the cherry trees, the green fields, the long red hill

"Road to Uxbridge"

road, and far over to the southwest the great clump of white wild cherries in the woods by Lovers' Lane. I saw all the incredible, indescribable, clear, dewy delicacy that thrilled me in those olden twilights. And for that one moment I shuddered with a pang of fierce homesickness.

Monday, April 30, 1923

I went to Toronto Thursday to attend the convention of the Canadian Authors' Association. Had a very nice time and several nice social stunts, including a reception at Government House and a dinner at the Arts and Letters. At this latter function I saw for the first time in Canada women smoking in public. Of course women have smoked in Toronto for some time but I never saw them do it before at a dinner. I didn't like it. Not that I thought it the least "bad" or "fast" or even unwomanly. But it is *ugly*. Few women are so beautiful and charming that they can afford to divest themselves of any portion of their charm; so they are very foolish to do so by smoking. It doesn't matter about men. Men look ugly and silly, too, when smoking. But it isn't beauty that matters with them—only strength....

One thing amused me at the convention. Invariably the least successful authors had the most to say and evinced the most determination to run everything and dictate all policies.

We had a breeze over the newly passed Copyright Bill. Nobody can understand it. I believe it will kill out our young Canadian authors altogether and in the end our Canadian literature. Under the terms of it publishers will be afraid to accept the work of unknown authors.

Personally, I sat quiet and took it all in. But I did not find it unpleasant when Dr. Logan of Halifax came up to me and said,

"Hail, Queen of Canadian Novelists."

Yes, I like it.

I came home feeling anxious and fearful, as I have come home every time for four years, and especially this winter. Ewan seemed pretty well, however. But when we got home and went into the library he said, "I have news for you. There is to be a new trial."

My heart seemed to stop beating. I thought of course, that he was referring to Marshall Pickering and that he must be bringing suit for conspiracy or something like that. I turned absolutely sick. And then I heard Ewan say, "There's Rollins' letter." I snatched it, read it, and gasped with relief. It seems French has appealed to the Supreme Court for a *rehearing* of their libel suit. This was nothing like as bad as I had supposed. I didn't think it was possible to get a rehearing but it seems so. Rollins says there is no need to worry etc.

Yes, but I suppose it will mean more expense for me and that is what the Pages want....

Tuesday, May 1, 1923

We went over to Wick manse to tea tonight. It is so delightful to be able to ride in our car again after the long cold winter of bad roads. One feels as if one had got out of prison. And Dodgie is a splendid car. Every time we go out in her we feel better satisfied with her.

I saw Dr. Shier today. He said he had never been so tickled over anything in his life than over hearing that Pickering hadn't been able to get a cent.

["Dodgie" and Ewan]

Wednesday, May 9, 1923
Leaskdale, Ont.

Ewan left for the Island tonight. We are in desperate confusion—the whole house torn up for the paperhanger. Owing to that detestable soft coal the paper all over the house is ruined and five rooms must be papered.

May has so far been cold and wet—today we had two inches of snow. A letter from Mr. Rollins informed me that French's petition for a rehearing had been refused. So that's *that*, and no bother or expense for me. But there will be plenty of both before the other suit is finally settled—if it ever is! Rollins said he had been talking to Judge Hammond *re* the case and the Judge said that it was in Nantucket parlance, a "whale of a case" and that he had got intensely interested in it.

Sunday, May 13, 1923

As today was Communion at Zephyr I went over with Captain Smith who is supplying for Ewan. Of course Mrs. Will Lockie gave me a slam—or rather Ewan through me. She never fails to do it. When I said Ewan was so sorry to miss his Communion service Mrs. Curl said "Yes, and we missed him, too." But Mrs. Lockie said, "Oh, well, we had a very good sermon. Captain Smith seemed to take so well with the young people."

Of course that *is* a weak point with Ewan. He doesn't understand young people and never did, even when he was a young man himself. He never seems to know what to say to them and tries to carry off the situation by a misplaced jocularity. It is impossible for him to take them seriously as adolescence demands to be taken. But in Leaskdale where we have plenty of young people I fill this lack for I feel more at home with the young fry than with the older folk. And in

Zephyr there are almost *no* young people. This is a fact. I never saw such a church. There are only about half a dozen "teens" in the congregation. Two of them are Mrs. Lockie's own and I don't think either Ewan or I "take" with *them*. Nor would we want to. They are as unattractive as their mother and the only two young people in both our congregations with whom I have never been able to "mix." I feel in their presence just the same feeling of secret enmity, dislike and resentment I detect in their mother. That woman *resents* any superiority in any-one—of education, dress, circumstances or personality. She resents my keeping a maid—having a car etc. It seems a personal matter with her. Of course she isn't normal—they say she is quite a bit "off" at times—but she is none the less dis-agreeable for that....

Friday, May 18, 1923
The Manse, Leaskdale, Ont.
Poor Aunt Annie is in trouble again—no money to pay hired man's wages and buy clover seed. Here is where little Maudie's purse must come to the rescue once more. Well, I am very glad to open it to poor Aunt Annie. Only—I smile a bit, remembering certain things of long ago, when Aunt Annie's Clara and Stella were so often flung in my teeth because they were such splendid cooks and housekeepers and general hustlers. Yet today those same smart girls can't help their mother with a cent. It is to the despised dreamer she must turn for financial help. But while I do not forget this, I do *not* forget that Aunt Annie was the only one of my mother's brothers and sisters who ever treated me like a human being, took my part, or seemed to have a spark of affection for me. She might condemn me herself as a foolish chaser of bubbles but she would not let anybody else "pick" on me and stood up for me valiantly. I remember a tale Frede told me. One day Uncle Leander and his second wife, Aunt Annie Putnam, and Uncle Chester and Aunt Hattie went to Park Corner for a visit and carried there some false yarns about me which had been told them by that old hypocrite, Aunt Ann Maria. They took their tales to the wrong market. Aunt Annie rose up in her majesty and told them soundly that if they were going to listen to "Ann Maria's lies about Clara's child they need not come to her house to repeat them"—and so sharply did she manhandle Uncle Leander that that gentleman actually dissolved in tears and admitted that he was wrong. He must have got a sound drubbing to surrender like that. But Uncle Leander *had* some genuine family feeling behind his autocratic exterior. Uncle Chester had none—though he was a more agree-able man exteriorly. But he seemed to have absolutely no affection for his sisters and brothers, even his father and mother. The *clan spirit* was totally lacking in him as in all the Woolners.

He might have been a different man if he had got a different wife. Aunt Hat-tie's selfishness raised a barrier between him and his kin which there was noth-ing in him to surmount....

Monday, May 21, 1923
A letter from Ewan. Things are worse than we dreamed of down there. Alec is dying. Leavitt, who was running the store, has got them in for $13,000 liabili-

ties. Worse still, he has helped himself to $1,500. of the post office money and has had to abscond to Boston. That is a penitentiary offense. Luckily Jack Whear, the Postmaster General for the Island, is married to a cousin of Christie's and he has covered the matter up, on condition of Christie's paying the money back.

Ewan has addressed himself to the mess. He has induced the creditors to compromise for $9,000, is raising five thousand by a mortgage on the farm and asks Angus for $2,000 and the remaining from me. I have to sell out some Victory bonds to get it but of course it must be done for poor heart-broken Aunt Christie's sake. My heart aches for her. Beside such crushing troubles as her husband's fatal illness and Leavitt's scandalous behavior what are my worries— apart from Ewan's mental trouble at least. But I could horsewhip Leavitt with a right good will. To get his parents into a mess like that! He has disgraced his family and all who have the misfortune to be connected with him. But I must not be too harsh. I don't know how my own boys will turn out yet. The immediate thing is to save what we can out of the wreck for Christie.

Ewan seems wonderfully well. His mind is so occupied with this that he cannot brood on his old dreads. It is as it was last fall during the trial. 'Tis an ill wind that blows no good.

I have been rushing around all day arranging for the sale of the bonds etc.

Thursday, June 7, 1923
I am really almost forgetting what Ewan looks like! He isn't back yet and won't be till next week. Meanwhile I write, garden, and run the affairs and societies of the congregation. As for the garden, alack! Tuesday morning my garden looked nice—rows of everything up beautifully. Tuesday evening it was a river of mud—the middle washed out. I have simply got out of patience with these Ontario thunderstorms. Every spring it is the same old story of washouts and floods, drat it! I have toiled for weeks in that garden and now I must toil weeks more to repair the damage.

Monday, June 11, 1923
The Manse, Leaskdale, Ont.
We had a Dominion Alliance man here this Sunday—a Methodist yclept Rev. Ryerson Young. He is clever, deaf, *Methodistic* and egotistic—the most egotistic man I have ever met I think. He is an unceasing talker and spent most of his time telling me all the wonderful things he has done in his career. He *has* done them too, I think. He is a veritable dynamo of energy—quite often misdirected—as, for instance, when he went out unasked and cultivated my aster bed, uprooting the ring of sweet alyssum I had planted around it under the impression that it was weeds. I think that incident extremely typical of the man. Before his sermon he gave me a horrible ten minutes by informing the congregation that the only reason he had come was because he wanted to see "L.M. Montgomery" and telling them they ought to be a highly cultured and bookish people when they had a "world-famous authoress" among them. If Jenny Geddes' stool had been handy I would have thrown it at him with a right good will. Anything like that

makes me wretchedly uncomfortable—it is in such bad taste. I never sped a parting guest so willingly for between his egotism and his deafness I was tired to death....

Tuesday, June 12, 1923
The General Assembly has voted for Union in the teeth of a large minority. I think it is a shameful thing and the coercive legislation which they are going to attempt to push through parliament is outrageous.

From all points of view I think it is a tragic blunder. The stately Presbyterian church, with its noble history and inspiring traditions, has been forced to commit suicide. The result will be strife, trouble and confusion for ministers and churches for twenty years. Nor, I believe, will the eventual result justify this wholesale uprooting. "Men and money" may be "saved" but the church will not be the gainer thereby. The money will stay in the pockets of the people and the men will go—forced to go—into other callings. The "United church" starts life with a combined deficit of nearly half a million. That will not be speedily made up by disrupted congregations half of whom are angry and sore over this compulsory "Union."

Personally, I refuse to worry. Union will probably complicate our problems here and if we are "squeezed out" and Ewan cannot get another suitable congregation we have enough to live on. Hundreds of poor ministers who trusted their fathers' church will be in a far worse plight. But I resent the high-handed way in which the so-called "leaders" have forced Union on to save their faces and I resent the feeling of "homelessness" it has brought me. I feel that I have no longer a church. My Presbyterian Church has gone—I owe and feel neither love nor allegiance to its hybrid, nameless successor without atmosphere, tradition or personality. I wish I were free to go over to the Anglican communion. It has always attracted me and I would feel more at home in it than I can ever feel in "the United Church of Canada"—a bumptious and arrogant title which it has no right to assume. Why should it call itself "the church of Canada" when Baptist and Anglican denominations are not in it?

Saturday, June 16, 1923
The Manse, Leaskdale, Ont.
Ewan got home today. He seems very well—if it would only last. He had a strenuous time down east but engineered things very cleverly. If Ewan had energy and ambition equal to his diplomacy and shrewdness in dealing with people he might have gone far. But he has always preferred to "take things easy" and for the past four years his mental disorder has intensified this to the point of apathy. He is capable of a big "*tour de force*," such as the remodelling of the old graveyard in Cavendish or inducing our congregation here to assume the support of a special missionary; but when it comes to steady routine work he does not like it. The missionary business has long since petered out for instance....

Speaking of the Mustards reminds me that Rev. John's son—who has always been a selfish, unmanageable boy—has broken his parents' hearts by suddenly without a word or warning, presenting them with a French Canadian Catholic wife whom he picked up in the mining regions up north. It is a disgraceful way in which to treat his parents. He might at least have told them beforehand. It makes one feel that it is useless to toil and sacrifice for your children who may treat you with such ingratitude in the end—or disgrace themselves as Leavitt has done. Will Chester and Stuart break my heart thus?...

Monday, June 18, 1923
I had a rare and real pleasure tonight. We went to call on a family up north and after I had done my duty talking to a woman who is in Milton's expressive phrase "stupidly good" I decided to run over to the next farm and call on two women living alone there. I took a short cut through the orchard and across two clover fields and for fifteen minutes I was alone with nature again as I have not been, I think, for five years. It was unbelievably lovely....Too soon I had left my fairyland behind me and was listening to the rather weird conversation of an old lady whose mind is not quite rational where religion is concerned. I had to listen to her minute account of the death and illness of her husband—who was a miserly old curmudgeon, of no use to God or man, who never had a thought above the dollar sign in his life and would have sold his soul, if he had one, for thirty pieces of silver any day—and her reasons for believing that, in spite of all, "his name was written in the Lamb's Book of Life." There was something pathetic and tragic in her efforts to convince me—and herself—that it was so. She was afraid in her secret heart that her husband had gone to hell—as logically he should have if the convictions she has held all her life were true—and she was also afraid that public opinion would think he had, which was a humiliating thing, even if he were really "saved." So the minister's wife must know how she had read the Bible to him and how he had said "Yes, ma," when she told him that these were the words of eternal life. No, I didn't laugh—even to myself. I didn't feel at all like laughing. I repeat that I found it pathetic and tragic; and I wondered what the God with whom I had been in close communion half an hour before on that windy green hill of clover would think of it all. Would He not have said, "Ye are all my children, blind, helpless, stumbling, mistaken, torturing yourselves with the creeds and dogmas of your own invention. In death I open a door and give you rest."

Thursday, June 28, 1923
....I am very busy preparing for a trip to the Island. I don't feel enthusiastic about it some way.
....I have been reading Strachey's *Queen Victoria*. Lord, how he smashes our old idols! When I was a child and young girl the Victoria myth was in full flower. We were brought up to believe that "the queen," from babyhood to old age was a model for all girls, brides, wives, mothers and queens to follow. In those days every home boasted a framed picture of the queen—a luridly colored chromo, sent out as a "supplement" by a popular weekly. There was a crown and lace veil on her head, a broad blue ribbon over her breast, and jewels plastered on thickly everywhere. But the face! I looked at it in distaste and said, "Why, she's just a fat common looking old woman!" I shall never forget the look of

horror on Grandfather's face. Talk of blasphemy—*lèse majesté*! I got a scorching rebuke, being told among other things that I should be ashamed of myself. I don't think I was. I only had an uncomfortable conviction that if Queen Victoria was really as "good" as she was said to be I must be very bad because I thought her ugly.

Strachey's book rather justifies me to myself. Poor Victoria hadn't any chance to be bad even if she wanted to be—and I *do* think she got tired at times of being so exceedingly proper. Prince Albert curbed her because she was unlucky enough to fall deeply in love with him. Mentally she was of very mediocre mould indeed, as anyone who read her published journals could see. But she had some qualities that helped to save her empire where a cleverer woman might have wrecked it. Her reign was a very wonderful epoch and its wonder made of a dumpy and dowdy little woman a symbol for a people who cannot do without symbols.

"Heart's Desire," Brighton, P.E. Island
Sunday, July 15, 1923
Monday night at seven o'clock we left Leaskdale manse. Wednesday night at about the same time we arrived at *Heart's Desire*—Fanny Mutch's summer bungalow at Brighton. Our trip down was pleasant and uneventful. But one curious meeting befell me on board the car ferry.

I was crossing the lady's cabin when an elderly woman came up to me and said,

"I suppose you don't know me, Mrs. Macdonald."

For a moment I did not. I looked at the dowdy dress and hat, the untidy twist of gray hair with one forlorn end sticking out, the wrinkled, baggy face—and the cold, prominent, faded blue eyes. Where had I seen those eyes before? Then—I knew! One couldn't forget those eyes. They were bound up with some of the most disagreeable memories of my childhood.

"You are Mrs. Warren," I said, "once Miss Robinson."

For it was she—that woman whom I have hated so bitterly for her old injustice and sarcasm. I had never seen her since she left Cavendish. She sat down beside me and talked to me all the time of our crossing. I had a queer feeling of unreality—I felt as if I had been hating a phantom—a creature that never existed. This shabby bent old woman was not—could not be the bustling bitter young woman I remembered. I had a feeling that I had expended a great deal of passionate feeling on a very futile object. In brief it did not seem worth while to have hated her for over thirty years. My ancient grudge suddenly crumbled to dust.

At the same time I was feeling wickedly amused. This woman had evidently chosen to forget certain things and remember others which never existed. She spoke as affectionately of "dear old Grandmother and Grandfather" as if she had not bounced out of dear old Grandmother's house one night with Parthian insults, and talked of both Grandfather and Grandmother afterwards in the nastiest fashion. She referred to my writing in those early years as if she had fostered my youthful talent and foreseen my future success before anyone else—she who had never noticed my scribbling save to sneer over it. As she maundered on with these insincerities, lavishing on me in twenty minutes enough compliments and praise for a lifetime, I was impishly recalling certain incidents of long ago and certain things she had said of me to others—"Her Satanic Majesty Maud"—"I never saw a child I disliked so much"—"one cannot teach one of her stripe anything"— and so on. I wonder what she would have said if I had suddenly mentioned these things. Denied them, probably. I have no doubt she utterly forgot them years ago. But she could not have forgotten that she left Grandfather's house in a senseless tantrum over a trifle and that he never let me go to school to her again. So one would have thought that some sense of shame or at least awkwardness would have prevented her from forcing herself upon me.

Fan met me at Borden and Margaret got on at Breadalbane and came as far as Hunter River. She looks well but hasn't been at all well this past year—nerves bad etc. The menopause, in all likelihood.

Fan is big, fat, and as jolly as of yore. Her family are almost all grown up. I always liked Fan and she never changes.

Her little bungalow is beautifully situated, just where the North River empties into Hillsborough bay. The sunset last night up North River was of a kind seen only in P.E. Island. We are situated here between two range-lights that burn enchantingly through the twilights, pearl-white against the ethereal skies. Down the harbor there are more range lights and the big lighthouse and far out, seemingly in mid-harbor, shines the far-off light on Point Prim—a beacon "in fairylands forlorn."

Next to us is a vacant lot full of daisies—a place of haunted loveliness in the twilights—and over the river daisied hayfields are as white as snow. I always come back to a realization of the Island's beauty with a certain amazement. I have always forgotten that it really is *so* lovely. There is nothing like it in smug opulent Ontario. I slip down to the shore sometimes in the late dusk, feeling how beautiful it is to be alone with the night again, with the stars all in their right places again over me and the white fields over the river lying lonely and lovely in the dim light, and gaze on water and field and hill with eyes that would devour them. In such exquisite moments I am a part of the sky and the night and the daisies blowing in the elfish wind.

The boys go bathing in the river and Stuart is much intrigued with two adorable kittens of the establishment whose mother is named Nebuchadnezzar!! He takes them to bed with him and in the night I waken to hear old Nebby at my door, softly calling to her children in that nice throaty sound only a mother cat can make—really one of the nicest sounds in the world. The two kits answer— old Nebby springs up on the bed, and there is a glad and gay family reunion, with no end of the same pretty love-sounds. Then when the kittens have had their lunch away goes Nebby quite satisfied that her babies are in good quarters.

No doubt it is terribly unhygienic. Theoretically I sternly frown when Stuart pleads to have the kittens with him. But I notice that he has them for all; and I myself don't know of many nicer things than to waken up in the night and put out a hand to feel a soft, warm, velvety purring little flank in the darkness.

Thursday evening we motored out to Winsloe to see Mary Campbell. We had a merry evening; but there was something sorrowful about it. Dear old Mary looked so miserable. Her face haunts me. Truly it seemed to me like the face of a woman not long for this world. She has been ill for over a year—some kind of heart attacks. She is fretting too over her son Roland going west. He can't get on with his father—small blame to him for that—but he should not break his mother's heart. Youth never realizes—never understands.

We had 'phoned out to Mary in the afternoon that we were coming and Maud had picked wild strawberries for us. They were delicious. And I had my own reasons for enjoying them doubly.

Saturday we went out to Earnscliffe with a picnic party. The rest went digging clams and oysters but I simply sat on the river's bank and drank in the loveliness of the landscape, especially across the river with its high steep red banks and beyond them sheet after sheet of daisies and clover. Such clover! The red ones were as big as roses.

Oh, my Island is matchless—matchless. I feel that I did some violence to my spirit in leaving it. I *belong* here. It is *mine*—I am its own. It is in my blood. There is a part of me that *lives* only here. And to think that I did not really want much to come! How could I have been so insensible—I have been here only a few days but it seems as if I had never left it. Ontario—Leaskdale—they are dim and distant as a dream. This only is real—this colorful little land of ruby and emerald and sapphire.

Fan and I picked daisies for an hour today and knew we were *not* middle-aged mothers but gay, crazy college girls again, just loose from old P.W.C. ....

Cavendish, P.E. Island
Friday, July 20, 1923
How very natural it seems to write that.

Last Monday we went out to Kinross and stayed there until yesterday morning. I had had a very nice time at *Heart's Desire*—and yet I was in nowise loth to leave!

Why?

Because both the children and myself were almost starved to death!

One could not believe, unless one had seen, the sketchy dabs of food that Fan called meals. She put on the table for ten people about enough for four—and most of it bought or canned stuff at that. I was in a state of chronic, gnawing hunger every moment of the time I was there. I could have endured it with a grin myself but it was dreadfully hard to manage the boys. They had the ravenous appetites of all sturdy boys and they were hungry all the time. I used to take them down to the shore—one dared not try to whisper in that thin, partitioned bungalow—and impress on them with threats of dire penalties that they must not ask for "pieces" or second helpings. They obeyed—but Stuart would sit at the table and look at me with the eyes of a hungry dog and sometimes whisper imploringly when Fannie had gone to the kitchen, "Mother, isn't there *anything* else?"

Had we been up town I would have sneaked them out to a hotel and fed them up or bought enough cakes to keep them in "pieces." But we were too far out of town for that and the "free-for-all" rooms of the bungalow precluded any private caches. So there was naught to do but endure. It spoiled my visit. I never want anything but plain food when I am a guest but I *do* want *enough* of it.

I don't know just where the blame lies. R.E. Mutch has the reputation of being very mean. Fan is not mean but she is rather easy-going and does not try to make the most out of what R.E. allows.

The day we went to the picnic Fan took one small leathery lemon pie as her contribution—and there were eight of us. But the other cars took generous hampers and we had a feast. I was positively *faint* from hunger when I sat down to

"Aunt Christie's" [P.E.I.]

that picnic spread and I was ashamed of the way I ate. The boys got a filling up which enabled them to exist patiently until we got to Aunt Christie's Monday. Aunt C. had cold chicken and roast meat and biscuits and strawberries and cream—and she must have thought that Ontario people had awful appetites....

Cavendish, July 21, 1923
Saturday
There is an amazing crop of kittens on the Island this year. Everywhere we go we find them—fat, fluffy, enchanting. Myrtle has a dear thing called—ye gods!—*Savonarola*. This beats even Nebuchadnezzar.

This evening was exquisite and I stole away for a walk. I find life here this summer easier than it has been in any of my previous visits. The boys are old enough to look after themselves....

So this evening I went over to the graveyard and kept tryst with my dead. The old spot was beautiful in the sunset light, with its plots snow-white with clover. And I did what sounds rather dismal but which did not seem dismal to me at all—I selected a plot for my own resting place. I want to be buried in Cavendish graveyard when my time comes. I want to lie among my kindred in the old spot I love so much better than any other spot on earth. As a minister's wife I shall not likely live long enough in any one place to make me feel that I want to be buried there. Certainly I do not want to be buried anywhere where a Pickering could walk over my grave!

No, I belong here—this old Island gave me birth—it must give me a tomb. Here only can I rest at last— here it is fitting I should be buried. And it is fitting that Ewan should rest here, too. Cavendish was his first charge and it was he who converted the graveyard from the old jungle it once was into the orderly, well-cared

"Stuart with 'Savonarola' and Lorraine Webb"

for place it is today. One could say of him, buried there, as it is said of Wren, "If you seek his monument look around."

I selected a plot on the crest of the hill, looking down on the beautiful scene I always loved—the pond, the shore, the sand-dunes, the harbor. On innumerable summer eves I have stood there and gazed on them, longing for some diviner speech to express what I felt. I want to feel that my last resting place is in sight of them.

It is rather odd that this plot should be vacant. It is one of the most desirable in the graveyard and all around it are taken up. I think it was predestined for me.

"Entrance to Lover's Lane"

There, sometime I shall lie and the wind will creep up from the sea to sing over me and the old gulf will croon me a lullaby....

Gartmore Farm, Cavendish, P.E. Island
Saturday, July 28, 1923
....There's nothing in all the world like a sea wind. But one poetry has vanished from the gulf forever. It is never now dotted with hundreds of white sails. The fishermen now have motorboats which chug-chug out in the morning and chug–chug back at night and are not on speaking terms with romance. One evening I went down to Hamilton Macneill's and told him I wanted to see the old place. Poor Hamilton was quite delighted. We sat awhile in the old sitting room where everything seemed exactly as it was forty years ago and therefore made me feel that I must be still a girl. Then he took me through the old garden and gave me a bunch of the old fat cabbage roses that I remember so well. Amanda used to bring bouquets of them to school to decorate our desk and old Aunt Caroline always carried one to church. But the garden was overgrown and neglected—and full of ghosts....

Saturday afternoon, Aug. 4, 1923
Gartmore Farm, Cavendish, P.E.I.
We have had I believe even a nicer week than the one at Myrtle's. At least, I have enjoyed it even more for May and Alec are old cronies of mine, whereas Myrtle belongs to a generation a step removed from mine. Therefore there is more color and vivacity in our talks and we can discuss family folklore with the zest and spice possible only to genuine contemporaries....

Our luck in kittens attends us. They have three beauties here of which one is the most oddly and beautifully marked cat I have ever seen—silvery gray with jet-black marks. The marks on his sides resemble a clover leaf with an M inside it and I said he would bring good luck so Chester suggested we call him that. I am going to try to take him home. I will not likely ever have such a chance again. Besides I want another cat from Gartmore Farm. The breed is good!....

I have always been glad that I possess the capacity to find the most intense pleasure in little things. Yesterday I was prowling about with my camera and I looked upon the little hill road east of Alec's and had one of my "flashes" of rapture in its beauty—rapture so poignant that I wrung my hands with the exquisite pain of it. It is in such moments as this that I know I can never die.

One night I had supper with Hammond and Emily down in that old remote house by the Cove. Had a lovely time and came home around by the shore. I never felt happier than I did on that lovely evening by that blue majestic ocean. My own, own land!

When I reached Alec's Cove I heard gay voices up in the shore field and found the boys there helping Alec coil hay. I waited till they were through and then we went home in the clear afterlight with a little lad clinging to each hand.

But, as always, the pleasantest hours of all were when the day was ended and the boys off to bed. Then May and Alec and I would get into the dining room and sit for a couple of hours around a lavish supper table—May is certainly a queen cook!—and eat and talk and laugh. Oh, laugh! It was delightful to be free to laugh with boon companions again. One evening in especial we laughed until we could laugh no more.

Alec produced a "diary" his father had kept for several years and we read it together. I don't think I ever read anything quite so delicious in my life.

"Alec's place"

Charles Macneill was an odd sort of a man, whom as a child I always loved because he was so kind to children. But I think that both as a neighbor and a father he left a good deal to be desired. He inherited from his mother—his father was not one of "our" Macneills but his mother was—a queer streak of the Macneill literary knack—a tiny thread of gold running through the slag of a very commonplace character. It flashed out here and there in the diary in several naive, satiric entries which were so artless and spontaneous that I could actually hear old Charles Macneill uttering them. We laughed until the tears poured from our eyes.

Apart from the unconscious humor of the diary it gave me the keen, sad delight of a vanished world re-created. It made old Cavendish live again—the Cavendish of my childhood and girlhood. It was all there in those little shabby notebooks as no deliberate attempt at description could ever produce it. Men and women long dead lived there again as in yesterday. The little affairs of church and state in a remote P.E. Island farming community were reflected there as in a mirror. I looked in it and saw the world of my teens pass before my eyes again. Oh, yes, we laughed—but behind the laughter was a sigh—and that is the difference between the laughter of youth and the laughter of middle age….[*Handwritten volume 5 ends here.*]….Alec has discovered from some old papers of his father's that this was the original name of this farm. There are various spellings—Garthmore—Gartmoor etc. I like the custom of naming farms. It seems to give them a personality. It is a custom which has never obtained in P.E. Island—which is odd, because most of the early settlers came from Scotland and England where all the farms are named. And they named theirs to some extent—but their descendants dropped it.

My week at Gartmore Farm has been almost wholly delightful. The only annoyance has been the carloads of callers—generally perfect strangers—who have come to see "L.M. Montgomery" and have more than once upset plans May and I had formed. One of these, a severe maiden lady from Ontario, named "Bentley," informed me that she had a crow to pluck with me. It seems in one of my books "Miss Cornelia" mentions a man named "Bentley" who was a drunkard! Miss Bentley was pleased to inform me that "no Bentley ever was a drunkard."!!!!!

Another caller was a Mrs. Stirling McKay. I had a letter from her recently—very nicely written on correct stationery but signed with the damnatory signature of "Mrs. Stirling McKay." She wanted me to go to Summerside and spend a week with her! Considering that she is a total stranger to me I thought this an odd request. I had heard of her husband, Stirling McKay, a wealthy business man of S'Side and a friend of John Stirling's. But of her I knew absolutely nothing. I wrote back, courteously explaining that I had so little time to spend with my old personal friends that I could not include a visit to Summerside.

Well, the family came today in person. Mrs. McKay said she wanted to give a lawn party in my honor when I was at Breadalbane and have me and the Stirlings in. I said I did not think I could go—I had only two days at Breadalbane etc. Oh, Mrs. McKay had already been to see Mrs. Stirling and had talked it all over with her. She did not exactly say in so many words that Margaret was eager for the party but she certainly contrived to give me that impression. So I yielded for if Margaret, after her shut-in winter among the aborigines of Breadalbane, was hungry for a little social diversion who could wonder? I told Mrs. M. I would go to her party and sent her away quite happy.

And now my visit in Cavendish is at an end. I go tonight to Park Corner and for the first time in my life I am dreading a visit there. It has been so beautiful here. And I know I will be lonely at Park Corner.

Everywhere I have gone this summer I have heard fulminations against Uncle John for tearing down the old home. The Charlottetown people were especially indignant. They said it was the only "literary shrine" the Province possessed and it was a shame to destroy it.

For my own part, though I know as everybody else in Cavendish knows, just what Uncle John's motive was, I am well content that it should be torn down. It would not please me to think of it being overrun by hordes of curious tourists and carried off piecemeal. The Bentley party had their car full of some old junk they had retrieved from the cellar!

I have never seen the vacant place. When I have been anywhere on the road where I could see it I have averted my eyes.

Uncle John and Aunt Ann Maria look old and she is very failed. Ern has had a great deal of trouble with his wife. She is a nice little thing but her mind was badly affected for several years. Since the birth of her first child a year ago she has been much better. Lucy is a *grandmother*. The thought dazes me. Her only son married when he was seventeen and they did not know it for months. He has been a wild fellow, I understand. Ben Simpson's son would have small chance of being a model character, I suppose. But one never can tell how children will turn out. One of my sons may break my heart, too.

Sunday Night, Park Corner
August 5, 1923
....Last night was painful to me. I found Aunt Annie looking so thin. She seems fairly smart again and is beginning to sleep and eat well; but she has failed greatly since I saw her last.

And George's family are almost grown up. Dan is a man, Amy a big girl of twelve looking fifteen. Handsome—jolly—naive! Jim is a smart chap. He and Chester announced that they were going to sleep in the back bedroom and did so. They talked until three o'clock.

Maud is a very nice child and Georgie seems bright and sharp. Oh, they are all nice youngsters—but where are Clara and Stella, Frede and George? When I

"Children at Park Corner" [Georgie, Maudie, Amy, Stuart, Chester, Jim Campbell]

went to bed I was so lonely I cried half the night and couldn't sleep. Oh Frede, Frede, how I missed you last night! Here was the mirror that had reflected your face! Where were you? Where was the savor and vivacity of your speech? It seemed to me that I could *not* stay at Park Corner—that I must rush away in the morning—anywhere, away from this agony of loneliness.

Today was bearable however—days always are. Aunt Annie and Ella are so glad to have me here that their gladness surrounds me with a warm pleasant feeling. Old Park Corner is still beautiful—the birches down the lane and behind the barn are as white and stately as of old. There is an eternal triangle in birch trees—you so often see them growing in groups of threes.

Tuesday, Aug. 7, 1923
Park Corner, P. E. I.
....I had tea with Aunt Eliza today and found Ellen Montgomery there—an old friend not seen for many years. She is seventy now but very bright and smart and full of the old, unmistakable, inimitable Montgomery flavor. I was always very fond of her and it was a pleasure to see her again.

Heath is a fine looking fellow. And he is going to make a wretched misalliance. It is too bad. He is going to marry a girl...with no family or background. When I heard it I thought that perhaps she was pretty—or at least buxom and colorful....I can't imagine what possesses Heath. He is a man who could take his pick; and yet he is going to put [her]...in the place of all the dear stately ladies of the old house. His mother, Aunt Eliza, is odd enough; but she is a lady....It is enough to make the old Senator turn over in his grave....

Every night poor Aunt Annie trots into the pantry and gets up a lunch for me. It pleases her so much that I make no protest though I am seldom hungry. I do

"Aunty and her hens"

not eat it in the pantry—I can't bear to. But I sit in the dining room *alone* and eat it and try to keep the tears back that Aunty may not see. For these solitary "snacks" are very bitter when those who once shared them with me are gone....

Wednesday, Aug. 8, 1923
Park Corner, P.E.I.
This afternoon I shut myself in the parlor and looked over a pile of old photographs of the vintage of puffed sleeves and pompadours. Nothing has a more ghostly pleasure than this. One photo I came across was of Ed Simpson taken some thirty years ago. Ed, by the way, has recently been on a tour around the world. His wife caught smallpox in Calcutta but has recovered. I heard this in Cavendish but nothing more except that Ed is very gray. Well, we are all getting gray but it must make a great change in Ed whose hair was so thick and dark. Poor Ed. The whole tale of that old affair seems so faint and far-off now that it has ceased to be anything more than a mere memory....

Tonight Life Howatt motored me up to see Aunt Emily....I found Aunt Emily not very well. She struck me as being very lonely.

Sometimes when I visit Aunt Emily she is so nice that I wonder why I ever thought she wasn't pleasant to visit. Other times she stings and slues until I

"The old back yard" [Park Corner, P.E.I.]

come away thinking I am justified in hating her. Tonight was one of her nice times and I enjoyed my chat with her.

It seemed nice to come back to Park Corner. After all, as long as Aunt Annie is here Park Corner will seem home to me.

Thursday, Aug. 9, 1923
Park Corner, P.E. Island

This morning when I wakened I found Stuart bending over me and saying in an eerie tone,

"Mother, we won't both live to get back to Ontario. We won't both step together into Leaskdale Manse."

The thing haunted me all day though I laughed at him and myself. I suppose he was worried because I was going away for the day. Stuart has been a haunted child ever since that night I spent at Amanda's. It was the first night he and Chester had been left without both Ewan and me away from home.

It seems he dreamed that night that the house where I was staying had been burned and me in it. Myrtle said he stood out in the yard next day and watched the lane all day until I came home. Since then he seems to dread my going anywhere and worries till I get back.

I went to Bedeque today to speak to a camp of C.G.I.T.s there this afternoon. The camp is in a lovely spot and at first I felt as if I envied those girls. But on consideration I do not. I don't believe I'd care to be one of a camping crowd. I never liked a mob; and to live in the woods with several overseers to watch every step wouldn't please me at all. To be there alone with Frede or Bertie—oh, that would be the right sort of camping. To bask on the clover in the sunshine—bathe in the flaming river at sunset—loaf on the bracken in the woods—sit at nightfall by a camp fire—tell the stars at midnight over the dark woods—and feel always near at hand, within touch or call, the comrade who understood!

I spoke my piece—on *Friendship*—posed before twenty cameras—chatted with visitors—answered innumerable questions—and now and then looked across the river to Lower Bedeque and the fields of the old Leard farm. But those ghosts, too, are laid....

I found a letter from Margaret. It seems Mrs. McKay has hoaxed us both. She made Margaret feel that *I* wanted the party, so Margaret, who *didn't* want it, yielded for *my* sake. Well, Mrs. McKay has attained her object. She is a climber, I understand—Stirling McKay's second wife—and so far has not been able to induce the old S'side families to be her guests. She is going to dangle L.M.M. as a bait and has worked the affair very skilfully.

Monday, August 13, 1923
Little Hugh would have been nine years old today had he lived. I wonder what he would have looked like.

Thursday, Aug. 16, 1923
The Manse, Breadalbane, P.E.I.
Tuesday was my last day at Park Corner. I felt very badly. In some ways my visit here has been sorrowful and yet there has been much pleasure and sweetness in it. And I felt so keenly over going away because I can never feel sure now that Aunt Annie will be here when I come again. She is 75. And at the best I cannot have many more visits with her in this dear old place. I might never have even another.

And she feels so badly over my going. She and Ella gave themselves up on Tuesday to preparing banquets for us, as if that were the only way they could express their feelings, poor souls. A dinner of wild ducks—a supper of chickens—the old table groaned as of yore.

Stella and Clara want Aunty to go out and spend the winter in Los Angeles and Clara has actually offered to send her money for the trip. Friends of hers are going, too. I have been urging Aunty to go and promised her I would give her $100 to pay for her clothes. I don't know whether it is a wise thing. Certainly, once she was there, it would be splendid. She would escape the cold winter and get rested and built up. But such a long journey for an old woman who is liable to sudden attacks like hers is a serious thing.

Yes, Aunt Annie *is* an old woman. I can never believe it but it is true.

It was a hard parting. Heath motored us to Breadalbane. Margaret and I talked most of the night. On Wednesday the McKays motored out for us and Mrs. McKay's reception came off. Over 300 people came—the "old families" to a woman. So she had her wish and was quite happy. Margaret and I had our own wicked private fun out of it all.

Among the guests were Oliver Macneill and his wife who are living in S'side now. Oliver has changed a good deal. It was very funny to recall that the last time I saw him he was down on his knees imploring me to marry him—and that one part of me wanted to while the other part of me laughed at him. His wife is quite nice looking and the best dressed woman there.

When we were leaving Mrs. McKay gave me a parcel which she entreated me to accept as a "souvenir." As there was a crowd around I did not want to make a scene by refusing but I did not like to take it. It was as if she were trying to pay me for coming to her house. Margaret got a plate and Doris a vase and the boys balls and Mr. McKay sent a pearl handled knife to Ewan!!

When we got home I opened my parcel and saw cup, saucer and two plates of what I thought at first glance was Crown Derby but on looking at the hallmark discovered to be Crown Aynsley. By an odd coincidence it is the same pattern as a slightly larger plate of real Derby I have at home. I doubt if Mrs. McKay knew the difference.

Today Margaret and I had a delightful day of sheer *talk* and tasted every minute.

Tomorrow I leave P.E. Island. I shrink from the thought.

St. John, N.B.
Friday, Aug. 17, 1923
We left Breadalbane this morning of fresh August sunshine and reached St. John at seven. Had a hurried dinner, dressed hurriedly and went to a reception Mrs. Raymond, president of the Canadian club, gave for me. It was very delightful and I had a good time. As I went into the reception room I heard some woman behind me gasp,

"Oh, doesn't she look just like Queen Victoria!"

Her enraptured voice seemed to imply that she meant to be complimentary— but a glance at Queen Victoria's picture casts a shade of doubt on the matter!

Sunday, Aug. 19, 1923
St. John, N.B.
....Aunt May came to see me this evening and I enjoyed our chat. She has changed little save to get gray. We talked over those old Cavendish days. She brought me a real treasure trove—a letter written by my mother to Uncle Leander which she found in one of his boxes after his death. I was overjoyed to get it. I never had a scrap of mother's composition before. The letter was undated but must have been written when she was a very young girl, as she was going to school. It is a rather stiff little epistle, such as a letter written to a much older brother away at college or already in the ministry would be apt to be. It doesn't express any of mother's real personality but it is delightful to have it.

Saturday, Aug. 25, 1923
The Manse, Leaskdale, Ont.
....We came home yesterday. Last Monday I spoke in the Imperial Theatre at St. Johns and left for home that night, so exceedingly tired that I promptly took a bad cold, as I always do when tired. We had to stay overnight in Montreal so in the evening I took the boys to a movie. Just as we went up the hill from the

Queen Hotel my heart gave a sudden painful throb. There was a church on the corner and in a corner of its grounds, raised from the street by a terrace of stone was a certain tree. Under that tree Frede and I once stood for hours, waiting to see Balfour and his party pass in the spring of 1917....

The next day we came to Trenton and stopped off to visit Ralph and Laura. Ewan arrived there the same night. He seems very well and this is a great relief for I had dreaded coming home and finding him dull and depressed.

We motored home from Trenton yesterday. On the way we were held up for a few minutes by some work on the road and one of the men came up and began talking to Ewan. Finding out who he was he said, "You're the man that was in that lawsuit last year. How did you get along?"

So I am back in the Pickering atmosphere again and must expect these reminders, like acrid stings....

Still, it is nice to be home. And yet I'm horribly homesick for the Island and my friends there.

Wednesday, August 29, 1923
Leaskdale, Ont.
Emily of New Moon is out. I got two reviews today, both very favorable.

[Chester, Stuart, Maud, Ewan, Aylsworth children]

The cover design of *Emily* is the prettiest one on any of my books I think. The little girl really does look as I imagined "Emily" looked. But there has been one weird mistake. The moon in the picture is an *old* moon, not a new one! *Absit omen!* The U.S. artist should really take a course in nature study.

I very seldom draw a character "from life"—"Peg Bowen" in the *Story Girl* is almost the only instance heretofore. But "Miss Brownell" of *Emily* is the Izzie Robinson of my own childhood. I gave myself that little bit of satisfaction!

New Moon is in some respects but not all my own old home and "Emily's" inner life was my own, though outwardly most of the events and incidents were fictitious. If poor George Campbell had lived to read *Emily*—or be told of it, for George never read anything—he would have laughed over the incident of the poisoned apple. He nearly frightened poor Heath Montgomery to death one evening when Heath was a small kidlet by telling him a big apple he had been eating had been poisoned for rats. That was George's idea of a joke.

The English edition of *Emily* has a plain cover but a pictured jacket. Somehow there is a certain eerie quality about the English artist's conception of "Emily" that I like. It is more *Emilian*. The English do these things better than the Americans.

I have been suffering all the week with an ulcerating tooth. It makes me homesick for heaven.

I began work again on *Emily II*. Find it hard to get back into the stream of thought.

Thursday, Sept. 13, 1923

....I have just finished reading *Les Misérables*. Oddly enough, I never read it before. I can hardly explain why. I heard about it when I was very young. I knew it was one of those books everybody ought to read—one of the acknowledged masterpieces of the world. Several times I had an opportunity of reading it but could I prevail on myself to begin it. I always meant to "some day" but the some day never came. What was the reason? I do not know.

But this fall I said, "Now, I'm going to *make* myself read *Les Misérables*." I *made* myself read the first few chapters. Then there was no further making. Or rather, the difficulty lay in making myself stop. I read hours when I should have been sleeping. One part of me enjoyed the book, another part shuddered in pain over it—but always it was fascinating. I am through with it—I don't think I'll ever want to read it again—but I would have missed a wonder out of life if I hadn't read it.

I have a busy fall before me. The Guild young people are going to get up a play and have asked me to attend the practices and stage manage the affair. I didn't feel that I could refuse them but I do grudge the two evenings out of every week that I shall have to give to it. I will hardly have an evening at home for two months.

Saturday, Sept. 29, 1923
The Manse, Leaskdale

The mad rush has begun. Last Monday the township school fair was held in Leaskdale. Stuart was one of the competitors in the speech making contest and won first prize although the three other speakers were much older than he was.

I had ten people to tea that night and Elsie and I were dog tired when the last dish was washed up. Tuesday night we began to practise the play. It is a rather funny thing, simple and crude. It would be no use to try to get up anything else with the material we have or for the audience we will play to. Wednesday I went to Uxbridge, had company to tea and went calling once on the Fifth in the evening.

Thursday I had a wire from Ella telling me that Aunt Annie was starting for California next Thursday. I knew she would likely go and I am glad but it gave me a horrible lost lonely feeling. Park Corner without Aunt Annie—without one of those who used to be there! It made me so lonely and homesick that I went to my room and cried.

Went to practice at night. Friday evening we were out calling. This is my first quiet home evening this week and I have answered a stack of business letters.

Saturday, Oct. 6, 1923
The Manse, Leaskdale

....Last night there was a hard frost and my garden went. The glory of the cosmos has departed. It has been very beautiful.

This morning we went to Uxbridge and brought home a vociferous gray kitten in a small wooden box—Good Luck....Really, he is quite the most beautiful cat I ever saw. His markings are unique. Pat looks quite faded and ordinary beside him. Pat is very much peeved about this interloper and his language is terrible. Luck is quite willing to be friendly but Pat only growls and spits....

Saturday, Oct. 13, 1923
The Manse, Leaskdale
Still rushing, Monday evening practice—Tuesday evening pastoral calling.

Wednesday was a lovely day. We motored in to Toronto to hear Lloyd George in Massey Hall. I had not expected to be able to get tickets but Mr. McClelland pulled wires and got a couple for me. There were 3,000 tickets and 180,000 applications!

I suffered all night from an attack of bowel trouble and for any other person than Lloyd George would I never have got out of bed, much less motor to Toronto. But I was determined to see him if I could go at all, so I went with a jaw swelled out of all proportion by reason of that blessed tooth. We saw and heard the "little Welshman." I don't think he is as tall as I am—"from the neck *down*." He was hoarse and we could not hear all his speech. What we could hear was not so very wonderful. But it was the man himself—the man of the Great War. I think Lloyd George is and will always be considered one of the greatest men in the world and one of the most intriguing characters in history. He is essentially a fighter. He is lost without something to fight. He did more than any one man or score of men to win the war. But I think his day is done. He is not a constructive statesman, such as is sorely needed now. But he *had* his day—and did his work—and it was for this that we all sprang to our feet as he came out on the platform and shouted and hurrahed and clapped and stamped and *cried*—and would have flung ourselves down and let him walk over us if he had wanted to.

We stayed in all night. I felt better in the morning and spent the day shopping. We came home in the evening and I was so tired I would have given much to be permitted to go to bed. But I had to go to practice—and without anything to eat, as Lily, with her usual entire lack of foresight had gone to practice without leaving a thing ready for us to eat....

Friday night we had our Guild social. Today I had the Mission Band and tonight we went to Zephyr to attend a W.M.S. social where an address and present was given to a departing member. (N.B. I wrote the address last night after I came from Guild!!)

Of course, in all this I have little time for *living*. I cannot read, except for half an hour after I get into bed at eleven. I *should* go to sleep—but I have to read a little bit. By these half hour snatches I have just finished re-reading *Hypatia*. I always like it.

Thursday, October 18, 1923
The Manse, Leaskdale
Haven't been well this week. Feel dull and headachy all the time and my ulcerating tooth still bothers me. But business as usual!

Today I had a letter from Ila—who is in Oklahoma at present. Being a civil engineer's wife, there is never any knowing where she may or may not be. Her letter was about Carl and made me feel sick.

She writes:—

"You were talking about Heath Montgomery's probable marriage. I don't suppose you know that Carl married a girl about three years ago and we never knew until Kate accidentally discovered it this year. It was a nasty shock. He has a little girl two years old, named Ila May after me, very sweet looking in her picture. They are not living together and it is all a horrid mess...."

I should think it was a mess! Oh, and such a shame! Carl was such a dear—I feel wretchedly over the whole thing....It's probably best to get a divorce—but divorces are not exactly part of our family traditions.

Well, as Ila says, we can't live other people's lives for them. For that matter most of us find it is about all we can do to live our own.

But this question of divorce is looming up as one of the problems of our age. I do not approve of lax divorce laws. But I do think our Canadian divorce law errs on the side of over strictness. Adultery is the only ground for divorce. To this I think two others should be added and two only—incurable insanity and desertion for a period extending over three years.

Friday, Oct. 26, 1923
The Manse, Leaskdale, Ont.

Today was beautiful—warm, sunny, with a faint grape-like bloom over distant hills and fields. Lily and I spent most of it planting our bulbs and blanketing our perennials for the winter. It was delightful working out on the lawn, in the golden weather with the pussy cats frisking about us.

Pat "first endured, then pitied, then embraced" Luck. They are very good friends now and play together in the most comical fashion. But Luck plays awful tricks on poor old Paddy. There is one especial chair both cats like. When Paddy is asleep in it Luck will jump on him and bite him all over, tearing great mouthfuls of fur out of poor Pat. Pat being older and fat and clumsy can't move quickly enough to defend himself so after a few vain attempts he flies leaving Luck in possession of the chair. Luck will look around with the most angelic, innocent expression and then curl down and go to sleep.

We are all crazy over Luck. He is the most *lovable* cat I ever had—even more lovable than Daffy II. He has the most engaging little ways and is a beautiful purrer. Old Daff was a most enchanting devil-cat and very dear to me for old sake's sake. But he was not at all the winning pussy Good Luck is....

Luck is beautifully striped. I don't care a hoot for any cat that isn't striped. I never saw any markings like his, especially on the back. And his gray is so silvery that he makes Pat look brown and faded....

Saturday, Oct. 27, 1923

This evening Ewan and the boys and I motored down to Uxbridge to hear the radio. We hear music in Chicago and a speech in Pittsburg. It is a very marvellous thing and will probably revolutionize the world in another generation. But it made me feel a little unhappy and unsettled some way....

Wednesday, Oct. 31, 1923
The Manse, Leaskdale, Ont.
Sometimes this fall when I am rushing madly from one job to another, with never a moment to rest, read, or dream I feel rebellious and ask myself if this is the kind of life I was intended for....

Tuesday, Nov. 6, 1923
....Last Sunday Ewan exchanged with Mr. Turkington of Whitby. I went to Zephyr with Mr. T. and listened to a good sermon which Will Lockie praised unstintedly. It was a *very* good sermon—and it was taken word for word from a book of sermons, a copy of which Ewan has in his library! Of late years I have come to know that there is an immense lot of this done. Even Dr. Smith, the president of Westminister Hall, preached a sermon here which we found verbatim in a book we had. It is no wonder the pulpit is losing its influence over the pew. I really seldom enjoy a sermon nowadays. I'm always wondering if it is merely a recitation. It is this which makes the "calling" system such a farce. Turkington got the call to Whitby I suppose by preaching a borrowed sermon. So he has a town church and a splendid manse with electric lights and bathroom and hardwood floors. To be sure his people criticize his preaching as "dull." It is one thing to borrow another man's coat. It is another thing to wear it gracefully. Sometimes it doesn't *fit*.

Thursday, Nov. 22, 1923
We had a big audience and our play went off with a bang. Everybody was delighted. What was odd was the way the performers waked up at the last. All at once they seemed to recall my instructions and act on them, with the result that, with exception of one or two absolutely hopeless ones, they all did amazingly well. When it was over George Kennedy came up to me and said, "Well, certainly, Mrs. Macdonald, we owe you a debt of thanks for all the trouble you've taken with us. You were very patient."

So I felt somewhat rewarded but I don't think the reward was quite enough to compensate me for all the extra work I've had. And I thought my feet would never be any more good. They ached so I couldn't sleep. Wednesday I had to let Lily go and help clean the church, so I did all the work at home, carrying everything back, washing almost all the dishes I possessed and putting everything back in place. I dared not stop a moment for fear I simply wouldn't be able to start again. My only comfort was those two blessed cats—it actually *rested* me to look at those two peaceful unhurried creatures lying on their cushions in ease and grace. It made me feel happy to think that there really were creatures in the world who knew what leisure was. It gave me a feeling of comfort to stroke Luck's satiny coat as I scurried by. He has the softest silkiest fur I ever touched in a cat—Pat whose coat has always seemed fine, is positively rough by contrast.

When people ask me what on earth I want to keep two cats for I tell them I keep them to do my resting for me. But there are times when I wish I could borrow a pair of their legs....

Have been reading, in the half hour before I go to sleep *The End of the House of Alard*. Sheila Kaye-Smith is a favorite of mine. She reminds me of George Eliot. But her work is tinged—I had almost said tainted—with the pessimism of most present day writers of power. They reflect their age. It is hard to be hopeful today when one looks at the weltering world.

Tuesday, Dec. 10, 1923

Zephyr had its anniversary on Sunday. I had as usual the visiting minister to entertain and then spent Monday packing up all our play "properties" on the forenoon and helping arrange Zephyr church for it all the afternoon—and all the evening prompting and stage managing generally.

We ended up the play both in Zephyr and here with a very pretty tableau showing our two brides and their attendants. I got out my wedding dress and veil for Margaret Leask, who looked very pretty in it. My dress looks very nice still, only the cut steel trimming on it has turned dark. I must replace it with something else. It quite spoils the look of it.

I couldn't get into that dress now. The disgraceful truth is that I'm getting terribly fat. Just at present I'm not *too* fat—but I've gained nearly forty pounds in the last two years and where will it stop? I must diet if I go much further. I was very plump in my teens. But I got thin that unhappy winter in Bedeque and never picked up again.

Today I came across an old letter from "Pastor Felix." I had sent him a picture of Stuart at ten months and he wrote. "He has drunk himself full of sunshine and radiates it everywhere around him." Nothing could describe Stuart more happily. He does indeed radiate sunshine—the dear happy fun-loving, loving little lad.

I began writing again today. I haven't been able to write a line for over four weeks. I wanted to finish *Emily II* by Christmas but I can't now.

Thursday, Dec. 12, 1923
The Manse, Leaskdale

This evening I finished reading *The Mill On The Floss*. I had actually thought Sheila Kaye-Smith was almost equal to George Eliot. Foolish creature! She has nothing of the breadth and power of George Eliot and cannot challenge comparison with her in regard to character drawing. *The Mill On The Floss* is my favorite among George Eliot's books. It is one of the few books which end sorrowfully and yet leave the reader with a feeling of satisfaction.

Friday, Dec. 21, 1923

The S.S. concert is over. The Zephyr concert comes off next week and then all such contrivances of the devil will be over for this year. But no doubt something else will come up to worry me....

And there is Luck, lying on the sofa, purring rapturously, a vision of beauty and grace, with his little stomach full of liver and not a care in the world. I could almost find it in my heart to wish I was a gray cat with a clover leaf and the letter M. on my side!

Tuesday, Dec. 25, 1923
Officially Christmas! Luckily we had ours yesterday. Otherwise I fear we should not have had nearly so pleasant a Christmas day. Chester was ill with an upset stomach, Stuart suffered all day with toothache, I had a stiff neck. It didn't hurt me except when I turned my neck, but then I kept *wanting* to turn my neck. It was moreover a chill and melancholy day, so dark that we had to light lamps at half past three.

Our friend, Greig, too, shot a tiny barb of malice into the day in the shape of the following letter:—

"Rev. E. Macdonald:

Dear Sir:—

I was wondering if, at this Christmas season, you could see your way clear to dispense some happiness by way of a contribution toward the amount of the judgment and costs which my clients, Mr. M. Pickering and Mrs. S. Pickering hold against you.

Yours faithfully,

Willard Greig."

It was beyond doubt Greig's amiable intention to embitter, so far as he was able, our Christmas day. As we had our Christmas yesterday he failed; but the fact that he tried shows what his psychology is. A man who had any insight into human nature would not have antagonized the people he was making a request of by doing such a spiteful thing.

But it was in every way an extraordinary letter for a lawyer to write. Does Greig imagine that we are so anxious to "dispense happiness" towards a man and a woman who hounded us with an unjust and iniquitous claim and swore to falsehood after falsehood in the witness box?

Then there was a letter from Ella. Dan had quarrelled with the hired man— Dan has no patience and his father's bad temper—the hired man had gone and they had no money to pay his wages. Would I "lend" them a hundred? Aunt Annie had told them when she went away "if they had any trouble to write to Aunt Maud!"

I wonder what they would do if there was no "Aunt Maud." I will send the money—that will be three hundred for 1923—but I am beginning to think that it is pouring water into a sieve to try to save Park Corner....

Between Greig and Ella I feel old and depressed tonight. But maybe my neck has a good deal to do with it.

Monday, December 31, 1923
The Manse, Leaskdale
Today we went to Uxbridge with the horse. I expect the car season is finally over. We ran Dodgie longer this year than ever before. I hate to give her up. It is so comfortable and quick in cold weather. But needs must. We had tea with Mrs. Hugh Mustard, who lives in Uxbridge now. She was always a good friend of

ours. At the supper table she was talking about *Emily* and the humor in it and remarked, "I often say to the girls, 'We never see the funny side of L.M. Montgomery'"—*apropos* of some joking remark of mine to the girls that a minister's wife didn't get invited to parties!

There are a good many of L.M. Montgomery's sides they don't see! ...

1924

Saturday, Jan. 5, 1924
The Manse, Leaskdale, Ont.
....Today a letter came from Mr. Rollins. I opened it with a grim determination to hear we had lost the appeal. I don't know but that that would have been better than what it really contained....Here is the gist...
Mr. Rollins to me:—
"....They have...started proceedings for libel against you in New York, getting jurisdiction there, or trying to, by attaching the sums due you from Stokes for royalties.
I suppose that it will be necessary to employ a New York lawyer now to defend this New York suit"....
There doesn't seem much to say except that there is apparently no end to the devilry the Pages will attempt and no end to the kinks in the U. S. law that enable them to do it. It is an iniquitous law that permits a person's property to be attached before a case is even tried. There is no end to the injury such a proceeding might work to an entirely innocent person....I swear that I will fight them all my life before I will allow them to thus bully me. Before the other suits were settled French told Rollins they would drop their suit if I would drop mine. Of course I refused. No doubt their motive is the same now. But their first shot has missed fire.

Monday, Jan. 7, 1924
Another letter from Rollins—a very reassuring one:—
"For your comfort of mind I may say that such investigation as I have made into this burst of activity on the part of our friends leads me to infer that the Pages will not get along in New York any better than they did in the United States courts. I find it stated in an authoritative book that the New York courts refuse to retain jurisdiction of an action of tort between non-residents on a cause of action arising outside of the state unless special reasons are shown to exist which make the retention of jurisdiction necessary and proper etc"....

Thursday, Jan. 10, 1924
An oft-quoted proverb is that "It is always the unexpected that happens." The unexpected *has* happened—not only the unexpected but the unthought of!
This doesn't mean that Louis Page has withdrawn his suit or written me a humble letter beseeching forgiveness. Oh, no, that is beyond the realm of even unexpectness.

155

No, what has happened is this. *Mr.* Marshall Pickering has been in the hospital in Toronto for nearly three weeks *taking the insulin treatment for diabetes.*.

It is really an almost incredible thing. If it had been *Mrs.* Marshall, it would have been only what everyone has been predicting. But that *he* should have diabetes!....

He swore on the stand that his wife had a "little diabetes" at one time but had been wholly cured by "some patent medicine from the States." Now, why couldn't he have cured himself by the same means and saved himself the expense of the insulin treatment?

For it *is* rather expensive. No wonder Greig wanted us to "dispense some happiness" in the shape of cash. But Marshall Pickering is a well-to-do farmer and is quite able to pay his own bills. *We* did not compel him to go to law.

"The mills of the gods grind slowly"—but it can't be denied that they do "grind exceeding small."

Friday, Jan. 11, 1924
The Manse, Leaskdale

Chester and Stuart have got the results of their Christmas Exams. Stuart led his class with an average of 80 5/7. Chester also led his class but had an average of 68 2/9. This was not really so good as last year but it must be considered that this year he wrote on questions taken from old High School entrance exams, which were therefore much harder in proportion. The odd thing is that he made 82 in arithmetic which has always been a poor subject with him, and only 58 in Literature. I suppose the improvement in Arithmetic is due to the fact that for two years I have worked with him in the evenings helping him with it. It is odd that a son of mine should be poor in *Literature*. But Chester is like his father in this respect. Ewan has absolutely no feeling for or understanding of literature at all. I think I never met anyone so absolutely lacking in it—at least, among educated people. Chester seems to lack it, too, in spite of his fondness for reading. But possibly it may develop in him later.

Chester is beginning to mature physically—too young I am afraid. It will be a reason of anxiety for me. If he has inherited Ewan's tendency to melancholia it will probably show itself during the years of puberty. I have had to talk to Chester lately about certain habits to avoid. His

['Dixie,' Stuart and Chester]

father should do this but he is not a man who can do it, so, as all else, it falls to me. I have always tried to talk simply and truthfully to my boys about sex matters when they came to me with questions. The way in which such matters were treated in my childhood disgusted me. I was told all manner of silly lies. I was *never* told anything of the truth. All sex matters—the basic matters of life—were taboo—evidently something too vile and shameful to be spoken of. What a conception to plant in a child's mind concerning such things. A certain "doctor's book" in the house, a clean, sensible volume, where sex was explained excellently, was forbidden to me sternly. It should have been put into my hands. Of course I read it by stealth and I have never felt that I did wrong to do so. I know I learned things there that safeguarded me and saved me in many situations of after life and spared me many a worry.

The present generation has saner views of sex and its presentation to the young. There are several excellent books which make a parent's duty somewhat easier. I gave one such to Chester today. I hope he will be guided by its teachings.

Sunday, Jan. 20, 1924
The Manse, Leaskdale, Ont.
We have had a great deal of gray depressing weather.

Tuesday I had a letter from Mr. McClelland. He said he had heard that N.Y. courts were "years behind" in their judgments and consequently it was unlikely they would take jurisdiction of my case. This is comforting—or meant to be. But through some twist of French's infernal ingenuity they do take jurisdiction. My royalties will be tied up at least two years and likely three or four. Well, I have my dreams to comfort me. They foretold all this and they were distinctly comforting.

Had a very nice letter from the editor of *The Delineator* this week, saying that *Emily* was "the most charming story she had read for years."

Thursday I finished *Emily II.* I haven't decided on a title yet. By dint of writing three hours per diem whereas I formerly wrote only two I am getting a bit ahead of my work and losing that hateful feeling of breathlessness I have had for years. Of course *Emily II* isn't half as good as *New Moon.* The second volume of a series, especially if it deals with a very young girl, is the hardest for me to write—because the public and the publisher won't allow me to write of a young girl as she really is. One can write of children as they are; so my books of children are always good; but when you come to write of the "miss" you have to depict a sweet, insipid young thing—really a child grown older—to whom the basic realities of life and reactions to them are quite unknown. *Love* must scarcely be hinted at—yet young girls in their early teens often have some very vivid love affairs. A girl of "Emily's" type certainly would. But "the public"— one of the Vanderbilts once said "Damn the public."

I'm just saying what one of the Vanderbilts said. I'm not saying it myself.

I can't afford to damn the public. I must cater to them for awhile yet.

Friday I went to a Presbyterial meeting at Lindsay—drove seven miles to Blackwater station over wild rough roads—then home at night again. I was tired by now—"the way was long, the wind was cold"—I was expecting a letter from Rollins and dreading it. I found the drive dismal and courage ebbed low. But there wasn't any letter—and there were two rosy little sons and two adorable gray cats—and a volume of Hume's history which I am finding very interesting.

But the letter from Mr. Rollins came yesterday along with one from Mr. Von Briesen—on the whole comforting....But Page's vindictiveness is abnormal and will carry him to any length, since he is rich and can afford it....

Ewan *is* very well. I realized this very clearly tonight at the supper table. We were, as usual, playing the game of "The Clergyman's Cat." Stuart loves this and I encourage it because I think it is a very effective way of stocking the boy's vocabulary of adjectives. We were in "d" and had used so many adjectives that the supply was running low. Finally when Ewan's turn came he said with a deprecatory grin, "The Clergyman's Cat is a *damned* cat"—and joined in the laughter that followed.

Now, if any trace of his melancholia still lingered in him he would never have said this and if anyone else had said it he would have flinched as if a deadly sore place had been touched. He would have felt, not the normal distaste of a mind averse to vulgar profanity, but the abnormal horror of a mind to whom the idea of "damnation" was too real and awful to put into words.

But our cats are not damned! They are elect animals.

Saturday, Jan. 26, 1924
The Manse, Leaskdale, Ont.
This has been a week of bitter cold and storms—also of unpleasantnesses. Monday I was ill all day—it stormed—and there was the Annual Congregational meeting with its usual tale of deficit. Thursday we visited in Zephyr and had supper with a family who are ignorant and narrow. Really, only one thing they said was interesting! That thing being that our friend M.P. is home for two weeks, at the end of which time he has to go back to Toronto to begin taking the insulin treatment. He has been on a diet hitherto. Of course, this is a "judgment" on him. We hear that everywhere. It is odd how firmly the idea of "judgments" is lodged in the mind of the average man. I don't think there is any judgment in the matter; but I daresay that Pickering's worry and sense of humiliation in failure has so affected his system that he has fallen an easy prey to disease. A good many "judgments" are doubtless of this nature....

On Wednesday came news of the death of Lenin—one of the most extraordinary men of any age. He made the most tremendous experiment ever attempted and shed the blood of millions ruthlessly to further it—and failed. Even Lenin could not conquer or change human nature. Matters in Russia are pretty much as they have always been. One tyranny has been substituted for another, that is all—a tyranny just as merciless as the former, it would seem.

In Britain they have a Labour Government—which some, of course, regard as the end of the world. But I am sure it cannot make a worse mess of things than recent governments have made and may easily do better. As for the end of the world *that* came in 1914—the end at least; of one world—and those who shut their eyes to that fact are blind and foolish.

I have been reading Mrs. Moodie's *Roughing It In The Bush*. This is one of our Canadian classics which I have been told repeatedly "I ought to read." There seems to be something in me that resents being told I "ought to read" a book. I find that I never buy or seek out that book; but if it is put into my hands I read it to get rid of it. Mac sent me a new edition of it in his Christmas parcel and I find it delightful from cover to cover—fresh, witty, vivid. I shall put it on my shelves to read again when opportunity offers. When I read of Mrs. Moodie's trials and difficulties I am ashamed to grumble about mine. But, really, she was never persecuted by demons like the Pages!

Sunday, Jan. 27, 1924
The Manse, Leaskdale
It was 28 below zero this morning! But then there are no mosquitoes!

Good Luck belied his name this evening. The little devil contrived to knock down and smash to bits three pieces of my treasured bric-a-brac—one was the little bronze statuette of "The Good Fairy" which was Frede's first wedding present, and one was one of my beautiful Bristol glass candlesticks. The odd thing is that both these things were broken before but a magician in Toronto mended them so beautifully that you wouldn't have known it. And now they are broken again. Is it predestination? Or devilment? On the chance of it being the latter I'll have the Good Fairy mended once more but I fear the candlestick is done for. I could spank Luck with a shingle!

"The candlesticks" [and Brass Fairy, Frede's first wedding present,
broken by "Lucky"]

Monday, Jan. 28, 1924

I don't recall so "gray" a January even in Ontario. We have hardly had a day of sunshine. This is very characteristic of an Ontario winter and I always find it has a very depressing effect on me, especially when I am worried. There is something in a storm that stimulates and provokes to combat, but dull, unvarying grayness soaks into and colors your soul....

This has been a hard year on our farmers round here. Buying prices very high—selling prices very low. As a result half of the farmers in Scott are financially embarrassed and a few are utterly down and out. This of course reacts on church work and finances.

Wed., Jan 30, 1924
The Manse, Leaskdale

....I had a letter from Alexina Wright. In it she says;

"Poor Laura is, I guess, a busy woman. She is still in Saskatoon. Andrew lost his position there and came down here to secure work. So he is clerking for Joe Kernaghan in the hardware business. I feel so sorry for them....They find it pretty hard getting along and their boys have been anything but a help to them. Gerald and Jack particularly are pretty wild and give their parents many heartaches...Laura at present has her house full of boarders and roomers. I feel sorry for Andrew having to live away from home at his age."

All this sent me upstairs to cry. It is a shame that dear Laura, who has always been a most unselfish and generous and hard-working creature, should be in such a position at her age and through no fault of her own. I feel ashamed of worrying over my own troubles. They are not as bad as hers. But then she had nearly forty years of happiness and freedom from care and I never had that. Oh, well, I must stop growling. But then it's a relief to get it out of my system in this journal. Nobody ever hears me growl outside of it.

Sunday, Feb. 3, 1924
The Manse, Leaskdale

This has been a mild day—but of course *gray* and sunless. I had a white night and had to take veronal but today I feel calmer and able to *endure*. Endurance! That has been my life since 1919. But no doubt it also expresses the lives of a good many people besides me.

Lately I have been corresponding with Mrs. Hotaling, editor of a N.Y. magazine regarding a curious case of parallelism. She wrote me a distracted letter several weeks ago, saying that the editor of *Modern Priscilla* had recently written her that one of his readers had written him that her story "Avis Lindsay" published in the January *Priscilla*, was simply the plot of *Anne's House of Dreams*. Mrs. Hotaling was in a bad way, and assured me she had never even read *Anne's House of Dreams* and had taken the idea of her story from a news clipping regarding a shell shocked soldier. I knew quite well that there could be no plagiarism for Mrs. Hotaling is quite incapable of that and besides, morality apart, has too much sense to steal a story from so recent and well-known a book.

I wrote her and assured her that I believed in her entire innocence. And I do still. Yet, when I read the story—she sent it to me—I was almost "dumfounded." It *was* a deadly parallel sure enough, and I do not wonder that the unknown reader who protested thought it must have been stolen. Not only was the central idea the same but setting and characters had a marked resemblance. Perhaps Mrs. Hotaling's subconscious mind fished my ideas out of the pool of world subconsciousness!!...

Monday, Feb. 4, 1924
A bad bad day every way. It was cold and east-stormy. In the morning I wrote and felt fairly. But a letter from Mr. McClelland upset me. He said he was going to mail me a check for my royalties at once lest Page attach my Canadian royalties also. I felt desperate and hopeless. If Page can do this I shall have to surrender. I can hardly believe it. I have always understood that in Canada no attachment can be made until a debt actually exists—in a case such as this, until the case is tried and a verdict for damages obtained. I think Mac *must* be mistaken and yet he ought to know....

Tuesday, Feb. 5, 1924
The Manse, Leaskdale, Ont.
How hard it is to hear little worries where we have big ones! When I have no big worries my smaller ones sit lightly on me—Lily's inefficiency, gray stormy days, getting up before dark on cold mornings, coal oil lamps because my gas lamp is balking just now, a furnace with water pan burned out, a front door that *won't* shut and a storm door that *won't* open, green wood for the range and so on and so on. Normally I "say Oh and let it go." But nowadays these midges annoy me unbearably. I want *all* my endurance for the big worry....

Wednesday, Feb. 6, 1924
The storm is over and the mail came. We even had half an hour of sunshine. So I felt better and was able to work and write.

This evening I went down to the rink to see Chester and Stuart skate. There is an open air rink in Leaskdale this winter. I had never seen them skate before. They do very well. It seemed quite wonderful to see Stuart darting about in the crowd like a bird. I felt an odd wistfulness as I watched them. I used to wish so much when I was a girl to be able to skate but I never had any chance to learn. I walked back home in the dark and snow, with the laughter of the skaters ringing behind me and felt very lonely and hopeless. *I* have no friends here—no congenial companionship of my "race of Joseph." When I am not worried I find enough pleasure in my household interests and books; but just now I can enjoy nothing.

Friday, Feb. 8, 1924
....This forenoon the *bailiff* appeared again and handed a legal document to Ewan which proved to be a notice that on Feb. 19th Greig would ask Judge

Ruddy of Whitby for an order to summons Ewan to a second examination "touching his means and estate since last examination."

I should have known this was coming. One night not long ago I dreamed that Lily asked me if Greig had "sent a service" and when I said "no" she said, "Well, it's coming soon." Two days later the Page service came and I thought the wires of the subconscious had got crossed and the warning referred to this. So I was woefully upset. Of course, it is nothing like to be dreaded as the first one was. Ewan has got nothing but his salary and has used it for our living expenses....

I may be mistaken but I believe the psychology behind this second attempt is this. Rumor persists in asserting that Greig has never yet been paid by Pickering. Last week in the *Times*, one of the Zephyr "notes" was that M.P. had been in the hospital for diabetes. Now, M.P. is a man who is never willing to admit that there is anything the matter with him or his family and I feel sure he has never told Greig that he is ill. Greig has seen this "note" and is afraid that M.P. will drop off some of these days, leaving his debt to Greig unpaid. Then Greig, to get it, would probably have to *sue* the widow and family—something he would be very unwilling and ashamed to do. Hence he is making a desperate attempt to get *something* from Ewan while Pickering is still living.

Today was dreadful. The Session met here this afternoon and the wives came also and stayed to supper. By chance or God's grace the bailiff came in the forenoon. If he had come in the afternoon when they were all here it would have been unbearable. As it was, we had a little time to recover our outward composure. But I was busy with preparations for supper—was making a salad when the bell rang—and I found it exceedingly difficult to go on with my compounding and planning. Then the mail came and there was a big fat letter from Rollins. Its corpulency alarmed me. Something, I thought, must be amiss when he had to write so long a letter. Of course I did not read it then. But the knowledge that it had come and must be read before I went to bed haunted me all day. Between the two things I was almost crazy.

But I finished my salads and preparations. I made a pretence of eating dinner. I dressed myself. I received my guests. I sat and talked to them the whole afternoon. I set the table and presided over it. I don't think any of my guests noticed that I wasn't eating any supper. Then I sat the evening through and talked small talk to those four good dull women.

I am not sneering at them. They *are* good—I like them. It is not their fault that they are dull. The lives they lead necessitate that. Usually I can chatter away to them of small local happenings, fancy work, house plants and hens, and find it easy, though not stimulating. But today it was torture. And this evening it was really dreadful. They were talked out—they were tired and waiting impatiently for their husbands to go home. But said husbands were having a fine time talking politics and Church Union in the library and wouldn't budge. I thought the evening would never end. But of course it did and at nine they went. Lily and the boys were out skating. Ewan settled down to read. I flew to the spare room and determinedly opened Rollins' letter.

But it, at least, was almost reassuring....

Saturday, Feb. 9, 1924

I had a good sleep last night so felt better able to grapple with my dour fate today. Ewan left in the morning for Stouffville to interview McCulloch on this new development. I spent the morning writing in full to Rollins and the afternoon conducting the Mission Band. A letter from Margaret was a pleasant thing, bringing with it a breath of comradeship and P.E.I. peace. I spent the early evening reading a delightful book Mr. McMillan sent me at Christmas, *Between the Larch Woods and the Weir*, by the author of the book which delighted me so last year, *The Flower Patch In The Hills*.

"A corner of the parlour"

Then Ewan came home. McCulloch says that the order may not be given by the judge. He says E. cannot be taken for a second examination "except for good cause"—and no good cause has arisen since the last time. But Greig may trump up some assertion to influence the judge. I know he wants to get a chance to badger Ewan with questions in the hope of getting some hold on him. Fortunately Greig is such a fool he can't devise much devilry. He can't do anything without a mistake, it seems. In the document he sent E. he wrote *Thursday*, the 19th of Feb. The 19th of Feb. is on Tuesday....

I have often felt, as I did after the trial, that it would have been wiser, despite the humiliation and rank injustice, for Ewan to have let me pay the $3,600 involved and be free from worry henceforth. But he never would or will. Nothing can move him when he has made up his mind. And if it were not for my own problems I would be quite ready to help him fight to the bitter end. But I confess that so much piling up all at once has rather broken my *morale*.

It is an odd coincidence that both Ewan and I should have so much trouble with litigation....

Sunday, Feb. 10, 1924
The Manse, Leaskdale
Reading *Adam Bede* today I found a sentence:—"There is nothing that is not bearable as long as a man can work." That is absolutely true....

We had something for supper tonight I never had before, and never expected to have—a roast of buffalo meat! It is a portion of the buffaloes slaughtered in the Government's park in Alberta last fall. It was delicious—tender and of excellent flavor—very like beef with just the merest suspicion of wildness....

Monday, Feb. 11, 1924
The Manse, Leaskdale, Ont.
....I have to go to Kitchener this week to address the Canadian Club. I wish I did not have to be away this week of all weeks. I had been looking forward to it all winter but now all pleasure in its anticipation will be gone. Perhaps I *will* enjoy it, though, if I do not get any bad news before I go.

I have learned that Page *cannot* attach Canadian royalties so *that* worry has vanished.

Saturday, Feb. 16, 1924
Wednesday morning I left for Kitchener. No word came from McCullough on Tuesday, so if I had no good news there was at least no bad. It was eighteen below zero and the roads were very heavy so that the drive to Uxbridge was not very pleasant. Ewan, too, talked constantly of Pickering and the injustice of the trial. When anything occurs to recall it he canvasses it as if it had happened but yesterday. This hurts me—it is like opening an old wound.

But I *did* have a very nice time in Kitchener and was too busy to think of my worries. I stayed with Mrs. Kaufman, whose husband is a manufacturer of Kitchener and must be very wealthy for they had one of the loveliest homes I was ever in, with every comfort and luxury. I came back yesterday. On my way through Toronto I called to see McClelland and Stewart. The result was rather depressing. They have had a very poor business year and have lost money—instead of making any profits. They are reducing their staff and lopping off everywhere possible. And it is said most of the other Toronto publishers are in even a worse plight. The business depression of the last two or three years has had a very marked effect on the publishing trade and better things cannot be hoped until the country is past the crisis—and no one can predict when that will be. I grew rather nervous as I listened. What if they were to go bankrupt? Well let us hope things will brighten up a little in 1924. It is never forbidden to hope.

As I drew near home I dreaded what I might have to hear. But as Ewan took my grip he said with a laugh, "I have something to tell you," and I knew that whatever news there was was not bad. McCullough had sent the copy of Pickering's affidavit. *Such* an affidavit. When I got home and read it I laughed too. Laugh! One might howl over it! Surely nobody but Pickering and Greig could concoct such stuff.

But it was no laughing matter to get home. It was bitter cold—twelve below zero—and such heavy roads that Teddy could only walk. I grew woefully tired—for on roads like that I am always trying to *help the horse.* At least, that is the only way I can describe my feeling. I seem to be making a continual mental effort to *push the sleigh,* and it tires me almost as much as if I were actually doing it.

When I got home, got warmed and fed I settled down to enjoy Pickering's affidavit. Here are the choice portions:—

I. "Since the date of the said examination I *am informed and believe* that the said judgment debtor has been *bequeathed certain property, estate or effects* by a friend or relative in *one of the Maritime provinces.* I am further informed and believe that the said judgment debtor has been making away with his property in order to defeat and defraud his *creditors in general* and myself in particular.

II. That I am further informed and believe that the *wife* of the judgment debtor is *paying for the upkeep* of the judgment debtor's house and in other ways relieving the said judgment debtor of his domestic financial obligations in order that the said judgment debtor may have more money *wherewith to enjoy himself* and to spend in *unnecessary ways.*"

The italics are of course mine.

I suppose Pickering has been hearing some irresponsible gossip born of Ewan's trip to P.E.I. last spring when poor Alec died! Poor Alec, who died thousands of dollars in debt and to whose widow I had to lend money to help her out!

Creditors in general! Who are they I wonder. Ewan doesn't owe a cent to a soul in the world. But perhaps this is merely a necessary legal phrase.

The cream of the whole thing, however, lies in the last paragraph. Really, it is hard to believe a lawyer would draw up such a nonsensical statement for anyone to sign. Why, don't the fools realize that if I *were* trying "to defeat and defraud" I could do it quite legally and safely by making Ewan pay *all* our expenses, as far as his salary went, and then *giving* him as much of my money as I wanted to to enable him "to enjoy" himself. In fact, this is exactly what our arrangement has been and there isn't a legal flaw in it. A man is bound to support his family—*I* am absolutely free, as far as Marshall Pickering is concerned, to spend my money exactly as I choose.

That phrase "enjoy himself" will be another family joke, on a par with the *Leaskdale bank.* Henceforth, I shall tell Ewan sternly, when I see him having a good time, that it is illegal for him to enjoy himself as long as Mr. Marshall Pickering can't get that $2,600 he is yearning for.

The affidavit is a great relief to us. Knowing how unscrupulous both Pickering and Greig are we were afraid Pickering would swear that the salary was unpaid or something like that. And in doing so he would have made it awkward for us, because Zephyr is two weeks behind....

Monday, Feb. 18, 1924
The Manse, Leaskdale
Today was fine but bitterly cold. However, we got the house comfortable by

night and had a nice home evening, reading in the parlor—the boys, Ewan and I, Pat and Luck. Not that Pat and Luck read. But they slept and purred and played and added greatly to the pleasure and *homeyness* of our evening. We use the parlor as our "living room" in the winter. Carpets and upholstery suffer but that is a minor consideration. The library is too cold in winter and the dining room too small and crowded. So we use the parlor. Tonight we were cosy and happy. The moon shone bluely on the frosted window pane and outside was a cold, white, beautiful, austere world; but inside was warmth and light and laughter.

I was re-reading *Zanoni*. I have not read it since I was married. When I was a child I read it until I could repeat whole chapters off by heart. The book was one of the few novels in the house at that time—Uncle Leander had left a paper-covered copy there. It had an incredible fascination for me. When I took up *Zanoni* I seemed to open a magic door and step at once into a world of enchantment.

I did not expect tonight to find much of the old delight or magic in the book. For one thing, I was so *saturated* with it in childhood that I expected to find it palling. For another, so few of Lytton's books have stood the test of years with me that I felt afraid I would find *Zanoni* wanting, too.

But I did not. I read the book with just the same pleasure as in those old years—with just the same sense of enchantment. The magic door still swung open and through it I still made my escape from the real. I loved and joyed and sorrowed with the characters as keenly as ever; and as ever the pathos of that last interview between "Zanoni" and "Viola" in the prison cell of the Terror left me in a passion of tears. Much of the pathos in many of Lytton's books is false and strained. But *that* scene rings true.

Zanoni entered largely into my childish life. I was always *living it*—reconstructing parts of it to suit my wishes. Sometimes I was "Viola"—but not the Viola of the book, whom I always thought a foolish weak creature, utterly unworthy of "Zanoni." I adored "Zanoni." *He* was always my dream lover. I could never forgive "Viola" for her desertion of him. Nothing could excuse it. In my dream we were parted but not through any fault of our own—and at the last we met again, escaped the Terror and "lived happily for ever after."

Just as often I was not "Viola" but myself—not in love with "Zanoni" but the pupil of "Mejnour." I quailed not at the "Dweller On The Threshold"—I failed not in any of the tests—I attained the Great Secret—the first woman who ever "passed the ordeal."

Sometimes I re-wrote certain parts of the novel. For instance I made "Glyndon" survive the ordeal and win the boon for which he thirsted. Then I always added a codicil in which "Mejnour" suddenly appeared in the last chapter, when "Viola" is found dead, adopts "Zanoni's" child and brings it up to be a second "Zanoni." It always worried me terribly to think of that poor baby alone in the world—especially the world of the Terror. I used to lie awake at nights in that old look-out room—I was sleeping in the look-out room in the years from nine to twelve—and rescue it and build up a wondrous life for it.

I have read no book which influenced my inner life as did *Zanoni*. There were some sentences in it especially which, in themselves and quite apart from their context, held an indescribable charm for me. They hold it still—I found them tonight as subtly delightful as of yore—as full of romance, suggestion, poetry, gramarye!...

Tues., February 19, 1924
Today was very different from last night. I was not the bride of *Zanoni*—the Mistress of the Stars—but the harassed mistress of a very cold country manse. It has been a miserable day—bitterly cold and raw, with a wild penetrating east wind. We *couldn't* get the house warm....

Sunday, March 2, 1924
....I've been reading "Vanessa"—Marjory MacMurchy's story—this week. It is not bad reporting but Marjory cannot create. Still, of its kind, it is quite well done.

Had a letter from Stella on Wednesday. Lots of complaints as usual. But still I do like to get a letter from old Stell. Between the complaints there's always a lot of the true Josephian flavor which is to me as manna to a hungry soul.

One bright spot in all these drab days is the fact that Ewan is so well. It will soon be a year since his last serious attack of headache and depression. Almost I dare to hope that he will remain well—at least for some years....

The snow is piled up all around us. I feel like a prisoner. One has to be young to enjoy winter.

Sunday, Mar. 9, 1924
The Manse, Leaskdale, Ont.
This has been a bitter week.

Ever since Ewan took his first attack five years ago I do not think it has once failed that if I venture to express to myself or write in this journal the hope that he was permanently well, another attack would follow immediately. On Monday Ewan seemed perfectly well; on Tuesday I went into the library and found him sitting there, a handkerchief tied round his head, his eyes wild and terrified, his face repulsive with the vacant almost imbecile expression so characteristic of these attacks at their worst.

It is very disheartening. I feel as if I had not, and could not, gather together enough courage to undergo the weeks before me. Ewan will *never* be well. Why was I so foolish as to hope it? But it seems harder to bear after the comparative happiness of the past six months.

I have felt better myself this week—have not been troubled by dizziness. But I feel uneasy about the fact of Chester's development. On Monday, when Ewan was well, I wanted him to consult a doctor about it but he pooh-poohed the idea. *He* had matured at twelve, therefore it was all right for Chester. But this fact, which assures him, alarms me. I am afraid that Ewan's early maturity may be linked up with his constitutional tendency to melancholia. Chester is not delicate physically. He is robust, rosy, and sturdy. But is there any lurking mental unsoundness? The next six years will answer that question.

I had a letter from Bertie on Monday which filled me with delight. She is coming east this summer....

The Missionary Tea came off Tuesday—and it was very hard for me to have it that day of all others. My mind was preoccupied with Ewan's condition when I wanted to concentrate it on the problem of *feeding* thirty guests. I never *enjoy* the Tea and always have a sigh of relief when it is over. But I find a certain enjoyment in doing everything necessary competently and efficiently—making a success of it, in short. But this year I longed only to have it over, to get them all away, and be alone to face the facts of existence.

One of the facts was a disappointing report from McClelland. I had expected it but not quite so discouraging a one. *Emily* sold only about 8,500 copies where *Rilla* sold 12,000. As *Emily* has done just as well as my other books in the States it can't be because it wasn't an *Anne* book but simply because of the rotten business conditions prevalent in Canada for the past year. I must share in the general slump of course. But it isn't exhilarating coming along with everything else.

The hardest thing about this week was that we had promised, before the attack came on Ewan, to go out to tea on three consecutive evenings, being anxious to overtake our allotted "visiting" before the spring break-up. We went but the evenings were torture. I tried desperately to keep talking, to conceal Ewan's silence and depression; and he himself always tries when out in company, to affect cheerfulness. I think the effort is good for him; but there is always a reaction as soon as we leave. The drives home, over the bad roads, have been dreadful, the horse plunging in the holes of the track, Ewan sitting beside me in unbroken silence. Friday night I cried silently all the way home. My nerves had been under such a strain all the evening, trying to talk brightly and naturally, that it was a relief to cry it out in the dark. Ewan never suspected my tears. He was wrapped in his own gloomy meditations to the exclusion of all else.

Well, in a few days I shall have adjusted myself to these conditions again and be able to endure them calmly.

Yesterday I finished my second revision of *Emily II*. It is now ready for the typist. I have called it *Emily Climbs*—a vile title, but the only one I can think of which includes "Emily's" name. It has been hard to do these revisions when ever since New Year's I have been so upset and worried. And yet, whenever I forced myself to sit down to it, I found solace and escape—I was free from my bonds and torments and roamed in an ideal world—coming back to reality at the end of my three hour's "stint" with renewed courage and "grit."

Ewan has been very miserable today and made a mess of preaching. But he did well to preach at all. Yet he is always better when he forces himself to do his work. When he gives himself over to inactive brooding it intensifies his conviction of his "lost" condition.

A curse on the devilish theology that implanted such ideas in his consciousness! But had he been a normal man they would not have taken such hold on him; and I suppose if it were not this delusion it would be something else.

I read two books this week—*Waverley* and *The Blind Bow Boy*! The gulf between them is as wide as the gulf between sanity and degeneracy. The latter book is an incredible compound of stupidity, vacuity and nastiness. Yet is has been praised in reviews as "exceedingly clever and brilliant." I should class it with the dull, dirty things obscene little boys scribble on the walls of water-closets. Faugh! I flung the thing into the furnace when I had finished it and washed my hands to get rid of the atmosphere of putrescence. To turn from it to *Waverley* was like coming out of a pigsty to a blue moorland hill swept clean by the winds of heaven.

It is a dull day but mild. The afternoon is a symphony of beautiful grays and smokes and pearls. One feels that spring is hiding around the corner. Oh, if it were only here.

I am writing with Luck curled up on my lap. We are all quite silly over that cat. He is so *lovable*. I never in all my experience with cats have known one so much so. Everybody who comes to the house raves over him. The girls who were here Tuesday burned incense at his shrine. I suppose something will happen to him erelong. I have grown so cringingly afraid of fate that I dare not hope that anything so beautiful and charming as this little purring cat will long escape the devil.

Sunday, Mar. 16, 1924
The Manse, Leaskdale, Ont.

....Ewan has been most miserable since Wednesday. I do not think he was ever worse even during his first attack five years ago. It has been most difficult to conceal his real condition from the community and the congregation. I do not know what to do.

He made a dreadful mess of preaching today. He was absolutely puerile. In these attacks his mentality seems to be that of a rather backward boy of about twelve. I writhed in humiliation and came home at the point of tears. I found Ewan in the library in a very bad condition. As usual in these attacks he was convinced that he would always be like this. Nothing is more curious than the way he forgets, in these attacks, the fact that he has recovered from many similar attacks during these five years—nothing, except the way he forgets, when he is well, that he has ever had such attacks at all.

But he wanted to "resign"—"get away." Now, as far as I myself am concerned, I would be very glad if he did resign. It would mean escape from the many intolerable conditions of recent years. And then, too, I have a large income, quite enough to support us all, in vastly greater comfort and amid far more congenial surroundings than is possible here.

But this is the trouble:—if Ewan resigned and then became quite or almost well again in a few weeks or months, as is quite probable, he would be most unhappy to find himself with no occupation and living on his wife's earnings. He would be miserable until he got to work again and then, even if he secured a congregation even as good as this one, it would be just the same thing over again.

I literally do not know what to do. The manifestations of Ewan's malady are so unaccountable that it is impossible to see what is best to be done....

When Ewan was well we had planned a motor trip in August to Kentucky to see the Mammoth Cave—something I have always wanted to see since childhood, when I read a most amusing story the scene of which was laid in Mammoth Cave. I wrote and asked Bertie to go with us. Now I don't know what to do. We *must* make our plans soon, in order that Bertie may arrange hers. If Ewan's malady runs on, more or less, all summer as it did in 1921, there would be no pleasure in going. I can never forget those miserable motor trips to and from P.E.I. And yet it is just as likely he may be quite well in August—or at least well enough to go and enjoy it.

The suddenness of these attacks is so uncanny. Two weeks ago Ewan was well, jolly, and care free—a fine looking man with a pleasant, open face and friendly, twinkling eyes. Yesterday he sat or lay all day—unshorn, collarless, hair on end, eyes wild and hunted, with a hideous imbecile expression on his face. I cannot describe how repulsive he appears—I can hardly bear to stay in the same room with him. I can conceal this feeling but I cannot banish or control it. I am almost tempted to believe in that old theory of devil possession. There *is* an alien personality in Ewan during these attacks. He is an utterly different creature from the man I married. The touch of his hand on me seems like the profanation of a stranger.

I wrote once in this journal that I did not mean to write anymore concerning my feelings during these attacks. But I find it too difficult to keep this resolution. I have no friend—no confidant. I find that "writing it out" here helps me to endure. When I feel that I have come to "the end of my rope" I write it here—and find at the close of writing that the rope has lengthened a little and I can go on.

And yet—to face years, perhaps, of this life, never knowing what day the malady may recur! But one must not think of it. When I do I feel that I can't face it. When I *don't* think about it I can go on.

There are thousands of other people far worse off than I. But I have never been able to find much comfort in this fact.

Life has, of course, gone on this week in spite of its dreadfulness. The routine of existence doesn't stop because one is miserable. There have even been some moments not altogether bad.

Last Sunday evening I was sitting in the parlor feeling that, somehow, I just couldn't go out to Guild—just couldn't, that was all. Then Luck and Pat got up on the rocking chair and began one of their funny performances, half-play, half-fight. Pat was so indescribably comical in his antics that I burst into laughter—and laughed until the tears stood in my eyes. Suddenly I was able to go to Guild and read my paper.

Stuart has begun "writing stories," modelled—bless us!—on "Peck's Bad Boy." And they are quite good, too, much better than I could have written when three or four years older than he.

And yet I don't think I want him to be a writer—at least, not primarily. I know too well the difficulties and discouragements of such a career. The reward is brilliant when success really comes—but it often seems a mere toss-up of fate whether it comes at all or not. I have always loved my work—I have been happy in it—I would not have exchanged it for any other. And yet I hope that Stuart will not be possessed, as I was, of the *cacoethes scribendi*.

Tuesday I wrote a little poem—"Canadian Twilight." When I write such poems I am always back in Cavendish. It was twilight on the old St. Laurence Gulf and the sand-dunes that I was really describing.

It has been bitterly cold these past four days. Nothing springlike in the air or landscape yet. Oh, for spring. When Ewan is able to get out in his car he will be better. And I will have some temporary escapes, too, that will help over the dark hours.

I read a weird "story" about myself in a Toronto paper lately. It ran as follows:—"When L.M. Montgomery, author of *Anne of Green Gables*, lived as a child at Prince Albert, Saskatchewan, she had not then decided whether to be a great writer or a great actress. The actress career had a little the best of it, owing to the copy of a thrilling melodrama having fallen into her hands.

One day a citizen heard the most blood-curdling screams coming from little Miss Montgomery's father's woodshed. Now the Canadian woodshed has long enjoyed a prominent place in the correction of children's misdemeanors, so that such sounds from such a place were not unusual. But so awful were the shrieks of terror the man was sure no childish crime required such punishment. Hurrying, bent on interfering, you can imagine his surprise at seeing a little girl of twelve alone in the shed.

The villain had dragged the ragged heroine to the precipice and was about to cast her over so that he could inherit the Montmorenci millions. So intent and wrapped up in the part was the maiden that she never noticed the intruder. He retired, amused instead of horrified, but ever since has felt that even if literature gained a successful author, the stage lost a wonderful emotional actress."

There isn't a word of truth in the yarn. My father never had a woodshed and I never did "stunts" like that anywhere. I never had the slightest hankering for the stage and my dramatic performances were confined to humorous dialogues for school concerts, which I never practised alone. However, the fake anecdote is harmless if silly. But it annoys me to have misleading things like that published about me....

I had a letter from Myrtle Thursday—rather depressing, too. They are having very hard times on P.E.I. and she writes as if they might have to give up farming and try something else. Times are hard everywhere. Conditions here in our community have been very bad these past three years. The farmers are going to the wall everywhere—especially those who bought farms at war time prices. Something *must* give way before long. Either prices for machinery and clothes *must* come down or prices for farm products *must* go up. This state of affairs has made our work in the church much harder for two or three years. And it worries us to see people we like and are interested in, as is the case in regard to most of our families, crowded to the wall.

I had a letter from Irving Howatt this week. He is still on the rocks. I think I might as well wipe the four thousand I lent him and Mort off my books. He has never been able to pay a cent of interest on it and I feel sure I shall never see a cent of the principal. What is worse, Stella made her mother send the $400 she inherited from Grandmother's estate to Irving for investment and I doubt if she ever gets any of it back. Yet, if I would lend her the money, she would be into some wildcat investment tomorrow. She never learns anything from past mistakes....

Sunday, March 23, 1924
The Manse, Leaskdale, Ont.
....This has been another wretched week. Ewan has been most miserable. This is by far the worst attack he has had since the initial one five years ago.

Oh God, if he is going to go like that again!

He has not slept well all the week. Some nights he could not sleep at all. I have kept up the treatment advised by Dr. Garrick but I never can see that it has the slightest effect. The attack runs its course and, as far as I can see, the treatment neither helps nor hinders.

We had a retired Methodist minister from Uxbridge take the services today. And of course every soul in the church came up to me and asked me if I "had tried this or that." Everyone has a remedy that cured *him* or *her* of headaches! As if we had not tried everything over and over! But of course they mean well and they do not guess that headache is but a symptom of Ewan's malady. If his torturing thoughts would vanish his head would be all right.

This has happened at the worst time of the year. The roads are all but impassable. Mr. Edmonds started with a buggy today and had to exchange it for a cutter en route. The ground everywhere is mud and slush—the landscape hideous. Ewan cannot get out to divert his mind in any way. *I* can't get out to gain a brief release from nervous strain.

Last Monday, on the last of the roads, I went to Uxbridge and read a paper before the Hypatia Club on "Problems of History." I haven't been anywhere since. Yesterday and Friday I was miserable physically—felt a nasty *tight* heavy feeling in my head all the time and could not take an interest in anything. I feel better today however.

Eight years ago the symptoms of the menopause began but the menopause itself did not come until two years ago. During those years, in which a woman should be free from worry and strain, I had the worst worry and strain of my life. Yet I never had better health. The menopause was absolutely normal with me. I had no disturbing symptoms of any kind. I hated to see it come—I think a woman always does. It seems as if a gate were shutting between her and youth forever. But at least it brought me no suffering of any kind.

But, although the actual menopause occurred two years ago, still regularly every month I experience certain symptoms which always characterized the monthly period. I always have a "sick headache" and I always have one, or sometimes two days, when I feel "blue," depressed, nervous and indifferent. When not aggravated by any worry or strain these feelings are not *very* marked or uncontrollable; but when, as this week, they happen to synchronize with worry and trouble they are very hard to bear and I found it almost impossible to endure them. *Everything* seemed dark, dreary, hopeless and I could not bear looking forward to years of life such as the past five years have been. I lived them all at once, so to speak. But today these symptoms have vanished and I feel more courageous.

In *Anne of Green Gables* I made "Anne" exclaim once, "Isn't it a splendid thing that there are mornings."

Just at present I can't feel that anything is "splendid." But I am thankful that there are "mornings." Every night this week I have gone to bed feeling "down and out" but always in the mornings I find it possible to go on.

I read two books this week, a new one, *The Gods of Pegana* by Lord Dunsany and an old one, *Ardath* by Marie Corelli.

I don't know what I thought of *The Gods of Pegana*. I don't know whether I thought it very clever or very foolish. But when I shut it up I thought, "Oh, if I could only talk this book over with Frede!"....

I always liked to read Corelli's earlier books. She had almost every conceivable fault as a writer but she could tell a story. In her later books she repeated herself and grew very shrill and hysterical....

Mingled memories came to me with *Ardath*. It recalled Cavendish and the friends to whom I lent it and with whom I discussed it. It was not so pleasant to remember Edwin Simpson. The book was full of him. I lent it to him that spring of 1897. I was then at the stage when one underlines books violently. I had much underlined *Ardath*. What I didn't underline Ed did. On every page some sentence he had marked flashed out at me with a sardonic reminder.

I wonder what Ed's life has been. I think likely it has been happy, though his childlessness must have been bitter to him. *I* have certainly had little happiness. But still I have never at any time been as unhappy as I would have been as Edwin Simpson's wife.

One sentence I had marked was "*Fame—fame—next grandest word to God!*" I was very ambitious then. Ed did not agree with me. He said it should be *truth* instead of *fame*. I retorted by saying *God* and *Truth* were synonymous.

Well, I no longer think *fame* a grand word or fame a very important thing. It certainly does not confer or increase happiness or goodness or usefulness. My work has brought me fame of a sort but the real reward of the work was in the pleasure it gave me to do it. And the fact that my name and my books are household words in all English speaking countries doesn't make it a bit easier for me to shake the furnace down or keep my patience with Lily's forgetfulness and untidiness!

For four winters I have had to look after the furnace—and it is really no job for a woman. But it was harder to get Ewan to do it than to do it myself. But this winter until three weeks ago Ewan always attended to it and it really was a great relief. But since his attack came on he has not done it. He won't get up until the middle of the day and he goes to bed too early. So I do it; but after all that is a trifle in itself. The trouble is there are so many of these trifles, each so inconsiderable in itself that one is ashamed to mention it, yet the cumulative effect of them all is not inconsiderable....

Stuart has discovered that he likes my books and has been greedily reading them all these past two weeks. He is such a comfort to me—the dear, bright, merry little fellow. He has never been anything but a joy to me from the moment of his birth....

Monday, March 24, 1924
The Manse, Leaskdale

Ewan slept fairly well but wakened early from a horrible dream. He said he dreamed that he was sitting at a table beside James Mustard and that he suddenly found himself *cutting James Mustard's throat.* Surely a horrible dream indeed. To me, the worst horror of it is that I fear this dream was caused by a self-destructive impulse trying to struggle up from the sub-conscious mind into the conscious, and being there converted, by that very "cowardice" Ewan confessed to me in his November attack of 1921, into a murderous attack on his best friend.

It is a curious fact that Ewan seldom dreams when he is well. It is only when these attacks come on that he dreams. I read not long ago that a total lack of dreams was a sign of a tendency to mental disorder.

Ewan was very dull all day and had a restless spell in the afternoon. I tided him over it with a bromide.

Tuesday, March 25, 1924

This has been a terrible day. Last night was also dreadful. Ewan could not sleep and two doses of chloral had no effect on him. This makes me feel very apprehensive. Never before has he been so bad that chloral would not make him sleep. What shall I do if it continues to be inoperable?

At six o'clock this morning he had the worst attack he has ever had at any time. He got so restless he insisted on getting up and going down to the library "to be by himself." I hardly knew what to do. I was afraid to insist on going too, lest he turn violently against me. So I let him go down alone. But in a few minutes he came up again. I never saw anything look like him. His face was absolutely livid, he was shaking from head to foot, his eyes were glaring like a tortured creature's—he said he was "almost gone"—his heart had "almost stopped beating"—"he was *lost*," he was going to everlasting perdition.

I would have been terrified to death had I not seen him almost as bad as this in Dr. Garrick's office five years ago. That time I *was* terrified; and even the doctor was alarmed. He sprang up and tried Ewan's pulse, then said, rather sternly, "Mr. Macdonald, your pulse is strong and normal. There is nothing the matter with your heart. This is just the effect of your nerves."

In a few moments the fit passed and Ewan was comparatively normal. Remembering this I took courage. I got the distracted creature into bed, got him warmed, gave him bromide *and* encouraged him to talk all his terrors out. Usually it is very hard to get him to do this. Ewan has always been unable to face any unpleasant reality, or what he thinks is a reality. He evades it in every way possible and if compelled to put it into words, clothes it as euphoniously as possible—as, for instance, "I am becoming a fatalist"—"My work will not be accepted" and so on. But this morning he was so wild with terror that it all came out—he was going to be lost—God hated him—he was doomed to hell. It was dreadful to listen to this string of mediaeval superstitions which to him at the moment were hideous realities. It almost made me physically sick. But it did him good to drag them into light and face them. In a few minutes his shakings ceased, the livid hue left his face and he was calm.

I sat all day by his bed, talking to and trying to encourage him. It was a dismal task for reason has no influence on insanity. At nine, at twelve and at three he had restless spells but an early bromide got him past them without any repetition of the awful experience of the morning.

His kidneys are not acting right, as is always the case in these attacks. His breath reeks with urea. I have begun giving him kidney pills and making him drink water copiously. I think his liver is disordered, too, for his skin is such a bad color. It is strange that his stomach and digestive apparatus never go out of order, even in his worst attacks. He can always eat quite normally. I read recently in a book on insanity that melancholiacs *never* had a good appetite or proper digestion. But he has.

The roads are bad, the weather gloomy, and there is no stirring out. But I suppose this is just as well. It prevents people from coming to the manse which is certainly a blessing just now. It would be almost impossible to conceal the real cause of Ewan's indisposition if people saw him.

I dread the night. I am so very tired after last night's sleeplessness and the unceasing watchfulness and anxiety of the day.

Wednesday, Mar. 26, 1924
The Manse, Leaskdale, Ont.
Last night the chloral made Ewan sleep, much to my relief and I got a little rest too. But he was very miserable all day. Had many restless spells and was tortured with his dread of having committed "the unpardonable sin." He stayed in bed till noon and then got up. He could not read. Generally in these attacks he can, except during his restless spells, read light fiction and divert his thoughts a little but this time he cannot. At six this evening he was much better and I knew by experience he would be all right for the evening. So I went out for an hour and called on an old couple in the village. They are futile, uninteresting creatures and it was hard to talk to them. But the atmosphere about them was sane and normal and did me good. I escaped for a breathing spell from the poisonous miasma of poor Ewan's horrible phobias. I came home feeling a little more courageous. Ewan seems fairly well now. Perhaps the worst is over.

I grasp at certain hopes. I know they are almost certainly illusory but we must get strength somewhere, if only from an illusion. I tell myself that since this is by far the worst attack since the initial one, five years ago, that it may be the *last*—the final "kick" of the departing demon. And I recall, too, a mysterious dream I had about the first week in February—one of my vivid, symbolic dreams. I dreamed we were visiting the Taylors. There was a house across the road and just as we were coming away Mrs. Taylor said, "Aren't you going over there to see your mother, Mrs. Macdonald? She is very ill." I said, "Why, Mrs. Taylor, my mother died years ago." "Oh, no," said Mrs. Taylor, "that is your mother sitting over on that veranda. She has been there quite a time and I do not think the people she is with are very good to her." Accepting the fact, as one

176

does in dreams, I went over and said to the sick woman, "Mother, I never knew you were here. I thought you were dead."

"No, I am not dead but I am dying," she said. "I have only a few months more to live." "Why didn't you send me word?" I said reproachfully. "I would have come and taken you to my home. You must come right home with me now." "Then you must take me away from these people or they will not let me go," she said.

I awoke and puzzled a good deal over this dream. I have had dreams of this type before though different in content. For instance, a few weeks before the Pages entered suit in New York I dreamed that I held in my arms a child I thought dead and presently found it living. I have come to understand that such a dream invariable means that *something I have thought was at an end* is coming up again.

In this instance it evidently foretokened a resurgence of Ewan's malady. What then? *It is dying.* There will be an end of it this time, perhaps at the close of the "few months" mentioned in the dream.

One hugs *anything* that promises a little relief from horror!

Thursday, March 27, 1924
The Manse, Leaskdale
A dreadful night followed by a *hellish* day. Undoubtedly the worst day I have ever had in my life. If Ewan is no better tomorrow I must have assistance. I dare not remain here alone with him if he continues like this. The responsibility is too great and the strain too awful.

Ewan could not sleep all night nor of course could I. I gave him two doses of chloral. They might as well have been water. He stayed in bed till eleven when he got up and went out to feed the horse. (Since Mr. Cook's death we have no neighbor to help us out in this matter.) When he came in I was alone in the kitchen. I saw at once that he was in the throes of another attack. He was shaking from head to foot—his work was done—he was lost forever—God hated him—he might drop dead any moment. He walked up and down wildly.

Fortunately Lily was upstairs. I shut the door, hurriedly got a bromide ready and made him take it. In half an hour it took effect or the spell was over and he was calm. I got him to lie down. After dinner he dozed off a little but woke at three very restless. Lily had gone to visit friends for the afternoon and evening and I was most thankful she was out of the house. From four to six Ewan was terrible. It was the worst attack he has ever had—nothing five years ago was comparable to it. He walked the floor—he could not rest—finally at six o'clock he declared he must get out—he could not stay in the house another moment. I had to let him go. The roads were a mass of mud and slush—I could not go with him and I knew he did not want me to go. I let him go—I watched him stride in along the side road in the dull March twilight as if pursued by furies—I got the boys' supper and ran every few minutes to the front door to see if he were coming back. I was cold from dread and worry. At last I saw him coming back. I knew then how frightened I had really been.

He came in—still hunted—still frenzied. He was dying—he couldn't live longer than a few minutes! I felt his pulse. It was strong. I got him into the library where the children couldn't see him. I thought I must 'phone for Dr. Shier. He isn't much of a doctor—none of the Uxbridge doctors are. And if he came the secret we have tried to hide—the secret Ewan wants to hide as much as I do when he is in his senses—would be the property of common gossip. But I felt I could bear this alone no longer.

Then, all at once Ewan's mood changed. *He burst into tears!* This is something that never happened before. For a little while he cried bitterly. Then he seemed almost normal. The demon left him wholly—for a time at least. He lay quietly on the sofa all the evening. His breath was suddenly quite wholesome. He even spoke of things he must soon do—have his teeth attended to, etc.—this from a man who twenty minutes before had believed himself dying!

These "spasms" of Ewan's are something I can never quite understand. I have read a great many books on melancholia and neurasthenia in these past five years and it always seems to me that his attacks are more like neurasthenia or, indeed, hysteria than melancholia, which seems generally to be a fixed idea, remaining about the same all the time. Dr. Garrick himself told me that it was very difficult to diagnose Ewan's case. If it were not for the notion about the unpardonable sin, which is the hall-mark of melancholia, he would be inclined to think the malady was neurasthenia. Myself, I believe it partakes of the nature of both. Whatever it is, it is devilish and nothing more terrible, both for the sufferer and his friends, can be imagined.

Oh, what am I to do if this goes on? How can I face tonight? And tomorrow?

Friday, March 28, 1924
The Manse, Leaskdale
Hell is absolute but heaven is comparative. There is only one degree of torture that constitutes hell—the unbearable. But there are scores of degrees of heaven. Therefore, today, *compared with yesterday*, was heaven. The torture was *bearable*.

Last night at nine I gave Ewan chloral. No effect. At eleven I gave him five grs of veronal. He went to sleep and slept till seven. I slept too, and so gained a little strength and energy. But before I slept I suggested to Ewan, "à la Coué" several things, repeating them softly over and over into his ear—"You will have no more headaches"—"You will sleep well every night"—"You will always feel well and happy"—"God loves you and all will be well with you." It can do no harm and may do good.

Ewan seemed better this morning but took a restless spell at 10. Very bad till eleven but nothing like yesterday. He would not get up and I thought it best not to urge him. I sent round to Dave Lyons to come up and feed Teddy. Ewan lay in bed all day and read very fitfully....

I spent the day sitting in the hall just outside our room, doing routine bits of sewing and mending and watching him closely. Today has been much much better than yesterday. But what about tomorrow?...

Saturday, March 29, 1924

A day or two ago I read in a book on neurasthenia that *blue pills* had a good effect sometimes in regulating the liver. I knew E's liver was in a bad state so I sent to Uxbridge for blue pills and gave him one last night. Also, I gave him 5 grs. of chloral and he slept 1 1/2 hours. But this was not enough. I knew if he lay awake all the rest of the night thinking he would be worse again today. So I gave him veronal and he slept till 8.30. Today he got through the whole day without either restless spells or bromides. This *is* an improvement. But his teeth have been troublesome all day. In a way though, this seems to divert his thoughts from imaginary horrors. I kept hot applications to his face all day, as this was the only thing to bring relief. There is no cavity in the tooth—he had it examined by a dentist two weeks ago. Probably the trouble is an abscess at the root caused by pyorrhea.

But in spite of the improvement I have found this a horrible sort of day. I had hardly any sleep. And the weather has been terrible. Dense black clouds—so dark we had to light the lamps in the afternoon—high, violent wind, bitter cold—showers of sleet—and, of all things, a wind-up this evening of thunder and lightning. This means at least two weeks of cold backward weather.

I see nothing from any window but a frozen hideous landscape. I am spiritless. I wish just *one* little pleasant thing would happen to give me a fillip. As it is I feel down and out.

Today Lily's constant muttering to herself nearly drove me distracted. She has developed the habit in the past two years and is growing worse all the time. I can seldom catch a word, though I have often tried to. I don't mind a person *talking* to herself as she goes about her work—I do it myself a little. But indistinct muttering is a very different thing. I don't suppose she is abusing me and my method all the time, though certainly she does part of the time, thus working off resentment she dare not show openly. I think she is railing at everybody and everything in her ken. Anyhow, it is unbearable just now when I have so much to contend with. I have mentioned it to her once or twice, jokingly, but she only stares and denies it. One can't do anything with a person like that. A young fellow has been going with her all winter and I have been hoping he would marry her. But he seems to be cooling off. Nobody can really endure her long. She is always being dropped and it doesn't improve her nerves or her disposition. I ought to pack her off of course. But it is so hard to get any kind of help here; so I put up and put off. But there are times when I would like to turn my sulky, muttering madam over my lap and give her a sound spanking.

Sunday, March 30, 1924
The Manse, Leaskdale

Last night E. slept an hour and a half without any drugs. This is the best for a week. Then his teeth wakened him and I gave him veronal. He has suffered greatly from his teeth all day but seems quite cheerful—laughs a little at jokes and shows some interest in affairs. This is a good sign. The blue pill has cleared his skin certainly—the livid dusky hue has gone and his face is clear and wholesome looking.

This morning, though, he complained of "hearing voices inside his head" whenever he shut his eyes. One voice said "A house divided against itself cannot stand." I do not like this....

Tuesday, April 1, 1924
Last night I 'phoned Dr. Shier and asked him if it would be safe to give Ewan seven grains of veronal. He said it would. As a result Ewan slept well all night but this morning his teeth were so bad that we had to decide to go to Uxbridge. I dreaded the drive both for him and myself. The wind was high and bitter and I thought the hard frozen, only half bare roads would be terrible. But we went—and positively I enjoyed the drive! The buggy top protected us from the wind, the roads were smooth and good; even the wild showers of snow that swept over the landscape at intervals weren't so bad. The dentist found a cavity in E's tooth after all, treated it and relieved him promptly. All the drive home Ewan was quite cheerful—even joked about Pickering. This evening he read all the evening.

Wednesday, Apr. 2, 1924
The Manse, Leaskdale
Both Ewan and I got a good sleep last night. He has been quite calm and rational all day, though his head troubled him somewhat. I feel such a relief. Life seems almost sweet once more.

But I can't yet settle down to do any writing. I feel barred out of my kingdom when I cannot write....

Chester told me tonight he had decided to try the entrance....I am afraid he will fail the arithmetic, though he has been doing much better in it lately.

It seems but as yesterday when *I* was taking the P.W.C. entrance and worrying because I feared *I* had failed in arithmetic. I recall the summer night down by the shore that evening after the results came out in the paper. How very happy I was! This has brought the past back to me with a quick rush, and a sweetness it did not possess even at the time.

Saturday, April 5, 1924
No doubt Ewan is *much* better. He went to Uxbridge today for another treatment of his tooth and has seemed quite cheerful. But now that the worst of the strain is over I feel the reaction. I have been terribly tired all day—just as if I had been *flattened down* to earth by some terrible beating storm. And my soul is washed empty of every wish and hope and desire except just to be *let lie there*—not to have to get up again and stagger on. House cleaning, gardening—all the spring "jobs" are looming up before me and I haven't strength or energy for them.

Read *Life and Confessions of a Psychologist*. Very interesting in some parts—very dull in others.

Wednesday, Apr. 9, 1924
Ewan has been keeping better—and I feel better. Pleasure in my work is coming back to me—at least in the mornings—but as the day wears on I get very tired

and discouraged again. The weather keeps so cold and dark. Ewan went to Toronto today and will stay till tomorrow. He is quite well enough to go now and I think it will help him. And, to be candid, *I* was glad to have him away for a day or two. When he is home, the house is, so to speak, saturated with him—or with the abnormal exhalations of his present personality.

Thursday, Apr. 10, 1924
The Manse, Leaskdale
I had such a glorious good unbroken sleep last night. But today was not easy, somehow. It was a dull cold day with showers of snow. I did some work on a book I'm trying to write, *The Blue Castle*, but couldn't get in the proper mood. And I rather dreaded Ewan's return home. I know he meant to see McCullough and did not know what he might hear. And I thought perhaps he might go to a specialist to have his heart and kidneys examined. They were all right five years ago but sometimes I have thought they were not as they should be. I have often suggested to him that he have them tested but when he is well he laughs at the idea and when he is not well he has not the energy to decide on doing it. But a few weeks ago when this attack first came on he promised me he would when he went to Toronto....when he came home he was quite cheerful. He *hadn't* seen any doctor however. But he had seen McCullough who said he had sent Ewan's affidavit to Greig as soon as he got it but had never heard a word since. I really believe we will hear no more of it—though I suppose as soon as we think that pop will go the weasel again.

I looked at Ewan as he sat at the table tonight eating his supper—a fine look-ing man, with a clear healthy skin, cheerful, rational, talking interestedly of domestic things—and contrasted him with that livid, shaking, terrified, haunted creature of exactly a week ago. It seemed impossible that they could be one and the same. Of course, Ewan is not well yet—and he will likely have relapses. But, if one can judge from past experiences he will not be so bad again during this attack at least.

Sunday, April 20, 1924
Ewan had a slight relapse the first few days of the week. Could not sleep without veronal and was dull and "heady." Heard voices "inside his head" again. But the past three days he has been quite better again and preached a new sermon today quite well. I am feeling better, too, and have had several temporary escapes that helped me.

We have got Dodgie out again and Wednesday evening we went over to Zephyr to visit and "tea" with a family. The roads were splendid and it was delightful to spin along them. I felt as if I had got out of prison again. Ewan, too, as always felt much better. I think the car gives him a sensation of *escaping* from his haunting demons.

But our sojourn with the Walker family was not a good thing for him. Mrs. Walker is the woman who once told me all the tales of women who had died in childbirth before Chester was born. Tonight, by a sort of devilish felicity, she chose the very subject of all others I dreaded to have Ewan hear discussed—viz;

suicides of the unsound in mind! Mrs. George Longhurst of Zephyr took Paris green Saturday and was saved only by the fact that she took too much. Mrs. Walker went into all the gruesome details with a relish. When she finished I tried to turn the conversation but she had found a congenial subject and meant to run it down. Next came a meticulous account of the suicide of "a cousin's daughter" who drank carbolic acid and an uncle who hanged himself! Ewan got so restless that he had to get up and go out while I sat in nervous apprehension. However, he soon came back and as Mrs. Walker could not think of any more horrors just then I got the conversation switched to something more agreeable.

We heard that Mrs. Marshall Pickering is also in the hospital now being treated for diabetes! The woman who swore that she never had diabetes! She must be pretty bad when she would give up and admit it. Pickering himself it seems is not taking the insulin treatment but is dieting.

Well, they will be able to compare symptoms!...

Sunday, Apr. 27, 1924
The Manse, Leaskdale, Ont.
Monday night I went to Toronto for my semi-annual orgy of household shopping. It was not enjoyable but it was a change of tribulation....

I brought home a minute puppy for the boys—a smooth-haired Airedale. I wanted a chow but couldn't get one and I have been putting off the boys too long. Boys should have a dog. Stuart particularly is fond of dogs. Our cats don't like "Dixie" any too well but must resign themselves to him. We have quite a menagerie.

I have never had much to do with dogs. When I was a child we had an old black smooth-haired dog called Gyp—a nice old fellow. After his death we never got another. I was very fond of "Rex" the beautiful Gordon-setter we had in Prince Albert, and of "Laddie," a Scotch collie belonging to one of the men in the *Echo* office,—beyond question the finest and most beautiful dog I ever knew. I like big dogs; but in our small lot a big dog wouldn't do. My own choice would be an English bull-dog; but what would the congregation think?

I am reading *Youth* by Conrad. The first thing of his I've ever read. He has some compelling qualities but overloads his stories with detail. I fancy the more one reads him the better one likes him; and I think I will enjoy *Youth* when I read it the second time much better than I am doing it in the first.

Sunday, May 4, 1924
The Manse, Leaskdale
....Everywhere we go this spring people are putting in hardwood floors. I cannot help contrasting them with the miserable floors in this manse—soft wood, worn, warped, cracked, stained and disfigured in every way, necessitating constant painting. No idea of putting hardwood floors in the manse ever occurs to them. I've been painting and staining floors all the week and I'm so tired of it that I'm disgusted with congregations!!!

On Tuesday I read in the *Guardian* of Aunt Hattie's death. She has been ill for three years with internal cancer. I never liked Aunt Hattie—none of us did, for that matter. Yet I felt oddly sorry and downcast to hear of her death. I think this must be because it seems, somehow, to remove that old life, of which she was a part, still further away. It doesn't seem to me possible that it is nearly forty years since that summer evening when Uncle Chester brought his bride to the old home in Cavendish for her first visit. I can see her very clearly as she stepped out of the buggy—tall, handsome, very fashionably dressed. Aunt Hattie was always in the forefront of the fashion and every fad that came along was eagerly adopted by her. In spite of her imposing exterior she was a child in heart and brain. She had neither intellect nor charm. She was, I think, the most absolutely selfish and coldly calculating being I ever knew and I have not one single pleasant memory connected with her personally.

Nevertheless it spoiled the day for me when I read of her death.

I read a most absorbing book this week—stealing time from sleep for the reading—*Glands Regulating Personality*. It is an amazing thing. I cannot agree with all the writer's conclusions and theories. Even those that are very likely correct will take a great deal of proving. But the *facts* concerning the endocrines are marvellous enough, all deductions apart.

I feel that we are on the threshold of a new and amazing revelation. The world needs it. The older revelations have exhausted their mandate. I believe the next one will come through science. What form it will take I cannot guess....Two thousand years ago Jesus burst the bonds that were stifling the human race. Now those bonds are tightening around us again—outworn dogma, dead superstitions. It will take something as tremendous as his message of spiritual freedom to destroy those bonds again. But it will come. The whole world is chaos; the Spirit of God again broods upon the face of the waters; and presently there will be light.

I think I found in the book a clue to the mystery of Ewan's personality. I believe his thyroid and pituitary glands are sub-normal. The symptoms given in the book have always characterized him. Possibly, too, it is some disorder in these glands that causes his periodic attacks of melancholia....

Saturday, May 10, 1924
The Manse Leaskdale
....I had a doleful letter from Ella on Monday. I had sent her a hundred dollars to get a new buggy—their old one being completely done. She was very grateful, poor creature, but thought she ought to tell me that Dan is pretty wild and may not "make good." I did not need her letter to tell me this. I saw enough last summer....

It is a pity Jim is not the oldest. He is a real Macneill—a worker and manager. He would bring back Park Corner prosperity and revive the old traditions. But he is only twelve and Aunt Annie and Stella are besotted on Dan—whom they have helped to spoil.

Sometimes I think our Dixie dog is an unmitigated nuisance. We have had an awful time teaching him to eat. And at night, until recently, he has howled for hours, "like a lost soul in agony" as Stuart gravely declares. (Unluckily he got this off before poor Ewan on whose morbid mind it fell like the flick of a whip on a wound.) Then the little beastie is so dirty, never having had any training. I have never had anything to do with bringing up a dog in the way good dogs should go but it is never too late to learn. There is something—comical, wistful, entreating—about the little dog's face that makes me love him in spite of his nuisances and indicates that he has the root of the matter in him in spite of appearances. Luck has kissed and made friends but Pat swears vilely whenever poor Dixie toddles near him. Pat for some mysterious reason has lately taken to sleeping at the foot of our bed—something he never would do before. But Luck has ousted him from the boys' bed and downstairs smells, I suppose, of dog. So Paddy comes to us. Last night he came up before we put our light out and took one of his weird "dancing" spells. I laughed until the bed shook. I never saw a cat go through such a performance before. There was really something weird about it; it was quite indescribable!

We have been housecleaning all week, hampered by the bad weather. Tonight is fine, so perhaps we will have a few nice days now.

Why have some lines of poetry a potent and indescribable influence over us—an influence that is not conditioned by their merit? There are four lines of Mrs. Hemans which have always, from the time I first read them as a child, opened the doors of magic to me.

> "The sounds of the sea and the sounds of the night
> Were around Clotilde as she knelt to pray
> In a chapel where the mighty lay
> On the old Provençal shore."

Today they recurred to me and I shivered with profound delight. Why? They are not great poetry—they do not possess the intrinsic sorcery of Keats' "magic casements" or Milton's "airy tongues." These latter thrill my mind and fancy. But Mrs. Hemans' lines make my *heart* ache with a supernal fleeting ecstasy. Is it because of the picture they paint? Is it because "the sounds of the sea and the sounds of the night" were around me in childhood? Is it because of the romance always associated with "the old Provençal shore"? It does not seem to me that the secret is in any of these things. It goes deeper still—to some former life and some intense moment in that life—perhaps!

Tuesday, May 13, 1924
I am reading, in that precious hour between ten and eleven, Guizot's *History of France*. It is very interesting. But a prolonged dose of history like this always breeds pessimism in me. The unceasing succession of crimes and brutalities and treacheries and horrors that make up "history" make me feel that it is impossible that there can be any "personal" God—or any Power that can or will protect or defend the individual. I can, of course, see clearly in all history a certain Force struggling upwards out of darkness and horror into light and sanity; but it seems to me a blind, impersonal force to whom the individual is nothing. And when I feel this I descend into the deeps.

Friday, May 16, 1924

I see by *The Guardian* that John Stirling has been called to Montague. This will be so nice for Margaret. She has been buried alive in Breadalbane, with no congenial friends or pleasant surroundings.

We had Guild this evening. Some of our Guild meetings are good and encouraging. But this one was a failure. The subject was "John Keats" and nobody cared anything about it. The readings were dull. Ewan read his paper wretchedly—when he is melancholy he reads as badly as a schoolboy of eight. I felt ashamed and humiliated. I wanted to throw a book at him and howl. But of course I didn't. I sat decorously, read my own paper—and came home alone. It was a beautiful night though cold—moonlight, clear sparkling air, luminous stars. The beauty soothed and calmed me....

Sunday, May 18, 1924

One thing today made today worth living and writing about. It poured rain until two. Then it cleared and became clear and bitterly cold. We all went to Zephyr and after service got Mrs. Rob Shier and went up to Belhaven to visit a former Zephyr family. We stayed there until eight then came home. Nothing in all that, except a dull day spent amid stupid people, shivering with the chill of fireless rooms most of the time. But when we dropped Mrs. Shier at Zephyr, Chester and I sat together in the back seat and talked all the way home. *Real* talk. Chester's mind is developing rapidly just now. We flew along. The moon flooded the bare spring hills with light. The pine stump fences writhed up along the roads like the stark skeletons of creatures that had died in torment. We talked. Chester discoursed on transmigration and told me some remarkable dreams he had had as we cuddled together in the dimness with our arms about each other. I cannot describe the charm of it all—you cannot photograph starlight. But we were perfectly happy for a little while. "What a nice little mother you are," said Chester.

Sunday, May 25, 1924

....The Church Union bill after being the storm centre for weeks in Ottawa has been given a two years hoist. Meanwhile, "the courts" have to decide on the constitutionality of it. If they decide against it that is the end of it. If they decide for it, it becomes law in July 1926. There's a nice muddle for you. It won't please anybody. But a good deal of water will flow under the bridges in two years and the ghost of Mr. Micawber broods over the troubled waters.

Monday, May 26, 1924
The Manse, Leaskdale, Ont.

This morning I resumed work on my third *Emily* book and this afternoon Lily and I cleaned the horse stable. I have been at Ewan all the spring to clean it but he kept saying "Yes, yes" and never doing it. It has never been cleaned since February—in other words since the inertia of his melancholy came upon him. As our horse was here until May 1st its condition may be imagined. It *had* to be cleaned before we could put our setting hens in it so today we did it. To do Lily justice, she never balks at a job of this kind. She seems, indeed, to like it, having had plenty of it to do on the farms where she worked before coming here. But it was a hard, dirty and unpleasant job. But we did it thoroughly and tonight, though my back aches and my feet moan, I feel the satisfaction of "something attempted, something done." It has certainly "earned a night's repose" but whether I shall have it or not is a question. I am too tired to sleep, I fear.

Of course I put on, for the task, clothes that couldn't be materially injured by it; and as, arrayed thus, I carried out forkful after forkful of manure I grinned to myself as I wondered what my readers—ay, and my publishers, too, for that matter—would think, if they could see me. Judging from the letters I get, my readers, at least the young and romantic portion, seem to imagine that I never do anything, except sit, beautifully arrayed, at a desk and "create" "Annes" and "Emilys"! They might admit that I sometimes washed dishes or dusted a room but I'm sure they'd never think I cleaned horse stables!

Wednesday, May 28, 1924

Yesterday afternoon we motored to Newmarket where I was to give an evening of readings for some C.G.I.Ts. It was a warmer day than we have had, the young leaves and blossoms were coming out, Ewan seemed fairly well and so I enjoyed the drive. It was certainly much pleasanter than cleaning the horse-stable!

We had supper at the manse. Mrs. Mann is one of those very gushing prayerful women whom I find fearful bores. While we were sitting in the church—which is a very nice one—she whispered to me her tale of woe regarding her first Sunday there. She was aghast to discover that the stairs, leading from the schoolroom up to the church were "excessively narrow." This was terrible. She did not see how she could endure it. "Oh, Mrs. Macdonald," she whispered fervently, "you don't know how I felt! Only my habit of constant prayer carried me through. As I went up and down those terrible stairs I kept saying over and over, 'Oh, God, help me to be brave. Oh, God, help me to be brave.'"

I found it hard to repress a whoop of laughter in the good lady's face. If she had come to a manse with no sanitary conveniences—if she had to clean out horse stables because her husband was too melancholy to do it—I wonder if she would have thought narrow stairs required so much courage. The stairs, by the way, are gone. God—or Mr. Mann—put it into the heads of the congregation to do them over and widen them. Who says prayer is never answered?

I wore my batik silk dress and my black and gold lace scarf. After the programme the girls gave me a beautiful bouquet of roses. As I held my roses and bowed I saw a picture of myself in the "rig" of yesterday popping in and out of that stable with unending forkfuls of manure. The contrast struck me so forcibly that I grinned—and Mrs. Mann assured me afterwards that never had she seen so charming a smile as that with which I rewarded the bouquet givers!

Thursday June 5, 1924
The Manse, Leaskdale

Last Saturday, just as we were leaving to attend a ball game up at the north school I got a letter from Stella saying that her mother, after being perfectly well all winter and gaining 25 lbs. had had another of her bad attacks and had been so ill that she alarmed them, but seemed getting better and they hoped the worst was over....We went to Uxbridge after the game and while there I got a wire from Stell:—

"Mother very very ill. No hope of her recovery. General break down of the mucous membrane of stomach and bladder. Chills, high temperature and hemorrhage. Let me hear from you."

I don't know how I got home. The drive was like a nightmare. But when I got here I found that a very curious thing had happened. *I had ceased to feel.* I can only express it that way. I never felt just the same in my life before. It was just as if something in me had said, "I refuse to be hurt. I *will not* suffer more pain." Fancy continued to picture the further impoverishment of life if Aunt Annie died, mind suggested a hundred problems and perplexities in regard to that helpless family at Park Corner—but nothing gave me pain. I wept no more. I went to bed. I did not sleep, it is true; but there seemed no reason why I could not. I was calm and composed and—detached. Ay, *that's* the word, exactly. Some vital connection between perception and feeling had been cut—whether temporarily or permanently I could not say. All day Sunday the numbness continued. It was merciful—and yet I did not like it. Not only the ability to feel pain seemed gone but the ability to feel anything....

Today's wire was:—"Cannot see much change but she is holding her own well. Temperature still high."

It may be she will again recover. But I doubt if she will ever again be able to return to Park Corner. And that, for me, will be just as if she had died.

Ewan left Monday morning for P.E.I. He will be away a month. I have to say that his going was a relief. For three months he has just hung around gloomy and unhappy, casting a blight on everything. Sometimes lately, when I have been so tired and over-worked I have felt as if it were the last straw to sit down at the table and look at his dull downcast face without a trace of interest or animation in it. This is the bitterest thing in mental disorder. In physical illness our household intimates are still the same; but in this they are changed into alien personalities.

Besides, the trip and concentration on Christie's business troubles may help him. I thought it did last year: but that may only have been coincidence.

Of course, compared to what he was in March Ewan is almost well. He sleeps well and is quite cheerful in company. He is just dull, and lifeless day in and day out at home and seems to think everybody else should feel as dull as he does. He has no affection at these times for either the children or me. We mean nothing to him. He has no interest in any of the things we are interested in. Poor, poor Ewan! Why should he be cursed with such a fate?...

Friday, June 6, 1924
The Manse, Leaskdale
....Marie Corelli is dead. The news affected me somewhat. When I was a girl she was in her hey-day and her books always made a tremendous sensation. The critics abused her lavishly and everything they said was true. But she could tell a

story and her books were read by millions. I used to read and discuss them with my friends so that Corelli's name was linked with much of the happiness of youth and her death seems therefore to have a personal meaning for me.

This evening I was reading *The Diary of Marie Bashkirtseff*. This book came out when I was a young girl and made a tremendous sensation. It was discussed in all the reviews. I longed to read it but books like that never penetrated to Cavendish and I could not afford to buy it. Recently a new edition was brought out and I sent for it. If it were published today for the first time it would hardly cause a ripple. We have had book after book of these intimate chronicles far more frank and sensational than poor Marie's passionate longings for fame and success. The diary is interesting at first but one tires of it as one reads on because it is just the same all the way through. It is a pitiful tragic record....

Monday, June 9, 1924
The Manse, Leaskdale, Ont.
On Saturday a letter from Mr. Rollins came. I felt sure that it contained news about the New York suit and I decided not to open it until today. Mr. Lord was coming that evening to preach and I did not want to be upset while he was here. Nevertheless I worried about it all Sunday and dreaded this morning when it would have to be opened. I felt that, somehow, I really had not the courage and strength to open another of those missives that have come at intervals for four years. But I had a dream last night that made me feel that the news the letter bore was not bad. I have often had this type of dream when I was dreading something that turned out a mere scarecrow after all. I dreamed that the garage was on fire and Lily and I were trying to put it out. *We succeeded*. I woke and said "There is good news in that letter." Nevertheless I opened it with trembling fingers:—
"Dear Mrs. Macdonald:—
I have just received a telegram from Briesen & Schrenk, reading as follows:—
'Page vs. Macdonald dismissed for want of jurisdiction.'
I am glad we have been successful, but suppose the other side may appeal"....

This has lifted a tremendous weight from my mind, which is especially a thing to be grateful for just now when I have so many other troubles. Of course Page will appeal and my money will still be tied up....but that will not seriously inconvenience me and I have no fear whatever that the appeal will succeed.

So that's that, Louis P.!

Tuesday, June 10, 1924
This has been a lovely day—the most delightful day we have had since last summer. It was warm enough to be pleasant. We have had such a phenomenally cold spring. But then there have been no mosquitoes. During these last five years the mosquitoes have been dreadful and last spring we were almost eaten up alive. This year we have had no trouble. I hate mosquitoes. One mosquito in my room at night can keep me awaker than a bad conscience.

This has been a happy day of a peace and quiet long unknown to me. There was no word from Aunt Annie and in such a case as this "no news is good news." I finished a short story in the forenoon—"Some Fools and a Saint"—and spent the afternoon and evening working in my garden, enjoying every minute. People say:—"It must be a great deal of work to keep such a large garden." Of course it is; but then it is such delightful work—out in the open, under the lovely spring skies with the young green leaves unfolding on every hand. What a change from my prison of the winter.

And I have the best garden I have ever had. Everything came up and there have been no bad thunderstorms to wash it out—another advantage of the cold spring. I have rows upon rows of delightful possibilities—corn, cucumbers, poppies, gypsophila, cosmos, peas, asters, gladiolii, beans, sweet peas, parsnips, sweet sultans, radishes, balsams, zinnias, beets, carrots, pansies, egg plant, parsley, nasturtiums, watermelons, lettuce, onions, cabbages, cauliflowers and tomatoes. I prowl about, weeding, watering, transplanting. My cats frisk around me, my small dog, of whom I am getting very fond, chases the cats and gets his ears boxed—by the cats—for his pains. And we are all so temporarily happy together that life seems good....

Saturday, June 14, 1924
The Manse, Leaskdale
Ten o'clock, A.M.
I had a very remarkable experience this morning—so remarkable that I hasten to set it down here while it is still fresh in my memory. I have never had anything of the kind before. I have had strange predictive dreams but this was not a dream.

I wakened early—too early to get up, so I tried to go to sleep again. I was not actually asleep. I was quite conscious that I was lying there in bed, that the boys were talking down the hall in their room—arguing over something—and that Dixie was howling dolefully at the kitchen door. I seemed to be just on the border line between sleeping and waking. Suddenly I heard a voice. It was as clear and distinct and audible as any voice I ever heard in my life;—"*This is the last of the series of misfortunes that have come upon you like a rage*" was what the voice said.

I awakened up wholly as it pronounced the last word—wakened up with a strange peaceful feeling that has persisted ever since.

I don't know what to make of it.

But I believe it. I believe that my misfortunes are at an end—this "series" of them at least. But the conviction does not elate me. Because I know Aunt Annie is not going to recover. I feel sure of it.

"This" refers to her illness, I know, and it will terminate in her death, for otherwise it could not be called one of "my misfortunes." No, Aunt Annie is going to die and this is to be the last of the "series of misfortunes." *Series* is the right word. Whatever intelligence uttered that sentence was an artist in words, and it has indeed fallen on me "like a rage." For the past five years I have been smitten with blow after blow as if some angry Taskmaster were buffetting me. It began with Frede's death. Then came the terrible months of Ewan's first attack of melancholia; then lawsuit after lawsuit with the Pages; then the horrible year of the Pickering affair; then this attack of Ewan's this winter; and now dear Aunt Annie's illness—yes, and death.

But it is ended. Frede's death began it—her mother's will close it. Henceforth there will be peace—and desolation.

Tuesday, June 17, 1924
The Manse, Leaskdale, Ont.
The wire came this morning; as I was writing in the parlor the 'phone rang. I went to it. The station master—a telegram from Los Angeles:—

"Mother is gradually sinking. Everything is being done but without avail"....

The strange numbness which has possessed me since the Saturday of the first telegram suddenly broke and was swept away in a torrent of sorrow and desolation. Aunt Annie dying! Impossible! Aunt Annie could not die—*could not*. I had a bad afternoon. Oh, these bereavements are hideous things.

This evening I sent a night letter to Stell; "....You must bring your mother home. I cannot face Park Corner alone or attend to the business there. I will pay your expenses."

Stella has written in one of her letters that she did not know what they would do if Aunty died. Clara is running a big private hotel and could not leave it; and she—Stella—could not afford to come. This was a hint for me, of course. And of course I took it. I would do anything in my power that dear Aunty would like me to do. Oh, how thankful I am that I have always helped Aunt Annie with money cheerfully and ungrudgingly. She never came to me for help in vain. I made her last six years on earth tolerable.

And I cannot—I *cannot* go to Park Corner for that ordeal alone. That helpless family—the ghastly loneliness with no Aunt Annie! *No Aunt Annie at Park Corner.* I cannot realize it. I cannot picture Park Corner without her. She has always been there—she was always the centre around which everything revolved—even at an age when other women are relegated to the chimney corner. I could scream at the very thought of going to Park Corner and not finding Aunt Annie there. I was never there in my life that she wasn't there....

It is dark, the house is quiet—the boys asleep. I am writing in the library. I dread to stop, for then the pangs of my grief will pounce on me like wolves again. With the exception of Frede's death this is the most bitter sorrow that has ever come to me. It will take more out of life than anything else, save Frede's loss, has taken. Oh, but I lived through *that*—so I can live through *this*.

I lifted up my eyes at supper time and saw the picture of Park Corner on the wall. There it was—the big beautiful, orchard-bowered house that was the wonder castle of my childhood, where Aunt Annie reigned as queen, dispensing the lavish and gracious hospitality for which she was famous. And she will never be there again—never....

The Manse, Leaskdale, Ont.
Wednesday, June 18, 1924
Last night was possessed of a devil in Leaskdale manse. I went to bed very tired and hoping for a good sleep which might give me enough strength to carry on

with. I was just falling asleep when I heard Lily calling out agitatedly, "Where's the flashlight? There's some kind of an animal in the yard." Inwardly cursing Lily and her mare's nests I roused up and got her the flashlight. Was just lapsing into slumber again when Lily returned, announcing that she could not see anything. Once more I wakened and once more I fell asleep. Re-enter Lily; agitation more marked: the mysterious animal had returned and had got into the hen pen; she believed it was a fox after the hens; wouldn't I dress and go out with her—she was afraid to go alone.

I got up, dressed and went out. If it really were a fox my hens must be saved. As we approached the hen-pen an old yellow dog, who had been gnawing a bone flung to the chickens dashed madly off in terror. I returned to bed, thinking things not lawful to be uttered.

Again, for the last time, I grew sleepy and was just "off" when I heard an anguished meow. The next moment a little distracted animal landed on my bed, still piteously entreating. I put out my hand—touched it—what on earth? I sprang out of bed and lit the lamp. I saw a sight that doubled me up with laughter. Poor Luck had evidently got into the pantry, got caught in and pulled down the long sticky "fly stop" hanging there; then he had got it wound around and around him from tail to nose. I had to separate the poor cat from that miserable girdling. His fur is coming out and it pulled off in big bunches. Then most of the mucilage remained on him and made the remaining fur stick out all over him in grotesque spikes. By the time I had finished I was past sleeping....

Friday, June 20, 1924
It is ended.

This morning at eleven the message came. Aunt Annie died yesterday June 19 at 12.30.

I spent the afternoon writing letters and telegrams. Sometimes I had to walk the floor in bitter tears and sorrow, mingled with the stubborn incredulity with

"Swimming pool" [in Leaskdale woods, with Chester in it]

which we always face the fact of death. Aunt Annie could not be dead—she *could* not.

Saturday, June 21, 1924

A busy day—pierced through every little while with stabs of anguish so dreadful that if I am alone I shriek aloud. Between these stabs I am numb and calm.

This afternoon I went back with the boys to their swimming pool in Leask's woods. It was a beautiful afternoon and for a brief space I didn't believe any more that Aunt Annie was dead. So I was quite happy.

Stuart is quite a fish. He can swim and dive amazingly. Chester, of heavier and less elastic build, doesn't do as well. Can't swim yet without a plank under him.

It was beautiful there in the sunlight and shadow. But this evening was hard.

Monday, June 23, 1924
Walker House, Toronto

I came in today to see Mrs. Meloney, the editor of *The Delineator*. She is much in love with "Emily" and I am to arrange four stories from the first and second *Emily* books for publication next year. For these four stories, which are already written, I am to get sixteen hundred dollars! Yet twenty years ago I wrote many stories just as good—better—for which I was glad to get fifty or sixty apiece. Mrs. Meloney was nice but couldn't realize at all just what my life is and couldn't understand why I couldn't get time to write more short stories etc. I gave up trying to explain. She is an inhabitant of a different world, and we do not talk the same language. I could not tell her the nature of my husband's illness or make her see the necessity for my doing so much church work.

And, of course, I didn't tell her I ever cleaned horse-stables!

Thursday, June 26, 1924
The Manse, Leaskdale, Ont.

Am very busy getting matters arranged so that I can go away with an easy mind. I don't know when I will have to go until I hear from Stella. Mrs. Alec Leask was down this evening and I walked up the hill with her. It's odd about Mrs. Leask—she has spasms of exasperating foolishness—she is eaten up with unholy curiosity about everything that doesn't concern her—I wouldn't trust her around a corner—and yet there is a tang of the race of Joseph about her....

Friday June 27, 1924

After all the Church Union Bill is passed—the "Coercion Bill" as it has been well named. The Commons disregarded the recommendations of the Committee completely and passed the bill *in toto*. Well, we will see what will come of it. No church, founded on such a deed of injustice will ever prosper.

Monday, June 30, 1924

The end of June. It has been a strange month. In one way a time of bitter suspense and grief; in the other a peaceful, pleasant month. It seems a horrible thing

[Road scene]

to say that a month has been peaceful and pleasant because my husband was away. Yet it is true. Those months before June were so terrible—the whole house seemed so saturated with that repulsive personality which replaced Ewan's normal self—that it was a relief when he went away. I have read and worked and slept, free from that sense of an ever-present strain and horror. Ewan's letters lately have been quite cheerful. He seems much better.

I packed for my journey today. I leave next Thursday night. Stell wants me to go down and help Ella with the arrangements....

Park Corner, P.E. Island
Sunday, July 6, 1924
I am here again in the dear old spot, so changed and lonely for me. I had a hot, unpleasant journey down. Life met me at Kensington last night and we came down the old beautiful road, fragrant with the wild-fern scent of a warm summer evening. There were a few terrible moments when I reached Park Corner and Ella came to meet me—but no Aunt Annie—for the first time in all my life no Aunt Annie.

Since then I have got on fairly well. Last night I slept alone in Stella's old room upstairs. I had expected it would be a ghostly night. Last summer I felt and recorded it in this journal, that at night the old house was thronged with phantom presences. I felt it so keenly that I almost was compelled to believe it. And I feared it would be even worse now. But there was absolutely no such sensation, though I lay awake for a long time. *The ghosts were gone.* They came only because Aunt Annie was here. She is not here now—and they come no more. They will never come again. This sounds very nonsensical—but it is exactly what I feel. And who knows?

This has been a dull day. Ella and I planned out everything. I think it is well I came. Poor Ella is so helpless and inadequate. It is farcical to see *her* in Aunt Annie's place. And yet I am fond of her and sorry for her. It is not her fault that she is only a grown-up child. It was a grim joke of Fate to cast her for a part which requires unusual powers of organization, will and judgment. Anything so helpless as Ella in the midst of the problems that surround her could not be imagined....

I went over to see Aunt Eliza tonight. As usual she told me how beautiful my mother was and added that I didn't look a bit like her!! Heath's wife is there and, from all appearances, is not going to let the family die out.

Park Corner
Wednesday, July 9, 1924
Yesterday afternoon Heath motored me over to Cavendish, and I stayed there until this evening. A brief visit but a very pleasant one. I stayed last night at Webbs' and had a delightful walk through Lover's Lane and Deep Hollow last night....

One thing depressed me very much—Cavendish is getting so shabby. Almost all the houses are unpainted and dowdy. Alec's looks nice and snug but everywhere else the places seemed down-at-heel. Times are hard, of course, but I fear there are other reasons—indifference, the dying out of the old families. The manse in particular looks dreadful and gives a poverty-stricken look to the whole landscape around it. No one has lived in it since the Stirlings left and the people are quarrelling over the question whether to build a new one or repair it. There is something wrong somewhere.

Thursday, July 10, 1924
I had a restless night. Today was very hot, made hotter by the frying of a big batch of doughnuts. I had excellent luck and was pleased. The funeral baked meats must not disgrace the old traditions. I found the pantry lamentably empty but I went to the local store and stocked it up. This evening I copied some recipes from Aunt Annie's old cook-book. It spoke very eloquently of her. Never was such a cook as Aunt Annie. Almost every page recalled some feast of the past.

I had letters from Chester and Mrs. Meloney today. Chester thinks he passed. Mrs. Meloney writes me that, after all, she dare not use the "Father Cassidy" story in the *Delineator*. Because of the Ku Klux Klan she is afraid to publish a story in which the "hero is a Catholic Priest!"

Yet we live in the year of grace 1924! Well, it would seem as if, in spite of all our vaunted democracy, nine tenths of the human race must always be in bondage to some form of tyranny.

This vexes me. I shall have to write a new story to fit into that particular place in the series. And this will be very difficult to do, much more so than writing an independent story. Besides it will take a good deal of time.

Sunday, July 13, 1924
Park Corner, P.E.I.
It is all over. "Ashes to ashes and dust to dust." Aunt Annie sleeps with her own.

Friday evening Cuthbert took me up to Kensington. Almost everybody in Park Corner went up....

We gave supper to twenty five people that night. I do not say it was for the sake of that supper so many went to Kensington and attended us home. No, I believe they would all have gone even if they had known they would have no supper. They were kind neighbors who loved Aunt Annie and were all anxious to help us in every way they could. But they enjoyed the supper for all that. Ella and I had seen that it was a good one—cold chicken a-plenty, biscuits, preserves, pies, cakes galore. Even Aunt Annie herself would have accorded it her approval I think. I had an uncanny feeling that Aunt Annie herself should be sitting at the head of the table, pouring the tea and smiling on the circle as she had always done of yore....

Aunt Annie, lying in her steel casket in that softly lighted old parlor was the most beautiful thing I ever saw. There *was* a change—the change from age to youth. She looked like a young girl. Her dark hair, in which there was hardly a thread of silver, was waved over her forehead as she always wore it. There was not a wrinkle on the peaceful face; and she wore a little dress of white silk.

I do not remember Aunt Annie young. As far back as I can recall she was a stout middle-aged woman, with a lined face, soberly clad in dark dresses. Now I saw her as a girl. Beautiful—I was thankful to see her once again and so lovely. And yet it is not as that marble-white bride of death that I shall remember Aunt

[Geddie Memorial Church, P.E.I.]

Annie. No, I shall think of her as an old woman in a gingham apron coming out of her pantry or feeding her chickens. Aunt Annie always seemed to be feeding *something*—human beings or animals. She was always *giving*. She had had much sorrow in her life and many disappointments but nothing had ever broken her spirit or embittered her heart. Death gave her back her old beauty and—perhaps—her old happiness. At least, peace and rest....

The funeral was yesterday. There have been eight funerals in that house, since it was built about fifty years ago—and only one wedding—mine. Aunt Annie never saw one of her daughters married. I was the only bride of that old house....

The Manse, Leaskdale, Ont.
Tuesday, July 22, 1924

I am thankful to be home again. Though I am conscious of a bitter desolation.

Last week was a sorrowful one. Stella and I went over the old house, where everything was linked with the old life and dreams. We left things pretty much as they were. Everything looked as it always did. It seemed to me so inadequate that everything should look so much the same when Aunt Annie had gone forever. But she had gone—and the old home was *dead*. Its soul went with her.

"Stella and Life" [Howatt]

We tried to solve the "problem of Dan." Stell soon saw for herself, and Life emphatically told her, that Dan would never make a farmer. We decided that she should take him away with her, for a year at least, and see how he gets on at something else. If he likes it and doesn't want to come back some arrangement can be made to tide matters over until Jim can take hold. I feel that I can do no more from a financial point of view for Park Corner. I have given Aunt Annie hundreds of dollars since George died. I am glad I did—glad that she never came to me in vain and that I always gave it to her freely—glad that I often sent her money unasked. But I cannot keep this up....

But I thank God for all those years of Aunt Annie. Nothing can take *them* from me.

Dan drove me to Kensington that evening and I spent the night with Tillie Bentley. Sunday morning I reached Montreal and spent the day with Fred Macneill and his wife who are living there now. Mrs. Fred is by way of being a bit of a freak. She is trying desperately to simulate a youth that has passed away. She has a fretful faded face and perhaps it was the contrast with what she saw in her mirror that kept her exclaiming at intervals all through my visit, "Oh Maud, you look *so happy.*" "You *do* look so happy."

Well! I suppose I do look happy—partly because I have always determined that the world should not know of my troubles and trained my face to wear a smile, partly because I have trained my muscles to look pleasant; but after all perhaps it may be—a little or a great deal—because under everything in the core of my heart I have always had and been conscious of a certain subtle happiness the world never gave me and could not take away. With the exception of a few tortured hours now and then it has always been with me, sustaining and nourishing. Kingdoms illimitable, starry or stormy, have been mine in that secret realm of imagination and insight. Even when fears and worries have dogged me like wolves I could find escape from them there. And so perhaps in spite of all the tragedies and sorrows of my life, I am, at heart, happy.

Ewan and Chester met me in Toronto in Simpson's rest room....

We got home in the evening and though I had only been away a little over two weeks I had the sensation of having been away a long long time. I found my cats, dog and garden fine and dandy. It is nice to be home again....

Wednesday, July 23, 1924

Zephyr had its garden party tonight. I spent the evening washing dishes for the gorging crowds, inwardly resentful of the fact that I must waste my time thus, when I had so much work to do of my own. A church that cannot pay its way without an annual garden party is a farce.

But I had a delightful drive home with my two kiddies.

Ewan says he thinks Zephyr will go Union. The Senate by the way amended the bill, to allow congregations to vote on the question whether they should go in or stay out. Zephyr is an unaccountable place. Three years ago when Ewan and Mr. Roach tried to bring about a co-operation arrangement whereby the two Zephyr churches should join and Leaskdale and Sandford unite—a really good arrangement for all concerned—the Zephyr Presbyterians voted it down. Now they have swung around to Union—at least a good many. This will leave Leaskdale in the air, no matter whether it votes in or out—and we will be on the road. Well, let it come....

From now on the Union Question will be the burning one everywhere. I dread all the talk of it. The feeling in Ontario is very intense. No matter what happens our Presbyterian church can never be what it was. We have to choose between staying in a broken, crippled church—which would be my choice were I free to choose—or going into a hybrid nameless "United Church."

Sunday, July 26, 1924
Leaskdale, Ont.

Last night we motored down to Uxbridge to meet Bertie. She has changed a good deal and looks older than when last I saw her—a good deal older. Only when she laughs youth pops out through her eyes and flashes over her face. Bertie has a wonderful smile.

Sunday, August 17, 1924

....On Monday morning, July 28, we left for our motor trip to Kentucky. We arrived back Thursday evening, Aug. 7, after a very delightful motor trip of 1817 miles. Yes, it *was* delightful, though there were hours and moments in it when I was ready to vow I would never, no, never go on a long motor trip again. But there were other hours and moments which made up for everything.

Our first day was very pleasant. We went from Leaskdale to Sarnia—a good lap....A few miles out of Sarnia a heavy thunderstorm came up. We popped into a barn close by the road, with a handy open door and stayed there for half an hour. Then the shower being over we made Sarnia unhindered. And that was the only drop of rain that fell on us or near us in all those eleven days on those 1817 miles. This was such good luck as to be positively uncanny.

The only real drawback in the pleasure of our trip was the hot nights. The days were of course hot, too, but the motion of our car created a breeze that kept us cool and we felt the heat only when we stopped for meals. But at night we felt it severely. That first night in a small-roomed hotel in Sarnia was anything but pleasant. However, we were so tired that we slept and felt quite fresh and adventurous next morning. We crossed into the U.S. and got to Detroit for dinner. We got *into* Detroit easily enough but I thought we would never get out of it. We wandered round for what seemed like hours and really was one before we could find our road out of its swirl of traffic. This delay prevented us from reaching our objective, Fort Wayne, that night. Darkness overtook us at *Hicksville* and at Hicksville we stayed.

I don't know what Hicksville is like—I did not see much of it. It *may* have every virtue. In it people may live, pure of soul, lofty of aspiration. Mute, inglorious Millions may throng its streets; gems of purest ray serene may sparkle in its social galaxy. But for me Hicksville will always connote—*bedbugs*!

No, no, let me be just—exact. Let me not exaggerate. *One* bedbug.

Bertie and I discovered him in our room, peacefully traversing a pillow. Naturally we went mad. We fell upon that bed and tore it to pieces. I flew to Ewan's room and dragged everything off the beds there. But we found no more. Evidently that poor solitary creature had been left there by some traveller and when we appeared came gladly out for company. Bertie, however, would not get into bed but slept on the floor. I was too tired for even my horror of bedbugs to keep me awake. I flung myself on the bed and slept....

We reached Warsaw at noon and had dinner with Angus and Edith at their pretty summer cottage at Winona Lake. I had never been in Warsaw since the fall of 1916. My horror of Edith's fussiness was always so great that I could never bring myself to go back. But our brief visit was very pleasant and Edith gave us a delicious dinner. Though Bertie and I did have a laugh to ourselves over the fact that when we went into the spare room we found the bed carefully covered with newspaper—lest we lay some dusty profaning article on the spread, I suppose.

We left at three and got to Indianapolis that night. The scenery down through Indiana was monotonous. Any one place was pretty enough but

"En route"

it was all fatally the same—mile after mile of fertile farms and little villages with hanging baskets....

Beyond Camp Knox the Dixie Highway was closed being under construction. We had to make two detours...of hills and sloughs, bumps and rocks....The next day at the cave we heard lurid tales of what had happened to cars on that road. One party of tourists were out all night on it and had to be towed back to Louisville the next day!

It was ten o'clock when we got to Cave City....

I find it difficult to write sanely of Mammoth Cave. It cast a spell upon me and I shall be its prisoner forever, no matter where I live. I have been homesick for it ever since I left it. It cannot be described.

If Mammoth Cave were in the Old World what legends and myths would have pertained to it. Epics would have been written on it—operas composed about it....

The first thing to do was rent and don the "Cave costume." When I put mine on Bertie declared I had it hindbefore. Agreeing, I reversed it. But it was hindbefore-er than ever. So I turned it again. One bloomer leg was so loose it insisted on slipping down to my ankle. I couldn't be continually pulling it up so I went through Mammoth Cave with one leg up and 'tother leg down. I must have looked very weird. But everything there was weird and nobody cared what anybody else had on.

There were about forty in our party, with two guides—negroes. Each pair of us was given one of the odd little lanterns used in the cave. Some caves in that region are lighted with electric light. I am glad Mammoth Cave is not. Half its charm, I think, is due to those flickering little lights and the resultant shadows; and nothing in the cave impressed me more than that long line of lanterns strung out along a river bank in that Stygian gloom or winding up the long flights of rock stairs, or flickering through stately palaces of eternal night.

We went down the pine clad hills by flights of stairs to the steep valley where the mouth of the cave is. We went down another long flight of stairs to the grated iron door. Here a tremendous wind met us—a terrific wind, seeming by contrast with the sultry air of the Kentucky afternoon as icy cold as "the wind that blows between the stars"—and yet a clean, lovely wind. It is only just at the entrance you meet it. In winter, I understand, it blows inward. The temperature in the cave itself is the same the year round—54 degrees. It is just comfortable and the air is peculiarly bracing and pure—not in the least damp or mouldy as I think I half expected in a realm 300 feet underground.

I also had a vague idea that Mammoth Cave was simply one enormous cave with various avenues leading out of it. But it is a series of caves, all enormous, connected with each other by all sorts of passages—great shadowy, mysterious avenues—winding stairs cut out of solid rock—narrow passages—low passages—tiny slits through which you can hardly squeeze. On that first route we walked five and a half miles and it seemed but a stroll for the love we had for it....

All my life I have heard preachers and teachers holding up the fish in the rivers of Mammoth Cave as horrible examples of what happened to creatures who neglected to use and cultivate their powers—they lost 'em. The fish in Mammoth Cave are blind—eyeless. One variety has a place for eyes but no eyes; another variety, still further sunk in sloth and wickedness have not even a place for eyes. And they are quite white....

The moments I enjoyed most in the Cave were those when Bertie and I lingered a minute or two behind the others and stood together in silence looking about us. Then we "sensed" the Cave—its grandeur, its compelling charm—its magic—its devilry. For it isn't altogether holy. No, it is a very Pagan place. The old gods of the underworld rule it....

We had supper—a delightful meal of chicken and corn fritters and hot biscuits in a primitive dining room. We had chicken for every meal at Mammoth Cave. The hens in that region must go in terror of their lives. But it was delicious.

Our rooms were small and hot. But we slept, oh, yes, we slept. You sleep after you have been through Mammoth Cave. Stuart slept outside under the pines and I envied him but was not small enough to curl up on the seat of the car as he did. He was up bright and early and declared he was "hungry for the Cave." We all felt that way. Even Ewan was captivated by Mammoth Cave—and Ewan seldom seems to take much pleasure in the things that please others. I may say in passing that Ewan was perfectly well all through our trip and enjoyed himself....

We left the cave after dinner and motored to Hodgenville—almost every place in the south is a "ville." We went by the Jackson highway. It was not as bad as that detour but it was next to it in my Expurgatorious Index of awful roads. Most of it was the "cobblestone" variety. We toiled slowly over it, wondering how the natives put up with such roads at all. Once in a long while we would come suddenly and unexpectedly on a wee bit of new macadam or cement—perhaps a mile or two. We would pounce on it with a simultaneous yell of delight and tear over it like mad.

And yet those roads were unbelievably beautiful. I shall forget their awfulness before I forget their loveliness....

Wednesday we reached Buffalo and crossed over. "Ah, there's *something* in Canadian air," said Ewan exultantly as we "hit the pike." It was cool, at least, and that was delightful after the sultriness of Ohio and New York. We got to Niagara at sunset—and the gods handed us out another special favor.

A thunderstorm came up—the worst electric storm that has been known at Niagara for thirty-seven years. We saw another indescribable thing—the Horseshoe Falls by lightning....for half an hour Bertie and I sat there, spellbound, rapt, gazing on such a sight as we had never seen or deemed it possible to see—the great Canadian fall, lying under the ghostly shimmering blue-white gleam of that lightning while athwart the mist tore zigzags of living flame as if some god were amusing himself hurling thunderbolts into the abyss. No, I shall never see the like of that again. But I have seen it once....

The next day was fine, cool and altogether delightful. We motored home by lakes of faint blue loveliness and through contented old harvest meadows, mellowly bright and serene....

All along our route we were beset with signs offering hot dogs. None of us had ever eaten hot dogs and we decided that before the trip was over we *must* sample a hot dog. But we kept putting it off from day to day in hopes of cooler weather and now on our last day it was "now or never." Luckily the day was cool and we were quite hungry. So we pulled up by a roadside booth and ordered hot dogs for all. We enjoyed them too.

Does some incredibly ignorant great grandchild demand "What is a hot dog?"

A hot dog is simply a savoury fried sausage, smoking from the pan, imprisoned between the two halves of a fresh roll. I recommend them if you are hungry.

We got home Thursday night. And there was a big fat letter from Rollins for me.

I wonder if the time will ever come when it will be possible for me to come home from a trip without the dread of finding a letter about that miserable lawsuit....

It was a bill from Briesin and Schrenck for a thousand dollars for getting that suit dismissed. I really think that is exorbitant for so little work. What on earth would it have been if we had had to fight the suit? There was also another bill for $400 from Rollins but this was reasonable for the work he did.

Well, I can pay it, but it will leave me woefully short of ready cash for the year....

Monday, Aug. 18, 1924
Mr. Gray told Ewan yesterday that the feeling in Leaskdale was strong against Union. Also Will Sellers said there was a great deal of opposition to it in Zephyr. The fact is, each person interprets the situation in the terms of his own prepossession. It is impossible to say which way it will go....

Neither Ewan nor I try to influence the people in any way, either for or against, nor ever have. We believe they should be left free to decide for themselves....

Tuesday, Aug. 19, 1924
Leaskdale, Ont.
I began work today on that short story for *The Delineator.* This evening when we were out calling I noticed to my horror that Ewan's head was bothering him again. I gave him a thyroid tablet. Last spring I decided that Ewan has always been a sub-thyroid and that any depressing event or situation, as well as epochal periods in his sex life, interfered with the functioning of the thyroid gland still further and produced his attacks of melancholia. I decided that when his next attack came on I would try the effect of some careful doses of thyroid.

Sunday, Aug. 24, 1924
....Tonight we thrashed out the Union problem. Ewan said he had made up his mind to remain in the Presbyterian church. I was glad to hear him say this. I have never tried to influence his decision and have told him I would of course follow him whatever course he took. As a minister's wife, there could be nothing else for me to do.

There is some talk of Leaskdale uniting with Mt. Albert if Zephyr leaves it in the lurch. This would make a good strong congregation. The worst drawback would be the distance apart—twelve miles. And in any case, Ewan would probably have to resign. Mt. Albert would want to choose its own minister. So, no matter where I look, I can see no chance of anything save of being torn up by the roots. And that is a process that is always very painful to me. Especially when one hasn't the least idea where one will be transplanted to.

Monday, Sept. 1, 1924
The Manse, Leaskdale
This has been a very busy week filled with many small duties. I got a good idea for the second story of the *Emily* series early in the week and have been working at it. Ewan has been very well lately and does not say his prayers. Is it the effect of the thyroid extract or did it just happen so?....

Stuart is reading *Kilmeny* today and is very much absorbed in it. He runs to me every few minutes to read me some passage that has struck his fancy....

Thursday, Sept. 11, 1924
In 1892 or thereabouts, when I was a very young girl, the United States and Canada were convulsed over the famous "Lizzie Borden" murder case in Fall River, Mass. The papers were full of it and people all over North America who had never heard of Lizzie Borden took sides for and against her and thrashed the case out day after day. I remember some of the Cavendish boys driving home from prayer meeting one night singing that horrible quatrain which was broadcast at the time.

> "Lizzie Borden took an axe
> And gave her mother forty whacks,
> And when she saw what she had done
> She gave her father forty one."

Lizzie Borden was found not guilty and returned home. From that day to this I have never heard or seen reference to her. A few days ago something, I do not remember what, recalled her to my mind and I thought, "I wonder if she is living still and if she was or was not guilty." The very next day, by one of those curious coincidences that so frequently happen, I read a review of a new book bearing the idyllic title *Studies in Murder*, in which one of the cases described was the Borden Murder. I sent for it and this evening I read it.

There is no doubt in my mind that Lizzie Borden was guilty. Because there was simply no one else who *could* have committed the double murder. And yet it is almost as impossible to believe that she *could* have done it. It is one of the most remarkable—nay, *the* most remarkable—psychological problems I have ever read of. My own idea is that Lizzie Borden murdered her father and stepmother and that the servant girl, Bridget, was an accessory after the fact, being bribed by Lizzie to help her conceal or destroy all traces of the crime. This would account for the fact that no trace of blood was found on Lizzie Borden's clothing and no instrument discovered that could be shown to have inflicted the wounds. For there was really no scrap of *real* evidence at the trial to connect Lizzie Borden with the murder. One cannot blame the jury for finding her not guilty. Yet guilty she must have been.

She is living today, in a comfortable home, on the money inherited from her murdered father. She must now be about 64 years old. Will she ever confess? Has she ever felt remorse for her crime? I confess I would like to see this woman—talk with her.

Another interesting case in the book, "Mate Bram," had a double interest for me in the fact that the lawyer for the defence was my own dear Mr. Asa P. French. Really, Mr. French is to be congratulated on his clients. He seems to have a liking for defending scoundrels.

Friday, October 10, 1924
I went up to North Bay Tuesday and spent Wednesday there. Spoke to the girls in the Convent school in the forenoon. They gave me a bouquet of roses in a handpainted vase. The Reverend Mother and Sister St. John were very sweet and interesting women. In the afternoon I had a motor drive, spoke to the students in the Collegiate and then to the Canadian club. Left North Bay on the night train, expecting to be in Toronto by seven and catch the morning train out home— which I was very anxious to do, as I felt that I had so much work to do at home that I must get back as quickly as possible. So much for my plans.

A short distance from North Bay we came up to a disabled freight train, which had lost a wheel off its locomotive. We were hung up six hours and as a result never reached Toronto until twelve. There was no way of getting anything to eat till we reached Allandale at ten, when we were given a few minutes at a restaurant there. But by this time I was past eating and could not swallow a mouthful. By the time we reached Toronto I had a dreadful headache and the very thought of food nauseated me. I went to the Walker, got a room, took aspirin and went to bed. I fell asleep and slept till six when I woke up, feeling quite all right but inclined to be very disgruntled over missing my train home and losing a day.

Now, mark! Had I caught that train home I would not have had a wonderful pleasure.

After I got some dinner—the first food I had eaten since supper the evening before—I decided that I would go to see George Bernard Shaw's play, *Saint Joan.* I had been wishing to see it but had not supposed it possible. I saw it—and never did I have such an evening of enjoyment. Julia Arthur played Joan. The critics praised her but I cannot echo their praises. Joan was never such a pink-and-white golden haired, brilliant, beautifully clad person. Only when I shut my eyes and listened to her wonderful golden voice did I get the conviction of the Maid. But the rest of the cast—the Archbishop of Rheims, the Bishop of Beauvais, the Earl of Warwick, Parson Stogumber, the Chief Inquisitor and above all the Dauphin were exceedingly good. Oh, if Frede could only have been sitting beside me while I saw that play.

One thing impressed me especially—the beauty of the costumes of that age.

Even the suits of armour, which I had always supposed must be awkward heavy things were beautiful. In the epilogue when "a gentleman of 1920" appeared, clad in the conventional costume of today, with a high crowned beaver hat, he looked so absurd and eccentric that I joined sincerely in the laughter of the assembled ghosts at his appearance.

Shaw's play is a ripe and wonderful thing; but I don't think his Joan is the real Joan either. That Joan is still an enigma....

Sunday, October 12, 1924
The Manse
I have been re-reading Frede's letters. I have not read them since the winter she died. But I have been so hungry for her lately—especially since seeing *Saint Joan*—that I had to get out the letters. Last night when I went to bed I thought I would read just one. Then I said "Just one more"—and that went on till twelve o'clock. It was always "just one more." I was like a famished creature pleading for just one more bite of food.

In one way Frede was never as good a letter writer as Stella. She had not Stella's knack of filling in all the small details which are so interesting. Frede only "hit the high spots" where she was telling you about anything—her letters were impressionistic to the last degree. But she had, more than anyone I ever knew, the power of infusing her personality into her letters. Such letters have a terrible resurrective power. While I read them Frede sat before me in the flesh. I saw her smile, heard her ready laugh, heard her voice uttering those poignant sentences. It was impossible then to believe her dead—impossible not to feel that she was still somewhere in the world and that I was reading a letter that had just come from her, still warm with the touch of her hand.

There is a great sadness in some of her letters. When you met Frede she was always so bright and funny that you never suspected the undercurrent of unhappiness and sorrow. But it betrayed itself in her letters. Both Frede and I hated to wear our hearts on our sleeves—to take the world into our confidence. It was part of our code that we must always present a front of laughter and satisfaction. Even with each other, as a rule, we kept this up. Nay, with each other it was not pretence—it was reality. For so dear we were to each other, such pleasure and satisfaction we found in each other's company that for the time at least we *were* happy and joyous, knowing neither loneliness nor disappointment nor regret.

Sunday, Oct. 17, 1924
Today we motored to Stouffville, through a brilliant sunlit autumn landscape to have lunch with Mr. and Mrs. MacCullough. Dr. and Mrs. Freel were there too and we had a very enjoyable time. It is very nice to meet people now and then who can talk of something besides crops and Church Union.

I had a letter from Myrtle Webb when I got home. In it she said "About a month ago John F. Macneill was thrown from a truck wagon and very badly hurt. He is only now getting able to move a little."

The curious thing about this is that about a month ago I had a very vivid dream about Uncle John. I dreamed that he fell off his barn loft and was very badly hurt. At first they thought he was killed; then one of the men who were carrying him out of the barn said to me, "He is not killed, only badly injured." When I woke I told Ewan the dream and said I felt sure I would hear that Uncle John had met with some accident.

And yet there are people who will say there is nothing in dreams. Well, I thought that myself once. I used to laugh at it as mere superstition. But I know better now. I have had too many telepathic and predictive dreams to doubt....

Monday, Oct. 20, 1924
"How easy it is to spoil a day"—the line from an old bit of newspaper verse comes back to me. Today was spoiled for me by the fact that Chester made only 30% in his composition exam.—the lowest but one in the school. It is a bit of irony on Fate's part that the son of L.M. Montgomery should do so poorly in composition. Of course Ewan has no gift or knack of literary composition whatever—I don't think I ever knew a person who had less. But I had hoped that Chester would at least inherit enough of my power of expression to get along respectably in his classes, even if he did not possess it to the full.

Stuart has been reading my old short stories lately—the "pot boilers" I wrote so many years ago. He has just gravely asked if I will "leave them to him in my will."

Wednesday, Oct. 22, 1924
We have had an ideal October. So like my first October here thirteen years ago. Tonight was clear, crisp, starlit. The boys had raked up the fallen leaves and Lily was having a bonfire of them outside the gate. But Chester and I prowled up and down the road star-hunting. We re-found Aquarius, Fomalhaut, Aquila, Corona, the Pleiades and the Hyades....

I have been re-reading Mrs. Gaskell's wonderful life of Charlotte Brontë. It is a fascinating book. Perhaps because it is so full of mystery—the mystery of those three strange Brontë women—those "gray sisters" and their weird lives....

I can well remember the impression *Jane Eyre* made on me when I first read it—an impression that has remained and deepened with every re-perusal.

It is customary to regret Charlotte Brontë's death as premature. I doubt it. I doubt if she would have added to her literary fame had she lived. Resplendent as her genius was it had a narrow range and I think she had reached its limit. She could not have gone on forever writing *Jane Eyres* and *Villettes* and there was nothing in her life and experience to fit her for writing anything else.

Emily Brontë is a mysterious figure. The impression of her left from reading the *Life* is an unpleasant one. She seemed to have no friends. Yet Charlotte loved her devotedly and said she drew her character of "Shirley" from Emily. The picture drawn of her stubborn, gallant, senseless heroic fight against death is a wonderful one. Nothing in literature is more poignant and pathetic than her sudden, useless capitulation at the last moment—"If you call a doctor I will see him now." Too late—too late. But probably no doctor could have saved her. Her genius was really greater than Charlotte's—and even narrower. But the world did not know it when she died. Strange Emily Brontë.

There was a marked masochistic strain in Charlotte Brontë—revealing itself mentally not physically. This accounts for "Rochester." He was exactly the tyrant a woman with such a strain in her would have loved, delighting in the pain he inflicted on her. And this same tendency was the cause of her cruelty to "Lucy Snowe"—who was herself. She persecutes "Lucy" all through *Villette* and drowns her lover rather than let the poor soul have a chance of happiness. I can't forgive Charlotte Brontë for killing off M. Paul Emmanuel. I don't know whether I like "Lucy Snowe" or not—but I am always consumed with pity for and sympathy with her, whereas Charlotte delights in tormenting her—a sort of spiritual, vicarious self-flagellation.

Speaking of masochism:—I think that normally I am entirely free from it. But all through the years of my sex life there was always one day or two every month when I became very nervous and somewhat depressed. During this time a mental masochistic tendency made its appearance in me and I heaped all sorts of misfortunes on myself in imagination—*and enjoyed it.* At such times I could not bear to imagine the gay and brilliant adventures I ordinarily revelled in. Pleasure became pain and pain pleasure—as if my nature were turned inside out....

Thursday, Oct. 23, 1924
The Manse, Leaskdale
Today was one of mild excitement in our small burg. The plebiscite election was held. We are a pretty "dry" community—in more senses than one. Out of one hundred and twenty eight votes polled only sixteen were wet. We have been conducting an intensive campaign of exhorting and canvassing for weeks and I am glad it is over. Personally, I think it a pity mankind cannot be the master and not the slave. But since it is so weak we must sheer it up with props like the O.T.A. and similar measures....

Friday, Oct. 24, 1924
The O.T.A. has carried—though by a very much smaller majority than last time.

We are busy housecleaning. I keep wondering rather sorrowfully if this is the last time I shall clean this old manse....

I had a letter from Kate today. She is to be married on November 19 to a Scotchman named Sinclair McKay. Ila wrote me several years ago about their engagement. I don't think he is much of a match from a worldly point of view but he may be very nice. Kate is 36—just the age I was when I married. I remember how her mother used to gibe at "girls who didn't go off very soon." I cannot feel much interest in the marriage somehow....

Ewan and I motored over to Zephyr tonight. The drive was enjoyable. As we spun along people were burning piles of potato stalks in the fields and the night seemed full of magic and engaging devilry. Bonfires in the darkness are always pagan and belong to the old charming gods.

Something else belongs to them too—the thistles and mulleins along the road in the car-light. In daylight they are thistles and mulleins. In car-light they are troops of Pan. Such eerie, gnomish things and creatures flashing up out of the shadows and sinking back again as we go by. They make our autumn roads a continual procession through elfland.

Sandwiched in between these two drives were two or three calls where Church Union was the most cheerful subject discussed. Oh, for a lodge in some vast wilderness where the name of Union was never heard and the thought of Union never thunk!

Saturday, Oct. 25, 1924
These are the days of raking leaves and burning them at night. The boys rake them up when they come from school and throw them over the fence on the roadside. Then we burn them by starlight. Tonight we had a corn-roast and the boys had some of their boy chums over. We sat on boxes around the fires and ate our roasted corn and candy, told jokes, sang community songs and had a very hilarious time. Overhead the Eagle flew and off in the south Fomalhaut smouldered in the autumn mists. I wonder if around those mighty suns revolve planets whereon are inhabitants who have corn-roasts. But it was a nice bit of fooling and I enjoyed it and was as crazy as the rest of them.

Wednesday, Oct. 29, 1924
....I have been re-reading *The Gayworthys* by Mrs. Whitney. She had a great vogue when I was young but nobody reads her now apparently. Yet *The Gayworthys* is a very charming book. Mrs. Whitney preaches and moralizes too much but between the preaching and moralizing her stories are delightful. At least *The Gayworthys* is. I enjoyed it for three reasons. 1. It brought back the old days when I first read it many years ago. 2. It is clean, wholesome, entertaining; 3. Mrs. Whitney had the gift, for which all other shortcomings are forgiven, of making her characters live. You feel they are real people whom you know. Therefore every trivial fact about them is interesting. Mrs. Whitney is at her best in describing country life. She bores you when she takes to the sea and the town. "Hilbury" seems to me a place I have lived in. "Jane Gair" is a masterpiece. If Anthony Trollope or Jane Austen had created her she would be one of the famous women of literature, instead of being forgotten by all save a few who like myself read and loved the book of old....

Thursday, Oct. 30, 1924
Today I was amazed and alarmed by a bulky letter from the "L.C. Page Co." I opened it gingerly. It was a screed from George Page—Louis knows better than to write me!—asking me if I would "co-operate" with them in getting out a little brochure of my life and literary career, to be used for the information for customers seeking it.

I can't understand the psychology of those men. Here they have been hounding me through the U.S. courts for years and at this very moment have a suit against me in New York—a mere "spite" suit—and have tied up my royalties and worried me half to death. And yet they coolly ask me to help them get up something solely for their own benefit and convenience—for I get nothing out of it....

Wednesday, Nov. 5, 1924
The Manse, Leaskdale
Ewan is wobbling again in regard to Church Union. I expected that when his melancholia returned. He has never any energy then. Well, I am ceasing to care. What matter what church he is in? If he continues as he has been he will have to give up the ministry. I am so sick of the whole thing—the sordid struggle between "Unionists" and "Antis"—the ceaseless battle in the papers, the bitterness and hard feeling engendered. It is horrible and if God ever does laugh He must be laughing now. What things are done and said in His Name!....

Sunday, Nov. 9, 1924
The Manse, Leaskdale
I fancy that few people in Leaskdale will ever forget this Thanksgiving Sunday....

The church was full. The devotional exercises were over. Ewan announced his text; but his sermon has not been preached.

Reuben Harrison ran in, white-faced, whispered to his father and Alex Mustard who got up and went out. Already Reuben's entrance is become shrouded in myth and legend. Some people aver he had his hat on. Others aver he had not. Some declare he was "white as chalk." Others are equally certain he was "red as fire." So much for evidence.

A whisper flew over the congregation like a wind—or flame. "Will Cook's house was on fire." In two minutes the church was empty and a stream of cars was pouring in along the side road. Ewan got our car and we started, too, desperately hoping that the fire might be only in a small way and easily conquered.

Will Cook has been one of our problems for the last two years. Ever since the shock of his father's death he has been "melancholy." Very like Ewan in fact. Wouldn't work—worried over imaginary financial difficulties instead of theological ones. He was worse than E. in some ways—tried to hang himself once. Yet out in company nobody would have supposed there was anything wrong with him. His poor wife has had a dreadful life of it these two years.

About two months ago Will suddenly got well. He began to work and seemed entirely normal. We were all glad and relieved.

And now this! It would, we feared, set him back worse than ever.

As we whirled up the hill by the schoolhouse we saw the house, away up on the hill along the sixth. It was wrapped in flame—flames were pouring from the roof. Nothing could be done.

The contents were saved. We could do no good and E. had to go to Zephyr so we came home and I got E. his dinner. I was alone all the afternoon as Lily was over at Will's....

Sunday, Nov. 23, 1924
I went in to Toronto last Monday morning for a shopping spree. I enjoyed the

first three days very much. I like shopping. Those big department stores delight me. I like to buy pretty things and take them away from the glitter and noise to a real home. All this at first. Then I get tired and loathe the stores with their noise and mobs.

I went to Hamilton Thursday night and spoke to the Business Women's Club there. I had a very nice time. The reporters descended on me in swarms and all wanted to know what I thought of the present day girl, smoking for women—and *Flaming Youth*. I said that I thought the present day girl exactly like the girl of yesterday—the only difference being that the girls of today *did* what we of yesterday *wanted* to. I said I thought smoking was harmless but made women look ugly; and that *Flaming Youth* was a book haunted by the imaginations of hell. They reported me with fair accuracy except that one lady wrote me down as saying that smoking did no harm—in moderation.

One undertook to describe me and my dress: "Often when a woman carves for herself a definite and very prominent place in the world of art or literature the effort by which she has attained that position leaves its mark on her. Mrs. Macdonald is an exception. When she graciously permitted the *Spectator* to interview her at the Connaught last night the interviewer found her altogether a delightful person—rather above medium height, with thick hair slightly graying, which she wore waved and coiled becomingly about her well-shaped head. Her face was unlined and she smiled easily. She wore a frock of delicate lavender flowered silk, caught at one side with a rhinestone buckle. Her hat was of gold cloth with lace falling softly over her face. An exquisite scarf of gold lace was about her shoulders and her brown satin slippers were buckled with rhinestones. The large pearls which she wore in her ears accentuated the clear whiteness of her skin."

Now, over and against the above ought to be set a description of me cleaning out the horse stable last spring or "rastling" with the furnace this fall!!

Friday I lunched with Messrs. McClelland and Stewart and spoke to the girls at McMaster. Yesterday I came home and went to bed with a horrible cold. When I got home I found—of course—a letter from Rollins. But it was only to say he had just argued our case before the Supreme Court that day....

Mon., Nov. 24, 1924
....The Union battle rages wordily still. I am sick of it. I am training a lot of boys and a lot of girls in two dialogues for the S.S. concert. And I am sick of that. I cough and sniffle constantly—and I'm sick of that. There are some things I am *not* sick of however and one of them is Jane Austen's novels. I've been reading *Emma*. When I think of it and *Flaming Youth* the contrast is as between a mad-house and a decent home.

Wednesday, Nov. 26, 1924
Was busy all day preparing to have the Dyers to supper tonight. He is the new minister at Greenbank and we have hitherto liked them both quite well, though Mrs. D. is shallow and he is a conceited youth who has no aversion to giving

advice to older and more experienced men. I like entertaining and I looked forward to a pleasant evening. It was a nightmare. Dyer spoiled supper by arguing furiously with Ewan about Union through the whole meal. Dyer is an apostate. He was a strong Anti while he was in Mt. Albert, an Anti congregation. Now that he is in Greenbank, a Union charge, he has turned his coat and like all renegades is determined that everyone also should follow his example. He did more to confirm Ewan in his Anti-ism than all the Anti arguments have done. Ewan has no liking for being herded along a road, willy nilly, by brash young ministers who "know it all."

The Dyers brought 3 children under six and I thought they'd tear the house down. Mrs. Dyer and I simply could not converse at all and finally I gave up the attempt. Dyer sat calmly there and preached Union without making the slightest attempt to control or check his riotous offspring until they wound up by smashing literally in pieces one of my good Hepplewhite parlor chairs. Then he rebuked them mildly. I was thankful to see the last of them, and I am so exhausted that my thoughts are flying around in my head without order or sequence. I know I shall not sleep.

Thursday, Nov. 27, 1924
I have been giving Ewan thyroid for a month—three tablets a week. He still keeps dull and I cannot see any effect whatever. But it is possible that he might be much worse without them. I am going to stop giving them for a month and note if there is any change in him, either for the worse or better. I dread the winter so. I am so afraid he will have another attack like last year. I *cannot* face it....

But it is a nice thing to feel a dainty little cat jump up on your bed in the dark and snuggle down beside you, purring. That happened last night. And there are some other nice things. I am finding much pleasure writing my new book *The Blue Castle* and getting ready to write Emily III. All these things help. But sometimes it seems to me as if my life now were little else than a search for anodynes. There is always some gnawing mental pain or anxiety to be temporarily obliterated by an opiate.

Saturday, Nov. 28, 1924
This evening after everyone was in bed I read over a packet of Will P.'s letters—and could not believe they were written thirty years ago by a boy who died twenty seven years ago. There was for me a bitter delight in them. They brought back all those laughing boys and girls of the long ago. They were full of our old jokes and phrases and catchwords—that have no meaning now to anybody in the world but me.

Saturday, Dec. 6, 1924
The Manse, Leaskdale, Ont.
This has been, I think, the "darkest" week I ever put in. I mean it literally not figuratively. Almost every day has been so cloudy that it was absolutely

necessary to light the lamp at eleven in the forenoon to see to write—and at four in the afternoon to see to do anything. This of course is not stimulating and disagreeable things are harder to bear in the absence of light.

We are practising for our annual nightmare—the S.S. concert. I go on Saturday afternoons to the general practice at the church to help generally and keep the children in order. Not an easy task. There are three or four boys from poor and ignorant families that are as bad and "nasty" as they can be and incite the others to riot. The girls of the concert committee can't do a thing with them so I have to go to overawe them. Which I do effectually.

Then I am drilling the girls in one dialogue and the boys in another. They meet here alternate evenings to practice and hammer nails in my coffin. The boys are doing fairly well. Perhaps because Chester and Stuart are in it and, knowing by grace something of acting, incite the others to emulation. But the girls seem hopeless. The only two who have any idea of expression and acting have such weak voices. It seems wasted time to work with them. And I have so much to do....

Ewan had a Session meeting Thursday evening to arrange for the Vote on Union. He says he thinks there is no doubt Leaskdale will go Presbyterian. I wish we could feel as sure of Zephyr. Counting vote by vote we think Union will lose. But I will not hope it. Hope has fooled me too often. The Session in Z. are for Union. But that does not matter especially as they are men who have always been out of sympathy with the congregation on every point and have little or no influence over it. They have blocked Ewan consistently and persistently ever since he came in any effort to build up the congregation or inspire it. They don't believe in prayer-meetings or special meetings of any kind. They never approved of our Guild. They are bitterly "down" on Christmas trees or Sunday School concerts. This year I offered diplomas in Zephyr S.S. and the result has been an increased attendance but that does not allay their opposition. The Leaskdale Session has always been so different. Ewan has found it a pleasure to work with them.

I have been re-reading *John Ward, Preacher.* It is years since I read it. I enjoyed it. The parts I like best are those dealing with the Ashurst life and people....The theological bogies she destroys are powerless nowadays but once they were of power and she should have recognized her position. But then Margaret Deland would have had no story.

Hugh Walpole's *The Old Ladies* is a very gripping book and I enjoyed it. Its truth is painful. There must be thousands of just such unhappy women. I feel honestly ashamed of my growls. But for how long will I be ashamed?

Sunday, Dec. 14, 1924
The Manse, Leaskdale

It is snowing thickly today and is very cold. I fear winter is really settling in. I wish it could have kept away until all the concerts are over.

Today the announcement of the meeting to consider the vote was read in church. It must come in two or three weeks now. As Ewan said the other day,

"Isn't it like a nightmare?" It truly has been. The bitterness and controversy—the unbridled letters from both sides filling the daily papers. It is all disgusting and disheartening. The Unionists have been up to some very dirty propaganda in this Presbytery. There is no doubt that the Unionists, whether they realize it or not, are trying to establish a clerical domination over the people of the church, who are simply to do what they are told and make no protest. In all old established churches there is always a tendency to this and in the "United Church" the drift is very pronounced and will become intensified. But it is too late in the day of history for that. The human mind will not submit again to such tyranny. Nevertheless the condition of our disrupted church is deplorable.

I wonder if it would be such a terrible thing if "the church" ceased to influence people at all. I do not think so. The Spirit of God no longer works through the church for humanity. It did once but it has worn out its instrument and dropped it. Today it is working through Science. That is the real reason for all the "problems" we hear so much of in regard to "the church." The "leaders" are trying to galvanize into a semblance of life something from which life has departed....

The Manse, Leaskdale, Ont.
Sunday, Dec. 28, 1924
These past two weeks have been one of those nightmares of which the recent years have been so full. Nothing in 1924 was worse except those terrible two weeks with Ewan last March.

Monday, Dec. 15 led off in the dance of devilry. It was a bitter cold day and we went to Uxbridge in the morning. Passing the window of a drug store I saw a *Delineator* hanging up with my name on the cover as a noted contributor. That is the first time it has happened in magazinedom. How it would have delighted me twenty years ago! "The wished-for comes too late."

After dinner the mail came. For me there was a great brown full envelope from Mr. Rollins—exactly the sort of parcel I would expect the decision of the Supreme Court to be enclosed in. I took it for such and decided I must not open it that day. If the news were bad it would upset me mentally and render the school concert that night a misery. So I locked it away in the desk and tried to forget it but could not. It spoiled the afternoon and evening for me....

Tuesday Ewan went to Presbytery. At first I had decided not to open Rollins' letter until Wednesday morning, as I had to go to the Zephyr Sunday School concert at night and take part and did not wish to be unnerved for it. But after dinner I suddenly resolved to open it and learn the worst. It was unnerving me as it was, rendering me unsettled and apprehensive and quite unable to settle down to work. So I got out the packet, reminded myself that even if I had lost the appeal the affair would be ended and that would be a blessing—gathered up my courage—slit it desperately open.

What did I find?

A copy of the *Boston Evening Post* with a marked paragraph regarding a certain book which Mr. Rollins thought I might find interesting!

So much for my twenty-four restless hours and my desperate resolution!...

I might here mention that the crossword puzzle infection which has swept like an epidemic over North America has at last struck Leaskdale manse in its most virulent form. Chester developed the first attack. For several days he worried me to death with appeals for "words" and as I had a thousand things to do I felt I could not spare the time to puzzle over them. Then, all at once, the germ laid *me* low. I became as idiotic as Chester and stole time from eating and sleeping to solve crossword puzzles. It is maddening to find oneself the slave of such a silly craze. But I suppose the fever will run the course and leave me convalescent. I really think it is a capital amusement for children. It must have a tendency to enrich their vocabulary and fasten a great deal of information in their minds which might never otherwise be obtained. But for such as me crossword puzzles are a device of the devil!...

Thursday, Dec. 18, was fine and coldish. I had a letter from Ella at last—the first since I was in Park Corner and full of complaints and some innuendoes. Oh, I *would* like to get a real cheerful letter from *somebody*! I am getting that I am afraid to open a letter—*any* letter. I get rather "fed-up" with having everybody's troubles heaped on my own. This is what comes of a certain resolution I made when I was a very young girl. To wit:—that I would never inflict the tale of my woes and worries on other people, who had plenty of their own to bear. I wrote them out in this journal but to the world and to my friends I invariably presented a smiling front. Now, the consequence has been that I am supposed never to *have* any troubles or anxieties—I never get any sympathy—and everybody hastens to dump their own upon me. No, in my present mood of discouragement and protest I aver that it doesn't pay to be invariably cheerful.

Neither do I altogether believe that it is a wholly desirable thing to have a sense of humor. Most women have not and the lack saves them. The few who possess it have no refuge from the merciless truth about themselves. They cannot think themselves perennially misunderstood. They cannot revel in self-pity. They cannot comfortably damn everyone who differs from them. No, we women with a sense of humor are not to be envied it!...

Lily took to bed with "tonsillitis"!?

She was in bed for three days. I had everything to do and her to wait upon. Ewan being away I had to attend the furnace. By Friday night I was too tired to sleep. Lily wanted the doctor in the afternoon—she had about a dozen different diseases besides "tonsillitis"—a new one every half hour. The doctor came—said there was no tonsillitis about her—merely a sore throat and a slight temperature. She was to stay in bed a few days and she would be all right....

Sunday night my throat was worse and I had a bad night with cystitis. It is years since I have had an attack. It came on suddenly as it always does and all the week I have been most miserable with it. It seems a year since last Sunday. I have never had any ailment which makes me more abjectly miserable for the time being. Ewan had to go away again Monday morning on church business and did not get back until Tuesday night. Lily got up but only wandered around complaining of everything. The day was gloomy and cold, and the night most wretched. I could not sleep and my ailment got on my nerves to an unbearable extent. All Tuesday forenoon I was most miserable and when at ten a 'phone came saying that a couple of men from Toronto were on their way to see me re the reorganization of an insurance company in which I am shareholder, I felt that I could *not* see them. Yet it was necessary that I should. Fortunately I felt much better in the afternoon and got my conference over without too much misery. When they had gone Ewan came home and opened a letter that had come in the mail for him. It proved to be from a certain George Furness in Toronto inviting himself out for Xmas. Neither of us knew him. He is the brother of the husband of Ewan's niece on the Island. Ordinarily it would have been all right. I would have been glad to have him come. But now it seemed the last straw. We had been planning since we were both so miserable that we would have a Xmas tree for the boys and postpone our dinner to the last of the week. But now we would have to have it.

By this time I was quite miserable again but had to go to the concert. It was necessary for me to go but it was not necessary for Lily who would have been much wiser to stay at home. Go she must, however. The evening seemed like a long nightmare to me. The concert was good after all in spite of all our trials. The boys did splendidly in their dialogue; and so did the girls. They no longer giggled and ogled but applied themselves to the business in hand and seemed to remember all at once all my hints and instructions. The famous rooster drill was a huge success; but I asked myself if it had been worth while to have all the trouble and worry I had had about it to give that audience five minutes of laughter; and I emphatically answered "no."

Ewan had driven us up and back in the car; but nevertheless I must have caught cold for I had a dreadful night. My throat got so bad it was agony to speak or swallow and at dawn I had the worst attack of cystitis I ever had. Nevertheless I had to get down to work and get the house put in order for the coming guest. After dinner I had to rest awhile, being utterly exhausted. Then I got up, resolved to make a batch of doughnuts, as we had no cake in the house. I planned to begin at two and get through at five but a caller came and stayed an hour. It was almost dark when she left for the day was very cloudy. But I set my teeth and went to work at the doughnuts. Finished them at six. Then supper had to be got ready. I was holding myself to the task by sheer will power but the special demon who had been set to plague me that day had another trick up his sleeve. He must have been a young devil, on probation and very anxious to win promotion. It was not enough that I should have a throat that made every word a torture and that nerve-wracking cystitis besides. I developed a strange sore foot. The soft muscle at the side of the Achilles tendon began to pain me. At first it felt exactly like a bad bruise though I had not hurt it in any way. It got worse rapidly. By the time I had supper ready I could not bear my shoe on. A phone came saying that the train was late and they would not be home till ten. I took off my shoes, lay down and fell asleep at once. When I was wakened by the car coming in I sprang up but fell back with a cry of pain. I could hardly endure to move my foot. Again I set my teeth, welcomed our guest, sat at the supper table, helped wash and put away dishes, then decorated the Xmas tree and put out the presents—all the time hardly able to move. It was now twelve. I got a pail of hot water, soaked my foot for an hour and then went to bed. I do not recall a harder and more exhausting day in my life. I had had no sleep for three nights and I was "all in."

For a mercy I slept well but at seven the cystitis returned and from then till ten I was in misery. My throat was still bad but the pain was gone from my foot which was only very stiff. It was the most peculiar seizure I ever had and I cannot understand it.

Christmas day was bitterly cold. We got the dinner. Then had just time to get dishes washed up before we had to get supper. At nine o'clock I sat down for the first time that day, except at meals. It was a terribly cold night with a high wind—the coldest Christmas we have had for years. I have never put in a more miserable one physically.

But we did not get any Xmas card from Friend Greig. I had been expecting it would come, to add to the enjoyment of the day. But it came not. The little devil had done his best but he forgot that....

1925

Saturday, Jan. 3, 1925
Yesterday at supper Lily who had been in a vile temper all day took something very like a fit of hysterics. I told her I thought she had better go home for a month and have a good rest. I also told her to go to her room and lie down and I would wash the supper dishes. She flung off to her room but she neither rested nor lay down. She strode about her room for two mortal hours, doing I know not what, and then went out somewhere till eleven o'clock.

This afternoon Ewan took her to see the doctor at Sunderland, who couldn't find anything wrong with her. Told her her nerves were bad and to take a rest. She came home and though she could not wash the supper dishes she could go to the rink and skate till eleven o'clock. She told me she only looked on and did not skate but the boys told me she skated all the evening. Chester also overheard Gerald Collins asking her why she hadn't been down to see the hockey match that afternoon and madam responded, "I was in bed while the hockey match was going on," whereas she had been to Sunderland. The fact is one cannot believe a word she says. She has got so on my nerves lately with her tantrums and her dozen new symptoms every day that I shall be heartily glad to get her out of the house. The real secret of her "nerves" is that she has no "beau" and cannot get one apparently. I would really feel sorry for her if she would behave herself but it is difficult to feel much sympathy for such a creature....

The Manse, Leaskdale, Ont.
Monday, Jan. 5, 1925
....This evening I was glancing over some of my old schoolbooks and smiling—a little bitterly I fear—over some of the things scribbled on their fly leaves. I was a shark for writing on my fly leaves in those days. A blank sheet of paper was always a temptation I could not resist. In particular I was addicted to mottoes. There were two I had adopted as my own and I wrote them on the fly leaf of every schoolbook I owned. Well, they were very good mottoes and I believe I can say I have lived up to them. One was,

"In everything you do aim to excel
For what is worth doing is worth doing *well*."

The other was,

"Never say that fate's against you,
That you cannot conquer luck,

> For there's no such thing as either,
> *All* depends on work and pluck."

But I no longer believe whole-heartedly in the latter. I am convinced that there *is* such a thing as "fate" and that sometimes it brings all "work and pluck" to naught....

Thursday, Jan. 8, 1925
Exceedingly busy, getting ready for Guild executive which meets here tomorrow night. I swept and baked cake, cookies and date loaf. And worried over the Union vote at Zephyr and at large. I dreaded the coming of the mail in the same miserable suspense I used to await the war news. But the news was reassuring. The pendulum is swinging our way. And the first congregation in our Presbytery to vote has voted out. Kensington on the Island has voted in. I fear the Island will go mainly Union. They are so far away from the centre of things and do not understand the tremendous issues at stake. But the vote was very close at Kensington and the "antis" are going to organize a Presbyterian church of their own. This is one of the dreadful things about the disruption that has been forced on our church by impatient "leaders" "drunk with sight of power." Congregations torn up or rendered bitter and sullen, old friendships broken, old ties sundered. I could "weep my spirit from my eyes" as I think of it.

Monday, Jan. 12, 1925
Elsie Bushby came last night and will stay with me till Lily can come back. This morning I took up work on my *Blue Castle*....

Tuesday, Jan. 13, 1925
Today the ballotting closed in Leaskdale which voted to remain Presbyterian by 63 to 11. I don't think any of the eleven will leave the church. They are not cranks and there has been no bitterness. But Zephyr is a different matter....

I had a letter from Hattie Gordon Smith today, telling me that she had had to divorce her husband, who had ruined her life by his dissipated habits. I had been thinking for several years that there was something agley there for she has never mentioned him in her letters and recently she has been living with a brother in B.C. "Dear, oh dear," is there no happiness anywhere? Yes, of course there is. Only it doesn't seem to come to me or my friends. Hattie's family—two daughters and a son—are grown-up and married, so she is practically alone in the world.

Tuesday, Jan. 20, 1925
Zephyr voted out—23 to 18. Ewan is very jubilant tonight but I cannot feel so—though I am glad we have won out, technically at least. He thinks the Pros will accept the situation. I cannot think so. Armstrong will never forgive the fact that Ewan prevented him from getting his own way and there are at least two other families who will follow him. If the church could afford to lose them it would be much better off without them for they have always been wet blankets in every

respect. But it cannot—and what will be the result! The church will dissolve—Leaskdale will be left in air—we will have to move. Of course it will not be hard to get a congregation in the Presbyterian church. But I hate the thought of leaving Leaskdale. It is home to me now and though I know there are many nicer places to live, yet *we* cannot be sure of getting one of them.

Stuart, when told that Zephyr had voted out said, "Hurrah! Now we won't have to leave." Stuart is like me. He gets deeply attached to his home spot and dreads the thought of being uprooted. I am sorry for it. I wish he had taken after his father in this respect, instead of me. He would likely be so much happier in his life—unless he can select his home and stay there—what I can never do.

The Guild fry want to get up a play and have asked me to be "coach" again. I must help them—but I dread it, when my mind is so constantly worried and my spirits depressed....

Saturday, Jan. 24, 1925
We all suffered a terrible disappointment this morning—a disappointment in which we had goodly fellowship. For the first time in a very long period Ontario was to have a total eclipse of the sun. It was total in Toronto but not quite so here. It seemed extremely aggravating to be so near a total eclipse and miss it. Had it been summer we could easily have motored in. But the roads and weather are so terrible that I reluctantly gave up the idea of going in by train the night before—as was necessary, as it began at eight.

Alas! Thick clouds covered the sky the whole forenoon. At ten it was so dark in the house we lighted a lamp. Outside it was twilight. That was all. We sorrowfully put away our equipment of smoked glass for the next eclipse—which is due in about a hundred and thirty-five years or thereabouts!

Sunday, January 25, 1925
It is six years since Frede died....

Sunday, Feb. 1, 1925
....I have been reading Dr. McMechan's *Headwaters of Canadian Literature*. One thing in it amused me very much. He said my writings plainly showed the influence of my having "married a minister." I raised a laugh over this. My "marrying a minister" had absolutely no influence in any way upon my writings. Critics generally imagine a good deal of nonsense.

Tuesday Feb. 3, 1925
I sometimes feel like giving up this diary altogether. It seems such a monotonous record of worry and sorrow. But it is the only outlet I have.

I slept poorly last night and could not write today. I had a letter from Mary Beal, full of woes and asking for a further loan of $300. I *would* like to get a cheerful letter from *somebody*. Of course I must lend her the money. But I am miserably short just now of ready cash and this will further inconvenience me. She has not paid the last interest on her former loan yet. But she got a new car last summer!

Well, she is the only congenial friend I have anywhere near me and I want to help her if I can.

Sunday, Feb. 8, 1925
....On Wednesday I finished a novel, *The Blue Castle*—a little comedy for adults. I have enjoyed writing it very much. It seemed a refuge from the cares and worries of my real world. I shall still have a good bit of work revising it....

Tuesday, Feb. 10, 1925
The Manse, Leaskdale
....Today I began a certain bitter task. To wit: making out a list of the things I must do and get for Chester when he goes away to school next fall. It hurts me horribly but it must be done. And it seems so brief a time since he was my wee white baby of that happy summer.

I *do* resent one thing keenly and that is that almost all the years of my boy's childhood which should have been my happiest years I have been so unhappy and worried over Ewan's malady. It has poisoned everything for me. And now Chester must soon go and will never belong really to the home again. Only coming home for vacations.

Sunday, Feb. 14, 1925
Ewan has seemed better again. But I have had a sort of break-down and a return of the condition of mind and nerves I suffered so many years ago that terrible winter down home....

This afternoon Lily phoned over and said she could not come back this week. I asked her bluntly when she expected to come. "Oh, she didn't know—wouldn't be any use if she was here"—and similar vague statements. I hung up the receiver, knowing at last what I have suspected all along. Lily is not coming back—and had no intention of coming back when she left. She has taken this way—and a mean way it is—to get away. I knew she was discontented ever since Earl Thompson stopped driving her around last summer. One day she said to me half jokingly that an aunt of hers had sent her word that she was staying too long in one place—that she'd never "get a man" if she didn't go to a new place.

Well, if poor Lily but knew it I would have been very glad if she had said she wanted to go. I have been wishing she would go for some time. But I feel hurt that she should behave in this way for she has been very well treated here and I had a right to expect squarer dealing from her. But one should not expect anything else from her class. If I can only get another maid all will be for the best. I will keep Elsie if she can stay, though I fear she is not overly strong.

Saturday, Feb. 21, 1925
Had a poor night. Today was dark with showers of rain. I worked at the revision of *The Blue Castle* but always with such an undercurrent of unrest and depression that I could not enjoy it or forget myself in it....

Thursday, Feb. 26, 1925
The Manse, Leaskdale
....Yesterday I got a letter from Lily...In it she said I had "better not depend" on her coming back. So that is settled.

It is best. Lily had been here quite long enough. Yet one cannot live seven years with a person and not feel some pain at parting—at least, I cannot.

Elsie is going to stay. I think she will do fairly well but I do not expect to find her altogether satisfactory. In some ways she will suit better than Lily, in others not so well. And I will have to teach her a great deal. But then she seems very willing to learn. She will not, I think, have the tantrums and cranky spells of Lily but neither will she be the good company Lily was *between* her tantrums. Lily had an almost Josephian sense of *jokes* and was not at all bad company when in good humor. And so devoid is my life of all congenial companionship that even this was a boon and was the strongest reason why I put up so long with other things that were very annoying. So her letter added a little to my depression of yesterday....

I worked all the afternoon at revising *The Blue Castle* but could not lose myself in it or enjoy my work. I tried to sleep but could not. There were no letters—nothing pleasant at all to break the dead monotony of bad weather, worry and neurasthenic wretchedness. I have been most miserable this evening and have felt that it is simply impossible to go on living. I am literally obsessed by the Zephyr situation and the Union mess. My intellect tells me it is nonsense to take it so seriously and presents a score of reasons why it need not worry me at all. But this has no effect on my feelings. I am exactly as I was that miserable winter down home so many years ago. Not quite so bad yet—but I soon shall be if this goes on.

Friday, Feb. 27, 1925
....Mrs. Harrison of the store—a notorious gossip—asked Elsie today if she got up before I did. She said Lily had told her that she was *always up and had all her work done before I got up.*

I have always known Lily told falsehoods but it is hard to believe she could have told so brazen a one as this. She never, since she came here, got up before I did. I have *always* been the first one up, rising at 7.15 and calling Lily. Then I got the boys' school lunches ready while she got breakfast. The rest of the work had to wait until she had gone down to the store and stayed there for the most of an hour gossiping.

It is well she is gone. But I suppose she will tell all kinds of falsehoods about me and my household all over the country. In my present state of nerves this worries me more than it should. But everything worries me now. I am terribly morbid. When I lie awake at night everything looks dark. I cannot see a ray of hope anywhere. I cannot believe that life will ever become livable again. I can see nothing before me but worry of one kind or another all the rest of my life and it takes the heart out of me.

Saturday, Feb. 28, 1925

....We had a slight earthquake shock tonight. At 9.30 I was sitting by the dining room table reading when I felt a queer sensation. I thought "Am I dizzy?" Then I realized that it was my chair that was wobbling, not me. At the same moment the dishes in the cabinet behind me began to rattle and jingle as if someone had collided with it. This went on for several seconds. I wondered if it were an earthquake but was not sure until I 'phoned to Uxbridge and found out that reports of it were coming in from all over the country.

Earthquakes—eclipse of sun—disruption of the Presbyterian church—what further signs and wonders in this year of grace 1925?

Sunday, March 1, 1925
The Manse, Leaskdale
I have felt better today than for a long while. But there is nothing especial to write of and I am going to spend the afternoon and evening copying into this journal for preservation Charles Macneill's old diary. It is such a curious record of the life of a farmer on the North Shore of P.E. Island thirty or forty years ago.

"Old Cavendish Church"

As such it will have a certain value in the future. May lent me the old notebooks when I was home last summer but I have never had time to copy them and I must soon send them back to her....

Monday, Mar. 2, 1925
The Manse, Leaskdale
Elsie and I worked hard all this cold, blustery day, preparing for the big annual missionary "Rally Day" tea here tomorrow. I have rather dreaded it with a new

maid but I think we have got everything pretty well in hand. By night I was very tired but I had to brace up, as we had play practice here tonight. I was a nervous wreck when it was over—and so discouraged. They don't begin to know their parts even yet and what with drilling, prompting, and reading absentee parts I felt exhausted when they left at 11.30, leaving a house all torn-up which had to be put in order before I could go to bed. It is now 12.30 and I have that big day ahead of me tomorrow.

Tuesday, Mar. 3, 1925
Thanks be, it's over. And well over, too. Elsie did very well in spite of inexperience. We worked all the forenoon getting things in readiness. A blue letter to Ewan from Scott of Cannington, bewailing the loss of fifteen Unionists who had left his church in a body and gone over to the Methodists, owing to the interference of outside Unionists, contributed the accustomed note of worry and depression to the day but I had no time to think of it when the women began to come. We had forty here and served three tables. When they were finally gone, the dishes washed and put away, I thought I might have an evening's rest. But I am one of those in whose stars no rest is written. I found old Miss Lindsay on my hands for the night—a wandering old maid of endless tongue who had missed her chance to her interim home and had to stay all night. She talked incessantly until bedtime and I tried to sit quiet and listen. But at moments it seemed to me that I *must* break loose—and run to the end of the world to escape this horrible existence.

I never felt more utterly weary and hopeless in my life than I do tonight. I am like a creature caught in a trap. I cannot get out and somebody is always poking sticks at me through the bars.

Thursday, Mar. 5, 1925
Tuesday night I had to take veronal in order to get a little sleep. So I obtained a few blessed hours of forgetfulness. I spent yesterday morning cleaning the house up. Mail came. A letter from Rollins. No doubt the long-deferred judgment of the Appeal Court. But I dared not open it for I had to go to Zephyr to attend the prayer service of the W.M.S. there and I dared not risk being upset by it.

To Zephyr I went. The service, owing to the Union situation was a period of mixed sensation for me. But outwardly everything went off very well, though I had, as I always have in Zephyr and never anywhere else, the feeling that everyone was looking at me through a microscope.

We had to stay over for the evening for a presentation to some people that are leaving Zephyr, and got home at twelve, played out as usual. However, I had a good sleep and felt better this morning though very tired and fibreless. It would take a score of good sleeps to put me on my feet. And one cannot sleep well if one is always afraid of tomorrow.

As soon as Elsie and Ewan got off to Uxbridge and I was alone I opened Rollins' letter:—

"The Supreme Court has just handed down its decision in your case against the Page Co. The opinion is by the Chief Justice himself and uses up ten type-written pages. He says there is no ambiguity about the contract and that it did not give the defendant the right to publish its 1912 copies; furthermore, that having used the wrong material the defendant should account for profits. The defendant's exceptions were overruled. In other words you are completely successful."

I had a half hour of exhilaration after this but I am too thoroughly depressed for it to last long and soon slumped again. Page and French will only hatch up some new devilry to prolong the agony. It will never be ended....

Friday, March 6, 1925
The Manse, Leaskdale
....I read tonight in a delightful book of astronomy by Camille Flammarion. He is a poet as well as a scientist and his book is charming. As I roamed with him among the stars I felt that, after all, Zephyr is not the universe.

But a pea held close to your eye can blot out the sun! And a grain of dust *in* your eye can make you temporarily oblivious to the Milky Way and the Orion nebula.

Never mind! If Ewan only keeps fairly well I shall not succumb to worry over the Union question. It is only its possible effect on him that worries me.

Oh, I am so tired—tired—tired! I was out this evening to see the trousseau of a bride who is to be married Wednesday. As I looked at her pretty things and her radiant face I wondered if I had ever been so hopeful and happy. It seems so long since I dared to feel hope about anything.

Her mother said to me, "I hope Mary's married life will be as happy as mine has been," and I found myself looking at the woman with a sort of wondering awe. She is a stupid, narrow-minded, selfish woman. Yet she has been happy! Why should she have had a happy life and I such a miserable one?....

Tuesday, Mar. 10, 1925
The Manse, Leaskdale
I have been feeling better of late. The weather has been mild and springlike and has had a good effect on me. I have finished revising *The Blue Castle* and have it ready to be typed. I am sorry it is done. It has been for several months a daily escape from a world of intolerable realities.

Ewan came home from Presbytery tonight feeling very unhappy. The way the Unionist ministers have acted has been terrible. The rankest injustice and under-handed devilry has been practised. Several of them have lost their congregations by reason of the latter voting to remain Presbyterian, and seem determined to destroy what they cannot carry with them. The United Church will be fortunate in her men. But where in all this is there any spirit of the Master they profess to follow? Thank God, they will be out of the Presbytery after June 10. But meanwhile old friendships are torn asunder and bitter heart burning, and resentment substituted.

Mr. Macdonald of Wick, who for six years has been a fast friend of ours is an enemy now because he has taken it into his head that Ewan tampered with the

Anti-Unionists in his congregation—something Ewan never dreamed of doing. Indeed, when some of them came to Ewan to ask his advice in regard to taking the matter into the courts Ewan tried to dissuade them. But I understand they are going to do it. Wick voted in by a majority of two because Mr. Macdonald would not let several people vote who had an indisputable right to vote. He simply removed their names from the communion roll without any authority whatever. I am amazed that Mr. Macdonald could stoop to such a dirty piece of work. The bitterness in Wick is dreadful. It was one of the nicest rural congregations in Ontario and now it is ruined whichever church finally gets it. And that is the story everywhere.

Sunday, March 15, 1925
The Manse, Leaskdale
Things have been going on as usual—hard work, much driving about on bad roads—bitter cold after a false promise of spring, great tribulation drilling the play-actors, many unsettling "Union" rumors, a few minutes escape into a fascinating volume, *History of Religion*—ice-storms—Mission Bands—fairly good royalty report from Mac—a bit of encouragement in that Ewan seems very well again and preached today as he has not done for a long time....

Wednesday, March 11, 1925
This morning I tried to write a little again and succeeded. To my joy, I was able to *lose myself* again in my writing and forget reality. As long as I sat there writing I knew that though my body might dwell amid these distractions of time my spirit inhabited Eternity. This cheered me up a little. I have had a horrible feeling lately that I would never be able to write again.

But the rest of the day I felt very flat and toneless. I went to Mary Oxtoby's wedding and seemed like a weary ghost among mundane revellers.

In the evening I went to play practice but not a quarter of the cast was there. The rest had gone to the station to see the wedding party off. The remainder might as well have gone for all the good they did. They could talk of nothing but the wedding and the practice was a farce.

Wednesday, Mar. 18, 1925
The Manse, Leaskdale
This was a Zephyr day which means I am a discouraged creature tonight. I went over to a meeting of the Zephyr Women's Institute this afternoon, having promised to read a paper. Of course, it is undenominational but I felt surrounded and inhibited by Methodists who are very "sore" at Ewan and me because we haven't "gone in" with them. No matter what I say they make me feel it is the wrong thing.

And the Unionists poisoned the atmosphere worse than the Methodists. I *sensed* their resentment like a tangible thing. *And*, that nothing might be lacking, that sister of Satan, Mrs. Marshall Pickering, and her three daughters were there.

But did I wilt in this air? Not I. I "hilt up my head" and kept my flag flying. Chatted pleasantly and composedly with everyone—except the aforesaid P's.

Read my paper coolly and impressively. And wished myself a thousand miles away.

But I had one inward snicker of genuine amusement. The Roll Call was to be answered by the name of "a famous Canadian woman." When Mrs. Julius Rynard's name was called she promptly answered with "L.M. Montgomery." Mrs. J.R. is a Methodist but rumor has it that there is no love lost between her and Mrs. Marshall P. And I firmly believe she answered with my name to annoy that amiable lady. If such was her friendly idea she succeeded admirably for the Pickering countenance was exceeding grim....

Thursday, Mar. 19, 1925

....Last night there came an awful storm of rain with a wind that was bound to get inside. It clawed at the windows, shrieked at the eaves, and rattled and banged at the shutters the whole night. I could not sleep. Took an attack of cystitis and was more miserable. Towards morning fell into a very brief nap and had a horrible dream of Luck coming home with his tail cut off! Got up feeling useless and felt so all day. Ewan was rather dull and heady, too.

In the evening we had to go over awful roads to a wedding reception on the fifth. It was a dull affair for us and we had a wretched drive home in the pitch black night, especially through a long swamp where the road was half under water and so narrow that when we met a couple of buggies we had a serious time getting by. Luckily I had my flashlight or we should all have gone into the ditch.

Monday, Mar. 22, 1925

This has been a bad day. I could not sleep last night and all day I suffered from nervous restlessness without cessation....There was nothing cheering anywhere and a letter from Mr. Rollins did not lighten the gloom. He thinks the N.Y. appeal will be argued in April and he says,

"I assume that you want me to go ahead on the accounting for profits. I suppose that this will be contested as stubbornly as the rest of the litigation to date. No doubt the defendant will seek to charge against the book its proportionate share of travelling salesmen, income tax, rent and everything else they can think of, and what the result will be I do not profess to say"...

Play practice was to be here tonight. But for the first time in my life—as far as I can remember—I have flunked. I simply could not face the prospect of drilling and prompting from nine to twelve. So I have told Elsie to tell them to go ahead and practice in the parlor and I am going to bed.

The Manse, Leaskdale, Ont.
Friday, March 27, 1925

I do not sleep. Some nights I fall asleep about three but waken at dawn and lie there in the grip of silly, senseless, gnat-like worries. We had a terrific thunder and lightning storm last night and heavy rain.

I forced myself to work all day but my nerves were sick. I feel as if there were no escape and never could be any escape from "the wheel of things." I never felt more unhappy and hopeless in my whole life than I did today. This is a real attack of neurasthenia and if I cannot soon recover from it I do not know what will become of me.

I would soon recover if only Ewan were well. It is the long-drawn out agony of the past six years and the biting dread of this winter that he would get as he did last March that has brought me to this. He was very miserable today. Lay around and chanted mournful hymns. His eyes stared into vacancy with a distraught look. Sometimes, watching that fixed, almost maniac glare, I could hardly keep myself from screaming aloud.

When, as now, I cannot work I realize how hideously lonely my life is. I have no friends here—no sympathy—no companionship. Nothing to divert my thoughts and give my nerves a chance to heal up. And I can't go away for a change. It would be impossible to leave Ewan as he is just now.

I suppose there is no use writing in this strain. But it helps a little. This journal seems like an understanding friend and to confess my worries in it is like talking them over with such a friend.

Saturday, April 4, 1925
The Manse, Leaskdale
Last Tuesday I came down with flu and have been terribly bad with it. This is my first day up. I am as weak as a baby and of course the nervous depression that generally accompanies influenza has intensified my wretchedness. But I am thankful to be able to be up. To lie in bed, sick and helpless, and think of nothing but worries was very dreadful. Ewan has been canvassing Zephyr this week to try to find out who will leave and whom we can depend on....

The Legislature has awarded Knox College to the Presbyterian church. This will be a bitter pill for the Unionists....

An item sent me today by a clipping bureau states that half a million copies of *Green Gables* have been sold, that the original plates are completely worn out and the publishers are having a new set made. This would please me if I could feel pleasure in anything.

Ewan has seemed a little better this week. Oh, for one *real* friend to come in and talk to me for a little while!...

Monday, April 6, 1925
I had a good sleep last night and felt much better this morning. It was a nice bright sunny day, too. We motored down to Uxbridge in the afternoon and saw Marshall Pickering going into Greig's law office. This significant conjunction of malign planets upset me again and I spent the rest of the day in agony. Not ameliorated by Miss Bowman, the teacher, flying into Ewan publicly before several people about Chester's misbehavior in school. Miss B. has been a miserable failure as a teacher and cannot keep order at all. Chester, even according to her, has been guilty of nothing worse than talking in school when she had ordered him not to. Of course he should have obeyed. But it seems a small thing for her to make an insulting fuss about. She is the first teacher who had any trouble with Chester....

Tuesday, April 7, 1925
The Manse, Leaskdale
Ewan went to Zephyr. Saw Mrs. Jas. Lockie who raved insultingly about several things. I don't think that woman's mind is sound just at present....

Then he went to see Mrs. Warren who is the new treasurer of Zephyr. He asked her if any of the Pickerings had been trying to find out about the state of the salary. She said, no, so we feel a little easier. For it *is* behind now, of course, nearly $200. and if Pickering knew he could and would make trouble for us.

I am worried about Elsie, too. The child's appetite has been wretched since she had the flu. She is not strong, having been troubled for three years with what her doctor tells her is chronic appendicitis....

Wednesday, April 8, 1925
I slept well and felt better all day. Finished reading proofs of *Emily Climbs*. Got one nasty little scare when a car stopped at the gate and a strange man came up the walk. I had a moment of sickening fear that it was some minion of Greig's. But it was only a harmless agent.

We all went to an amateur play in Sandford tonight. It was very good and we laughed so much that it did us all good.

Thursday, April 9, 1925
Today seemed like an eternity and tomorrow will, I suppose, be just as bad. My mind goes around and around in a miserable circle and I get nowhere.

Early this morning before breakfast Mrs. Warren phoned over. I knew before she said a word that something was wrong or she would not be calling at that unearthly hour. She said she "wanted to see Mr. Macdonald about the matter they were discussing the other day"—i.e. the Pickering affair. I could eat no breakfast. Ewan, as soon as he swallowed his went right over. I shut myself in my room and walked the floor on tenterhooks till he returned.

It was as we feared. Pete Arnold, Pickering's son in law, had been asking Herb Warren about the salary and saying that if any was owing they would garnishee it. Herb said—or says he said—that it was all paid up as far as he knew.

We did not know what to do. We could not go to Will Sellers now to arrange matters. And could we trust anyone else? We had to. Ewan went to see Wm. Weldon and had a little talk with him. The result was that Weldon as manager agreed to *lend* the church the necessary sum to pay the salary up to the end of June. So that is that. But if Pickering does as Pete Arnold told Warren he would do—take both Ewan, the treasurers and the managers all into court it may be a very nasty mess. Of course if Herb Warren really told him what he said he did Pickering can have no "good cause" for getting such an order. But did he? Warren is not a man on whose word you can rely.

I am sick of it all. I wish Ewan had let me pay that money long ago. Unjust as it was, it would have been better than this ever-recurrent worry & humiliation....

Monday, April 13, 1925
Today I felt better. Was able to work and *forget*. Mr. Garvin of Toronto called in

the afternoon on some literary quest and the chat I had with him did me no end of good. Heartened me right up. After all, there *are* some people in the world besides the Lockies and the Armstrongs and Zephyr is not the hub of the Presbyterian church in Canada.

Tuesday, April 14, 1925
The Manse, Leaskdale
Not so well today. Nervous and restless. Hands tremble. Put in a miserable day. But Ewan came home from Toronto with good church news. Six hundred churches have already voted out and a strong Presbyterian church in Canada is assured. We will not belong to a mere sect. The general outlook is encouraging and I feel better and hope to get a good sleep tonight.

Sunday, April 19, 1925
....Have been busy housecleaning and getting on much better than I had feared. Ewan, too, has been very well this week—perfectly well to all seeming. He has tackled the job of clearing up the yard—something he has never done since

"Snow scene this morning" [Leaskdale Manse]

1919. The springs have hitherto been very bad times with him. I am very glad of this for I have been wondering how I would get the yard done. Other springs I had Lily to help me but Elsie is not strong enough for it. However, it has proved one of those bridges we never have to cross....

Monday, April 20, 1925
I slept well last night and that always makes the following day bearable. It was fine but cold today and I went down to Uxbridge over the sloppy slushy roads to give a talk on the Mammoth Cave to the Hypatia Club. I had a nice time. Companionable women—nice supper. I felt quite cheered up....

Wednesday, Apr. 22, 1925
The Manse, Leaskdale, Ont.

....Yesterday I was busy housecleaning all day and went to play practice tonight. It seems to me that we will *never* get that play up. Most of the performers don't *try* to get it up. They never study their parts—they make the same mistakes over and over again and *over* again. Last practice night I made Bert Collins repeat six times a short, two-sentence speech where he always went wrong. Tonight he made the same mistake again!

I came home wretchedly tired. Found Ewan in bed and half-asleep, he having got home before me from a Zephyr meeting. He roused himself to tell me that Marshall Pickering was confined to his bed with a paralytic stroke.

I admit candidly that I did not worry much over this. Instead, I went to bed with a distinct feeling of relief. If Pickering and Greig have not already set some devilry in motion it is not likely they will do so now. Pickering will have something else to take up his attention.

Thursday, Apr. 30, 1925
The Manse, Leaskdale

A queer little incident happened today. It shows what Unionists will stoop to.

We are members of the local Ministers' Association. Mr. Watch, the Methodist minister of Uxbridge is President, Mr. Dyer of Greenbank is Secretary. Dyer has been very bitter against Ewan, I understand, because he would not go in for Union and blames him for Sonya and Uxbridge voting out. Ewan certainly did what in him lay to influence Sonya and Uxbridge. He did not have to ask Mr. Dyer's permission to do the work he was asked to do by the Presbyterian Association. But Dyer is bitter with the bitterness of defeat because in spite of his efforts Lindsay Presbytery has gone strongly for Union.

Dyer's own record in regard to Union is a curious one. When he first came to Mt. Albert, a weak congregation, he was for Union and tried to arrange a Union between his church and the local Methodist church. All went swimmingly until Mr. Dyer discovered that the Methodists would not have *him* as minister in the United Church. Then he turned his coat out of hand and became a bitter opponent of Union. Last year, however, he got a chance to become minister of Greenbank United Church. Presto, the coat was turned again and Mr. Dyer fairly foamed at the mouth in his efforts to aid the Unionist cause. I am wasting a lot of perfectly good space detailing all this unimportant stuff but it makes clear the reason for what happened today.

Last fall when the programme was being made up Dyer asked me to take the May meeting—a meeting that nobody wanted because it came right in housecleaning time and, as supper has to be served, means a lot of extra work. I didn't want it either but Dyer solicited so earnestly I agreed. And this past week in addition to housecleaning like mad to get at least upstairs finished I have been planning and arranging my menu, ordering the necessary supplies etc.

Today Mr. Watch called here on the 'phone. Ewan was away so he had to tell me the burden of his soul. He began by the rather extraordinary question,

"Would it inconvenience you, Mrs. Macdonald, if we had the meeting in Uxbridge instead of Leaskdale next Monday?

Why he though it might "inconvenience me" to have the burden of such an entertainment taken off my list only the mind of a Unionist could explain. But I "sensed" the situation at once. Dyer's fine Italian hand was very plainly in evidence. Poor old senile Watch was merely his tool.

"Not at all," I said promptly and crisply.

Watch maundered on, trying feebly to explain. It was the last meeting of the season—they wanted a good turn-out—and the ministers were "all so *busy*" that they couldn't "spare the time" to come to Leaskdale.

This was absolutely nauseating. With the sole exception of Dyer every rural minister in the Association is much nearer Leaskdale than Uxbridge. And as half of the Uxbridge ministers are retired Methodist ministers I didn't think *they* were so exceedingly busy. I cut Watch's puerilities short by a curt repetition of my statement that it would not matter to me at all and hung up the phone.

I am glad enough to be rid of the meeting but I resent the insult. I know quite well that Dyer and Watch have cooked this up between them, for with every other minister in the Association we were on good terms, despite the Union question, with the exception of Macdonald of Wick who might not want to come here but who hates Dyer, so is not very likely to have been a party to the plot.

This evening I walked up the hill in the owl's light to see Mrs. Alex Leask. Lucky went with me half way up and then, becoming frightened by a car, ran into the bushes by the side of the road. Three hours later I came down the hill, enjoying the cool, starry darkness of the spring night—one cannot be altogether hopeless in spring—and not thinking of Lucky at all, supposing that he had gone home long ago. But as I passed that very clump of bushes I heard a little meow and the next moment out popped a purring, delighted little cat who had been waiting patiently there all that time for my return. I gathered him up and snuggled him against my neck; and then—since it was so dark that the parish could not be scandalized—I carried him home, singing his song of triumph. The love of even a faithful little animal is very precious. What care I for old Granny Watch and conceited Dyer? I snap my fingers under their very noses. They simply do not exist in my world at all. They have never entered its magic gates—they never can.

Sunday, May 3, 1925
The Manse, Leaskdale
There are two girls in my Sunday School class whom at times I feel tempted to take by the scruff of their necks, knock their silly giggling heads together and throw them out into the horse sheds—and think I did God service. Of course I never do. I smile and smile and am a villain still. But I don't know how much longer my patience with them will hold out. They cannot be shamed or inspired to better behavior, it seems, and of course it would be of no use to scold or satirize them. Wow!

But I felt better today and had a nice quiet restful afternoon of reading—

though Ewan came home from Zephyr discouraged as usual. That goes without saying.

Monday, May 4, 1925

In Uxbridge today we met Mr. Baldwin, the Baptist minister, who is a member of the Association. He is boiling with indignation over the removal of the meeting from us. He had never been consulted about it but Mr. Taylor, the Anglican, who is Vice President, was. Watch told him first what he told us—that the members thought it "too far" to go to Leaskdale. Taylor said he did not want it changed—that he had been looking forward to going and wanted to go. Then Watch, seeing that Taylor was not coming to heel properly, told him the truth—or rather, the truth as far as he and Dyer were concerned. "That the ministers didn't want to go to Leaskdale because of Mr. Macdonald's *views on Union.*"

So it seems that the Rev. Mr. Watch, Methodist minister, told *me* a deliberate *lie.* Verily, Wisdom is justified of her children.

Taylor gave in then—which he should not have done—but was so disgruntled that he would not go to the meeting. Baldwin did not go, either, partly because of the affront to us, partly because of the way Watch and Dyer had used *him* in regard to something last winter. Rev. Mr. Edmonds, a retired Methodist minister who has sometimes supplied for Ewan, telephoned up this evening in great agitation to assure us that he had never been consulted and had nothing to do with it. Of course he hadn't. Nobody had but Watch and Dyer—who are worthy of each other.

I went to practice again this evening and am deadly tired.

Thursday, May 7, 1925
The Manse, Leaskdale

Our play came off last night. We had a capacity audience and made sixty dollars. The thing went off fairly well. Much better than I had dreaded, although they made plenty of mistakes and omissions.

Not one of the performers said a word of thanks to me for all my trouble. At the end of our last play George Kennedy thanked me. But there are none of his type in this lot. I own I felt it. They simply did not think of it. But one would like a slight show of appreciation. Of course "the minister's wife" has nothing whatever to do but work for other people!

Ewan came home from Zephyr tonight with an astonishing piece of gossip. Unpleasant? Of course. Could any other kind emanate from Zephyr?

It is said *Jim Lockie* is going Union.

This, in a way, seems almost incredible, if it were not so characteristic of the Lockies. Jas. Lockie is one of the elders and as cranky as all the Lockies are. He and all his family voted against Union. But of course they thought when Union was voted down that all would stick. When at the annual meeting last winter Will Lockie and Armstrong "acted up" it was found hard to get a new treasurer. Jas. Lockie was not there. Although an elder he never does go to an Annual Meeting. He always stays away and then growls at everything that is done. Someone moved that he be elected treasurer. His own wife said that it was no use to put him in as he would not act. In the disorganization caused by the Unionist stampede it was impossible to get a male treasurer so Mrs. Warren was put in as treasurer. Jim Lockie nearly went off his head about this. He raved to us that awful evening we spent there about "a woman treasurer." Anyone would imagine it was a terrible disgrace. Most people think he wanted to be treasurer himself. I believe it is simply because he did not want Mrs. Warren to find out how little he, an elder and "leader," gave.

Anyhow, he has never come to church since. An elder, the very man who should have stood by his pastor and backed him up and helped him out in this crisis. And he has simply done nothing but sulk. Now he is reported as going Union. Well, it's the best place for him but if we lose that family with all the rest the church will have to close. And I would be sorry to see that for Leaskdale's sake and also because Armstrong and Will Lockie would rejoice and triumph.

The whole petty squabble is nauseous. I despise myself that I cannot help suffering from it....

Tuesday, May 12, 1925
I had a miserable night. Couldn't sleep until nearly six when I fell into a brief doze and had a most delightful dream—a dream I have often had all my life but not a dream that ever turned out to have any special significance. In it I suddenly discovered a door never before seen in my house. I opened it and went in—found a most beautiful suite of rooms with open fireplace and electric light. I was so delighted; and so oddly disappointed when I woke.

Had a busy day. Housecleaned the parlor and went to the Missionary meeting at Mrs. Leask's. We had to disband and reorganize as an Auxiliary of the Continuing Presbyterian church. A disagreeable necessity. But it was very easy here compared to what it is in some societies. Here we are all of one mind. Nobody is leaving us. So all went smoothly. Nevertheless, something about it all hurt. It emphasized the passing of the old order and the beginning of the new.

Thursday, May 14, 1925
The Manse, Leaskdale
I am worried over Ewan again. He was dull, grumpy, contrary all day. This see-saw of persistent hope and dread is wearing my life out. Went to Guild tonight and conducted a programme of "Canadian Humor." Did not feel humorous.

Friday, May 15, 1925
An unsettled restless sort of day. Had a headache and touch of cystitis again. Cleaned all the dishes and silver in the dining room. A letter came from Rollins enclosing a big bill for over a thousand dollars, and with a disheartening forecast of the length of time and work yet to come on that interminable case. Stuart had toothache all day.

Anything more?

I have concluded, however, that Greig is not going to do anything. If he had intended he would have shot his bolt before now. So I am easier on that score.

The papers carried the announcement of Rider Haggard's death today. I heard it with a feeling of personal loss. When I was a girl his fine tales of adventure and magic were a great delight to me. Are yet, indeed, in certain moods when the humdrumness of a constantly worried life gets on my nerves. Of course, they weren't even reflections of "literature," but they were "darn good yarns." I didn't care for his later stories. The magic had gone out of them.

Wednesday, May 20, 1925
....Had another rather gloomy letter from Rollins today. I don't know just what it means but I think he and French are both tired of the case and have put their heads together to end it. French tried, I know, to induce Page to quit but of course failed. So now they want subtly to discourage me. But what can I do? It would be absurd to drop the case now it is won, all but the accounting....

Tuesday, May 26, 1925
Whether I am accursed by the God of the Unionists or whether I am just a plain fool who doesn't have sense enough to take care of herself I know not. But I suspect the latter. Because I know I have been foolish; and because I think it likely the Unionist God has his hands full just now keeping the Unionists in order and hasn't time to bother tormenting me.

Friday night we had such a thunderstorm all night that I couldn't sleep. Saturday was cloudy, damp and bitter cold. I worked hard all day, was tired at night, and *should* have gone straight to bed. Instead, I suggested to Ewan that we make a call we have overlong been promising to make. So we drove over to Vallentyne to call on the young Methodist minister and his sister, who are friendish to us and rather nice folks. Mr. Newell is a Unionist but not an offensive one, so I hardly think he infected me with any germs of malice prepense. But at three o'clock Saturday night I woke with a dreadful cold. Such a kind of cold as I never had before. I could not get my breath at all—just lay there, gasping. Of course I should have stayed in bed and not got up at all. But I did get up and went to Sunday School and taught my class. Came home from church and went to bed, blue and discouraged. It was bitter cold and gray. Long icicles formed on the roof—and this the last week in May. I had a dreadful night and had to stay in bed all day Monday. It was Uxbridge fair day and Ewan, Stuart and Elsie went. I would have been very lonesome had it not been for Luck, who grows in beauty day by day, and who curled up on my bed the whole day and never left me for a moment. A blessing on all good gray cats, say I.

I managed to get up today and work but feel terribly shaky and have what old folks used to call a "graveyard cough."

Sunday night John Blanchard told Ewan that he had been talking to John Lockie who told him that he didn't think Will Sellers or Will Rynard would leave our church. As John Lockie is going himself he ought to have a pretty good idea who is or is not going. This has encouraged us greatly for we have been feeling woefully sure that both those families meant to go.

Yesterday I had a letter from Mary Beaton. She thinks of coming up to Toronto to the Presbyterian Congress and coming out for a visit. I am glad and have written urging her to come. But I do wish it was any other time. My enjoyment of her visit will be spoiled by the Union situation. It will coincide with the worst time of all—the final scenes of the tragedy. And I would wish to be alone then to bear my suffering unseen of even the friendliest eye....

Saturday, May 30, 1925
I had a wretched night Thursday night and felt so miserable all day yesterday that I stayed in bed till four. I should have gone on staying there but I got up, dressed, and went to the play at Udora. The performers thought they couldn't get through with it if I wasn't there. It's hard to see how much worse they could have done if I hadn't been. They simply made a frightful mess of it. Of course, the unfamiliar stage and setting made them nervous. Then Bert Collins made a fool mistake and spoiled a whole scene. This rattled them all; they lost their grip and went to pieces. Moved and spoke like puppets—forgot their points—oh, it was a nightmare! It was hot and close—I was ill—mortified at seeing my performers do so badly in a strange community. Perhaps it seemed worse to me than it really was; but it *was* bad.

Anyhow, that is the end of the devilish thing!...

Sunday, May 31, 1925
A warm, showery, breathless day. Had a poor night. Poorer day. Cough very bad. Weak and depressed. Couldn't help crying all the afternoon when I was alone. Can't eat. Have a horrible taste in my mouth. Feel like a walking patent medicine ad. before taking.

Ewan is dull, too.

Well, May is ended....*Everything* has been so hard—so *many* pestiferous, gnawing, malignant little worries like a multiplied cancer of the soul.

But the worst of the agony will soon be over at least. The fatal tenth of June will soon be here. We shall *know* the worst then—know where we stand—know who will or will not leave. This hateful suspense will be over. We will know who are with us and those who are not with us will have gone out from among us. There will be a desolation called peace.

The Manse, Leaskdale
Saturday, June 6, 1925
....I expected Mary on the Montreal train but she did not turn up. I felt much disappointed and came home by train very blue. But when I reached home there was a phone from Toronto that she had missed the first train but had come on the next and would be out to Uxbridge in the morning. So this morning we went down to meet her. I was shocked at my first sight of her. She was so thin—so haggard—her eyes looked as if they had wept unceasingly for a year.

And perhaps they have, poor soul. She told me all her troubles this afternoon. And they are no light ones. Her daughter Maud has been behaving the past year as if possessed of the devil. Up to then she was such a nice girl, devoted to her mother and liked by all. Engaged to a fine fellow, able to give her a nice home.

All at once she changed utterly. Broke her engagement and began running around with all kinds of riff-raff. Deceived her mother, quarrelled with her brother. Wouldn't work. Would leave home and stay away for weeks—oh, space and time forbid me to tell of all her kididoes. Mary is heartbroken and can't understand it at all. Neither can I—unless, as I strongly think, the girl is not in her right senses. Archie, it seems, was quite deranged in his mind for two years, a few years ago. I did not know this until Mary told me today. It was in the years when our correspondence had lapsed. So it is quite likely Maud is not quite sane. But she has all the cunning of such minds and contrives in a dozen ways to make Mary's life wretched....

Monday, June 8, 1925
The Manse, Leaskdale
Yesterday was a ghastly day. Intolerably warm. We went to Zephyr. Ewan spoke nicely to and about the Unionists from the pulpit, saying that he wished them well, etc. Of course Ben Armstrong and Will Lockie weren't there. They gave up going several Sundays ago. Will Sellers and Mrs. Will were there and gave no sign of any emotion of any kind, whatever they felt. But the thunderbolt came after the service. As I went down the steps Mrs. Jas. Lockie said to me, "Mrs. Jake Meyers voted Union and is going into the Union Church."

I was dumbfounded. Mrs. Meyers has always been one of our few intimate friends in Zephyr. She always talked against Union. Everyone supposed she voted against Union. When Ewan went to them they signed $25. to the new salary list and never said a word to lead him to suppose they would leave. And now!

"Mrs. Lockie, that is almost incredible," I gasped—quite conscious amid all my dismay that Mrs. Lockie had spoken almost triumphantly.

"She just told me so herself," said Mrs. Lockie. "And Maurice McNelly and Julia Madill are going too."

Two more that had promised to stay and signed E's paper! Is there any such thing as honor known to anyone in Zephyr? I turned and went to our car where Ewan was waiting. As I went I heard Mrs. Lockie say to someone, "Oh, I don't know whether I'll be back next Sunday either."

Before I could get into the car Mrs. Meyers came up to me and began to cry. All I could disentangle from her incoherent utterances was that she "would never have left if her husband had been a member of the church"—whatever that meant. I was so hurt that I permitted myself one bitter expression.

"I thought we could have depended on you, Mrs. Meyers."

She caught my hand and wept bountifully.

"Oh, you'll still come to see me as usual, won't you, Mrs. Macdonald?"

"No," I said. "You will belong to another congregation."

"Oh, that won't make any difference," she wailed.

"It will—to us," I said coldly. I got in. We drove away. It was a bitter drive home. After all our efforts. Well, that is the end of Zephyr Presbyterian church. It really deserves no better fate. But it is hard to be so humiliated before Ben Armstrong and Will Lockie who are our enemies simply because we have remained Presbyterian. They will exult in winning the victory. The strange part is that every one of those people who are leaving have been grumbling for years at Armstrong and Lockie and complaining that they were killing the church. Well, they have killed it. But perhaps God has yet something to say to Ben Armstrong and Will Lockie.

Not *one* of these people who are leaving are going because they sincerely believe that Union will "hasten the coming of the kingdom of God." Not one. We know the motives that have actuated everyone and in not one case is it a right motive.

I went all to pieces when I got home and cried bitterly. It is Leaskdale I am worried over. What will it do now? And we have built up such a good church here. It was a miserable congregation when we came—torn by feuds and cross–purposes. Now it is harmonious and flourishing, full pews, lots of young people coming into it every year—all a church should be. But it is not strong enough to stand alone....

Wednesday, June 10, 1925
The fatal date. When our beautiful Presbyterian church is torn asunder by those who swore to protect and cherish her. It has been a terrible day for me....

Thursday, June 11, 1925
The Manse, Leaskdale
Again a hard day after a poor night. The papers are full of flamboyant accounts of the "birth" of the Great United Church. Well, perhaps so. But in Nature the births of living things do not take place in this fashion and history does not show that great movements came into being with such clash of cymbals and clamour of trumpets.

No, 'tis no "birth." It is rather the wedding of two old churches, both of whom are too old to have offspring.

Davies and Taylor of Toronto called here this afternoon re the Torcas Co. We had a hot debate on the Union question. Taylor is a rampant Union-Methodist, although he has completely discarded "the supernatural" in his religion. It was funny. He dared not say anything that would anger me, for fear I wouldn't buy his stock. So he had to take all my slams good-humoredly and smile as if he liked it. "Goodness, isn't mother trimming him?" whispered Chester to Elsie in the kitchen. But it did me heaps of good. I got something poisonous out of my soul that has been festering there ever since Sunday. Because of that and because it did me good to talk for awhile with some intelligent educated people I felt much better the rest of the day. Yes, one is all right when one *can* fight. But to lie in the dust and take kicks from people like the Zephyrites requires more of the grace of God than I have ever had or ever will have.

Friday, June 12, 1925
Last night I slept better and got back a little of my sense of proportion. Tonight in Guild Mrs. James Cook told me how, when they used to live in Zephyr 30

years ago, they had such terrible times with the Lockies of that day—the father and uncles of Will and Jim. They would do and say the most dreadful things in the church and had to have their own way in everything. It does me a lot of good to hear someone abuse the Lockies!!!! And *say* just what I've always thought of them but dared not say.

Saturday, June 13, 1925
I felt better today with less nervous unrest but certainly not good for much. I found it hard to have the mission band and concentrate on sewing patches. But Ewan and Mary came home this afternoon in such good spirits over the splendid Presbyterian Congress and the assurance of a strong continuing Presbyterian church that it cheered me up by reflection. Ewan had to go to Sonya tonight so, though it was raining heavily, Mary and I went with him. In the car we did not mind the rain and we enjoyed the twelve mile drive through the cool, wet darkness. I love the sound and scent and freshness of rain in the dark.

And we found, too, that, given half a chance, we had not lost our olden power of making fun for ourselves.

Sunday, June 14, 1925
In spite of our pleasant drive I did not sleep well. This was a fine cool day and Leaskdale church was filled to the doors....*So far as we know* not one person is leaving Leaskdale church....

Then Ewan went to Zephyr. I spent the most miserable afternoon of suspense yet. I simply *dreaded* his return because of what news he might bring. But his news was much better than we had dared to hope. After all Mr. and Mrs. Jake Meyers have stayed with us. The reason why is funny. Jake is not a member of the church. He was brought up a Mennonite and believes in Baptism by immersion. He came to our church with his wife, but would never join. Mrs. Meyers is evidently one of those women who believe that if a man is not a church member his chances of heaven are small but if he *is*, he is all right, no matter how or in what fashion he became so. It seems that she got into her head the extraordinary notion that if they went into the Union church he would automatically became a member. When she found out this was not so her chief reason for "going Union" disappeared. This explains her mysterious cry last Sunday. Besides, it seems her daughter did not want to leave our Sunday School. So back they are. All Jim Lockie's family were there except him—and after all his kididoes he has not gone to the Union church....

Wednesday, June 17, 1925
....Elsie's side is bothering her lately. She has often complained of pain in it but of late it has been almost continual. Her complaints do not irradiate life. I endured Lily's for years. They were unpleasant but did not worry me much because I knew the most of them were imaginary or pretended. But Elsie's *do* worry me because they are real. The girl is not well and I am afraid she will hurt herself in some way, lifting or reaching....

Tuesday, June 23, 1925
Yesterday Ewan, Mary and I motored in to Toronto. We had a beautiful drive through a world of clover and for a time I felt much better. Mary and I had a pleasant time in Toronto and I saw her off on the Montreal train this morning with real regret. She has gone back to her problems, poor soul, and I have come home to mine. She told me last night of her hard life with Archie. He drank heavily for years and almost ruined them.

Ewan was in good spirits when I came home and *seems* perfectly well. As long as he keeps like this let the Unionists do their worst!

Wednesday, June 24, 1925
The Manse, Leaskdale, Ont.
I feel very much better all day. I began writing again this morning and found I could carry on. This evening we were out calling and as we sped along the pleasant dark June roads, with the shadows and the stars I heard again the whisper eternal and found my way back to my dear world of fancy. I have been an exile from it for many moons and had oft times feared I should never be able to re-enter it. But I have found again, "the ivory gates and golden" and so long as they keep open for me there is nothing I cannot bear. Freedom is a matter of the soul.

Friday, June 26, 1925
....I am sleeping better but always waken too early—at three or four—and then cannot sleep again. I feel very dull and vapid most of the time. But that is better than active torture.

Elsie is very miserable. The doctor says it is chronic appendicitis and she must have an operation.

I have a nice thing to relate of our small black Dixie. It is the joy of that little dog's life to accompany anyone who goes down to the Post Office. Yesterday I went down and Dixie bounded after me, every curve of his body quivering with delight. Luck also decided to follow and the two, who are excellent friends, trotted along behind me to the middle of the creek-bridge. Then a passing car alarmed Luck who bolted into the shrubbery and would not come out. What did Dixie? Did he come on with me and leave Luck to his fate? Not he, though his whole being yearned after me. That gentlemanly little dog sat right down by the trees into which Luck had disappeared and remained there until I had gone to the P. O. and returned. Then Luck took courage to emerge and he and Dixie trotted home with me. Loyalty and courtesy incarnate in a small black body with a tail like a sausage. Dixie, I salute thee. Thou art of the household of faith.

Sunday, July 5, 1925
Elsie went home today. She is to be operated on tomorrow. Myrtle Taylor is coming to help me until Elsie can return.

Elsie cried when she went away. "I have had six happy months here, Mrs. Macdonald," she sobbed. Poor child, I hope she will get on all right.

Monday, July 6, 1925
Elsie was operated on this morning and got on very well.

Mr. Fraser was here today. We have all outlived the coolness generated by the Brooklyn affair and are good friends again. I am glad because I always found J.R. an agreeable companion. He is very unhappy just at present. He has always been bitterly opposed to Union but he thought there would be no Presbyterian church worth while left and so went into Union and induced his church to go too. Now when he finds there is still a strong Presbyterian church he is homesick and regretful but cannot retrace his steps after influencing his congregation. Well, J.R. is a bit of a time server. He doesn't believe in the immortality of the soul, the Virgin birth, the deity of Jesus. Yet he pr ˄hes in a church which requires such belief. I do not blame him for not believ...g them. Very few thinking people do believe in miracles now—though most of us believe in some kind of immortality. But he should not be preaching them when he doesn't believe them. *That* is the canker at the heart of all the churches today. It will kill them. But equally of course preaching the falsity of belief in the supernatural will kill them, too. So either way the church, as it exists today, is doomed and will eventually die. Though something that has lived for 2,000 years will take a long time in dying.

But suppose it does die. What matter? It has served its day as God's instrument. He is using another now—Science. Through Science the next great revelation will come. I may not live to see it in this incarnation but I am as certain of its coming as I am that the sun will rise tomorrow morning.

We heard in Zephyr today that only three of the Unionists who left our church were in Zephyr United church last Sunday evening though it was a lovely evening. It would seem that they are no better to go there than to their own of yore.

As for me I am slowly but surely recovering my wholesomeness. My secret spring of joy is bubbling up in my heart again....

Thursday, July 9, 1925
The Manse, Leaskdale
This afternoon I went to a W. M. S. quilting in Zephyr church. There is something about the homely old art of quilting that I like. I could sit and quilt happily for hours. But the afternoon was spoiled for me by the presence of that devilish woman, Mrs. Jas. Lockie. She always seems to poison the atmosphere. Mrs. Ben Armstrong was there too, wife of the great and only Ben. What brought her I cannot imagine. Probably a desire to play the spy. At all events she made us all feel uncomfortable.

When it was over the rest of the day was pleasant. Ewan and I motored to the induction at Port Perry....Ewan preached the sermon and did very well. It is always a dreadful strain on me when I know he is going to preach in a strange church. Sometimes, as tonight, he does well. But sometimes, when his black dog rides him, he does miserably and puerilely. And one can never be sure which it will be....

Will Lockie and Ben Armstrong have, I understand, reiterated their decision to "smash the Presbyterian church" and "give it two years in Zephyr." I am sadly afraid their prediction will come true. I really can't see any prospect ahead for Zephyr church, unless something very unforeseen comes to pass.

Wednesday, July 15, 1925
The Manse, Leaskdale, Ont.
....Yesterday we motored to Kirkfield and spent the day with the Burkholders. Very pleasant but of course, for me, marred by the ceaseless talk about Union and its results which made an otherwise excellent dinner a meal of bitter herbs.

Kirkfield is where father was married to his second wife. The old MacKenzie house, where the reception was held, is still there, across the street from the manse. A beautiful place which has been shut up for years. The ceremony was performed in the old church which has been torn down. We went for a walk through a most beautiful long lane of lombardies on the MacKenzie estate. It was the part of the day I enjoyed the most. How I miss out of my life now the long intimate walks through woods and secluded fields....

Today I canned cherries and had splendid luck. I also wrote two hours at a series of short stories I am trying to get done for *The Delineator*.

Thursday, July 16, 1925
Today I read an article in which the writer spoke of a book he had once hoped to write and never would. This set me thinking of the books *I* planned to write—but never did. There were several of them in my early teens, all carefully "thought out" and quite complete in my mental storehouse. Many a night I lay awake in that old farmhouse by the eastern sea—many an evening I walked alone in the afterglow of autumnal sunsets—composing them and a jolly good time I had of it.

One was to be called "How We Ran the Farm." This was an amusing story about two girls who, by some twist of circumstances, were left with a P. E. Island farm on their hands and determined to show all and sundry that they could run it. They had any number of adventures, especially when they daringly attempted to shingle the stable and build a "snake" fence. I really think it would not have been a dull little yarn.

Two other projected novels were very serious affairs. One centred around the fortunes and misfortunes of a young French Canadian—whose name was Louis—who was "only a hired man" but had endowments and aspirations beyond the rank and file of his race. He was to fall in love with his employer's daughter and she with him and the course of true love was to run deviously and turbulently and alas, to no happy haven. For in the end he was to go back to the forsaken sweetheart of his own race.

Another novel was to have been a chronicle of life in a country church. A minister well stricken in years was to be set aside in favour of a young man. A faction adhered to both and the story was to deal with the intrigues and counter-intrigues of the said factions. At last, in a very dramatic scene—my eyes used to stream with tears as I pictured it—the two ministers became reconciled.

I think I could have written these books quite well. I shall never write them now but at times their "frustrate ghosts" loom reproachfully in the offing as if demanding why I called them into spiritual being yet refused to give them incarnation.

But I *did* write a book whereof no record remaineth. It was back I think in '99 or '00. I intended it for a "Sunday School Library book"—thinking that if I could get it accepted by one of the religious publishing houses I might make a few hundreds out of it. I modelled it after the fashion of the "Gypsy" and "Pansy" books of my childhood and had no idea of attempting anything beyond a pot-boiler. It was called *A Golden Carol*—a title punned from the name of the heroine, "Carol Golden," who was a girl at Halifax Ladies' College when the story opened. Summoned home suddenly by the death of her mother she had to stay there, rebelliously, to keep house for her father and young brother "Bobbles," who supplied the comedy relief to Carol's struggles and trials—said struggles of course culminating in a victory over self and a determination to live up to the college distortion of her name and make life "a golden Carol." It was all laid down on thoroughly conventional lines and would have passed any censor. Yet, *of its kind*, it wasn't a bad story. I thought then—and think still—that it was every whit as good as nine out of ten of the Sunday School stories that found publishers. I sent it away to the Presbyterian Board of Publications in Philadelphia and when they refused it I sent it to the Congregational Publishing Society of Boston. Back it came. I never sent it out again.

Probably if I had kept on I might have found a publisher. I am exceedingly thankful I did not. To have had that book accepted would have been the greatest misfortune that ever happened to "my literary career." I could never have risen above it; and it would probably have committed me to a lifetime of writing "series" similar to it.

But I did not realize my lucky escape at the time. The cloud of disappointment seemed to have no silver lining and I cried myself to sleep for a week over the downfall of my humble little castle of dreams.

Eventually I boiled the book down to seven or eight chapters and sent it out to several Sunday School papers in the hope of having it taken as a serial. To condense it thus I had to cut out three quarters of it and as this included the "Bobbles" stunts all the salt and savour it had possessed utterly evaporated. Nobody would have it at any price and finally I burned it, vowing that never again would I try to create a Sunday School heroine. It was the re-action drove me to "Anne" and probably kept me from making a dummy of her.

I have several "unborn" books in my head yet. I hope they will some day come to birth. Perhaps they will; and perhaps not. It will all be according to predestination.

Monday, July 20, 1925
The Manse, Leaskdale
Last night Ewan left for the Island going down to make a third attempt to settle up Aunt Christie's tangled business affairs and get the store property sold. I shall have to do without a vacation this year. What with Elsie's illness and preparations for Chester's going to St. Andrew's I can't get away. But a certain kind of

a vacation I mean to have while Ewan is away. I am excused from all "visiting" because I can't drive the car. *That* in itself constitutes a vacation. And though I shall have to work hard all the time I am going to work only at "jobs" I enjoy doing. And I'm going to rest and read as much as I can. I had a splendid day today full of steady pleasurable work.

Thursday, July 23, 1925
A lovely day. Fine and cool. And I was alone. Myrtle was away, Stuart went off to visit a chum. I found it very agreeable and restful for a change.

I went down to the Post Office in the forenoon and as I crossed the bridge I looked over to Mr. Leask's hayfield on my left. Wave after wave of sinuous, glistening, wind-shadows were going over it. I have not seen just that exact effect for years. A flood of ecstasy washed through my soul. The mystic curtain fluttered and I caught the glimpse of Eternal and Infinite beauty which "Emily" called her "flash." I fairly trembled with the wonder and loveliness of that supernal moment. Only a moment. But worth years of ordinary existence.

Then I went into the Post Office and bought two cans of peas and a packet of Cream of Barley. The body can't live on shadow-waves and flashes.

Sunday, July 26, 1925
A Mr. Noble came last night to preach today. Young, clever, a bit conceited. Eloquent but stentorian preacher. I think he could easily have been heard a quarter of a mile away. I went to Zephyr with him and after the church service we went up to the Decoration Service held in the cemetery. The Women's Institute arranges this and it is undenominational. Some of the ex-Presbyterian ladies came and spoke to me. Some did not. Mrs. W. Sellers, among the latter, though she smiled and bowed slightly across an open space. I think she is really shamefaced.

Lily Shier found a chance to whisper to me, "Have you heard about the fight in the Methodist church?" I said "No," and she said, "The ladies of the Institute are getting into sad messes." She had no chance to tell me more so I must suffer the pangs of deferred but candidly confessed curiosity for a season.

Janet Myers, whom I had not seen since that dreadful Sunday in June, came up to me in church, crying again. "I couldn't live without you, Mrs. Macdonald," she sobbed, "so I stayed."

Fudge! She stayed because her daughter made a fuss and because she found that her husband couldn't automatically become a church member and sure of heaven. I know my Janet. Though I think she likes me and did really feel badly when she purposed leaving.

I have a vaseful of Shirley poppies before me as I write. Exquisite things! Enough to compensate for Zephyr. Shirley Poppies always make me think of Myrtle Webb. The first Shirley poppies I ever saw were in a bouquet she brought over to me long ago, one evening in Cavendish when she was a newcomer to the place. I can see that lovely bouquet plainly yet. It is nearly a quarter of a century since that evening and those frilled things of rose and snow have been dust as long. But they bloom still in my garden of remembrance.

Wednesday, August 5, 1925

There has been a terrible tragedy in Zephyr. Mr. Barron, the night operator of the C.N.R. there, was lighting a fire with coal oil. The stove exploded, house and contents were burned, and Mr. Barron so badly burned that he died this morning. The Barrons are Methodists so that it touches us only in so far as they are fellow creatures and human beings—which is far enough. The whole thing seems nightmarish and Zephyrian.

The house they lived in was right beside our church. The sheds caught fire and the church was only saved by the fire brigade from Mount Albert. I am sure the Unionists, especially Will Lockie and Ben Armstrong, must think that the prayers of the righteous did not avail for once, or the detestable building would have been removed by fervent heat from their midst.

Emily Climbs is out. My twelfth book.

I am sleeping splendidly now. I seem to be getting pretty well back to normal in this respect. For one thing, I suppose I am not disturbed by E's sighs and groans in his sleep. Even when he is pretty well in daytime he seems distressed in his sleep. He is having a nice time on the Island and I believe he is really going to get the store property sold at last. If so that will be one of our minor burdens removed.

A funny thing happened tonight. The phone rang and Myrtle came out. "Mount Albert is calling you." I had been expecting a call from Lily Shier in regard to a missionary meeting. So I was thunderstruck when I heard a voice saying, "This is *Ham Pickering* speaking."

For a moment a wave of sickening apprehension went over me. Ham is Marshall's brother and very bitter against us—although up to the time of the accident he hadn't been on speaking terms with Marshall for years. What devilry was afoot? And in any case why should Ham phone *me*??

"Do you want any more of *them* raspberries?" demanded Ham. In considerable relief I realized that he had got the wrong number so I told him so, adding, "This is Mrs. Macdonald of Leaskdale," and hung up. I rather think the Mount Albert operator would get a calling down. Ham would feel a bit silly.

Sunday, Aug. 9, 1925

....Elsie came back tonight. I would rather she had not come back so soon but she seemed so anxious to come that I did not like to say a point-blank "no." But I am sure she cannot be fit for work yet and it worries me. Of course on Monday I will run the washing machine and bring in the pails of water and I will help her with all lifting but still there is a danger of her hurting herself....

Monday, Aug. 10, 1925
The Manse, Leaskdale

....We have heard all about the "row" in the Methodist church. The Pickering girls started it and made things pretty hot for Mrs. John Lockie and Mrs. Will Sellers. The whole thing is too sordid and petty to detail. I fancy Mrs. Sellers will realize that Ewan told her the truth when he told her the Zephyr Methodist church would be the same church for petty fights and squabbles for the next 20 years that it is today.

Tuesday, Aug. 11, 1925
It was cool today. Such a blessed relief! Ewan is still dull but slept fairly well last night. I spent the forenoon making sandwiches and putting quilts in the frames in the church. This afternoon we had the quilting and served tea. It was a rather hard day and it can't be said I enjoyed any part of it. But among all the forty women who were there there is not *one* with whom I feel ill at ease or who has the same effect on me that Mrs. Jimmy Lockie has. I felt that everyone there was my friend.

Thursday, Aug. 13, 1925
....We got up at five and motored into Toronto for a day's shopping. On our way home we stopped at Columbus manse and had tea with Mr. Fraser and Margaret. I looked over the manse with a rather bitter curiosity. Had it not been for Fraser I would have been living in that manse for the past five years. We would have

"The side road"

been spared the wretched Pickering affair and I think Ewan would not have been so melancholy. The manse is a very nice one with electric light and I felt a little of the old resentment surge up when I thought of the trick by which Fraser had got it. Well, I suppose it doesn't matter much now. These things are settled by fate.

The evening was a nightmare to me. When Ewan is normal his ordinary conversation in social intercourse while never brilliant or even cultured is a passable average. But when these spells come on him he talks like a child of twelve using a new language which he has learned very badly. I writhed in humiliation all the evening. Fraser must have thought him an ass. And his eyes looked so wild and hunted that I could hardly bear them. I had to clench my hands and grit my teeth in order to sit still while I talked to Fraser. On the way home I was tired out and only avoided tears by taking refuge in a new and vivid dream life which I have been living very splendidly all summer and which, by reason of the temporary escapes it has offered me, has been the only thing that has made it possible to endure. It is a curious thing that all through my life when some great strain or crisis came and all my old dream lives, lived so often that they had at last grown stale and flavorless, failed to give these escapes, some new, vivid, and exhilarating dreamlife would come into being. For months I have been a member of a party seeking in the mountain deserts of South America the jewels hung on a stone god in a great underground cavern. I have gone through the most amazing adventures, risks, terrors, hardships, have found the jewels, outwitted foes and traitors and returned in triumph. How silly it all seems written down. Yet it has been a wonderful, breathless, exciting existence as lived, and seems now in retrospect as *real* as life I have actually lived. "The Hill of The Curse" is visible before my eyes. I know its geography by heart—every curve in the river at its foot beyond which on the one side were the deserts and on the other the mountains. I know every corner of that terrible underground cavern—every curve in "The Stairway of a Thousand Steps"—every mile of that dreadful, solitary journey back across rocky plains, subsisting on sun-cooked fish caught from the river, with the jewels of the plundered god twisted around my body under my ragged garments. All the others dead by the curse of the god—I, the sole survivor.

These dream lives are altogether different from the stories I "think out." When thinking out a story I am *outside* of it—merely recording what I see others do. But in a dream life I am *inside*—I am living it, not recording it. I do not know whether other people generally possess this power. All these various dream lives are just as real to me as if I *had* lived them and were looking back on them. And in these lives I am never hampered by facts and probabilities as I am in a story. Everything happens as I will whether it is possible or not. I don't know whether a river of bitter waters, containing edible fish, could really flow through a desert where no plant life is found. But it could and did in my dream journey. No difficulty at all about that or anything else! Oh, it has been fun.

Saturday, Aug. 22, 1925
The Manse, Leaskdale
Ewan seemed a little better today—a bit *cranky*, which is a good sign. This evening we took the boys down to Uxbridge to see a movie. This is an occasional treat we give them. And tonight it was a treat not only for them but for me. After a day packed full of many and, under present circumstances, carking routine duties, I was *thirsty* for something different—something that would take me for a little while into a different existence. The film was a good one and the "comic," detailing the adventures of a cross-words puzzle "fan" was the most excruciatingly funny thing I ever saw. I laughed until my cheeks ached and I felt young again. I am thankful I have never lost "the power to become a child again at will." We were just three kids together there tonight. Ewan didn't go. Never goes. Doesn't like movies. Spent the evening reading and brooding in the back room of Willis' drug store. If he had gone with us and had a good laugh over that irresistible comic it would have done him more good than many prayers.

Well, we had a good time, howling over it, and a lovely drive home, the three of us in the back seat, and had almost as much fun talking the movie all over again.

Saturday, Aug. 29, 1925

....Bertie McIntyre was in Trenton on her way from England to Vancouver. She could not come here. Our one chance of meeting was to go to Trenton. We must go and come in one day as on Saturday I had people coming to supper. We left here at six in the morning and covered the hundred miles to Trenton by 10.20. We certainly smoked along. I admit there *is* a witchery in speed. We had a delightful drive and the effects of the early morning mists along the creek and river valleys were more exquisite than any I had ever seen....

"Souvenirs of a happy day"
[Ewan, Laura, Chester, Stuart, Bertie, Ralph Aylsworth]

Bertie and I talked our souls out and dipped into all the affairs of the world once more. We had a merry, happy dinner party at eventide. Ewan so well, everybody smiling and jesting, laughter sparkling from lip to lip. We left at 8 and got home at one, after a pleasant and uneventful drive. But this morning— wow! It was the morning after the night before with a vengeance. We had the Baldwins to supper tonight and I'm dead—just about. I feel like the old man who said he must have all eternity to rest in.

But here's a joke:—

The carpenters who are working on Will Cook's new house under Jim Lockie have been complaining to Will of "the way Jim Lockie swears at them."

Yet James Lockie is, or was, an elder in the church, a self-appointed and intolerant censor of conduct and morals, a man who thinks no one but himself fit to fill any office in the church. Is it any wonder Zephyr church died under the rule of such men?

Since the Lockies and Ben Armstrong left the church we have been hearing so much about them that people never dared tell us before. We always *felt* that they were not what they professed to be, but we have never discussed our people to the others, so we did not *know* a great many things we are finding out now.

Saturday, Sept. 5, 1925
The Manse, Leaskdale
On Wednesday we rose early, motored into Toronto and spent a long day on the Exhibition grounds. Took in the Midway stunts, stayed for the grand stand and fireworks at night, left for home at eleven in a pouring rain, had a flat tire, took nearly an hour getting on our spare, and did not get home till two, dead tired. We go through all this for the boys' sake, repaid because they enjoy it so. But Chester is beginning to outgrow the midway. This year he did not care for many of his old delights. For Stuart however, it is still fairyland.

On Thursday we motored to the induction at Gamebridge. On our way there we had the narrowest escape from death, or at least from serious injury to ourselves and destruction to our car that we ever had. It is too long and involved a story to tell here. It was nobody's fault—the trouble began with a pair of frightened horses bolting in a narrow road where the ditch was frightfully deep and steep. We escaped and finally rescued the car also, which a man had prevented from turning turtle into the ditch by letting his horses go and grabbing the side of our car. But the incident took more out of me than a hard day's journey. I am not quite over the effects yet. The odd part is, that, just at the critical moment, when I felt sure that we were both going to be killed I was not in the least alarmed or apprehensive. When all was over and we were safe I sort of went to bits. Began to tremble, shiver, and want to cry. I didn't cry—but I think it would be better for me if I had.

Today we went down to see "the gardens" at Port Perry. A wealthy Toronto man is making a hobby of his gardens there. It is a wonderful spot, especially the "Italian garden" and as I roamed about in it and drank my fill of beauty life seemed a different thing and childhood not so very far off. One felt safe from the hungry world in that garden. I came home with a fresh stock of courage and endurance.

Ewan has seemed fairly well, this week, too.

Sunday, September 6, 1925
This is Chester's last Sunday home. The last Sunday he will ever be here as a real member of an unbroken household. Henceforth he will come only as a guest on holidays. This bitter thought has been with me all day, like a dark cloud darkening still more gloomy hours of cloud and rain. This evening I took Chester into the parlor in the twilight and had a serious little talk with him, giving him some good advice and warnings, in such tone and language as I thought would win his co-operation instead of repelling him.

I have tried to teach and train Chester as wisely as possible in these past years—as wisely and well as a woman can who has no assistance or co-operation whatever from her husband. I know I have been too impatient at times—I know I have fallen far short in many ways. But I have done my best. And now he must fare forth into the world to sink or swim. I am glad he will be under masculine influence henceforth—and, as I hope and believe, good masculine influence. He has come to the age when he needs it. He cannot, alas, get it here. But at least I am thankful I can afford to send him where he can get it. My little little lad. He is so young to go so far away.

This evening I read an autobiography by Corra Harris, a writer of some note in the U.S. In one striking respect her experience was very like my own. She was the wife of a minister who fell a prey to religious melancholia. She says:—

"I have written out in another place the life we lived during this period but not the terror and silence that fell upon me. That cannot be set down in words. The frantic efforts I made to save him from himself and to protect him from that terrible world in the church. I know where the spirit of all tragedies dwells—in the silence which you dare not break by even one call for help. I contracted the habit of holding my breath in those years of suspense. Even when my body slept it seemed to me that my heart was forever sitting up with Lundy in the dark hours of the night...I used to wish I could find relief in a real battle, see the dreadful face of my enemy and feel his wounds rather than face the powers and principalities of Lundy's terrible darkness."

Oh, true, true! "The silence you dare not break by one call for help." It is as if my own heart had uttered that moan. And "holding my breath in those years of suspense." Yes, how often have I held mine since that ghastly spring of 1919.

Monday, Sept. 7, 1925
....This evening Miss Imrie came unexpectedly—an old maid of Zephyr who spent her youth in Leaskdale and occasionally comes over for her "vacation." Just why she chose to make this her headquarters I cannot say for I never asked her. But at any other time I would have been glad enough to see the poor soul and give her as decent a time as possible for I don't think her lot has ever been a very bright one. But she is one of those who feel, if they do not think, that no Christian woman should be beautiful—or interesting. And I did secretly resent her coming at this time and spoiling for me Chester's last days at home.

I didn't let the poor lady see this however. And she gave me lots of amusing gossip about Zephyr people as we sat in the parlor and crocheted. I found out several amusing bits. Ever since I knew Will Lockie and his wife I have *felt* that neither of them were normal. And now I find that my feeling was correct. Will Lockie's mother was quite out of her mind many of the earlier years of her life. This accounts for the odd streaks in both Will and Jim. And Mrs. Will Lockie herself has been quite "off" several times. I have always suspected this. Indeed, I don't think she is ever wholly "on." Then, too, I found from Miss Imrie that Ben Armstrong has always been considered an unbearable sort of a man by all the rest of the people. Nobody could ever get along with him. He domineered and dictated. Heaven help everybody concerned if they dared to differ from him. Miss Imrie expressed surprise that Ewan had been able to keep him in order for fifteen years.

Ewan has a knack that way. But perhaps if he had fought Armstrong out and put him in his place it might have been better for the church today. If Armstrong had left it years ago he could not have made the trouble he did in regard to Union.

The Manse, Leaskdale
Wednesday, Sept. 9, 1925
Today I packed Chester's trunk and valise. It does not seem very long since I used to be packing my own for school and college flittings....

Friday, Sept. 11, 1925
The Manse, Leaskdale
On Wednesday night I went in as usual to see the boys before I went to sleep. Dear little fellows lying there. Never separated before. Always to be separated henceforth save for fleeting holidays. After I went to bed I lay awake for hours crying. Every time I had scolded Chester for some boyish peccadillo came up and reproached me. Hadn't I been too exacting with him? I felt as if I had—as if I had fallen terribly short of my ideal of motherhood.

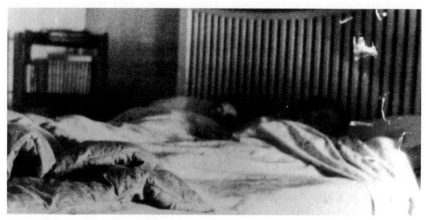

"Two little fellows lying there" [Stuart and Chester]

We left at 6.30 yesterday morning and had a pleasant drive in. The world is always young again for just a little while at the dawn. The day was beautiful and "the flash" came so often that it made life worth while again. As if there were a great cistern of beauty in the universe from which we all may drink and be filled.

We left Chester at St. Andrew's—all alone among a crowd of strange boys. He was plucky but I think he felt pretty blue at parting. "Thanksgiving will be Thanksgiving for the first time in my life this year, mother," he said.

We got home at 9.30. Poor Stuart would not go to bed until we got home—he was too lonesome. Then he went with his dog. When I went up he was asleep and Dixie was lying on Chester's pillow. Only one little boy where the night before there had been two!

I couldn't sleep for a long time. And when I did drop off a tremendous thunderstorm wakened me. All day I have missed Chester terribly. When we sat down to supper tonight and saw Stuart in Chester's place both Elsie and I broke down and cried. I miss Chester in so many ways. His kisses—he never passed me without stopping for a kiss and asking his old baby question "Do you like me?" His music—he was always putting on Victrola records. His "mother dear-wums." His rosy healthy face! Oh, I suppose I'll "get used to it"—as I have got used to so many seemingly intolerable things. But just now it seems as if I couldn't....

Sunday, Sept. 13, 1925
A pouring rainy day. The long drought of August and early September has broken with a vengeance. I wrote Chester today. Henceforth this will be a weekly item. Of late years my personal correspondence has dwindled. Only very few regular correspondents remain out of the dozens with whom I used to exchange voluminous epistles thirty years ago. But now I shall have more letters to write again and receive.

Stuart wrote, too, and I laughed over two sentences in his letter. Speaking of a family that has had a great many operations he wrote, "Seemingly an operation is all in the day's work there" and in regard to the rain, "I guess the weather is sorry over your going away." Stuart has my gift of writing easy letters. Chester hasn't. His letters are stiff and stingy.

Monday, Sept. 14, 1925
The Manse, Leaskdale
....I was amused tonight over something Mary Shier said. She knows the woman for whom Lily is working in Toronto now. Meeting her in Simpson's she asked her how she liked Lily. "Oh, fairly well," said the lady "but for a girl who had the responsibility she had she doesn't seem very capable of going ahead with things."

Responsibility! I could have howled. I suppose Lily has been telling her new mistress that she "kept" my house *in toto*. Poor Lily! Yet the thing annoys me—it is so untrue and grotesque. And false impressions travel as fast and last as long as lies.

Wednesday, Sept. 16, 1925
The Manse, Leaskdale
The School fair came off at Sandford today and of course we had to take Stuart and endure a day of boredom. Of course the children enjoy it so it is justified but for me the low descending sun of the school fair always counts for a day lost....

But Stuart had a jolly time and got second prize for table bouquet. And Ewan picked up some amazing bits of gossip with which we regaled ourselves on the way home.

Item 1. William Lockie has been declaring publicly that "it is no harm for a Christian to swear!"

I wonder if he learned that in the Unionist church! It does not sound to me like Presbyterian doctrine.

Item 2. Will Lockie and Ben Armstrong never would stand in the Presbyterian church while the "Amen" was sung at the end of a hymn. They did not "approve" of "Amens" at the end of hymns, so as soon as the last word of the hymn was sung down plumped the two gentlemen promptly on that part of their bodies the good Lord made for plumping. But in the United church they stand for the Amens without turning a hair.

Item 3. On the Sunday *following* Union Ewan spoke a few words in Zephyr church to the effect that now those who thought differently about Union had gone out those of us who remained were "of one heart and one soul etc." He spoke nicely and there was nothing in what he said to offend anyone. Mrs. Will Sellers is going about saying that if he hadn't said that she "might not have left the church." Now, the fact is that when he said it Mrs. Sellers had already left the church and at that very moment was over in the Methodist church joining it. So Mrs. Sellers seems to feel the need of justifying herself. It is a pity she has got a little mixed in her dates....

The reviews of *Emily Climbs* are coming in. They are mostly very good. Many reviews say it is "equal to my best." But I can't get excited over reviews as I once did.

Tuesday, Sept. 22, 1925
The Manse, Leaskdale
I had a really dreadful night last night. The difficulty of breathing caused by my cold prevented me from sleeping and I got badly depressed and Zephyr-obsessed. But I feel better today. And I had a little note from Miss Devigne, the St. Andrew's matron, saying that Chester was getting on nicely.

This evening I have finished reading *Charlotte Brontë and Her Circle* by Shorter. Hitherto I have thought that the fascination Charlotte Brontë's life and personality held for me was largely due to the literary charm of Mrs. Gaskell's biography. But it is just as strong in this book so I have concluded that it is inherent in her.

Charlotte Brontë made only about seven thousand by her books—not a tenth of what one of the flimsy and ephemeral "best sellers" of today would bring in. It seems unfair and unjust.

What I admire most in Charlotte Brontë is her absolute clear-sightedness regarding shams and sentimentalities. Nothing of the sort could impose on her. And she always hewed straight to the line.

I have been asking myself "If I had known Charlotte Brontë in life how would we have reacted upon each other? Would I have liked her? Would she have liked me?" I answer "no." She was absolutely without a sense of humor. I could never find a kindred spirit in a woman without a sense of humor. And for the same reason she would not have approved of me at all. All the same, had she been compelled to live with me for awhile I could have done her whole heaps of good. A few jokes would have leavened the gloom and tragedy of that Haworth parsonage amazingly. Charlotte would have been thirty per cent better for it. But she would have written most scathing things about me to Miss Nussey and Mrs. Gaskell.

In one of her letters she speaks of "the canker of constant solitude." Ah, truly. If we could have had no soul contact in the House of Mirth we could have come together in the House of Lonely Years.

People have spoken of Charlotte Brontë's "creative genius." Charlotte Brontë had *no* creative genius. Her genius was one of amazing ability to describe and interpret the people and surroundings she *knew*. All the people in her books who impress us with such a wonderful sense of reality were drawn from life. She herself is "Jane Eyre" and "Lucy Snowe." Emily was "Shirley." "Rochester," whom she did "create" was unnatural and unreal. "Blanche Ingram" was unreal. "St. John" was unreal. Most of her men are unreal. She knew nothing of men except her father and brother and the Belgian professor of her intense and unhappy love. "Emmanuel" was drawn from him and therefore is one of the few men, if not the only man, in her books who is "real."

Thursday, Sept. 24, 1925
I finished today a series of four stories I have been working on since July, with an eye to the *The Delineator*,—"What's In A Name?," "The Magic Door," "The Bobbing of Marigold" and "Her Chrism of Womanhood." They centre around a new little heroine and I have been very happy in writing them. I think they are very good specimens of their *genre* and "Marigold" seems very real and enchanting to me. Perhaps I'll write a book about her sometime.

We were over to J. Meyers for supper this evening. I loathe visiting anywhere in Zephyr now. I always have the feeling that I am walking over a powder mine, even in the houses of our friends. And nearly always something is said that hurts our feelings or worries us, though it may not be so intended at all.

Friday, Sept. 25, 1925
The Manse, Leaskdale
I am tired tonight. Today seemed to be infested with a multiplicity of small duties. But—I am going to see Chester tomorrow—tomorrow—tomorrow. It has been singing itself in my heart all day.

Saturday, Sept. 26, 1925
We rose with the lark—only there was no lark—and had a lovely drive into Toronto under the coral of the morning sky, with faint violet or white plumes of smoke going up everywhere on the crystal air. When I ran up the steps of the Lower House there was Chester smiling down at me, looking the picture of health with his rosy face. He is getting on finely now. Has got acquainted and is quite happy. This is such a relief to me. When Ewan was a boy he had an attack of his malady whenever he went away from home—when he went to P.W.C. and again when he went to Dalhousie. No doubt this was brought on by the loneliness of change and strangers. I have always dreaded that it might be the same with Chester and that if the seeds of his father's melancholy lurked in his system it would make its appearance when he first went away from home. But now one dread has been removed from my life and I realize how oppressive it was by its sudden lifting.

We had lunch at Simpsons and then I took Chester to a movie. Chester has been at St. Andrew's only two weeks but already it has put its stamp on him. He is a "public school" boy and talks the jargon of his guild as glibly as if he had been talking it for years. He got through his "initiation" in fine shape. One stunt was that he had to push the football over the gym floor with his nose. I had warned him before he went to take it all in good part. He did, with the happy result that the boys pronounced him "a good little kid."

He has scars on face, elbow and knee from football but displayed them proudly as badges of honour. I am not without anxiety. They play Rugby at St. Andrew's and it is a rough game. But I do not voice my anxiety. Chester must take his chances. I am glad he is interested in sports. Ewan never went in for any kind of game or sport in his college life and realizes now what a mistake he made. On the other hand there is a danger that Chester may give more of his mind to sports than studies. However, it is on the knees of the gods. The older I grow the more convinced a fatalist do I become. I think we "fash" ourselves uselessly over things. It is all written. We cannot by any pleading or effort erase the future any more than the past.

On our way into Toronto we stopped for a moment at a shabby little house on a poor road because Elsie's grandmother lived there and she wanted to see her. Out came her uncle with her—a big, rough-looking man who proceeded to tell me that he had "read every one of my books he could get his hands on." He seemed from appearances the most unlikely person in the world to read anything much less books like mine. I can't decide whether it was a compliment or not.

Thursday, October 1, 1925

Tonight we were at Tommy Marquis' to tea. When I was taking off my wraps in the little spare room off the dining room I happened to glance out of the window. Before me lay a long beautiful double row of spruce trees, with moonlight falling through them in enchanting shadows. Instantly I was swamped in a wave of homesickness for Park Corner, of which the scene reminded me—why I do not know, for there was nothing very like it at Park Corner. Perhaps because it linked up in some way with an old memory of a night when Frede and I were driving along a spruce bordered road back among the Irishtown hills and she remarked to me on the beauty of tree shadows in moonlight....

I read a brief biographical sketch of myself in a paper today where it was stated that I "lived as a girl in Saskatchewan where my grandfather was the postmaster of Avonlea."

Truly, I have come to believe that "history is a narrative of things that never happened."

Friday, October 2, 1925

Ewan was not very well today. It poured rain all day and evening. Ergo, the preparatory service in Zephyr did not take place. Poor Zephyr. There has always seemed a doom on it.

But I have a dish of marigolds before me that are so lovely that I can't believe the world is wholly delivered to Satan.

Wednesday, Oct. 7, 1925
This is Stuart's birthday. He is ten years old. Soon I will have no child at all.
I wonder if Chester is warm enough in bed these cold nights.

Thursday, Oct. 8, 1925
I had two odd dreams last night. One was that I was in Cavendish, sitting down to supper with Grandma, Aunt Annie—and Mrs. George Harker! Of all women! The latter was a woman of no significance to me who died thirty years ago and of whom I don't believe I have thought since. But at that gruesome supper table three of the party were *dead.*

I wakened, slept, and dreamed again—an odd dream this time of Mr. James Mustard telling me "what a happy life he had had." When I came down I said to Elsie "If there is anything in the old saying, 'Dream of the dead and you'll hear of the living' I'm going to hear some special news today."

Sequel:—Presently the phone rang. It was a message to tell me of the sudden and dangerous illness of Mr. Jas. Mustard. The mail came. An envelope in Mary Beaton's hand. Containing an invitation to Maud's wedding—to the young man she was engaged to and threw over. This was what Mary worried so over in the summer. She liked Albert Middleton so well and wanted the match. I hope this indicates that Maud has come to her senses and that Mary's troubles are over as far as she is concerned. But Maud may have had a case too....

Saturday, Oct. 10, 1925
A dreadful day of wind and cold—the coldest Oct. 10 for fifty years it is said. The leaves are frozen on the trees.

This evening I felt a bit blue. I had listened to eight sermons this week and I felt rather fed up. So I asked Ewan to take Stuart and me to Uxbridge to see a movie by way of counter irritant. I put it on the ground of Stuart's wish—he had been promised a movie for a birthday treat—but I really wanted a change of any kind. And they get very good movies in Uxbridge. The comic was so funny I laughed consumedly, felt ever so much better, and my theological indigestion vanished.

Ewan has got Lena Lockie into Normal, having moved heaven and earth to accomplish it. It is too long a story to go into here. But she owes it to him. *I* wouldn't have bothered myself about it had I been he, after the way Jim and Mrs. Jim have acted. They don't know the meaning of gratitude—but I think Lena *is* grateful.

Monday, Oct. 12, 1925
The Manse, Leaskdale
The Ministerial Association held its first meeting of the season at Rev. Taylor's, Uxbridge, today. And thereby hangs a tale—regarding that meeting that was to have been here last spring and was not.

We knew perfectly well that Dyer and Watch were at the bottom of it but we were not sure if they were the only ones. So, after leaving the matter fallow all summer we had decided that we would have it cleared up this fall. If Dyer and

Watch were solely responsible for it, well and good. *They* did not matter an old shoe to us. But if any of the other members of the Association would not come here because of our Union views it was not well or good. We resolved to ferret out the truth. If Dyer, as we had very good reason to suspect, had contrived to make the Association shoulder the action of his own personal spite, he must be shown up.

Shown up he was. Oh, we cut the comb of that pompous young ornament of the United Church *be-yew-tifully*. In good old expressive Scotch he got his breeks warmed.

The members of the Association turned out well. Dyer, who was secretary, came early, swelling like a little turkey cock, fraternizing markedly with a couple of Ex-Methodist ministers and discussing some of their own conference doings and plans as if on him and him alone depended their carrying out.

The election of officers proceeded. Mr. Robinson was nominated for secretary. The president said, "Any other nomination?" Dyer at once got up and said *he* didn't want to be re-elected. It was not necessary. Nobody wanted to re-elect him. He *felt* this and saved his face by declining a re-election before it was (*not*) offered him. The significant fact is that he had not declined it when nominations were first called for.

Robinson was elected secretary, Mr. Taylor president, Mr. Baldwin vice. So far, good. Here rose Ewan. He told simply of what had happened. Said Mr. Watch had told me that the members of the Association were too busy to come to Leaskdale. But that we had learned later from *reliable authority* (of course we couldn't drag Taylor's name into it as he had spoken to us in confidence) that the meeting was changed because of Ewan's views on Union. Ewan said he simply wished to know the truth. If, as Mr. Watch had said, the ministers were too busy to come that was all right. If on the other hand, the reason was Ewan's stand regarding Union, then we must know if the Association members were behind the Executive in this action. If they were, we, of course, could not continue in the Association.

During the progress of Ewan's remarks I had been watching Dyer. At first his expression was one of lofty indifference. Then, as the significance of Ewan's speech dawned on him, the most comical change came over his countenance. It was quite indescribable. And he did what a guilty person naturally would do—he looked at me. Then he was done for. I was gazing straight at him and I wickedly continued to gaze. Dyer was like a fascinated bird. He would look away—then look back at me at once—to see, I suppose, if I were still looking at him. I never saw a mortal look more guilty or more exquisitely uncomfortable. If he were innocent he would not, of course, have found any special significance in the fact that I happened to be looking at him.

When Ewan finished Mr. Taylor said *he* had nothing to do with the change. In turn all the other ministers present got up and disclaimed any share in it. Dyer, seeing everyone was looking at him got up and stumbled through a jumble of confused remarks. He was utterly unprepared and made an ass of himself. He said all he knew of it was that Mr. Watch had rung him up and said, "What about the meeting at Leaskdale?" "And *I* said, 'Oh, I'll go anywhere'." (Who had suggested anything else to him?) And that was all *he* knew of it, dear innocent little man.

Down he sat. And if he had kept his head and said no more he would have won a kind of victory—for of course we could not *prove* anything, as we could not betray Taylor's confidence. Then one member moved that the Association express its regret that the Executive had seen fit to change the meeting etc. Dyer, realizing, I suppose, that this would go in the minutes and that if Watch ever heard he had thrown all the blame on him the fat would be in the fire, got up and blurted out the truth—the very opposite of what he had said before. He said the meeting had been changed because "Mr. Macdonald had been interfering in my pastoral work" and had "refused to shake hands" with him at a Presbytery meeting. That is to say, he himself had been the sole cause of changing the meeting on the ground of his own personal grievance but throwing the onus of it on the association—something which he had no business whatever to do and which most of them properly resented.

Now, in regard to the things Dyer had said:—

Ewan, of course, never had anything to do with Dyer's own congregation of Greenbank. But Dyer was interim moderator of Uxbridge up to the time of the "Union." He was determined that they should hear no speaker on the Presbyterian side but he himself propagandized on every hand. He could not, however, prevent Uxbridge from taking a vote but he got the session of Quaker Hill (which is part of Uxbridge congregation), three of whom were Unionists, to decide that they wouldn't have a vote. The Presbyterian Association wrote to Ewan and asked him to try to see what he could do towards getting a vote for Quaker Hill. Ewan went to see all the leading men of Quaker Hill church who were opposed to Union and got them to sign the necessary request for a vote. And Quaker Hill and Uxbridge both voted Presbyterian by large majorities. Poor Dyer was furious and at once resigned the moderatorship.

At the last meeting of Presbytery before "Union" Ewan did not exactly refuse to shake hands with Dyer but when Dyer came up to the group and began to shake hands with the other men Ewan turned and walked away.

This meeting was *three weeks after* the Association meeting and the reason why Ewan turned away was that he was not going to greet as a friend a man who had refused to come to our house.

And yet Dyer got up there and said that it was because of this that he had changed the meeting. Verily, the prophets are not all dead yet!

Now, if Ewan had just been quick enough to catch on to this, as I did, he could have exposed Dyer then and there for what he is—a cowardly little liar. But he did not. He thought at first that of course Dyer must be referring to the meeting of Presbytery *before* the May Association. And he knew he *had* shaken hands with Dyer then. I remembered him coming home and telling me that Dyer had not seemed to make any difference because of the Quaker Hill affair but had shook hands with seeming friendliness.

At this point Mr. Baldwin pressed the motion and it was carried unanimously. Dyer as secretary had to write it in the book himself and Ewan expressed himself as satisfied. The meeting ran its course and was closed. Dyer did not stay for the social part. He simply faded out of the picture. Nobody seemed to miss him. I am sure he could have eaten us all up alive.

Well, it had to be done and I do not regret that we did it. The thing had to be cleared up if we were to continue as members of the Association. But I hate such ructions. I fight well when I am at it, giving and asking no quarter, but when it is done I sicken over the necessity. In a sense this has spoiled the Association for us at least for a time. I have been sad and unhappy all the evening over it.

We are to have the next meeting. Dyer will certainly not be "among those present." In fact I fancy he will leave the Association. He must feel that the Association condemned his action and that, to one of his overweening conceit, must be a bitter pill.

It was a pretty severe lesson and the young cockerel deserved it. He had offered a pointed insult to me. Whatever Ewan had done on the battleground of Union *I* was guiltless of all offence towards him. I was the hostess, whom Dyer himself last fall entreated to take the May meeting. I do not choose to be made the butt of the petty spite of a creature like Dyer. But I regret the necessity of soiling my hands and vexing my spirit over him. It seems to leave more of a feeling of degradation than any exultation of victory. One certainly cannot feel proud of having stepped on the head of a venomous little snake.

Friday, Oct. 16, 1925

Yesterday Mrs. Leask and I went to the W. M. S. at Wick. Mrs. Leask had to read a paper and I felt that I ought to help the Wick women a bit in their present uncomfortable chaotic condition. We had a pleasant time but I grudged the time.

Today there was in the papers some wonderful news—or what should prove wonderful news. France and Germany have sworn "perpetual peace" at Locarno. Said peace being guaranteed by England and Italy. As far as man can dispose this ends at last the war begun eleven years ago in 1914. I certainly hope that it *does* end it and that henceforth distracted Europe will set its face to a new day.

This evening at 6.30, when I rose from the supper table I said to Ewan, "Let's run over and call on the Brydons this evening."

Mr. Brydon is the minister inducted some months ago in Woodville. To call on them is a duty that has been postponed too long. But the point I wish to bring out is this:—Woodville is 26 miles away. To "call" on the Brydons meant a run of 52 miles. Ewan said casually, "All right" and we went.

Suppose thirty years ago, I had got up from the supper table in Cavendish and said, "Grandpa, let's run in to Charlottetown tonight and see So-and-So." The good old gentleman would have thought I had gone crazy. And he would have been right.

The world moves faster now. But is it any happier a world?

We went but it was not the pleasant drive it sometimes is. We called at Cannington and took the Scotts along with us. I like Mrs. Scott but she is not entertaining. She talked during the whole drive of the doings at the last Presbyterial and kindred subjects. I get very tired of endless missionary diet. Then at Woodville it was Union—Union—Union. The subject of Union has more bite than that of missions but I am horribly fed up with it too. I don't deny that Brydon is a comfortable person to hear about Union. He is a man of first rate intellect and sees very clearly. His sizing up of the situation was masterly and his account of some of the doings of Unionist ministers very adequate. But it poured rain all the way home and we had a flat tire. So it was two when we got here and I was very tired. Mrs. Brydon did not consider it necessary to offer us even a cup of tea after—and before—our long drive. And so I think things were just as well thirty years ago!

There is absolutely no autumn pomp this year—the first time I recall such a thing. This part of Ontario is usually very gorgeous in the fall. The bitter frost that came early in October actually *froze* the green leaves on the trees. I never saw such a bedraggled and melancholy landscape....

Thursday, Oct. 29, 1925
The Manse, Leaskdale
I have been in Toronto for a week. For a whole week I have been where I never heard the abominable word Zephyr and where nobody expected me to attend a missionary meeting. I had a very nice time and it has pepped me up for the two months that are before me—the hardest and *worriedest* months in the year.

We motored in last Wednesday. It was a lovely day with a crisp sunshiny air— a rare event this fall when it has rained or frozen almost continually. The most abominable October since I came to Ontario—and indeed in my whole recollection.

My main occupation was shopping but I had some very pleasant teas and luncheons. Friday afternoon I went up to St. Andrew's to see the Junior saints play the Appleby boys and win. When I sat on the bench and tried to spot Chester in his team I couldn't do it. Not till he came up to me was I able to recognize him— due mostly to the fact that he had a helmet on—and it made him look absurdly as he looked when he was two years old, wearing that bearcloth cap with the earlugs.

Mr. Tudball, the Lower School headmaster said Chester ought to make a good football player when he mastered the points of the game because he had just the build for it.

I felt sad as I sat there and watched them play in the cool gray autumn afternoon. I was thinking of Frede and how she had once said she would give anything to see Chester's first football game. When she said that it seemed such a far-off thing. Why, it would be years—long years—before that little white, dimpled baby would be playing football!

After the game the boys rushed into the tuckshop and entertained the defeated visitors. I came away and left Chester there, carousing with his mates and very happy I think.

One evening Mary and I went to see *Three Live Ghosts*. It was the best comedy I ever saw and we laughed unceasingly all through it. How pleasant it would be to live where I could see a good play once a week—or even once a month.

Yet, in spite of my pleasant week and in spite of many rather delightful pomps and vanities and in spite of Zephyr and missionary meetings, I was glad enough to come back to my own orderly comfortable home. I got home last night through a wind pursuing tormented wreaths of snow over the hills. Today was bitter cold. Only 11 above zero! And this in October.

It was election day too. I voted for the conservative candidate. No Liberal ran in this riding and I would not vote for the U.F.O. man—an ignorant creature who is not fit to be in Parliament.

I had a letter at last from Margaret Stirling. It is over a year since I wrote her. She and John are in the Union church. He was always a fanatic on the subject but Margaret used to be bitterly opposed to it. Of course she had to go with him—and now, I hear, she out-Unions the Unionist. Of which fact the psychology is tolerably clear.

I am sorry we are in different churches. There will always hereafter be a subject we cannot discuss. We have had many good laughs together over the various idiosyncrasies of the members of Presbytery and our mutual ministerial acquaintances. But never again! I *cannot* joke to Margaret of Unionist ministers and I *will* not of Presbyterian ministers. She will be in the same predicament and half our fun will be absent.

But our friendship has been too pleasant. The devil had to spoil it in some way. For some reason he could not kill Margaret as he did Frede so he just brewed up Church Union to spoil it.

I had another letter also but I have not opened it yet and will not till tomorrow. It is from Rollins—and I don't want to be worried until I get this house set to rights and all my belongings restored to order. I have been hard at work all day.

Ewan seems a bit dull and heady. But there is *one* encouraging bit of news in Zephyr. A certain Mr. Smith has bought one of the stores there and he is a Presbyterian. They are very nice people especially Mrs. Smith but have no family— at least none with them. Which is a pity. A few young people and children would be such an encouragement.

Last night when I came home I thought Dixie would go mad. He simply lay down before me and howled with joy. I could not get upstairs until Ewan dragged him away by the collar. The poor little dog seemed utterly out of his head. Luck was more dignified as became a cat, but he sat on the table and never took his eyes off me for a moment the whole evening. It seemed almost uncanny. Generally he sleeps all the evening beside me but last night it seemed as if he were afraid to shut or move his eyes lest I vanish again. Well, it is good to feel that my cat and dog won't rise up against me in judgment, at least.

This evening after nine—I stop working at nine. No eight hour days in my scheme of things—I was re-reading *The South African farm.* It made a tremendous sensation when it came out over thirty years ago. It would not make any now. But there is a charm about the book still. Whatever its faults, the people in it are *real*, so you are interested in them. I found myself disagreeing with a good many passages I had marked in agreement formerly. But in regard to many I could draw a second score of intensified agreement.

Friday, Oct. 30, 1925
The Manse, Leaskdale
A day distractingly full of small things as well as the big one of getting the

house into order for the Association meeting Monday—helping Stuart get his Hallowe'en Jacky Lantern ready—helping a young couple get dressed up as nuns for the masquerade at Sandford, writing a long letter re the contracts for *The Blue Castle* and so on and so on. When things were pretty well done I went upstairs and opened Rollins' letter. It was short, enclosing one from Briesen and Schrenk as follows:—

"It gives us great pleasure to inform you that we have just been notified by the Clerk of the Appellate Division of the Supreme Court of the State of New York that the order of Judge McGoldrick dismissing the complaint in the case of L.C. Page Co. V. Macdonald has been affirmed unanimously and without opinion. This action, under normal conditions, brings the litigation to a definite end. There is still the possibility that counsel for the Page Co. may apply for re-argument or for leave to take the case to the Court of Appeals, which is the court of last resort in our state....For the time being we entertain the somewhat justifiable hope that the case will not be permitted to be taken to the higher court...and that Mrs. Macdonald...will actually receive her money that has accumulated with the Stokes Co"....this heartened me up a bit for the day and a letter from *The Delineator* was another burst of sunshine. Mrs. Meloney wrote that she "loved Marigold" and would give $1,600 for the four stories.

And the first year I wrote seriously I earned $75, writing ten times as much!

But I admit there was a difference in the quality.

This windfall set my mind at rest concerning a financial problem or two.

Today I read an account of Maud Beaton's wedding in the *Guardian*. It seems about three or four years since I read—having first written it—the account of her mother's wedding. In one way. In another way it seems a thousand years. There was really less vital change in the thousand years from 800 to 1,800 than there has been in the world during the last thirty years....

It has been my misfortune to be a born conservative, hater of change, and to live my life in a period when everything has been, or is being turned topsy turvey, from the old religions down. My aunts and grandmothers lived practically their whole lives in an unchanged world. Changes came to them in the natural course of life but never were the foundations of their lives torn away from beneath their feet. For myself I have my own foundation and I stand firmly on it, unalarmed and unhurt by the crash of creeds and systems. But I cannot help being affected adversely by the changes in the world around me and the unrest and misery of an age that has thrown away everything because it has lost some things, and is itself lost and floundering now....

Thursday, Nov. 5, 1925

A day of rain and wind so dark we had to have the lamps lighted all day. Ewan talked, too, of resigning when and if Wick is joined to Leaskdale. Of course I realize that it is the proper thing to do but it disheartens me to think of it. I cannot bear the thought of leaving Leaskdale. And why? Leaskdale is a very average place. Life here has been growing intolerable for three or four years owing to the Church Union cleavage, the Zephyr situation, the Pickering misery and several other things over which we have no control. And yet how I love this old manse where my children were born and where I have tasted such rapturous happiness and endured so much hideous agony. I love its very faults. I love my garden and my trees and the pretty leafy corner of the side road and the sunsets over Mr. Leask's bush. I don't want to have to leave it all and go away to some new strange place among strange people. I shrink from the thought even while I know I must face it. I have long felt the coming change as one feels snow in the

"*Leaskdale Manse*"

air before it comes. I went through all this years ago in Cavendish. I cannot bear to anticipate going through it again. Especially do I dread Ewan having to "candidate" again in his state of mind. If he found it hard to get a call what effect might it not have on his mental condition. Of course just now calls are easier to get. But not to the *desirable* places, for which everyone is striving.

Well, well, I really believe that everything is foreordained and that it doesn't matter what we do or don't do to bring it about. But when what is foreordained is quite as likely to be unpleasant as pleasant and more so it is hard to say to Destiny "Thy Will be done." Of course my attitude is more or less the outcome of the past terrible seven years. I have become convinced in my subconscious mind that nothing good can come my way again—that all my life I must live just as I am living—or *worsely*—that any change must be for the worse. And I can't reason myself out of it try as I will....

Wednesday, November 11, 1925
The Manse, Leaskdale
Friday Ewan went to Toronto and brought Chester home for Thanksgiving. We had him till Tuesday morning. It seemed heavenly to have our big boy home again. Saturday it poured rain all day and all night. Nevertheless we all went down to Uxbridge. We had promised Stuart and Chester that we would take

them down to see a film that night and the promise must be kept though the heavens fall. We seemed to be motoring through a river there and back but in the little Jew theatre itself we spent hours in another world. The film was *The Birth of a Nation* and was very fine. We were three children together in our enjoyment of its thrills and laughter and agonies....

Monday, Nov. 16, 1925
Yesterday was Zephyr's anniversary and it poured from dawn till dark. Poor Zephyr! Whatever has ever been attempted there seems doomed. Ewan went to Cobourg to preach and Tom Goodwill came here. He is a good preacher and an agreeable guest. I hadn't seen him for over thirty years. Then he was kicking up a fearful and unreasonable quarrel in the Mock Trial at P.W.C. From all accounts he has been repeating that performance in most of his congregations.

I had a letter from Ella today, at last enclosing Maud's boot bill....

Monday Nov. 30, 1925
The Manse, Leaskdale, Ont.
We had a near-tragedy here last week. On Thursday evening our beautiful and beloved Good Luck went out about six o'clock for his usual evening prowl—and did not return. We went out for tea at five-thirty, leaving Luck sitting on a chair in the dining room, looking his beautiful*lest*. I bent over him and said jokingly, "Luck, you are *too* dear entirely. You will not escape the Jealous Power which will not tolerate perfection. Anything as delightful as you will not long be permitted to exist in this world."

When we returned at 9.30 Luck had not come back, nor had he returned at 11. I went to bed, somewhat worried because Luck, in cold weather, had always come home early. I left the cellar window open but when I got up Friday morning Luck had not come home. I did begin to worry in right good earnest then, for I knew something had happened but what? If I had been sure he was dead I would have paid my little pet the tribute of a real grief and some sincere tears. And then I would have said, "He is gone. His little life was perfectly happy while it lasted and I must not fret over his loss." But the uncertainty tortured me. Was he shut up somewhere cold and starving? Had he been poisoned and died alone in anguish? Was his little body lying stretched somewhere in the snow, stiff and stark, his bright, almost human eyes glazed and dull? Or—most hideous thought of all—had he been caught in some trap and held there in agony long drawn out, perhaps not even yet mercifully dead?

If grouchy old Pat had disappeared we would not have minded so much. But our charming Luck with his adorable ways and graces!

I made a frenzied search in every barn and outhouse and stable in the village save one. No Luck. Everybody was concerned for everyone in Leaskdale is fond of Luck. I went to the door every ten minutes to call despairingly. I watched from every window in hope that I would see him coming. Elsie was as bad as I was.

I went to Social Guild that night and conducted the program very miserably. Hurried home after it, still hoping that when I came in Luck might run to meet me with his plumy tail waving, or that I might find him rolled up into an adorable ball in his favorite parlor rocker. No Luck.

I had a bad night with the miserable conviction that everything I loved, human or animal—but Luck *was* half human—must die. My love was doom to them.

Towards morning I slept and dreamed that I found Luck in a stable. I could not think of any stable I had not searched but I looked through several again. Then Stuart and I searched through the cedars along the brook, thinking we might find his body and *know* what had become of him.

After dinner I was in the library drearily concluding that it was time to go to that abominable practice, when I heard Elsie say "Mrs. Macdonald." I looked up. Elsie stood in the doorway with Luck in her arms.

We just made two fools of ourselves. I won't tell what we did or said. And I'm sure Luck never will.

We did not find out where he had been until last night when we discovered he had been shut up in John Lowrie's stable, the only one I hadn't searched because I had forgotten the Lowrie boys had a stable.

How he got there is a mystery. The Lowrie boys are two old bachelors who keep no horse and Jack says they hadn't been in it for weeks. He happened to go to it Saturday, looking for a tool. As he opened the door a gray streak shot past him and tore down through the back yards of the village.

I was so delighted I was perfectly happy for awhile, all worries, conscious or subconscious, ceasing to sting for a time. I went gaily to practice, and found it quite easy to keep my patience under all provocation....

Today was my birthday. I got more presents than I have had since I was ten years old! Stuart gave me a centrepiece he had embroidered himself. Elsie gave me an apron. Ewan a box of chocolates and Mrs. Mills a cushion. An *awful* cushion of log cabin silks in *purple* and *green*—the purplest purple and the greenest green—with a full, wide frill of glowing scarlet! The thing would put your eyes out. And yet the gratitude behind it made it of value and I was absolutely sincere in my expression of appreciation. But I shall stow it away in the same box with the autograph quilt Zephyr W.M.S. gave me and the other autograph quilt the Mission Band gave me. There are certain things one cannot have before their eyes all the time. I have endured considerable these past years. I may and fear I am fated to endure a good deal more. But I will *not* endure that green and purple and scarlet nightmare.

Sunday, Dec. 6, 1925

....Had an odd dream last night—the same dream of pregnancy I have had so often when a call was hoped for or attempted. But there is nothing of the sort in the wind just at present....I feel it portends a change of some kind.

Later On.

A strange thing has happened. When Ewan came home from Zephyr he suggested that we go to Uxbridge to the evening anniversary service. Glad of a chance to get out of rather depressing surroundings I agreed. We had tea at the manse and then we met Rev. Mr. McKay, the Anniversary preacher. After supper he and I were talking in the parlor when he suddenly said, "Have you and

Mr. Macdonald any idea of making a move some of these days?" I said it was possible we might, once the Wick affair was settled. He then said he was moderator of a very nice charge, Norval and Union, about thirty miles west of Toronto on the highway. There was a nice manse with electric light and bathroom and Norval was on a radial line etc.

I did not say much but I recalled my dream with a shock. Was this what it heralded?

On the way home Ewan said Mr. McKay had spoken to him about it and he had promised to preach on Dec. 20th.

I feel a strange and unhappy conviction that my life in Leaskdale is near its close. And I cannot bear the thought.

Sat. Dec. 12, 1925

On the whole, a depressing week. Peevish weather and such a multiplicity of small duties that I feel despairingly that I am a slave of time and must always be so. Then, too, three of the girls who were to take part in the S.S. concert have "got mad" and announced that they will not take part at all. I have no connection with the cause of their anger. They are furious because they are not in the "drill." Margaret Leask and Mary Stiver are getting that up and very properly concluded that it was no use to ask any High School girl to take part in it, as she could attend only one practice a week when three were absolutely needed to get it up in so short a time. Behold three badly disgruntled damsels! Now, these girls are in my S.S. class and for years I have tried to teach them high ideals of conduct and behavior. Two of them have seemed to respond, too. But now, at a purely imaginary slight they are acting like spoiled babies.

Ewan was at Jim Lockie's Friday to hear the usual disheartening gossip. Mrs. Lockie is certainly never happy except when she is putting tacks in somebody's tires.

Today with considerable regret I discarded my windowfuls of geraniums. Ever since I was twelve years old I have had geraniums and loved them. Lately I have decided that I cannot longer spare the time to care for them. I *must* cut out a few more non-essentials. Yet I disposed of them with a bitter feeling that the time spent on the beautiful things was better spent than the hours I am compelled to use training silly children or presiding at dismal guild meetings and mission bands.

Thurs., Dec. 17, 1925

On Tuesday night they sent down for me to go up to see Mrs. Jas. Blanchard who has been very ill all the fall and has lately quite gone out of her mind, poor thing. I stayed all night and had a rather terrible time. Sometimes she was very violent. At other times I had a little influence over her. She never stopped talking for a moment. She has turned against everyone, after the sad custom of the unsound in mind. It is a dreadful thing to look into the eyes of a friend where the light of reason is replaced by the glare of madness.

Yesterday I was agreeably surprised to get a letter from Stokes enclosing a check for all the long-withheld royalties. So that litigation is actually ended at last. Page had evidently been unable to find any loophole for a further appeal. I can hardly credit the good news. It has lighted up an otherwise dark and depressing week.

Last night I should have gone early to bed but instead must go to the school concert, else Stuart would have been heart-broken. It was a poor affair, compared to other years, and I was grievously tired. Also something Mrs. Alex Leask told me she had heard someone in Greenbank—evidently one of the Dyer Clique there—say about me,—a very nasty something—did not heighten my enjoyment at all. It was quite unnecessary for her to have told me. It did not atone for it that a few minutes later she told me that she had heard a gentleman who knew me say that I was "the most perfect woman he had ever known!" Mrs. Leask is a paw-and-claw friend. First a scratch, then a pat, I would prefer to dispense with both. But just now everything jars on me. I seem to have no resiliency of spirit. Ewan who has been pretty well all the fall, has been putting his hand to his head again this week—a gesture which always fills me with horror and foreboding.

Monday December 21, 1925
The Manse, Leaskdale
Ewan went on Saturday to fulfil his Norval engagement. He did not return until tonight. He came in about eight in high spirits—a fact which told me all before he said a word. He had found Norval and Union a very nice charge and from what was said to him in both churches he feels it very probable that a call will ensue. I went over to the practice at the church with very mixed feelings. And I found, too, that all at once I felt *outside* that circle of young people. I knew something they did not—yet a something that concerned them. The knowledge gave me a queer, half-guilty feeling as if the secret were a barrier between us. If we go I shall be sorry to leave these young people. I have worked among them so long—have seen them grow from children to young men and women.

After practice Ewan and I had a long talk—a veritable domestic council. He wishes to go if the call comes. I believe it *will* come—my dream foretold it. He says the manse is a fine large one and both church buildings very nice. The advantages seem to be many. No doubt there will be disadvantages also. One is apparent already. Both churches are very large—built in the day of big families, much too large for the families of today. Half the seats empty is not a nice thing to confront a minister every Sunday. And there is a United Church in Norval and great bitterness arising from the Union cleavage. Half of the Norval congregation left and went over to the Unionists. But half the Mount Pleasant people came in when their church went Union so that Norval is as strong as ever. Still, the situation will be a difficult one. Yet I suppose we will go. I could not dare urge Ewan to decline—though I feel no enthusiasm regarding it.

Wednesday, Dec. 23, 1925
I spent last night at Mrs. Leask's and this forenoon getting the Sunday School diplomas ready. When Ewan came up with the mail be beckoned me into the

library and handed me a letter from Mr. McKay. It stated that Norval and Union wished to call him and that it would be unanimous.

So it is settled. I felt very strangely. I looked around my beautiful library. Already it seemed to me to wear a reproachful air. My home that I have loved. And I must leave it.

We had our Xmas concert and tree tonight. I have taken part in fourteen such concerts since I came here. And this would be the last one. The knowledge haunted me all the evening and I moved among the gay folk and happy children like a ghost moving among revellers it has outgrown.

Thursday, Dec. 24, 1925
The Manse, Leaskdale
We celebrated Christmas today—as Elsie goes home tomorrow. We had our tree and our dinner. In reality it was a sorrowful day for me. Our last Christmas in Leaskdale manse!

My thoughts kept going back to our first one here. Frede and Stella were with me.

But Chester and Stuart were not.

In the evening came word that Mr. James Mustard had died. A sad ending to a day that was joyous outwardly.

After supper George Leask took the big, old-fashioned wood sleigh and carried a load of us—Ewan, myself, and half a dozen performing boys over to help the Zephyr Sunday School concert programme out. We had a good evening, too—church well filled and no thanks to Methodists or Unionists either. We have not had so many concerts in Zephyr as in Leaskdale—it is only within the past four or five years that the Zephyr folks dared defy Ben Armstrong to the extent of having a Sunday School concert. But the same feeling of sadness existed for me.

The boys and I sang old songs all the way home along the dim moonlit road, between the old gray fences in the softly falling snow. On the surface I enjoyed it but underneath—oh, how I hate the thought of leaving! And the thought of new places and people. I paused for a moment at the front gate as I came in. Will I have such a pretty view from my gate in Norval? The beautiful woods behind Mr. Leask's, the leaf-hung corner of the side-road, the lovely hill field beyond with the elms on its crest. I love these things and grieve to leave them. But what has my life been but a succession of leaving things I loved?

Ewan seems to have no feeling about the matter. He is more devoid than anyone I ever knew of any capacity for attachment to places or things. They mean nothing to him. I do not think it will mean more to him to leave Leaskdale after sixteen years than it would mean to leave it after so many weeks. Well, I suppose it is the best way to be. He does not have the agony of losing. But oh, neither does he ever have the exquisite pleasure the love of them can give. It is a question of price. Is it worth it? I say yes—after all—yes, verily.

I remember as if it were but yesterday the first time I suffered the anguish of losing a *place* I loved. I was less than seven, for it was before Aunt Emily was married but how much less I do not know. Between our two hill fields was a narrow strip of grassland with a few little spruces in it where I often went to pick strawberries. It was full of ferns and red leaves and blue-eyed grasses and birds' nests and little winds and cloud-shadows—a most delectable place.

Grandfather decided to plough it up. To me that came as a calamity. I cried myself sick over it and pleaded wildly and vainly with Grandfather not to plough it up. I think still he might have granted my bitter prayer. The strip of grassland was very narrow and short—scarcely would it yield a bushel of grain or a bag of potatoes. It would have meant little to him—and it meant so much to me. What a kind and grateful remembrance I would have of him today if he had said gently, "Well, since you want it so badly, you can have it. I won't plough it up." But he refused—and refused harshly. The strip was ploughed up—and the hurt is in my heart today. The old scar aches when I touch it.

Monday, Dec. 28, 1925
....Tonight I happened to glance out of the kitchen window and noted how the frost-diamonds were glittering magnificently over the yard. Instantly I recalled—and saw—our old orchards in Cavendish where there used to be such a show of fairy jewels on frosty moonlit nights. And I saw the old dear trees and the firs beyond and the white hills I loved, lying in a great austere silence....

Wednesday, Dec. 30, 1925
The Manse, Leaskdale
Today Mr. McKay wrote that he had moderated in the call. So the thing is a certainty. There is a certain resulting peace and comfort when a thing becomes irrevocable.

This being the case I decided that Elsie must be told. I had an idea that she would be much delighted at the thought of going to Norval....She was tremendously excited and quite overjoyed at the news.

I do not know if I am doing a wise thing in taking her. As a maid she does very well and is improving all the time. She knew almost nothing when she came here but she was willing and eager to learn and she has learned. And she admits freely that I have taught her all she knows. As far as her capability for service goes I am quite willing to take her.

The trouble is....to take a girl...away from home where her parents can keep some kind of tabs on her is a rather heavy responsibility.

However, it is highly likely she will be too homesick and lonesome to stay long and it will mean much to have someone I know to help me move and get settled. So it is decided that she is to go with me.

Thursday, Dec. 31, 1925
We have decided that, as the Toronto road is still passable for cars, it would be better to take ours in at once and leave it in a garage there. Then we can take it out to Norval whenever we need it whereas, if we kept it here, we could not get it to Norval until late in the spring. So Ewan took Dodgie today. I watched him

sadly. The last time of many that old Dodgie will be backed out of our lane and go off down the road. From now on the days will be full of "last things" each with its own little ache.

Ewan has been very well lately. Probably the excitement evoked by the Norval call has reacted favorably. But it is a whole year now since he has had a *bad* attack of melancholia. This is the longest time he has been free since the first one in that terrible spring of 1919. I wonder if it is possible that the change will cure him completely. I suppose it is too much to hope for.

1926

Friday, January 1, 1926

The last year to be spent in the old Leaskdale manse is gone.

Ewan was in Zephyr tonight, at Warren's, and heard a bit of disquieting news. We had hoped that no whisper regarding Norval would get out for some time yet. But the birds of the air *do* carry things.

Warrens had heard about the call. It seems that Ella Arnold, a Zephyr girl, now home for the holidays, once taught in or near Norval and is engaged to a young man there. This young man 'phoned up to her the other night and told her Norval congregation was calling Ewan. She told her brother Pete Arnold who told Warren. And the said Pete Arnold is married to one of Marshall Pickering's daughters and has always been very bitter against us!

It worries me to think that his sister's lover lives down there and might possibly hear things in regard to the salary—which of course is not paid in advance in Norval—yet,—and tell them. It is only a remote contingency I suppose but I do not like it. Norval is 70 miles from here and I had hoped we would get completely out of the Pickering zone.

Elsie's ceaseless gush about Norval is getting on my nerves. Morning, noon and night she talks of it, "hoping" this and that about manse, church and village. It jars on me, for I am not so eager to get out of Leaskdale as she is....

I told Stuart and Chester about Norval today. Both seemed to feel badly over it, especially Stuart. He is fretting over leaving his chums here. But he is so young. He will soon forget and form new friends.

Today the old, shabby, inglorious, outlived calendars came down and the new ones went up. What will they dot off for us?

Sunday, Jan. 3, 1926
The Manse, Leaskdale

We drove over to see Gladys Cook tonight. Her condition is serious and we are all worried about her. But I enjoyed the drive through the mild night and the old charm of the white road, where every turn was a friend, and of the dark trees. Trees always take such funny shapes in the dark. A huge lion prowled in Alec Leask's field. A rooster strutted on George Leask's fence. A very devil with horns and tail squatted behind Cox's barn. An old man peered out of the swamp. I ached with fantastic delight as I recognized them afresh. All that had once made magic made it again for a little while.

But I felt very sad all day.

Wednesday, Jan. 6, 1926
This has been a hard day. Gladys Cook died this morning. She leaves three little motherless girls. I have felt upset all day and Elsie's foolish chatter about Norval became so unbearable that I had to rebuke her for it.

Then, in the minutes of Toronto Presbytery, published in the Globe, the Norval call is mentioned. So everybody will know it now and, somehow, I dread that foolishly.

Ewan, who went to Toronto yesterday, returned this evening, having been out to Norval and got a plan of the manse. It seems to be a very nice one. We sat in the parlor late, talking and planning. And I recalled another night when we had been late in that room—fourteen years ago, when we were trying to get it ready for callers the next day.

Friday, Jan. 8, 1926
The Manse, Leaskdale
Today I began packing. It will be such a tremendous task that the sooner a beginning is made the better. I packed my little old trunk full of things that will not be needed here again. I did it in the gray twilight of the winter evening, with a lonely wind sighing around the eaves. And I did it with a heavy heart, recalling the hours of happiness that have been mine here and forgetting the hours of agony.

Tuesday, Jan. 12, 1926
I took Chester back to St. Andrew's yesterday and then looked at some furniture. I think we must sell our parlor set. It is a small design, too small for the big Norval parlor and one chair is lacking—smashed last fall by Rev. Dyer's cavorting youngsters. I am loath to give it up but it is best. We must have new dining-room chairs too as our old ones are done, scarred and chipped by many kicks from little boyish feet.

I was packing all day today and thinking of the other times I packed—in Cavendish and again in Park Corner....

This old manse hurts me. I love its very uglinesses and inconveniences as well as its virtues, just as one likes better the wrinkled face of an old friend than the smooth face of a stranger.

Today I was sitting on the dining room lounge with Luck—whose beautiful coat is in full bloom now—in my lap and did not notice that Dixie lying beside me was trying to attract my attention. Finally he gave up in despair and I suddenly heard the most human kind of a sigh as he lay patiently down. Poor little black dog. He got the petting he wanted.

Thursday, Jan. 14, 1926
The Manse, Leaskdale
I packed all the morning. Mrs. Albert Cook came in and cried. Hoped we would not go. This afternoon I went to the W.M.S. in Zephyr. A nice meeting as Mrs. Jim Lockie was not there. Not a word was said about Norval but I felt they all knew.

By the way, the Methodists are saying that "the Presbyterians sent their cranks over to us." Ben Armstrong and Will Lockie, I suppose.

It is to laugh. They were very eager to get them. They can't tell *us* anything about their crankiness.

We had a nice drive home in front of the gentle storm, through a dead-white, fascinating unreal world. We called in at Will Cook's. His mother said to me, "Are you going to leave us, Mrs. Macdonald?" "I don't know but I am afraid so," I replied. Mrs. Cook began to cry. "Oh, don't go—don't go. We'll never get anyone like you again."

It is very hard. And yet there is certain secret relief in the thought of getting away from some things that have become almost intolerable here. The old galled spots have become *too* sore. It may be easier to bear new ones.

Friday, Jan. 13, 1926

I dread going anywhere now. Tonight at Guild Mrs. Richard Oxtoby began to cry, pleading with me not to go. "I thought you'd never leave Leaskdale," she said.

Bitter—bitter! And yet an inconvenient sense of humor in the back of my mind made it hard for me not to smile. Mrs. O.'s complacency was so amusing. I am very sorry to pull up my roots here because I am one of those unlucky people who send roots so far down that the process is always extremely painful. But there is really nothing about Leaskdale in itself or the people here that would lead anyone to suppose we ought to be glad to spend all our years here. Most people have always thought we were "buried alive" here. I have never felt so because I have my own world of fancy and adventure and beauty wherever I dwell. And in these long years of Ewan's mental trouble I have been thankful we were "buried." But to have anyone take it for granted, as Mrs. O. does, that we were perfectly satisfied here *is* funny.

Saturday, Jan. 16, 1926

I packed all day—mostly books. We have dismantled the parlor and taken down the curtains to use it as a packing room. I felt sad over this wiping out of my parlor. It has been the dearest room in the house to me—a room which in my life here took the same place as my little bedroom did in my Cavendish life. It was *my* room. It was a beautiful room with a pleasing outlook. I wrote all my books here from *The Golden Road* up. I came here to read my letters and to dream. And I came here to be alone in hours of anguish and dread. How often have I walked up and down it and fought for strength and composure. Frede and I used to sit here and talk—how she dies afresh in this destruction of a room full of memories of her.

Stuart, when he was two and three years old and found himself shut out of the parlor when "mother" was writing would sweetly and patiently lie down on the hall floor outside and "throw kisses" to me under the door, desisting not until I had thrown him a kiss back, then going away contented. This room has been a friend to me and now it has vanished out of existence—and in its place is merely an apartment strewn with boxes and barrels and straw and newspapers.

Poor Mrs. Warner is taking our going away very deeply to heart. Stuart found her crying when he went in today. "Oh," she sobbed, "Gladys Cook's death was a shock but it was nothing to this." Mrs. Warner is too old to make new friends. She will miss us. And we will miss her. She has been, in the old phrase, "a good neighbor."

I went up to see Mrs. Alex Leask this evening. I was tired after packing all day and my walk rested and refreshed me. A new moon hung low in the west and flawless stars were gleaming over fields thinly white with snow. Above me Orion shone out over a goblin market of wind-tossed trees. Suddenly I *felt* my immortality. For a space my spirit was *free.* I had "an authentic glimpse of eternity." I felt what Emerson calls "A sublime hope that in other regions of universal power souls are now acting, enduring and daring which can love us and which we can love"....

Tuesday, Jan. 19, 1926
The Manse, Leaskdale
Have been packing steadily. The house is by now so upset that I begin to feel I have no home. Last night I was too tired to sleep and the whole thing assumed the aspect of a nightmare. Just then I would really have given much to find the whole thing a dream and my torn-up, reproachful home in its old order again—the pictures back on the walls, the books again on their shelves....

Zephyr had its annual meeting tonight and for the first time Ewan came home from it in good spirits. Everybody was in good heart—all was harmony. They have subscribed as much for next year as the whole church paid last year. It does seem impish that we are going just when things have taken such a turn for the better. And they are all so anxious for us to stay.

Wednesday, Jan. 20, 1926
The Manse, Leaskdale
Packing all day and very tired. Brought down my own old trunk today and packed it—the trunk that has accompanied me in all my wanderings. I thought of all the many times I packed and unpacked it in girlhood days of college and teaching.

Mrs. Alec Leask told me today that my leaving was "the greatest misfortune that ever happened to Leaskdale." But I think she is speaking from her own point of view in losing a friend. I think Leaskdale will get on as usual. It will not miss me as much as I miss it.

Mrs. George Leask is very blue, too. She says she and Mr. Leask can't sleep at nights for thinking of it.

Friday, Jan. 22, 1926
Today I began packing the dishes—a huge task. Got all my good set packed and have a sore back as a result. We had Guild tonight and I read a paper on Marjorie Pickthall—the last one I shall read here. I recall the first one, "A visit to Shakespeare Land." I sat down and wrote *it* amid the confusion of unpacking boxes and barrels to get settled here. And now I write the last amid the

confusion of tearing up and unsettling. What a fourteen years these have been! Not merely for a poor worm like myself but for all the world.

Monday, Jan. 25, 1926

This morning seven years ago Frede died. It seems but as yesterday. I can never believe that years have passed since then. It seemed one of those events which *must* stop time.

Is it well with thee, beloved, in that far land to which you have gone? You, who lighted my life like a friendly, beaming candle. How dark the world grew for me when you went out of it. I have grown used to its dimness now. But sometimes I suddenly remember what it was like when you were here....

Friday, January 29, 1926

Tuesday I went to Brantford to speak to the Canadian club there. I had a nice time and a needed rest from packing. I felt cheered up and more hopeful. On my way back I stopped in Toronto and bought some furniture—a reed set and a nice, comfy, "overstuffed" set for the parlor. I think they are rather ugly, clumsy things but oh, how comfortable they are. To sink into the depths of one of them before an open fire. The thought is a rest.

But it was sad to come home to a dismantled house. And it would be the last of many times that Ewan would meet me at Uxbridge station.

I packed all the afternoon so am as usual tired and disheartened.

But we *did* hear one heartening thing today. At the Governor General's annual levee, the Moderator of the General Assembly was given his old, historic place as representative of the third oldest church in Canada. And this in face of the protest of the United church! Verily, there is a bit of satisfaction left in life. The Presbyterian church goes on. And the gates of hell shall not prevail against it....[*Handwritten volume 6 ends here.*]

The Manse, Leaskdale
Saturday, Jan. 30, 1926

Packing goes on apace. We are really getting on exceedingly well. We have got all the books packed—forty-two boxes—and labelled, "Rev. E. Macdonald, *Norval*." I have written it so often that I begin to feel as if we belonged there. And I finished packing all my fruit jars out of the cellar cupboard. Our library is stripped to the bare bones.

Sunday, Jan. 31, 1926

Ewan went to Uxbridge today and Mr. Robinson came to preach here and read the formal citation. I felt almost unbearable emotion while he read it. And all the women and some of the men were crying.

"The bottom seems to have dropped out of everything," one woman said to me.

Tonight is windy and the shutters are banging dismally. After supper Stuart said to me, "Mother dear, *do* go to bed early and get a good sleep. You look so tired."

It gave me an odd sensation. It is so long since anyone said anything like that to me—since anyone tried to take care of me. Not since Frede died. I found my eyes filling with tears over the unaccustomed sweetness of it.

Ewan is never unkind. He simply never notices. In all the fourteen years of our married life he has never once said to me, "You look tired" or "You must be tired. You have had a hard day." It just never occurs to him.

Well, it doesn't matter much—it's a little thing—but it *was* sweet to hear Stuart say that—to realize that the child noticed I was tired and wanted me to have a rest.

Thursday, Feb. 4, 1926
The Manse, Leaskdale
Ewan began crating furniture today. We are beginning to live rather from hand to mouth now. I have all my dishes packed except the granite camping set—eleven barrels. I do hope they will go safely....

Monday, Feb. 8, 1926
Dick Colwell and Dave Lyons were here all day crating. Neither of them has ever seen any reason why he should hurry. They got only thirteen pieces done. I planned out the meals for the week—no joke just now—and we spent the evening at Mrs. Jas. Mustard's. A very hard time. "You'll never know what you have meant to us," said poor Mrs. Mustard weeping, as we came away.

The Manse, Leaskdale
Tuesday, Feb. 9, 1926
Mr. Colwell was here all day crating but got on very slowly. This afternoon the W.M.S. had its annual rally-day tea. For fourteen years I have had it in the manse. But today it had to be held in the class-room. All the women of the congregation were there. I was presented with an address, a Life Membership in the W.M.S. and the gold badge pin. I appreciated the affection behind it even if the Life Membership did not rapturize me.

It has been our custom to answer roll call with a verse and when one member responded today with "Thou wilt be missed because thy seat will be empty," I could not repress tears. It was all a terrible emotional strain on the one hand—and on the other a nerve-racking repetition of the same questions from everybody. I came home exhausted.

Wednesday, Feb. 10, 1926
I went to bed too tired and overwrought to sleep and fell to a helpless worrying over everything, especially the crating. I figured up a thousand times over how many pieces could possibly be done per day but by no juggling could I get all those things crated by Saturday night. And it was all quite unnecessary—as so many worries are. For three men came today and got on swimmingly. I packed boxes of kitchen utensils and odds and ends. The whole house is an indecent orgy of straw, paper, saw-dust and chunks of wood. Elsie and I got dinner under distracting difficulties.

Two boys came and took away a couple of loads of the things we are selling. I hated to see my parlor set go—and the old hanging lamps that have shone on many a gathering of friendly faces.

We went to Uxbridge after dinner and made some farewell calls. Our things sold well but how I hated to see them sprawled all over the street among a mob of strangers.

We had our last cold drive home from Uxbridge—and no nice home awaiting us....

We took up the stair and hall carpet this evening. The house seems as it did on the first night I came to it. Tonight as I went up I paused on the landing to look down at the oblong of light falling across the lower hall from the open library door, and an old memory came suddenly and sweetly back to me. One autumn evening thirteen years ago, I had turned there and looked down—so—and in that oblong of light Chester was standing, having recently learned to trot around alone—in his little tan linen romper with the blue binding. I could see him there as plainly as I did thirteen years ago, the pretty little baby-man with his curly head and chubby face.

Thursday, Feb. 11, 1926

Remorselessly the days ebb away. Today was fine but very cold. Three men were here crating and I had a wild morning of getting ready for them. A thousand things all insistent to be done at once. In the afternoon we went to the W.M.S. in Zephyr and from there to tea at Warrens—where we heard that Marshall Pickering had recently cut his first wisdom tooth! What a pity he hadn't cut it five years ago!

There was a farewell "reception" at the Zephyr church at night. They gave Ewan a hymn book and me a gold fountain-pen. I had never expected to feel sorry over parting with the Zephyr people. But the ones I disliked are gone out and the remaining ones are friends I have always liked. Mrs. Jim Lockie was the only woman who did not tell me she was sorry I was going. She was not sorry. In her heart she really felt a vast relief....

And I shall never have to visit her any more! Oh, beautiful freedom!

Then we came home. The last of our many long cold drives over those hills. But it was a nice drive. Frosty, crystal air—the pale fires of the northern lights—exquisite beauty of leafless trees against a starlit sky. As we drew near Leaskdale all the trees were rimed with white frost—an unreal, magic world.

As we drove into the yard I looked up as always but there was no light in "the boy's room." Stuart had gone to stay with friends. He will sleep no more in the old manse.

Friday, Feb. 12, 1926

Last night we slept on the floor—that is, our mattress was on the floor. We had no men here today but were very busy. Tonight we had another ordeal—a congregational reception in the church, with the usual addresses and regrets. As we stood up to hear the address read I recalled the night of our "reception" when we came here after our wedding. I stood up then, a slim bride, wearing my wedding dress and Hugh Mustard read the "address." He is dead now—and many others who were there that night.

The Guild gave me a casserole dish and the congregation gave us $100 in gold. Everybody seemed and I think really were very sorry over our going. And yet here and there, under it all, one sensed a little of that curious resentment some people feel when they discover that you can get along without them!

Saturday, Feb. 13, 1926
....I packed odds and ends madly all day. We had tea at Richard Oxtoby's. When we went in "my" hall lamp was shining redly in their hall—they bought it at the sale. A little thing—but it suddenly brought home to me the reality of change. I had a most odd, utterly unreasonable feeling of resentment. What business had they with *my* lamp!!!

When we came back to the manse I finally opened Rollins' letter. There was, thank heaven, nothing startling in it but some interesting items. Briesen and Schrenck write him that they think I have a perfectly clear case against Page for all my expenses in the New York suit and want to know if they may go ahead. I don't like the idea of another suit but Rollins advises me to bring it. He is so cautious that it must be reasonably sure and it would be very nice to get back the $2,000 that suit cost me.

Sunday, February 14, 1926
I do not want ever to go through such another day. My last Sunday in Leaskdale. And of course I recalled the first—that rainy morning when all were strangers and everybody was looking curiously at me to see the bride—and the minister's wife—and L.M. Montgomery.

I bade my Sunday School class good-bye. I was somewhat sorry and sorry that I wasn't sorrier. They all seemed to feel badly but when I saw that the two girls who had given me the most trouble with their whispering and inattention howled the most dismally I permitted myself a cynical smile. The church was of course crowded. Ewan preached very well and in good taste. There were endless farewells. We had dinner with the Oxtoby girls. I called at Cox's in the afternoon & had tea at Alec Leask's. As soon as Ewan came from Zephyr he went to Wick where there is a farewell service and presentation tonight.

I am alone in the manse. It is our last night here. By this time tomorrow night everything will be gone. I am terribly tired but perhaps I will have a better sleep than I had the first night I slept here—on that extemporized couch of sofa pillows in what was afterwards the boys' room. At least, my bed tonight will be level and not one of hills and hollows. I hope I shall get a good sleep for this has been the hardest week I ever lived through from the point of view of hard work.

And this is the last entry to be written here. I can write no more until we are moved and settled. What a comfort this journal has been in these past fourteen years with their griefs and problems and terror! What would I have done without it? I am here all alone with my two faithful fat gray pussies. Stuart is over at Mr. Stiver's. Sometimes I wander about the stripped rooms with my memories of vanished days. I have a very dreadful feeling of "lostness" and emptiness—as if all emotion were drained out of me and the resulting vacuum were more dreadful to bear than pain.

Good-bye, old life. Tonight I forget your terrible hours and think only of your bright and pleasant ones.

Farewell.

The Manse, Norval, Ont.
Sunday, Feb. 28, 1926

....We are in Norval. But I must go back to that last night in Leaskdale manse. After I finished writing I went up to my big empty room, undressed and lay down on the bed, so tired that I fell asleep at once. I slept about an hour—all the sleep I was destined to get that night. I wakened when Ewan came home and sat interestedly up to hear the news from Wick. But the news I heard was not about Wick.

Ewan had been handed a letter by Mrs. Warren at Zephyr. A dramatic epistle, informing us that "our enemies were on our trail." Pete Arnold, who is married to a daughter of Marshall Pickering, had been telling a deal of stuff to Herb Warren. It was evident that plenty of devilry was afoot. Our "moving expenses were to be garnisheed." And the young man to whom Ella Arnold was engaged was a member of our congregation in Norval and Arnold's were going to have him as a spy to find out everything. Finally Mrs. Warren exhorted us to ship everything in my name as there was also some scheme afoot to seize the railway car if it were in Ewan's name.

I was literally aghast. We have heard nothing of "moving expenses" but some congregations do pay them and it is possible Norval is doing it and this beau of Ella's has told the Arnolds. However, I didn't see what Pickering could do about *that* since, if it were so, it is only a voluntary offering which could not be garnisheed because it was not "owing." So this did not worry me. But the fact that Ella A's beau is a member of our church!! He will indeed be a spy. He will be our enemy. And he can and will tell Pickering the salary is not paid in advance and I foresaw endless complications and shame over the matter—in a new place where people will not know what Pickering is like nor the real truth about the whole affair. It sickened me. One of the things that have reconciled me to going was that we were getting, as I hoped, far away where nothing of all this would be known and Pickering could not find out anything about our affairs.

We decided that Ewan would have to ask the managers to pay his salary monthly in advance as here—something we both hated to do. And we also decided that we must go to work at once and change the address on all the tags from "Rev" to "Mrs." So *that* was how I spent my last night in Leaskdale manse—we worked till four o'clock, reflecting on the general cussedness of things. Then I lay awake the rest of the night till the stars went out one by one in the dawn.

Monday was a hideous day. I rose as soon as it was daylight. A house always looks desolate and unfriended at dawn—how much more when it is stripped and packed. Racked with worry as I was there was a score of "last things" to be attended to—and I felt exhausted to begin with. I finished packing the big box in the garage with bedclothes and mirrors and had it and the last barrel finished when the teams came at nine. For two hours all was a confusion of loading and I gave directions and explanations calmly, with that gnawing worry coiled up in my mind like a snake. Luckily it was a very fine mild day, for the doors had to be taken off and left wide open. After the last team left Elsie, Margaret Leask, Mrs. Cook and I swept the whole house over and burned the rubbish. By four all was done and the others went home. I was so glad to be left alone. It was a relief to shut the doors and *give way* for awhile. I *did* give way and cried for an hour over everything—the prospect before me and my beautiful lost home. Those empty rooms were more than I could bear. But the cry relieved my tortured nerves....Ewan went over to see the Warrens and find out what he could but it was not very reassuring. They declared the Pete Arnold's were exultant, believing that they had a strangle hold on us at last, and were going to "make it hot for us." It seems they are quite sure of the aid of Ella's fiancé—whose name is John Russell. We shall never escape from the shadow of that sordid affair.

But it all had to be faced. We put the thing behind us and went over to the manse to crate our cats. We nailed each of them up in a box with a supply of meat. Luck took it as meekly as the dear thing takes everything, but Pat fought and snarled and clawed viciously. We left them in the manse all night.

Wednesday morning was mild but gray and squally, with a chill wind pursuing tormented wraiths of snow over the hills. We left at nine, in three cutter loads. The neighbors were in to bid us good-bye. As we drove off I turned and watched the old manse in that gray stormy winter morning as long as I could see it. It was gone. It was no longer my home—the big, ugly brick house where I had been so happy and so wildly unhappy.

Elsie joined us at the station and we came on to Toronto by train. We attended to business all day and at five met Mr. and Mrs. Barraclough of Glen Williams at the Walker, they having come in to pilot us out to their home where we were to stay till after the induction. They are the nicest people in our congregation and—which is neither a cause nor a consequence—the wealthiest. He owns woollen factories in Glen Williams and has a lovely home there. Mrs. Barraclough is a darling.

We proceeded to have dinner. The stimulus of pleasant company and surroundings—the realization that the worst of leaving Leaskdale was

"Right Worshipful Bro. E.Y. Barraclough"

"The Barraclough house"

over—cheered me up and I was enjoying my dinner when the blow fell—the most devilish blow of all those which fate has dealt us, in connection with the Pickering affair.

Ewan asked Mr. B. some carefully casual question regarding John Russell and Mr. Barraclough remarked with genuine casualness, "Oh, he is the treasurer of Norval congregation."

The rest of the night was like a nightmare to me. I continued to sit at the table and force myself to swallow food that was nauseous to me. I forced myself to talk; and all the time I was foreseeing the trouble and worry and scandal ahead of us. The salary garnisheed. The tempest of gossip and exaggeration let loose. The exultation of the bitter Unionists who had left the church and hated us for coming to it. The shame of our people who would not understand. The being dragged through the hideous sordid affair again. The whole country would ring with it.

And what a special devilishness in the fact that, out of all the Presbyterian congregations in Canada, we should have been called to the very one where a close friend of Marshall Pickering's was treasurer!

After dinner we got our boxes of cats in the back of our car—it being quite possible to motor to Glen Williams on the highway. My only conscious wish was to get somewhere—anywhere—where I could be alone with Ewan and talk over this ghastly development. But the fates were verily against us that night. Scarcely had we left Toronto than Mr. B's car began to "act up" and continued to do so. At no less than six garages did he have to stop. At each one the man was sure he had located the trouble and assured Mr. B. that there would be no further bother. Then in a mile or two Mr. B's car would stop again. Of course, we had to stop too. We didn't know the road—we couldn't leave the B's—and there was no one at Mr. B's house if we could have. I was so tired and nervous and worried that I couldn't keep from crying—though I didn't let the B's see *that*. The black intolerable night dragged on. But at last about one o'clock a garage man in Brampton did really find the trouble—or else Sathanas wanted a nap—and from that on we travelled. As we came down the hill into Norval and through it I roused myself from my stupor of misery to take a faint interest. But there was little to see. An odd light high in air—as I discovered later the light on the top of the mill which goeth not out by night—and a long, dark, silent village street. At one point Mr. B. stopped and came back to us. "Have you anything you'd like to leave in the manse?" he said. "It's back there behind those trees." I peered out, curious to see the stage of the next scene of my martyrdom, but I could see nothing, not even trees. Nothing but dense blackness. So on we went again and at two finally arrived at the Barraclough house in Glen Williams—a village that in summer must be very beautiful, with the Credit winding through it.

We got in—got supper—went to bed. Oh, wasn't it nice to stop smiling!

My first words when we were alone were, "Ewan, let me pay that Pickering judgment. I can't face this."

"You shall not pay it," said Ewan. "Let him garnishee the salary if he likes. He'll only get the chance to do it once."

It was in vain I urged all the consequences of this—either Ewan could not see them or they did not influence him. He said he would ask to have the salary paid in advance and all would come out well. I couldn't see it so but I was past worrying and in spite of everything fell asleep.

The next day was a snowstorm. But the church at Union was filled and the induction was a successful function as inductions go. The church at Union is old but a very beautiful one of white stone and quite nice inside. The whole thing had for me the seeming of a grotesque dream. I smiled and shook hands with everybody and talked automatically and was presented with a bouquet. And all the time I was see-

"Union Church"

ing these same friendly, delighted people in a few weeks when the scandal would burst. My body was there but my soul was far away in a dark torture chamber of its own.

We met John Russell there—a young fellow with a pleasant face. He seemed friendly enough and they told us he was one of the most ardent Presbyterians and bitterest hater of Unionists in Norval. This gave me the first faint ray of hope. If this were so he might not want to have his minister disgraced in the eyes of the Unionists. After all, things mightn't be impossible. But the hope *was* very faint. And in any case, he is in love with Ella Arnold and she will be able to pick anything out of him. He strikes me as being amiable and weak.

What a relief it was when the service and "banquet" was over, the mobs of people gone, and we back at the Glen.

I had hoped to be able to run over to Norval that evening to see the manse but it was too cold and stormy. Next day after dinner we started but could only get as far as Georgetown in Dodgie. So we came to Norval by radial, getting here in the dusk of a gray winter afternoon—the most dismal time on which to see anything.

"The radial station at Norval"

We alighted at the radial station up on the hill. Before us was a road leading down to the village but of the village itself we could see absolutely nothing except the top of a church spire apparently sticking out of the ground. But as we walked down the hill the little village on the bank of the Credit unfolded itself.

Norval is considered one of the beauty spots of Ontario. I am sure it must be very pretty in summer. But in winter all such villages are pretty much alike.

I saw a long straggling street, with some places that must be nice in summer and some that couldn't be nice anytime. There was a general store, a

"A long, straggling street"
[No.7 highway—Presbyterian church spire in background, Norval]

hardware store, a bank, a butcher's shop—the usual equipment of the country village. We walked up the street for a short distance—and the church and manse were before us.

My reason told me that the place must be lovely in summer. But in that cold, dim hour of late winter afternoon, miserly of its light, I was not in a mood to be pleased with anything.

The church is a large one of red brick. The caretaker, Mr. Williams, took us through it. It is a very nice church inside and the newly installed electric lights are beautiful.

My first view of the manse was from the back. We went into and through it. A forlorn sight. Every room was full of crates and boxes and barrels. Nothing in the house seemed related to me. It was so big I felt lost in it. I felt hopeless,

"Sideview of manse"

unhappy, unreasonable. I hated the place—I was homesick for Leaskdale manse—I was not able to see anything good about it.

Of course this mood was the result of my secret worry. My nerves were so raw a palace wouldn't have pleased me. Karnak would have seemed a hovel.

It is really a splendid manse—far ahead of Leaskdale in most respects. And now that we have got it fairly hospitable I can see its good qualities without having to try to. But that evening I couldn't see any—all was confusion and cold and disorder and ugliness.

We went back and by the time we got up to the radial station it had begun to snow and drift. Before us was a dreary white unknown land in a wild winter wind—a *black* wind. Winds *have* colors.

I was glad to get back to the Glen, where at least there was warmth and light and luxurious surroundings. I sank into the soft chesterfield before the open fireplace with a sigh of relief....

I must not forget our animals. Dixie having Stuart with him asked no more. It was quite another thing with Pat and Luck. We had turned them loose in the B's cellar and kept them there, allowing them up in the evening. At first they roamed about fiercely and alienly. But Luck, dear thing, soon began to settle down, especially when he could snuggle on my lap. Pat remained distrustful and anti–social. Saturday morning Ewan went over to Norval to uncrate the furniture. I wanted to go, too, and make a beginning at getting settled but was overruled by much good advice from the hospitable Barracloughs, who insisted on my waiting till Monday. From their point of view it was sensible advice. But they did not know my secret worry and unrest which made it torture to sit still and do nothing. I thought Saturday and Sunday would never end. When Monday morning dawned fine and cold I was determined to get to work. Elsie, Ewan and I came over by radial and Mr. B's man brought over a sleigh load of grips and

["Lucky"]

cats. Also a box Mrs. B. had most thoughtfully packed with supplies. I had got some steak on the way over and while Elsie cooked dinner I tackled the job before me. The first thing was to get eating facilities in order. The next beds up. We worked hard all day and in the evening went over to the "Union" meeting—corresponding to our Guild. The young people's society here is composed of both Anglicans and Presbyterians. I was surrounded by a depressing assembly of strangers. A Mr. Milman gave an illustrated lecture on Japan. The usual banal stuff—and I was so besottedly tired I could hardly keep from falling asleep. Too tired to be even homesick. The only longing I had was to get to bed. But our first night in Norval manse was not a comfortable one. In spite of the fire being on all day the big house so long unheated was cold

and everything in it was cold. In spite of all our bedclothes we were a-cold. Poor Luck was so cold that he snuggled down on the bed between Stuart and Dixie. I worried all night and was so tired in the morning I felt aghast at the day before me. Nevertheless I got up and tackled it. Stuart started off to school. We got the manse warm. Our cats, discovering their own especial cushions, which no doubt smelled of Leaskdale, seemed quite contented. I got our room "organized" that day. If I had been free from worry re. the Russell-Pickering complication I would have enjoyed the task of "getting settled." Even as it was I did enjoy it in spots. Sometimes I would forget temporarily and think only of the pleasures and fun of "finding my things again." On that Monday morning when the teams took them from Leaskdale I felt as if all my household gods were gone—vanished out

"Norval School"

of existence. And it was delightful to find them again. Packing them had been sad but unpacking them was joyous—like meeting dear friends again. Out of the whole eleven barrels of dishes only *one* thing was broken—a little coffee-cup saucer. Oddly enough it was the first thing I unpacked and thought, "Heavens, if this is the beginning what will be the ending?" But not another thing was broken. I feel quite proud of my packing.

All Tuesday I was worried but at dusk a reaction set in. I suddenly remembered something I had forgotten—that strange voice which had told me in the spring of 1924 that my series of misfortunes was ended. So far it has proved true. No terrible thing has happened since. Especially Ewan has had no bad attack. And if it was a true portent we will not have any trouble over the R-P matter. I could not *see* how we could help having it; but when I remembered that "heavenly voice" I did not believe we *would*. For a time at least I felt tranquillized and that night it seemed to me that I was going to like Norval. I was coming down the stairs and I looked out of the hall window. The moonlight on the grounds, on "the dark church tower" and on the lovely dim things that were a hill of pines beyond was a thing to remember forever.

Ever since I have been working day

"The dark church tower"
[Draper Street side]

and night. Elsie has been of no use as far as getting things in order go. But she has got us our meals and for the rest we have really got on amazingly. All that first week I was unpacking and arranging and stowing away. I am sure I went up and down the garret stairs a thousand times. At night I would be too tired to sleep and worry, that had been drugged through the day by hard labor would waken into wolfish activity and gnaw at me, despite my desperate clinging to faith in my vision.

This morning I was in Norval church for the first. I felt very strange and lonely and wished myself violently back in Leaskdale church, knowing everyone who came in.

Tonight I feel sad and lonely. But it is a comfort to get back to my old journal again.

Now that I am beginning to find my feet I realize that we will have a very nice home here. Architecturally, Norval manse is much more attractive than Leaskdale manse—which was, it must be admitted, a very ugly one—at least until my vines screened it into beauty. In plain fact, this is absolutely the first

"Manse & church"

time in my life that I have a home I need not feel a little apologetic for when strangers come. For many years before leaving Cavendish the old home had gone down so much that externally it was a very shabby place and Leaskdale manse left much to be desired externally. Norval manse is well designed and situated. It is of red brick. The kitchen is much larger and more convenient than the Leaskdale one. We have the soft water pump in the kitchen which is a good item, and there is a back staircase.

We still have to go through the dining room to reach the rest of the house—*that* seems to be my fate. But the room itself is a splendid one. The Leaskdale dining room was the most unsatisfactory room in the house, small and inconvenient, with a wretched view of back yard and stables. Our dining room here is large and light with a big bay window at the end and a door opening on to the veranda through which we can see the beautiful pine wood on the hill behind the village. An exquisite grove—which alack! belongs to John Russell! The only thing I miss in the dining room is the convenient little wall cupboard of Leaskdale.

The front hall is large and very like the one at Leaskdale. The parlor is a nice room too—very large with a large bay window. It has not the pretty view my Leaskdale parlor had—it looks out on a huddle of small and stupid little houses and an ugly United Church. But in summer the trees will screen that and in one corner we can see that same hill of pines.

"View from parlour window"

The least satisfactory room is the library behind the parlor. It is too small. But we have managed by putting my books in the parlor and so it serves Ewan very nicely as a study and is a cosy room, though it will never be like our beautiful Leaskdale library.

I do not like the stairs here. They are steep, with an inconvenient twist at the top instead of a landing. But there is one compensation—that hall window whence I can see every time I go up and down some outer beauty—the dark magic of those pines or the lovely creaminess of the snowfields at sunset.

The upstairs hall is not as nice as Leaskdale hall. I shall miss my handy little "sewing room." And while the four front rooms are all nice and of a fair size not one of them is really large enough for Ewan and me. I miss our beautiful large room at Leaskdale. But every room has a closet and the other three rooms are much nicer than the corresponding ones in Leaskdale. And the views from all the windows, looking out on wooded hill and river must be exquisite in summer.

Lying in bed I can see the hill of pines, dark against the dawn when the black night turns to silver, mysterious under the stars or weaving magic with moonlight.

The bathroom is above the kitchen and behind it is a nice tiny room which I shall fit up as a sewing room. There is a good linen closet at the head of the back stairs. *And* a splendid garret where all sorts of things can be stowed away. This was always a problem at Leaskdale which the little "trunk room" only partially helped to solve.

On the whole I am well satisfied with my new home and will be more and more so as days go by and it becomes home in reality.

I *do* like the electric light. It is an odd thing that last fall was the first time that I ever felt a longing for electric light. I had always been used to oil lamps and never felt that I wanted anything else. I had a gasoline lamp which I used for reading and sewing and I like it better than electric light. Do yet for that matter were it not for the trouble of fixing it up. And our flashlights were a great convenience. But all at once, last fall, long before I knew there was such a place as

[Pine wood: "Russells' Hill"]

"View from back hall window"

Norval I began to feel suddenly tired of coming in and fumbling in the dark for matches—tired of wrestling with wicks that no maid *ever* got straight. I felt that I'd like to have hydro. And here I have it. And after two weeks of it I wonder how I ever did without it! It gives me such a nice, omnipotent feeling to press a button—"let there be light and there *is* light."

Norval is in Esquesing township in the county of Halton. Across the river is Chinguacousy township in Peel county. In childhood days I had to learn all the counties of Ontario off by heart—a geography lesson of the value of which I am to this day ignorant. Most of the lists were very long and hard to memorize. More than one hot summer day I had to stay in at recess and learn them. But there was one dear group that was easy to learn—short and rhythmical. We could always chant it glibly—"Lincoln, Wentworth, Halton, Peel. I had no idea then that "Halton, Peel" would ever mean anything to me but a name. And now I am living in one on the borders of the other.

Well—tomorrow will bring another day of hard work and worry.

Monday, March 1, 1926
The Manse, Norval
I slept poorly last night. Woke too early—worried and homesick.

I miss *Frede* heart-breakingly these days. I seem to be reminded of her at every turn. While I was fixing up Leaskdale manse I was constantly thinking, "Will Frede like this?"—"What will Frede think of that?" She can never come to Norval manse—she can never sit with me before our open fire. *How* we would have enjoyed that, with our cats toasting their furry flanks beside us. I am haunted by these thoughts and I suffer.

Ewan called on the Russells today and liked them. Mrs. R. is a widow with three sons, John, Jim and Don. Tonight at our social Guild I met John again. He seems like a real nice young fellow and I cannot believe he is our enemy. Yet even so Ella Arnold will likely be able to wheedle all his secrets out of him.

But the social tonight helped me. I got really acquainted with a lot of people and did not feel so much like a cat in a strange garret. And I am on the committee of the St. Patrick concert and Banquet. It is just as well to make up your mind to do the things you have to do. I suppose the galled jade must get into harness again.

Luck, loveliest of little lovely cats, is quite happy and contented. He *is* the dearest thing, half human. I don't know what I'd do without the purring, restful little creature.

Thursday, Mar. 4, 1926
Elsie has been up home yesterday and today to a wedding so I've been very busy. Yesterday I got the parlor in order and hung the pictures. Whenever the pictures in a room go up I seem to feel at home in it.

Yesterday afternoon we were over to Union W.M.S. and saw the famous view of Norval from the long hill. It is charming now and must be trebly so in summer.

I like the Union women. They seem a nice harmonious group—very different from the Zephyr ones. I felt more contented last night than any night yet. If only life would stop nagging me!

Tuesday, March 9, 1926

There is one thing I like about our library—its little reading lamp. Tonight for the first time in months I had a cosy, undisturbed evening of reading in one of my comfy new reed chairs in the library corner. It was delightful to have a "good read" again, with that heavenly feeling of leisure and tranquillity which

"Corner of library"

has been lacking so long. But I am feeling very tired. These past six weeks have been very hard, physically and mentally.

Today I finished hanging the last of the pictures—a big job in itself. It is nice to have them all around me again.

Sat., March 13, 1926
The Manse, Norval

Am beginning to live an orderly life again and, being a little rested, I don't feel so down-hearted. Today I put the stair carpet down and the kitchen oil-cloth. The house is really beginning to have a homelike appearance.

Sunday, Mar. 14, 1926

We had special services today morning and evening to celebrate the putting in of the new electric lighting. Shades of Knox and Calvin! However, the services were agreeable and the music good. I was secretly worried by John Russell's absence. Is he away to see Ella Arnold? And what will he tell her?

Tuesday, March 16, 1926
The Manse, Norval

Forty-eight hours ago I was a worried, harried creature. Tonight I am so light hearted that I feel like a stranger to myself. And all the worry of this past dreadful month has been utterly unnecessary. My vision did not lie.

Yesterday we were busy all day preparing for the St. Patrick banquet and concert in the evening. I worked in the church all the morning, miserably worried under external composure because I had learned that John Russell was really away to see Miss Arnold. There were moments when I was so utterly sick at heart that it seemed as if I must throw everything down and fly to some vast wilderness. But I went on decorating and arranging tables and exchanging jokes and banalities with my fellow workers.

When I came home at noon I found that Ewan had been up to see Mr. Laird, chairman of managers, and had asked if it were possible to have the salary paid monthly in advance. He received the somewhat astonishing reply that that had been the intention anyhow.

This relieved me considerably. Of course there was still this element of danger. There are bound to be times, just as in Leaskdale, when the salary will fall behind temporarily and if John Russell told the Pickering clique they could make trouble. But I felt so much better that I found it possible to carry on and enjoy the evening. Mr. and Mrs. Dodds came over. They are at Dixie now. We knew them well when they were at Sonya. I have always liked Mrs. D. and found her good company with a marked Josephian flavor. Yet very few people seem to like her. She is English and decidedly outspoken. Also quite "temperamental," I fancy. But we seem to hit it off for all that.

We had a very good programme. I gave a couple of readings and was presented with a bouquet by the congregation. Later on, down in the basement, John Russell, who had turned up, came up and whispered "We are proud of you both." The Dodds stayed here all night and we had a jolly talk after we got home. I noticed Ewan seemed to be in very good spirits. And when the Dodds had gone up to bed he told me an astounding tale. Briefly it amounted to this.

John Russell had come to him in the evening and told him the following facts. Just before we came to Norval Greig had written to *him*, asking him how the salary was paid—in advance or not. I suppose Greig fondly believed J.R. would gladly tell him all about it. And what did John Russell, whom we had so dreaded and on whom the Pickering gang were so fatuously counting, do? Off his own bat he summoned a meeting of the session and managers and told them the whole story. He said he knew all about it and that it had been a framed-up job to extort money from us and that the Leaskdale congregation paid the salary in advance. The Norval people promptly decided to do the same and John at once wrote Greig that the salary was paid in advance.

"And it will be," John wound up. "Don't you give another thought to this. Your managers and session are behind you to a man."

What a difference this has made in everything! For the first time since that dreadful last night in the old manse I am happy. The intolerable dread of scandal and slander which has been hanging over me like an ever-present menace vanished in an instant. All things became new. I went to bed far too happy to sleep. But to lie awake for happiness is a very different thing from lying awake through worry or dread.

It is curious, too, that the very thing we thought the most terrible—that John R. was treasurer—was the best thing for us. If the treasurer had been a man who knew nothing of the situation he might have fallen into Greig's trap—or at any rate couldn't have so easily convinced the managers of the justice of our cause.

Today we went to visit the Townsends of Union—a lovely drive through glen–like curves that must be beautiful in summer. The whole day seemed a delight to me. My world was transfigured. Coming home we saw the lights of Norval sparkling along the white valley—a beautiful sight....

Saturday, March 20, 1926
The Manse, Norval

Ewan went up to Leaskdale Thursday to attend the funeral of Mr. Urquhart, a good friend of ours who has been ill for a long time. He returned tonight. I have been very busy and happy. Had a letter from Mrs. Rob Shier yesterday saying that a tale had been all around Zephyr that Marshall Pickering was going to have a lawyer to "stop the induction" and how worried they all were. Very unnecessary for in any case neither Marshall Pickering nor any lawyer could do that.

When Ewan was in Uxbridge he was talking to John Smith who told him that Greig had been planning to "seize our furniture" when it was put up for sale. But I had foreseen *that*, and the sale bills were in my name so he could do nothing. No, my Greig, we are not *quite* so blind as that!

Wednesday, March 24, 1926

At last I have put everything in order. And I am very well satisfied with my new home. I don't *love* it yet. It doesn't *belong* to me. No atmosphere—no traditions. I am only visiting here. But that will come.

I have a great deal of painting and staining to do yet but can do it gradually. I admit I feel tired. The past three months have been very strenuous ones in every way.

Saturday, March 27, 1926
The Manse, Norval

Tonight, standing on the back veranda I thought I had never seen anything of its kind more lovely than the moonlight behind the tall church spire. It was exquisite. And there is such a darling double echo here. I was calling Luck and as I called "pussy, pussy" *pussy-pussy* came back liltingly from the church wall and a second later from away down near the river came another echo, fainter, more fairy-like—the echo of an echo as if some goblin pussy were being summoned "thin and clear" from the dark pine woods beyond.

Sunday, Mar. 28, 1926

This very cold fine evening Elsie and I went to service in the little Anglican church up the side street. I enjoyed the service—I have always liked the Anglican ritual. The rectory is just across the street from us. Dr. and Mrs. Kyle are very nice and congenial. The Reverend Douglas of the United Church is anything but nice. I disliked him on sight and he seems to be detested by everyone, even his own people. His wife, who people say is nice, has never called on me.

"Norval Church" [Anglican]

"Rectory"
[of Church of England: St. Paul's]

Both of them confidently expected to be living in this manse now and hesitated not to state it publicly and exultantly last year. However, Mr. D. has been asked by his people to resign so they will be going in June. The bitterness in this village between the Presbyterians and Unionists is very extreme. And it cannot be wondered at, after certain things the latter did. But some of the manifestations on both sides are very petty.

Tuesday, March 30, 1926
Evidently Greig is determined to leave no stone unturned. Today Ewan got a letter from Dr. A.S. Grant, the Presbyterian minister, who is head of the Committee of Supply in Toronto and who has a reputation for wanting to play the Pope and rule everyone. I think he deserves it. Why Greig should write to him I don't know. Dr. Grant has no more power than any other minister over the matter of a congregation calling a minister. He is not even Clerk of Presbytery. But perhaps because he has in hand at present the business of finding supply for our many vacant pulpits Greig has imagined that he has some power over us. It must be from Greig he obtained his information because it was couched in legal terms and contained certain information none but Greig knew. The letter said briefly that he had been informed that a judgment existed against E. that several attempts to collect it had been made and that he "thought it should be paid at once." And E. was to communicate with him instanter—or words to that effect.

Now this letter upset us both not a little. Not because of any fear it provoked. Grant can do nothing even if he tried. But what annoyed me was the curt dictatorial tone of the letter, asking for no explanation but coolly ordering us to pay, as if he had any shadow of right to call E. to account or meddle in the matter at all. I felt so angry over it that it has quite spoiled my evening. However, there is one consolation. Greig must feel that he is at the end of his legal bag of tricks when he tries such a foolish one as this. It is probably the last shot in his locker.

By the way, John Russell told Ewan recently that it was Greig who put Marshall Pickering up to the whole thing—that Pickering didn't want to go on with it but Greig urged him on and wouldn't let him drop it. John also said he believed Greig had never got a cent for his services—that his payment was conditional on his getting it out of us. I hope this is true. Much as I detest Pickering I hate Greig much more. We've always felt he was at the bottom of the whole affair and I am very glad if he hasn't got paid.

Thursday, Apr. 1, 1926
We have had a terrific two days' ice-storm—the worst in years. The Hydro is off and we are very thankful to get out our old kerosene and gas lamps. Ewan went to town yesterday and brought Chester home for Easter. He also saw Dr. Grant and told him politely that the matter between him and Pickering was none of his business. Grant pulled in his horns and apologized. When he heard that the "judgment" was the result of an automobile collision he seemed amazed. Probably Greig had given him the impression that it was some debt for value received. He would not say where he had got his information—but we know quite well. So that's that. But I suppose there will always be pinpricks over the dirty business.

Friday, Apr. 2, 1926
Got out my MS. of *Emily 3* and read it to get into the spirit of it again. I *must* get down to work. Haven't done a thing since November. The book will be poor stuff I fear. My heart is not in it.

Wednesday, Apr. 7, 1926
....I had a letter from Mrs. Warren today. She says that before we left Greig went around to all the Uxbridge banks to find out if Ewan had any money in them.

He didn't try "the Leaskdale bank"! Dear Greig! Excuse me if I weep!

Had a weird letter from some woman in the U.S. who thinks I must be "obsessed with birthmarks" and gives me a fearful calling down for endowing "Mr. Morrison" in *Emily Climbs* with a blood-red hand. She adjures me to stop and think what untold harm I may do to future generations by putting such things in my stories! And winds up by declaring she has forbidden her granddaughters to buy or read the book. Poor dear! She'd better stop reading my books and give her granddaughters *Simon called Peter* and *Flaming Youth*.

I feel like an old Scotch woman Frede met once. "I can stand wickedness but I cannot stand foolishness."

We are enjoying our open fireplace. Every evening we are home we have a fire there and sit by it to read or work. I never at any time before lived in a house where there was a fireplace. But we had an old stove in the sitting room at home which was every bit as good, when the "blowers" were opened wide. Until Grandfather's death we always sat there in the evening and the glow of that lovely "open fire" shines over the winters of childhood....

Tuesday, Apr. 20, 1926

So much milder that one feels spring *may* come sometime. Yet some things made today sad. An item in the *Guardian* stated that Wellington Nelson, my old childhood playmate, had recently died in Minnesota. I had not heard of or about him for years. He was married but left no family. He was my age within a week. My birthday was Nov. 30, his Dec. 6. And he is dead. Our jolly old days are buried under the snows of over forty yester-years. We would probably never have met again had he lived to be an old man. Yet the news of his death cast a chill and a gloom over the day....

The Manse, Norval
Saturday, Apr. 24, 1926

Yesterday Ewan was putting his hand to his head again. My heart is very heavy. Even in his lightest attacks he becomes so very listless and lazy. One has to *make* him do everything. I shrink from it here, where all is new and I know so little of the people or the work. I feel I have no strength to cope here with the problems I managed to solve in Leaskdale. What a hell any form of mental disorder makes of life!

Wednesday, May 12, 1926
The Manse, Norval

I began setting out some shrubs today—ivies, spireas and forsythias. I can't do without them. And I suppose when they get to be beautiful I'll have to move on and leave them.

Ewan is very dull and glare-eyed these days. I feel so anxious and harassed under my spring activities.

Tuesday, June 1, 1926
The Manse, Norval, Ont.

I have been exceedingly busy the past two weeks, gardening, painting and visiting—the first delightful, the second tolerable, the third as abominable as ever—especially as Ewan is far from well, though not so bad as he sometimes is.

Stuart is delighted that there is a good swimming place in the river down by the dam. I suppose it is safe enough—and he is such a wonderful little duck in the water. But I am never very easy when I see him starting off with his bathing suit.

Chester was home for another week-end.

There have been no outstanding occurrences to record—at least, none that seem so. One never knows what may come out of seeming trivialities. If, on that Sunday when we collided with Marshall Pickering, the collision had *not* occurred, I would never have thought of writing in my diary the fact that Mrs. Jake Myers had asked us to go over to tea from the church. It would have seemed too trivial to record. Yet if they had *not* asked us all the misery and worry that followed would have been averted.

Friday, June 11, 1926
A good deal may happen in a week. Last Friday if I had been told that in less than a week Elsie would have gone and another girl here in her place I would have thought it a very unlikely prediction. Yet it has come to pass—I am sorry to say....

I at once wrote to an agency in Toronto to see if I could get a girl from them. I knew it was almost hopeless to try to get one around here. There are almost no girls who "work out" and the few who do go to the woollen mills in the Glen....The Employment bureau said they had a girl for me—a middle-aged Scotch girl just out and "well recommended."

I did not like the idea of a Scotch girl at all. She would be so unused to our ways—so different—so apt to be lonely and homesick....

Ewan...is not so well and I am anxious and worried about him. We were visiting Wednesday evening and it was an evening of misery. Ewan never left his head alone for one minute. He clutched at his forehead, he tied his arm around his neck, he rumpled his hair till it stood on end— and then he began all over again. Even as a mannerism, a whole evening of this would have got on my

"View of Credit River"

"Chester & Dix"

nerves. But when I knew it betokened mental unrest which *might* run on to another bad attack—just as it *might* pass in a few days—I could hardly sit there and endure it....

Yesterday morning I rose at four, finished the dining room, got breakfast and

"Elsie [Bushby and "Paddy"]

motored into Toronto. We brought Margaret McKenzie out. I shall say nothing of her until she has been here some months—if she stays so long. But my first impressions are decided unfavorable. I do not believe I'll ever like her. And I have a sort of instinct she won't like us, either.

I miss Elsie very much, poor misled girl....

Sunday, June 13, 1926
The Manse, Norval, Ont.
Mr. and Mrs. Barraclough were here this evening. She is really a dear creature. One such woman in the congregation makes a world's difference....

Thursday, June 17, 1926
The Manse, Norval
Chester came home today. He failed in one exam—history. To be sure, his teacher, saying that he had done well in it all the year, gave him a second exam. He passed it and so will go into the next year but that is not the same thing and I feel badly about it. Chester should not have failed. He has a good memory, so must have failed because of some weakness or lack somewhere. I, somehow, believe he does not study as hard as he should. He trusts too much to "luck."

He has grown tall for his age and is in long trousers.

Margaret cannot cook at all—at least, in terms of Canadian cookery. I shall have to teach her everything. She never made a pie or cake in her life. And I don't think she will be easy to teach. She is stupid and "set" in her ways. I feel nettled. I am paying her thirty dollars a month—eight more than I ever paid before—and I told the Bureau I wanted a girl I did not have to teach. I have been teaching maids ever since Mrs. Reid got married and I'm getting tired of it. Now I have to begin all over again, with this dour old Scotch maid. Well, it's my kismet.

Ewan seems better. His attacks are very mild affairs now. But there is always the haunting fear that he may have a bad one. And he is seldom really *well*—just melancholy enough to have no ambition or energy.

Monday, June 21, 1926
Chester's year's report came today. And a very good one on the whole. Conduct good, some marks splendid, all tolerable. So perhaps I did not well to be so cast down by his one failure. But there are some things about Chester that make me anxious in regard to his future.

Monday, June 28, 1926

This has been a hectic week but there were many pleasant things in it. I went to Toronto last Monday to attend the Triennial. We crammed into three days enough festivities to do for a year. The first evening there was a reception in the club rooms and who should pop in but Edith Russell, my old co-worker on the *Echo* in the early days of the century. I have never seen her since I left Halifax, twenty five years ago—though I put my foot in it by saying so, as Edith did not like to be reminded that she had been Miss Russell for so long a time! We corresponded for several years but I have not heard from or of her for a long time. She is as odd and unattractive as ever, yet with something likeable about her. She ran around to all the affairs in an outmoded blouse and skirt, with a startling beflowered petticoat showing two inches below it. But that would never worry Edith. She has got fat and at first glance I could see nothing of the girl I knew but eventually the old likeness came out.

Toronto fêted us royally. The newspaper men gave us a luncheon at the King Edward, the Ontario Government gave us a dinner, the Toronto Press Club gave us a luncheon, some other body gave us a reception at the Grange, Lady Willison—Marjory McMurchy who married seventy-year old Sir John last winter and is consequently a *grandmother*—gave us a tea, and the Royal Canadian Yacht Club gave us luncheon in its club house on the Island—all very pleasant affairs. I think I enjoyed the Government dinner as much as anything—though I had to answer the P.E.I. toast. Premier Ferguson told someone afterwards that my speech was the best of the lot and Mrs. John Garvin told me it was "perfection"—witty, appropriate and not too long—a virtue certainly not possessed by some of the speakers who talked till everyone was tired. Here is a copy of mine.

"I feel that it is a great honor, privilege and pleasure to represent 'the Island' here tonight. No true daughter of P.E. Island ever outgrows her affection for it. It is now fifteen years since I left Prince Edward Island and they seem to me but a few days for the love I bear to it. Therefore I am indeed proud to answer 'adsum' tonight when P.E. Island's name is reached on the roll-call.

"Prince Edward Island is the smallest province in the Dominion—the diamond in the coronet of our colonial empire. 'Tis a colorful little land of ruby and emerald and sapphire—its bright-red, winding roads, its green uplands, its blue encircling sea make a combination that cannot be forgotten from the point of view of natural loveliness. It is a land where nobody is very rich and nobody is very poor. A land which, being somewhat out of the beaten track, is, it may be, a bit old-fashioned. A land where you are born into a certain political party and live and die and go to heaven in it." (*Premier Ferguson*: Which party? *Speaker*. Oh, I'm not telling *that*). A land where you can still find real grandmothers and genuine old-maid aunts. A land where it is still held to be a great feather in a family's cap if it has a minister among its boys; a land that has a trick of raising university presidents and international ambassadors for export; a land where the ten commandments are still considered fairly up-to-date; but a land where it would be safer to smash all those commandments at once than to be caught without three kinds of cake when company comes to tea. From this land where English and Scotch and Irish are all beginning to be blended into something that is proud to call itself Canadian I bring you all tonight greeting and good-will."

I came home Friday, very tired to prepare for our Anniversary on Sunday. Edith Russell came Saturday for the week-end. I asked her out for I think the poor thing has a rather hard life of it and finds it hard enough to make both ends meet. Mr. Jamieson, our anniversary preacher was also here. I got up at six yesterday morning to complete my dinner preparations and we had fine anniversary services.

Edith Russell remarked that Stuart had "a face like one of Raphael's cherubs." When he was three he had. But I hardly think his roguish, laughing face is very cherubic now. Edith, poor thing, is a fearful bore and I could not help feeling relieved when she went today.

Ewan and I spent an evening of boredom visiting. He seems pretty well again.

Wednesday, June 30, 1926
The Manse, Norval

Yesterday was the day of the annual garden party which is always held on the manse lawn, while the platform for programme is built on and from the veranda. I rose at six and made cake, candy etc. All day and all night I nearly ran my feet off. There were a thousand people on the grounds and the house was over-run with the

"Edith Russell"
[former co-worker from Halifax Echo*]*

"Lawn prepared for party"

performers, and somebody wanting something every minute. I was too tired to sleep and today had to be devoted to putting things straight. I am awfully tired but I seem seldom to have been anything else since last November. But I had a quiet evening home alone tonight and it was heavenly. Also I began work—again—on *Emily III*. I wonder if I shall *ever* get that book done!....

Friday, July 2, 1926
The Manse, Norval
Today I was again saddened by a letter telling me of the death of Rev. A. J. Lockhart—"Pastor Felix." He was an uncle of Nate's and we have corresponded ever since *Anne of Green Gables* was published. He was a delightful correspondent and I shall miss his letters much....

Sunday, July 4, 1926
Yesterday morning I again rose at six to prepare for company. Cuthbert and Ada spent the weekend with us and have just gone. Cuth is as dear as ever, but Ada leaves me with the feeling of being scratched all over.

She has her knife into Laura and Bert also and I can't tolerate that. She always gives me a feeling that whatever I say to her it is the wrong thing.

I feel tired and submerged tonight. There is nothing more tiring than trying to entertain someone with whom you have no point of contact whatever.

"*Ada & myself*"

Saturday, July 10, 1926
A week crowded as usual—and, for the most part crowded with things that, as I believe to the bottom of my heart, were not worth while.

Monday was very warm and busy. In the afternoon Douglas Armstrong, his wife and two children got themselves and car ditched in Norval on their way to Toronto. We took them in until their car could be fixed which was not till Tuesday evening. Meanwhile I was busy preparing for our annual Auxiliary "picnic" on Tuesday. Got up at six Tuesday morning to make sandwiches, etc. Miss Dickie, our speaker, came. We had ten for dinner and as Margaret is very little use yet—I doubt if she ever will be much—I had a busy forenoon and was "all het up" and tired when we went to the picnic at Mrs. Ismond's. Luckily I could sit through the meeting and address, also the feast that followed. So the time was not wholly wasted for I got a little rest. Next day I went to Union Missionary picnic—a similar function—where I ate the most delicious strawberry short-cake I ever tasted. It would praise its maker in the gates.

"The Manse, Norval"

Thursday I had a truly blessed day—I was home all day and got a little of my own work done and some of my garden weeded. I am beginning to have some flowers of my own again....

Today I did up 18 boxes of berries, taught—or tried to teach—Margaret how to make pie crust, and did a score of odd jobs. I ought to be dead tired tonight but somehow I'm not. Only my feet burn terribly.

Dr. Kyle, the Anglican rector, is going away. I feel sorry for Mrs. Kyle has been a very nice neighbor and nobody knows who or what will come in their place.

Saturday, July 17, 1926

Tuesday I painted the kitchen floor and tidied up the garret.

A Mr. Simpson is going to Leaskdale for the summer—an old man but a good preacher. I'm glad they have got even a temporary supply for they have had very poor candidates. Men are so scarce just now that it is hard to get anyone to go to back country places like Leaskdale.

On Wednesday I gave the kitchen another coat, wrote 2 hours, with endless interruptions—Norval being a haunt of agents—I was so tired at night I felt as if I could never get rested. Thursday, with all else, I stained the kitchen floor and worked till 11.30 at night. I feel as if I could *never* catch up....

Had a very adoring letter from a young girl in Acton yesterday. She vowed that if I were in Acton instead of Norval she and the other young girls would form a guard around me to keep me from all annoyances and guard me like a saint in a shrine etc. etc.

How n—i—i—c—e!!

She also was sure my husband must be "idolatrously proud of me."

Oh, me!!!

Well, what does it matter!

Saturday, July 24, 1926
....A letter came from Ila Thursday. She is in Winnipeg with three children and is coming to spend a week with me in August on her return trip to Virginia. He is a civil engineer and they wander about terribly.

In one way I want to see Ila. In another I dread it. I was so horribly disappointed in Kate. If Ila is like her I would rather never meet her. To be sure, Ila's letters have always been very different from Kate's. And people who know them both have told me that Ila was so much nicer than Kate. Still, I dread her visit.

In a way it's quite romantic—expecting a visit from a sister you've never seen!....

Monday, August 2, 1926
Are all the weeks of summer to be like this? Monday evening we had company till late. Tuesday we had a stream of callers and in the evening had to go to a garden party at Dixie. Wednesday I had to go to a lawn social in Georgetown and give readings. (Because we want the Georgetown people to come back and help *us* in our programs.) Thursday I cooked all day and visited in the evening. Friday I made jelly roll, cherry pies, tarts, cookies and date loaf for a Sunday School picnic—and visited in the evening. I was ghastly tired and E. was "headachy" and I was overcome with a sense of the impossibility of life. Saturday I rose at 6, made sandwiches and lemonade, then went to Stanley Park for a long, bored day. Came home in evening and found Mr. and Mrs. Robinson of Uxbridge here for the week-end. They went this morning....

Ewan left today for P.E. Island. He has a month's vacation here. Much better than Leaskdale's beggarly two Sundays. And for the last three years not even that. He had the Sundays but paid for the supplies himself....

I am not going anywhere this summer. I have too much to do. But I am going to try to get a rest—the rest I want. E. being away I won't have to visit—oh, bliss! I am going to try to catch up with my book (which would "rest" me more than anything else), read a few books, get some letters written,—in short have a little bit of *real* enjoyment.

Tuesday, August 3, 1926
Intensely hot and humid. A kind old lady brought me in a basket of gooseberries. None of us like gooseberry jam but I had to take them or she would be offended. And for the same reason I'll have to do them up. Otherwise I'd pour them into the river. But suppose later on she were to find out I had no gooseberry jam? People have such a devilish knack of finding out things like that. Then I pickled beets. So my rest is not yet begun. But I did have a lovely evening of reading.

Wednesday, Aug. 4, 1926
The Manse, Norval
I went to Georgetown today to return some calls. No rest about that—in one way. In another there was. Because I got them off my list and it rests me to feel

I'm catching up a bit. This constant haunting sense of being behind with *everything* worries me like a snapping dog.

This evening I looked forward to another pleasant evening of reading. But in comes a maiden lady of mature vintage "to keep me from being lonesome"!!!

She stayed the whole evening—is terribly hard to talk to—and left me thinking "lonesomeness" the most beautiful state on earth. Solitude does not bore me but gossipy old ladies do.

But one thing darkened the day. In the *Guardian* was the news that Fannie Mutch's only son had been drowned in the Yukon. Poor poor Fannie! What are

"Nestling in a loop of the Credit"

my little worries compared to this? Frank Mutch was about 21. It seems but a few years ago that I was in Ch'Town for the Exhibition and went up to see Fannie and her new baby. She was lying in bed and flung back his little blanket to let me see the wee lad beside her....

And now he is drowned, thousands of miles away from her. And I fear there was some bitterness over his leaving home. They wanted him to go to college but he wouldn't. He and his father did not get on well. I remember a story Fannie told me the summer I was at Heart's Desire. Frank had done something that annoyed his father—taken out the car and injured it slightly I think. R.E. gave him a sharp calling down. Frank was so angry that he never spoke to his father for two weeks. *And his father never knew it.* He simply took so little notice of his son and had so little in common with him that the fact that his son was never speaking to him did not dawn on his consciousness!

What terrible little silent tragedies there are in life!

Thursday, Aug. 5, 1926
My *Blue Castle* came today. It has a make-up different from all my other books. Not so pretty. A plain cover.

I have been painting floors and doing up fruit and pickles. It has been very hot.

Saturday, Aug. 14, 1926
The Manse, Norval

Wednesday night I went to "camp fire" at the Girl Guides' camp to tell them some stories. But I really enjoyed that—though I was a little envious of their good times. They put up a little impromptu program and I told them stories of the old North Shore—the days of the Marcopolo etc. And it took me back to happier years beside those old smiling or stormy seas and I came home rejuvenated because of it.

But the week has been as busy as any other. I had a letter from Myrtle. She is coming up for a visit when Ewan returns. I longed so much to see some of the old gang that I wrote and sent her a check for a hundred and told her to come. It was not generosity—just selfishness. But she has worked hard there for 20 years and brought up a fine little family so she deserves a bit of a party. I do hope we'll have a pleasant visit together.

Stuart was sick two days this week. Ada and Pat McIntyre spent Friday here. Ada grows no more likeable. Pat is a perfect beauty but has little soul beauty. Yet Chester was quite taken with her. Chester is by way of being in love with every pretty girl he sees just now. It may pass over harmlessly. Or he may make a mess of his life on those rocks. It's no use worrying about it. I must fall back on foreordination for comfort.

"The mill at Norval"

Chester has been working in the mill here most of the month. It is good for him and should keep him out of mischief. But I question if all the men and boys he meets there are just the best companions for him. There are almost no "nice boys" of his age here....

Saturday, Aug. 21, 1926
....Ila came Monday with three kiddies and left Friday. She is one of the race of Joseph. I loved her at once and loved her better every day. She is a real Mont-

gomery with just the same taste in jokes as our clan. I had that instant sense of "at homeness" which marks the kindred spirits.

If Ila and I had been brought up together we would have been devoted friends as well as sisters. Even yet if we were to see much of each other we would come to mean much to each other. But we have no mutual past and we can have no mutual future. Still, I am very glad to feel that I like her so much and that in one of my father's daughters at least I can find congeniality. As far as Ila was concerned I enjoyed every minute of her stay. But the week was hot and muggy and three small kiddies all under 6 made life rather strenuous. I was really terribly tired when they left. But it was worth it.

"Ila & 'Me'"

Mary, Ila's daughter, is not quite 6. I did not fancy her. She is my stepmother over again. But Charlie and Billy were entirely delightful—"specially Bill."

I discovered that Ila could never "get on" with Kate. She said the year she and Kate lived together in Winnipeg they had a cat and dog life. Poor Carl and his wife are divorced. Ila fears Carl has taken up with just such another girl again. It is a shame. He is such a dear in some ways. But he has his mother's obstinacy and it is ruining his life. Where he gets his low taste in wiving I cannot understand. *That* can't be blamed on his mother.

Ila said little about Bruce. Somehow I feel she does not care for him as for Carl.

Jessie Leask arrived unexpectedly on Wednesday and stayed till Friday. It was annoying. She is an uninteresting girl at any time and it spoiled Ila's visit to a certain extent. But Chester took her off my hands considerably. Also he amused the children who tagged after him like young puppies. It is a new development in Chester and one I am glad to see. But I have some worries over Chester this summer that make life rather bitter. I feel very helpless. And tired! Oh, so tired.

Tuesday, Aug. 31, 1926
The Manse, Norval

August is gone—my month of "rest." There has been no rest. But these past ten days have not been quite so strenuous as the earlier part of the month. We have had almost unceasing rain.

Last week was made unhappy for me by Chester's behaviour. He told me such a petty cowardly lie about a small matter. Somehow it broke up my morale entirely. Wednesday he asked my forgiveness and we were at one again but it will be long before I can forget it.

I had the missionary meeting here and got a lot of "jobs" done that have been crowding me all summer. And I had one or two nice quiet evenings that rested me. If I could have a week of such evenings I would feel like a new creature. But there is no use in wishing for the moon. I must simply take a tallow candle and be thankful.

Yesterday we had the "Missionary Quilting." Today I began work—again—on Emily Third—the last section.

Thursday, Sept. 2, 1926

I have had a miserable night and day. Last night I discovered that Chester has been smoking cigarettes. It was not the mere fact that upset me—it was his deceit. I had asked him long ago to promise me that he would not smoke anything until he was 25. After that he could please himself. And he had promised.

I felt sick at heart—broke down altogether—cried chokingly. Chester seemed very repentant. Went of his own accord, brought a Bible, and swore he would never do it again. But can I trust him again? I could not sleep all night and I could not work today. This has spoiled everything for me.

Friday, Sept. 3, 1926
The Manse, Norval

Chester and I went to town today to get his school outfit for the year. It would not have been an unpleasant day but for one incident. A nasty thing. Some people are such fools.

I met John Smith in Simpsons and stopped to speak to him. He is an Uxbridge man and a good friend of ours. Another man passing had stopped to speak to him at just the same time. The notorious Greig! Now, John Smith knew the whole story and why he did what he did I cannot understand—unless on the theory that he had temporarily forgotten the whole affair. He introduced Greig to me!! Greig put out his hand but I bowed coldly, ignored it, and turned away from him to Smith. But the gods had certainly made Smith mad. He went on to explain to Greig who I was. "This is Mrs. Macdonald—wife of the Rev. Ewan Macdonald who used to live in Leaskdale."

Greig needed no information on that point. No doubt he was cursing John Smith as heartily as I was. I was so enraged over the whole stupid, silly, embarrassing encounter that if I could have fried the Smith in boiling oil I believe I'd have done it....

Sunday night. Sept. 5, 1926

I felt thankful tonight because a little harmless pleasant life I love and which means much to me has been spared. Friday night when I came home from Toronto I thought Luck seemed very dull and Margaret said he had refused to eat all day. All day yesterday he refused to eat and lay on my bed. At dark—an early dismal dark for it had poured rain all day—he began to vomit. He seemed so much like that beautiful old Daffy the Second of twenty years ago that I thought he was going to die the same way and I felt bitter. Must I lose even this pretty little creature with the engaging ways that do so much to make my harried life bearable? No Lucky to run gaily, tail up, across the lawn to meet me—no Lucky to jump on my lap and purr—no Lucky to snuggle down at my feet in the black of night. I phoned a Georgetown vet. and he told me to give Lucky subnitrate of bismuth every half hour. So I sallied down street in a starless dripping night and got some from Dr. Webster. Then I sat up all night last night and gave Luck half hourly doses. The poor little cat took them so meekly but looked at me reproachfully afterward as if asking why I was torturing him. He never slept—

"Dr. Webster's"

just lay on my bed and stared into vacancy. But when I stroked him the poor little cat tried his best to do as he always did—roll over on his back and hold up his little paws to give me a free chance to tickle his "bunkie" gently. He always loved that but he could not put any heart into it last night.

However, the vomiting stopped and he seemed better this morning. But he neither ate nor slept all day till 6 o'clock this evening when he ate a little and tried to groom himself up. About eight he climbed in my lap and went to sleep for the first time in 36 hours. I cried with relief. He is such company.

Ewan came home yesterday. He seems fairly well but still a little "heady." Now for congregational harness again.

Monday, Sept. 6, 1926
The Manse, Norval
For a wonder it didn't rain. We have had almost constant rain for a month. I do hope it will be fine when Myrtle comes. Had another depressing letter from Rollins today.

"You may be interested to hear that the Page Co. are contending that the expense to it of purchasing the stories from you should go in diminution of the gross profits....

I think that we shall have to admit that our opponents are ingenious & resourceful."

306

Thursday, Sept. 9, 1926
We motored to Guelph this morning to meet Myrtle who has been spending a few days with an aunt. It was *good* to see one of the household of Joseph again. While Ewan had the car attended to we "did" the grounds of the agricultural college. A beautiful place. And doubly beautiful with a friend who could share my delight in it. It is one of the grievous lacks in my life that Ewan has no feeling whatever for beauty in nature, art or literature.

Myrtle and I had a delightful afternoon there. Tomorrow we go in to see the Exhibition. I mean to take my "vacation" while she is here and let pastoral visits go to pot.

"Myrtle & I"

Thursday, Sept. 16, 1926
The Manse, Norval
Tuesday morning we took Chester to Aurora where the new college is and left him there while we went on to Leaskdale. I wanted Myrtle to see it and the School fair was that day where I knew we would see lots of old friends. We had dinner at Geo. Leask's and then went over to the manse where Mr. Simpson has his study in the parlor. The whole place depressed me. The grounds were overgrown with weeds and grass. Surely the congregation might have kept it decent. And those bare, deserted, reproachful rooms hurt me.

The fair was a fizzle owing to heavy rain. And by the fatality which always seems to attend us when Ewan parked our car in the circle around the sports grounds we found ourselves cheek by jowl with Marshall Pickering's car. He himself was not there but old Mrs. P. was, glowering at us, like Milton's "blue meagre hag" from its interior. This of course did not add to our pleasure....

We went to tea at Beatons' in Wick and had to stay there all night because of the rain. Today we came to Toronto and Myrtle and I stayed there to see *Ben Hur*. Very wonderful. About the only movie of a book I have not been disappointed in. The chariot race was amazing as was also the fight with the pirates. Yet the *atmosphere* of the book was lacking and "Esther" was a pretty movie doll ludicrously unlike the "Esther" of the book.

Saturday, Sept. 18, 1926
Stuart and I are a heart-broken pair. The fate that hates everything I love, having missed its bolt at Luck, shot another at poor Dixie.

When we came to Norval Dixie was a happy dog. He found a friend and companion in Otto, Dr. Webster's dog. Otto was a beagle, a small dog, and he and Dixie did have splendid times together. But alas, they roved too far from home and began chasing Mr. Laird's sheep up on the hill. They never hurt the sheep and were only in fun but they frightened them and Mr. Laird came down this morning and insisted we must either kill Dixie or send him away. Had he not been one of our people I would have told him flatly I would do no such thing unless he could prove Dix had harmed the sheep but we would keep them tied up. But we can't fight with one of our people. Poor Stuart cried pitifully and I was not much better. I would have preferred to chloroform poor little Dix rather than send him away to dear knows what treatment. But Stuart could not bear the thought of this so we have decided to send him up to Mills. They have no sheep and I know they will be good to him. And there is a faint possibility that if he is where he isn't tempted to chase sheep for a year he may be broken of the habit and we may have him back. At least, I tell Stuart this to help him over the first bitterness.

I was all upset and it spoiled the day for me. We were out to tea at Alf McLaughlin's and he took us down to show us the most delightful and fairylike scenery around the Credit that runs by his farm. But it could not delight me. My thoughts were with a poor little dog I have grown to love. "A sheep's life is worth more than a dog's life," said Mr. Laird. Not to me, Mr. Laird. It all depends on the point of view. Does anybody love one of your sheep as we love our dog? Mr. Laird was no doubt within his legal rights but when we promised to keep Dixie tied up at home I think he might have given him a chance. Dr. Webster is going to chloroform poor Otto so two happy little dogs who meant no harm have come to sad grief.

Wednesday, Sept. 29, 1926
Sunday was that rarity—a fine warm day. In the afternoon Myrtle and I had a delightful walk over the west branch, through the woods on its banks and out to a little point on the river opposite the manse, with a wonderful view. How long is it since I had a walk in woods with a "kindred spirit"....

Monday we went up to the Dale Greenhouses in Brampton—the largest in the world. Certainly it was an entertaining visit. Myrtle and I both love flowers so much. Tuesday afternoon I had the W.M.S. here and that duty being done

"View from point"

Myrtle and I tore off like a couple of girls to the radial and went to Toronto. Ewan had gone in in the morning with Barracloughs and they met us and we went to the induction of the new Principal of Knox College. Then we came home in their lovely car, had supper at a road house and a very delightful companionable time. Only the pinprick was not missing of course. I had a grumbling toothache which while not bad enough to spoil my fun certainly diluted it.

This afternoon we had a delightful drive up to Belfountain—one of the beauty spots on the Credit. The Credit is really the most picturesque river I have ever seen and Belfountain, the play-place of a wealthy man, is a fairy dream. Oh, for one *idle* week in such a place, with no callers and letters and missionary meetings!...

Sunday, Oct. 3, 1926
The Manse, Norval

These past few days have been rather devilish. Myrtle's visit came to an end on Thursday much to my regret. I shall miss her terribly. It has been *good* to have a real companion who could enter into passing jokes. I think I gave her a nice time, too, and these three weeks will always shine pleasantly in my memory...

I had a bad time with my tooth Wednesday night but by dint of taking capsules all Thursday I was able to stand in the evil day. Had I not had to go away I would not have taken them, for they only delayed the process of ulceration which had to come finally. But I had promised to go to Montreal with Myrtle who was nervous over travelling alone and I had to do something to render it possible and tolerable. We went into Toronto Thursday morning and had a pleasant day, with an exploration of Simpson's, a movie, dinner with a friend at the Walker, and Pantages at night to see Blackstone, the conjuror, do things that would be unbelievable if one had not seen them. In one way they affected me unpleasantly. If these things were not real, how believe that anything was real? Is the whole Universe the trick of some Master Juggler?

But an ulcerating tooth makes one pessimistic.

My tooth was bad all night and the way to Montreal Friday was a Via Dolorosa of toothache and headache combined. The capsules lost their effect and I was very miserable. Saw Myrtle off on the Maritime Express—the very name always makes me homesick!—and then endured in the waiting room till my own train left. I had a wretched night but towards morning fell asleep and awoke free from pain but with a grotesquely swelled face and feeling utterly played out.

Nevertheless I had to gather up a little courage and go to see a specialist about my ear.

Last spring I began to feel something wrong with my right ear—a curious sensation of fullness. But the hearing did not seem affected and I never seemed to find it possible to go to Toronto and see about it. Lately, however, I have realized I soon must—the sensation of fullness grew worse and I began to have constant shooting pains in it. I have always been afraid of getting deaf in middle life. Grandfather Montgomery was very deaf for years before his death and though none of his children became so, a thing like that often crops out in the second generation. I got Mr. McClelland to put me in touch with a good ear specialist but when Myrtle came every day was so full that it seemed impossible to get away and I kept putting it off to a more convenient time. Then last Tuesday I went suddenly and absolutely deaf in that ear. So I knew it must be seen to at once. I had a pretty good idea that the trouble was hardened wax and when I went to Dr. Royce I found I was right. The canal was filled with it. Hard as a stone. So hard that I could not endure the pain of his attempt to remove it. So he gave me drops to use for a week and then I have to go again.

I came home yesterday on radial. Very tired, with a full, nay, a jammed week ahead. *And* Amos Eagles coming Tuesday for a visit.

Flatly, he isn't welcome. I never liked him. He wasn't nice to poor Flora. He is also an unmitigated bore. And I do so want to get down to literary work. I am wretchedly behind-hand with it. And I have had such an unending stream of company this summer....

Tuesday, October 5
The Manse, Norval
Yesterday was filled with many things. One was an amusing letter from a very adoring girl who signs herself "your devoted slave."

"Exquisite shadows"

His Amosship came tonight. I see no change in him since first I saw him. Certainly he isn't any more interesting. And he tells us over and over again all his troubles and squabbles with his neighbors. We have no idea how long he means to stay and it leaves all our plans in the air.

The reviews of the *Blue Castle* are coming in. Most of them are much better than I expected. One reviewer says, "the best little yarn I have read in a year"....

Wednesday, Oct. 13, 1926
Really, I wonder what it would be like not to feel tired.

Sunday evening the drops Dr. Royce gave me for my ear had a very queer effect when I used them. I turned so dizzy and seasick that I could not stand or sit but had to lie down. My ear began to ache and I put in a most miserable night but felt normal in the morning.

Monday night I had to go to Limehouse to read for their anniversary concert, not liking to refuse Mrs. McLean when she asked me. It was nearly one when we got home. Yesterday morning I actually finished writing *Emily's Quest*. Of course I have to revise it yet but it is such a relief to feel it is off my mind at last. I've never had such a time writing a book. Thank heaven it is the last of the Emily series....

"A view of fairyland"

And today while emptying a box of "dump" into the river Mr. Williams opened a jealously locked door in the shed to let me do it—and it was like a door into fairyland. There was a wonderful view down the blue river below the autumnal maples. It made me feel that life wasn't half bad....

Tuesday, Oct. 19, 1926
We took Amos to Toronto today on his way home. We sped the parting guest right willingly. But, to give the devil his due, he did a lot of little jobs for me, having a liking for pottering round. He cleaned up the garage and helped me clean up the garden. I don't know how I'd ever have got the time to do it by myself. So I suppose it's rather a good thing he came....

Wednesday, Oct. 20, 1926
....I am literally persecuted by endless requests to go here and there to give read-

ings. Of course I refuse most of them. But some I cannot, for various reasons, refuse. Yet I have neither the time nor the energy for them....

Sunday, Oct. 24, 1926
The Manse, Norval
....Ewan and I went to Georgetown to hear Rev. J.K. Fraser of Galt who was preaching the anniversary sermon. He was my old teacher "Mr. Fraser" of long–ago days in Cavendish. He boarded with us and we little tots adored him, though the "big boys," some of them older than himself, almost ran him out of the school. The sermon and music were fine and we went over to the manse after it and had a pleasant two hours with Mr. Fraser and the McLeans. This was *real* social enjoyment and rested me as much as sleep would have done. Also it gave me some spiritual grit to face the on coming week—which is another crammed one. Georgetown fowl supper tomorrow night where I must give readings—paper hangers here Wednesday. Thursday and Friday preparing for our own fowl supper which is Friday night.

Monday, October 25, 1926
....When I began to dress for the Georgetown concert I realized that I should go to bed instead. I was so tired that I *cried* when I couldn't find a hairpin. I am committing a *sin* when I overwork myself to such an extent. But I went over, ate a "fowl supper" jammed at a table between two strangers so tightly that it was misery, gave two readings and came home. Dead beat? Not at all. I suppose the reserves had come up. At all events I felt rested, relaxed, courageous.

Wednesday, Oct. 27, 1926
Last night I spent *at home*. It was as much of a treat as an evening *out* would have been twenty years ago. It is always either "a feast or a famine" with me—or rather, a surfeit or a famine. Today I had paper-hangers doing over my room. It looks very nice now. The new paper is so dainty and restful—soft gray with little branches of white ferns over it. It has transformed the room.

Tonight we had a meeting to re-organize the Young People's Society for the winter. They meet every Monday night. I dreaded it, recalling executive meetings in Leaskdale when we had to do practically everything ourselves. But things are different here. The young folks here are used to doing things for themselves, evidently, and there are some excellent natural leaders. So everything went on finely and we hadn't any more of it to carry than the rest.

Saturday, Oct. 30, 1926
So tired again. Same old story. Thursday and Friday I baked and brewed all day, making cake, jellies, salads, mock chicken etc. for the supper. Thursday night we went to tea in Union with a dull stupid family who gave us half cooked sausages for supper. Most of the Union families are nice cultured people who set excellent tables, but this is one of the few poor ones.

Last night our fowl supper came off and was a big success, as such things go—good night, big crowd, and lots of shekels scooped in. The decorations were really pretty. The basement was a bower of autumn leaves, black cats and jacky lanterns. One of the jacks belonged to Stuart; it was a beauty and some woman deliberately stole it. Walked off and out with it. Mr. Williams saw her but did not know her.

Mrs. Sam McClure brought a turkey which she kept secreted and after the concert all we performers ate it.

Things like this are really pleasant when one is not too tired to enjoy them. The folks who come to the suppers are not out every night or many nights so they can enjoy them. But we wretched "minister and wife," who are on the go all the time are too fed up to enjoy them.

I have one and one only keen desire just now. It is to go to bed and stay there for exactly one week, seeing no one, going nowhere—never smiling—not even eating!

Monday, Nov. 1, 1926
The Manse, Norval
....I had such a blessed evening home tonight. Got some letters answered. And when 9 o'clock came I experienced once more the secret thrill that comes when you open a new book. I had two delicious hours of reading—a feast after a famine—well, not a feast exactly but at least one good bite.

"Norval Manse"

The trees are all bare now—the rainstorm today has stripped them—of all save a few lonely yellow leaves falling in autumn dusks. So Norval has lost much of its beauty. But the pines remain and I am consoled for the going of the leaves by the fact that now they are gone I can see the pine grove on Russell's hill again—lie in bed and look at it, a delicate, unreal, moonlit world—wake and see it talking to the sky against the fires of sunrise.

Wednesday, Nov. 3, 1926

Last night we were visiting in Union and as Ewan was organizing a Guild it was very late when we got home. They have had no Guild in Union and there are a lot of young people there so though it means more work for us and more going out I think it should be done. Today I went to Terra Cotta to a Missionary meeting. I enjoyed the drive. The day was mild and brooding and the scenery back at Terra Cotta is wild and eerie. Rolling hills of leafless trees,—purple distances, loops and glimpses of the Credit, which is really the dearest and most fascinating little river I have ever seen....

Friday, Nov. 5, 1926

This was a lovely day. I was out in the afternoon planting bulbs and talking to the pines on the hill. Chester came home tonight for Thanksgiving. Looking well and with a good report. All this was pleasant. But it was not pleasant to hear that Alf McLaughlins had sold out and were going away.

"The Boys" [Chester and Stuart]

Four or five families have sold and gone since we came. To be sure, up to this, another family has always come in their place. But the newcomers are not as good financially and now the McLaughlins are going and an Anglican has bought the farm. So I feel a wee bit blue tonight. It would be nice to have a congregation sufficiently strong not to mind a removal now and then.

Saturday, Nov. 13, 1926

....I had the old recurrent dream I have had so often all my life. A vivid dream—yet I have never been able to solve its significance if it has any. It is always the same in outline—I suddenly discover a beautiful and unsuspected suite of rooms in a house I've been living in for years. They are always full of beautiful things. I run through them delightedly, wondering why I have never before known they were there—and wake up disappointed in the midst of my wonder and delight. I fancy it is merely an effort on the part of my subconscious mind to escape from the narrow confines of my harassed life.

Sat., Nov. 20, 1926

....This morning I dragged up. Finished revising *Emily's Quest* and mailed it to the typist. I can hardly believe I've really got it off my hands at last. It is no good. How could it be? It seems to me I'll never be able to write anything worth while again. But perhaps if I could get rested—and had a few unbroken spare moments!

Sunday, Nov. 21, 1926
The Manse, Norval

In sorting out the garret today I was freshly amused by the titles of the foreign editions of my books, as I packed them away in a box. Some sound fairly well, others strike me as being very uncouth. *Regnbuedalen*, Swedish for *Rainbow Valley*, sounds quite well, but the Dutch *Het Ryenbougdal* is outlandish. *Anna Pa Gronkulla* seems to be Swedish for *Anne of Green Gables* but in Dutch the book is called *In Veilage Haven* which cannot be a translation of *Anne* etc. *Emily Van de Wienuwe Maan* sounds oddly, but *Anna Van Avonlea*, *Anna Van Het Eiland* and *Rilla Van Ingleside* are quite recognizable.

The cover design of the Swedish *Green Gables* has always been one of the joys of my life. Anne is depicted as an exceedingly weird creature, carrying an enormous carpet bag with hair of a literal *scarlet*—not red or auburn or carrot but a bright glaring scarlet.

Grandma Woolner's old jug stands again in my parlor. Someone not long ago told me what I knew very well myself. That if I took the jug to a certain place in Toronto they would take it apart on the old break, remove the smears of white lead placed there 80 or 90 years ago by Great Grandmother Woolner and re-join the pieces in such wise that the break would hardly be noticeable. Very true. But I don't want the white lead removed. There in one place is Grandmother Woolner's thumb-print clear and distinct as when nearly a century ago she pressed the white lead down along the line of cleavage. To me that finger print is part of the old jug's charm. I wouldn't have it removed for anything. As long as the old jug holds together so long shall the white lead remain as it is. If it ever shows signs of coming apart I shall reluctantly have it professionally mended.

The old jug is one hundred years old this year. It was made in 1826 as the date shows. What a hundred years! If Harriet Kemp were to waken from her sleep of nearly a century what would she think of the speed-mad world today? Would she thankfully go back to her long slumber?

Monday, Nov. 22, 1926

These are attic days. Again this afternoon I was in the attic looking over some old scrapbooks. I had gone up to look for a certain paper to be read at a Missionary meeting; but the ghostly charm of the old books seized hold of me and I stayed longer than I should—seeing that there are only twenty four hours in a day and many heathen yet unsaved!—turning over their yellowing pages. Such a hodge-podge as they are, dating back to early girlhood days. Many of the "souvenirs" mean nothing now—I have forgotten their very significance. But on the first page are three that are not forgotten. One is an old calendar Willie P. sent me, with a little dot marked on every day when I had an especially good or happy time. The early pages of my scrapbooks teem with these calendars. In this especial calendar 76 days are marked with the significant little black dot. If I were so to mark one of my calendars today I wonder how many dots would appear. Sadly few I am afraid.

I looked over the list of names of the old P.W.C. entrance of July 1893—a thing that meant so much to me at the time. *Did* it mean so much? As far as my worldly success is concerned I do not think now that it did. But from another point of view—well, supposing I had never "passed for a teacher" just exactly what difference would it have made in my life? I would never have suffered the anguish and humiliation of my engagement to Edwin Simpson. And on the other side of the ledger I would never have known that sweet and terrible love for Herman Leard. *That* is a thing I could not have blotted out of life. So it was well, after all, that I passed that old "entrance"—an entrance truly into worlds undreamed of.

In those old scrapbooks are some fashion plates. I looked critically at the first one I came to—of the vintage of that same '93. It was the time of hats that sat on the top of the head, of high collars, puffed sleeves, belted waist line and long skirts. Many obsolete fashions are very laughable and ugly but this did not strike me as being so. Indeed, compared to the fashions of today it seemed to me dignified, beautiful and becoming. There was nothing extreme or exaggerated about it. The pretty hat showed the becoming frame of hair. The sleeves, not yet the monstrosities they afterwards became, lent slenderness and grace to the figure. It looked rather good to see a waist again and the long skirt with a dainty little toe peeping out had something that the knee skirts of today haven't—reserve, mystery. I smiled to see the left hand holding it up in the back. We always had to do that, else the "tail" became muddy and draggled. I suppose it was inconvenient. But when we were accustomed to it we did it automatically and I cannot recall thinking of it as a nuisance. No, I do not think the girls of '93 needed the rather scornful pity that is sometimes meted out to them by the scantly-garbed damsels of today. We were just as pretty, just as graceful, just as well-pleased with ourselves.

That early scrapbook is well filled with newspaper accounts of weddings: and my latest scrapbook of today is filled with the weddings of the children of those gay brides and bridegrooms!...

Among many wedding notices Hattie Gordon's reads ironically now, with the divorce aftermath of its "happy couple."

A series of cards with a mock programme of the Literary nights brings back the memory of the winter Nora Lefurgey was with us and Literary the one dependable function of the winter. We had much fun at those meetings—though the real joy of such things was beginning to wear very thin for me. And there was an account of George Campbell's wedding—very flowery, with all the time–honored expressions—"a very pretty wedding"—"lavishly decorated with cut flowers"—"bride charmingly gowned in white silk"—"beautiful bouquet of roses and maidenhair fern"—"charming flower-girls"—"large number of beautiful presents" and so on. To me, who knows so well all the years of tragedy and wretchedness that followed that gay wedding it has a very bitter tang. George's funeral notice is somewhere in the scrapbook, too—the end of a foolish, futile life flung away in blind obstinacy.

There is one item:—

"The Rev. Edwin Simpson of Illinois and Burton Simpson of Acadia College are visiting in Bay View. The former occupied the pulpit of the Cavendish Baptist church on Sunday evening."

A very harmless, commonplace note. Yet there was much behind it for me of unpleasant emotions. I often wonder when reading similar notices in the papers today what is behind them all of human passion and joy and fate. It would not be a bad idea for a series of stories, eh?

For example, Nettie Millar's wedding notice on the next page. I happen to know that Nettie never wanted to marry Austin Ramsay but was literally harried into it by her parents. Helen Leard's marriage is here, too—and the other day I pasted into the scrapbook of the present a notice of her husband's death—"so runs the round of life from hour to hour."

When I taught in Bideford a certain Toronto Magazine was running a department devoted to reading character from handwriting. Daisy Williams and I both sent in samples of our writing—she under the nom-de-plume of "Night's Eye," I, under "Psyche." Here is the result of mine. I think it is very true. I have often wondered what "the other things" were that might have been revealed. I hope there was no dark and terrible mystery of iniquity hidden in them.

"You are of a rather domineering disposition but knowing how to master yourself as well as others are very controlled. You are very fond of elegance and luxury, of aristocratic manners etc. *You know how to suppress and hide your internal thoughts and feelings to such an extent as to appear utterly different from what you really are.* You can be extremely amiable, affable and obliging, especially in society. You have a will of your own. You like comfort and ease. You are very economical, very politic and diplomatic, suspicious and distrustful. I could tell you a great many more things from your very interesting handwriting."

The italics are mine. I consider that the underlined sentence marked me out and foreordained me for a minister's wife!!

On one page I found an old poem, "The Fringed Gentian," published in *Godey's Lady's Book* over forty years ago. I don't think I ever knew the author's name. It is only newspaper rhyme—and yet through all my childhood and girlhood it was more of an inspiration to me than all Milton's starry splendor. It seemed to me then to express all the secret feelings and desires of my being—especially the last verse.

The Fringed Gentian

Lift up, thy dewy fringed eyes,
Oh, little Alpine flower,
The tear that trembling on them lies
Has sympathetic power
To move my own, for I, too, dream
With thee of distant heights
Whose lofty peaks are all agleam
With rosy dazzling lights.

Who dreams of wider spheres revealed
Up higher near the sky
Within the valley's narrow field
Cannot contented lie.
Who longs for mountain breezes rare
Is restless down below
Like me for stronger, purer air
Thou pinest, too, I know.

Where aspirations, hopes, desires
Combining fondly dwell,
Where burn the never-dying flowers
Of Genius' wondrous spell.
Such towering summits would I reach
Who climb and grope in vain,
Oh, little flower, the secret teach
The weary way make plain.

When whisper blossom in thy sleep
How I may upward climb
The Alpine path, so hard, so steep
That leads to heights sublime.
How I may reach that far-off goal
Of true and honored fame
And write upon its shining scroll
A woman's humble name.

There is an envelope pasted on one page addressed to Lucy M. Montgomery, Charlottetown, P.E. Island. *The Ladies World* is printed in ornate flourishes in one corner. In it is my first acceptance—of "The Violet's Spell." I remember the sunny autumn day I got it in Charlottetown P.O. I wonder if I could feel so happy now over anything. Truly, the happiness certain things give us is never to be measured by their worldly importance.

A report of a concert mentions that "Miss Montgomery was encored over and over again." Well, I'm still at it—and bored to hatred by it now where once I loved it. When one *has* to do a thing—when it becomes a *duty*, farewell to delight in it....

And there is a wedding notice of a certain Hugh Miller and Grace Noble. I knew neither of them. But Ewan was once engaged to the said Grace's sister!! In his student days on one of his Home Mission Fields. She was much older than he and when he found himself back in college he wakened to the fact of his foolishness—and eventually escaped. She was close on thirty-five and it would be nearly five years before he would be able to marry....

There are many Leaskdale notes in the later scrapbooks—some with pleasant associations, some not. And a picture of the lilacs at the gate of Park Corner orchard. Won't Aunt Annie slip through them with her basket of apples? And Frede smiling at me—and some faded flowers from my wedding bouquet—souvenirs of our wedding trip—blue bells from Melrose Abbey—Frede and Miss Ferguson and Daffy on our Leaskdale lawn. All three dead. I looked no further. I shut the old book and came back to thoughts of the foreign mission field. Eheu!

Thursday, Dec. 2, 1926

There has been an odd resurrection of *Kilmeny of the Orchard* lately. Page recently brought out a reprint edition—he has been issuing reprints of all my old books, I think with the idea of swamping "the trade" with them and so spoiling the market for my new books. I have been getting letters from all over lately, adoring *Kilmeny*. So I hunted it out and read it myself. It seemed as if somebody else had written it. I had no feeling of maternity about it at all. And I found it interesting!!!

Saturday, Dec. 11, 1926

For a few minutes this week I have walked with the gods. The first time was Friday afternoon when I was on my way to the United Church Bazaar. I passed by

"Pine Grove" [Russells' Hill]

the pine hill and looked up at it, lying there in its dear silence. There were those god-like trees rising majestic out of the white sweep of snow with the pale fallen banners of sunlight between them. I know that pine grove well. It is as old a friend of mine as the spruces on the hills of home. How and when I became acquainted with it I know not. All I know is that when I first saw it a year ago I came to it as no stranger. And the message I got from it yesterday went with me, even to the United Church bazaar when I bought an apron I didn't want and some doughnuts that proved uneatable and was whispered at hostilely by several Unionists who hate me because I am a Presbyterian. The former Methodists are quite nice and friendly. But the ex-Presbyterians are very much the reverse.

Then tonight I walked down the street to make a call. There was a half-moon over the pines—an old friend of mine—not too bright for stars. And under the stars the shadows of the pines on the snow. And the line of a poem read long ago came into my mind,

> I will go home to the evening star
> To the light on the edge of the world."

So I went down the street hand in hand with delight. What a pity you can't photograph starlight! Yet—is it? Isn't it just as well there is something that cannot be caught?

Item: I was almost talked to death by the lady I was calling upon.

Saturday, Dec. 18, 1926
I went to Aurora today and brought Chester home, so am tired out—especially as we went to the Sunday School concert at Union last night. The concert lasted till twelve and then our car acted up—as well it might at fifteen below zero—and we did not get home until two.

The W.M.S. met here Tuesday. I was elected President—not having enough to do without it! However, since I *am* President I mean to put a little life into the society. It has been almost moribund under Mrs. McLaughlin.

1927

Saturday, Jan. 1, 1927

The last week of the old year has not been a very pleasant one. On Tuesday a letter came from *Greig*. He and M.P. have been very full of silence for a long time but evidently they feel moved again to utter a few yowls. This was the precious epistle:—

"Dear Sir:—

Re Pickering.

Without Prejudice.

We have been consulted by Mr. Pickering with regard to the judgment which he has against you and on which you have done nothing towards making a settlement. Mr. Pickering *has allowed this matter to run for some time now* and he now feels that unless you make some honest endeavour to settle this judgment he will be obliged to take steps which might cause some embarrassment to you. We do not wish to take any drastic steps without giving you an opportunity of making an amicable settlement. Your attitude however in this matter, has been one of indifference and Mr. Pickering does not feel that *any more leniency should be allowed you.*

Unless we hear from you with some proposition of settlement forthwith we will be obliged to take the matter up with the church authorities of the Presbyterian Church in Canada and have them take the matter up with the officials of the church where you are preaching and in that way probably a settlement can be arrived at.

We are also advised that the salary which you are receiving is more than sufficient to support your family so we have alternatives to the proceeding set out in the last paragraph—namely, of having you examined again as a judgment debtor or garnisheeing your salary.

We would be pleased to hear from you as soon as possible."

The italics in the letter are mine. The idea of Mr. P.'s "leniency" is very funny. I suppose neither he nor Greig have any idea that we know all about the different schemes he has tried every little while to bring Ewan to book and failed. They must imagine that we are under the impression that Pickering really has "let the matter run" since his abortive attempt three years ago to have Ewan examined a second time.

This letter would not have disturbed us at all had it not been for one thing. As far as the threat to take the matter up with the Presbyterian church goes, it is merely to laugh. We know—though Greig does not know we know—that he has already tried that and failed. And even if he had not the Presbyterian church does not take on itself the functions of a law-court to compel its ministers to pay "debts" when they have no money to pay them. But the second threat *did* worry us a bit at first.

Although the salary is supposed to be paid in advance as a matter of fact it is not. At the present moment Norval owes Ewan about three hundred dollars. We have been puzzled about this for we know by the "check-treasurers" that the money has been paid in. Ewan has never liked to ask John Russell for the money. And a week ago John went up to Mt. Albert to spend the Xmas season with his fiancée, Miss Arnold.

Had John—perhaps unconsciously—*let slip the facts of the situation?*

This worried me a bit until I had time to think it over. Then I realized that if such were the case Greig would not write a letter and tell us what he was going to do. He would do it without warning. The whole letter, so full of threats, was a gesture of defeat. One threat would have meant more than so many. So I have not worried much over it. Nevertheless it has spoiled my week.

Tonight when I went in to kiss Stuart good-night he murmured drowsily, "Mother, did I put my boots together under the bed?" I said "Yes." "Then it's all right," he said. "I always like to put them together so that they can be company for each other."

So often Stuart's speeches sound to me like echoes from my own childhood. That is so like some of the ideas I had then. I personified everything and dowered it with human feelings. For instance, when washing dishes I always observed a certain procedure and attributed feelings of envy or disappointment to the dishes that were not washed just when they thought they should be. There was one pert cup I did not like and I always left it till the last, rage as it might. It was really fun to see that cup glowering at me.

Tonight at Mr. Gollop's I had an interesting moment. Many years ago—before I was married—a lady in England—a Miss Macirone—who had been a concert singer in her day—sent me the music of an air she had composed to the words of a poem, "The Wild Cherry Tree," by an author whose name I do not just now recall. She said that in the music she had tried to express the "charm and atmosphere" of *Anne of Green Gables* and she dedicated it to me.

"*The Gollop place*"

Naturally I wanted to hear it sung. But as it was a difficult thing, requiring a baritone voice I have never met anyone who could sing it until I came to Norval and met Mr. Gollop's son George who was here on a visit to his father and is a fine singer. He took the song away and tonight he sang it for me. I was rather disappointed in it—except for the concluding bars which are very fine. Yet I fancy it is a song one would like better every time one heard it.

For a good many years now I have been supporting a little boy named Temple Parsons at St. Anthony's orphanage in Newfoundland. Recently he has grown old enough to leave school and work for himself. So for a change I have taken on a little girl, Flossie Roberts. I chose her out of several pictures sent me for the inadequate reason that she looks like Maud Campbell.

[Flossie Roberts of St. Anthony's Orphanage, Newfoundland]

Friday, Jan. 7, 1927
I had a letter from the editor of the *Delineator* today asking me to do a series of four stories for them and offering two thousand dollars for the four. Of course I shall try to do them. But I detest writing stories to order knowing that they must be done by a certain time. As far as my literary work goes I was far happier years ago when I was a "free lance" writing what I would as I would. I made less money then with a hundred stories than I do now with four. But independence was very sweet.

Saturday, Jan. 8, 1927
The Manse, Norval
Thank mercy, I am going to get rid of Margaret. She has seemed like an Old Man of the Sea for the past five months. Last fall I realized that I really could not put up with her indefinitely. I was killing myself trying to do all my own work and half of what I was paying her to do. And yet I hated to send her away. I knew she would never get—or at any rate—keep a good place and I was sorry for her, a stranger in a strange land, middle aged, unattractive and unadaptable. So I put off telling her to go out of pity and now I'm glad to say she has saved me the trouble.

From the start I did not like her either as a person or as a maid. She had the most disagreeable personality imaginable. Always hunting for a grievance—

always looking for slights where none was intended—always apparently smelling a bad smell—not an unpleasant odour but a bad smell! She looked like a gargoyle—a face that was half forehead and straight bobbed hair. We have all detested her and felt that she detested us and despised all our Canadian ways. I never said a thing to her without feeling immediately that I had said the wrong thing.

To say what good could be said of her she got up in the morning without being called and she kept the house fairly neat—only fairly. In nothing else was she satisfactory.

I discovered as soon as she came that she could not cook. I tried to teach her but it was hopeless. So after a few weeks I gave up the vain attempt and when I expected company or had baking to do for church festivities—which was about all the time—I did the baking myself. She resented this and I always felt like an intruder in my own kitchen. When she came we did everything to make her feel at home and happy. We treated—or tried to treat—her just as one of the family. We took her everywhere we went, to movie or concert or little car excursions and paid her way. I may say, too, in passing, that never once did she express one word of thanks for this or one word of appreciation of anything. Not even when we took her to Niagara. Not one word did she say about it. And she certainly spoiled all our outings with her dour, contemptuous personality.

She had been here about a month when I saw something that made me realize that I had a strange creature in my house. One evening at dusk I went into the sewing room for something and happened to look out of the window, through the muslin curtain. It was quite dark in the room and no one outside could see me. But in the garden below it was still quite light. Margaret came into view walking down the path to the house. Suddenly she lifted her face and *made a face at the house*. That is exactly what she did—just as a child would grimace at some thing or person it disliked. It may seem a small thing but to me it was very significant. It was quite natural that Margaret should be lonesome and homesick during her first weeks in a strange land. But we were not to blame for that and we had done everything in our power to help her over the first hard weeks. So the spirit revealed in that petty spiteful act was appalling. From that moment I never felt easy with her in the house.

She was no good as a laundress. Her ironing was heart-breaking. I tried to teach her how to sprinkle and iron the clothes damp so that they would be smooth. But it was no use. She resented any attempt at teaching her anything. She was sure she "knew it all." As for her slowness I never saw anything like it. Elsie was not a fast worker but Elsie could do in one hour what Margaret took four to do. As a result she never overtook her work and some of it was either left undone or I had to do it. She had a vile temper and was constantly going into black rages, nobody knew why. But until today she never *said* anything—just banged things around. I would take no notice of her and eventually she would get over it.

It was impossible to make any kind of a companion of her. She was the only maid I ever had I could not work with. And she took no interest in her work—

she did what she had to do and never saw anything else to do. She was slightly hard of hearing and did not catch what was told her unless she was expecting you to speak to her. She went about looking like a scarecrow. She smashed some valuable dish every week. She hated the cats. She served up cold, undercooked or overcooked meals. And with it all, such a complacency, such a calm assumption that she knew everything and had nothing more to learn. All in all she was the most puzzling composition I ever came across. And I really think the thing that annoyed me most with her was her aggravating way of dismissing everything that was said to her with a contemptuous "Yais—yais."

Stuart declared he could not stand her habit of licking her lips at the table and Ewan was driven to protest over her habit of burning bones in the stove, whereby the house was made to smell like a glue factory. I told her to throw them away in the back lot but she coolly disregarded this, as she did all my directions unless I insisted on them.

Then why did I keep her on? For two reasons. First, as I have said I was sorry for her. Secondly I knew if I sent her away too soon, especially after Elsie's kididoes, some yarn would get around that I was a crank and I might find it hard to get a maid at all. So I was determined that I would put up with her for a year if possible. Though lately I have felt that it would not be possible. I thought with dread of the spring housecleaning. How could I ever get through with it with that creature?

A lady who was here in the fall said to me, "Mrs. Macdonald, you are making a mistake in treating that girl as you do. A Canadian girl would understand it but those Scotch girls don't. They are not used that way in the Old Country and if you make so much of them they think it is because you are afraid they will leave you and they take advantage of you."

I realize now that this was the truth. She also said that in the Old Country people generally kept two maids to do what one maid does here and paid the two of them just what we pay one. She said the Scotch girls came out here expecting to get the big Canadian wages for the same amount of work they did back home.

Shortly before Christmas I got so "fed up" with Margaret's incompetency and peculiarities that I felt I would have to get rid of her. But I waited till after the Xmas season was over. Then I kept putting it off and putting it off. I hate to tell a maid to go. I never had it to do before, and luckily today she saved me the trouble. So, though I am disgusted with her insolence I am mightily relieved. The very thought of being free from her makes me feel young again!

Last Monday she went in to Toronto to see a friend who had recently come out. I suppose they cooked it up between them. Or else—as some things lead me to suppose—Margaret simply thought she'd stage a play for higher wages. Now, it would only be natural for her to like to be near some of her compatriots. She never made up with anyone here. It was impossible to make friends with her though our women heartily tried. So she must have found it lonely and if she had said pleasantly and respectfully that she wanted to make a change both of us would have been suited.

When she came home last Monday night I noticed a change in her. I had the

Sunday School officers in for a business meeting and when Margaret came home I went out to the kitchen and found her reading a letter which had come for her that day. I said, "Well, how did you get along, Margaret?" "Oh, very well, thank you," was the reply in a very stiff tone. "Did you get your letter?" I asked. "Yes, but there should have been a great many more. I don't know what is happening to my letters." I was amazed at the insolence of her tone. And I should not have tolerated it. But I did not want any fuss with company in the house so I merely said "Well, that is all that came for you" and went on to say that I wanted the kettle boiling at ten o'clock and returned to the parlor.

When I came out at ten o'clock there was no sign of Margaret and no kettle on. I set my lips, put the kettle on and proceeded to get lunch myself. I had it half done when Margaret came down. I said not a word nor did she and we served the lunch. It was always my custom to help Margaret wash the dishes after a late lunch but this night I was so annoyed with her that I didn't. All the week she has seemed grouchy but I was too busy to bother much over her.

This morning when I came downstairs I saw she was in a bad humor though I could guess no reason why. Stuart has been up late a great many nights lately owing to unavoidable circumstances and the child was so tired that I told him to stay in bed till dinner time this morning. This did not mean anything to Margaret since he did not want any breakfast and if he had I would have taken it up to him as I have always done. But when I said Stuart would not be down to breakfast Margaret said snappishly if she had known that she wouldn't have made toast for him—it was a pity to waste it!! I should have told her it was no concern of hers if it was wasted. But—as always and foolishly—I ignored her impertinence—and ate the extra slice myself—not to save it from being wasted but because I really wanted it. After breakfast was over I told Margaret to make a couple of pies for the weekend and I would make a pudding. I had by dint of much patience taught her how to make piecrust after a fashion though it was never very good. I went out to the kitchen and began my preparations when Margaret suddenly turned and blazed out—and in a rage I think she was the most repulsive object I ever saw—"Mrs. Macdonald I might as well tell you that there is too much work here and I'm going to leave."

If she had said pleasantly that she wanted to make a change I would have been only too delighted. But for her to speak like that, after the way she has been used here annoyed me.

"Work," I said. "You are doing about two thirds of the work my poorest Canadian maid ever did and you are paid ten dollars a month more."

"*Young* girls get $40 a month in Toronto," she flashed.

I smiled. "A few get that in wealthy places but not for the quantity or quality of work you do. Girls who get forty dollars are good cooks."

"I've always been considered a good cook," she retorted.

"You cannot cook at all by Canadian standards," I said. "And you can go just as soon as you like."

I never saw such a change come over anyone as came over her. She simply collapsed. I feel sure it was the last thing she expected me to say.

"I shall never forget how kind you have been to me, Mrs. Macdonald," she said, "and I'll stay till you get suited with a maid."

"You can please yourself about that," I said and left her.

An amusing corollary was that she would not touch her helping of pudding for dinner, though commonly she had a quite tremendous appetite and ate everything!

Well, I may have some trouble getting a maid but nothing matters so long as I am rid of her!....

Monday, Jan. 10, 1927
The Manse, Norval

Tonight we had an Old-Timers' concert in our guild here. It was capital. Everybody—that is, all the performers—wore old-time costumes—big sleeves—bustles—crinolines—bonnets, veils, etc. Some of them looked funny but most did not look funny at all. Charlotte McPherson in a dress and hat of the vintage

[Old Timers' Concert Party]

of 1912 looked graceful and pleasing. And Kate McPherson in her mother's black silk dress, with long-tailed basque and apron-draperied skirt, dressy little lace bonnet and lace veil looked *sweet*: I looked from her to a woman of 60 sitting in a front seat, with skirts to her knees and bobbed hair and believe me the contrast was not in the latter's favour.

In many ways the costumes made me curiously homesick. When I was a young girl the pews of the old Cavendish church were filled with middle-aged women dressed like Kate McPherson—women who were not afraid to grow old. Grandmother had a dress and bonnet very like hers.

Myself, I wore a widow's dress and veil and recited "The Widow Piper."

Saturday, Jan. 15, 1927

I went to Guelph yesterday and spoke to the Women's Club there. Had a nice time and met a lady—I forget her married name but she was once Martha Thompson and went to school in Prince Albert with me. Oh, yes, the name has just come to me—Mrs. Petersen. It seemed like a voice from the tomb to see her again. Though she was far from tomb-like—a plump jolly lady.

Today Ewan got a letter from Rev. Mr. McNamara of Toronto who is clerk of the General Assembly. Greig has shot his bolt. Mr. McNamara wrote a very courteous letter—very different from Grant's dictatorial screed of last winter—saying he had received the letter and wishing to talk it over with Ewan before he took any steps in such a delicate matter. Mr. McNamara knows Ewan well and we are not much worried. Nevertheless, there is always a possibility of something embarrassing and I feel nervous and dispirited.

This reminds me that by some oversight I have never written of the astonishing sequel to Greig's letter. When John Russell returned from his two weeks' sojourn with his beloved he came down here one afternoon, asked for Ewan and was closeted for a long time with him in the parlor. Finally Ewan came up and I heard the tale.

Before beginning it however I might say that John told Ewan that Marshall Pickering came to see him in Mount Albert and asked him if Ewan's salary had been paid up. "Yes," lied John cheerfully. "I paid him up to the hilt just before I came away." So M.P. then said "Well, I suppose all I can do now is get the officials of the Presbyterian church to take it up."

I have never been able to understand why John Russell espoused our cause so vehemently and to such good purpose last winter before we came. He did not know us, so it could not have been personal friendship. He *did* know and was engaged to a sister of Pete Arnold. Why then should he be on our side and not on theirs? It never seemed to me a satisfactory solution of this problem to say that he, being a Presbyterian—did not want his minister to be involved in a local scandal, because of the gloating Unionists. But now we know it all. John confessed all today; and it is rather sickening too. John has been borrowing from the church funds to *the extent of five hundred dollars*. Expecting to pay it back when he got certain "compensation" due him for injuries received in a paper mill he was working in last year! This has been going on a long time. No wonder John didn't like the prospect of his books being hauled into court last winter. And no wonder our salary is three hundred in arrears! This also explains certain other mysterious things that have been puzzling us and the managers for some time.

Well, John was "up against it at last." The annual meeting was due in a week. He has to present his statement—and he has no money to replace what he "borrowed." So he wanted to know if I would "lend" it to him!!

Of course I could do nothing else. In the first place, John has certainly helped us out of a tight corner, whatever his motive. In the second place it would never do to have such a scandal explode in the church. It might wreck the congregation. Certainly there would be an awful scandal. At any cost the thing must be hushed up. So I lent him the money on his note—which is worth about the paper it is written on!—and nobody will ever know what John has done. It will bind him to us, too. No fear *now* of his ever telling anything to Pickering.

John does not seem to have the slightest realization of what he has done. He was only "borrowing" and meant all right. I suppose dozens of others have done the same and paid back their borrowings and hid their tracks. But such a man should not be a church treasurer.

Saturday, Jan. 22, 1927
The Manse, Norval
Last Monday morning I rose early and caught the 7.30 radial to Toronto—a fact memorable for a very delightful solitary walk up to the station just before dawn when a red full moon was hanging low in the *west* just over the wooded hill to the north of us. I had never seen a full moon in just that position before in all my life and it seemed uncanny and weirdly charming—as if I had suddenly landed on a planet where full moons rose in the west.

I went into Toronto to see a woman who had answered my ad. I had several answers but hers was the only one I liked. I was very favorably impressed with her and she agreed to come. She is a young widow named Mrs. Mason, nice, lady-like, well-recommended and of a very pleasing personality. A good cook and a neat housekeeper. And why is such a paragon as this willing to leave the city where she could command any situation and come to a quiet country place? There is a reason—a two year old baby girl. In my eyes this fact, which most people consider a drawback, is an asset. She will be more contented, knowing how hard it is for a woman with a child to get a situation. The child itself, little Helen Mason, is a pretty little thing, seems good and in this big manse a child more or less does not matter at all. So I shall make the experiment and see what comes of it. Mrs. Mason is a Canadian born and knows our ways so I will not have to teach her from the ground up.

Tuesday Ewan went to Toronto to see Mr. MacNamara *re* Greig's letter. I awaited his home-coming rather anxiously and even walked the parlor floor a bit when the radial was due. Everything was satisfactory of course. McNamara when he heard the facts of the case said he would write Greig that the Presbyterian church did not meddle with matters under the jurisdiction of the civil courts. So that's that!

Wednesday morning Margaret went. I could have howled with joy when I saw the last of her. I did do a war dance round the kitchen. She is the only maid I ever saw go without the least regret. When she shook hands with me at parting she said "Thank you for all your kindness to me, Mrs. Macdonald." But as I thought she had requited that kindness very poorly by her insolence when telling me she was going to leave I said nothing but a cool goodbye. If she had told me pleasantly and respectfully that she wanted to make a change I would have sped her graciously, asking her to let me know how she got on and also telling her to come back and visit us whenever she would like a trip to the country. But as she had spoken as she did I never wanted to see her or hear from her again.

I spent a busy day getting the house ready for a new maid and in the afternoon

Mrs. Mason came. She has been here three days and we are better acquainted with her now than with Margaret after 6 months. I think she is going to be splendid—the best maid I have had since Lily Reid. Speaking of Lily, I had a letter from her recently. Our friend Wm. Lockie seems to have strayed far since he left the Presbyterian fold. He has got into trouble gambling in wheat stocks in Toronto, has had to put his farm in his wife's name and he himself is living in Toronto—and *going to a Presbyterian church.* He was always odd and I think he must be a little out of his mind. What a come-down for such a chosen vessel of the Lord.

I had the session here for supper last night—men and wives, twelve in all. So I am tired. But there was such a difference between Margaret and Mrs. Mason when entertaining company. Margaret always resented my helping to set the table and arrange things, though she could not do it properly herself. I have always helped my maids when there was any extra work and they were always glad of it. But Margaret always made me feel very much out of place. There is nothing of that about Mrs. Mason. She is a woman I can work with.

I had a nice letter from Mr. Stokes today re *The Blue Castle.* They have done so well with it that he wants me to write another similar to it as soon as possible. This is gratifying because they were, I felt, very dubious about it at first.

Tuesday, January 25, 1927
The Manse, Norval
This is the anniversary of Frede's death....

Eight years! And the pain still aches and throbs whenever I think of her and all the remaining glow and color goes out of life. Oh, Frede, Frede, our friendship affronted the gods and they severed it. If you could come here—if we could sit by my fire and talk as of old—I must not think of it. The pain unfits me for everything else....

Wednesday, Feb. 2, 1927
My friend Mrs. Dodds of Dixie died yesterday after a brief illness. The world seems all at once to have got very dark. She was the only "ministerial chum" so to speak that I had in Ontario and I shall miss her very much. It seems rather fatal to be a friend of mine. But of course that is a foolish remark, prompted by my present unreasonable bitterness of loss.

Saturday, Feb. 5, 1927
Some of the young fry of the Guild want to get up a play and have persuaded me against all my common sense to direct it. I think I am quite mad to consent—but they pleaded so hard. They have had no experience in plays and I know perfectly well what it will mean—two more nights a week out at practices, late coming, non-attendance, drudgery, disappointment, etc. etc. etc....

Monday, Feb. 7, 1927
Today came a letter from Rollins with the long-deferred Master's report on the

accounting. The Master gives me the profits of the book and interest—nearly sixteen thousand in all. But will I ever really get it? The Pages will appeal of course. There is no end to this thing!

Wednesday, Feb. 9, 1927
The Manse, Norval
I passed an hour this evening as terrible as any I ever passed in my life—nay, more so.

Every evening as soon as school comes out Stuart and a village boy, "Sparky" Bignall, have been going skating down on the river by the mill. Everybody skates there and everyone said it was quite safe so I have never worried over it. Stuart always turned up at supper time, smiling and rosy.

But this evening at 6 o'clock there was no small son asking questions. I thought he was fooling about downtown with Sparky and was not uneasy but after supper I asked Ewan to go downtown and send him home. A quarter of an hour later he returned, saying that Stuart was not to be seen anywhere. Becoming alarmed I sent him over to Bignalls. When he came back he said Sparky had never come home either.

Alarm at once passed into terror. It was now past seven and pitch dark. The boys would never be skating now. What had happened to them? I had a sickening vision of Stuart at the bottom of the Credit. I rushed down town and already a crowd was collecting at Barnhill's store. The boys had been seen going down to the river at 4.30 and nobody could be found who had seen them since. Eventually, Jack Rankine turned up with the information that he had heard them say they were going to skate down the river to Huttonville. I don't know if this news was a relief or the reverse. If it were true it solved the mystery of their disappearance. But it was only three miles to Huttonville. If nothing had happened they had ample time to have got there and returned. A dozen people had cheerful yarns about the "whirlpool" half way down and the holes all along the river left by ice-harvesters. Nevertheless the news gave me a little hope and helped me over the dreadful half hour that followed. Some thought the boys would come home from Huttonville on the radial so we waited for it to come in before taking further steps. It came—and they were not on it.

I gave up hope then. Ewan decided to go by car to Huttonville and see if anything had been seen of them there. A band of men were to walk down the river with lanterns. I stood there pleading to be allowed to go with them. I could *not* wait there in that hellish suspense till they returned. Ewan would not let me. All at once there was a shout up the road—a boy came running—"they are back— they walked home from Huttonville by the road—Stuart has gone home round by Bignalls."

In the heavenly reaction of relief I could hardly stand. My legs trembled under me as I hurried home. I met Stuart running to meet me and in my joy and relief I really could not be as hard on him as he deserved for such a naughty trick as going to Huttonville without permission. They had thought they could easily go and return by supper time. But what with cat ice etc it took longer than they thought and it was dark when they got there. They had sense to know they had better not attempt to skate back, so came home by the road, two pretty cold, tired and hungry boys.

After Stuart was asleep I went in and kissed his dear rosy face. What would I have felt like if I had seen it cold and white and dripping from the Credit's icy waters?

Saturday, March 12, 1927
Have been in Toronto for a week—a blessed rest from the ceaseless rush of the past months. I had a quite nice time with a good movie or two. But poor Mary and Norman are having a hard time financially. He can't get on his feet after the bankruptcy and they are finding it difficult to get along at all. I have lent them more money—a foolish thing from a worldly point of view I suppose. But there are other points of view than the worldly one.

Monday, March 14, 1927
Two letters today were rather interesting from vastly different reasons. One was from Margaret. She wrote to ask me for a "reference." Said she had intended to ask me for one before she left but "forgot." This is a fib. She dared not ask me for one after the way she had spoken. She thought her Old Country references would be all that was necessary. She has found out the difference. She said she had been in "a place" since going to Toronto but it was not "suitable" and she was leaving it and going to stay at the Canadian Girls Hostel till she could get "a better one." This I feel quite sure is a fib also. She has simply been told to go. She also informed me that she was taking cooking lessons at the Y. every Wednesday afternoon. Why she should tell me this after her indignant avowal that she was a good cook I don't know. It is very unlike her to back-water like that. Perhaps she thinks I would not give her a reference unless I knew it. And there was something about the letter that made me wonder if she wouldn't like to come back and was feeling her way. I have written a brief reference saying I found her honest (which she was) industrious (which was stretching it pretty well) and a good housemaid (which also was making the truth go as far as it possibly could). So I hope I have heard the last of her.

My other letter was a pleasant thing if it ever comes to anything. Mr. Stokes writes that a theatrical manager in New York has purchased an option on the *Blue Castle* and wants to bring out a play from it if it can be managed. Of course, as Mr. Stokes is careful to warn me, there is many a slip etc. and many options are never taken up at all. But it is a pretty little dream to play with. Yet I hardly see how a good play could be made from *The Blue Castle*. There is nothing very dramatic about it. However, we will see.

I see by a newspaper clipping that *Anne of Green Gables* has been issued in a French edition. This is interesting. I wonder how the Latin mind will react to Anne. I rather think it should be favorable.

Have read two new books this week. *This Believing World* and *Elmer Gantry*. The former is most interesting. Through what dark and devious paths has the mind of man crept in its terror! As for *Elmer Gantry* it is a putrid sordid thing with a sad amount of truth in it. Yet as a whole the book is untrue and unjust. One feels on reading it that one has spent a smothering hour in a badly neglected latrine.

Wed. Mar. 30, 1927
The Manse, Norval
....I've had a most terribly and ceaselessly busy year. And yet it has been the happiest year I have had since 1914. Hard as it has been physically I have been free from all serious worries and from a great many nasty little things that embittered life in Leaskdale. Yes, it has been a happy year. To be sure, thirty years ago I would have thought the life I live was an intolerable sort of existence. But after the years since 1919 the peace and comparative freedom of this year has seemed wonderful. And I have always had my own ideal world of dream and fancy to roam in—my "secret garden" where my soul dwells and quenches its thirst at unknown, enchanted springs while my hands are painting floors....

Tuesday, April 19, 1927
The Manse, Norval
Have had a busy two weeks, housecleaning, painting, papering, play-practising etc. Chester has been home for Easter holidays. He has done pretty well so far in his studies this year. Is third in his class. Just now he has a notion to go in for civil engineering. Can't say I like it. For one thing, it is such a Wandering Jew sort of life. For another I think it has been overdone. However, he may change his mind a good many times yet. I believe in letting children decide for themselves what they want to be. And yet they are quite as likely to decide wrongly, led away by some superficial attraction in some profession or opening....

Chester

Saturday, April 23, 1927
We spent last Wednesday night at Jas. Mustard's and it was rather pleasant. And it was pleasant to motor along the old 6th again. We went to dinner at Will Cook's Thursday—a rather amusing experience. Lily Meyers is keeping house for him. As soon as she heard of his wife's death she gave up her job in Toronto and came home. Will had a housekeeper then but she did not suit him so he sent her off and got Lily last fall. It's rather an odd thing—and some of the weaker brethren are much scandalized. His people don't like it. I predict a wedding erelong. A frightful jolt to the Cook pride. But I fancy it will come off. Lily knows how to play

332

her cards. To hear her talk one would think she was the mistress of the house now. She took me all over it—it is a new house—and every room looked as if it were stirred up with a stick. But there was always something rather likeable about poor Lily, in spite of her untidiness and her endless tongue—which did not always speak the truth. And, apart from the matter of family, she is quite good enough for Will who is a dull stupid fellow....

We spent the next day calling in Leaskdale and had a nice time with several funny asides. The dear old manse looks terrible. The veranda is literally falling down. However, they are going to put up a new one and also put in a bathroom. The minister told them they would have to or he would not come. They realize at last

[Maud & Mrs. Barraclough]

that they will have to fix up the manse or they will never get a minister....

We came home last night. Today I housecleaned and went to an afternoon tea in Georgetown. While housecleaning I came across a box of my old photos. I showed Stuart one I had taken at sixteen. "Oh, mother, weren't you pretty!" he exclaimed.

Well, that was a long time ago. Eheu!

Monday, April 25, 1927
The Manse, Norval
....Tonight I had a strange experience. I have an old daguerreotype of mother's taken when she was a young girl in her early teens. The black backing has worn out and I was experimenting tonight with a piece of black velvet. All at once, as I was holding the bit of glass at a certain angle to the light and with its back towards me, a most extraordinary change took place in it. Owing to the way in which the light struck it it was the face of an old woman. The black hair was white, the plump cheeks were hollow as were also the eyes. The mouth looked thin and slightly puckered. And I *knew* that I was seeing the face of my mother as it would look if she were living today at 74! It gave me the strangest, most indescribable feeling—as if she had suddenly become real and alive—as if this picture of her must just have been taken the other day.

The illusion was perfect. And another strange thing was the resemblances which came out in that old face—which though old was still beautiful and attractive. With the slightest shift of angle it was a feminine edition of old "Speaker" Macneill's face as I have it in a picture taken of him in his old age. And there was a look of Grandmother too—and again a look of old Great Grandmother

Woolner—and now and then a hint of Aunt Annie. Also, there were differences in the apparent age. At one angle mother was a woman of forty; at another she seemed about sixty. Still another and she was seventy. I think these effects were due to the coating of shellac or varnish on the back of the picture because I could not produce them on the right side.

It fascinated me. I sat there for nearly an hour with it. Somehow I hate to think of putting the black velvet behind it and shutting it up again in its frame. For then that strange illusion cannot appear.

If mother were living she would be seventy-four. Only twenty-two years older than I am. And I know now exactly what she would look like. Did a trick of chance ever give anyone a stranger gift?...

Saturday, April 30, 1927
The Manse, Norval
We had dress rehearsals Tuesday and Wednesday nights. Tuesday they did so miserably I came home in despair, yearning for the delight of giving somebody a wigging. Wednesday they pulled up a bit and Thursday night our play came off.

And it was a big, unqualified amazing success. We had a packed house, made $78 and everything went with a bang. My players did splendidly. And Gordon Leslie who seemed so hopeless for so long—he could *not* memorize his part and until he did he was just a puppet—was the star of the cast. He had learned his part at last and then he suddenly was able to act it splendidly. He brought down the house. The audience was in a gale of laughter from start to finish. For a couple of hours we were in a nice smiling world where everyone was happy.

When I supposed it was all over I was asked to step out on the platform—and presented with a basket of lovely roses as an expression of gratitude on the part of my players. I was completely taken by surprise. Somehow such a thing had never entered my head. In Leaskdale I directed ten plays. After the first one George Kennedy came up to me privately and thanked me for my trouble. George was not in the next play and after my weeks of drilling not one of the cast ever as much as said, "Thank you, Mrs. Macdonald." So I had not thought about it here at all and it came as a mighty pleasant surprise....

Tuesday, May 3, 1927
Another letter from Mr. Rollins today contained two things—another big bill and the news that Geo. Page has retired from the firm! I wonder what is behind this. Mr. Rollins says it may be because of his health—that he has looked rather badly of late.

Saturday, May 13, 1927
The Manse, Norval
I was in Toronto yesterday to see Mac about the play contract. And I was shocked and grieved to be told that Mr. Stewart, who has been ill for some weeks, is hopelessly so and has only a few weeks to live—he has what used to be called galloping consumption and is now being called miliary tuberculosis and is equally fatal whatever it is called.

I feel very sad. Mr. Stewart is my favorite of the two men and we have been very good friends.

I have felt miserable all day with a sore throat. Seem to be taking grippe.

Thursday, May 26, 1927

Was very busy on Monday and Tuesday as Mrs. Mason was away and Miss Carroll of *The Delineator* was coming Wednesday. So I was making cake, pudding, mock chicken etc. Miss Carroll came and stayed till today—a very charming and delightful young lady. She carried off four *Marigold* stories with her which I have managed to finish at last.

We went to Georgetown tonight to practice since we put on our play there tomorrow night. I came home hoarse as a crow. Since I had grippe the least exertion plays me out.

A letter from Mr. McClelland that they have had a lung specialist to see Mr. Stewart and that he gives them some hope. The disease seems checked. I do hope he will recover.

Norval is so beautiful now that it takes my breath. Those pine hills full of shadows—those river reaches— those bluffs of maple and smooth-trunked beech—with drifts of wild white blossom everywhere. I *love* Norval as I have never loved any

"Miss Carroll" [of The Delineator*]*

"A river reach" [taken from Hillcrest Cemetery]

"Wild white blossoms"

place save Cavendish. It is as if I had known it all my life—as if I had dreamed young dreams under those pines and walked with my first love down that long perfumed hill.

Wednesday, June 1, 1927
The Manse, Norval, Ont.
Several more days of prancing about as usual. Our play came off excellently at Georgetown. They did better than any time yet. We had anniversary services at Union Sunday and I've been busy gardening. Norval is so beautiful now in its June blush. The views up and down the river are entirely delightful and satisfying.

Yesterday I began work on a new book about a new heroine—Marigold. I don't think I'll love her as well as Anne and Emily—so likely the public won't.

In the *Guardian* yesterday I saw a notice of the death of one of Lou Dystant's daughters—a little girl of ten—and wrote him a note of sympathy. He has two other daughters—no sons, I think. How very long ago those Bideford schooldays seem. Yet how vivid in my book of remembrance.

Tonight Norval seems misted everywhere with wild blossom. I can never believe in June that the world is millions of years old.

The Manse, Norval, Ont.
Thursday, June 2, 1927
Today I had a letter from Mr. Rollins saying that George Page was dead. I felt a queer regret. He was once my friend.

Saturday, June 4, 1927
Yesterday I got a very extraordinary telegram from Louis Page.

"Since, *as advised,* you like a good fight, you will be interested in knowing that George Page was buried today."

Then, today, I got a letter from him couched in the same words and enclosing a duplicate of the telegram; so that in all I have received three copies of this precious message.

I cannot understand the psychology of a man who would send such a thing. But then Louis Page's mentality was never normal. I can't understand what he meant. I certainly never said or wrote to him or anybody that I "liked a good fight." I abhor fighting and avoid it whenever possible—though I *can* fight when the spirit moves me. Somebody—French or Rollins—must have said it for me. What then? Suppose Page does believe I said it and is not just pretending he thinks I said it to introduce his message? Does he then mean to imply that our "good fight" has caused Geo. Page's death? I hardly think it did! Of course, this suit must have cost the Pages nearly fifty thousand dollars already, with the prospect of paying out another fifteen thousand or so. But I can't quite think that George worried so much over it. However, if he did, he asked for it. He could have avoided it altogether if he had done what was fair. And he could have stopped it long ago if he had wanted to—or if Louis had let him. I refuse to feel conscience-stricken because of George's death.

I wonder if the real inwardness is this? Had Louis Page a real affection for his brother? Does he feel a secret remorse for forcing on and keeping up litigation that may have worried him? And does he think he can shift some of that remorse upon me?

No, no, Louis. But I *do* think Providence has made a mistake. He should have sent *you* to your own place and spared George. But I suppose Beelzebub doesn't want any rival in Hades.

Yet that telegram hurt me. It seems a gratuitous slap in the face from a man who has done me a great deal of injury and whom I once thought of as a friend.

If Louis Page had simply sent me a notice of his brother's death, I would have written him a conventional note of sympathy. But I shall ignore this insult.

Ah me! When I received that delightful letter from the Page Co. years ago, accepting my book, I did not dream that one day I would get such a telegram. What a pity it has all been. And if Louis Page had only been honorable I would have been with his firm yet. It has always hurt me that I had to leave them.

Friday, June 10, 1927
The Manse, Norval
Today was very pleasant. I went over to Glen Williams this morning to spend a whole day and take photographs of that charming spot. I prowled about with my camera and captured beauty on every side....There was one spot in the grave-yard that gave me my old flash of supernal beauty—a great drift of white spirea

"The Glen"

"The Credit"

with a pine and a lovable spruce in the background. I took a picture of it—but not likely it will do more than suggest the peculiar eerie, magical charm of the spot. Pine trees never photograph well. They lose all their purring pluminess in a picture and come out lean and crone-like against the sky....

Saturday, June 11, 1927
I spent this cloudy evening, fresh and sweet, setting out plants in the garden and enjoying life. I am well again. Ewan is well. We are free, just now at least, from any biting anxieties or worries. This spring has been a pleasant and happy one....

Tuesday, June 14, 1927
I called on the Boyds this evening—the new Anglican rector and his wife. I don't think I shall like her or find any friendship in her. I did not enjoy my call and came away feeling rather messy. But as I came into our own lawn I turned and saw what brought my soul into harmony with itself once more. Up on the hill were two young spring-clad elms. And right between them, floating in a sky of silver, a great pale golden full moon. To the right were those dark haunting pines.

I stood entranced and gazed at it for as many minutes as I dared snatch from a waiting committee meeting. Emerson says somewhere "If we are silent we may hear the whisper of the gods." I heard it—and what it told me can never be expressed in symbols of earth. But even the committee meeting could not banish its echoes from my soul.

Thursday, June 16, 1927
The Manse, Norval
We rose early and motored in to Toronto—spinning along the smooth highway at an ungodly rate. There *is* a witchery in speed. Why? Is it because it gives us the subconscious feeling that we are *escaping*?

All the thorn trees along the way were a-snow. And there were so many of them. In one little curve of the Credit there was a veritable wild orchard—a garden of wildwood gods. There is something exquisite about thorn-bloom; it is so virginal....

June 17, 1927

This was not a nice day. A good many pinpricks of worry over the coming Anniversary and its attendant functions. And one big disappointment. It seems that the *Blue Castle* play is not going through after all. The negotiations have been going on and the contracts were all ready, waiting to be signed. But the manager who was interested has got involved in a law suit over some other play he was producing and is not going ahead with any more just now. I feel very blue about it. It may be just as well. The play might have been a failure and that would have been far worse. But I can't feel that way about it just now.

Saturday, June 25, 1927

A very busy week with little of diary interest. One of the weeks when I exist and work but do not live.

Yesterday Chester got word that he had passed in all his subjects and is third in the honor list. This pleased us all.

Tomorrow is our anniversary Sunday and today I made a certain pudding which I make on special occasions—and on special occasions only, it being rather merciless on the eggs. It is an old Park Corner recipe and as it was nameless I have christened it "New Moon pudding." It is delicious and is, for me, associated with old banquets at Park Corner and those who meet there no more. I'm going to copy it here, that it may not be lost from the earth. And I can cordially recommend it to my descendants—if I have any and if they are not sustaining existence on chemical tabloids alone.

New Moon Pudding

Into one quart of milk put two full cups of bread crumbs, 2/3 cup sugar, the rind of one lemon grated, the slightly beaten yolks of six eggs and 1/2 tsp salt. Bake in oven until a silver knife comes out clean. Beat the whites of the eggs stiff with 1/2 cup white sugar and the juice of one lemon. Spread on top. Return to oven and brown. Serve cold with cream.

Cream! We have hard times getting cream here. That is one of the things that make me think wistfully of Leaskdale.

Saturday, July 2, 1927
The Manse, Norval

I think it would do me an enormous amount of good, just to go out and yell at the moon.

This has been a nightmare week. In the first place it has been terribly hot; in the second place I've been ill half the time; in the third place it has been an unceasing scramble.

On Monday Mrs. Alec Leask suddenly popped in. I had had no word of her coming, and was up to my eyes in preparation for the Missionary Picnic next day. Neither did her advent fill any aching void in my soul. Tuesday morning our speaker Mrs. Adams came and in the afternoon we had our "picnic" at Thos. Early's. In the evening Mrs. Leask went home and I, exhausted, betook myself to bed—at eleven o'clock.

Wednesday was very hot and I was ill with intestinal trouble—which in older, cruder days we called "the back-door trots." But I made candy for the Garden Party all the forenoon and went to Barracloughs for supper in evening. I had better have stayed home for I could not eat and had to lie on the sofa all the evening. Nevertheless, the visit did me good. That house has, somehow, an agreeable personality. You feel the better for being in it, just as you feel the better for meeting some people.

Thursday was vilely hot. I iced cakes and prepared the house for the garden party, which came off at night and was quite a success of its kind. But on Friday I was so ghastly tired that I felt I could never get out of bed again. I did, of course. Mrs. Mason was away, the house had to be put to rights, it was boiling hot, and I had to get ready to leave for the Island Monday.

I feel better today and have got pretty well ready. I do not feel any enthusiasm about going "home"—I am too tired—there will be such changes, and I hate to leave my garden and my pussy cat. My poppies are just beginning to bloom and everything is in its most interesting stage.

But I know when I get down I will be glad I went.

Kinross, P.E. Island
Saturday, July 9, 1927
Home again! And the same old miracle has taken place. The moment I set foot on the red Island soil it *was* "home"—I had never been away! And oh, how lovely and—lovelier—and loveliest—it is. How *satisfying!* . . .

We reached Ch'Town Wednesday evening and spent the night at Fannie's. She has grown much older in these four years. The tragic death of her son has grayed her hair and deepened the lines on her face.

We attended the reception given Lord and Lady Willingdon who happened to be on the Island just then. To stay over for this Mr. Mutch said he would motor us out to Kinross in the evening and the boys had to go out on the afternoon train. It was the first time the two of them ever started off on a train alone. Chester is fifteen and when I was sixteen I travelled practically alone from Prince Albert to P.E.I. Yet I felt as if I were sending two helpless infants on a trip around the world. In youth I used to be annoyed because *my* elders never seemed to realize that children grew up. But I shall have to "watch out" lest I become just as bad myself....

I had left Ontario hoping that I would have a month's freedom from everlasting missionary meetings and doings. And at Aunt Christie's I fell right on another one. And the minister's wife was determined I should "address" them. In vain I pleaded my cold and the fatigue of a long journey. She was inexorable.

I "must," that was all there was to it. *I* should have been inexorable too. I should have snubbed that selfish inconsiderate woman and flatly refused. But I have never been good at snubbing people and I weakly gave in. I got up and, wiping my dissolving nose at every sentence, I gave an old talk on the Women of the Bible.

The odd thing is that the minister at Kinross and the husband of this lady is George Grant—the "Bashful George" of Dalhousie days. I had never met him since that gruesome night when he thought it his painful duty to walk home with me from the Y.M.C.A. at Dalhousie. I wonder if he remembered it. He is just as morbidly shy and bashful as ever. I cannot understand how he ever got married. Possibly the lady told him, smilingly and inexorably as she told me that he "must" marry her. He would have to do it, if she did, I feel quite sure of that.

Yesterday evening John Stirling came and took us over to Montague where we stayed till this evening. I had rather dreaded going. Margaret and I had never met since Union and I fancied there was a constraint in her letters. But when we met it disappeared. We frankly agreed not to discuss a subject so provocative of bitterness and to be just the friends we always were....

Monday, July 11, 1927
Kinross, P.E. Island
I have not slept very well since coming here. Possibly because Aunt Christie's spare room bed has a valley in the middle of it. My own wonderful bed at home has spoiled me. I seldom find any bed comfy after it.

But it was not the inequalities of the bed that kept me awake last night. I don't know what it was. I was lonely and sad and haunted. I watched the dark tops of the spruce trees down the lane against the moonlit sky and thought of nights long ago when I had been possessed of the silver madness of moonlight. I thought of friends who had walked in the moonlight with me and walk no more on earth. I thought, unwillingly and under the compulsion of my night hag, of all my problems and perplexities, of all my old humiliations and stabs and heartaches. And under it all the happiness of being once more in my own dear land....The Island roads *are* so beautiful. And while, for this haste-mad age, the auto is the only thing, it *is* a delight once more to get into a buggy behind a horse and just *poke* along, driving for the sake of driving, in no hurry to get anywhere. We drove along red roads with daisies blooming along them, past little hollows full of scented fern, past little pole gates under spruce trees, past stonedykes hung with wild strawberries and over looping blue rivers, by fields girdled with woods and through valleys where amber brooks called—and always the fragrance of dead fir coming unexpectedly every little while—that fragrance which is as the wine of old romance to me and always opens some flood-gate of my soul.

We passed a high hill covered with a maple wood and Mrs. MacLeod told me a bit of tragic local history which had happened seventy-two years ago in her father's time. She had heard the story from him. Just beyond that hill was a hollow and in this hollow a woman of the neighborhood was found murdered. She had either been killed with an axe or stabbed with a knife, I forget which Mrs.

MacLeod said and her face was terribly mutilated. The murderer was never discovered. It was a case which gave the lie to the proverb "Murder will out." And yet—there were suspicions. The murdered girl had been one of those who love much; a certain man was known to be infatuated with her and his wife was half mad with jealousy. It was whispered—

Well, the body was taken to the schoolhouse that evening and by candlelight everybody in the community had to come to the school, lay his or her hand on the dead body and swear innocence. It is hard to realize that this "ordeal" was practiced in P.E. Island only seventy-two years ago. But those old Highlanders retained old customs and superstitions generations after they had died out elsewhere.

Among the rest came the suspected woman. Coolly she laid her hand on the mangled body and swore like the rest. The wounds of the dead *fille de joie* bled not. For no one's touch did they bleed.

What a scene! The old superstitions may have been foolish indeed but with what drama they invested life. Is it well to grow too wise and scornful?

After supper I walked back to Aunt Christie's alone, up the railroad tracks—walked loiteringly and lovingly as I have never walked since I was on the Island before. To walk so, with no hurry to get anywhere—how pleasant, how restful.

Cavendish, P.E. Island
Wed. July 13, 1927

Yesterday morning we left Kinross—regretfully. It is possible we may not be at Aunt Christie's again. Her boys don't seem cut out for farmers and I suppose she will have to sell sooner or later. She is a dear soul and I love her. And she has had it terribly hard these past six years.

We came to town and out to Winsloe. Mary still looks poorly. Archie is an old, gray, *bleached*, silent man. He seems nothing but a cipher. Roland is running the farm. Maud has quite recovered her mental balance and is her old pleasant self. She is a very nice-looking woman—quite beautiful indeed and her husband is a nice fellow.

Mary sent for Ida who came out and spent the afternoon. It should have been quite idyllic—the re-union of three old chums. But to tell truth I was a bit bored. Mary and Ida are, mentally, just what they were thirty-four years ago. And we had nothing in common save our memories of the past.

Still, there was some pleasure in it. We laughed a good deal. We can all laugh still. Not quite so gaily—not quite so spontaneously perhaps. And Mary had wild strawberries for supper....

This afternoon Albert Middleton motored us up to Cavendish. Mary and I took a walk through Lover's Lane this evening. I did not want to take her there—it hurts me to have any outsider see the old lane now with almost all its beauty gone. Almost—not *all*. There are some beauty spots left....

Mary wanted to go up to the old place but I would not go. I have never been there since the house was torn down and while I might have borne to go alone I could not dream of going there with Mary of all people. Mary is an old friend for whom I have an affection. But she has not a spark of sentiment in her make-up and she could not have the slightest understanding of my feelings about that old spot, sacred to me even in its ruin and degradation....

Thursday, July 14, 1927
Cavendish, P.E.I.
A day I love—windy, with an occasional stinging shower. I walked in Lover's Lane—I walked in the "old orchard" where there are as many white birches as there are apple trees—I picked and ate wild strawberries.

And I got a letter from the Hon. Stanley Baldwin, Premier of Great Britain! A nice letter—a letter that made me purr. And I am glad it came to me *here*—at home!

"19th June, 1927
10 Downing St
Whitehall

Dear Mrs. Macdonald:—

I do not know whether I shall be so fortunate during a hurried visit to Canada but it would give me keen pleasure to have an opportunity of shaking your hand and thanking you for the pleasure your books have given me. I am hoping that I shall be allowed to go to Prince Edward Island for I must see Green Gables before I return home. Not that I wouldn't be at home at Green Gables!!

I am sincerely yours,
Stanley Baldwin"

Yes, I think he would. Evidently the Hon. Stanley Baldwin is one of the race of Joseph!!

I took the letter with me to Lover's lane and read it—read it not to myself but to the little girl who walked here years ago and dreamed—and wrote her dreams into books that have pleased a statesman of Empire. And the little girl was pleased.

I should never have supposed Stanley Baldwin would have time to read novels, much less mine.

I am afraid I won't see him, though. He is not to be on the Island until mid-August and I cannot stay till then....

Friday, July 15, 1927
This has been one of the days and nights, that shine out in memory like fixed stars. It was a cool pale-gray fragrant day—the kind of day I love—the kind of day we never have in Ontario. It belongs solely to the Maritimes. And I picked strawberries along the road from here to the church the whole afternoon. The sides of the roads and the old dykes are red with them. I was perfectly happy and—what is more than and distinct from happiness—perfectly *satisfied*. My soul was home. I was young again—a girl again—it was the old Cavendish I picked strawberries in. The breeze that blew over the clover fields was as the very water of life to me—old joy was mine again such as I knew in the beautiful days before I had learned the bitter lesson that joy could die. This afternoon alone was worth coming to P.E. Island for....

"Lover's Lane"

Sunday, July 17, 1927

This morning I went to the "United Church." It is a bitter thing to me that there is no longer a Presbyterian church in the old historic congregation of Cavendish. Many of the people are bitterly discontented. They voted early for "Union" having been told by their minister that there would be no Presbyterian church for them to belong to! Some of them have left the United Church altogether....

And the old manse is gone! They are building the new one almost on the very edge of the road. Who was responsible for such a weird idea I know not—nobody seemed willing to father it—"somebody else" was always blamed whenever I asked about it. The old site was much nicer in every way. But there! *I* haven't got to live in it ever and perhaps the minister's wives who do will like all the

"Cavendish Church" [New one]

dust of the road blowing on their veranda and the doings of their back door under the eyes of every passer by....

This evening was an illustration of how very difficult it is in this world to do as one wants to do, even when what one wants is simple and righteous and entirely one's own business.

Mrs. Florence Livesay of Toronto, a writer of some repute and a Press Club friend of mine, happens to be spending the summer in Cavendish—or rather Bay View—and is boarding at "Young" Will Graham's, whose wife was Mary Moore. I had promised her I would go up and see her and I had promised myself a lovely walk there. I *wanted* that walk—wanted it badly. It is only two miles. I would go up the pretty road to the forge, turn down there through the blueberry barrens and follow on down the long red road through the spruces until I came to the farmhouse down near the harbour. And when my call was over I would walk back again, with the stars for neighbors and beyond those seaside meadows the old beauty of my moonlit sea.

Oh, I simply wagged my tail when I thought about it.

But I couldn't do it. I wasn't let do it. Harmless, lovely, desirable, as it was, I wasn't let do it. Will Greens' couldn't think of letting me walk all that distance! Alone! So a young lad with a car who was visiting them drove me up. I thanked him with my lips and cursed him in my heart. And when my visit was over "Young" Will Graham wouldn't "let" me walk home. He got out his car and drove me. May jackals sit on his grandmother's grave!

In between I had a pleasant visit with Mrs. Livesay who is delighted with the Island but, I fear me, supposes that Mary Graham represents the natives of Cavendish. She informed me that she had been wondering how I ever got a start here where there seemed to be nothing whatever of literary atmosphere or background. I came very near telling her crisply that she need not suppose Mary Graham's back yard was Cavendish or that the Graham background was mine. I think the "literary atmosphere" of the old Macneills and Simpsons would not have been too rarefied for even Mrs. Livesay to breathe. To be born a Macneill was to be born to the purple in Cavendish and in those days the Moores and Grahams were very "poor white trash" indeed. I admit it nettled me that Mrs. Livesay should coolly assume that I had no other background than that in which she found herself. Even today, one would think, she might clearly see that the Grahams were not in the same class as the rest of Cavendish.

Still, I suppose she cannot see what I see in Cavendish. And it *has* changed sadly since those far-off days. The old families have died out. There used to be twelve families of Macneills in Cavendish. Now there are only six and four of those have no children. In fact "our" Macneills are almost extinct....

Monday July 18, 1927
Cavendish, P.E.I.
A gray windy delightful day. A letter from Ewan bore the satisfactory intelligence that Stuart had passed his entrance with honors. Not so bad for the kid. But he is to stay in Norval another year yet. I *can't* let him go away so soon. But will it be any easier next year!!

This evening I made calls on Wilbur, Fred and Darnley Clark. A nice half hour with all. Fred and I were talking of all our old friends "who were changed and who were gone"....

And I *had* the delight of walking home alone. I paused when I came to the hall and went in. It has been in a state of disrepair for many years but now they are doing it over. I opened the old book-case and looked over the books of the old library. Most of them are gone—taken out and never returned. A shame. It was a good little library in its day. I found—and took!—an old bound volume of MacClure's in the 90's. It is too out of date to be of any value today and if ever they start up the library again, properly looked after, I shall send some modern volumes in its place. After I came home I looked it over with a sudden keen realization of how the world had changed. One article intrigued me greatly. A sort of prophetic symposium of the views of many distinguished men as to what was going to happen in the next thirty years! Most of the prophets are not even names now. Some prophesied wisely, some

[Maud in the garden]

foolishly. And one said that in the next thirty years war would be abolished—there would never be another great war—the world had grown too wise for it—or words to that effect. Ah, did not the shadow of 1914 fall across his paper as he wrote!!

Tuesday, July 19, 1927
Cavendish, P.E.I.

Today I walked through Lover's Lane and across the fields to the road where the old Baptist church once was....

I called in to see Lizzie Stewart Laird. She is better than on that dreadful evening when I called there some years ago but she is not herself—never will be. One of the little unheard-of tragedies of life.

It seems to me that living with Everett Laird would—and should—drive anyone insane. He is the grossest and most repulsive creature I ever saw.

Then I went on to Amanda's and had a not unpleasant afternoon. When I arrived George was throwing a fit in the back yard and Amanda was petrified in the kitchen. Why? A distant cousin was there on a visit—a girl who had recently graduated from a U.S. Hospital. She was waiting for her father to motor to the shore to bathe—she was writing at the table—she had on nothing but her bathing suit—and it was "nothing much before and rather less than half of that behind."

Amanda and George will never get over it. If she had sat there stark naked they couldn't have been more horrified. And why should they, indeed?

I have seen too much of such array in late years to be either shocked or disgusted. But as I looked at those two enormous white legs I confess I thought them ugly. And therefore indecent. And what seems fitting on a sea shore seemed positively obscene in that prim little room. I think if I had been Miss Cameron I would have flung a kimono around my nakedness for the sake of beauty. But I am sure she enjoyed shocking George and Amanda. And I am sure she thought she was proclaiming her emancipation from—something. I don't know what and neither did she.

After she went away Amanda gradually recovered the power of speech and we had a limited chat. She gave me her photograph. It has no place in the world save in this diary so here I put it.

Tonight Myrtle was complaining that skunks were about and she feared for her chickens. Whereby hangs a grievous tale.

When I saw *Anne of Green Gables* in the movies I was disgusted because she was depicted as picking up a skunk on the way to a picnic. And skunks were—then—absolutely unknown in P.E.I. Never tell me that coming events do not cast their shadows before!

Several years ago, when the fox boom was at its height some one conceived the idea of starting a skunk ranch. Accordingly the ranch was built and the skunks imported. The venture did not succeed financially. And instead of dooming the skunks to death or exile they were simply turned

[Amanda Macneill Robertson]

loose with the fiendish result that they are over-running the Island. Moreover, an imbecile Government has passed a law for their comfort and protection. They are not to be killed but allowed to replenish the earth. In spite of this, indignant farmers *do* kill them. More power to their elbows. The fragrance of skunk on the crystal air of a P.E. Island summer evening is *not* a sweet savour unto the Lord.

Saturday, July 23, 1927
Gartmore Farm
We came down to Alec's Thursday evening. He is a little better. I have managed to make him begin taking a tonic. He sneaks into the pantry before meals and swallows a spoonful hastily and furtively. It was always a curious characteristic of Charles Macneill's boys that they would never admit that they were ill—never go to a doctor or take medicine until they were driven to it. They seemed to con-

sider it a deadly disgrace. Alec is full of this. You couldn't insult him worse than to ask him in public if his medicine was doing him any good....

Tuesday, July 26, 1927
Gartmore Farm, Cavendish
....I went up to Myrtle's and along Lover's Lane and through the woods and fields beyond, over little hill and wood paths that were never made but just grew. I was happy—content—at peace. I was neither young nor old—I was ageless. The past and the present were one and there was no future. I moved in an enchanted circle beyond which there was no time and within which there was no change.

I came out on the hill—I went down the hill. Which is growing beautiful again, after its desecration of some years agone. I picked wild strawberries along its dykes and talked to the spruce trees—because I understand their language and they mine. And then I went up the old school hill to where the old gate used to be.

I wanted to get a picture of the trees that surrounded the old front garden. They are much thicker than they used to be but the general outline is not changed. So I climbed the fence and went over to the middle of the potato field and took it. Then a sudden desire seized me to go up to the corner where the cherry trees used to be and look at the old place. I have never gone there since the old house was torn down. But I went today. And when I reached the corner I stopped still feeling as if a blow had been struck in my face.

It was not that the house was gone and the old cellar filled up with a rank growth of wild raspberry. I had discounted that in imagination and it looked about as I had expected it to look. No, it was the complete change in everything—*everything*. If I had been set down there without knowing where I was I really doubt if I should have recognized the place at all. If I had it would have only been by reason of the old back orchard which alone retains some aged semblance of what it used to be. I found it hard to believe that even sixteen years could have changed a place so much. The old hen house was gone and the spruce grove behind it as well and the place of both was occupied by a thick grove of young birch. Over the old well a little house had been built which hid it completely. The old barn and granary was gone and another birch grove was in their room. The spruce grove behind the granary and the one behind the "new" barn were gone—not a tree remained and nothing had taken their place. The poor old "new" barn in its bareness had nothing at all familiar about it.

But the change that hurt me most was in the old front orchard—that once so lovely spot which I loved so well and which was so entwined with the joys and dreams of childhood and girlhood. It was completely grown up with young trees as thick as a jungle. I picked my way into it and found the old apple trees still there. Even the old old tree that was old when I was a child and must be at least eighty now and maybe nearer a hundred. There it was smothered amid that intruding growth. I wonder if it felt my kiss on its gnarled trunk and if its aged sap coursed with a momentary quickening at the step of its lover.

I took the risk of going into the back orchard, too—the risk of being seen by some of Uncle John's. I did not wish to be seen by any of them. I can find in my heart no diminution of my bitterness against them for their treatment of me. The further I get from it in years the more clearly and distinctly does it loom up—the indescribable meanness and pettiness and selfishness of it, the treachery, the underhandedness. I wonder if they ever regret it. I wonder if when innocent strangers overrun them looking for souvenirs of *Green Gables* and pestering them with a thousand questions about me they ever wish they had acted differently. It must really be very awkward for them. For their own sakes they must wish that they had not taken it so calmly for granted that their poor, obscure, insignificant orphaned relative would always remain so and might be persecuted and brow–beaten with impunity.

No, I did not want to be seen by them on this exploration. There was something of sacrilege about it. Yet I ventured into the orchard a little way. And there I found a strange thing. Long ago when a child I was told that two little square plots in that orchard that always kept their shape though overgrown with grass were my mother's old flower-beds. In one of them grew a perennial that was always found in old-fashioned gardens though I never see it now and cannot find it in any catalogue. A low-growing plant with leaves something like the rowan and bearing a plume of fluffy, creamy-white flowers. They had never spread any in my time. But now I found that they had spread over a large plot of ground, made a vigorous growth and were a cloud of the feathery bloom, surviving many a thing that had come and gone since mother's girlish hands planted the roots there over half a century agone. Which thing is a symbol.

Then I came away, feeling not too sad. After all what matters it? The old place is as it ever was in memory's halls. Nothing can bar me from it or keep me from revisiting it there....

So I feel tonight that I have had a strange beautiful day.

Friday, July 29, 1927
Park Corner, P.E.I.
Geographically the same. In all else changed.

Yesterday was my last day at Alec's. Poor May brought out a cup and saucer and plate of her bridal set and begged me to take it. It would have hurt her not to take it—so I did. Treat it lovingly, you to whom it comes in after years. Many a merry table has it graced, with laughter echoing from lip to lip. May brought it a quarter of a century ago to that farmhouse where she was a happy young bride looking forward to be a joyful mother of children. They were never born. From our point of view it seems a shame. But so twisted and tangled is heredity that it may have been better.

Yesterday evening Alec and May motored us over here. We arrived in the shadows of a misty evening and were greeted with hilarious delight by the children. At first I thought I could not endure it, especially after Alec and May had gone. But one *does* bear things.

I slept last night in "Amy's room." The last time I slept in it was on the night before my wedding day, sixteen years ago and under the same roof slept Aunt Annie and Uncle John and Frede and Stella and George....

For a few minutes today I burned with unholy flames. A certain Rev. Cleveland and wife from Fall River, Mass., have been touring the island and came here to see me. They said nice things about my books and had they left it so all would have been well. But after I had said that I came back to the Island whenever I could Mr. Cleveland said coolly, "It is certainly very splendid of you to remain so faithful to your old friends here."

Can anyone believe he said it? He did! I was so furious I could hardly speak. I was even more furious than with Mrs. Livesay. Oh, I longed—I burned to say;—

"Sir, these friends of mine in P.E. Island to whom you are surprised I should be "faithful," are infinitely superior to you. They are far more interesting to talk to. They are far more agreeable to look at. They are probably better born than you and they are certainly better bred. Never has one of them bored me as you and your wife have bored me for the past hour. Avaunt!"

But what is the sense of being annoyed at people like that: They can't help it. I said as courteously as possible that my friends here were all very dear to me and that life held no greater pleasure for me than to see them and talk with them, and left it at that. P-u-u-gh!

Saturday, July 30, 1927
Park Corner, P.E. Island

I find there is an amusing rivalry between Cavendish and Park Corner "ponds" as to which is the original of "The Lake of Shining Waters." Jim Campbell is ramping with rage because some summer tourists laughed at him when he told them "his" pond was. They told him the Lake was in Cavendish.

Well, Jim was right and they were wrong. The Park Corner Pond was in my mind when I sketched the Lake of Shining Waters. Though many of the effects of light and shadow on Cavendish pond were blended in the picture.

Mary Johnstone motored us all up to Malpeque this afternoon to see Aunt Emily, who makes her home now with her daughter Charlotte—Mrs. Percy MacGougan, down on what used to be called "King Street" long ago. We had a lovely drive and a nice visit. Aunt Emily looked well and young, with hardly a gray hair in her heavy brown locks. And she was in a very agreeable mood—perhaps because she and I are both "Presbyterians" and so had at least one subject on which we were in perfect accord. Besides, she is the only aunt I have left now. And though you may fight with your kin and sometimes even dislike them there is a bond between you for all that. Your very nerves and sinews are twisted with them someway.

One thing Aunt Emily said amused me a little—and hurt too, striking too sharply on an old secret dream. She had been to Cavendish this summer for the first time since Grandma's death and was horrified at the state she found the old place in. (I'll warrant she gave John F. a bit of her mind about it, too.) And she said, "It was a terrible pity that father did not leave the old place to you. I don't know what we were all thinking of that we didn't get him to."

Well, I smiled inwardly. None of them ever thought of such a thing or would have suggested it to Grandpa if they had, least of all Aunt Emily. And if anyone had, Grandpa would have thought her crazy. Not any great wonder either I admit. It *would* have seemed silly on the face of it. I had nothing to keep up a house on then. But if he had had the inspiration and faith to have done it it would have turned out all right. And what a difference it would have made to me and Grandmother during those thirteen years that followed. I would have kept the old place up and beautified it—and gone there to spend my summer vacations. I've often and often dreamed it out. It would not look as it does today. But it is idle to wish things had been done differently.

We came home by Kensington, called at Long River and home by roads where we saw a new moon and evening star over mysteriously lovely groves of white birch. We spent the evening at Heath's and enjoyed it fairly. Aunt Eliza got off some of her usual felicities. Ella happened to remark that she thought I looked so much like "Aunt Bib." "Oh, no, she doesn't look at all like Aunt Bib," said Aunt Eliza. "Bibby had such beautiful eyes. I never saw anyone with such bright eyes."

Ella and I howled to each other in the pantry after we got home about it. Aunt E's speeches of that sort are among the family jokes....

Sunday, July 31, 1927
Park Corner, P.E. Island
....We leave tomorrow. Marian Webb is coming back to Ontario with me for a visit. She has not been well and the change may do her good. Besides it will be nice to have company when Mrs. Mason and Ewan are away on their vacation.

Sunday, Aug. 7, 1927
The Manse, Norval
We spent last Monday night in Kensington where I had a good soul-satisfying *Presbyterian* talk with Tillie Bentley. Next morning we left the old Island in a pouring rain and had a pleasant uneventful trip to Toronto where we arrived Wednesday and left Marian with some friends. Ewan met us and brought us home where it was exceedingly nice to be again. My garden is wonderful, the phlox a drift of snow; and trotting across the lawn to meet me on his little silver gray legs a dear pussy desiring to be remembered. Luck seemed positively delighted to have me back. He kept at my heels everywhere I went and every few seconds would give my leg a fiendish little bite. I think it is his way of giving a kiss but it is very hard on silk stockings.

It was nice to get home especially back to my own comfortable bed. I really haven't slept in what I call a comfortable bed since I left. My own mattress has spoiled me. It is the best I have ever slept on. This isn't just because I'm used to it. I have the same kind of mattress on my guest room bed and visitors constantly ask me where I got such a bed. And then to lie there and look out to my darling pines on Russell's hill and the big maples crowding around the manse.

When I reached home I found an invitation to meet "His Royal Highness" at the garden party at Gov't House on Saturday! I fancy Premier Baldwin's wish to meet me was behind it and I was glad that I should have an opportunity of seeing him. Ewan couldn't go as he was leaving for his vacation on Friday so I went in to Toronto on Friday to get me a new hat. I'm sure His Royal Highness'

[Invitation to Chorley Park Garden Party]

feelings would have been hurt if I had gone in my old hat! Luckily I had a very nice new dress which I got just before I went away of cocoa-colored lace and georgette.

Saturday afternoon the great event occurred. I went with the Hatheways. We got out at the gates of Gov't House and took our place in the queue that extended clean up to the house. We crawled along a few inches at a time for about an hour in the broiling sun. A lady behind me kept lamenting that her rouge was coming off in the heat.

Presently an aide-de-camp came up and asked if I were Mrs. Macdonald and said Premier Baldwin was asking for me. I could not leave my place in the line until I had been presented to the Prince. Eventually that took place—Governor Ross—the Prince—Mrs. Ross—Prince George. "The" Prince did not look like the newspaper pictures of the "Smiling Prince." I saw a thin, tanned, smileless, tired, bored-looking young man who shook hands with me and looked up at that never ending queue as if to say "My God, how many more of them?" I don't wonder. Fancy facing that every day of his tour. Bored—blasé—I should say so. Prince George looked much happier and more interested. It was a novelty to him. He was a nice-looking boy but how the ladies present raved about him. "The *sweetest* thing" I heard one exclaim enthusiastically with clasped hands and uplifted eyes.

Then I had *my* thrill—I met Premier Baldwin and Mrs. Baldwin and had a delightful chat with them. Mr. Baldwin spoke enthusiastically of the pleasure my books had given him. Mrs. Baldwin was a very pleasant plump round-faced lady with ankle skirts and a hat that sat up on top of her head as was the vogue twenty years ago. But she looked the great lady for all that.

I never saw so many pretty dresses at one time in my life before. And some that were anything but pretty. My own looked as nice as any of them.

When it was all over I hurried down to the Walker, met Marian and her friend, had dinner there and came home—back to my garden and my pines and little cats that curl and purr and chew your legs.

It's really quite funny—the local sensation my being asked to "the Prince's party" has made.

In church today John Clark, an elderly man, shook hands with me, went off to a group of men and heard about it, came back and said, "Is it true you were asked to the Prince's party?" I said "yes." He stuck out his horny paw once more. "Will you shake hands with me again?"

I did.

"Costume I wore at Garden Party"

Sunday, August 28, 1927
The Manse, Norval

This has been a very busy fortnight as Mrs. Mason was away for her vacation. There was an Institute tea and our Bible Class picnic—the latter to LaSalle Park where the beauty of smooth blue-silk water and dark purring pines atoned to me for much of the boredom inseparable from such an affair—for me—now.

There has been much that was pleasant in these two weeks too—a re-reading of Omar Khayyam—which made such a sensation thirty years ago and should live forever because of one verse if no other.

> "The Moving Finger writes: and having writ
> Moves on: nor all thy piety and wit
> Can lure it back to cancel half a line
> Nor all thy tears wash out a word of it."

Not one word!

And there was one devilish thing—so devilish that it turned me physically ill and has haunted me ever since with an anguish that will not cease.

I was in the garden one afternoon picking cosmos when I heard the agonized shrieks of some poor cat. In terror lest Luck had been caught by a dog I rushed across the lawn to the fence but was met by Luck tearing around the house, his eyes nearly popping out of his head with terror. The dreadful cries still went on but seemed to be over near the Norval garage owned by a man named Beamish. I ran out into the street but by the time I got to the corner the cries had ceased and as I didn't know where to look I came home again. Next day Stuart came home and said, "Mother, a dreadful thing happened yesterday. That young Beamish kid took his kitten and *sawed its head off.*"

And yet people say there is no devil. What then is the source of horror such as that? That child is about seven years of age. "If they do these things in the green tree"—

I rose from the table, went out and—was sick.

Thursday, Sept. 1, 1927
The Manse, Norval
I took Marian in to the Exhibition today. Was haunted all day by a strange and vivid dream of last night. In it I had gone out to Prince Albert to marry Will Pritchard, having, it seemed, been engaged to him for some years. Laura and Will met me at the station and I walked home with them through the snowy streets to Laura's home. When she left Will and me alone in the living room he took me in his arms and kissed me. Oh, such a terrible kiss—the icy cold, clammy lips of the dead! I suddenly remembered Will was *dead*—shrieked— tore myself from him—wakened. I could not shake off that horror all day—I could feel that vampire kiss on my lips for hours.

Among much else we saw the pussy cat show—and among all the pussies *one* that I coveted. A beautiful cat but no more beautiful than some of the others. But such eyes! I never saw such eyes in a cat's head—not even in Luck's, whose eyes are his great beauty spot and *almost* as wonderful. This cat had great golden eyes, surrounded by a jet black border, *with a soul looking out of them.* It was quite unmistakable. One felt, instantly, the difference between this cat and the others....

When we got home Lucky ran to meet me with his tail at full mast. And I repented me that even for a moment I had thought another cat's eyes more beautiful. They weren't!

Tues. Sept. 6, 1927
We went to the Ex. again today as I had to represent P.E.I. at a luncheon there and also give a talk before an assemblage of women. After it was over a woman came up to me and told me she had known and loved Frede in the old Macdonald days. We had a little talk about her and she told me that the Institute of Quebec had founded and endowed a scholarship at Macdonald in her memory. I had heard once that this was to be done but I had never heard that it really was done.

I have discovered that certain Norval people have been trying to pump Mrs. Mason in regard to "how much money I have." No doubt it is a great worry to them.

Wed. Sept. 14, 1927
The Manse, Norval
Chester returned to Aurora today. I went as far as Toronto and when Ewan returned we had a look at some cars. I want to get a really nice closed car. Old Dodgie has grown shabby. A minister's car, out in all weathers and in all kinds

of roads, can't be kept spic-and-span. And yet I hate the thought of forsaking Dodgie—though we are going to keep her on for rough roads. It seems disloyal. She has been such a splendid old car. We have never had a bit of trouble with her from any fault of hers. After that unspeakable Grey-Dort she was a wonder.

We have about decided on a Willys-Knight.

Fri. Sept. 23, 1927

Yesterday Ewan and I took Marian to see Niagara and stayed till night to see "the illuminations"....

Last Friday I had a letter from Hattie Gordon saying that she was going to Philadelphia to visit her married daughter and would pass through Toronto, so that if I liked she could arrange to spend a day or two here. At first I was wholly joyful—and still am glad. But a chilly little doubt has crept in. It is thirty-five years since I bade Hattie Gordon farewell on the sunlit evening road at our "red gate." A very long time. I could not expect to see *that* Hattie Gordon again. All these years of correspondence. I have kept the illusion of her; but when we meet will it not be destroyed and I be the poorer? After so long a separation would it not be better never to meet—because we must both be a kind of stranger to the other. Still, I am glad she is coming....

Sunday, Sept. 25, 1927
The Manse, Norval, Ont.

I had such a nice quiet evening of reading tonight. I was reading an old book— and probably for the last time. So many new books are coming out that one has to read—life is so crowded—and so far-spent!—that I begin to feel that there are certain books I can never spare the time to read again. It is a sad conclusion for they are old friends and I enjoy them more at every reading. But it seems to have become inevitable.

Friday, Sept. 30, 1927

Marian left for home today. I shall miss her very much. She is a very nice agreeable girl to have around the house. She is much better than when she came— quite well in fact—and I think she had a very good time here.

Tuesday, Oct. 4, 1927

I have been much worried and upset since last Saturday. When I was in Toronto with Marian on Friday I saw and loved and bought a dear little cabinet—a sort of revival of the old-time "what-not" which, despite its mid-Victorian implications was a very useful bit of furniture. Saturday afternoon I was mentally numbering the bits I would put in it when I got it home—and suddenly I remembered that I could not recall seeing my mackerel reamer of "Franklin Dexter" romance since coming home. I flew down to the living room where it had always lain on the mantel since coming here. It was not there. Nor was it apparently anywhere else. I have searched the house from attic to cellar—I have searched the lawn and garden microscopically—and I have cried over it. But I have not found it.

The last time I can recall seeing it was when I was getting the living room ready for the garden party in June. I remember looking at the reamer and thinking "I wonder if it is safe to leave that lying round tonight!" Then someone called—and so far as I can remember I never thought of the reamer again.

Now, did someone *take* that reamer that night, intrigued by its oddity? The house was open to all and sundry. The troupe that gave the programme dressed there. Several women took babies in there to put them to sleep.

Or, did Helen pick it up and carry it out sometime through the summer and drop it on the lawn? She has done that repeatedly with spoons, knives etc. It seems to me the most likely explanation. But in that case why did no one see it and pick it up? It is not so small that it could not be easily seen. And the lawn was mown every week.

Or, did I myself put it away somewhere and forget where? I was so terribly sick that day that it is a mere nightmare of recollection and I might easily have done so. Yet I have looked in every place and receptacle in the house I think and cannot find it.

I feel terribly about it. There is not a thing in the house, not even my old Woolner jug, that I would not sooner have lost. The only thing of its kind in the world—absolutely unique, reeking with romance and mystery—its disappearance seems to me a veritable calamity. Money cannot replace it.

If it really be somewhere about the grounds it *may* turn up. That is my only hope. My greatest fear is that Helen may have dropped it into the big waste-box in the kitchen and that it has been burned. I have raked the place of bonfire in the vacant lot, even with my fingers. But the wood of it would burn and the lead run to a shapeless lump.

We have got our new car—a Wyllis-Knight sedan....And the dramatic club have begun re-practising *Safety First* for fall performance.

Friday, October 14, 1927
The Manse, Norval
On Wednesday morning we motored to Toronto to meet Hattie Gordon and found her in the ladies' room of the new station. After thirty-five years, during which the whole world has changed we met again.

I knew her at once. In the dim light of the waiting room I thought she had changed very little. In the less kind light of the street I saw change. Her face was covered with fine lines. Her once so-pretty wavy golden hair had faded to a neutral brown—less beautiful than if it had become gray. And it was bobbed which did not at all become her.

She stayed till tonight and we had a very nice "visit." And of course talked Cavendish exhaustively. It gave me a shock, when we counted up the people who were in Cavendish when she was there and are there still to discover that there were only *twenty-five* of them. Hattie asked after everybody in Cavendish—except Geo. R. So there must be some old soreness there still. The last year Hattie taught in Cavendish George R. "beaued" her round and everybody thought it would be a match. Nor was there any good reason why it should not have been. It would have been an ideal marriage, seemingly. I have good reasons for believing that they were engaged at one time. But why it was broken up and who was responsible I do not know. From a bitter sentence in an old letter of Hattie's, written soon after she went to Oregon, and from her absolute silence regarding him during this visit I somehow feel it was George's fault. And yet—there was Aunt Jane. Hattie once asked Grandmother if she thought it was possible to live with Aunt Jane. Grandmother told her truthfully that she did not think it was. Nor was it. To picture Hattie Gordon and Aunt Jane under the same roof is unthinkable. Perhaps this was the rock on which she and George split. It was all a pity. She would have made George a good wife—he would have made her a good husband and become a normal citizen instead of developing into an eccentric old hermit of no use to his community. They would have probably had a clever family, some of whom might have kept the Macneill name and brains in Cavendish. And Hattie would not today have been a homeless, husbandless woman, subsisting on a brother's charity. Well, it was not to be.

I enjoyed Hattie's visit. And yet I was conscious of a sense of loss, just as I expected. The balance of things seemed oddly reversed between us. I was no longer the adoring schoolgirl looking up to a semi-divinity whom I thought wonderfully clever—and I regretted it. Yes, I had lost something.

We took Hattie to Toronto tonight and saw her off on the Philadelphia train. I saw the great gates swallow her up sadly. It is so unlikely we will ever meet again. And yet—the girl of 1892 and the woman of 1892 have not met again. They do not exist. And in that realization lies my loss.

Sunday, October 16, 1927
The Manse, Norval

This evening we went to Toronto in our new Wyllis-Knight car—"Billy" for short. It is certainly a very comfy one, though whether it will do us the good service faithful old Dodgie has done is doubtful. I paid about $2,000 for it—the price being $2,100. In olden days I have seen a good P.E. Island farm bought and sold for that.

We took Mr. and Mrs. Gollop in and went to hear the notorious Dr. Shields, who is at present doing his best to split the Baptist church in two. Well, we heard him; and his church has the distinction of being the only one—so far—in which I was threatened with the Police!

We were a little late. A prayer was being prayed when Mr. and Mrs. G. and I went into the porch—Ewan having gone on to see a sick parishioner. We halted behind the little group of people at the inner door until the prayer should be over. The church was packed, with a row of people standing all around it in the back circular aisle. When the prayer was over Mrs. Gollop and I stepped quietly just inside the door. Immediately up bustled an usher who had just stepped out of a Dickens' novel. He was about sixty, about up to my shoulder, with an underlip that stuck out like a shelf. And you could tell by the look of him that he was a Fundamentalist who would call every opinion that clashed with his own damnable heresy. "Here, you, step back," he whispered savagely to Mrs. Gollop and me. "Don't you see you're blocking the aisle." We had *not* seen this but we saw at once that we were and stepped back at once quietly. But old Self–Importance had evidently caught a whiff of unorthodoxy about me, for he stuck his face close to mine and said insolently, "If we call the police in they'll put you out pretty quick."

I looked him in the eye and quailed not. He would have made a lovely inquisitor but the days of rack and faggot are past. I said quietly, "If we are not welcome here we will go without your having to call the police."

This gave him to think. Perhaps he was an honest though stupid old ass. At any rate he pulled in his horns a bit and explained more politely that it was against the law to block the aisle of any building. Which we knew already.

Well, well, maybe he thought we were McMaster spies. A man with an under-lip like his could think anything. Dr. Shields began to "preach" at 7.30 and when we left at ten he was still busy saving the world and damning McMaster. We stood most of the time. At 9.30 the aforesaid usher—who had been standing behind me with his wife—I know she was his wife. No other woman in the world would ever have married that man—and having a glorious time shouting Praise-Gods and Hallelujahs all through the sermon (?)—gave me a fierce dig in the ribs with his thumb and whispered that a seat had just been vacated which I could have. "Thank you, I prefer to stand," I said icily. But a few minutes later when another usher pointed out the same seat I smiled graciously and took it. But I was neither tired nor bored. I never was so amused in my life. There's nothing dull about Dr. Shields, especially when he is calling MacMaster names and sending everybody to hell except himself and the members of Jarvis St. church. Oh, no, it wasn't dull; but neither was it religion. I felt soiled and stained when I came away—and ashamed of myself for having been so amused at such a desecration.

Wednesday, Oct. 19, 1927
The Manse, Norval
I had a letter from Miss Carroll today that tasted bad. Last winter she asked me on behalf of Mr. Loren Palmer, editor of *The Delineator*, to write some more "Marigold stories" for them, offering five hundred dollars for each one accepted. I wrote several and they selected three and paid me $1,500 for them. Also Miss Carroll wrote me that Mr. Palmer said that one of them "Red Ink or—" was the best story of its kind he had ever read, not even excepting Booth Tarkington's *Penrod*. The stories were to appear in the Jan., Feb. and March issues and I had so told several friends.

And now! There has been an upheaval in the offices of *The Delineator*. Mr. Palmer has gone and a new editor is in power—a Mr. Oscar Graeve who is evidently a very new broom indeed. He has decreed that my stories are not "sophisticated" enough for *The Delineator* and he is not going to use them.

It is an abominable way for him to treat me. I suppose he thinks because I have been paid for the stories I have no reason to feel injured. But I submit I have. I did not write those stories for money but for the kudos their appearance in *The Delineator* would give me. As far as money goes, I could almost have written a new book in the time it took me to do them, because I put so much work and time on them. I feel very bitter and indignant....

Sat. Oct. 29, 1927

....Mrs. Livesay has been capitalizing her Cavendish summer in the *Toronto Star*. Some of her paragraphs are going to make the C. people rise up and howl. And some of them tempt me to do so. One in particular:—the utterance of Mrs. Warren—Izzie Robinson. She told how "dramatic" I always was. "One of her most cherished memories," it seems, was of coming into school at the close of recess and finding me standing on a desk, flapping my arms and crowing like a rooster, by way of practising a recitation I meant to give that evening!

Oh, I remember *that* incident very well, too well, dear Mrs. Warren. And I remember just as well your mincing look of horror and the unmerciful and sarcastic calling down I got before the whole school for my "unladylike exhibition." Do you really think I have forgotten it? And have you?

Izzie concluded her speech by saying "We are very proud of her and always have been."

Oh, Izzie, Izzie, do you know where little girls go who tell lies? Have you quite forgotten and do you think I never knew that you told your bosom friends that you "hated" me and that your favorite name for me was "her Satanic Majesty, Maud."

I cannot help feeling furious over this matter. That this creature should dare to pose as my early "guide, philosopher and friend" when she was my bitterest enemy. I wish she knew that she served as the model for "Miss Brownell" In *New Moon*. I don't think she would go about then posing as my early and always admirer. It is foolish to be vexed over it, I know, but I am vexed.

And Mrs. Livesay remarks further that among my old friends I am always know as "Lucy Maud." This is quite untrue. I know not what the Grahams and Moores—who were *not* my early or late friends—call me behind my back but I was never called Lucy Maud by any of my friends or relatives after I left babyhood behind. My friends all knew I disliked the two names together. Mrs. Livesay also has her article illustrated by a picture of the old Cavendish manse labelled my "early home"!

I think I will give up believing anything I see in "de paper news" about anybody!

Thursday, Nov. 17, 1927
The Manse, Norval

....The young folks of Union want to get up a play this winter and have asked me to help them. I cannot refuse, after helping Norval, but I dread having to direct two plays. I feel it will be too much for me.

The Humane Society is going to take up the case of the Beamish boy who tortured the cat to death. I reported him—I was determined a deed like that should not go unpunished. He is said to have killed another one the same way.

Our Hallowe'en supper came off last week. The next day I was so tired I did not know what to do. I felt desperate—driven—hunted. But in the evening I went down to take some jars of fruit to a poor woman of the village and coming home alone in the dark I saw something that suddenly rested me—the pines on the hill dark against the starlit sky. Oh, there was the way, the truth, the life. Sheer ecstasy above the world possessed me—re-youthed me. I was no longer tired or worried or driven. There was peace—eternal calm—on that waving hill. And it was mine.

The seventh of November was Thanksgiving. Mrs. Mason was away so I cooked our duck dinner. My hand has not lost its cunning for Stuart said bliss-fully "Mother, *no one* can make gravy like you" and "Mother, why don't you always do the cooking?"

Well, I wish I could for I love cooking when I have time for it. Mrs. Mason is a good cook but she hasn't "the knack" in some things. All the Montgomery's had it and our family of Macneills through the Woolners. Grandmother Macneill knew naught of calories and vitamins or balanced rations but she was the best cook I ever knew in my life. Aunt Annie was also a wonder and all her girls inherited the gift. We can all "make things taste good" as Stuart says. We know by grace and not by law just how big a "pinch" to put in.

Tonight I thought I should have an evening of reading—and I had. But it was spoiled for me. I was reading *Your Cuckoo Sings by Kind*—a story I had picked up on a Toronto bargain counter. I liked it. It was a simple little story about a child—dear, wholesome, understanding. And then right in the middle of it came the most hideous, loathsome bestial incident—the vilest thing I ever read in any book. Not more than half a page long as far as words go but reaching down to the primeval slime of crawling things. I flung the book from me, as if I had touched a red hot coal. It turned me sick—ruined the whole evening for me. I think what hurt me worst was that it was so unjustifiable. There was no *need* for it—it didn't *belong* to the book. Pugh! Shall I ever get the taste out of my soul? I am no prude. I have read a great many books where sex played a prominent part—great books which I enjoyed. But I have no use for the filth that is being spewed out by the presses of the world today. It is *not* sex—it is plain dirt. This was worse than dirt—it was verminous. I poked it into the fire and held it down with the tongs and watched it burn with delight. Nothing but fire could purify it.

Why did the author put such a thing into what else would have been a charm-ing book. Was she afraid of the laughter of her world if she wrote a wholly decent book? Then why didn't she pour pornography over every chapter and omit that damnable half page?

The Manse, Norval, Ont.
Wed. Nov. 30, 1927
....It has not helped me any to discover a few days ago that Stuart has that horri-ble disease—the bugbear of old schooldays—"the itch." It seems the school is full of it—a "home boy" having infected it. A short time ago I noticed a rash on Stuart's wrist. Had I taken it in hand then it would have been well. But I never thought of such a thing—just supposed it to be eczema, to which I am subject myself occasionally. I treated it with zinc ointment but as it did not avail I took

him to the doctor last week and discovered the fell truth. So now confronts me weeks of rubbing Stuart's whole body night and morning with sulphur & carbolic ointment and seeing that all his clothes etc. are sterilized. He has such a dose of it that I fear it will take a long while to eradicate it completely.

I had been looking forward to today—we had planned to motor to Aurora in "Billy" to see the Prize Day doings. Chester won third prize for last year. But it has all been a disappointment. It poured rain in torrents all the way there—and when we got there it was to find that Chester was in the infirmary with *mumps*. I could not even see him, as I have never had mumps. We stayed for the exercises but it was no longer very interesting to us. And we had a *dreadful* drive home, through a storm half snow half rain that kept freezing on the windshield. I have come in, swallowed a jorum of hot tea, poured out my woeses in this journal—and am now going disgruntedly to bed.

Thursday, Dec. 1, 1927
I am very happy tonight. I was *not* happy all day. I was tired, neurasthenic, pessimistic. And I was oddly haunted by the loss of my reamer. I kept thinking about it constantly as I flew about all day, getting house and food ready for "company to tea." The McLeans were coming. At a quarter to six all was in readiness and Mrs. Mason and I were putting the finishing touches to the table—which with its flowers and rose-shaded candles looked very pretty. Ordinarily it would have given me pleasure but tonight nothing pleased me. I only wished supper was over, the McLeans gone home and I alone—not needing to talk and smile. We needed a certain set of spoons that I have not used for a long time. I told Mrs. Mason to get the box containing them out of the sideboard drawer and went out to the pantry to get the cream. I heard Mrs. Mason call out "Mrs. Macdonald!" in an excited tone. I ran back. She had the box open. And there with the spoons lay my reamer!!!

Nobody knows how it got there. Some of us, probably myself, must have dropped it in there for safekeeping the day of the garden party. If it were I, I was so ill and miserable that day it is no wonder I forgot. But there it was, safe! I was so delighted that everything changed and became beautiful. I enjoyed my supper, enjoyed the evening. And after they were gone I kissed my dear relic and joyfully put it on the shelf of my cabinet. Nobody knows how glad I am to have found it. It seems to me that a part of my childhood was bound up in that and was lost to me with it.

Wed., Dec. 14, 1927
The Manse, Norval
Last Friday Charlotte McPherson and I went to Toronto and bought a hundred presents at Woolworth's for the Xmas tree. A hard day's work and one that somebody else could very well have done. But then the minister's wife would have nothing to do!!

Yesterday I entertained the W.M.S. and in the evening Charlotte and I labelled the gifts.

Fri., Dec. 16, 1927

We had our Sunday School concert tonight and the boys of my Bible Class did a lovely thing—they presented me with a big basketful of roses.

But in a way I wish they hadn't. Because Ewan didn't like it. He never made any reference whatever to it. I brought the basket home and set the roses in all their splendor on the table under his very eyes. He turned away without a word or glance.

This would have hurt me terribly once. It no longer hurts me so much but it *humiliates* me. I hate to realize that my husband has such a petty streak in him—it makes me ashamed of him.

How easy it is to spoil things!

Sat. Dec. 17, 1927

Chester came home today. He has quite recovered from the mumps. Last night I was amused to find in *Saturday Night* a column long article by Austin Bothwell on my dedication of *Emily's Quest* to "Stella Campbell Keller of the tribe of Joseph." The mystery of it seems to have intrigued him greatly. However, he read a good deal more into it than it could carry—and he did not understand it fully because he knew nothing of its origin—he did not know that Frede had invented it as her definition of "kindred spirits." And he is quite, quite wrong in saying that the real members of the race of Joseph do not *know* they are members. They jolly well know it. No fooling the members who are sealed of that tribe.

How Frede would laugh over that article if she were alive to read it. How bitter its flavor was to me because I kept thinking what its flavor would have been had she shared it with me. Oh, Frede, Frede!

I have lately been reading Wilson Macdonald's poems. They are very beautiful. But the day of great poetry is, I fear, over. Humanity has to pay some price for growing up and becoming wise and rich and comfortable. It loses the power to write great poetry, which is a thing of youth. We are just entering, I believe, on the age of Science—an age of wonderful discoveries and development. We will *do* things that are hardly as yet dreamed of—but we will not write great literature or paint great pictures. We can't have everything at the same time. We will fly around the world and solve the secret of the atom—but there will be no more Homers or Shakespeares. They went out with the gods.

Fri., Dec. 23, 1927

Have been busy preparing for Christmas which we celebrate tomorrow as Mrs. Mason is going away for Xmas. Tonight I called on some of our people across the bridge and then walked home alone, past the dark pines that were shivering in the chill night wind. And as I went I was haunted by Nora Holland's dear poem "The Little Dog Angel" which I re-read recently and loved again. The last two lines sang themselves over and over to me,

> "The little dog angel's eager bark
> Will comfort his soul in the shivering dark."

Well, many a worse thing might meet us "without" than the welcoming bark of a jolly little ghost dog. I wonder if the spirits of all the pussy folk I have loved will meet me with purrs of gladness at the pearly gates.

I have been re-reading Macaulay's *Lays* lately. Not literature of course—oh, dear, no! But I am Philistine enough to prefer them to modern hysterics. What a swing and fire "Horatius" has, what dramatic intensity from first to last.

> "How can man die better than facing fearful odds
> For the ashes of his fathers and the temples of his gods?"

The pacifists have not invented any conclusive answer to that yet. But then there are no longer any gods. And our fathers were only mistaken old fools who didn't know beans. Why die for their ashes? Far better make fertilizer out of them.

Nowadays the flat roof of the bay window outside my room is a daily rendezvous for birds. Stuart—who always wants to be feeding some poor starving thing—puts rations of bread and suet there for them and the tidings thereof have gone abroad through birdland. It is very interesting to watch them.

Stuart has a very tender little heart—too tender I fear for his own good in this brutal world. I remember when he was four or five up at Leaskdale our yard was haunted by a big black and white cat whom we called Abraham, because he had belonged to a family of that name who had moved away. Stuart wanted to feed him but I would not let him because Abraham was very fat and sleek and evidently well-fed and I did not want to encourage him hanging around, having suffered many things in my early Leaskdale days from One-eyed Oxtoby and The Dweller On The Threshold. But one cold winter night as we sat at supper Stuart looked up into my face with his great shining blue eyes and said pleadingly, "Mother dear, *can't* I give poor Abraham a bone?"

Abraham got his bone, with plenty of meat on it....

Saturday, Dec. 31, 1927
The Manse, Norval

....Today I came across a long lost old picture of Nora Lefurgey taken long ago on Cavendish rocks looking out to sea. It brought back that lovely day we spent at the shore bathing and kodaking and picturing—one of the very few *perfect* days in my life. I do not even know where Nora is now—but I see her as in the picture, tall, black-eyed, standing against those old rocks looking out over the blue waves of that eastern sea.

Have re-read *Undine*. What is there in books like this that never grows old or stale? Yet it is the simplest tale. And a fairy tale at that, which the modern world sneers at. But we all need some kind of fairy tale else we cannot live.

What a strange belief that old persistent belief in the land of faery was. It is found everywhere in some guise and lasted for thousands of years—nay, lasts yet in some lands. Verily, there are moments when I cannot believe that it had no foundation whatever.

1928

Saturday, Jan. 21, 1928
Play practices in Union and Norval—entertain the Boys' Bible Class here one evening—got a letter from Rollins saying that the appeal was to be heard Thursday. That is all there is to say of the week except that I found time to read Wallace's *Wooden Ships and Iron Men*, a very fascinating book in which I found to my delight a picture of the *Marco Polo*. There she was, just as I remembered her—and again I saw a far-off shore where breakers boomed and a big black ship lay out among them.

Tuesday, Jan. 24, 1928
We went to play practice at Stirratt Leslie's at Union tonight—without chains, as the roads were all right when we left here. When we started home we found it was raining and freezing but we got along until we came to Copeland's Hill—a steep hill with two twists. Suddenly Dodgie skidded into the ditch—struck the bank with such force that she was flung clean across the road into the other ditch. As we crossed the road I thought, with great apparent deliberation, "We are going to be killed." But nothing happened to us. Dodgie stopped in the ditch with her front axle doubled up under her. We got out and walked home on that wet ice in a pouring rain, feeling rather nasty after the shock.

This night nine years ago I sat in anguish by the death-bed of the woman I loved best in the world. How the anguish comes back!

Sunday Feb. 12, 1928
Last night I was in Toronto giving an address to the Canadian Authors Association. Had a pleasant time, meeting some nice people. John Garvin was there—the husband of "Katherine Hale." It always makes me feel a wee bit *bitter* to meet him. He is *so* proud of his wife and her literary attainments, so whole-heartedly pleased over her successes.

Ewan secretly hates my work—and openly ignores it. He never refers to it in any way or shows a particle of interest in it. I certainly wouldn't want him to go about boring people publicly with his appreciation. But I would like him to *feel* a little. I have *never*, since I was married, neglected *any* duty of wife or mother because of my writing. I have done it at odd hours that were squeezed out of something else by giving up some of my own possible pleasure and *all* my leisure. So he has no justification for this attitude.

However, let *me* be just. Would I want Ewan to be like old John Garvin in other respects? I certainly would *not*. Therefore let me not howl with indignation because he is not like him in this.

He is really funny—J.G. I mean. He came up to me last night and whispered mysteriously "I'm going to tell you something you don't know." There are many things I do not know so I uncorked my ears and smiled. I was going to learn who knew what of wisdom or secret lore. "*I* was the means of getting the Canadian edition of *Anne of Green Gables* accepted," he said. "Really?" I responded brilliantly. "Yes." Mr. G. tapped me paternally on the shoulder. "They gave it to me to read and asked me what I thought. I said, 'Take this book. It will sell in tens of thousands.' And they took it."

J.G. tapped me again and went off, hugely pleased with himself.

The only trouble with this nice little yarn is that there never has been a Canadian edition of *Green Gables*! Page never offered it to any Canadian firm. But I didn't tell Mr. Garvin this. I think he believes the yarn himself now. Its evolution is an illuminating little commentary on the growth of legend. Years ago when he told me this story first it was merely that when he first read *Anne of Green Gables* he said to the friend who loaned it to him, "This book will sell by the thousands." If he keeps on and lives long enough he will probably be telling that he wrote it.

Tuesday, Feb. 14, 1928
....They are carrying the mails over to P.E. Island now by aeroplane. A wonderful bit of progress—or would be if the letters so carried were any the sweeter or more vital thereby.

Stuart has just made and brought me in a cup of cocoa—fit for the gods. There are few things Stuart cannot do when he tries. And he has inherited a bit of the old Montgomery and Woolner knack of cookery. He can make the best cup of cocoa I ever tasted.

Saturday, Mar. 10, 1928
Stuart came down with mumps last Monday. He has not been very ill and is up today but I suppose I will have them. And what will the play-folk do then, poor things?

I do not often nowadays think about travelling in far and storied lands. All my old desires and dreams thereof have for years been so sternly repressed and inhibited that I had deluded myself into thinking they no longer existed. I knew better last Monday when a letter came from Dr. Allison of Manitoba university inviting me to join an excursion trip he is arranging for the members of the Authors Association. To last six weeks this summer and cover the most of Europe and Palestine.

Oh, if I could but go. And with all those congenial folk who will comprise the party. If it were not Stuart's last summer at home I think I would make a frantic attempt to compass it. But as it is—no.

Last Saturday evening we spent at the Barracloughs—the first time I have been there since October. It was like a return from exile. And a delight to see Mrs. B. again. I do love that woman. And I have been so worried about her all winter. She has been ill with mumps and I could not go as they were quarantined; she was terribly run down when she took them and could not seem to throw them off. Indeed she is very far from well yet but I do hope she will improve from now on. It seems fatal for me to love anyone....

Tuesday, Mar. 13, 1928
I was amused today, reading of a recent "parade" in a Toronto store where all the fashions since 1860 were passed in review and "shrieks of laughter" greeted them all, especially the "absurd" puffed sleeves and long skirts of the 80's. Well, laugh on. Twenty years from now flappers will be laughing at the "absurd" knee length skirts and eye-eclipsing hats and shapeless coats of today. I remember in the 90's we laughed at the bustles of the 80's and the crinolines of the 70's. It is always youth's privilege to laugh at its grandmother. And always the gods of one generation are the derided idols of the next. We *have* to laugh at something and we dare not laugh at ourselves.

The other day I noticed two young girls who called themselves "friends"—and may be. I noticed the way they caressed and kissed each other—with mouths, by the way, which looked as if they had been making a meal of blood. A lip-stick is really a vampirish thing.

It suddenly occurred to me how little I and my friends were ever given to physical caresses—even in emotional youth. To me, it has always been positively abhorrent to kiss or caress one of my own sex. I cannot recall a single instance when Frede and I ever kissed each other. When we met we shook hands with a joke or a yelp of pleasure—when we parted we waved an off-hand farewell. The only chum I ever recall kissing frequently was Laura Pritchard. She had been trained in the convent to "greet her friends with a holy kiss" and she was a demonstrative girl. She always flung her arms around me with an energetic kiss and hug combined—from which I emerged rather thankful, much as I loved her, that *that* was over....

Thursday, Mar. 22, 1928
Monday night we had our dress rehearsal of the Union Play with the usual confusion and despair. Tuesday night the play itself came off splendidly. We had a full house and everybody was delighted.

The next day I had to go to Toronto. I never felt, I think, quite so tired in my life. It was a positive obsession. I went about Simpson's all day shopping and thinking, "*Oh, if I were only in bed.*" Yes, I thought in italics about it. I had only one wish, thought, desire, aspiration left in my soul—to get into bed. Eventually I got through the day, got home and *got* into bed. Never shall I forget the deliciousness of it. To lie there—to stretch weary limbs out between the warm blankets—to know that I could lie there for nine unbroken hours—to hear the storm wind rising—rising—rising outside and know it couldn't get at me—to hear the cars honking past on the highway and know I didn't have to go anywhere in one of them—to hear a raptured pussy cat purring at my feet—oh, nothing in the world could have tempted me out of that bed. I had a *good* sleep, the first in weeks and felt all through it that I was having it.

Saturday, March 31, 1928
The Manse, Norval
Fate dealt me a mean little wallop last Monday when I slipped on a bit of orange peel on a street in Toronto and fell violently. I twisted wrist, knee and ankle nastily and they have troubled me ever since....

Last Wednesday my heart stood still with horror. Ewan had a headache! He has had no trace of headache for over a year and a half. Oh, surely, surely that horror is not returning.

He has not been troubled again since Wednesday. But I feel sick with apprehension. When I look back on those dreadful seven years during which his melancholia persisted my very soul shudders within me.

Have been re-reading Renan's *Life of Jesus* lately. It has always been one of my favorites. Though I doubt if Renan's "Jesus" is very much like the historical one and his treatment of the miracle problem is unsatisfactory. Nevertheless it was the first book which ever made me *feel* that such a person as Jesus had really existed, taught, suffered and failed.

Monday, April 2, 1928
We had an electric range installed today. The oil stove was done and since I had to get something I decided to get an electric range. I think I shall like it. It is clean and convenient. But if I had my choice of a cookery beast I'd choose an old "Waterloo Stove" with plenty of good hardwood!

It's odd to think we are cooking by the grace of that thunder of waters eighty miles away.

Saturday, April 7, 1928
....Chester's report for the winter term came today. For the first time he leads his class. It has just occurred to me that Chester is now just the same age *Nate* was when we were playing at first love. I thought of Nate as grown-up. I think of Chester as a child. So much for the point of view....

Wednesday, Apr. 18, 1928
Leaskdale is certainly unlucky. Their new minister Mr. McCullough died Sunday of cancer in the throat. He preached only eight Sundays after induction.

By a curious coincidence Lawyer McCullough died yesterday after an operation. I was sorry to hear it; and a bit worried, too. He knew so well all the ins and outs of our lawsuit with Pickering and if any further trouble comes up a stranger would not understand. But I hope we will not have that. Pickering seems to have given up with the failure of his attempt to put the ecclesiastical screws on.

Friday, Apr. 27, 1928
This is the first evening I have had home since Sunday. Monday we had our dress rehearsal in the new Anglican Parish hall and they made a ghastly muddle of it. Gordon Leslie does not know his part at all. I came home and cried. Tuesday we practised again. Wednesday night I went with the Union Players to

Acton. Last night we put our Norval play, *Turning the Trick* on here. And it went off splendidly in spite of Gordon's shortcomings. We had a packed audience and took in over a hundred dollars. Some of the players did splendidly....

Wednesday, May 2, 1928
Last night I had a curious dream of being sent for to Boston "to see the end of the eight year suit."

That seems too good to be true. That suit will *never* have an end. The appeal was heard in January and there has been no word of any decision since. Rollins says it is most unusual. But time is apparently no object to the U.S. legal mind.

As for the suit which Briesen and Schrenck advised me to enter in New York two years ago in February, there has been no word of that either. Of course the New York courts are years behind. I wonder if, a hundred years hence, when this "evil" has been remedied people will think we lived in the Dark Ages, to submit to such a state of things. *I* can do nothing but submit. But surely somebody or some band of somebodies could do something about it if they wanted to.

I have managed lately to steal enough time from my scanty sleeping hours to read two very delightful books. One was an old favorite *Our Sentimental Garden*, by Agnes and Egerton Castle. It is one of the few books I *love*, in contradistinction to the multitude of books I *like*. All the charm and loveliness of old-fashioned gardens is in it and "Loki" is a pal of mine. A most refreshing book.

The other book *The Mystery of Shakespeare* is a very well written and stimulating book on the question "who wrote the plays of William Shakespeare?" It is a book calculated to make one dizzy. There are so many "claimants" to the plays and such a good case can be made out for everyone.

A short time ago some British magazine ran an interesting series of letters on the idea: "If you could meet the ghost of some famous person what question would you ask him or her?"

A great many questions were asked. Many of the writers wished they could meet Shakespeare and ask him if he really did write his plays. Well, there is one question I would like to ask Shakespeare but it is not about his plays. I feel absolutely certain that he *did* write them and the so-called "difficulties" worry me not a whit. One cannot measure a demi-god with a yardstick.

No, if *I* met Shakespeare's shade I would ask him "*Why* did you leave your wife your second-best bed?"

Controversies have raged over this. Some say it was a mark of contempt—a veiled insult. Some say it was a token of affection. I should really like to know.

What a pity Shakespeare didn't keep a diary. Fancy the worth of such a volume. But then the gods do not keep diaries. And we are not permitted to know too much about them. So nobody will ever know the truth about that second best bed nor what Anne Hathaway thought before she went to sleep in it....

The Manse, Norval, Ont.
Saturday, May 26, 1928
The hardest week of a hard spring has gone where old moons go. In addition to ceaseless hurry and toil I have had a bitter heartache all the week. Last Sunday

Ewan came home with what was for me really terrible news. Barracloughs were going to sell out and move to Toronto.

I cried all night about it, bitterly and rebelliously. For fourteen years I lived in Leaskdale with no real friend near me—no society except stodgy, unimaginative farmers' wives whose sole interest seemed to be in hens and butter. I had got so used to it I said—and believed—I didn't mind it. But in the two years we have been here, finding such pleasure and congeniality in that lovely home in Glen Williams I realize that I *did* mind it and realize how much was lacking in my life. And now it is to be torn out of my life again.

Besides, not only my own personal loss worried me but the loss to Union congregation. It will be a terrible blow.

I have dreamed and thought so much of Frede this unhappy week. Always in "the haunted spring" the thought of her comes to me with renewed vividness and longing. I had to get out and re-read her letters to stifle a little my anguish of longing. And to dull the pain of life I dreamed a waking dream after this fashion.

Frede did not die of pneumonia in the infirmary of St. Anne's. Instead she was on a wrecked train which took fire. No trace of her could be discovered save that one of the charred, unrecognizable bodies held in its hand a hand-bag of hers. We were forced to conclude it was she and have mourned her as dead all these years. Then one day I receive a letter. I start—grow pale—feel my head whirling. The letter is addressed in Frede's handwriting and post-marked from some obscure village in Québec.

I tear it open. I read the first lines "Dear Maud"—I rapidly scan the pages—and then I fall on my knees, sobbing out my gratitude to God.

Frede did not die in the wreck. The unknown woman who must have clutched her hand-bag was not she. Frede was so to speak shell-shocked. She lost her identity—wandered for miles, until at last, reeling with fatigue she came to this little French village and fell unconscious at the gate of a simple kindly French family. They took her in and nursed her back to health—but not to memory. Nothing of her past could she remember. There was nothing about her that could give a clue. They never thought of connecting her with a train wreck seventy miles away if they ever heard of it. The local priest made some inquiries but discovered nothing. Frede stayed on with the old couple, taking the place of a daughter in their household, content, helpful, wistful.

And then one day memory suddenly returned—and with it the awful realization that nine years had passed. *What had happened to her world?* Was her mother living? Was *I*? She wrote to me at once, half distraught. Was I still alive? Could I come to her?

I read the letter and called Ewan. In a few minutes I was on the way to Toronto. The next afternoon I got off the train in the little French village and sought out the house where Frede was. She met me at the door. After years of anguish we were together again.

I brought her home. I helped her link up her past with the present. Will Sutherland, a convenient *widower*, comes to see me—the old blighted romance puts forth a second blooming. Frede is happy—and I—I wake!

It all sounds very silly and childish. But it is not so, lived in vivid fancy. And it helped me through this otherwise intolerable week of spring loneliness.

Last Tuesday night we gave the tenth and last performance of our Union Play in the Anglican parish hall. I moved among the players like an unhappy ghost. Wednesday night we gave our Norval play in Woodbridge and Friday night in Caledon—the last of the season. I am so thankful it is over. I am tired completely out.

We finished the garden and the housecleaning this week also—and I feel as if I were finished too. I have no heart for anything.

"Parish Hall" [Norval]

Saturday, June 3, 1928
The Manse, Norval
....It has been a lovely week of rest and quiet evenings and old beloved books in twilit rooms full of dicentra—the old "bleeding heart" of old-fashioned Cavendish gardens now come back into favor and fashion. I have always loved it and for the first time in my life I really have enough of it. I could never grow it in Leaskdale but I have some lovely clumps here and the gem-like sprays welcome me in every room.

Sunday, June 10, 1928
This week has been rainy and cold but it has been a nice week for all that. I have *rested*. Ewan left Monday for Regina to attend the General Assembly and so there has been no visiting. I have stayed home; my "resting" has been trying to catch up with over due work but that in itself is a kind of rest; and in the evenings I have read—and even loafed a few minutes now and then and let my thoughts ripen and grow mellow.

The Union Dramatic Club cleared $305 on their play. I think that is good.

Yesterday I had a wire from Briesen and Schrenck. It is so long since I heard anything about that New York suit that I had almost forgotten it. It was two years last January since it was entered. The wire was to the effect that the National Surety Co. (who went bond for Page) offered $2,200 in settlement of suit and as this was a little more than we had sued for they advised settlement....

I have been reading a most amazing and fascinating book this week, *Exploring the Universe*. I can hardly describe the effect it has had on me. It made me feel both infinitesimal and infinite. And a little dizzy—....

Sunday, June 17, 1928
The Manse, Norval
A busy pleasant not too hurried week...Yesterday I got Briesen and Schrenck's bill—for twelve hundred! I think eight would have been ample. However to get back a thousand of what I paid is better than not getting anything. And the N.Y. affair is definitely closed and I am free from further anxiety on that score.

I can't imagine why the Boston suit has not ended before this. The appeal was heard last January and I never expected the Court would take this long to decide. But time and eternity have always been one in this endless litigation.

Saturday, June 23, 1928
We have had a great deal of rain all through June. The whole house is getting damp and blue-mouldy, doors and drawers sticking, cake & bread moulding. I always resent June being spoiled. Every other month may be but June *should* be exempt.

I was in Toronto for a couple of days this week—stayed over night with Mary and saw some good films. Also had dinner with Mr. McClelland and a salesman of Little Brown Co. who was formerly with the Pages and could tell me a few interesting things. Louis Page, it appears, fought with George until the latter had to get out of the firm altogether. Poor Mrs. George worried so much over it that she went out of her mind and is now in an asylum. When George died—his illness being probably caused or heightened by his worries—Louis went to the funeral but would not sit with the other mourners but off by himself.

In view of all this that telegram he sent me last year becomes amusing. I wish I had known these things then. I would have answered it with an epistle that would have raised a blister. All these years, I have, on Rollins' advice, rigidly held myself in and refrained from "sassing back." But I would have done it—by the three wise monkeys I would!

Chester's report came this week. A good one. He has led his class in the Honours List, took a special prize for general proficiency—he could not take the regular prize because he missed the Xmas exams owing to the mumps—and the Ashton medal for English.

Chester's brains are all right. It remains to be seen what use he will make of them. There are times when I cannot help feeling very anxious about Chester in some respects....

Ewan came home yesterday. Mrs. Donald Simpson died recently. I heard the news with regret. She was a woman I always liked—with her smiling round brown eyes. Like her I did—yet, until I learned a certain trick—I would have dodged around any corner to avoid shaking hands with her. She would give the most unmerciful grip—a grip that would make a little thread of a gold ring I always wore cut into my flesh and leave my bones aching for the day. A hearty handshake is excellent. Preserve me from the flabby soulless handshakes I have known. But Mrs. Dan's were *too* hearty. One day I happened to come across an item in a paper to the effect that if, when you were about to shake hands with these people you *gripped* their hand quickly and firmly before *they* could get a stranglehold, they would not hurt you. I tried it on Mrs. Dan the next time we met—successfully. Never again did I dread her handshake. Perhaps she dreaded mine....

Wednesday, June 27, 1928
....Yesterday evening Ewan went to the Barracloughs' and I spent the time in very miserable suspense for I knew he would likely find out whether they were really going to leave or not. When he came home and told me that the deal was not going through after all I was too happy to sleep. And today we went over to dinner there and had such a nice time that I am afraid there will be a price to pay. Unless Alf Simpson's visit may be considered payment. I'm sure it was anything but a pleasure.

Just after dinner at the Glen I was called to the phone and heard a voice, "Is that you, Maud?" I could not imagine who was calling me "Maud" but soon found out. It was Alf who—of course—was in Toronto attending the big Baptist Alliance Congress and had come out to Norval to see us. We came over and saw him. He is the same ungainly, awkward, nervous Alf, with the habit all that family had of asking you a question and giving you the impression that they are not paying the slightest attention to what you are answering. Alf said he had come up because Fulton was determined to come & it was not safe to let him come alone, as he has some serious heart condition which might terminate fatally at any moment. Fulton did *not* come out to see me, nor did Ed and his wife who were also in Toronto!! Alf himself was over in England last year, a member of some agricultural delegation who went over. They had an audience with King George in Buckingham palace. Alf *may* get over it in time but he will certainly never be the same again!

After he left we went back to the Glen and finished our visit.

Sunday, July 22, 1928
The Manse, Norval
The Manse, Norval, has been an unhappy worried place for the past three weeks. They have seemed more like three years—a hellish three years both for us personally and for the community at large. It is a long time since so much torture has been packed for me into three weeks.

Now for rack and thumbscrew.

The first few days of the week after my last entry were peaceful but it was very hot and I was very busy and very tired. On Thursday Ewan and I had some trouble with Chester—something nasty and worrying that embittered life for many days and filled us with deep-seated fear of his future. There is no use to write much about it—no use tearing open a wound that has begun to skin over. But I have been very wretched over it and I cannot think about it without agony. And then Friday evening a new worry crashed down on us. A lawyer from Milton served Ewan with a notice that a garnishee order had been served on Mr. Wiggins, the Norval treasurer (who succeeded John Russell a year ago) in regard to any part of E's salary that might be owing him. Old Pickering had struck again.

Of course it was all very nasty. By an extraordinary bit of good luck Mr. Wiggins had paid Ewan only *two days ago* not only all that was owing to him but his July money in advance. So Mr. P. was just two days too late! If the order had come two days earlier he would have got two hundred and twenty-five dollars! And the money would have been the least of the evil. The scandal and gossip and general dreadfulness would have overrun the congregation and community like a wave....

To make it harder for us our lawyer Mr. McCullough died a few weeks ago—which fact may have influenced Pickering to make another attempt. We could not endure the thought of getting a new lawyer, who would not understand the truth behind the case or Pickering's perjury and schemes. Luckily, there was John McCullough of Toronto, "our" Mr. McCullough's brother, who was associated with him in the case and knew all about it. Ewan wrote to him and he sent word back that he would go to Milton but he was not especially comforting in regard to the questions Greig might be allowed to ask. It all depended on the view the judge might take of the case, he said. So here was something for me to think about when I woke up in the night!

On the same day the board barrier across the dam broke and Stuart and several boys who were swimming in the mill pond were swept over the dam. They might have been killed—stunned on the stones & drowned. Some of them were badly bruised and Stuart came home with a dreadful abrasion on his hip where he had been dashed against some cement work. But I was at least thankful amid all else that he had escaped so easily.

On Monday came a letter from Rollins. Of course it would come at a time like this. I do not think there has been a time, during these past eight years, when I was undergoing any particular stress and strain, that a letter from Rollins *did not* come, as a sort of last straw. I made up my mind I would not open it until Wednesday was over, for I had to keep some measure of calmness for the missionary picnic and the Anglican garden party. Thursday morning I decided I might venture to open it.

The suit was ended at last—after eight years. At least Rollins said it was. And I had won! The Page appeal was refused.

It seems quite unbelievable. I feel quite sure French and Page will produce some devilment yet.

But the news was a pleasant variety to what had been happening all the rest of the week and gave me a bit of "pep" to carry on. And yet my instinct was a true one. Friday another letter came. French had applied for a "re-hearing." And as the Supreme Bench won't meet again until the fall his request will not be refused or granted till then. Rollins says it is his opinion it will be refused. But Page is determined to put me to every particle of expense and worry he can and French will take advantage of every twist the law of the U.S. offers him—and it seems that there is no end to them, when any unscrupulous person wishes to find them.

That night Chester asked forgiveness and we had a little talk that helped us both and poured a little healing into my sore heart. But it will be many a day before the wound is fully healed.

And then, on Saturday July 14th there was a ghastly accident up at the radial station.

Just a few houses down the street George Brown and his wife lived, with three children—Jimmy aged 10, Betty aged 8 and Phyllis aged five. They were not our people but we knew them well. On Saturday morning George Brown started in his car for his farm up the road and took the three children for a drive. At the crossing they were struck by the noon radial. Jimmy and Betty were killed instantly; Phyllis died two hours later; and Brown was taken to the hospital unconscious and in a serious condition.

Again one wonders just where in all this one finds a good God!

We were all stunned. It seemed like some awful nightmare. Nobody knows why George Brown did not see or hear that car. There was nothing to prevent him. He has the reputation of being a reckless driver.

I could think of nothing but the poor mother! How could she endure to live!

Poor Stuart was one of the four boys who witnessed the accident. They had been out on a bicycle hike and were waiting for the radial to pass. After the crash he and Jack Rankine lifted up the top of the car and dragged poor dead Jimmy out. No fit sight for children—the poor child's head was split open and his brains plastered over his face!

We all went about in a daze for days. I felt as if I could never enjoy life again. It was a fearful sight to see those three dead children lying in their coffins around the little parlor. The funeral was on Monday. They were buried in one grave. Their little playmates were pall-bearers. Stuart was one of them, looking unaccountably *old* in the long trousers of his new suit. It hurt me to look at him. I had lost my baby too. And I felt it was wicked to feel this, when I thought of the poor mother, lying in a drugged sleep in the room above.

"Stuart in his first long trousers"

That night I thought would never end. It was breathlessly hot—my nerves had been racked to breaking point by the tragedy—and I was worried about the next day. I could not sleep at all and arose in the morning, sick physically and mentally.

Ewan and Mr. Wiggins went to Milton. E. said he would be back by one o'clock. He did not come at one—or two—or three. I walked the floor of my room in unrest. Finally he came—and I learned that all our worry had been quite needless. Greig was not there at all. Hutchison, the lawyer who had served the summons, got up, said he had no personal interest in the case, would not even swear Wiggins and asked, "Is anything owing Mr. Macdonald?" Wiggins said "no." "How is the salary paid?" "Monthly in advance." He sat down. That was all.

Well, one can't be sure in advance so it is impossible *not* to worry. The fact that Greig was not there shows that he expected nothing of it and that the idea was Pickering's alone. Mr. Wiggins will keep his own counsel and nothing will get out for local gossip.

I slept that night for the first time in nearly two weeks. Next day Mr. and Mrs. Ephraim Weber came, motoring from Battleford to Quebec. He is my old literary correspondent for nearly thirty years. We had never met before—and I do not feel that we have really met yet. We met more fully in our letters, where our real selves are expressed without fear of conventions. Mrs. Weber is nice. They stayed until Thursday and we enjoyed their visit....The inquest on the Brown tragedy was held in the parish hall Friday evening. Stuart was one of the witnesses—and the look he gave the county attorney, Mr. Dick, when the latter was so "insulting" as to say, "I suppose you are too young to estimate the speed of the car" sent everyone in the hall into shrieks of laughter and Brown's lawyer and the Radial Co.'s lawyer, who had been calling each other names ten minutes before, roared and clapped each other on the back. But Stuart will never I am sure forgive that lawyer.

Sunday Aug. 5, 1928
The Manse, Norval

....Our house and garden are all torn up. We bear it cheerfully because the congregation are putting in a real bathroom and a hot & cold water system for us. But it makes everything rather difficult temporarily and it hurts me to look at my poor garden.

We did not ask for the bathroom. They decided of their own accord to

[L.M.M. & Ephraim Weber]

give it. I cannot keep thinking of the difference between Norval and Leaskdale in this respect....

Tomorrow we start with the Barracloughs for a week's motoring trip through Muskoka and up north. I am glad. I need a change of some sort and a rest.

Sunday, August 12, 1928
The Manse, Norval
We have had a delightful week with so much of beauty and pleasure packed into it that it seems like a month. It has really done me whole heaps of good. I am sleeping and eating well again and life does not seem quite so difficult.

We left last Monday morning and motored up to Orillia, from there on through Muskoka as far as Sundridge....Tuesday morning we motored to North Bay and from there on through the sixty miles of virgin forest where the new "Ferguson Highway" cuts through the Government Reserve. To me every moment of it was a delight; and the greatest delight of all was the innumerable lakes starred with water lilies—the most exquisite things blooming there in the wilderness—untouched, untouchable—for they never grow within reach. One must look at them—desire them—and pass on. We went as far as New Liskeard that night—passing through Cobalt where mines of richness are. Such a desolate, unlovely town surrounded by ghastly leprous hills. I could not live in such a place if I discovered a new gold or silver mine every morning.

In the morning we turned homeward and reached Sundridge again that night. Somehow that night stands out in memory as a particularly lovely one. The little hotel on Lake Bernard was so full that only one room could be had. We let the Barracloughs have that and Ewan and I slept in a tiny cabin right down on the sandy shore of the lake. Before I went to bed I sat for an hour on a log out on a little sandy point in the dreamy August twilight. To my left was a beautiful little cove, where the shadows of trees in the rose and silver water were even lovelier than the trees themselves. I held communion again with my dear friend that night after the fashion of old years. The darkness was like a cool draught to drink—some magic brew that for a little space brought youth back. I was lapped

"Our sleeping cabin"

round by an exquisite silence. And I slept in that little cabin room as I have not slept for a long long time—slept soundly, dreamlessly, refreshingly—and woke in the early morning to bathe my soul in dawn and love the mists that hung over the lake. Then the sun came out and performed its usual miracle; the beautiful lake horizons emerged from the silver glamor; and I turned away from it regretfully as one always parts from a fleeting glimpse of beauty one will not see again.

The next afternoon we reached Bigwin Inn and stayed there until the next afternoon. I have been in a good many hotels and summer resorts but never in any that delighted me so much as Bigwin Inn. It is a darling spot. The view from "the tower" is as beautiful as any I saw in England or Scotland—though, alas, it had no charm of history and myth.

The next night we stayed at Port Carling and came through Bala on our way home. It is as beautiful as I remember it, and full of pleasant memories of our stay there, six years ago. I've always wanted to go back—but it has never seemed to arrange itself....

Tuesday, Aug. 21, 1928

I don't know whether I am madder than I'm glad or gladder than I'm mad. Anyhow I'm very both.

Last autumn as recorded Stuart had the "itch." I went to work to clean him up—and I cleaned thoroughly. Every night and morning I rubbed him with sulphur ointment—every few nights I bathed him in creolined water—and I boiled and steamed his little duds continually. And, or so it seemed, in vain. In a few weeks *most* of the "itch" was gone, but it seemed impossible to cure it completely. A few spots kept coming here and there—here and there—all winter. I was in despair. Other people—even some dirty families in the village—seemed to have got rid of it completely. And I could not. I went twice to the doctor but he said I was doing all that could be done and I must be "careful to steam or boil" all the clothes he wore. He really seemed to think I must be careless in this matter and I was ready to gnash my teeth. In the spring I took desperate measures. I *burned* every stitch of Stuart's clothes—some of them real good ones—that I could not boil and got him a new outfit. And still the spots appeared. And remember all this time I was rubbing that child every night and morning—an ordeal alike for him and me.

When he went to Leaskdale he had only two or three spots and I gave him ointment and told him to keep them rubbed. But when he came home last Thursday his body was almost covered with spots again.

Well, I sat down and cried. In less than a month he was to go to St. Andrew's. He certainly could not go if he had "the itch." And I had done all I could do. Certainly "the seven year itch" seemed no old wife's fable.

I was literally in despair. McAllister was the doctor I had taken him to first but Dr. Paul was attending a neighbor across the street. In desperation I called him in and told my tale of woe. With the same result. Sulphur ointment—carbolic or creolin baths—boil or steam all his—

"Don't say it, Dr. Paul," I implored. "I really can't stand it. I'm going to call him down and have you look at him."

Dr. Paul peeled off Stuart's shirt and looked him over—took him to the light and examined him—then—

"That's not the itch he has at all, Mrs. Macdonald. That is only the pimples so many boys have at Stuart's age. It is not a skin disease at all—and is certainly not infectious."

I was so thankful I could have cried with joy. And with rage when I thought of the dreadful year I had put in....

Sunday, Sept. 9, 1928

....My nerves have been somewhat racked for the time has come to which I have looked forward with gooseflesh for several years. Chester has been learning to drive the car! I know he *has* to learn. And I have even gone with him, trying not to let him see that I felt I would never see home again. He has picked it up with ease of youth and really does very well. But I have seen so many things go wrong with a car, no matter who is driving, that I never see him starting off without a pang of dread.

This week will happen that which I have been dreading all summer. Stuart is leaving home for St. Andrew's—leaving home forever, except for holiday visits. It is such a terrible thought that I have never let myself look at it squarely in the face all summer, even while I was busy getting his outfit ready. But it has to be faced now. This is his last Sunday home. We had a serious little talk in the twilit parlor tonight in which I tried as best I could to warn him of some of the temptations he will meet in St. Andrew's.

Dear little Stuart. I have had him for thirteen beautiful years. And in all those years from the very night of his birth when he opened his big blue eyes and looked around the room as if he were two months instead of two hours old, he has never been anything but a joy and a delight and a comfort to me. I have never felt once ashamed of him—I have never had any reason to worry about him in regard to behavior or character. He has been the sunshine of the house and how I am going to live after he has gone I know not.

Sunday, Sept. 23, 1928
The Manse, Norval

....Last year Hattie Gordon suddenly emerged from the mist of years. And this year comes Nora Lefurgey!!

To my delighted amazement I got a letter from Nora last week, written from Toronto. The last letter I had from her years ago was written in Anyox, B.C. I had lost all trace of her, save for dim rumors by way of the Perkins family and Bertie M. And now she is in Toronto having taken a flat there while her two boys are going to Upper Canada College.

I was wild with delight; and yet when I went in Tuesday to see her I did so with considerable dread. It was twenty-four years since I had last seen Nora. A life-time lay between us. Could we clasp hands over it?

We could and did! Ten minutes after we had met the twenty-four years were not. We "clicked" as well as ever we did.

Nora looks older of course—some gray in her hair—some lines on her face. But otherwise unchanged—her bright black eyes as bright and black as ever— her smile as elfin. She has been out since for an afternoon. How we talked of those old times when we made every day an adventure for ourselves—our wild exultant dips in stormy waves—our walks together over shadowy hills—all the fool things we did for the fun of doing them. Apart from Laura Pritchard and Frede Campbell, Nora Lefurgey (who in some respects is much the same type of girl) is the only friend I have ever had before whom I could, in Emerson's fine phrase, "think aloud." The relief after nine years of unbroken repression is tremendous. I feel as if I had been smothered and were now drinking in great gulps of clear gay mountain air.

We drove out to Aurora just to see the boys for a moment. Stuart came running to meet us, introduced us to his chums and declared gaily he wasn't homesick. But when the other boys had gone and he was alone in the car with me, I said laughingly, "And so you're not homesick?" He suddenly snuggled his face against my shoulder and said with a near-sob, "Yes, I am—but I didn't want the fellows to know. I wish I could go home with you."

Well, I am glad he is homesick! It is not a good sign of a boy—or of his home—if he is not homesick when he goes away for the first time. But I hope he'll soon get over it and I think he will....

In a recent letter Ella Campbell says she was literally over-run this summer with people coming to see the house I was married in etc. My poor relatives on the Island must often wish I had never put pen to paper. The joke of it is, Uncle John's in Cavendish are likewise overrun by people who know nothing of the estrangement between us and take it for granted that Uncle John and his family must be among my intimate friends. I wonder "if yesterday were tomorrow" and if Uncle John could suspect that his obscure penniless niece would one day become something very different, he would have acted exactly as he did. I know his family would not!

Everyone in Cavendish says that Uncle John tore the old home down because he was jealous of the crowds who went there to see it. But I think it was quite as much because of the very considerable nuisance of it. Whatever his reason, demolishing the house did not help any. They still go to see the spot itself—that desolate, overgrown spot. And they carry off everything they can lay their hands on as souvenirs! One lady carried off a fat bulbous iron pot which Uncle John had over there at the well, boiling pigs' potatoes! *I* never had anything to do with the pot—I doubt if I ever saw it. But probably the lady in question will have it in her parlor and bequeath it to her heirs as L.M. Montgomery's porridge pot! Such is fame!!

Monday, Oct. 1, 1928
The Manse, Norval
Stokes' semi-annual report came today. Not a good one. My sales have been slipping a bit of late years. Well, I suppose I have had my day and must make

way for newer favorites. For twenty years I have been in the van and that is considered a long time for the fickle public to be faithful. Yet my publishers tell me there is another reason—and a rather flattering one. It seems the sales of my *old books* are keeping up *too well* and they cut the market from my new ones to a large extent. For example last year in Canada alone McClellands sold 13,000 or so of all my books. Now, anyone who buys an old book is not so likely to buy a new one, because the new ones are much more expensive. Now if 13,000 *new* ones were bought I, at the rate of 30 cents per book would make $3,900 on the Canadian sales alone. But at the rate of 5 cents a book which is all I get on the reprint books I get only $650 which is a big difference! The same principle is working everywhere. I should be proud—and I am—that my old books are selling so well. But I'd be considerably in pocket if they didn't because then people would be buying my new and higher-priced ones....

Life has seemed so *decentralized* since Stuart went. It has revolved around him so long; and now he is gone I am a lost planet adrift in space....

Wednesday, October 17, 1928
At last I have managed to finish my new book *Magic for Marigold*. I have never had such a hard time to get a book finished. I have been two years at it. "Marigold" is a nice little thing but I doubt if she will be as popular as "Anne" or "Emily."

Monday, Oct. 22, 1928
On Saturday came a long-expected letter from Rollins. When he wrote on the 23rd of September he said that the final decree would probably be entered that day and then French and Page would have three weeks to decide whether they would appeal from the "wording" of the decree or not. He did not think they would, because they could gain nothing of real value by it. But I could not share his optimism and I have been dreading to hear from him ever since lest he tell me they *were* appealing. When his letter came Saturday I turned physically ill—I actually did—when I took it in my hand. I felt that I could not bear to open it, for fear of what it might contain. And I decided I would leave it unopened until today, so as to get Sunday and its work over first. But the knowledge that it was in my desk pricked and teased me all the intervening hours. When I went out to make a call Saturday evening I felt good-for-nothing and dowdy and old! But the sudden beauty of a full moon breaking out of a dark cloud over the pines of Russell's hill suddenly rejuvenated me. What did it matter what was in Rollins' letter? Whatever it was it could not rob me of that kingdom of loveliness. It flooded my soul with all the sweetness of old days when I was just beginning to *realize* the beauty in sea dawns and hill twilights, silent mysterious ships, far out on the gulf, and full-mooned skies.

But today the letter had to be opened. I opened it—took in its contents at a glance—gasped and trembled in a "sober certainty of waking bliss"—a realization that this lawsuit *was* over *at last*. Finally and forever over. It seems almost impossible to believe it. For nine years—almost—I have dragged about a ball and chain. And now I am not only free—but victress!

The final decree has been filed—Page has at last accepted his defeat—and French told Rollins he would pay. Of course he has to, because if he didn't Rollins, who attached his property some time ago, would promptly take out an execution. *French's* bill, it seems, is not paid in full yet. And, believe me, it would be no small one. Rollins says that this suit has cost Page fully the profits of a year's business.

It is over! Over!! Over!!!

And—I—am—free!

Wednesday, Oct. 31, 1928
The Manse, Norval, Ont.
Yesterday Ewan and I motored up to Wick to attend a Fowl Supper by which the Wick Presbyterians were celebrating the fact that after three years they had got their church back. It was a delightful dreamy autumn day and we had a lovely drive up. There was an enormous crowd—they fed about 750 people—and *such* tables. They had 44 geese, 28 chickens and 15 ducks! Besides cakes and pies and tarts and cookies and jellies and pickles and salads beyond enumeration. We saw many Leaskdale folks and I enjoyed the evening as much as I ever enjoy affairs of that kind. They have no minister in Leaskdale yet. It is really too bad. I think they are too hard to please. It is useless of them to expect a very brilliant man for $1,800 a year and the privilege of living in Leaskdale!

Wednesday, Nov. 7, 1928
....Yesterday I went into Toronto and at night Dr. Charles Roberts, Arthur Stringer, Bernard Sandwell and I opened the annual Canadian Book Week by speaking in Convocation Hall to an audience of 2,000 people, after another thousand had been turned away. I had never faced such a big audience before and for a moment I came all out in goose-flesh. But they received me so rapturously that I forgot to be nervous and told my stories of the old north shore as to friends. I wound up by reading a little poem of New Year Wishes I wrote lately and as it seemed to capture the fancy of the audience greatly I will copy it here—partly for that, and partly because there is something about it that makes me very fond of it. Somehow, it seemed to "write itself" and gave me more satisfaction than I have felt for many a year.

> Friend o' mine, in the year on-coming
> I wish you a little while to play
> And an hour to dream in the eerie gloaming
> After the clamorous day.
> (And the moon like a pearl from an Indian Shore
> To hang for a lantern above your door.)
>
> A little house with friendly rafters,
> And someone in it to need you there,
> Wine of romance and wholesome laughters
> With a comrade or two to share.

(And a secret spot of your very own
Whenever you want to cry alone.)

I wish for a garden on fire with roses,
Columbines planted for your delight,
Scent of mint in its shadowy closes,
Clean, gay winds at night.
(Some nights for sleeping and some to ride
With the broomstick witches far and wide.)

A goodly harvest of figs to gather
With a thistle or two to prick and sting,
Since a harvesting too harmless is rather
An unadventurous thing.
(And now and then, spite of reason or rule
The Chance to be a bit of a fool.)

I wish you a thirst that can never be sated
For all the loveliness earth can yield,
Slim, cool birches whitely mated,
Dawn on an April field.
(And never too big a bill to pay
When the Fiddler finds he must up and away.)

After the affair was over I was literally mobbed by hundreds of girls, wanting autographs. One however did not ask for an autograph. She was content with a handclasp. "I just wanted to *touch* you, Mrs. Macdonald," she whispered, looking up with adoring eyes. Poor kiddy! Humanity can't get along without some god or goddess to worship. It is well that my young worshippers don't know what a very clay-footed creature their divinity is. Their lives would be poorer if they lost their illusion.

I wanted to meet Dr. Roberts and thank him for writing *The Heart of the Ancient Wood* but by the time I had got free from the girls he had gone. I met Arthur Stringer however, who told me I was "wonderful" and I told him I had enjoyed his Prairie trilogy and we were very well pleased with ourselves. Mr. Elson and another pillar of the Association whose name I've forgotten drove Nora and me home and as we whirled through the glittering streets I whispered to Nora, "Do you remember the night Henry McLure and Rob MacKenzie drove us home from the Literary in Rob's old pung sleigh, the two boys in front and we two behind? It wasn't as splendid as this—but it was really more fun."

Nora and I sat up and talked till two. It was satisfying; but it is twenty years since we could do that with no score to pay the next day. I came home today feeling very ragged. But found a letter from Boston with a check of $15,000 dollars in it.

Page really paid eighteen thousand and two or three hundred dollars—I forget the exact figures. But Rollins kept the rest for his services this past year. It seems a good bit but his charges are really reasonable when one considers the enormous amount of work he has put on the case in nine years. French would charge Page three times as much.

And now where do I come out? I have got a little over $18,000. The case cost me about $14,000. So I have about $4,000 for my trouble and worry plus the satisfaction of thoroughly beating a man who tried to trick me. *That* second item, not the first, makes me feel that after all it was worthwhile.

This money, coming in one big lump like this is very convenient this lean year. Wisely invested it will nearly pay Stuart's expenses at college and make things easier in many ways.

Sunday, Nov. 18, 1928
The boys came home a week ago Friday for Thanksgiving....

A busy week ended in a minor calamity Friday evening when I went to the fowl supper in Union church. When I was coming down from the platform after my last reading my foot slipped on the narrow steps and down I crashed. I jarred my whole anatomy rather badly and sprained my left arm and wrist very badly. I have it bandaged up in a sling and can't dress myself or comb my hair or cut my food. Of course I'm thankful for a number of things. That nothing was broken— that it wasn't my ankle or my right wrist....

Sunday, Nov. 25, 1928
The Manse, Norval, Ont
My arm is improving. Today I could do without the sling but it is painful and very weak yet.

Last Monday a letter came from Rollins and I almost passed out with heart failure when I opened it and saw that it contained a "copy." Because that meant that he had had some communication with French and was sending a copy of his reply.

French, on behalf of Page, had made two requests—or rather asked two questions. One was—would I be willing *now* to let Page continue publishing the *Further Chronicles*!!!

Long ago I gave up trying to understand Louis Page's mentality. Here I have been fighting tooth and nail for nine years to compel him to take that book off his list and now when I have succeeded he seems to imagine I will let him keep it on.

I suppose he thinks it was the money I was after and since I have got that will not care whether the book is left on his list or not—in which case he could save his face before "the trade."

But Louis understands my psychology as little as I understand his. I never went into that case with the idea of getting money. I went into it solely to get that book, with its ridiculous reduplications, off the market. And it stays off....

Mr. Rollins has sent me all the documents relating to the trial, including an enormous pile of type written evidence. I have been reading it over and find it as enthralling as a serial novel. Really, as I read my own evidence, I am quite well pleased with myself. I don't think I came off at all badly in that long duel with one of the best lawyers at the Boston bar. He didn't, as the slang phrase goes, get much change from me. When reading the evidence of George and Louis Page, and noting all their twists, evasions and downright lies I wonder how I could ever have won the case. And Mr. Nay, a brilliant and able lawyer, says one thing in direct examination and the very opposite on cross-examination.

In one place Louis Page—or George—says that the picture on the cover of *Anne of Green Gables* was taken from an old calendar or picture hanging in his office. This in direct contradiction to my statement that the original was a picture hanging on the wall of his library which he pointed out to me as "Our dear Anne."

And yet I have in a former volume of this diary the photograph Paul Marcone took during that visit to Boston of the very wall of Page's library with this identical picture coming out on it too plainly to be mistaken. At the time I thought of trying to have the photograph sent to me and put in evidence. But it was in my diary—locked up in a trunk in Leaskdale manse. I didn't want to send the key home and have anyone open the trunk and have access to those diaries—I didn't want to risk losing the diary in transit by mail or express. And I was so sick at heart and so sure the case was irretrievably lost, that I hadn't the grit to go home and get the diary and bring it back. And it's just as well I didn't bother....Only— I *would* like to have seen Page's face—and French's—if I had produced that picture after Page had given his evidence.

Reading those pages brought everything back very vividly—the long table snowed over with Titian prints—Mr. French striding blackly up and down objecting—the Master's thin, non-committal face—the Pages' uneasy and furtive glances—Mr. Rollins, calm, smiling, imperturbable—as day after day dragged its slow length along.

George Page's revelations, during the accounting, of the business end of the firm were very interesting. And significant. In 1921 the receipts were close on half a million. By 1926 they had slumped to about $250,000. Probably this was what George and Louis started quarrelling about.

Louis is odd—odd. On Thursday at dinner the 'phone rang. When I went to it Toronto was calling. A telegram from the Page Co. of Boston. I almost dropped in my tracks. More trouble? No, only another of Louis' unique wires:—

"Mrs. George Page lost her mind after her husband's shocking death. She never recovered. She died yesterday."

Well, I was sorry to hear of the death of Mrs. George Page. I saw her only once but she seemed a very sweet woman. But I quite refuse to accept the implication of guilt which Louis seems anxious to lay upon me. *I* am not responsible for Mrs. Page's illness or her husband's death. Louis does not know what his former salesman told me about that matter or he would not make himself ridiculous sending such telegrams. I happen to know that Mrs. Page went insane—and I think it was *before* her husband's death—through worry over the trouble between him and Louis. Also why "shocking" death? George Page did not hang or poison himself. He died rather suddenly from heart disease which would give his family a "shock" certainly but can hardly be classed under the head of "shocking" demises.

I find I have forgotten to chronicle that Louis sent me a telegram a few days previous to this one. "I have paid your attorney over eighteen thousand dollars."

Louis Page has always been obsessed with the entirely false idea that Mr. Rollins "put me up" to that lawsuit—incited and encouraged me to begin it and persist in it. He cannot believe that I, a woman, could have done it and persisted in it off my own bat. As a matter of fact Mr. Rollins did nothing to induce me to bring the suit and at two different times as it dragged its slow length along he told me he thought we'd better try to settle it. After Nay's first evidence he told me that it was no use going on with it after that. I told him that no matter what Page and his lawyers swore to I did not believe any fair-minded Master or Judge would believe that I would contract to go home and go to all the work and bother and expense of re-writing sixteen stories and having them typed, if I had been told that the Pages had the 1912 copies of those very stories in their possession. As a matter of record the Master found against me on that point but Judge Hammond saw it instantly and it really won the suit for me.

But to return—Page, not knowing this, thinks Rollins did it all, in the hope of getting money out of it. So I suppose he thought he'd better inform me just how much Rollins had been paid, so that the latter couldn't cheat me at the final accounting! Much as Page hates me he hates Rollins far more and since the money was gone, he was not going to let Rollins get more than his share! At least, I cannot imagine any other possible motive for the telegram.

Mr. McClelland in a recent letter says a Boston salesman told him the other day that Page has discharged several of his staff and lengthened the working hours of the others on the plea that he has to economize! Possibly because of the money he has paid me and French—although the latter's bill is not fully paid yet. But the salesman aforesaid said Page had lost a lot of money recently in gambling. This may be true, too—several years ago Page incurred some very heavy gambling debts.

But what a pity it all has been. There is and always will be a soreness in my soul over it. If Page had been an honest, straightforward man—if he had treated me justly—I would still have been with his house—we would still have been friends. I would never have left him, even for higher offers from other publishers. Well, well—"if" is the biggest word in any language. But I am sorry—sorry. It could so easily have all been different....

Sunday, Dec. 9, 1928
The Manse, Norval, Ont.

Have been too busy and rather miserable. My arm seldom ceases aching and I get nervously exhausted very easily—have ever since my unlucky trouble which evidently "jarred my slats" rather more than I thought at the time. Thursday of last week Charlotte McPherson and I spent at Woolworth's buying the hundred odd "presents" for the S.S. Xmas tree—a job I dread all the year. The crowds were terrible and my arm ached all day. But the welcome night came at last—I crawled into bed early with a new novel, *The Case of Miss Annie Spragge* and stretched out my toes luxuriously. "The longest day weareth to evensong."

We are having practices for the Sunday School concert and most discouraging play practices at Union—discouraging because an epidemic of flu is raging over there and several of the cast are missing every night because of illness.

The news that Mr. Alec Leask is dying of stomach cancer darkened this past week. Another of our good old Leaskdale friends gone.

But there was at least one delightful thing. The "Avonlea Institute"—composed of the Cavendish and North Rustico women—sent me as a Christmas present two water color paintings of Cavendish shore by Helen Hazard of Charlottetown. They are beautiful. And one is the view from the old "Watch-Tower" that I have loved so much all my life and could never get a picture of because it was too large for any camera I had. There is the sandshore with a wind blowing along it and the white-capped waves: the sea-run; a glimpse of Clark's pond; New London Harbour; *and* New London point with its revolving light, the old point of my childish dreams beyond which was the land of Lost Sunsets. Looking at the picture I can almost hear the heart-breaking call of the sea that has called for a thousand years.

The other picture is just turning around on the Watch Tower and looking east instead of west. My old home shore of red rock and surf-worn headland, Cawnpore—the Big Lane—Cape Leforce. The old shore where I played as a child, knowing every kink and curve and cove and rock of it.

I shall have the pictures framed and hung in the dining room where I can look at them whenever I eat. So shall soul be nourished as well as body.

Today has been, what is a rather rare thing here—an absolutely quiet and restful Sunday. No visitors—no callers. Some letters written—this old journal scribbled in—a book read at leisure. Such a Sunday rests me up for the week ahead and when I don't have it I miss it all the seven following days.

Sunday, Dec. 23, 1928
The Manse, Norval

As usual a busy crowded week. A trip to Hamilton Monday night—in a pouring rain—to have dinner with friends—a play practice at Union Tuesday night— rather discouraging because of the flu epidemic that is raging there—Mrs. Mason and I both with bad colds the rest of the week. And there have been sad things and worrying things—and a few wonderful moments that came Tuesday night when we returned from Union.

It was a windy night. I got out of the car at the garage and walked across the lawn to the side door where I paused for one of the rare splendid moments of life—which always come when we are not looking for them. The wind was singing in that garden of the wild gods up on the hill which prosaic people called "Russell's Pines." Its volume and surge seemed tremendous—as if the gods were veritably sweeping through it. And perhaps they were. *Some* spirit moved there; and my soul caught its call and I stood mute and rapt as in some vast temple of the night. I was born again: and life, that a few moments before had seemed a tawdry thing of shreds and patches became something more than "delicately balanced organic chemistry"—a march in the triumphal procession of the universes.

My love for pines has always been a very deep and vital and strange thing in my life. I say strange because there is nothing in my life—or *this* life—to account for it. There were no pines in my early home. Very few pines in P.E. Island at all. One or two each in the woods. Yet I always loved pines better than any other tree. And I wrote scores of poems about them; and now that I have come to live in a place that is rich in pines I find that those old poems were *true* and expressed the charm and loveliness of pine trees as well as if I had known pines all my existence. I came to them as no stranger but an old friend—"music aeolian of wind in the boughs of pine," "Sounds all soft and sonorous, Worshipful litanies sung at a bannered shrine"—I knew them all long long ago.

And Albert Macneill is dead. I feel this. An old family friend of whom I was always fond—who was always a part of the old Cavendish life....

The boys came home Thursday, with a good record in exams. Stuart leads his class, Chester is second and would likely have been first save for an accidental happening. It is *living* to have them home again. Stuart got a tree yesterday and is looking forward to Christmas.

But there is a shadow in my heart which I cannot share with anyone. Stuart casually mentioned when he came home that for a month back he "couldn't sleep well."

The words fell on my ear like clods on a coffin. Is it possible that Stuart has inherited his father's fatal taint and it is beginning to manifest itself, as it did with Ewan—at the approach of puberty?

I have never felt worried over Stuart. I *did* worry over Chester who is so like his father physically and tempermentally. But he has passed through the crisis with no trouble of this sort. Stuart is so like me and my father—joyous, healthy of outlook, full of fun and humor—that I have never thought of any danger of melancholia for him. Yet it is quite possible the taint may be there—his sole inheritance from his father's side. That would just be the sort of trick fate loves to play.

On the other hand it may just be that the strain of exams has made his brain a bit over-tired at night. He *does* sleep the latter part of the night—he just "can't go to sleep till late." Nevertheless, I shall not feel easy about him for several years. It is the only uneasiness he has ever given me, the dear boy. Since his birth he has been the sunshine and delight of my existence....

Sunday, December 30, 1928
The Manse, Norval
This has been a mixed week—something pleasant about it—a good deal unpleasant. Stuart was ill with flu Sunday and Monday, but able to be about Xmas and enjoy our scrumptious turkey dinner—some good friends having sent us in a huge turkey for Christmas. We haven't had turkey for a blue moon—not being millionaires. We had a nice Xmas. A pretty tree in which I was as much interested as Stuart. I *love* Christmas trees, all hung with colored balls and twinkling "icicles."

I spent Xmas afternoon reading *Strange Fugitive*—a much be-trumpeted novel by a new Canadian writer Morley Callaghan, who takes himself very seriously. Nora sent it to me for Xmas and I began to read it from interest—and forced myself to finish it because it was a gift. It was the deadliest dull thing I ever tried to read. Some "sex" novels are interesting and stimulating, whatever may be thought of their wisdom or unwisdom. But Callaghan's idea of "Literature" seems to be to photograph a latrine or pigstye meticulously and have nothing else in the picture. Now, latrines and pigstyes are not only malodorous but very uninteresting. We have a latrine in our backyard. I see it when I look that way—and I also see before it a garden of color and perfume—over it a blue sky—behind it a velvety pine caressing crystal air—a river of silver and aquamarine—misty hills of glamor beyond. These things are as "real" as the latrine and can all be seen at the same time. Callaghan sees nothing but the latrine and insists blatantly that you see nothing else also. If you insist on seeing sky and river and pine you are a "sentimentalist" and the truth is not in you.

Callaghan is no newly risen star. He is not even a meteor. Merely a Roman Candle shooting up sparkously and then sputtering out into darkness. He has neither vision, imagination nor insight. And he is deadly dull....

I had one bad day because of Chester this week. And I have to bear these things alone. Ewan, who is really a most pathetic futility as far as real fatherhood is concerned, is of no help to me. He hasn't the faintest idea how to train or direct or deal with an adolescent boy.

Stuart has seemed all right this week, though a little languid after the flu. He appears to be sleeping normally—something I am not doing and haven't done since my unlucky tumble down Union steps in November. I go to bed and lie awake for hours—seeing everything in the darkest hues, past present and future. After what seems a score of these ghostly hours I fall asleep for an hour or two and wake feeling that if a fairy gave me three wishes they would be 1. Sleep. 2. More sleep. 3. Still more sleep.

The mothers of this generation have a new terror. I realized this one day this week when Chester and Stuart both announced that as soon as they had a chance they were going to join a flying corps. Of course I said "Oh, no, you won't. It's too dangerous" as mothers have said all down the ages....But "what is to be will be." I have come to believe that, ever since that mysterious voice of four years ago....

One day this week I had two letters that weren't pleasant. Poor Ella, in a spasm of worry over what is to be done with the farm—Heath won't rent it again and everything is going down. *I* don't know. I've carried Park Corner on my back for ten years and helped them financially to the tune of thousands but I'm at my wit's end now. What advice to give her I don't know.

The other letter was from a fanatic "pacifist" in New Zealand who calls *Rilla of Ingleside* a "beastly book" because it "glorifies war." God rest her simple soul. Can't the poor moron realize the difference between offensive and defensive war. I wrote *Rilla* not to "glorify war" but to glorify the courage and patriotism and self-sacrifice it evoked. War is a hellish thing and some day it may be done away with—though human nature being what it is that day is far distant.

But universal peace *may* come and *may* be a good thing. But there will no longer be any great literature or great art. Either these things are given by the high gods as a compensation—or else they are growths that have to be fertilized with blood.

1929

1929. Nowadays when one says "the year one," it means 1901. When *I* was a girl "the year one" meant 1801. And I bethink me that I knew a woman who was born in the year one—old "Mrs. Jack" of Cavendish road. She was born in Scotland—and was fourteen years old when the battle of Waterloo was fought! It rather staggers me when I think that I have known a woman well who was a contemporary of Napoleon!

So far the New Year has been very like the old—crowded and hurried....

Sunday, February 24, 1929

....Since last September I have been too ill to work for *seven weeks*—adding them all together. Of course I know what the matter is—I am overworked and do not get enough sleep. And I cannot see any way out....

That Union play is riding me like a nightmare. Every practice night seems like a nightmare. I come home from it utterly discouraged, beaten, spent. The cast *will* not come till late—we never get underway before nine—the practice is never over till 12.30—then they must have lunch—and it is two when we get home. They are not taking the same interest in it as last year—two of the cast in particular are hopeless—dead, indifferent; and they cannot or will not learn their parts. One of them is an especial disappointment; everyone thought he would be good and I gave him a good part. He doesn't know it *at all* after a winter's practice. There is seldom a practice at which everyone is there. As soon as they have stumbled through their scene they rush off to the other room to play whist and "neck" until their cue comes again. Last Tuesday night my patience gave way. The practice was in the church basement. I was half-sick and terribly tired. My throat was sore; my head ached. And that group was simply fooling away the time. I threw down the book and said, "Young people, if you don't want to get up this play *I* don't. Suppose we drop the whole thing."

That woke them up. They had apparently thought my patience literally inexhaustible. I suppose it suddenly occurred to them that they would be the laughing stock of the community if they let the play drop now. They sobered up amazingly, decided to have two practices a week and get right down to work. A little late, I am afraid....

I stayed in bed till eleven next day—a very new thing for me when not actually sick. But the Barracloughs were coming in the afternoon to take us in to see *John Bull's Other Island* and I had to have some rest first. I rather enjoyed the excursion in spite of my languor and headache. The day was cold but brilliant, with fine faint blue shadows everywhere on the snow, and pleasant companions add much to a drive. Shaw's play was quite good but not nearly so good as *St. Joan* and the accent of the English cast made it difficult to follow the dialogue. We stopped at Cooksville on our way home and had dinner at a delightful little road house. If I had been well I would have enjoyed the day very much....

The boys were home for a week end two weeks ago. Stuart is sleeping all right again & seems all right. Chester spoiled the holiday for me by sulking because he could not get his own way over something.

Three weeks ago I was in Toronto and spent the night with Nora. I took in those old comic "diaries" we wrote while she was with us in Cavendish and we sat before her open fire and read them over—and laughed until we nearly cracked our ribs and the people in the flat below must have thought us drunk or mad. That was one of the two pleasant things of this past month. The other was the "Old Tyme Concert" the older members of the Guild put on in the parish hall three weeks ago. Everyone was supposed to wear an old-fashioned costume. I had none I could get into so I went to Malabar's in Toronto and hired one for the night—"a court costume of Mary Queen of Scots." Believe me, I made quite a sensation. It was a gorgeous affair. A skirt of crimson velvet trimmed with gold braid and ermine. A bodice of velvet with a "diamond" stomacher, square cut, with a lavish adornment of pearls, and loose hanging sleeves of yellow lace. *And* a ruff of lace, besprinkled with diamonds and edged with pearls. A devilish thing to wear but *so* becoming. I wore my hair high, with a sparkling little crown, and I really did look very well. I recited "Mary, Queen of Scots" and "Curfew must not ring tonight" for an encore.

It is curious—the effect clothes have on us psychologically. When I put on that dress I *was* Mary of Scotland—and I hated to put it off—in spite of the fact that its weight was simply tremendous. But it *felt* so rich and splendid and romantic. And it was *so* becoming. I really looked beautiful for once if never before or again. I wish I could have been photographed in it but that was impossible as the dress had to go back the next day.

We closed the programme with a tableau "Old Tyme wedding." Alice Lesley wore my wedding dress and veil and nobody would believe I had ever been so slender. I could not believe it myself....

Ewan, Mrs. Mason and I also had a dialogue which was very funny. But the whole affair has cost me a great deal of extra work and worry and has no doubt added to my present prostration. But really, the thrill I got out of "Mary" was worth it....

Sunday, March 3, 1929
The Manse, Norval, Ont.
So little that is of real interest in a diary occurs just now that an account of our recent fright—or *my* recent fright—over that proud and saucy and wholly delightful puss, Good Luck, may make a colorful page amid so many drab records of play practices and guild programs. For me these past three days have

been truly terrible—as any lover of cats will understand and as nobody else will or can understand.

On Thursday evening we were up at Arthur McClure's for supper and session meeting. Arthur's are renowned for the banquets they put up and this was no exception. We had as pleasant an evening as could be expected after such a repast and reached home at eleven. I found a note Mrs. Mason had left on the table to the effect that Luck had not come in.

Ordinarily I would not have worried over this. Luck occasionally stays out all night. He goes mousing in McPherson's barn in daytime when it is open, gets shut in there at night and can't get out till morning. Or he goes to sleep in our barn and doesn't wake up till the wee sma's. Then, if I have left a window open, I will likely be awakened by a soft body landing plumpo on my stomach and a vociferous purring proclaiming through the darkness that the prodigal has returned.

But Thursday night I *was* worried. Two weeks ago Luck came in one evening with a wire rabbit snare tight around his neck. He had evidently been caught in one but had been able to break it and escape. I have felt very uneasy ever since, for another time he might not succeed in getting loose. I asked Bob McPherson about it and he said he knew the Watson boys had rabbit snares out in the vacant lot beside their house and along the river bank, not only below their house but up along the West Branch. Now,

"'Good Luck,' 1929"

when Luck had not come home, I was anxious lest he had been again caught in a snare. So I took a flash-light, slipped down street and looked all over Watson's vacant lot but found neither cat nor snare. I plunged about in the soft snow till I was out of breath and came home gasping. I left the library window open and went to bed but slept very little, so haunted was I by visions of my poor beautiful pet gasping his life out in some cruel snare or already stiff and stark on the snow. No furry body came to me through the night. At six in the morning I got up, slipped down and out and crawled along the whole river bank below the manse and the houses down the street before anyone was astir. But I found nothing.

By noon I knew *something* was preventing Luck from coming because he would never stay away from home so long of his own accord. McPhersons searched their barns—both the one on the home place and the other on their vacant lot down in the corner where the West Branch runs into the Credit—but found no trace.

Mrs. Mason and I hunted the whole afternoon. We went to the school and asked the children if any of them had seen him. Several had—all in a different place. The story that seemed most likely was that of a small boy who said he had seen him about five Thursday evening—just about the time he had gone out—crossing the river on the ice in the direction of the hostel. Mrs. Mason went over to the hostel to inquire but no one there had seen him. The hostel was filled just then with a bevy of wild lads from Scotland and I feared lest Luck had fallen into their hands. The Watson boys visited all their snares and declared they were all empty and none missing. But when night came again with no Luck I gave up hope of ever seeing him again. The uncertainty was the worst. If I only *knew* what had happened him! But if he were dying by inches somewhere in torture!

I left the window open that night again and about three I heard fierce cater-wauls below stairs. I sprang up and rushed down—to find two strange tomcats singing hymns in the hall. A third one was sitting on the library window sill!

I told the school boys I would give a reward to anyone who brought me the cat alive or dead. Yesterday all the boys in Norval were out hunting him. They combed every barn and outhouse in the village and all the woods around. Every half hour a group would arrive with a cat for identification. I had not believed there were so many million gray cats in Norval. Or perhaps they did not have the cat but wanted me to go down to the mill to see if a certain cat there were Luck. I could not believe Luck had ever got so far down as the mill but go I would with a string of youngsters tailing along behind me, only to find when I got there some thin faded mangy animal Luck would never have forgiven me for calling a cat.

Even the grown-ups searched—and talked. Many assured me with a superior smile that Luck would turn up—cats always went away this time of year! And the smirk seemed to add, "Haven't you sense enough to know why?" Those who knew Luck was a neuter and never went courting had each a different—and comforting—theory of his disappearance. Bob McPherson continued to assert that he had been strangled in a snare—you couldn't believe a word the Watson boys said. If they found Luck dead in a snare they would hide his body and lie out of it. Mr. Gollop insisted the cat had been kidnapped—why, two days ago a strange car-load of people had tried to kidnap Mrs. Black's dog! The butcher was sure he had been poisoned—Clary Hunter had sworn he would poison any cat he caught near his pigeon barn. Miss McPherson thought he had been chased into the woods by a dog and probably mangled to death—the new miller had a big dog who had been seen chasing a mill cat. George Sharp thought Luck had been run over by a car and had dragged himself under some hedge to die. And Mrs. MacPerson was sure he had been drowned in some of the holes in the river left by ice men.

There was enough probability in all of these theories to torture me, especially the poisoning one. George Sharp's suggestion so wrought on my mind that after supper last night Mrs. Mason and I took our flashlights and searched painstak-ingly under all the hedges in the vicinity—a back-breaking task and a fruitless one. We returned to find the two tom-cats of the previous night on our veranda and a shifty-eyed boy—one of the Wylies—up at the radial hill—explaining that he had seen a gray cat—with a "Valentine" on his side—coming down the radial hill—that he had caught him—that the cat had bitten him and got away—and taken refuge under the mill. I was rather tired of hearing about gray cats but his description of the cat's markings was so like Luck's—whose markings are very odd and quite unlike every other cat I have ever seen—that a little hope did spring up in my despairing heart. But it was of no use going to the mill at that hour.

Then George Brown phoned up. *He* had a strange cat there—could it be mine? I went down—found a sleek gray pussy with entirely orthodox stripes and no resemblance whatever to Luck. I came home, tired and despairing. Luck was dead. I would never see him again. And on that note I went to bed, not to sleep, but to cry bitterly. My dear little puss—so beautiful, so charming, so loving. Such company—so entirely adorable. What fate had overtaken him? Was I never to see him coming to meet me across the lawn with what Mrs. Mason calls his "proud little walk?" Was I never again to find a round velvet ball curled up on my pillow?

Then I heard a commotion below stairs. I sprang up, threw on a negligée and ran down. Ewan and Mrs. Mason were there in a state of great excitement. Both declared they had seen Luck. Ewan had been walking about the library declaiming his sermon when he saw a strange cat peering in at the open window. He went towards it—it leaped out and disappeared—but on the pile of cordwood just outside the window was another cat. He recognized it as Luck—called Mrs. Mason who reached the window just in time to see the back of the cat as it leaped from the wood in wild pursuit of the fleeing Tom. But she vowed it was Luck's back—she would know it in a thousand. I could hardly believe it—but it cheered me up a bit and I went to bed and slept. But although the window was open all night there was still no Luck in the morning. I was sure they had been mistaken. Then Mrs. Williams appeared and said that a cat was shrieking at an upper window in the McPherson barn down by the Branch. We got Andrew McPherson who went over and unlocked the barn. Mrs. Mason went over and brought the cat home.

It was Luck!

But for a couple of hours I found it hard to believe it was Luck and not some cat-demon in his skin. He seemed mad with fright: did not recognize any of us—ran from me, tore round and round the house, tried to bolt head first through the library window—would not eat—would not rest. And to crown it all with a grotesque touch, flew over the furniture, lifting his tail ever few seconds and *squirting* over everything that happened to be near him!!!

Finally the devil departed from him. All at once his brief insanity was over and Luck was creeping up on my lap, purring and entreating with mild, imploring eyes for pardon and love.

There are some mysteries about it all which I suppose we will never solve.

If Luck had been shut up in the barn—which is really no "barn" but only a small building where McPhersons' keep a few hens—ever since Thursday it could not have been he Mrs. Mason saw last night. But I can't believe he *was* there. That barn was thoroughly searched and moreover the doors were left open all Friday and yesterday. Again if Luck got in there of his own accord—and Andrew M. says there is no opening where he *could* get in—why couldn't he get out the same way? And why was he so crazy when we did find him? In all his six years I never saw Luck behave like that.

On the other hand, if it were really Luck that Ewan and Mrs. M. saw on the woodpile where had he been and why didn't he come in as of old instead of getting into the barn and shrieking like a lost soul at the loft window? I have a theory which may be utterly false. The aforesaid Wylies live in a house up on the radial hill. They are new Irish and there are a lot of children. I believe they kidnapped Luck. Or he may even have chased some Tom-cat up the hill, though Luck never went so far away before. But he hates strange cats and it is possible that he pursued one so far. The Wylies may have captured him and kept him prisoner. Perhaps ill-treated him which would account for his dazed, crazy condition. Then when they heard of the reward the boy may have started to carry him home and Luck got away from him and took refuge under the mill, coming home after dark to find another hated stranger in his very shoes so to speak. This is the only explanation that fits all the facts, though it does not explain how or why Luck got into that tight-shut barn. But I believe he was the cat with the "valentine" on his side which the Wylie scion declared he found on the radial hill. The term exactly describes the odd heart-shaped mark with the letter M. inside it which is on both of Luck's sleek velvety sides.

Anyhow I have my dear puss back and I am a happy woman tonight. Luck is curled up on my lap, purring and looking at me with adoring eyes, in nothing like the frenzied creature that was tearing around here this morning.

Friday, March 8, 1929

I made a big fruit cake today—quite a job, especially the baking of it, which is half the trick in a fruit cake. But I think it turned out pretty well. Somehow, making fruit cake always makes me think of Grandma.

Once a year, in the fall, Grandmother made a big fruit cake, which always lasted the year out. It was quite an event. The evening before the fruit was prepared, Grandma washed the currants and I proudly stoned the raisins—for there were no "seeded" raisins for the buying in those days. Next morning "we" concocted the cake. Grandma brought out the spare-room washbasin, washed and scalded it very carefully and used it to mix the cake in with her bare hand—which is really the only way to mix a fruit cake properly. I helped beat eggs and hovered around watching everything with fascinated eye. When it was mixed completely the big cake pan with the peak up the middle was brought out, lined with greased brown paper and filled with the mixture. Invariably two little "patty pans" were filled also—"to see what the cake would be like"—but *they* were always given me to eat as soon as they were cooked. Meanwhile I could scrape out and eat what was left in the mixing bowl. Despite its uncooked condition it was delicious—so thick was it with fruit and so rich with spices. I really liked it much better than the finished product. I have never been very fond of fruit cake except when eaten with soda crackers to take its richness off. But it is always a comfort to my soul to know there is a great juicy, plummy, spicy fruit cake in my cellar box lest "unexpected company" come. My last fruit cake lasted three years and was even better at the end than at the beginning.

Sunday, March 31, 1929
The Manse, Norval

....This week has not been a pleasant week though I expected it to be with the boys coming home for the holidays as they did on Tuesday. Stuart looked very well, jubilant over leading his class of over 20—he made 100 in French and had an average of over 80—and anticipating a lovely holiday.

Thursday Ewan and Chester went to Toronto in the little Dodge coupe for which we recently traded our old Dodge touring-car. On the way home just after leaving Dixie they saw a large sedan coming rapidly towards them. Just as it came up to them it suddenly without the least warning turned and dashed right over to their side of the road, collided with our car, knocked off a fender and a tire and bent one of the wheels two double at the axle, wrenched off one of its own wheels and then hurtled into the ditch. Luckily our car was not ditched and nobody was hurt....The driver of the car was a young man who, when he scrambled out of the ditch, couldn't explain what had happened at all. When I heard it I said he was probably drunk but the men say he was not. The only other explanation is that he had momentarily fallen asleep. His name was Woodbridge and he handsomely acknowledged that all the blame was his and that he would see that our car was put into the shape it was before and pay all expenses. Chester and Ewan got home in a friend's car, none the worse for their nasty experience. It shook me up a bit when I realized what a narrow escape they had had.

Then Friday night Stuart took ill with sore throat and was in bed all yesterday and today. I felt uneasy for scarlet fever is in Norval and a sore throat is one of its symptoms. So as he was no better tonight I had the doctor who said that Stuart had tonsillitis and that his tonsils were badly enlarged and should be taken out!!! So that's that....

Sunday, April 7, 1929
The Manse, Norval

....The only really pleasant thing in the week was our visit to Barracloughs this evening. And on the way home Stuart nestled up to me and said "I'm glad you're pretty, mother, and don't have to *make up your face* like other women."

We never lose our liking for a compliment! And besides, I haven't had one of that sort for a donkey's age.

Friday, May 3, 1929
The Manse, Norval

After housecleaning ferociously for a month we have finished and I shall now give up thinking housecleaning and think daffodils. The interval since my last entry has been as usual full of hard work, several pinpricks and some delights.

One of the pinpricks was a letter from Ella with an account of her troubles and worries, of which she always has enough, poor soul. She wants Dan to come home and take the farm and he doesn't want to. I do not think he would ever succeed as a farmer but I have been hoping Jim would feel like taking hold of it when he grew up. But Jim it seems doesn't want to farm—wants to go in a bank. If so—good-bye Park Corner. I cannot bear to think of it. I have tried in every way since George's death to hold that place together until one of the boys could take it and run it. But it evidently shares the curse that has always been over every spot I've loved. It must be torn away from me and pass into the hands of strangers. I feel as if it would kill me to see Park Corner pass thus. That beautiful old place which in childhood and girlhood seemed more of a real home to me than the old homestead in Cavendish!

Poor Uncle John and Aunt Annie, who loved it so and worked so hard there! Is that all to go for naught? I suppose *I* have loved it too much. It does not do to love anything too much in this world. God *is* a jealous God!

I have come to the time of life where I can rarely pick up a paper without seeing the death notice of someone I knew. Last Tuesday I read of the death of Fulton Simpson. Alf told me when he was here last fall that Fulton had a very serious form of heart trouble. How the ghosts of old passions arose when I read that notice! That dreadful spring in Belmont. That agony and humiliation! Those embarrassing capers of Fulton's all winter! What tragedy and comedy mixed up together!...

In reading one of George Eliot's books recently I came across the description of a set of china—"the best white fluted china with gold sprays on it." And I remembered Grandmother's set—the "best set" of my childhood, "fluted, with gold sprays on it." I thought it wonderful then—I think it beautiful still, quite as beautiful as any modern design. I gave that set to Aunt Emily and kept the brown set. I wish I had reversed it. I liked the brown set better because Grandma had said she bought it for me. But now I think very longingly and lovingly of that old fluted set....

Stokes' catalogue came today with the ad of *Marigold*. My fifteenth book. I feel very indifferent about it. Somehow I did not love writing it as I loved writing the *Blue Castle* and the *Emily* books. But that may have been because so much of it had been written before as short stories for the *Delineator*. It seemed like warming up cold soup.

I am working now on an adult story, centering around the old Woolner jug. But so far my heart isn't in it either. But I *have* a good idea for a story—one that really appeals to me—and I hope to write it when I get the present one off my hands.

I had an odd clipping sent me the other day, from an Australian paper—a girl's account of an "imaginary interview" with L.M. Montgomery. I should say it was imaginary. She pictures me as "tall and stately," with red hair and freckles like Anne!!

Sunday, May 12, 1929

....I was over at the Agricultural College at Guelph Friday night speaking to an audience of five hundred students or so. It is a beautiful place and I was haunted all the time by Frede at my elbow. She took a short course there once and wrote me all about it. So the two are linked in my memory and I thought she must be somewhere around....

When I was waiting in the radial station for the car to Guelph I was mentally and almost physically sickened at the vile obscenities that were scribbled all over the walls. I never read anything like them even in the old outbuildings of country schools—where, heaven knows, they were bad enough. What sort of animal is it who can write such stuff?...

Thursday, June 6, 1929
The Manse, Norval
Miss Stuart of Guelph was here to tea this afternoon—an old friend of Frede's whom I met when I was at St. Anne's just after Frede's marriage. We talked of her the whole afternoon—vivid, unforgettable Frede....

The garage man across the street has put a radio with a loud speaker in his garage. As a result the village is flooded with jazz music night and day. As I lie in bed at night the last thing I hear is jazz. The first thing I hear in the morning is jazz—curiously recalling the old prediction in *Looking Backward* of the man who was wakened in the morning by music. I am fond neither of radios nor jazz. But at this distance it is not unpleasing. Yesterday afternoon I weeded the garden to the accompaniment of music that came from New York and found it rather romantic and mysterious.

Tuesday, June 11, 1929
Had a nasty fright today. A ring at the door-bell—a neighbor gasping "The church sheds are on fire"—wild confusion—ringing up the Georgetown fire brigade—men running with ladders—frenzied snatching at pails and pans—anything that would hold water—a very bad twenty minutes—then safety.

Mrs. Mason had been burning paper in the vacant lot—a careless thing to do on a windy day. A bit of paper must have blown to the roof of the shed—the high wind and baking hot shingles did the rest. Luckily the aforesaid neighbor saw it as soon as it started or I turn sick to think of what might have happened....

Tuesday, June 18, 1929
The Manse, Norval
"The world of beauty is in deep distress"—Bliss Carman is dead. I feel a sense of personal bereavement. He always seemed to me like a survival from the Golden Age. In his youth he looked like a god. Yet he is dead and his music is silenced with him....

I have been re-reading *The Sentimental Garden*. The pictures in it drive me wild with envy—and *homesickness*. Homesickness for an old dream that will never be fulfilled. For *that* is the garden I have always wanted and can never have....

Tonight I re-read William Wilfred Campbell's "Mother" and recalled my ecstasy on first reading it when I was a child or very young girl and it appeared in—I think—the old *Summerside Journal*. Young as I was I felt when reading it as if I were pasturing in some divine field of starry air.

Thursday, June 27, 1929
The Manse, Norval
I wonder what it would be like not to have to "catch up" with anything.

Chester came home Monday. Tonight a Mrs. Brown, who was formerly a Miss Wilkie called. She was a friend of Frede's in that year at Red Deer. So the old wound was torn open afresh.

I am having a miniature of myself painted by a Miss Wrenshall of Toronto and go in every two weeks for a sitting. I was in today. It is interesting. I was amused to hear her say today, "You must have been a *very* beautiful girl, Mrs. Macdonald."

I wonder! I had the reputation of being pretty. But beautiful is another thing. I hardly think I could claim to be that. Miss Wrenshall also informed me that the fact that the Montgomerys originally came to Scotland from France probably accounts for the "scintillating" quality in my face—which she hopes she can get into the picture.

But maybe it's the Irish. I'm a queer mixture racially—the Scotch Macneills, the English Woolners and Penmans, the Irish of Mary McShannon (Hugh Montgomery's wife) and that far-off French descent....

Sunday, July 14, 1929
The Manse, Norval
Tonight I had a divine half hour when my soul was filled and satisfied with beauty, desiring nothing else.

I was alone in the manse, reading Herodotus. (I think I would have liked Herodotus very much, by the way. He is really an old duck.) I slipped up the street in the magic hour of mingled twilight and moonshine, through a gate in Mr. Leslie's back fence and across Russell's pasture up to the hill of pines. There I roamed for an exquisite space that was only half an hour by the clock but which seemed a sort of lifetime by some other computation. The lingering hues of a wonderful sunset were still staining the sky over the dark pine hill west of me. Lights of unending cars were swooping jewel-like down the Branch hill. Silence seemed to come through the pines to me like a Real Presence—hovering, enfolding, blessing. Those great tall trees around me were my brothers—my older wiser brothers. I stood for many minutes by one of them, my arm around it, my face pressed to it, breathing a prayer to the God of Beauty I have always served—a new re-consecration to Him. Fresh from Herodotus, I feel like the priestess of an oracle under her sacred pines. The Past was the Present. Frede came to me there—and a man I once loved kissed me again.

When I came reluctantly away I said, "This Sunday at least, has been a *holy* day for me." I felt rested—recreated. I shall sleep tonight. The utter calm of that grove has possessed my soul and given me rest.

There is a knoll in that grove where I would I could build me a tiny study and go there to write with the great dark silent pine-brothers all around me. Just one little room where no one could enter but myself. It is but a dream.

It is a real regret and disappointment to me that neither Stuart nor Chester seems to possess one spark of my love for and power of communion with the beauty of Nature. Ewan has not a gleam of it but I had hoped I might have given of it to my sons—because it is such a boon to those who have it. But perhaps they will not need it—perhaps it is given only to those who will need it. There have been many times when I could not have endured life without this power. And I would not exchange it for *any* earthly happiness or gift!

Friday, July 19, 1929
The Manse, Norval
I had to go to our Sunday School picnic in Stanley Park today. Couldn't get out of it. But for once I refused to be bored. I took two books along with me—Herodotus and *Tish Plays the Game*. I shut myself up in our car under the pines and read the whole afternoon. Had a gorgeous time! A chapter of Herodotus and a chapter of *Tish* turn about. It was like alternate bites of ham sandwich and ice cream—only you don't bite ice cream. Anyway, this atrocious literary mixture was capital. I laughed so much over *Tish* that the tears streamed down my face.

Wednesday, July 24, 1929
Today Chester started work in O'Neill's garage at Georgetown. He is to be there for a month. This was my idea. I wanted Chester to learn all he can about cars since he is now driving them. I had hard work to bring it to pass. Chester opposed it because he seems to have a dread of anything new—and Ewan, I think, just because I proposed it. But finally I have got Chester persuaded to try it. There is nothing here to occupy his time and a boy of his age with nothing to do is apt to get into mischief.

"Pat [Aylsworth] & Chester"

Sunday, July 28, 1929
This has been anything but a day of rest. The heat has been dreadful and my nerves have been bad. We had a houseful of company—Mrs. Mason's friend Jean Leslie, the minister who was supplying for Ewan who is away on vacation, and Donald Campbell.

Dan has been down home for a visit and is on his way back to Los Angeles. He is a good-looking chap with a pleasant personality. But there is a little too much of his father in him to please me. Happy-go-lucky—let-the-other-fellow-worry type.

Tuesday, August 6, 1929

Last Monday night came a very horrible experience—which might so easily have been much more horrible that it gives me a "grue" to think of it.

After supper I asked Chester to take us all for a drive so he did. He and Dan on the front seat—Mrs. Mason, Jean, Helen and I behind. We took a long rambling drive and enjoyed it. And finally on the home stretch came to the village of Erin.

As we approached I said to Chester, who was speeding along at a thirty-five mile clip, "Chester, slow down going through Erin. There are always children about."

Chester accordingly slowed down and went through Erin, or a part of it, at about fifteen per....

Half way through we saw an old—a very old—frail, bent man come out from a yard with a pail of water in either hand, apparently about to cross the street. Chester blew the horn loudly and the old man stopped so we went on. Then at the very last moment he dashed across the street right in front of us. Chester jammed on the brakes at once and the car stopped but not before the fender had struck the old man. Down he went, out of sight, and at the same moment a shower of drops flew over me. Sick with horror I thought, "We've killed him—this is his blood."

Somehow we got out. The old man was laying face down on the road in a horrible limp little heap. He looked as if every bone in his body was broken. I saw everything in a moment of horror. Poor Chester just at the beginning of his driving career had killed a man—the tale would spread abroad—nobody would ever believe that he had not been driving recklessly—there would be no end of talk and scandal—suits for damages (though the thought of insurance was a shield and buckler against this thrust) perhaps even an arrest, certainly an inquest!

Meanwhile Chester and Dan had turned the poor old chap over. He opened a bleary eye and feebly said, "Where is my hat?" Not all the tongues of men and angels ever uttered a sentence sweeter in my ears. He was not dead. But was he injured? The usual crowd had collected as by magic. The men carried Mr. McCaig—as we discovered his name to be—into his house. His wife met them at the door saying drearily "Well, I've been expecting this right along." Meanwhile I stood shaking against the fence. An elderly man came up to me. "Now, lady, don't you go worrying over this. We all saw the accident and it was all that old fool's own fault. He oughtn't to be out on the street alone anyhow—he's been childish for years. I guess if you *had* killed him his wife would feel relieved—he's been an awful trouble to her. She can't keep him off the street."

This was all very well. But I did not want Chester to kill a man just to save his wife from worry. And even though it was all his own fault that would not prevent me from feeling that we had all committed murder, if we had killed him. Another man said to me, "That boy of yours ought to have a gold medal for the way he handled that car. I never saw anyone stop a car so quick."

I thought the doctors would never come. When they did they were nearly an hour examining him. Then they came out and said that as far as they could see he was absolutely uninjured except for a very slight concussion which would pass off in a few hours. Then for the first time since that hideous moment I breathed—at least that is how it seemed to me!

Eventually we got away and came home. All of us knew we could not sleep so we spent most of the night making a table rap and doing stunts in the parlor—laughing a great deal with the hysterical mirth of people who have just been through an abnormal strain.

"If you had not made me slow down, mother, we'd have been through Erin long before the old fellow came out with his pails of water," said Chester.

Which was true. But it was written!

We got word today that Mr. McCaig is as well as ever. But this shock has not helped my nerves any.

The next night...I went to see—or hear—a "talkie." The first third I did not like it—the effort to hear what was being said interfered with my enjoyment of the picture. Then I suddenly found it easy to hear and enjoyed the rest. But I doubt if I shall ever like the "talkies" as well as the silent pictures. I like "legitimate" drama, and I like a good picture but I do not care for the mixture.

New inventions crowd on each other's heels—each more amazing than the last. But the trouble is—no one is happier or better because of them.

Notes

N.B. In the following notes, Lucy Maud Montgomery Macdonald is referred to as LMM. *The Selected Journals of L.M. Montgomery* (Volume I, Toronto: Oxford University Press, 1982; Volume II, Toronto: Oxford University Press, 1985) are referred to as *SJLMM*.

1921

April 8 GROTE. LMM's earlier journals record her reading of George Grote's study of Greek legends and history, published 1846-56, in 1914; she began her current re-reading in January 1921. EWAN. LMM's husband, the Reverend Ewan Macdonald (1870-1943), had been minister at Leaskdale and Zephyr Presbyterian churches since 1910. **April 12** "PREMONITIONS". Published in *Canadian Magazine*, November 1921, p. 72. UXBRIDGE. 7 miles south of Leaskdale, 35 miles north-east of Toronto. Population in 1921 was 1,456. MR. [Herbert] BENNIE (1887-1953). Rev. H.L. Bennie, educated in Dublin and Glasgow, held the joint charge of Chalmers Church, Uxbridge, and St. Andrew's Church, Quaker Hill, 1921-1924. MR. FRASER. Rev. James R. Fraser, M.A., held the charge in Chalmers Presbyterian Church, Uxbridge, 1898-1921. FREDE. LMM's cousin and beloved friend, Frederica Campbell MacFarlane (1883-1919). COLUMBUS AND BROOKLYN. Ontario hamlets, about 5 miles apart, each 20 miles south-east of Leaskdale and north of Whitby and Oshawa. THE MODERATOR. The Lindsay Presbytery (consisting of a minister and an elder from each church in the region) would elect one of its members as Moderator to direct regional church affairs for the year. LEET. List of candidates preaching for a call to a Presbyterian church. ZEPHYR. A hamlet 5 miles west of Leaskdale. Zephyr Presbyterian church was held as a joint charge by the minister of St. Paul's, Leaskdale. WHITBY. A town on Lake Ontario, incorporated 1855, about 25 miles east of downtown Toronto. SUBCONSCIOUS MIND. Intellectual capacity beneath the threshold of consciousness. Theories of repression, the sublimation of subconscious impulses, and the uses of psychoanalysis had been published in Sigmund Freud's major works, translated by Brill into English between 1912 and 1918; Carl Jung's *Collected Papers on Analytical Psychology*, translated by C.E. Long, in 1917. The topic of psychotherapy, not present in the 1911 edition of the *Encyclopedia Britannica*, was discussed at length in the 1922 edition. PINKERTON AND PRICEVILLE. Two Ontario villages around 150 miles northwest of Toronto, in the direction of Owen Sound and the Bruce Peninsula. MAY SINCLAIR (1865-1946). A prolific popular English novelist. LMM mentions *Mary Oliver: A Life* (London: Cassell, 1919) and *The Romantic* (London: Collins, 1920), a novel set in the 1914-18 war: Sinclair had served in a field ambulance unit in Belgium. AMELIA; JANE EYRE. In W.M. Thackeray's *Vanity Fair* (1848), gentle Amelia Sedley contrasts with ambitious, unscrupulous Becky Sharp; in Charlotte Brontë's *Jane Eyre* (1847), the plain, intense heroine endures hardship as orphan and as governess. **April 17** LILY. Lillian Meyers, daughter of John R. and Lillian Meyers of Zephyr, had come to work as a maid at the Leaskdale manse March 1, 1918, replacing her sister Edith Meyers Lyons. **April 21** THE BOYS. LMM's two sons, Chester Cameron Macdonald, aged 8 in April 1921, and Ewan Stuart Macdonald, aged 5. "THE TIGER IN THE HOUSE". Current novel (New York: Knopf, 1920) by prolific and popular Carl Van Vechten (1880-1964). BUBASTIS. Graecized name of the Egyptian goddess Ubasti: a mild feline goddess with the head of a tigress. **May 1** LONDON. An Ontario city, 70 miles west of Toronto. MRS. DR. HUGHES. Lillie, wife of Dr. Frank W. Hughes, physician and professor at University of Western Ontario, was president of the London Women's Canadian Club 1923-1926. The form of reference recalls a P.E.I. localism used by "Susan Baker" in *Rainbow Valley*: "Mrs. Dr. dear". MRS. MACGREGOR ("MARIAN KEITH"). Mary Miller MacGregor (1876-1961) had published her first novel *Duncan Polite* in 1905. Her new novel was *Little Miss Melody* (Toronto: McClelland, 1921). MISS WILSON ("ANISON NORTH"). May Wilson had just published *The Forging of the Pikes*, a romance of 1837 (New York: Doran, 1920). LONDON CANADIAN CLUB. The Women's Canadian Club had been founded in 1907 to introduce speakers on current social and intellectual topics. The London branch was established in 1910. GIRLS' CANADIAN CLUB. Established 1920 as a junior branch. GRACE BLACKBURN (1865-1928). Columnist and reviewer in the *London Free Press*, writing under the pseudonym "Fan-Fan"; had published poetry, mostly 1898-1902. She was the aunt of the owner of the Free Press. WOMAN'S PRESS CLUB. The Canadian Women's Press Club, founded in 1904. LMM had been vice-president of the Toronto branch in 1912. (The name of the club was changed in 1971 to the Media Club.) TORONTO. Capital city of Ontario, 60 miles southwest of Leaskdale; centre for shopping, entertainment, and post-secondary education for southern Ontario. CHEVROLET; GRAY-DORT. The Chevrolet car was manufactured in Oshawa, Ontario. The Gray-Dort automobile was manufactured in Chatham, Ontario; the Macdonalds' new car boasted white-walled tires with hand-polished wooden spokes and Spanish leather upholstery. **May 8** CAPTAIN [Edwin] SMITH. This long-time friend, four years younger than Ewan Macdonald, had been a Presbyterian minister before the War. He had a distinguished war record, fought at the Battle of Jutland, but returned from war with "shaken nerves". In Whitby, between 1920 and 1924 he acted as fill-in minister for Rev. Edward Turkington and also sold insurance. LADIES' COLLEGE. The Ontario Ladies' College at Whitby, founded in 1874, for young women aged 16-21; it specialized in vocal and instrumental music, domestic science, and arts. The school name was changed in 1979 to Trafalgar Castle School. LMM's lecture was reported in the Whitby *Gazette* and *Chronicle*. SCOTT'S "BETROTHED" (1825). The heroine, out of gratitude, becomes affianced to an older man, though she secretly loves his younger nephew. TRILLIUMS. A white three-petalled wildflower, the provincial emblem of Ontario. **May 11** STOKES. The Frederick A.

Stokes Company had become the American publisher of LMM's books with *Anne's House of Dreams* (1917). Stokes had granted reprint rights for this book to A.L. Burt of New York; the L.C. Page Co. meanwhile licensed Grosset & Dunlap to reprint the same book. This "fraudulent licensing" was one of the two points on which LMM sued Page in 1919. "THE NEW MOON SERIES". The first "Emily" book was begun in 1920, published as *Emily of New Moon* in 1923; the others in the series are *Emily Climbs* (1925) and *Emily's Quest* (1927). **May 16** ANOTHER ATTACK. Ewan Macdonald had been subject to severe depressions since adolescence. In the summer of 1919 he had consulted nerve specialists in Boston. MELANCHOLIA. Identified as a disease for centuries, melancholia was classified in the 1920s as a mild form of insanity, manifested by eating and sleeping disorders, memory loss, impairment of body functions, thought processes, common sensibility, ability to enjoy life, and in the case of religious melancholia, delusions of sin and unworthiness, and a tendency to commit suicide. STELL. Stella Campbell Keller (1879-1955), second oldest of the Campbell cousins of Park Corner, five years younger than LMM. *Emily Climbs* is dedicated to Stella. **May 18** QUAKER HILL. St. Andrew's Presbyterian Church was located at the north end of Quaker Hill, a rural area about 7 miles south of Leaskdale, just west of Uxbridge. THE MILLERS. The Rev. Thomas O. Miller (1869-1963) ended his 12-year ministry at Quaker Hill in 1921; after this the minister of Chalmers Presbyterian in Uxbridge also served the Quaker Hill parish. **May 31** NEIGHBORS: As a Maritimer, and as a writer for American publishers, LMM had habitually used the American spelling of this and other "-or" words. After moving to Ontario and transferring to the Canadian publisher McClelland, Stewart and Goodchild, she adopted the "-our" suffix form. Here she reverts to American usage. **June 16** MRS. JAKE MEYERS. Janet Brooks Meyers, wife of "Red Jake", farmer and Road Superintendent for Scott township. The Meyers family, of Mennonite background, lived one mile south-west of Zephyr. Mrs. Meyers' brother Robert Brooks, who was killed overseas in WW I (1918), was one of the three young soldiers to whose memory LMM dedicated *Rainbow Valley* (1919). MARSHALL PICKERING (1859-1930). Pillar of the Methodist Church in Zephyr: in 1886 Marshall Pickering had been on the building committee for the church (built on land once held by his father, Thomas, a pioneer farmer who had come from England in the 1850s). MRS. PICKERING. Mr. Pickering had been married twice. In 1921, his wife was the former Sarah Raham; his two daughters Flora and Cora were children of the first marriage. MRS. LAW. Edith Rebecca Mann, wife of W.O. Law, Ford dealer in Zephyr. **July 3** PRINCE'S "DISASSOCIATION OF A PERSONALITY". Dr. Morton Prince (1854-1929) published this biographical study in abnormal psychology (New York: Longmans, Green, 1906). He also wrote *Psychotherapeutics* (1910) and *The Unconscious* (1914) as part of a general popularizing of pre-Freudian theories, exploring the reality of "secondary selves". "HUMAN PERSONALITY AND ITS SURVIVAL OF BODILY DEATH" (1903). F.W.H. Myers' polemic on subliminal consciousness, summarizing the tenets of the British Society for Psychical Research, revived in popularity after WW I. **August 11** BRAINTREE. A village in Massachusetts, 9 miles south of Boston city centre. FLORA. Ewan's elder half-sister, Mrs. Amos Eagles of Braintree; in 1919

LMM stayed with her during the Boston law suit, and again while consulting Boston specialists about Ewan's mental health. QUINCY; WEYMOUTH. Massachusetts towns south of Boston. PORTLAND. A major seaport in Maine, about 120 miles north of Boston. BELFAST, BUCKSPORT FERRY, ELLSWORTH. Villages on Penobscot Bay, 85-100 miles north of Portland. ST. STEPHENS, NEW BRUNSWICK. Canadian border town, across the St. Croix river from Calais, Maine: about 125 miles north of Ellsworth. CAPE TORMENTINE. The point in the southeast corner of New Brunswick from which ferries crossed the Northumberland Straits to Prince Edward Island. ST. JOHN. Saint John, New Brunswick, a seaport-city on the Bay of Fundy; SACKVILLE. Near the neck of land between New Brunswick and Nova Scotia; the site of Mount Allison University. BREADALBANE. Prince Edward Island village where Rev. John Stirling was Presbyterian minister. He had performed the marriage ceremony for LMM and Ewan in 1911. Margaret Ross Stirling was a long-time friend of LMM's. (See *SJLMM* II, 8-9.) MARY CAMPBELL [Beaton]. A second cousin who shared boarding-house lodgings with LMM while at Prince of Wales College, Charlottetown. Her daughter Maud was named after LMM. WINSLOE. A village northwest of Charlottetown, in the direction of Cavendish. ALEC MACNEILL (1870-1951). A second cousin, brother of LMM's school friend Pensie. MYRTLE (Macneill). Mrs. Ernest Webb: her mother was the girl brought up by David and Margaret Macneill, the elderly brother and sister who lived in the house now known as Green Gables. PARK CORNER. On the north shore west of Cavendish, home of the Campbell cousins. AUNT ANNIE (Campbell). Sister of Clara Macneill Montgomery, LMM's mother. DAN (Donald Campbell). Son of George Campbell who had been Aunt Annie's only son. DR. AND MRS. MAHONEY. As a teacher, LMM had boarded with Mrs. Mahoney's parents in the Methodist parsonage at Bideford, P.E.I., 1894-5. "SONSY". Scotticism: healthy, plump, cheerful. COPYING MY OLD JOURNAL. In winter 1919 LMM had begun copying earlier diaries into volumes of uniform size, resolving to copy "exactly as it is written" but adding illustrations from her photograph collection. She was now working on Volume 3 of the recopied journals. **August 17** MR. ROLLINS. Weld Allen Rollins (1874-1952), educated at Dartmouth and Harvard, specialized in corporate law and included General Motors among his clients. LMM had been referred to him by B.H. Stern, Counsel to the Authors' League of America. Rollins had successfully pleaded LMM's first case against Page in 1919 when she sued the publisher for $1000 in withheld royalties, and for giving reprint rights to Grosset & Dunlap without her permission. In 1920 Rollins took on her second suit, when Page published *Further Chronicles of Avonlea* against her wishes. THE MASTER. The judicial expert to whom LMM's case against Page was referred for adjudication: Henry LeBaron Sampson acted as Master in 1920. THE PAGES. Lewis Coues Page (1869-1956) and George Page (1871-1927) were the sons of a distinguished Civil War journalist, later U.S. consul to Switzerland. Both graduated from Harvard and joined Estes and Lauriat, their stepfather's publishing company. Lewis left to join Joseph Knight Co., then in 1897 established his own firm, L.C. Page & Co., which eventually took over both the Knight and the Estes firms. George joined Lewis in directing the company. THE PAGE SUIT AGAINST ME. In May 1920 the Page Company had countered LMM's suit by suing her for libel in "malicious litigation". FRENCH. Asa Palmer French (1860-1935), the lawyer representing the Pages from 1920 on, was a former District Attorney for the District of Massachusetts and U.S. Attorney for the same District. SUPREME COURT. Pages' countersuit against LMM, for malicious litigation, first heard and dismissed in the Massachusetts Supreme Judicial court, could be appealed in the United States Supreme Court. **August 18** MCCLELLAND. John McClelland (1888-1951) co-founder with Frederick Goodchild of McClelland & Goodchild, 1906. George Stewart's name was added to the firm in 1914, and in 1918 Goodchild resigned. RILLA. The wartime novel, *Rilla of Ingleside*, concerned the activities of families on the home front. Rilla is the youngest child of LMM's major heroine, Anne Shirley Blythe. HODDER AND STOUGHTON. London firm which published the British edition of *Rilla of Ingleside* in 1921. CONSTABLE. Published the British edition of *Anne's House of Dreams* 1917. HATTIE HARRISON. The Harrison forebears, George and his wife Harriet Oxtoby Harrison, had settled in the Township in 1849; theirs was the fourth farm north of Leaskdale. **August 20** *EMILY OF NEW MOON*. The new heroine, like Anne an orphan, lives with unsympathetic relations; her obsessive sense of a literary vocation is stronger than Anne's. **September 11** CANNINGTON. A village between Leaskdale and Wood-ville, to the north-east. THE KENNEDYS. The Kennedys had come to Scott Township in the 1870s and farmed on the Uxbridge-Leaskdale Line. W.M.S. Women's Mission Society, founded 1825 in Prince Edward Island. By 1921 the Society supported work among Indians, hospitals and school-homes in the West, and educational centres in French districts. DR. SHIER. Walter Shier, M.D., son of Leaskdale area farmer James Shier, had an office on Main Street, Uxbridge. His brother had married Lily Reid, a young widow who had served in the Leaskdale manse as maid, 1912-15. VITAMINES. The term was coined in 1912 by German physiologist Casimir Funk in the mistaken belief that amino acid was the essential element in life-enhancing dietary substances. In 1921 three vitamins had been isolated: anti-scorbutic C, water-soluble B, and fat-soluble A. **October 1** WARSAW. A city in Indiana, 50 miles south-west of Fort Wayne, a 400-mile trip from Leaskdale. DR. [John] SCHOFIELD FROM KOREA. A retired missionary, on the supplementary roll of Sarnia Presbytery. UNCLE LEANDER. A distinguished Nova Scotia clergyman, Rev. Leander Macneill was brother of LMM's mother Clara Macneill Montgomery. REVIEWS OF "RILLA". Among favourable early reviews was one in the *New York Times Book Review and Magazine*, Sept. 11, 1921, and one in the Toronto *Globe*, Oct. 1, 1921. LMM subscribed to a clipping service. **October 3** *HOUSE OF DREAMS; RAINBOW VALLEY*. The royalties from *Anne's House of Dreams* (1917) were $3,903 in 1920, $1,130 in 1921; from *Rainbow Valley* (1919) they were $11,968 in 1920, $543 in 1921. LMM had no royalties from her earlier novels in these years because of the way her first suit against Page had been settled: in January 1919 she had accepted $17,880 in return for all rights to the books of hers published by L.C. Page Co. DEPRESSION. In 1921 industry in all branches declined in output because of lack of foreign demand, manpower depleted by war, and industrial disputes. Canada's net debt was $363,000,000 before the war; in 1920 it had risen to $2,248,868,623, because of war expenditures and huge advances

to Britain which could not be repaid. PRINTERS' STRIKES. 1921 saw the largest
number of industrial disputes leading to strikes or lockouts since 1912. **October
7** RICHARD OXTOBY. The Oxtoby homestead lay behind the Leaskdale manse.
EMULSION OF COD LIVER OIL. Cod-liver oil was a prime source of vitamin A. In
emulsion flavoured with malt extract the unpleasant taste was masked. **October
18** "[Old] GRANNY FOX". One of the "Green Meadow" series of bedtime stories
by Thornton Burgess (1874-1965) first published Boston: Lathrop, 1920.
MCCARTHY. Justin McCarthy, politician and novelist, published his Victorian history in 1877. **October 21** BIBLE SOCIETY COLPORTEUR. A book-hawker employed
by the Society to sell Bibles. The British and Foreign Bible Society, founded in
1804, did vigorous work in British colonies; the American Bible Society, established in 1816, had sold over 80,000,000 volumes by 1900. "TALMAGE'S SER-
MONS". The American Thomas De Witt Talmage (1832-1902), world-famous
dramatic preacher; his most famous published collections of sermons were
Everyday Religion (1875) and *The Pathway of Life* (1895). "PANSY BOOK".
"Pansy" was the pseudonym of Isabella Macdonald Alden (1841-1930), author
of pious, sentimental books for girls, including *Ruth Erskine's Crosses* (Boston:
Lathrop, 1879); *Judge Burnham's Daughters* (Boston: Lathrop, 1888). **October
24** A SHORT STORY. "White Magic" appeared in *Women's Century*, June, 1921.
"ONE OF THE FINEST". "Each in His Own Tongue", first published in *The Delineator*, 1910, received particular praise from reviewers when republished in
Chronicles of Avonlea (1912). **November 17** CANADIAN BOOK WEEK. Established
by the Canadian Authors' Association in 1921 as a device for publicizing Canadian authors and publishers. **November 18** 2 NINA AVENUE. The home of Norman
and Mary Beal, friends formerly of Uxbridge who had moved to Toronto in
1913. AUTHORS' ASSOCIATION. On March 12, 1921, a literary dinner was held in
Montreal, organized by Stephen Leacock, Murray Gibbon, B.K. Sandwell, Pel-
ham Edgar, and others to form a Canadian Authors' Association, discuss copyright and licensing laws, establish *The Canadian Bookman* and a Canadian Book
Week. LMM attended the first meeting of the Toronto branch of the Association. NELLIE MCCLUNG (1872-1951). The feminist author of *Sowing Seeds in
Danny* (1908) and other best-selling novels was on a speaking tour of Canada
and Great Britain in 1921. ARTS AND LETTERS CLUB. Founded in 1908 for people
professionally involved and also those interested in the arts, this men's club had
recently moved from 57 Adelaide to 14 Elm Street. The Canadian Authors'
Association held their early meetings at the club. BASIL KING (1859-1928). Since
1911, when LMM first met him in Boston, King had published eleven popular
novels, the most recent being *The Thread of Flame* (1920) and *The Empty Sack*
(1921). JAMES S. HUGHES (1846-1935). James Laughlin Hughes, Toronto poet,
essayist, biographer, and social historian, had published *The Child's Paradise:
Stories and Musings for Parents and Teachers* in 1919. **November 19** ROBERT
SIMPSON CO. A large Toronto department store at Yonge and Queen Street. PRESS
CLUB. Chartered in 1911, the Toronto Press Club was located on Toronto Street
in the 1920s; it had dissolved by the 1930s but was resuscitated in 1944 as the
Toronto Men's Press Club, located first on Yonge, later on King Street. JEN
FRASER. See the photograph of Jean Fraser with Frederica Campbell MacFarlane

in the greenhouse at Macdonald College, in *SJLMM* II, 304. HART HOUSE. Theatre in the students' centre at the University of Toronto, built as a war memorial
for Hart Massey, and opened in 1919. COMMUNITY PLAYERS OF MONTREAL. In July
1921 the *Canadian Forum* suggested editorially that Hart House Theatre and the
Montreal Players exchange performances. The Montreal Players were hailed as
the major Canadian example of the currently flourishing Little Theatre Movement. **November 21** CAM. Cameron MacFarlane had married Frede Campbell in
May, 1917. She died in February, 1919. JARVIS STREET COLLEGIATE. Central
Toronto secondary school, founded 1807 as York Home District Grammar
School; moved to 361 Jarvis Street 1871, and to a new building nearby in 1924.
Dr. MacMurchy, father of LMM's long-time friends Marjorie and Helen, was
Rector of Jarvis 1872-1900. I.O.D.E. Imperial Order Daughters of the Empire: a
patriotic and charitable women's organization, founded in 1900; comparable to
the Daughters of the American Revolution. PARKDALE. A west-end section of
Toronto, solidly middle-class in the 1920s. VICTORIA COLLEGE. The Methodist
college of University of Toronto, founded in 1836 at Cobourg. **November 22**
MOULTON COLLEGE. A residential and day school for young women and girls, at
34 Bloor Street in north central Toronto. QUO VADIS. Silent moving picture based
on Henry Sinkiewiecz's classic Polish novel of 1897: a first version directed by
Italian Enrico Guazzari had appeared in 1913: one of the films which established
cinematography as a major entertainment form. In 1920 in the USA daily attendance at motion-pictures reached an estimated 10,000,000. Gross receipts were
around $800,000,000. DUNN AVENUE. Parkdale Presbyterian Church dominated
this short, stylish street in west-end Toronto. **November 23** OAKWOOD. Collegiate at the corner of St. Clair and Oakwood, in north-western Toronto.
November 24 CARNEGIE LIBRARY. The central library in Vancouver. City Librar-
ian Robert W. Douglas (d. 1931) was the author of *How Books May Help You*
(1914) and *Bibliotheca Canadiensis* (1887). MRS. ROCHESTER. References to Mr.
and Mrs. Rochester appear in LMM's 1891 diary (see *SJLMM*, I, 58, 62).
November 25 CHESSY-CAT. The smiling Cheshire cat in Lewis Carroll's *Alice's
Adventures in Wonderland* (1865). RYRIES. Jewellery store in downtown
Toronto, later merged with Birks. HAMILTON. City on Burlington Bay, 42 miles
southwest of Toronto; population in 1921 was 114,766. LMM autographed
books at Cloke's Bookstore on Main Street West. **November 26** MR. STEWART.
Before joining the publishing firm of McClelland & Stewart in 1914, George
Stewart had worked as a salesman in the Methodist Book Room, Toronto. THE
NATIONAL CLUB. A private men's club on Bay Street, Toronto, founded 1874. MR.
AND MRS. BRADY. William J. Brady, a salesman for McClelland & Stewart, lived
on Indian Road, Toronto. SHERBOURNE HOUSE. A club for young professional
women, at 104 Sherbourne Street, Toronto. **November 29** BUSINESS WOMEN'S
CLUB. Located at 199 Yonge Street; founded 1917, became the Canadian
Women's Business Club in 1920, and later the Business and Professional
Women's Club. MRS. PANKHURST. With her daughter Christabel, Emmeline
Pankhurst (1858-1928) had led the militant movement for women's votes. She
had been President of the Women's Social and Political Union of Great Britain
since 1906. SUFFRAGETTE. The word was coined in 1906 for a female supporter

of woman's enfranchisement. In Canada, full woman suffrage had been passed in March 1918. LADY BYNG. Wife of Baron Byng of Vimy, Governor General of Canada 1921-1926. Lady Byng's novels included *Barriers* and *Anne of the Marshland* (Toronto: McClelland & Stewart, 1921). **December 7** LIBERAL. The 1921 national election brought W.L. Mackenzie King into office as Liberal Prime Minister of Canada, until June, 1926. CONSERVATIVE. Arthur Meighen, who led the Conservative party on a high tariff platform was defeated: Liberals: 121, Conservatives: 51, Progressives: 60. "U.F.O." United Farmers of Ontario, a political party founded in 1914, had won the 1919 provincial election and formed the current government of Ontario. HALBERT. Robert Henry Halbert, first president of the U.F.O., was elected Member of Parliament for the riding of North Ontario in 1919, and returned in 1921—although in the Leaskdale poll he had fewer votes than his Liberal-Conservative-Unionist opponent. LLOYD GEORGE (1863-1945). David Lloyd George, Prime Minister in the British coalition government since 1916, had become a hero for Canadians by his vigorous leadership during World War I. For Ireland he urged a "Dominion Home Rule", similar to that in Canada. **December 13** CLEVELAND, OHIO. American city on the south shore of Lake Erie, in 1921 the seventh largest city in the United States. LIPPINCOTT'S. A major American publisher based in Philadelphia. JAZZ. The word is first recorded in 1918, applied to "syncopated music, as played by negro bands in the United States". "NOR LEAVE MUCH MYSTERY". Lord Byron (1788-1824), "English Bards and Scotch Reviewers", 250. **December 24** A "RAILROAD". Battery-powered train sets by Lionel company of England were best-selling toys in the early 1920s. **December 29** FLASHLIGHTS. Photographs taken with flash-lamps, blowing magnesium powder through a small flame. AGNES MACPHAIL. The only woman elected to the Canadian Parliament in the first election in which women could vote, Agnes Macphail sat as a member of the Progressive Party, affiliated with the U.F.O. "LADY TREVANION". In E.A. Poe's "Ligeia", the blonde beauty is Lady Trevanion of Tremaine. LMM uses this memory also in *Emily of New Moon*, 328-9. "PITT'S REPLY TO WALPOLE". In a long-remembered debate in the British parliament, 1745, Horace Walpole sneered at William Pitt for his youth. Pitt's rhetorical self-defence became memory work for generations of school children: LMM learned the "Reply" from the Prince Edward Island *Royal Reader*. She substitutes "my sex" for "my youth". CECIL RHODES (1853-1902). British imperialist, South African politician and magnate. MIDSHIPMAN EASY. *Mr. Midshipman Easy* (1836), a novel for boys by Frederick Marryat. WILLIAM CLARK. The Clark family homestead was at the western end of Cavendish. DUNCAN MCINTYRE. Husband of Aunt Mary Montgomery, sister of LMM's father Hugh John.

1922

January 6 ANTI-UNIONIST. Opposed to the proposed union of the Presbyterian and Methodist Churches in Canada. THE KHAKI ELECTION. In the election of December 1917, Liberal Wilfrid Laurier who opposed conscription was defeated. Women with an immediate family member in uniform were allowed to vote (presumably pro-conscription): LMM had a vote because of her half-brother Carl's military service. TRANSMOGRIFIED. Grossly altered in form or appearance. **January 17** "SEEING THINGS AT NIGHT". Eugene Field's "Seein' Things", reproduced in many anthologies of recitation pieces. **January 27** FROUDE'S "ELIZABETH". One volume in *The History of England from the Fall of Wolsey to the Defeat of the Spanish Armada*, published by J.A. Froude, Victorian editor and historian, between 1856 and 1870. MARY STUART. Queen of Scots (1542-1587), imprisoned and finally beheaded on Queen Elizabeth's orders. "FARMER GEORGE". George III (1728-1820), King of England during the American Revolution, wrote letters as "Ralph Robinson, Farmer". "QUEEN BESS". Elizabeth I (1533-1603), Queen of England during the time of the Spanish Armada. "VICTORIA" (1819-1901). Remembered by LMM as the staid widow-queen of late 19th century propriety. **February 13** THE LADIES' HOME JOURNAL. Established in 1883 by Curtis of Philadelphia, the *LHJ* was edited 1921-28 by Barron Currie, who was changing its thrust to accord with new conceptions of women's interests. **February 28** MARGOT ASQUITH (1864-1945). Second wife of Herbert Asquith, British Prime Minister from 1908-1916; the publication of her *Reminiscences* (1920) was considered to have set back his reviving career as leader of the opposition. MASSEY HALL. Built in 1892 as the finest concert hall in Toronto and presented to the city by Hart Massey. MARKHAM AND CEDAR GROVE. The town of Markham lies 23 miles south-west of Leaskdale (toward Toronto); the hamlet of Cedar Grove is 3 miles south-east of Markham. UNIONVILLE. Unionville is 2 miles west of Markham, at the eastern edge of Toronto. Rev. Frank Rae was the minister there until 1925. MR. LAW. William Law, the Zephyr Ford dealer. His son Ivan married Pickering's youngest daughter, Daisy. **March 6** HANDS OF DESTINY. LMM later inserted the parenthetical comment, "(Yes. 1938)" at this point in the handwritten journal. **March 7** *BLOODY MARY*. Mary Tudor, queen of England 1553-1559, married the Roman Catholic King Philip of Spain and undertook counter-reformation of Protestants. SMITHFIELD FIRES. Fires in the Smithfield market in London, where Protestants were burned as heretics. **March 11** ELLA. Widow of LMM's first cousin George Campbell. (See *SJLMM*, II, 263-4). **March 18** MRS. WM. C. MACNEILL. A second cousin by marriage, mother of Amanda Macneill Robertson, LMM's best friend in Cavendish schooldays. AUNT CAROLINE. Wm. C. Macneill's unmarried sister. (See *SJLMM*, I, 229.) **April 2** JUDGE [Theodore Augustus] MCGILLIVRAY (1852-1925). Lawyer in Whitby 1890-1912, Registrar of County Courts at Whitby 1910-12, and Senior Judge of the Courts of Ontario County 1912-1925. MR. MCCULLOUGH. James W. McCullough of Stouffville was the son of a barrister who had been practising in Uxbridge since 1886. In 1916, Lawyer Sam Sharpe, preparing to take a battalion overseas, arranged for Lawyers J.W. McCullough and Button of Stouffville to help out in his Uxbridge practice—the firm of Sharpe and Greig. WANAMAKER'S. Large department store established in New York City in 1896. **April 3** ROYALTY REPORT. Total royalties from *Rilla* in its first year (1920) were $10,616; for *Rainbow Valley* in its first year (1920) royalties were $11,968. LMM kept very careful accounts of royalties from all sources. WM. LOCKIE. William D. Lockie and his wife Mary Minetta farmed east of Zephyr; their son Keith and daughter Ruth each married a Pickering. **April 16** AN ABRIDGED

VOLUME. LMM did in fact create a typescript abridging materials in the journals; her son Dr. Stuart Macdonald also began an abridged version based on her abridgement. Both these versions have been consulted by the present editors in conjunction with the handwritten volumes. **April 25** GREIG. Willard F. Greig (c. 1890-1964). Called to the Bar in 1915, became solicitor for the town of Uxbridge from 1919 until his death. His sister, Florrie Greig Gould (Mrs. R.H. Gould), became the mother of Glenn Gould the concert pianist. The family claimed relationship with the composer Edvard Grieg (note the different spelling). LMM consistently uses the same spelling as the composer's name. **April 27** YOUNG HORNER. Mason Horner (1899-1961), son of William Horner, a farmer of Zephyr, was articled to W.F. Greig, and called to the Bar in 1919; he practised law at Sunderland and became a Q.C. (Queen's Counsel) after WW II. **May 9** MR. [W.R.] AULD. Called to Markham, 1922-25. **May 10** LECKY. W.E.H. Lecky, M.P. for Dublin University 1895-1902, in his *History of European Morals from Augustus to Charlemagne* (1869) traced the rise of rationalism and tolerance in place of theological dogmatism. UTILITARIANS. The ancient philosophy, re-articulated by James Bentham and J.S. Mill in the mid-19th century, assumed that desire for happiness (specifically for the greatest happiness of the greatest number of people) is the motivating force for actions. "CHRISTIANS HAVE BURNT..." Lord Byron, *Don Juan*, Canto I, stanza 83. **May 20** OAKVILLE. A small town at the mouth of 16-Mile Creek, between Toronto and Hamilton. **May 22** EMILY II. *Emily Climbs* (1925) focuses on an adolescent's compulsion to write and on her experiences away from home, at high school. A large proportion of the book is in the form of journal entries. AN ADULT NOVEL. Eventually, *The Blue Castle* (1926). DWELLER ON MY THRESHOLD. An allusion to *Zanoni* by Bulwer-Lytton. Represents "Fear" or "Natural Horror" and is countered by "Faith". **June 8** DR. BOYNTON OF SUTTON. William John Boynton, M.D., practised at Sutton, a village near Lake Simcoe north-west of Zephyr, from 1899-1924. **June 13** CANNINGTON. A village about 20 miles north-east of Leaskdale. **June 20** THE WRIT. Legal document issued to the lawyer, directing him to prepare for trial in an action for damages: Pickering had not accepted the out-of-court settlement offered on April 24. **July 2** MR. [Carmen] DYER OF MT. ALBERT. Rev. C.E. Dyer (1891-1953) was the last minister (1921-1924) at Chalmers Presbyterian Church, Mount Albert (about 8 miles south-west of Zephyr); this church became part of Mount Albert United Church and Mr. Dyer went to Greenbank. **July 8** LADY JANE GREY-DORT. The hero of *The Blue Castle* calls his car (a Grey-Slosson) "Lady Jane". MCKAYS OF STREETSVILLE. Rev. and Mrs. Wm. A. McKay had moved from Wick, near Leaskdale, to Streetsville, a village west of Toronto (See *SJLMM*, II, 93). **July 15** JUDGE HAMMOND. F.T. Hammond of the Suffolk County Court, Massachusetts, heard Rollins argue LMM's case, requesting an injunction against continued publication of *Further Chronicles* and requesting an accounting for Page Company profits from LMM's books in the years before she broke away from them. SUPREME COURT. The Page Company's counter-suit against LMM for "malicious litigation", dismissed in 1920 in the Massachusetts Supreme Judicial Court, was carried forward in an appeal to the United States Supreme Court. **July 30** "ROSELAWN". Tourist home in Bala, a resort town on

Lake Muskoka. MUSKOKA. The area around Lake Muskoka, Lake Rosseau, and Lake Joseph, east of Georgian Bay in mid-northern Ontario, had been popular cottage country since the 1870s. MISS TOMS; MRS. BRACKINRIDGE. The first reference may be to Katherine Burgess, a daughter of the proprietor, Thomas (Toms) Burgess and granddaughter of Thomas Burgess, founder of Bala in 1878. Mrs. Brackinridge may have been another guest or an employee. MRS. PYKES. Fanny Walden Pike, an eccentric Englishwoman, formerly a Bala midwife, served meals to summer visitors. Her Bala house is being converted into a Muskoka museum. "CABINED, CRIBBED, CONFINED". Wm. Shakespeare, *Macbeth*, III, iv, 23: original has "cabin'd, cribb'd, confined"). JOHN MUSTARD OF DUDLEY. In 1891, Mr. Mustard was LMM's high school teacher in Prince Albert, Saskatchewan; he proposed marriage, to her discomfiture and amusement. He was now a Presbyterian minister in Toronto, holidaying at Dudley Bay, Lake Muskoka. EGLINTON VILLA. LMM's father had given his Prince Albert home a traditional family name: the head of the Montgomery family was the Earl of Eglinton. **July 31** STEVENSON'S LINES. From "Foreign Lands" by R.L. Stevenson, *A Child's Garden of Verses* (1885). "To where the roads on either hand /Lead onward into fairyland." MR. MACMILLAN. Correspondent George MacMillan of Alloa, Scotland; on her honeymoon, LMM met her long-time pen pal and took a thorough dislike to the girl he was engaged to. (See *SJLLM*, II, 70-5.) *Emily of New Moon* is dedicated to him. **August 3** POINT SANDFIELD [sic]. Port Stanfield is north of Bala. **August 4** EIGHT YEARS AGO. World War I began when Great Britain declared war on Germany, August 4, 1914. **August 6** "COMMISSIONED". A term applied to those authorized to ride a circuit as preachers. MOMMSENN [sic]. Theodor Mommsen (1817-1903) first published *Rome, from earliest times to 44 B.C.* in Berlin, 1858; though regarded as old-fashioned by historians in the 1920s, it continued to be re-issued. **August 26** "ORPHANS OF THE STORM". D.W. Griffith's motion picture epic was "novelized" by H. MacMahon (New York: Grosset, 1922)—an early example of the literary genre appearing subsequent to film form. **September 2** THE EXHIBITION. Fall fair at Toronto, begun in 1878 in the garrison reserve of old Fort York, had been officially named "the Canadian National Exhibition" in 1912. **September 10** THE PRISONER OF ZENDA. A major silent moving picture, based on Anthony Hope [Hawkins]'s novel of 1894. Rudolf was played by Ramon Novarro, Flavia by Alice Terry, Sapt by Robert Edeson, and Lewis Stone starred as the commoner-king. THE IROQUOIS. Toronto hotel, opened in 1899, at the corner of King and York Streets. **September 18** MR. [David] CARSWELL (1865-1956). Formerly a missionary out west, now on the supplementary roll of the Toronto Presbytery, i.e., not assigned to a congregation. TRILBY. George DuMaurier's novel (1894) concerns bohemian artists and their protégé, Trilby, enabled to sing by the hypnotist Svengali. LMM's early novel *Kilmeny of the Orchard* played with a comparable theme of the inhibition and release of artistry by psychic manipulation. TAMS. Scottish-style beret: short for "tam o' shanter". TOQUES. Small hat with turned-up or no brim; contrast children's knitted tubular toques. EMILE COUE (1857-1926). *Self-Mastery through Conscious Autosuggestion* (New York: American Library Service, 1922) spread the French psychologist's popular methods, and set thousands to murmuring,

"Every day, in every way, I am getting better and better." MR. [John] LINDSAY OF ERIN (1867-1946). Born in Scotland; had supplied in Cannington; Moderator of the Orangeville Presbytery north-west of Toronto. HILLSBURG[h]. In Wellington County, 30 miles north-west of Toronto. **September 23** VERONAL. Regularly prescribed as a hypnotic drug for treating melancholia, the chemical diethyl-malonyl-urea was first formulated in 1903. Veronal loses its effect if taken over long periods; overuse by insomniacs could lead to death. KISMET. Arabic term for destiny or fate. **September 27** MT. ALBERT. Next village east of Zephyr. Evans was a farmer, Wilson a blacksmith at the north end of the village. **October 1** CARCASS. The manuscript has "carcase", British spelling. **October 4** MISS BUCKHAM [sic]; OLIVE BLANCHARD. In the years when the Macdonald boys were public school students, no teacher stayed for more than a year in either of the two schools in the Leaskdale area. V. Buchman taught at Bethesda School, S.S. #4, Scott Township, and Olive Blanchard at S.S. #8, Leaskdale, September 1922-June 1923. **October 11** PHELAN. T.N. Phelan, Toronto lawyer representing Mr. Pickering, was a "K.C."—King's Counsel—a distinction awarded to prominent lawyers in the Governor General's annual Honours list. **October 13** LILY SHIER. Lillis May Harrison, widow of Arthur Reid, had left her position as maid in the Leaskdale manse in order to marry Robert Shier of Zephyr. DR. JOHNSON (1885-1939). Medical practitioner from Mt. Albert. MRS. HEATH. Mary Caroline Heath, a widow living in Zephyr. MRS. BURNHAM. Libbie, daughter of Mary Heath and wife of George Burnham. The Burnhams, Methodists, had come to Scott Township from England around 1850, at the same time as the Pickerings. VERNA PICKERING. Third child of the Marshall Pickering family, became Mrs. Howard Tiffin. HYPATIA. A literary club formed in Uxbridge in 1907. In 1912 the club had held an open meeting so that area women could become acquainted with L.M. Montgomery. LMM regularly presented papers to the club. The name of this Uxbridge literary club was taken from Charles Kingsley's novel *Hypatia* (1853), based in turn on the story of the neoplatonic Alexandrian philosopher-mathematician Hypatia (c. 370-415 A.D.). MINNIE GOULD. Daughter of Isaac and Rebecca Gould, and cousin of LMM's friend Mary Gould Beal. JACQUES LOEB. American university professor, served from 1910 at Rockefeller Institute for Medical Research. Author of *Comparative Physiology of the Brain and Comparative Psychology* (1900). **October 14** STOUFFVILLE. A town halfway between Uxbridge and Toronto. **October 15** MRS. ALEX LOCKIE. Sophia Lockie, widow of Alex, who had farmed a half mile south of Zephyr. THOMAS HARDY'S "TWO ON A TOWER". A novel (London: Sampson, Low, 1882) about a woman married to a notoriously unkind husband and her love for a young astronomer. **October 16** DR. MACCLINTOCK. Joseph A. McClintock, M.D., practised in Uxbridge from 1903 to 1946. He was Medical Officer of Health for 35 years. **October 17** JOE TAYLOR. Zephyr agent for Deering farm equipment since 1912; he sold his property to W.O. Law in 1924. **October 19** MRS. BINGHAM. George and Jennie Bingham ran the Zephyr Hotel at the village crossroads; George was a stone-mason. **October 20** DR. STEPHENS. Probably Dr. Wellington Stephens (b. 1874), Toronto surgeon. DR. JONES. Probably Dr. Newbold Jones, M.D., C.M. (b. 1880). HISTORY OF THE REFORMATION IN FRANCE. From 1835-78, Merle d'Aubigné (1794-1872) published a widely read 13-volume history of the Reformation which had remarkable success in English translation. AUTO DA FE. From Spanish, meaning "act of faith": burning of heretics after sentencing by the Inquisition. **October 24** AY, DI ME. Alas for me: Anthony Trollope's character Francis Arabin uses this expression. **October 31** MR. BUTTON. Mr. McCullough's partner in his Stouffville law practice. **November 6** LANCE COPELAND. Son of Peter Copeland, farmer and blacksmith, whose farm was on the road from Zephyr to Mt. Albert. HARRY RISLEY. Zephyr's first garageman, Risley had been blacksmith and wheelwright before he opened an auto repair shop in 1912. "Harry" (Percy) Risley had run away from his foster home at the age of eleven, and travelled across the continent and to the Philippines. JOHN URQUHART. A Zephyr carpenter. JOE PROFIT. A labourer in Zephyr. The Profit family had been in the Zephyr wagon-shop business since the 1880s. "HOME BOY". A boy from the London slums, brought to Canada under a scheme devised by Dr. Barnardo, and placed with a rural family in need of extra farm help. **November 10** MRS. TAYLOR OF SHILOH. There were several Taylor families in Shiloh, a rural area in Georgina Township about 6 miles north-east of Zephyr. **November 13** LAWYER ORMISTON. Wm. S. Ormiston, B.A., L.L.B., Q.C., practised law in Uxbridge from 1898-1936. **November 16** A ROMAN HOLIDAY. Celebration with gladiatorial contests and the martyring of Christians. **November 21** JOHN HALL. In 1922 John Hall was farming between Sandford and Zephyr; he moved to Sandford in 1923. **November 26** JUDGE RIDDELL. Mr. Justice William Renwick Riddell (1852-1945), of the Assize Court, Toronto. A distinguished lawyer, he published innumerable articles on a wide range of interests: history, science, theology;his papers and personal library are held at Osgoode Hall, Toronto. JOHN MCCULLOUGH. Brother of the Macdonalds' lawyer J.W. McCullough of Stouffville. DR. ROBINSON. Probably John Livie Robinson, M.D., C.M., M., CP&S., L.M.CC.(b. 1888). DR. POWELL. Probably Newton Powell (1856-1935), Professor Emeritus and former chair of Medical Jurisprudence and Clinical Surgery, Toronto General Hospital. DR. STEVENSON. Probably J.M. Stevenson, M.D., C.M. (b. 1862). DR. BANTING. Dr. Frederick G. Banting (1891-1941), co-discoverer of insulin with J.J.R. Macleod, C.H. Best, and J.B. Collip, announced the isolation of secretions of the pancreas and consequent new treatment for diabetes in October 1922. Judge Riddell either ignored or was ignorant of this widely-publicized discovery. GARNISHEE. Notice served on a debtor that money owed to a creditor will be attached, usually by intercepting wages. **December 2** JAMES MUSTARD. Lived on the farm south-west of Leaskdale which had been in his family since the 1830s. **December 4** GEORGE ALLAN SMITH. Farmed just north of Sandford, south-west of Leaskdale. **December 5** OSGOODE HALL. Since 1830 the centre of legal study and administration, on Queen Street, Toronto. **December 7** RICHARD CURL. A Zephyr blacksmith. **December 16** RADIO. Term first used in U.S.A. in 1915, short for radio-telegraphy: a wireless receiving-set. The technology, invented 1907-1913 by Marconi, De Forest, and Armstrong, accelerated in WW I. In 1921 there were only a dozen long distance radio stations in the world, but by 1923 the "crystal set" had become a household commonplace. ZEIT GEIST. Spirit of the age (usually one word in German). The term had come into popular usage in 1884. LIFE OF TEN-NYSON. Hallam, Lord Tennyson, *Tennyson, a Memoir, by his Son* (1897). CHATEAU YQUEM. A fine Bordeaux wine; LMM had enjoyed tasting Château d'Yquem in 1910 in Boston with the Pages. (See *SJLMM* I, 30.) **December 28** MR. BARTON. The Barton family had come from Ireland in the 1850s. They lived on the fourth farm north of Leaskdale. **December 31** ORMUZD AND AHRIMANES. Twin deities of Zoroastrian religion: the creative and the destructive principle. Mentioned in *Zanoni*.

1923
January 2 "THE HEART ASKS PLEASURE FIRST". Poem #536 in *Poems of Emily Dickinson* (1896). **January 8** KATE CARNEGIE [and Those Ministers]. A novel published in 1896 by "Ian MacLaren". Under this pen-name, a Scottish minister, Rev. John Watson, had published a series of best-selling novels beginning with *Beside the Bonnie Brier Bush* (1894); LMM had presented a paper on his work when she was a student at Dalhousie University. **January 19** JANE WELSH CARLYLE (1801-1866). Her letters were published in 1883; her husband was Thomas Carlyle. **January 21** DAVID GRAHAM. A farmer, living 3/4 mile south of Zephyr, on the far side from Leaskdale. **January 24** THE GREAT ARGYLE. Archibald Campbell, 8th Earl of Argyll (1607-1661), executed for high treason by Charles II. **January 28** THE ROYAL SOCIETY OF ARTS. Established in England in the 20th century to parallel the Royal Society of London for Improving Natural Knowledge, prestigious "invisible college" of science founded 1660. STRATFORD; MITCHELL. Small Ontario cities about 100 miles west of Toronto. **February 3** [Rev.] MR. AND MRS. FINLAY MATHESON. Minister of St. Andrew's Presbyterian Church, Stratford, 1914-1925. WINDSOR. A central hotel on Albert Street, Stratford, established 1881, renamed "22 Albert" in the late 1980s. **February 6** PONGEE. Soft, unbleached Chinese silk. DELAINE. Light woollen dress fabric. CHALLIE. Challis is a fine silk and worsted fabric without gloss. BERTHA. Deep-falling collar. ORGANDY. Very fine stiff translucent muslin. SATEEN. Cotton fabric with glossy surface. CHARMEUSE. Soft smooth silk dress fabric. HONITON LACE. Lace manufactured in the delicate style perfected in Honiton, Devonshire, established by Flemish immigrants in Queen Elizabeth I's time. POLONAISES. Woman's dress consisting of a bodice with overskirt opening from the waist downwards. SIC TRANSIT GLORIA MUNDI. Latin: So passes the glory of the world. **February 18** DALHOUSIE. In Halifax, Nova Scotia, Dalhousie University was the college attended by Ewan Macdonald as an undergraduate; LMM also studied there for a year. PRINCE OF WALES. In Charlottetown, Prince Edward Island, Prince of Wales College was the post-secondary college where young people studied to become teachers, or prepared for entry into off-island universities. "BRIGHT'S DISEASE". Granular degeneration of the kidneys. A FLOWER PATCH IN THE HILLS. Flora Klickmann first published *The Flower-Patch Among the Hills* in 1916 (London, New York: Stokes)—one of a long series of her home-centred self-help books. She was editor since 1908 of *The Girl's Own Paper* and worked from her country home, a model cottage among beautiful gardens. **February 19**

THE SUPREME COURT. Supreme Court of Canada in Ottawa; meantime LMM's case against Page was being appealed in the Massachusetts Supreme Court, and Page's case against her in the Supreme Court of the United States. **March 5** THE GODDESS PASHT. Alternate name for the Egyptian cat-goddess Bast, in the role of Destroyer or devouring Sphinx. See *Emily of New Moon*, 285. **March 12** MRS. WIDDIFIELD. Benjamin and Estelle Widdifield, and Ben's mother the widowed Emiline Widdifield, lived on a farm south-west of Sandford. An "old" family who had come in the 1850s from north of England via Pennsylvania. **April 1** THE KING EDWARD. Elegant downtown Toronto hotel on King Street, designed by Edward Lennox, architect of the old City Hall in Toronto. THE MAIL AND EMPIRE. The Conservative Toronto paper, established when the daily *Mail* and the *Empire* joined in 1896; merged in 1936 with the Liberal *Toronto Globe* to form the *Globe and Mail*. **April 2** BLACKWATER. A hamlet 6 miles east of Leaskdale. SHERIFF [John Franklin] PAXTON OF WHITBY. Succeeded his father as Sheriff of Ontario county in 1887 and held that position until 1931, with the longest service record in Ontario. **April 8** GERTRUDE [Horn] ATHERTON (1857-1948). *Black Oxen* (London: Murray, 1923) came from a prolific author. Her books included *The Aristocrats* (1902), on an English lady in the Great North Woods of Canada. **April 11** MR. COOK. Albert Cook lived in the house next door to the manse. **April 14** MEMORANDUM OF FINDING. Official note of judgement. CHRISTIE. Christie Macdonald McLeod of Kinross on the eastern part of the Island. TOMMY AND GRIZEL. A novel (1900) by J.M. Barrie (1867-1937), sequel to *Sentimental Tommy* (1896). Biographies of Barrie, speculating about his private life, did not appear until 1929. **April 30** STUNTS. The old meaning of "special effort, feat, or show, performance"; superseded by the meaning of "performance, especially acrobatics". GOVERNMENT HOUSE. Chorley Park, the grand Rosedale residence of His Honour Henry Cockshutt, Ontario's Lieutenant-Governor. It was demolished in 1959. NEW COPYRIGHT BILL. The Copyright Act of 1921 protects Canadian writers from unauthorized reproduction or performance of original work, during the life of the artist, and for fifty years after the artist's death. Amendments of 1923 clarified the licensing clauses in the Act. DR. LOGAN OF HALIFAX (1869-1929) Poet, essayist, social historian, and literary critic, had just published his biography of T.C. Haliburton. His *Highways of Canadian Literature*, with D.G. French, would appear in 1924. **May 21** JACK WHEAR (1867-1951). Charlottetown lawyer, Postmaster of Prince Edward Island (1904-1914), Post Office Inspector (1904-1933). His wife, Florrie Murchison, had lived in the same boarding house as LMM when they attended Prince of Wales College in 1893-4. **June 11** DOMINION ALLIANCE. Society "for the Suppression of Liquor Traffic". RYERSON YOUNG. His missionary father, Egerton Ryerson Young (1840-1909) had written boys' books about the north; Ryerson Young (1869-1962) also wrote boys' stories for the *Boys' Own Paper*, the religious Tract Society, the Philadelphia *Sunday School Times*, etc. METHODISTIC. With evangelical enthusiasm like the followers of John Wesley's breakaway Anglican group, the Methodists. JENNY GEDDES. Supposed to have inaugurated a riot in St. Giles's Church, Edinburgh, in 1637, against the introduction of Archbishop Laud's new form of church service into Scotland. **June 18** STUPIDLY GOOD. From Milton's *Paradise Lost,* IX, 465. **June 28** STRACHEY. Lytton Strachey, author of the controversial *Eminent Victorians* (1918), published *Queen Victoria,* an irreverent biography, in 1921. **July 15** FANNY MUTCH. *Née* Fannie Wise, a classmate at Prince of Wales College, now living at Brighton, the western end of Charlottetown. MISS [Izzie] ROBINSON. In *Emily of New Moon* (1923), LMM had created a devastating portrait of this unfeeling teacher in "Miss Brownell". Another Miss Robinson (Selena) became a friend during the time she taught LMM: she was in part, along with Miss Gordon, the original of "Miss Stacy" in *Anne of Green Gables.* "IN FAIRYLANDS FORLORN". John Keats' "Ode to a Nightingale", l.42: "faery lands forlorn". EARNSCLIFFE. Eleven miles southeast of Charlottetown; named in 1897 after the residence of Sir John A. Macdonald in Ottawa. **July 28** HAMILTON MAC-NEILL. Brother of Amanda and son of LMM's second cousin Wm. C. Macneill. **August 4** HAMMOND. Hammond McKenzie, son of LMM's great-aunt Margaret Woolner McKenzie and brother of LMM's late friend Tillie McKenzie Houston. CHARLES MACNEILL. Father of Alec Macneill, Pensie, and five others, friends and contemporaries of LMM's. Charles Macneill's mother (also a Macneill) was a sister of LMM's grandfather. (See *SJLMM* I, xvi.) DAMNATORY SIGNATURE. According to contemporary etiquette, a married woman should sign her Christian name and surname, with "Mrs. N or M" in brackets on the next line. LITERARY SHRINE. The site of the old home farm has been re-established by Uncle John Macneill's descendants as a shrine for LMM fans since 1985. MRS. STIRLING MACKAY (1877-1961). Ruth MacLeod MacKay, born at Stanley Bridge near Cavendish, was the second wife of a prominent Summerside lawyer. **August 7** HEATH MONTGOMERY (1893-1962). Heir to the Montgomery farm in Park Corner; LMM's first cousin, son of her father's younger brother James Townsend Montgomery and Eliza Montgomery Johnstone Montgomery (see *SJLMM,* I, 77). **August 8** ED SIMPSON. A Baptist minister, now a leader of the Temperance movement in the United States; LMM had been engaged to marry him in 1897-98. (See entries in *SJLMM,* I and II.) LIFE HOWATT. Eliphalet Howatt lived in French River, between New London Harbour and Park Corner. Long-time friends, members of the Howatt family had been among the 12 guests at LMM's wedding. **August 9** C.G.I.T. Canadian Girls in Training, an association for Canadian girls of 12-17, founded in 1915 by the Young Women's Christian Association and major Protestant denominations. BEDEQUE. Community on the south shore where LMM had taught in 1897-98; home of Herman Leard with whom she fell in love. (See *SJLMM* I, 201 ff.) **August 13** LITTLE HUGH. LMM's second son, who died at birth August 30, 1914. **August 19** AUNT MAY. Widow of LMM's uncle Leander Macneill, who had been a leading Presbyterian minister in Saint John, New Brunswick. LMM also visited Major McLaine of Rothesay during this visit to New Brunswick. **August 25** BALFOUR. British Foreign Secretary A.J. Balfour, who was in Canada to rouse further support for Allied forces in May 1917. TRENTON. Ontario city 112 miles west of Toronto; LMM's first cousin LAURA McIntyre Aylsworth from Charlottetown, married to an optometrist and with two children, Mac and Pat, had moved there from Toronto.

September 13 LES MISERABLES. Victor Hugo's novel first appeared in Paris in 1862; it was first translated into English 1893. **October 13** *HYPATIA* Kingsley's historical novel about Alexandria in the 5th century, for which LMM's Uxbridge club was named. Hypatia, expounder of Greek philosophy, disturbs the faith of a young Christian monk; she is torn to pieces by a mob of Christians. **October 18** ILA; CARL; KATE. LMM's half-sisters and half-brother, children of her father Hugh John by his second wife, Mary McRae Montgomery. **November 6** MR. [Edward] TURKINGTON (1869-1928). Presbyterian missionary in the Yukon Territory in the 1890s; called to St. Andrew's Church, Whitby, 1918. In favour of Church Union but outvoted by his congregation, he became associate pastor at Tabernacle United Church, formerly Whitby Methodist Tabernacle. **November 22** SHEILA KAY[e]-SMITH (1887-1956). *The End of the House of Alard* (London: Dutton, 1923) deals with tensions in an English county family; one plot thread concerns the revolt of a young woman against her family's snobbery and pursuit of wealth. **December 10** "PASTOR FELIX". Rev. A.J. Lockhart (1850-1926), American poet and essayist, and uncle of LMM's school friend Nate. *Emily Climbs* is dedicated to him. **December 12** THE MILL ON THE FLOSS. LMM consistently misspells George Eliot's name as "Elliot". The rebellious Maggie of *The Mill on the Floss* (1860) is misunderstood by her family.

1924

January 10 "THE MILLS OF THE GODS". Greek proverb, *Oracula sybilliana*, VIII,14; translated in H.W. Longfellow's "Retribution", "Though the mills of God grind slowly, yet they grind exceeding small". **January 20** *THE DELINEATOR.* Among the top five women's magazines in circulation (more than a million in 1920); founded in 1873 by Butterick to promote the sale of dress patterns and expanded to include fiction in 1897. Edited by Theodore Dreiser 1907-1910. MR. VON BRIESEN. Attorney of the Stokes Company of New York, publishers of LMM's American editions. Damages sought by Page in this renewed libel suit for "malicious litigation" were $30,000. While the trial was underway Page's lawyers sought to "attach", i.e., stop payment of LMM's New York royalties. LENIN. Vladimir Ilyich Ulyanov Lenin (1870-1924), Russian Communist leader from 1903 and President of the Soviet Government from 1921. LABOUR GOVERNMENT. Ramsay MacDonald formed the first Labour government in Britain, by linking with the Liberals to defeat the Conservatives. His ministry lasted nine months, until October 1924. MRS. MOODIE. Susanna Moodie (1803-1885) records her stubborn survival in *Roughing it in the Bush: or, Life in Canada* (London: Bentley, 1852). **January 30** LAURA. Laura Pritchard Agnew, friend from Prince Albert schooldays, and sister of Will Pritchard. (See *SJLMM*, I,72.) **February 3** *MODERN PRISCILLA*. American magazine for women (1887-1930); in 1894 after a move to Boston it enlarged its scope and specialized in fiction. **February 9** *BETWEEN THE LARCH WOODS AND THE WEIR*. Flora Klickmann's new book, a late example of Kailyard sentimentality. **February 10** *ADAM BEDE*. In George Eliot's novel (1859) an older man loves a gifted young woman. **February 16** KITCHENER. Ontario manufacturing city, 100 miles south-west of Toronto, founded in 1876 by Pennsylvania Mennonites, originally called Berlin, the name being changed before World War I. MRS. KAUFMAN. Alvin Ratz Kaufman, owner of Kaufman Rubber Company, lived at 35 Roy Street. His wife was the former Jean Hutton. GRIP. A valise or suitcase. "Gripsac" appears in the Oxford Dictionary as "a handbag". **February 18** ZANONI. LMM's childhood favourite, published first in 1842 by Edward Lytton, Baron Bulwer-Lytton. **March 2** VANESSA. The full title of this unusual and witty novel by LMM's long-time Toronto friend is *The Child's House: A Comedy of Vanessa from the age of eight or thereabouts until she had climbed the steps as far as thirteen.* (London: Macmillan, 1923). **March 9** BERTIE. Alberta McIntyre, LMM's first cousin from Charlottetown, daughter of Mary Montgomery McIntyre, LMM's father's sister. *WAVERLEY.* Walter Scott's first and most popular novel (1814) deals with the wanderings of an orphaned hero in Scotland at the time of the second Jacobite rising led by Bonnie Prince Charlie. THE BLIND BOW[-]BOY. Another novel by Carl Van Vechten, whose *The Tiger in the House* LMM had enjoyed in 1921. **March 16** "PECK'S BAD BOY". George W. Peck's *Peck's Bad Boy and his Pa* was a bestselling novel in 1883. *CACOETHES SCRIBENDI.* Scribbling mania, from the Greek *kako* (ill) *ethes* (disposition) and Latin *scribendi* (of writing). IRVING HOWATT. An old suitor from Park Corner (see *SJLMM*, II, 204-5). **March 23** LORD DUNSANY (1878-1957). Irish novelist and playwright, central in the "Celtic Twilight" movement, published *The Gods of Pegana* in 1905. MARIE CORELLI (1864-1924). Among the long list of popular novels by this purveyor of spiritualism, evangelism, amateur psychology, and romance, *Ardath: the Story of a Dead Self* (London: Bentley, 1889) ranked high, with a sale of almost 500,000 copies. Her last book was *Love—and the Philosopher: a Study in Sentiment* (London: Methuen, 1923). LOOK AFTER THE FURNACE: Coal furnaces had to be stoked twice a day, ashes taken out daily, clinkers cleared from the coal bed, furnace pipes cleaned twice a year, coal ordered, and brought by coalmen, after whom one had to clean up. **March 25** CHLORAL. A liquid formed by the action of chlorine on alcohol; commonly used to refer to chloral hydrate, a white powder resulting from the combination of water and chloral, much used as hypnotic and anaesthetic. Taking chloral can become a pernicious drug-habit. **March 29** BLUE PILLS. Mercurial antibilious pills. **March 30** "A HOUSE DIVIDED. . .". Holy Bible, Mark III:25. **April 5** LIFE AND CONFESSIONS OF A PSYCHOLOGIST. Grenville S. Hall (1844-1924), author of *Jesus Christ in the Light of Psychology* (1917), and other books on genetic philosophy and child study, produced this unusual autobiography (New York: Appleton, 1923). **April 10** THE BLUE CASTLE. A blend of biting social satire and romance, with a heroine named Valancy and a setting in the Muskoka lake region of Ontario. The book begins with the heroine consulting a medical specialist. **April 27** CONRAD. Joseph Conrad (1857-1924) published "Youth" in *Youth: a Narrative and Two Other Stories* (Edinburgh: Blackwood, 1902). "Heart of Darkness" was one of the two other stories. *Youth* had been reissued in Toronto by Doubleday, Page, in 1921. **May 4** GLANDS REGULATING PERSONALITY. Louis Berman (1893-) wrote this "study of the glands of internal secretion in relation to the types of human nature" (New York: Macmillan, 1925). **May 10** MRS. HEMANS. Felicia Dorothea (Browne) Hemans (1793-1835) published *Juvenile Poems* at fourteen. Separated from her husband, she supported herself by producing much-anthologized poems including "Casabianca" ("The boy stood on the burning deck"). **May 13** GUIZOT'S HISTORY OF FRANCE. F.P.G. Guizot (1787-1874), with Mme Guizot de Witt, first published this statesman's version of history; the first English version in America was published in Boston by Estes and Lauriat, 1877. **May 16** MONTAGUE. A well-established town toward the west end of P.E.I., near Kinross, home of Ewan's sisters. **May 25** CHURCH UNION BILL. Formal proposal in the Canadian Parliament to legislate the union of Presbyterian, Methodist, and Congregational churches. MR. MICAWBER. An ever-optimistic character in Charles Dickens' *David Copperfield* (1850). **May 26** MY THIRD EMILY BOOK. In *Emily's Quest*, Emily's urge to write is deflected by Dean Priest and Teddy Kent. **May 28** NEWMARKET. Town 20 miles north of Toronto towards Lake Simcoe. Rev. Mr. A.J. Mann continued as minister in 1925. **June 6** THE DIARY OF MARIE BASHKIRTSEFF. The *Journal* of this intense and gifted Russian artist, dead at 24, was published posthumously (1888) and in translation reached an international readership. **June 10** SOME FOOLS AND A SAINT. Published in the *Family Herald*, 20, 27 May and 3, 10 June 1931: a 7-year gap between writing and publishing. **July 10** KU KLUX KLAN. American secret society devoted to maintaining the purity of the white race and the Protestant religion. The "Father Cassidy story" is chapter 18 of *Emily of New Moon*; Emily finds an ally in a charming Roman Catholic priest. **July 13** CUTHBERT. LMM's uncle, Cuthbert Montgomery, her father Hugh's younger brother. **July 23** THE SENATE. The Canadian Senate, a non-elected body, ratifies, rejects or amends bills forwarded to it from the House of Commons. **August 17** MAMMOTH CAVE. The great series of caves in the limestone area of southwest Kentucky had been a major tourist attraction since 1809. **August 18** MR. GRAY. The Grays lived south of Leaskdale on the road to Uxbridge. WILL SELLERS. A farmer on lot 26, concession 4, just east of Zephyr. **September 1** *KILMENY*. Written before *Anne of Green Gables*, *Kilmeny of the Orchard* was published two years later, in 1910. **September 11** STUDIES IN MURDER. Edward Pearson, essayist and mystery writer (1880-1937), in this book (N.Y.: Garden City, 1924) marked the rise of the genre to best-seller lists. Mysteries by Agatha Christie and others became LMM's favourite light reading. **October 10** NORTH BAY. A city at the eastern end of Lake Nipissing, 216 miles north of Toronto. GEORGE BERNARD SHAW (1856-1950). *Saint Joan: A Chronicle Play in 6 Scenes and an Epilogue* (London: Constable, 1924), staged in Toronto at the New Princess Theatre, presents Joan as an obstinate visionary. **October 17** DR. AND MRS. FREEL. Medical doctor in Stouffville. **October 22** MRS. GASKELL. Elizabeth (Stevenson) Gaskell (1810-1885) wrote the biography of her friend and literary contemporary, published London: Smith, Elder, 1857. HAWORTH. The village in Yorkshire where the Brontë sisters lived and wrote. LMM visited it on her honeymoon. **October 23** PLEBISCITE ELECTION. A referendum held to determine whether Ontario communities should ban the sale of alcoholic beverages. O.T.A. Ontario Temperance Act of 1924, as drafted by Premier Ferguson (formerly anti-prohibition) legislated total prohibition of alcohol in Ontario, no compensation to former license holders, and no plebiscite on the issue. THE WETS. Those in favour of allowing the sale of alcoholic beverages in the community. **October 25** FOMALHAUT. A star of the first magnitude in the constellation *Piscis Austrinus*. **October 29** MRS. WHITNEY. Adeline (Train) Whitney (1824-1906), a New England author of books for girls including *The Gayworthys: A Story of Threads and Thrums* (Boston: Loring, 1865). **November 23** *FLAMING YOUTH*. Warner Fabian's torrid novel (London: Boni & Liveright, 1923) characterized the twenties' desire to shock moralists, and provided a catch-word for the period. MCMASTER. Founded in 1887 in Toronto as a Baptist college, McMaster had not yet moved from 273 Bloor Street to its later home in Hamilton. **November 24** JANE AUSTEN (1775-1817). *Emma* (1816) centres on the maturing of an intelligent, self-willed young woman. **November 26** DYERS OF GREENBANK. Rev. Carmen Dyer had moved from Mt. Albert at the time of church union; Greenbank is a hamlet 8 miles south-east of Leaskdale. **November 28** WILL P. In Prince Albert, LMM was very fond of Will Pritchard, brother of her best friend Laura. He died shortly after LMM returned to Cavendish. (See *SJLMM* I, 35-62, and entry in this volume, June 23, 1928.) **December 6** THE SESSION. Each Presbyterian church is governed by a session consisting of the minister and the elders. The minister is not accountable to the session. MARGARET [Campbell] DELAND (1857-1945). Author of *John Ward, Preacher* (London: Warne, 1887). HUGH WALPOLE (1884-1941). A vigorous, popular, prolific British author whose *The Old Ladies* (London: Macmillan, 1924) was praised by Virginia Woolf and E.M. Forster.

1925

January 12 ELSIE BUSHBY [Davidson]. The fourth maid at the manse. The Bushbys were farmers who lived between Leaskdale and Sandford. **January 13** HATTIE GORDON SMITH. Miss Gordon was a favourite Cavendish teacher, reflected in "Miss Stacy" in *Anne of Green Gables*. (See *SJLMM* I, 9.) **January 20** VOTED OUT. That is, voted not to allow their church property to be vested in the new United Church. A church-by-church vote determined whether Presbyterians would join the Union; the Methodist Church had made a national decision in favour of Union. **February 1** DR. MCMECHAN. Archibald MacMechan (1862-1933) was LMM's Professor of English at Dalhousie in 1895. In his *Head-Waters of Canadian Literature* (Toronto: McClelland & Stewart, 1924), MacMechan emphasized LMM's regional and Scottish qualities, her popularity in the United States and the British Isles, and her failure to find literary critics' approval. **March 1** CHARLES MACNEILL'S OLD DIARY. LMM devoted the next hundred pages of her journal to recopying this diary, a day-by-day matter of fact record of farm activities, weather, church events, and health in 1892-8. A sample: "March 20: Fine day. Roads very sloppy. Snow last night nearly gone. Russell gone to drive Mr. Robertson down to Rustico church....Me and Pensie done up the work. Laura Houston and Jenny was here tonight and Bessy. May Hooper is on the track. We will likely have another bawl soon." Charles Macneill's diary is indeed as LMM says, "tedious to read and unthinkably tedious to copy", but she concludes her transcription with several pages of reminiscences on the memories it evoked in her. **March 5** SUPREME COURT. The Massachusetts

Supreme Judicial Court, deciding on Page's appeal against LMM's suit, in which she charged Page with illegally publishing *Further Chronicles of Avonlea* in 1920. The U.S. Supreme Court had already ruled (also in LMM's favour) on Page's counter-suit for malicious litigation in April 1923. Page's appeal in the New York jurisdiction was still pending. **March 6** CAMILLE FLAMMARION (1856-1925). *Astronomie populaire* (Paris, 1880) was translated as *Astronomy for Amateurs* (New York: Appleton, 1904) and as *Astronomy* (New York: Doubleday, Page, 1914). ORION NEBULA. The cloud-like cluster around a brilliant constellation named for one of the giants of Greek mythology. **March 15** *HISTORY OF RELIGION*. Allan Menzies (1845-1916), *History of Religion: a Sketch of Primitive Religious Beliefs and Practices, and of the Origin and Character of the Great Systems* (London: Murray, 1895). **April 4** KNOX COLLEGE. The Presbyterian Theological college attached to the University of Toronto, established in 1844. The present College building on St. George Street had opened in 1915. In 1925 all Canadian Presbyterian college buildings except Knox and Montreal Presbyterian College came under control of the United Church. All the professors at Knox and most of the students were in favour of Union, and the faculty and student body had to be re-established. **April 6** MISS BOWMAN. Another one-year appointee, teaching in Leaskdale S.S. #8 in 1924-25. **April 13** MR. GARVIN. John Garvin (1859-1935), Toronto editor and anthologist. His collections, *Canadian Poets and Poetry* (Toronto: McClelland, 1916) and *Canadian Poems of the Great War* (Toronto: McClelland, 1918), were among indicators of a wave of literary nationalism; *Canadian Poets*, a third anthology, would appear in 1926. Garvin's wife, Amelia Warnock ("Katherine Hale", 1878-1956) had published a study of Isabella Valancy Crawford in 1923: LMM, who had earlier presented a paper on Crawford to the Hypatia Club, gave the unusual name "Valancy" to the central figure in her current book, *The Blue Castle*. **April 22** BERT COLLINS. Burton Collins owned the farm immediately north of Leaskdale. This family had lived in the original "Village of Scott" which became Leaskdale in 1857. **April 30** MR. WATCH. Of the Uxbridge United church, formerly Methodist. **May 3** I SMILE AND SMILE.... "One may smile, and smile, and be a villain." Wm. Shakespeare, *Hamlet*, I,v,106. **May 4** MR. BALDWIN. The Rev. J.R. Baldwin was pastor at Uxbridge Baptist church. WISDOM IS JUSTIFIED....Holy Bible, Matthew XI: 19. **May 7** AN ELDER. Presbyterian elders are elected for life and ordained as spiritual leaders of the church. MRS. WARREN. Herb and Winnifred Warren farmed 1/4 mile south of Zephyr. **May 15** RIDER HAGGARD (1856-1925). This popular writer was the author of *King Solomon's Mines* (1885), and *She* (1886), sensational favourites when LMM was an adolescent. **May 26** VALLENTYNE. A hamlet about 5 miles north-east of Leaskdale. JOHN BLANCHARD. Farmer; third farm south of Leaskdale. JOHN LOCKIE. Farmer, just south of Zephyr; the oldest son of Robert and Elizabeth Imrie Lockie. WILL RYNARD. Two William Rynards farmed on the Zephyr road. Two earlier Rynard brothers had married two Shier sisters; the family came from Ireland. **May 30** UDORA. A hamlet 4 miles due north of Leaskdale. **June 8** MAURICE MCNELLY. Farmer, 1/4 mile east of Zephyr. JULIA MADILL. Housekeeper in Zephyr; daughter of Robert Madill. **June 11** THE TORCAS COMPANY. The Toronto Casualty, Fire and Marine Insurance Company.

Davies and Taylor were agents, A.E. Dawson the general manager. **July 5** MYRTLE TAYLOR. A young girl from a family of ten in Shiloh. **July 15** KIRKFIELD. A hamlet about 26 miles north-northeast of Leaskdale, east of Lake Simcoe. Mr. Jenkins Burkholder (1873-1942) later moved to Morrisburg. FATHER'S SECOND WIFE. Mary Ann McRae. Her uncle, Sir William Mackenzie, who with Sir Donald Mann had built the Canadian Northern Railroad, was born in Kirkfield in 1849. **July 20** ST. ANDREW'S. Private boys' college school, founded in Toronto 1899, located in the Rosedale area of Toronto 1906-1926, when the school moved to Aurora, north of the city; enrolment in 1925 about 250 boys, mostly boarders. **August 5** THE C.N.R. Canadian National Railway trains had stopped at Zephyr, when flagged, since 1880. The station was completed in 1905, burned in 1916 and rebuilt 1917. **September 5** MIDWAY STUNTS. Sideshows, freak shows, and rides along the central avenue of the Canadian National Exhibition. THE GARDENS AT PORT PERRY. West of Uxbridge on the south shore of Lake Scugog. **September 6** CORRA [White] HARRIS (1869-1935). Author of some 20 works, including *As A Woman Thinks* (New York: Houghton Mifflin, 1925), *A Daughter of Adam* (New York: Doran, 1923), and *A Circuit Rider's Widow* (New York: Doubleday, Page, 1916). **September 7** MISS IMRIE OF ZEPHYR. Mary Imrie (1860-1941) came from a family of weavers who were among the founders of the Leaskdale Presbyterian church; they also helped establish the church at Zephyr. Her sister Elizabeth Imrie had married John Lockie of Zephyr. **September 22** MISS DEVIGNE. Senior matron at St. Andrew's College until the 1950s. SHORTER. Clement S. Shorter (1857-1926) wrote an introduction to a re-issue of Gaskell's book and also published *Charlotte Brontë and Her Circle* (London: Hodder & Stoughton, 1896), *Charlotte Brontë and Her Sisters* (London: Hodder & Stoughton, 1905), and *The Brontës* (New York: Scribner's, 1908). **September 24** "WHAT'S IN A NAME," etc. These stories become chapters in *Magic for Marigold*. **October 1** TOMMY MARQUIS. In 1959 the Marquis Hill on the Leaskdale sideroad was cut down as road improvement. **October 16** LOCARNO. A small town in Switzerland on Lake Maggiore. WOODVILLE. Village 15 miles north-east of Leaskdale. Rev. Walter W. Bryden (1883-1951), at Woodville 1912-21 and 1925-26, became lecturer on church history at Knox College, 1925-27, and eventually Principal of Knox, 1945-51. CANNINGTON. Between Leaskdale and Woodville. Rev. Robert S. Scott (1867-1935), born in Ireland, stayed in Cannington 1923-35. **October 29** THE APPLEBY BOYS. Appleby College in Oakville, Ontario was the traditional rival of St. Andrew's College. MR. [Barnston "Tuddy"] TUDBALL. Popular teaching master at St. Andrew's College 1908-1950. He had joined the 48th Highlanders during World War 1, gone overseas in 1916 with the 92nd Battalion, was wounded (gassed) and suffered a severe flu attack before returning to Canada in 1919. Stuart Macdonald remembered Mr. Tudball with affection. THREE LIVE GHOSTS. Charles Hampden's British Players presented this play by F.S. Isham (1866-1922) at the Comedy Theatre, Toronto; the script was published as "a comedy in three acts" (Indianapolis: Bobbs-Merrill, 1918). 11 ABOVE ZERO. That is, 12 degrees below zero Celsius. Canada converted from the Fahrenheit to metric system in 1972. THE SOUTH AFRICAN FARM. *The Story of an African Farm* (1883) by Olive Schreiner

(1855-1920), "powerful and original and fearless"—one of LMM's "wonder books". In *Emily's Quest*, a letter crucial to the plot is discovered in a copy of *The South African Farm*. **October 30** JACKY LANTERN. More commonly "Jack o' lantern": pumpkin carved into a face and hollowed out to hold a candle on Hallowe'en. **November 11** THEATRE IN UXBRIDGE. The Strand Theatre on Main Street was operated by Mr. Shulman who came to Uxbridge in 1920. BIRTH OF A NATION. Important in cinematographic history as the first to use orchestral accompaniment and other theatrical enhancements. **November 16** TOM GOODWILL (1872-1948). Son of missionaries, baptized by Dr. John Geddie of P.E.I.; educated at Prince of Wales College, Charlottetown, and Queen's; came from a charge in Kensington, P.E.I. to Cobourg. **December 6** REV. MR. [W.D.] MCKAY. Moderator for the Toronto presbytery in 1925, minister at Weston. NORVAL. A village in a valley at the forks of the Credit River and its west branch, 30 miles west of Toronto, with a grist and flour mill, a hotel, three churches, and a variety of stores. UNION. A nearby farming community to the north-west, with a large stone Presbyterian church built in 1835. Union and Norval were joint charges of a single minister. In February 1925 both churches voted against joining the Methodists to form the United Church. **December 12** MARGARET LEASK. Daughter of Alexander and Elizabeth Morrison Leask; later married Elmer Mustard. MARY STIVER. Mary Oxtoby, wife of Ronald Stiver; they lived on the Oxtoby farm behind the Leaskdale manse. **December 17** MRS. JAS. BLANCHARD. Zella Beatrice Murray (1881-1926) wife of James Blanchard, reeve of Scott Township 1913-15; elected Member of Parliament 1929. **December 21** MOUNT PLEASANT. Village east of Norval, toward Toronto.

1926

January 3 GLADYS COOK. Gladys Ferguson, first wife of William Cook, who later married LMM's former maid, Lily Meyers. **January 22** MARJORIE PICKTHALL (1883-1922). Toronto poet, short-story writer and novelist, published first book of poetry in 1913. Her *Complete Poems* were published by McClelland & Stewart in 1927. **January 29** BRANTFORD. A small city 60 miles south-west of Toronto, birth-place of Alexander Graham Bell. GOVERNOR GENERAL'S LEVEE. At Rideau Hall in Ottawa on January 1, the Governor General holds a reception: in the 1920s only high-ranking civic, military, and ecclesiastic officials were invited. **February 8** DICK COLWELL, DAVE LYONS. Labourers, Leaskdale. MRS. JAS. MUSTARD. Jennie, wife of James who farmed on the family lot south-east of Leaskdale. **February 28** NORVAL. The village was first called "Esquesing Mills", then "McNab" or "McNabbsville" after its founder; by 1833 early settlers of Norval, American loyalists originally from the Grampians in Scotland, renamed it from a line much quoted in school recitations, from John Home's play *Douglas*: "My name is Norval; on the Grampian Hills. . ." JOHN RUSSELL. With his brothers Jim and Don, John worked a large farm on the hill south-west of Norval. GLEN WILLIAMS. Originally Williamsburgh after its founding family, a flour- and woollen-milling village on the Credit, near Union and 5 miles northwest of Norval. MR. AND MRS. BARRACLOUGH. Ernest Barraclough (1874-1938) was general manager and secretary-treasurer of the Glen Woollen Mills. He had come to

Canada from England in 1904 and married Ida Stirratt (1874-1967) from nearby Union. THE WALKER. The Walker House Hotel, formerly at the corner of York and Front Streets, near the Union Station in Toronto. SATHANAS. Hebrew: the adversary. Term used to avoid saying the devil's name. THE CREDIT [River]. Flowing south, entering Lake Ontario at Port Credit, the Credit had supplied power to an important series of mills in early days. In the 1920s wheat was exported from Port Credit to the United States and distilleries such as Gooderham and Worts (originally at Norval) made other use of local grain. GEORGETOWN. Larger milling and manufacturing town 3 miles west of Norval. RADIAL. An electric railway: the Toronto-Guelph Electric Suburban Street Railway extended its line westward 1914-17, running through Norval, Georgetown, Limehouse, and Acton towards Guelph. The Norval radial station, taken over in 1923 by Canadian National Electric Railways, was on Adamson Street, southeast of the village. The radial line was closed in 1931. MR. [Charles] WILLIAMS. An Englishman who lived in a small house next to the Presbyterian manse. KARNAK. Ruins of ancient Thebes in upper Egypt consisting of temples and palaces of finest materials and workmanship. WE WERE A-COLD. "Poor Tom's a-cold": Wm. Shakespeare, *King Lear*, III,iv,151. SOFT WATER PUMP. A hand-pump in the kitchen, tapped into a cistern holding rain-water. THE ELECTRIC LIGHT. A household revolution in lighting since WW I brought "artifical daylight" into homes and public buildings. Experiments with carbon, cadmium, and mercury arc lamps had given way to silica glass bulbs enclosing twisted tungsten filaments, brought to incandescence by electricity—now available in some Ontario towns. The Georgetown dynamo was the first long-distance hydro-electric plant in the area. HYDRO. The Ontario Hydro Electric Power Commission was in 1921 the largest single electrical system in the world. Power drawn from turbines at Niagara Falls supplied cooking as well as lighting needs. **March 1** THE GALLED JADE. "Let the galled jade wince": Wm. Shakespeare, *Hamlet*, III,ii,256. **March 16** MR. [Alfred] LAIRD. His farm was at the top of the hill east of Norval, towards Toronto. In Presbyterian churches, elected managers run the business affairs and arrange physical upkeep. TOWNSENDS OF UNION. Farmers; in 1927 their daughter Margaret became the teacher in Norval school. **March 28** DR. AND MRS. [William] KYLE. The minister (1923-26) of St. Paul's, the Anglican church founded in 1845, was also a medical doctor. REVEREND [W.H.] DOUGLAS. Minister of the Norval Methodist church 1924-26; he was replaced later in 1926, by Rev. Neil MacKinnon, formerly a Presbyterian, after the church, built in 1890, was taken over by the new United Church. LMM does not mention Mr. MacKinnon in her journal. **March 30** DR. A[ndrew] S. GRANT (1860-1935). "Grant of the Yukon", a former missionary, in 1923 put in charge of organizing the work of the church in the event of separation from Union. Secretary of the General Board of Missions 1925-1935. **April 7** SIMON CALLED PETER. By Robert Keable (1887-1927), published London: Constable, 1921. **April 20** WELLINGTON NELSON. One of two brothers brought up as boarders in the Macneill family. (See *SJLMM*, I, 87.) **June 28** TRIENNIAL. National conference of the Canadian Women's Press Club, held every three years. ROYAL CANADIAN YACHT CLUB. Founded in 1868, the club had moved to an island in Toronto Bay in 1881, and had opened new premises there in 1922. PREMIER [Howard] FERGUSON (1870-1946). Conservative Premier of Ontario from Kemptville, elected 1923, re-elected 1926. MR. [Peter] JAMIESON (1876-1952). Minister in Port Stanley 1924-26. **July 4** CUTHBERT (McIntyre). LMM's first cousin, brother of Laura Aylsworth and of Bertie. **July 9** SCOTT SWAMP. Runs diagonally across Scott Township from southwest to northeast, between Zephyr and Leaskdale. **July 10** MISS DICKIE. Donalda Dickie (1888-1972), author of a series of school history books, including *When Canada was Young* (Toronto: Dent, 1925). **August 14** GIRL GUIDES CAMP FIRES. A "Camporee" or provincial gathering of Guides was held on the Noble property, organized by Marion Noble. LMM's compelling performance is still remembered in Norval. **September 9** GUELPH AGRICULTURAL COLLEGE. Founded 1874. The grounds were used as demonstration of landscaping and horticulture. LMM's cousin Frede had attended short courses in household economics at Guelph. **September 16** BLUE MEAGRE HAG. John Milton, *Comus: A Masque*, 434. WICK. This village had become the scene of a sectarian drama: the Presbyterians, locked out of their church, re-occupied it. BEN HUR. A Metro-Goldwyn-Mayer film, based on Lew Wallace's 1880 novel; starring Ramon Novarro and Francis X. Bushman; presented in Toronto at the Princess Theatre. **September 29** BRAMPTON. Town contiguous to Toronto, 6 miles northeast of Norval. Dale Greenhouses were advertised as "the largest area under glass in the British Empire". NEW PRINCIPAL OF KNOX COLLEGE. Thomas Eakin (1871-1958), born in Ireland, had been at Montreal Presbyterian College 1920-25; Principal at Knox 1926-44. **October 3** PANTAGES. Theatre on Yonge Street, opened in 1920 and ran vaudeville and other shows until 1932. Renamed the Imperial Theatre it showed films and occasional live performances; in 1988 a year-long renovation began and the Pantages Theatre re-opened restored to its original style in 1989. DR. [Gilbert] ROYCE. (1874-1939). Toronto throat and nose specialist; Col. Dr. Royce had a distinguished war record overseas with the Canadian Army Medical Corps. AMOS EAGLES. Ewan's brother-in-law in Massachusetts. **October 5** REVIEWS OF THE BLUE CASTLE. Early reviews appeared in *Saturday Review of Literature*, September 18, *New York Times Book Review*, September 26, *Times Literary Supplement*, September 30, and *Canadian Bookman*, October. **October 13** LIMEHOUSE. A hamlet to the west between Norval and Acton, on a secondary road. **October 24** J.K. FRASER (1864-1953). J. Keir Geddie Fraser, born in Alberton, P.E.I., educated Prince of Wales College and Dalhousie, did post-graduate work in New York and Europe, served at Knox Church, Galt (now called Cambridge) 25 miles south-west of Norval, 1915-26, then moved to Renfrew before retiring to Prince Edward Island. **October 30** MRS. SAM MCCLURE. Ethel Dolson McClure, the church organist, one of the Mount Pleasant continuing Presbyterians who had joined Norval church after their own church voted pro-Union. **November 3** TERRA COTTA. Village 10 miles north of Norval, up the Credit River. **November 21** GRANDMA WOOLNER'S OLD JUG. Lucy Woolner Macneill, LMM's grandmother, was the granddaughter of Harriet Kemp of Dunwich, England. The jug was eventually featured in *A Tangled Web* (1931). **November 22** *GODEY'S LADY'S BOOK* (1830-1898). A popular American women's magazine, arbiter of fashion in the 1880s.

1927

January 1 ST. ANTHONY. A port on the north-eastern tip of Newfoundland. The orphanage was run by the International Grenfell Association. TEMPLE PARSONS. Born 1909 in Williamsport; admitted to the orphanage 1917, discharged 1926 to his father's care. FLOSSIE ROBERTS. Born 1920 at Little Bay Islands; entered the orphanage 1924, where she appeared "friendly with all and motherly with her little sister." Discharged to her mother in 1937. Orphanage records in both cases note the support of Mrs. L.M.M. Macdonald. **January 8** OLD MAN OF THE SEA. In "Sindbad", *Arabian Nights*, the Old Man tricks the Sailor into carrying him. THE OLD COUNTRY. For many Canadians of British descent, a habitual phrase for referring to England, Scotland, Ireland, or Wales. **January 10** CHARLOTTE AND KATE MCPHERSON. The McPherson family, four sisters and two brothers, lived in the house next to the Presbyterian church, on the Guelph-Toronto road. LMM shifts in spelling their name from McPherson to MacPherson. **January 15** REV. MR. [J.W.] MACNAMARA, (1865-1948). Secretary of the Presbyterian Church Association, 1922-25, Clerk of the General Assembly, 1926-28, D.D., Knox, 1928. **January 22** MRS. MASON. Sixth of the women who worked for LMM as maids. GAMBLING IN WHEAT STOCKS. Wheat crops in the west had been excellent throughout the 1920s; speculative buying of wheat futures on the Winnipeg Exchange was handled by grain brokers in Toronto. The price of grain, at its peak in 1927, dropped however and was never so good again until after WW II. **February 9** "SPARKY" [George] BIGNALL. His father was a fireman at Dale's greenhouses; the family lived in the double house at the forks of the river, formerly a warehouse of Gooderham and Worts. BARNHILL'S STORE. At the corner of Adamson and the main street; run by the same family for three generations. JACK RANKINE. Grandson of Mr. and Mrs. Williams; the family lived on Guelph Street, the main street, across from the Presbyterian church. HUTTONVILLE. Hamlet about 3 miles down the Credit. **March 12** MARY AND NORMAN. The Beals from Uxbridge. **March 14** THE Y. Young Men's Christian Association, Y.M.C.A. THIS BELIEVING WORLD. Lewis Browne (1897-1949) presents in this book (New York: Macmillan, 1926) "a simple account of the great religions of the world". ELMER GANTRY. Sinclair Lewis (1885-1951) reflects a revolt against hypocrisy in the church; *Elmer Gantry* (N.Y.: Harcourt, Brace, 1927) satirizes a corrupt and self–deceiving Protestant minister. **April 19** WANDERING JEW. Legendary Ahasuerus, condemned to roam forever because he taunted Christ on the road to Calvary. **April 25** DAGUERROTYPE. Photograph produced by French painter and physicist Louis Daguerre's 1830s invention: fixing a latent image on a coated silver plate by focusing sunlight through a lens and then developing a positive image by immersing the plate in a chemical solution. "SPEAKER" MACNEILL. LMM's great-grandfather, Wm. Simpson Macneill (1781-1870). **April 30** GORDON LESLIE. The family farm was toward Ashgrove; Gordon later went to the Yukon. GEORGE KENNEDY. One of the 21 young men of Leaskdale church who subsequently joined the armed forces in World War II. **May 13** MILIARY TUBERCULOSIS. Granular, seed-like nodules formed within the lungs, leading to degeneration or pulmonary consumption. **May 26** *MARIGOLD* STORIES. About Marigold Lesley, LMM's new six-year-old character. **June 1** LOU

DYSTANT. A friend from Bideford days, 1894, and a persistent suitor until 1910. (See entries under "Dystant", *SJLMM*, I.) **June 4** BEELZEBUB. The devil (Hebrew); HADES. Hell (Greek). **June 14** THE BOYDS. The Reverend R.W.S. Boyd was the Anglican minister in Norval 1926-35. His wife, according to local history, "inspired conversation by sitting in front of the rectory smoking and reading novels while the neighbours went to church." **July 2** THOMAS EARLY'S. Farmer on the 9th line to the east of Norval, father of Harold and Chester, who took part in the play directed by LMM. **July 9** LORD AND LADY WILLINGDON. Lord Willingdon was Governor-General of Canada from October 1926 to January 1931. DALHOUSIE DAYS. LMM had attended Dalhousie University in Halifax, 1895-96. **July 11** MRS. MACLEOD. Sister-in-law of Ewan's sister Christie. **July 13** ALBERT MIDDLETON (1895-1964). Maud Beaton's husband, Mary Campbell Beaton's son-in-law; he operated a service station in West Royalty, on the outskirts of Charlottetown. IDA. Another friend from college days: Ida McEachern, now Mrs. George Sutherland. **July 14** HON. STANLEY BALDWIN (1867-1947). Prime Minister of Great Britain, 1923-24; 1924-29; 1934-37. **July 17** FLORENCE LIVESAY (1874-1953). A volume of her poetry, *Shepherd's Purse*, was published by Macmillan in 1923. The Canadian writer and poet Dorothy Livesay is her daughter. WILL GRAHAM (1881-1967) and MARY MOORE [Graham] (1892-1988). Lived at Bayview, just west of Cavendish. WILL GREENS'. Bertha and Will Green now lived in the old Baptist manse. **July 18** WILBUR, FRED, AND DARNLEY CLARK. "Brotherly chums" from schooldays: (see *SJLLM*, I, 318). **July 19** LIZZIE STEWART LAIRD. A friend who had been mentally ill: see *SJLMM*, II, 254-55. **August 7** TILLIE [Metilda Ellen] BENTLEY (1850-1931). A second cousin, daughter of great-uncle Daniel Macneill, first postmaster in Cavendish; wife of James T. Bentley of Kensington. "HIS ROYAL HIGHNESS." The Duke of Windsor (1894-1972); in 1927 the Prince of Wales, who became King Edward VIII on the death of King George V, January 1936. GOV'T HOUSE. Chorley Park, a Toronto residence in French renaissance château-style, set on 14 acres in North Rosedale. GOVERNOR ROSS. His Honour Wm. Donald Ross, banker and businessman, Lieutenant-Governor of Ontario. PRINCE GEORGE. Acceded to the throne as George VI after the abdication of Edward VIII, December 1936. The two princes opened Princes' Gate at the Canadian National Exhibition during this Toronto visit. JOHN CLARK. Norval farmer on the 4th line, north-east of the village. **August 28** LASALLE PARK. Typical Sunday school picnic: by train to Hamilton, by steamer to LaSalle Park on Burlington Bay. OMAR KHAYYAM. From Edward Fitzgerald, "The Rubaiyat of Omar Khayyam" (1859) stanza 71. LMM and her son Stuart quoted this frequently. BEAMISH. The garage was across from the Presbyterian Church. Winslow and Ernie Beamish both served in the armed forces later during World War II. **September 6** THE INSTITUTE OF QUEBEC. At Macdonald College of McGill University, Frede Campbell had co-ordinated provincial Women's Institutes. **September 16** A WILLYS KNIGHT. Willys, originally a bicycle manufacturer, was a pioneer in American car-frame manufacture, and Charles Knight of Chicago invented the "Silent Knight" engine in 1908. **September 23** THE ILLUMINATIONS. The play of lights on Niagara Falls. **October 4** MACKEREL REAMER. Odd-shaped knife for cleaning fish, saved many years earlier from the wrecked ship *Franklin Dexter*. **October 14** GEO. R. George Macneill, a distant cousin who farmed near the Cavendish crossroads. **October 16** MR. AND MRS. GOLLOP. George Gollop had retired in 1918 from business in the United States and Canada (he was director of sales, Canada Salt Company), returned to his birthplace, and bought a big house on the main street. DR. [Thomas Todhunter] SHIELDS (1873-1955). Pastor of Jarvis Street Baptist Church; later expelled by the Baptist convention for his attacks on McMaster professors. **October 19** BOOTH TARKINGTON (1869-1946). *Penrod* (New York: Doubleday, Page, 1914) is a comic boy's book in the Mark Twain tradition. OSCAR GRAEVE. After 1926 the *Delineator* became more sophisticated under the direction of Graeve. **November 17** *YOUR CUCKOO SINGS BY KIND*. Valentine Dobrée, author of this novel (New York: Knopf, 1927), also published an edition of *Wuthering Heights* with Knopf the same year. **December 14** WOOLWORTH'S. The "five or ten cent store" selling low-priced notions. **December 17** THE RACE OF JOSEPH. Frede's phrase for congenial people. *SATURDAY NIGHT*. Canadian magazine founded 1887; Hector Charlesworth was Editor, 1926-1932. WILSON MACDONALD. Canadian poet (1880-1967) who began publishing in 1915. In the 1920s he began touring Canada with poetry readings, visiting schools and colleges. **December 23** NORA HOLLAND (1876-1925). "The Little Dog Angel" is from her second volume of poems, *When Half Gods Go* (New York: Macmillan, 1924). MACAULAY'S LAYS. As a schoolgirl LMM memorized many of the *Lays of Ancient Rome* (1842) by Thomas Babington Macaulay (1800-1859), including "Horatius at the Bridge". **December 31** UNDINE. A fairy romance published in 1811 by de la Motte Fouqué. Undine is a sylph; her love is eventually fatal to the human knight who marries her.

1928

January 21 *WOODEN SHIPS AND IRON MEN*. F.W. Wallace (1886-1958) published this tribute to seafarers (London: Hodder & Stoughton, 1924). **January 24** STIRRATT LESLIE. Stirratt Leslie (no relation to the Norval Leslies) ran a big farm in Union. There were a number of Stirratts, including Mrs. Barraclough, in Glen Williams. WITHOUT CHAINS. Automobiles carried metal chains to be attached to the wheels to improve tire traction in icy weather. **February 14** MAILS BY AEROPLANE. The first authorized mail flight in Canada was instituted September 18, 1919, between Truro and Charlottetown. By 1926 bags were also being delivered by hydroplane from Victoria, B.C. to Pacific coast islands. **March 10** DR. ALLISON OF MANITOBA UNIVERSITY. Wm. Talbot Allison (1874-1949), poet and essayist, had published *Blazing a New Trail*, a study of Canadian writers, in 1920. **March 31** *LIFE OF JESUS*. First published by Ernest Renan (1823-1892) in 1862; translated C.E. Wilbour (New York: Carleton, 1864). In other entries, omitted here, LMM reports re-reading *The Life of Jesus Critically Examined* by David Friedrich Strauss (1808-1874), first published in Germany, 1836, translated by George Eliot, 1846. **April 27** PARISH HALL. On Adamson Street, above the Anglican church. **May 2** THE SUIT ADVISED. In February 1926 LMM had instituted a suit against Page for costs of the New York libel action: the seventh and last of the series of suits between LMM and Page. The U.S. system requires each party to pay its own attorney's costs. In Canada the successful party in an action is usually awarded about 50% of its attorney's costs. AGNES AND EGERTON CASTLE. Agnes Sweetman Castle (1857-1922) and Egerton Castle (1858-1920) collaborated on a series of bucolic books such as *Our Sentimental Garden* (Philadelphia: Lippincott, 1914). "LOKI". Character in Castles' book. Also the pen name of Professor Karl Pearson (1857-1936), author of studies on heredity and environment; a major book was on the influence of parental alcoholism on the physique of the offspring. **May 26** WOODBRIDGE, CALEDON. Villages north-east and north of Norval. **June 10** REGINA GENERAL ASSEMBLY. Each year 1/6 of the churches send a minister and an elder to the national assembly which moves from one region to another: in 1928 to Regina, the capital of Saskatchewan. The Moderator of the national church is chosen at the General Assembly. EXPLORING THE UNIVERSE. C. Henslow Ward (1872-1935), author of school texts on history and English composition, published this book, with subtitle "The incredible discoveries of recent science" (Indianapolis: Bobbs-Merrill, 1927). On July 1 LMM reported reading G.H.S. Harper's *Astronomy with the Naked Eye*, subtitled "A new geography of the Heavens" (New York: Harper, 1908). **June 23** LITTLE BROWN CO. Boston publishers of *Quo Vadis* and many other best sellers. A GOLD RING. A gift to LMM from Uncle Leander's first wife, given to Will Pritchard and returned after his death; a hand-written note in the journal, dated 1938, adds "I am still wearing it!" **June 27** ALF SIMPSON; FULTON. Brothers of Edwin Simpson. (See *SJLMM*, I, 175-7, 182.) **July 22** MR. WIGGINS. A former farmer who had moved to the United States but retired to Norval. Mrs. Mason later went to work for him. HUTCHI[n]SON, THE LAWYER. Thomas A. Hutchinson had come to Milton in 1920; remained to become a prominent lawyer and a K.C. EPHRAIM WEBER (1870-1956) had corresponded with LMM since March 1902. Her early letters to him appear in *The Green Gables Letters*, ed. Wilfrid Eggleston (Toronto: Ryerson, 1960). Mrs. Weber was the former Annie Melrose, school-teacher of Didsbury, Alberta. MR. [William Inglis] DICK. Milton lawyer who was Crown Attorney for Halton County from 1905 to 1949. **August 12** ORILLIA. A town 100 miles north of Norval, near the north end of Lake Simcoe, original of Stephen Leacock's "Mariposa". SUNDRIDGE. A further 100 miles north, on Lake Bernard. NORTH BAY. 40 miles further, on the north-east shore of Lake Nipissing. FERGUSON HIGHWAY. Now part of the northern branch of the Trans-Canada Highway to Nipigon. Premier Ferguson made highway construction to northern mining areas a major concern. NEW LISKEARD. Town at the north end of Lake Temiskaming, near Notre-Dame-du-Nord in Quebec. COBALT. Mining town 3 miles south of New Liskeard. BIGWIN INN. On the Lake of Bays, about 100 miles south of Sundridge. PORT CARLING. Between Lake Rosseau and Lake Muskoka, about 10 miles north-east of Bala. **August 21** THE "ITCH". Contagious disease caused by the itch-mite which burrows under the skin. DR. MCALLISTER, DR. PAUL. Both these doctors lived in Georgetown. Norval had previously been served by Dr. Samuel Webster (1842-1928), retired but until this year still living in a big house next to the McPhersons on the main street. His wife was Mr. Gollop's sister. **September 23** NORA LEFURGEY. Teacher in Cavendish 1902-3 (see *SJLMM*, I, 283-8). *Magic for Marigold* is dedicated to her. UPPER CANADA COLLEGE.

Private boys' school in Toronto, founded 1829, which owned a large property in Norval, where it had contemplated building new premises. **October 1** MY SALES. Total royalties in 1924 were $14,147; in 1928, $10,897. **November 7** CHARLES ROBERTS (1860–1943). Poet, novelist, translator, writer of animal stories, had lived in New Brunswick, Nova Scotia, New York, and London; he settled in Toronto in 1925. ARTHUR STRINGER (1874-1950). Author of crime adventure stories and of a trilogy of realistic prairie novels in journal form, based on his brief experience in Alberta; after living in Ontario until 1921 he had now moved permanently to New Jersey. BERNARD SANDWELL (1876-1954). Informal essayist and contributor to *Saturday Night* (which he edited 1932-1951). His current publication was *The Privacity Agent* (Toronto: Dent, 1928). CONVOCATION HALL. Formal assembly hall at the University of Toronto. THE HEART OF THE ANCIENT WOOD (1900). A romance that influenced *Kilmeny* (1910) and Gene Stratton-Porter's *A Girl of the Limberlost* (1910). ELSON. John M. Elson (b. 1880). Toronto poet and novelist, whose *The Scarlet Sash* had appeared in 1925. THE LITERARY. The Literary Society of Cavendish, founded 1886, sponsored meetings, debates, and a library. Re McLure and Mackenzie see *SJLMM*, I, 242, 313. WISELY INVESTED. Ominous phrase in the year of the stock market crash. **November 25** TITIAN PRINTS. Reproductions of works by Renaissance painter Tiziani Vicelli, used to establish whether the picture of "Anne" on *Further Chronicles* infringed a legal agreement. See *SJLLM*, II, 382. **December 9** "THE LONGEST DAY WEARETH TO EVENSONG". John Foxe, *Book of Martyrs* (1563), ch.7: "Be the day short or never so long,/ At length it ringeth to even-song." HELEN HASZARD (1890-1970). Charlottetown artist, trained in Boston; lived in Toronto in the 1920s, returning to P.E.I. in the summers; her work was very popular with tourists. LMM misspells this old Charlottetown Loyalist name "Hazard". **December 30** MORLEY CALLAGHAN (1903-1989). A recent law graduate who had been encouraged by Ernest Hemingway to follow a literary career; *Strange Fugitive* (New York: Scribner's, 1928), a hard-boiled story about a bootlegger, was Callaghan's first novel. FLYING CORPS. Aeronautic development since WW I was reflected in frequent news about American army flights around the world. The Royal Flying Corps was renamed the Royal Air Force in 1918, and the Royal Canadian Air Force gained separate identity in 1920.

1929

February 24 JOHN BULL'S OTHER ISLAND. First produced 1907: George Bernard Shaw's satire on Irish politics was published "with preface for politicians" London: Constable, 1909. Presented at the Royal Alexandra Theatre in Toronto by Maurice Colbourne's London Company. COOKSVILLE. A village now part of metropolitan Toronto's west end. MALABAR. A Toronto firm hiring out costumes for theatrical performances. "CURFEW MUST NOT RING TONIGHT". From a poem by Rosa Hartwick Thorpe, a favourite for school memory work. ALICE LESLEY [sic]. Sister of Gordon Leslie. Note variation in spelling: LMM was using the name "Lesley" for her new heroine, Marigold. **March 3** ARTHUR MCCLURE. A farmer on the 3rd Line, Mount Pleasant, an elder, cousin of Sam and Joe McClure. THE WEE SMA'S. Scottish slang: the wee small hours, i.e., very early in the morning.

BOB McPHERSON. Next door to the church, brother of Kate and Charlotte. WATSON BOYS. Mac and Lee Watson, aged 17 and 18, sons of Robert Watson whose grocery store was two doors beyond the McPherson house. WEST BRANCH. West Credit, tributary of the Credit River. THE HOSTEL. The big Adamson-Noble house, belonging to the former mill-owners, had been rented to the United Church and Y.M.C.A. for use as a hostel, called "Norval Farming School", for boys from Great Britain, in training for work on Canadian farms. MRS. BLACK. A sister of Mr. Gollop. Her husband ran the candy store and ice cream parlour next to Watsons' grocery in a house originally built as a hotel. CLARY HUNTER. A lad working in the mill. GEORGE SHARP. Worked at Barnhill's grocery; lived on Draper St. across from the manse. WYLIES. Lived first in a log house; after it burned down, they moved to a frame house farther down the hill. One of the boys was called "Hoot" Wylie. GEORGE BROWN. Lived two doors from the general store; sold insurance and also ran a farm. MRS. WILLIAMS. Next door on Draper Street, wife of the caretaker. **March 31** DODGE COUPE. A two-seater car; smaller than "Dodgie" which was a four-door sedan. **May 3** AN ADULT STORY. Eventually published as *A Tangled Web* (1931). **May 12** GUELPH. The Ontario Agricultural College, since 1964 a part of the University of Guelph, had offered courses on Canadian literature since 1906; visits by Canadian writers were regularly arranged. LMM appeared as banquet speaker at the Macdonald Institute, May 10. **June 6** MISS STUART. On the faculty of Macdonald Institute; like Frede Campbell Macfarlane she was a graduate in Household Science. *LOOKING BACKWARD: 2000-1887* (Boston: Ticknor, 1888). Utopian novel by Edward Bellamy (1850-1898). **June 19** BLISS CARMAN (1861-1929). The poet had been on a demanding reading tour; he died in Connecticut. A book by Carman was one of Ewan's first gifts to LMM: see *SJLMM*, I, 347. WILLIAM WILFRED CAMPBELL (1858-1918). Of Carman's generation, Campbell's first volume of verse was published 1888. "The Mother", an intense reworking of evolutionary theory, utilizing the myth of a mother returning from the dead to nurse and claim her baby, created a sensation when published in *Harper's* 1891. **July 14** HERODOTUS (484-424 B.C.). Greek historian, whose 9 volumes, named for the Muses, relate legends to documented facts on the enmity between Asia and Europe, Persia and Greece. REAL PRESENCE. The immanence of Christ's physical self in the Eucharist or Communion service. **July 19** TISH PLAYS THE GAME. A sequel (New York: Doran, 1926) by Mary Roberts Rinehart (1876-1958) to *Tish* (1916). **August 6** ERIN. Village 20 miles north-west of Norval, beyond Terra Cotta. A TALKIE. A new slang word of 1928, for an innovation introduced in 1927: "moving pictures" began to give way to "talking pictures".

List of deletions

All the entries that have been deleted, either in part or in total, are listed below. An asterisk after the date indicates that the deletion is only partial. Three dots indicate a deletion of less than a sentence, and four dots indicate a complete sentence or more has been deleted. When four dots come at the end of a paragraph, this usually means that a subsequent paragraph, often on a different subject, has been deleted.

1921: Apr. 8*; May 1*, 31*; Aug. 11*, 20*; Sept. 3*, 11*; Oct. 3*, 18*; Nov. 6, 19*, 25*, 26*; Dec. 1*, 13*, 22; **1922**: Feb. 13*, 19, 28*; Mar. 3, 18*, 25*; Apr. 2*, 5, 16*, 20*, 28*, 30*; May 10?, 13*; June 8*, 28; July 8*, 20*; Aug. 6*; Sept. 2*; Oct. 7*, 18, 19*, 24*, 27*, 28, 30*; Nov. 2*, 3*, 4*, 7, 8*, 9, 12, 14*, 17*, 20, 21*, 28*, 29*; Dec. 4*, 5*, 22*, 22*, 28*; **1923**: Jan. 2*, 8*, 19*, 21*, 24*, 25*; Feb. 8, 11, 18*, 19*, 22*, 28*; Mar. 5*, 6, 10, 12*, 17*; Apr. 1*, 8*, 9*, 11*, 14*, 18*, 20*, 24, 26*, 30*; May 13*, 18*, 27, 28; June 11*, 16*, 17, 21, 28*; July 8, 15*, 20*, 21*, 28*; Aug. 4*, 5*, 7*, 8*, 9*, 12, 18, 19*, 25*; Sept. 13*; Oct. 6*, 13*, 26*, 27*, 31*; Nov. 6*, 22*; Dec. 21*, 24, 25, 27, 31*; **1924**: Jan. 5*, 7*, 9, 10, 20*, 26*, 28*; Feb. 1, 3*, 4*, 5*, 8*, 9*, 10*, 11*, 16*, 18*, 19*, 20, 22, 23, 26; Mar. 2*, 9*, 16*, 23*, 28*, 30*, 31; Apr. 2*, 3, 4, 5, 10*, 20*, 27*; May 4*, 10*, 11, 16*, 17, 25*; June 5*, 6*, 9*, 10*, 16, 17*, 18*, 19, 26*, 30*; July 6*, 9*, 10*, 13*, 22*, 23*; Aug. 17*, 18*, 24*; Sept. 1*, 13, 20, 24, 26; Oct. 5, 10, 17*, 21, 22*, 23*, 24*, 27, 29*, 30*; Nov. 4, 5*, 8, 9*, 15, 16, 23*, 24*, 27*; Dec. 6*, 14*, 28*, 29; **1925**: Jan. 1, 3*, 4, 5*, 6, 9, 12*, 13*, 19, 20*, 25*, 27; Feb. 1*, 2, 8*, 10*, 11, 14*, 16, 18, 19, 20, 21*, 26*, 27*, 28*; Mar. 1*, 5*, 6*, 15*, 12, 15, 16, 18*, 19*, 21, 22, 23*, 24, 25, 28, 29, 30; Apr. 4*, 5, 6*, 7*, 9*, 10, 11, 12, 15, 19*, 20*, 22*, 23, 26; May 1, 2, 5, 7*, 11, 19, 20*, 21, 26*, 28, 30*, 31*; June 1, 3, 6*, 8*, 9, 10*, 14*, 16, 17*, 26*; July 6*, 9*, 15*, 27, 28; Aug. 2, 7, 9*, 10*, 13*, 17, 19, 20, 21, 24, 29*, 31; Sept. 7*, 9*, 11*, 12, 14*, 16*, 20, 21, 24, 27, 29, 30; Oct. 1*, 8*, 9, 14, 16*, 30*; Nov. 4, 5*, 11*, 16*, 30*; Dec. 5, 7*, 8, 13, 18, 22, 27, 28*, 29, 30*; **1926**: Jan. 1*, 7, 10, 12*, 16*, 19*, 25*, 29*; Feb. 4*, 10*, 11*, 13*, 28*; Mar. 6, 7, 10, 11, 16*; Apr. 7*, 19, 20*, 26, 29; May 2, 7, 11, 17; June 11*, 13*, 30*; July 2*, 10*, 24*, 20; Aug. 2*, 4*, 8, 14*, 21*; Sept. 3*, 6*, 9*, 13, 16*, 20, 21, 25, 29*; Oct. 3*, 5*, 9, 13*, 15, 18, 19*, 20*, 24*, 25*; Nov. 1*, 3*, 4, 6, 13*, 16, 17, 20*, 22*, 27; Dec. 20, 25; **1927**: Jan. 8*, 25*; Feb. 5*; Mar. 1, 29, 30*; Apr. 19*, 23*, 25*, 30*; May 7, 21; June 7, 10*, 11*, 16*; July 9*, 11*, 13*, 14*, 15*, 17*, 18*, 19*, 20, 23*, 24, 25, 26*, 27, 29*, 30*, 31*; Sept. 1*, 23*; Oct. 19*, 29*; Nov. 17*; Dec. 3, 4, 17, 21, 23*, 31*; **1928**: Jan. 14, 25; Feb. 1, 3, 11,

434

14*, 28; Mar. 10*, 13*, 31*; Apr. 7*, 27*; May 2*; June 3*, 10*, 17*, 23*, 25, 27; July 1, 22*; Aug 5*, 12*, 19, 21*; Sept. 9*, 23*; Oct. 1*, 15; Nov. 7*, 18*, 25*; Dec. 23*, 30*; **1929**: Jan. 13*, 20; Feb. 24*; Mar. 31*; Apr. 7*, 14; May 3*, 12*, 19; June 6*, 11*, 18*, 27*; July 13, 14*, 28; Aug. 6*.

List of Montgomery's errors in dating entries

L.M. Montgomery occasionally attached the incorrect day of the week to the date of the entry (or vice-versa) when writing up her journals. This happened periodically because of her method of jotting daily events on scraps of paper and then assembling them to write into her journals later when time permitted. Where the text of the entry supports a change (e.g., she says in the text that they went to Sunday School so we know the day was actually a Sunday, not a Saturday), we have changed her erroneous dates to the correct dates/days (shown in brackets). These corrections have been made by checking each entry against a perpetual calendar. When we cannot determine with absolute certainty whether the date or the day of week should be changed, we leave the text as it is and note it below.

When her life was particularly stressful, a considerable span of time may have elapsed between the date of the "jottings" and the date of the final write-up; however, the errors may have occurred strictly because of carelessness. In a few instances, she entered the same material twice, but with different dates; we have retained the entry which seems to represent the most accurate date, depending on internal evidence.

Saturday, May 8, 1921 [Saturday, May 7]; Sunday, Nov. 28, 1921 [Sunday, Nov. 27]; Wednesday, May 9, 1922; Thursday, May 10, 1922; Friday, May 20, 1922; Thursday, Oct. 24, 1922 [Tuesday, Oct. 24]; Wednesday, Feb. 22, 1923; Tuesday, Dec. 10, 1923; Thursday, Dec. 12, 1923; Sunday, July 26, 1924; Sunday, Oct. 17, 1924; Sunday, Feb 14, 1925; Monday, Mar. 22, 1925 [Monday, Mar. 23], Friday, Jan. 13, 1926 [Friday, Jan. 15]; Saturday, May 13, 1927; Wednesday, July 25, 1929.

Index